OCA Oracle Database SQL Exam Guide

(Exam 1Z0-071)

 *Oracle Press*™

OCA Oracle Database SQL Exam Guide

(Exam 1Z0-071)

Steve O'Hearn

 Mc Graw Hill Education

New York   Chicago   San Francisco
Athens   London   Madrid   Mexico City
Milan   New Delhi   Singapore   Sydney   Toronto

Cataloging-in-Publication Data is on file with the Library of Congress

OCA Oracle Database SQL Exam Guide (Exam 1Z0-071)

1 2 3 4 5 6 7 8 9 LCR 21 20 19 18 17

ISBN: Book p/n 978-1-259-58550-0 and CD p/n 978-1-259-58548-7
of set 978-1-259-58549-4

MHID: Book p/n 1-259-58550-6 and CD p/n 1-259-58548-4
of set 1-259-58549-2

Sponsoring Editor Lisa McClain	**Technical Editor** Todd Meister	**Production Supervisor** James Kussow
Editorial Supervisor Jody McKenzie	**Copy Editor** Kim Wimpsett	**Composition** Cenveo Publisher Services
Project Manager Dipika Rungta, Cenveo® Publisher Services	**Proofreader** Lisa McCoy	**Illustration** Cenveo Publisher Services
	Indexer Jack Lewis	**Art Director, Cover** Jeff Weeks
Acquisitions Coordinator Claire Yee		

*To Jim Bauchspies, who gave me my first Oracle job
and who has always been like a second father to me.*

Steve O'Hearn is a technology consultant with expertise in the design, development, and administration of various data and data-driven systems for such clients as the U.S. Defense Department, NASA HQ, the FAA, the World Bank, and many others. He first became an Oracle Certified Professional (OCP) in 2001 and is a certified Oracle Database SQL Expert. He has a degree in business administration with a specialization in information processing from George Washington University, and his postgraduate work includes advanced statistics and the completion of the Future of e-Government Executive Education training at Harvard University's Kennedy School of Government in 2003. He is a member of Mensa.

Mr. O'Hearn authored *OCE Oracle Database SQL Certified Expert Exam Guide (Exam 1Z0-047)*, the official certification exam guide for Oracle's first expert-level certification exam, and the critically acclaimed *OCP Developer: PL/SQL Program Units Exam Guide*, both from Oracle Press. He contributed to *Oracle Web Applications 101* from Oracle Press and *Oracle8 Server Unleashed*. He has been featured on Oracle TV and Oracle Open World/JavaOne. He has been published in a variety of publications, including the *Harvard Business Review* and the *Record* of the National Press Club, where he is an officially recognized subject-matter expert on the topics of database and information technology. He has been vice president and conference coordinator for the Mid-Atlantic Association of Oracle Professionals. He leads the official Java User Group (JUG) for the Baltimore Washington Metropolitan Area, possesses certifications in Java and other technologies, and loves working with his own Raspberry Pi and 3D printing devices.

Mr. O'Hearn provides Oracle and Java technology training and tutoring online. He blogs at Skere9.com. He invites any and all inquiries at soh@corbinian.com.

About the Contributor

Bob Bryla is an Oracle 9*i*, 10*g*, 11*g*, and 12*c* Certified Professional with more than 20 years of experience in database design, database application development, training, and Oracle database administration. He is the primary Oracle DBA and database scientist at Epic in Verona, Wisconsin. He is a technical editor for a number of Oracle Press books, including several certification study guides for Oracle Database 10*g*, 11*g*, and 12*c*. You can also find him on Lynda.com teaching Oracle Database fundamentals in bite-sized videos. He has also been known to watch science-fiction movies, tinker with Android devices, and refinish antique furniture in his spare time.

About the Technical Editor

Todd Meister has been working in the IT industry for more than 20 years. He's been a technical editor on more than 75 books ranging in topic from SQL Server to the .NET Framework. Besides technical editing, he is the assistant vice president/ chief enterprise architect at Ball State University in Muncie, Indiana. He lives in central Indiana with his wife, Kimberly, and their five bright children.

CONTENTS AT A GLANCE

CONTENTS

ACKNOWLEDGMENTS

First, I want to acknowledge you, the reader. Were it not for you, this book would never have been created. Because of you, because of your interest, because of your professionalism, and because of your demonstrable commitment to improving yourself and therefore the industry, this book was created. Were it not for you, there would not be an elite team of experts here at Oracle Press responding to your interest and your demand for quality material. So, thank you. Without you, we would not be doing what we do, nor would this book exist.

Speaking of this book that you are holding in your hands (or perhaps reading on your screen), it is a tremendous work and a valuable contribution to the industry. It represents a great deal of effort by a number of talented, persistent, and dedicated professionals.

This book originally started as a second edition to my 2009 SQL Expert book on the 1Z0-047 exam and was nearing completion when it evolved into this book, the first certification exam guide for the 1Z0-071 exam.

First, a special and huge thank-you to Hilary Flood. This book would not have happened without her. It was her bold, open mind and creative force that helped originally steer this ship through murky waters to its eventual goal. For her persistence, patience, expertise, and insight, I thank her.

Claire Yee was the editorial coordinator. She was consistently cheerful and encouraging and worked tirelessly to ensure each chapter or other section worked its way through the many editorial cycles, from original material through technical edit, copyediting, and beyond to final production.

Dipika Rungta was the project manager. As the various chapters and other sections exited the process headed by Claire, each moved to Dipika for additional review, work, and the many demanding details necessary to prepare the book for production. Dipika has been a joy to work with and is a tremendous asset to any book production effort.

Jody McKenzie was the editorial supervisor and stepped in to resolve some challenging issues at key times. Lisa McCoy was the proofreader and caught some of the most obscure typos imaginable. The copy editor was Kim Wimpsett and helped make sure some of my curious expressions or word choices were translated into understandable narratives. The production supervisor was Jim Kussow, who has managed the production and printing processes of this ponderous tome.

Thank you to Vasundhara Sawhney who contributed a lot of work in the earliest stages of this journey.

The acquisitions editor was Lisa McClain. Acquisitions editors lead the charge to put book projects together in the first place and stay involved to ensure those projects march forward to their destination. They make tough calls in the face of uncertainty and have to discern a path forward with sometimes limited information. Oracle Press has talented acquisitions editors, and Lisa McClain is one of the best in the business. She heralded this effort in the latter stages, and it has been a privilege to have served with her on this project.

Now let's talk about indexing. Indexing a book is a crucial job. This is true whether the book is in printed or digital form. I judge technical books by a few key indicators, including the quality and relevance of the index. I generally already have an idea of what I'm looking for in a technical book, so when I pick up a paper technical book for the first time, I flip to the index and check for particular subject areas of interest to determine whether the index correctly references them in the narrative. If yes, I buy the book. If not, I don't. That's often my only criteria when evaluating new books. That's how important the index of a technical book is to me.

If you're reading this digitally, you might be thinking, "So what? I can always do a word search. Why do I need an index?" There are many topics in books like this where the keyword isn't easily searchable. For example, consider the word *set*. It is used quite a bit in normal conversation and is likely in the narrative for various reasons. But *set* is also a key concept in this book with regard to SET operations such as UNION and INTERSECT. And that topic is completely different from the keyword SET in an UPDATE statement. All are in this book. So if you are searching for just one particular use of *set* in this book, then an electronic search on a keyword may slog you through all sorts of unrelated material. But a well-crafted index will get you where you need to go quickly, even in a digital version of the book.

For that reason, I am very grateful for the work of Jack Lewis, the indexer for this book. It's a great deal of work and often overlooked but never by me—neither as a consumer nor as an author. Thank you, Jack. I appreciate your work much more than you may realize.

A huge and special thank-you to my technical editor, Todd Meister. Todd has worked tirelessly to review and analyze hundreds of pages of code, and he has reverse-engineered a myriad of examples, illustrations, questions, and answers. He traveled down this long road with the rest of the team with style, grace, and amazing persistence. One particular challenge with this kind of technical book is that it doesn't lend itself to a consistently built application (for examples and illustrations) like some other books do. The nature of a certification exam guide is that it must cover a variety of syntax combinations, so rather than building an application as a project, this book requires you to understand all forms of certain syntax combinations. That is a challenge to the certification candidate; imagine the challenge to a technical editor. It is enormous. Yet Todd has done it brilliantly and with aplomb and professionalism. I will always have visions of his familiar "Todd Meister verified" annotations throughout the draft copies of the book as the various sections passed back and forth along the cycle of production. But note that the book has gone through a few iterations, so if you still bizarrely manage to find something in it that is less than ideal—and that's the case with virtually every publication—then that'll be on me. But know that thanks to Todd, the book is light-years ahead of where it otherwise would have been.

Also a big thank-you to Bob Bryla, an outstanding Oracle Press author in his own right many times over, who jumped in at the last minute to contribute a good number of questions and answers to the sample certification exam included with the book. Thank you, Bob!

To my very many friends and colleagues with whom I've had the pleasure of working and/or serving over the years at various locations and in various capacities, at such enterprises as Atrexa, LHR Digital Consulting, Corbinian, Sysorex, ISC, db-Training, MAOP, EOUG, Boeing, ORI, ARC, NPC, and elsewhere, including some who are still at those places and some who have gone on to other adventures—there is no way I could name everyone here who has been instrumental or contributed something important to my life and work. A partial list includes the following: Mark O'Donnell, Matt Hutchinson, Dave and Jackie Dougherty, John Cook, Tim Green, Jeremy Judson, Salam Qureishi, Nadir Ali, Wendy Loundermon, Athar Javaid, Dan Doherty, Tony Covert, Bianca Canales, Marlene Theriault, Kevin Loney, Michelle Veghte, Ardell Fleeson, Markus Dale, Karl Davis, Allen Shoulders, Ed Wolfe, Ashley Rubeck, Cindy Shiflett, Phil Hasse, Dave Gagner, Jon Feld, Jay Nielsen, Steve Smith, Edgar Kline, Dave Salmen, Oscar Wood, James Perry, Terri Buckler, Sarah Henrikson, Mark Tash, Steve Vandivier, Adhil Shaikh, Monique Tribolet, Ed Spinella, Dino Merkezas, Kathy Gardos, Bert Spencer, Karen Owens, Mike Ault, Graham Seibert, Vince Adams, Bob Schnetter, Josh Parreco, Craig Kasold, Jennifer Blair, Brett Simpson, Mike Gerrity, Dave Cooper, Ted Cohen, Steve Cummings, Jimmy Smith, Peter Dube, Ruthie Washburn, Kim Curl, Toni Boyd, Robin Ruth, Renee Battle, Danny Duong, Hung Nguyen, Drew Daffron, Ken O'Neal, Kim Miller, John Lauder, Bob Smout, Todd Stottlemeyer, Paul Leslie, David Wise, Dan

Rutherford, Laura Taylor, Laura Setliff, Trin Tranh, Wilson Dizard, Paul Elliott, John Metelsky, Don Knight, Art Garrison, Marshall Cohen, Mark Wojno, Bill McCarren, Jonathan Salant, Carole Feldman, Tammy Lytle, Sheila Cherry, Rick Dunham, Doug Harbrecht, Audrey Ford, Tim Aquilino, Debbie Beebe, Bill Simpson, Annette Taylor, Fred Wills, Carlesza Harris, Gardner McBride, Cindy McBride, Jim Flyzik, Rob Guerra, John Coffey, Lyle Beall, Bobbie Beall, and to Roy Patterson, who – with Jim Bauchspies - assigned me to my first Oracle project. And to Todd and Cindy Bauchspies, Mike and Kate Waters and Gavin, James and Claudia Waters, Phil and Charlotte Jones, Harriet Marin and Joe Motz, and Danna Henderson.

To those who are no longer with us: Aaron "Eppie" Epstein, Martin Kuhn, John Cosgrove, Mike Shanahan, Gordon Gustin, Helen Kamajian, Georgine Bauchspies, Eileen Waters, and Jack Henderson.

To Dan and Brenda Hinkle, who gave me outstanding opportunities and from whom I learned a great deal about Oracle and entrepreneurship.

To my very many outstanding Oracle students over the years, too numerous to mention here. I remember one class that gave me a going-away present of a small antique water pump, symbolic for how learning is as important to one's life as is water necessary for survival. That symbolic gesture was moving beyond words, and I have never forgotten it.

To my longtime professional associate and close friend Bill Bryant, who has mentored and coached me on many aspects of technology, business, the world, and life.

To my father, Don, a brilliant engineer, excellent project manager, published author, great professional, and great dad and to whom I dedicated my second book.

To my mother, Joan, the best mother in the world, who I love with all my heart and to whom I dedicated my first book.

A very special thank-you to Lisa, the love of my life, for being wonderful, sweet, patient, brilliant, so loving, and so very encouraging!

And finally, to Jim Bauchspies, who is like a second father to me in many ways, and to his late wife, Georgine, whose infectious laugh and warmth and love are treasured memories I will never forget. Jim gave me my first Oracle opportunity, as well as a great deal of advice on all things personal and professional over the many years I've been privileged to know him. It is to him I dedicate this, my third book.

Recently I attended a technical conference hosted by a leading big data vendor. I found myself speaking with an exhibitor about his startup company's NoSQL product. Now folks, I love all forms of data systems; they all have their place. Key-value pairs, dynamic schemas—they all have a use. But this particular vendor boldly declared that the relational database was useless and "SQL is dead." He described how his system could harvest text-based comments and infer sentiment across millions of records and support all sorts of clever use cases—all of which, incidentally, is doable with Oracle-driven SQL-based systems. But he was convinced that Oracle's relational database management system (RDBMS) was irrelevant.

So I asked him, "Let's say I place an order for this product of yours. Are you going to track that order in a NoSQL database? Or does your office rely on an RDBMS to capture orders?"

He thought about it. "Good point, that *is* a relational database system."

"OK, and how about your employees? When your company tracks your hours, what do they use?"

"True, true, that's a SQL database too."

"How about supply management? Shipping? General ledger and other accounting functions? Inventory management? And the other office systems?"

"OK, you got me—those are also RDBMS servers, all SQL systems, true."

"So anything involving orders, customers, employees, vendors, partners, products, inventory, manufacturing, payroll, and just about every other aspect of the business is a SQL system."

"True, it's true."

"But if I want to analyze comments on my web site, your company's product is a good choice."

"Yes! Exactly!" He seemed relieved to be back on familiar territory. "And we can analyze millions of comments per second."

"OK, so if I get millions of comments per second on my web site, I'd be interested."

"Yes. Twitter uses us."

"Cool. So if I want to perform some text analysis on a massive scale, I could theoretically still use Oracle but your product might be better optimized for massively large volumes of insert-only processing if I'm Twitter."

"Exactly."

"Awesome. One problem. I'm not Twitter. How many Twitters are there out there? Last I checked there was one. Now granted, I know other organizations have requirements to process millions of records per second. But who? Facebook? Or Google? So perhaps two, ten, or thirty web sites?"

"Well...probably more than that."

Sure, probably. And we all know that number is growing. But still—to suggest this means the death of Oracle?

And at this point I decided to really freak him out. "Your product is probably written in Java, isn't it?"

"Yes, it is."

"You know Oracle owns Java, right?" He looked horrified and denied that it was true.

Folks, I'm as excited about the big data revolution and the potential of the Internet of Things (IoT), machine learning, and all technology. I work in the world of big data systems and a myriad of exotic data modeling alternatives. I love cutting-edge developments. But at the end of the day, there is no question that the workhorse of all industry and government, the backbone of automated systems, the technology on which virtually all large organizations rely has been—and continues to be—the relational database management system. And the Oracle RDBMS is the best in the business.

I recently attended a technical session at a popular Java conference where the speaker presented something like 32 use cases for various situations where some new NoSQL system would perform faster or otherwise more optimally than Oracle's RDBMS. Each example was based on a unique and—to me—unusual (perhaps some would say contrived) use case. "So if you have this unusual combination of data structures and your business objective requires some particular type of analytics, sure, you could use Oracle, but if you want a shorter development cycle or faster performance, you should use this New NoSQL Open Source Tool #17." For one example, the SQL code required was 30 lines in length, but doing the same job with the alternative new tool required only 23 lines of code. OK, sure, so I'm going to learn, install, configure, code, test, and deploy a different tool each time for every one of 32 different use cases so I can type seven fewer lines of code. Yeah, let's do that.

Or not. How about I just use Oracle and be done with it?

Again, folks, don't get me wrong—all systems have their place. But even today, the most powerful information tool in the world is still the relational database. As of this writing, the official ranking at DB-ENGINES.com lists the top four database engines in use today as being of the relational database model, with seven of the top ten in use falling into that category (see http://db-engines.com/en/ranking). At the top of that list is the same database that has led the world for years now: Oracle's RDBMS.

Oracle's MySQL is number two.

The core language at the foundation of all Oracle products is Oracle's Structured Query Language (SQL), a language that is common to all major relational databases of all vendors worldwide.

Even many of the newer alternative data stores that aren't necessarily based on a relational database model are struggling to implement SQL-like languages, such as Cassandra's CQL or IBM's "SQL-like querying language HiveQL" (https://www.ibm.com/developerworks/library/bd-sqltohadoop2/) for use with Hadoop systems.

The relational database model is still the number-one database model in the world, and SQL is the only language common to all relational database models. It's also the standard against which new special-purpose database models pattern new language features.

This book is designed to help you become certified in this significant, powerful, important language at the core of the successful operations of governments and industry worldwide.

You have a made a brilliant choice to study and work with SQL and to use this book to work toward certification.

Welcome!

In This Book

This book is organized in such a way as to serve as an in-depth review for the Oracle Database SQL exam for both experienced Oracle professionals and newcomers to SQL technologies. Each chapter covers a major aspect of the exam, with an emphasis on the "why" as well as the "how to" of working with and supporting relational database applications.

On the CD-ROM

For more information on the CD-ROM, please see the "About the CD-ROM" appendix at the back of the book.

Exam Readiness Checklist

At the end of the introduction you will find an Exam Readiness Checklist. This table has been constructed to allow you to cross-reference the official exam objectives with the objectives as they are presented and covered in this book. The checklist also allows you to gauge your level of expertise on each objective at the outset of your studies. This should allow you to check your progress and make sure you spend the time you need on more difficult or unfamiliar sections.

In Every Chapter

I've created a set of chapter components that call your attention to important items, reinforce vital points, and provide helpful exam-taking hints. Take a look at what you'll find in every chapter:

- Every chapter begins with **Certification Objectives**—what you need to know to pass the section on the exam dealing with the chapter topic. The objective headings identify the objectives within the chapter, so you'll always know an objective when you see it!

- **Exam Watch** notes call attention to information about, and potential pitfalls in, the exam. These helpful hints are written by the author, who has taken the exam and received his certification—who better to tell you what to worry about? He knows what you're about to go through!

- **On the Job** notes describe the issues that come up most often in real-world settings. They provide a valuable perspective on certification- and product-related topics. They point out common mistakes and address questions that have arisen from on-the-job discussions and experience.

- The **Certification Summary** is a succinct review of the chapter and a restatement of salient points regarding the exam.

✓ ■ The **Two-Minute Drill** at the end of every chapter is a checklist of the main points of the chapter. It can be used for last-minute review.

Q&A ■ The **Self Test** offers questions intended to check your knowledge of each chapter. The answers to these questions, as well as explanations of the answers, can be found at the end of each chapter. By taking the Self Test after completing each chapter, you'll reinforce what you've learned from that chapter.

Some Pointers

Once you've finished reading this book, set aside some time to do a thorough review. You might want to return to the book several times and make use of all the methods it offers for reviewing the material.

1. *Reread all the Certification Summary and Two-Minute Drill sections,* or have someone quiz you. You also can use the drills as a way to do a quick cram before the exam. You might want to make some flash cards out of 3 × 5 index cards that have the Two-Minute Drill material on them.

2. *Re-read all the Exam Watch notes.* Remember that these notes are written by the author, who has taken the exam and passed. He knows what you should expect—and what you should be on the lookout for.

3. *Re-take the Self Tests.* Taking the Self Tests right after you've read the chapter is a good idea because the questions help reinforce what you've just learned. However, it's an even better idea to go back later and do all the questions in the book in one sitting. Pretend that you're taking the live exam. When you go through the questions the first time, you should mark your answers on a separate piece of paper. That way, you can run through the questions as many times as you need until you feel comfortable with the material.

4. *Take the practice exams,* timed and without your book, to see how you did. Make notes as you progress to keep a list of topics you think you need to study further before taking the real exam. (See Appendix A for more information about the practice exams.)

INTRODUCTION

This book helps you become certified in the Structured Query Language by preparing you for the OCA Oracle Database SQL Certified Associate exam, 1Z0-071. The objective of this study guide is to prepare you for the 1Z0-071 exam by familiarizing you with the technology and body of knowledge tested on the exam. Because the primary focus of the book is to help you pass the test, I don't always cover every aspect of SQL. Some aspects of the technology are covered only to the extent necessary to help you understand what you need to know to pass the exam, but I hope this book will serve you as a valuable professional resource after your exam.

Chapter 1 starts with a section that will provide you with some introductory information about the exam and the exam experience. The rest of Chapter 1 delves right into the topics of the certification objectives.

The book aligns to the certification exam's stated objectives, published by Oracle Corporation and stated by the company to be the topics from which the exam draws its questions. This book will not—and cannot—reveal actual exam questions or their corresponding answers. Those of us who have taken the exam are forbidden to reveal that information. But this book will focus on the topics that the exam addresses and will teach you the information that, as of this writing, you need to know about the exam.

This book is comprehensive and focused. Note that Oracle Corporation has made several manuals available online that describe the full functionality of its products. But those of us who have been in the business a while know that while these are valuable resources, they are huge—some are thousands of pages long— and sometimes they are overwhelming to navigate effectively within a person's professional lifetime without some sort of guide. This book is your guide, but it is much more than that; it is a self-contained study guide, complete with full descriptions, syntax details, sample code, self-tests, and practice exams that simulate the real certification exam experience. In other words, you are holding a treasure map to the nuggets of wisdom you need to know to pass the exam and win your certification. It is the product of years of experience, earned through hard work, tested among veteran Oracle professionals from around the world and with many backgrounds and strengths, and consolidated into one clearly organized format to empower you to prepare quickly and efficiently to become certified.

The book is designed to serve the following audiences:

- For the veteran who wants to zero in on topics on an *à la carte* basis, the book is categorized by certification objective. If you have already seen the published certification objectives and want to study up on a few areas, you can do that with this book—find the appropriate topic and study those chapters.

- For the reader who wants a more comprehensive review, the objectives and chapters are sequentially ordered to begin with the fundamentals and work up to the more advanced topics. You can study the book straight through and experience a complete presentation of the knowledge you need to pass the exam.

- For the seasoned practitioner who wants to jump straight to the exam experience, go straight to the back of the book, install the CD-ROM, and take the exam. Each question is tied to a topic in the book so that any questions you miss will quickly focus your time on the topics you need to study.

The 1Z0-071 exam has been validated against Oracle Database versions 11*g* Release 2 (version 11.2.0.1.0) and up to 12*c* Release 1 (12.1.0.1.0). For this book, I used Oracle Database 12*c* Release 1. For the screen shots, I used screen capture software to "grab" images of SQL statements as displayed in either SQL*Plus or SQL Developer. Note that in the SQL Developer's Script Output display, numeric data displays left justified by default, as opposed to SQL*Plus, where numeric data displays right justified by default. For the entity-relationship diagrams, I used Oracle SQL Data Modeler.

Good reading, study well, and the best of luck to you. Your feedback is invited and welcome: soh@corbinian.com.

Exam 1Z0-071

Exam Readiness Checklist

Certification Objective	Chapter	Page	Beginner	Intermediate	Expert
Oracle and Structured Query Language (SQL)	**1**	1			
Identify the connection between an entity-relationship diagram (ERD) and a relational database	1	16			
Explain the relationship between a database and SQL	1	25			
Describe the purpose of DDL	1	28			
Describe the purpose of DML	1	29			
Build a SELECT statement to retrieve data from an Oracle Database table	1	30			
Using DDL Statements to Create and Manage Tables	**2**	41			
Categorize the main database objects	2	42			
Create a simple table	2	46			
Review the table structure	2	54			
List the data types that are available for columns	2	56			
Explain how constraints are created at the time of table creation	2	63			
Drop columns and set column UNUSED	2	80			
Create and use external tables	2	86			
Manipulating Data	**3**	105			
Truncate data	3	106			
Insert rows into a table	3	109			
Update rows in a table	3	117			
Delete rows from a table	3	121			
Control transactions	3	122			
Restricting and Sorting Data	**4**	147			
Sort the rows that are retrieved by a query	4	148			
Limit the rows that are retrieved by a query	4	157			
Use ampersand substitution to restrict and sort output at runtime	4	173			
Use the SQL row limiting clause	4	182			

Exam Readiness Checklist

Certification Objective	Chapter	Page	Beginner	Intermediate	Expert
Using Single-Row Functions to Customize Output	**5**	201			
Use various types of functions that are available in SQL	5	202			
Use character, number, and date and analytical (PERCENTILE_CONT, STDDEV, LAG, LEAD) functions in SELECT statements	5	205			
Using Conversion Functions and Conditional Expressions	**6**	245			
Describe various types of conversion functions that are available in SQL	6	246			
Use the TO_CHAR, TO_NUMBER, and TO_DATE conversion functions	6	249			
Apply general functions and conditional expressions in a SELECT statement	6	264			
Reporting Aggregated Data Using the Group Functions	**7**	279			
Describe the use of group functions	7	280			
Group data by using the GROUP BY clause	7	293			
Include or exclude grouped rows by using the HAVING clause	7	303			
Displaying Data from Multiple Tables	**8**	319			
Describe the different types of joins and their features	8	320			
Use SELECT statements to access data from more than one table using equijoins and non-equijoins	8	321			
Join a table to itself by using a self-join	8	333			
View data that generally does not meet a join condition by using outer joins	8	335			
Using Subqueries to Solve Queries	**9**	351			
Define subqueries	9	352			
Describe the types of problems subqueries can solve	9	354			
Describe the types of subqueries	9	356			
Query data using correlated subqueries	9	357			
Update and delete rows using correlated subqueries	9	359			
Use the EXISTS and NOT EXISTS operators	9	363			
Use the WITH clause	9	364			

Exam Readiness Checklist

Certification Objective	Chapter	Page	Beginner	Intermediate	Expert
Write single-row and multiple-row subqueries	9	365			
Managing Schema Objects	**10**	389			
Describe how schema objects work	10	390			
Create simple and complex views with visible/invisible columns	10	392			
Create, maintain, and use sequences	10	407			
Create and maintain indexes including invisible indexes and multiple indexes on the same columns	10	412			
Perform flashback operations	10	424			
Using the Set Operators	**11**	449			
Describe set operators	11	450			
Use a set operator to combine multiple queries into a single query	11	452			
Control the order of rows returned	11	459			
Managing Objects with Data Dictionary Views	**12**	473			
Query various data dictionary views	12	474			
Manipulating Large Data Sets	**13**	497			
Describe the features of multitable INSERTs	13	498			
Merge rows in a table	13	514			
Controlling User Access	**14**	529			
Differentiate system privileges from object privileges	14	530			
Grant privileges on tables and on a user	14	542			
Distinguish between privileges and roles	14	552			

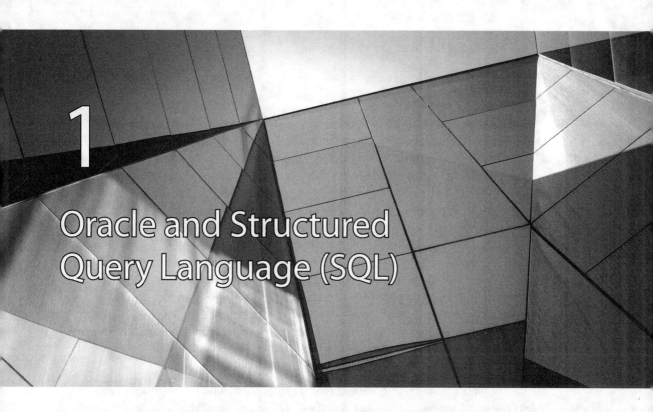

1
Oracle and Structured Query Language (SQL)

CERTIFICATION OBJECTIVES

Oracle Corporation's implementation of the Structured Query Language (SQL) is arguably the most powerful and most significant computer language used in the world of government and business today. This chapter begins the process of preparing you to successfully take and pass the Oracle 1Z0-071 exam, Oracle Database SQL Certified Associate. First, I'll discuss a few particulars about the exam and how it is different from other Oracle certification tests. You'll learn what you can expect on exam day. Next, I'll make some suggestions about study materials. Then I'll use the rest of the chapter to analyze the first exam objective, for which this chapter is named. In the first of the subobjectives, I'll discuss the concepts of a relational database management system (RDBMS) and explain entity-relationship diagrams (ERDs). Next I'll talk about the relationship between the RDBMS and SQL, and you'll look closely at two important subsets of SQL: Data Definition Language (DDL) and Data Manipulation Language (DML). Finally, you will learn how to build a SQL SELECT statement. This will complete the first objective and set the stage for the remainder of this book as you study each subsequent objective and prepare for the test.

If you are a veteran Oracle-certified professional who is already familiar with the exam process, you might skip the next section about the exam. In fact, you may choose to jump to only those exam objectives where you think you need study. However, I encourage you to review all the material in this book, even if you think you know it all already. The exam will challenge you on fine points and nuances, and it will try to trick you with concepts and keywords that almost sound correct but are not. You want your knowledge of the material to be rock-solid. For the purpose of the exam as well as to the benefit of your career, it is crucial that you maintain your SQL skills at the highest level, as this is what organizations in the world today require—and the exam demands the same from you. Be confident in your knowledge and you'll dramatically increase your odds of success on exam day and in your career.

Let's get started!

CERTIFICATION OBJECTIVE 1.01

The Exam: An Overview

The Oracle Database SQL Certified Associate is a demanding exam. It poses questions that test the full breadth of your knowledge of SQL syntax and processing and its application to business rules. A typical question on the exam might go something like this:

- You may be asked to review an exhibit, which could be a set of data output in a half-dozen columns and perhaps 20 or 30 rows—or it might be an entity-relationship diagram (ERD) containing as many as a half-dozen entities or more.

- You may be asked to review a related set of SQL statements that are intended to operate on the exhibit you were just shown, with a number of SQL statements in which there might be a series of nested scalar functions, aggregate functions, subqueries of various forms, and the use of different statements and clauses showcasing features such as very large data types, complex join conditions, and so on.

- Some of the code may be correct, and some may not. You'll need to recognize the difference.

- With the sample exhibit and SQL code in front of you, you may be asked to identify the resulting status of the database after the SQL statements execute.

- You may be asked to identify the internal workings of the Oracle database, in order, in accordance with the SQL statements you've been shown.

- The list of possible answers may include more than one correct response, and you must identify each of them.

Does that sound like a lot to do for a single question? Then consider this: for the entire exam, you are allowed 100 minutes to answer 73 questions. That is an average of 1.36 minutes per question, or about 82 seconds each.

exam

ⓦatch

Like many of Oracle's certification exams, the 1Z0-071 exam includes many multiple-choice questions that have more than one correct answer. In other words, a single question may require you to "select all of the following answers that are correct." The result: you must evaluate each individual answer. Once you find a correct answer, you aren't done—you must continue checking them all. On these types of questions, you can't rule out any of the answers based on the process of elimination since all answers are possible candidates for being correct. One question in this format is more like several questions rolled into one. The result is a more demanding test that requires you to be more knowledgeable and requires more of your time to answer. So study well. Review this book thoroughly. This is not a simple exam. But you can do it—equipped with this book, your odds of success increase dramatically.

Think you can handle it? Do you have what it takes to be a formally recognized and officially certified Oracle Database SQL Certified Associate?

Whether you do or not remains to be seen, but one thing is for certain. This book will prepare you, strengthen your knowledge, fill in the gaps, and dramatically increase your odds of success.

So get ready for a fun and rewarding challenge and an important milestone in your career. Get ready to enter the world of the technical elite, to join the crème de la crème, and to be ranked with the best of the best!

What to Do and What to Expect

Here is how to register for the exam and what you can expect as you go through the process.

Test Logistics

Here are instructions for how to register and take the exam. (Please note that Oracle's registration process is subject to change. Some of the specifics I describe here may have changed by the time you read this.)

To register for an exam, visit the Oracle Corporation web site (www.oracle.com), click the Certification link, and look for the 1Z0-071 exam page. From there, click the link asking to register for the exam. Your browser will navigate to the web site for the company that proctors the exam, Pearson Vue, at www.pearsonvue.com. From that web site, you can locate a local facility at which you can take the exam. Look for an available time—odds are you'll have to plan to take the exam at least one day in advance, if not longer, perhaps a week. Provide your credit card information for the required payment, and you'll be booked to take the exam at the precise time and location you selected.

When you arrive at the exam location, you may be asked to turn off your mobile phone and give it to a staff member. In my case, the staff member locked my mobile phone in a portable heavy-duty bag. The staff retained the key to the bag but handed the bag containing my mobile phone to me. I was told I would be able to take the bag with me into the testing room, unable to access it inside the locked container. I was told I could recover my phone after the exam.

You'll need to provide two forms of ID to the staff to complete your sign-in process. After that, you'll probably be escorted into a room with a desk with a computer, logged in to an automated testing system. If you want to take notes for use during the exam only, you may be provided with a few blank sheets of paper and a pen or a dry-erase board. (Note that whatever notes you might take, you will be required to turn them in at the end of the exam.)

Odds are you'll be left alone at that point, but note that the exam has not yet started. On the computer's automated testing system, you'll be presented with a series of disclosures and agreements to review, and when you're ready, you can click a button to initiate the timed exam. The timer will start with the first question. A timer on the screen will track your remaining time as you progress through the exam.

All the questions will be multiple-choice questions. Many of the questions will require you to click a button to display an exhibit. The exhibit—once displayed by you—will probably pop up in a separate window, automatically sized just big enough to show whatever the exhibit is displaying. The exhibit may be an entity-relationship diagram, or it could be a listing of data that could have been the contents of a table or the output of a report. Many questions include SQL code.

During my exam experiences, I have noticed that many questions are often accompanied by a good number of diagrams or code or data output not necessarily relevant to the point of the question. Most questions will present to you, for example, an ERD and a data listing, as well as a brief explanation of some business rules or background, and finally ask the actual question. You'll eventually realize that you can waste a good amount of the time analyzing details of exhibits before you finally read the question, only to realize that you didn't need to study the entire exhibit after all. Many questions, once understood, can be answered at a glance of the ERD. So do yourself a favor: when you encounter a new question, skip past the code and the data output (the report, exhibit, or whatever) and skip ahead to the actual question, which is often the final sentence just before the multiple-choice answers are presented. Read the question and then go back and quickly skim the preceding material; you'll find that you can identify the answer much more quickly this way than by reading all the background material.

The questions will be presented on the screen one at a time. Click Next to advance to the next question. You can skip questions; you aren't required to answer each question before advancing. To flag a question for later review, each question display has an optional Mark check box in the upper-left corner, which you can use to "mark" any question for future reference, whether you have answered it or not.

Once you have progressed through all the questions, you will reach a summary screen showing the number corresponding to every question of the exam in a singular tabular listing. The questions will be identified by number only, and next to each number will be the letter—or letters—of the answers you have provided. Any question "marked" will be indicated by a highlighted *M* next to it. Any question not fully answered shows with a highlighted *I*—for "incomplete"—next to it. You'll be able to easily review and complete the answers and review any questions, including those you have marked, before you indicate that you have completed the exam.

One nuance to keep in mind occurs when you encounter a question with more than one correct answer. To score those questions, you will have to provide the correct number of correct answers. The question may state "choose the two correct answers," for example. You will have to provide two answers. If you try to provide three, the automated system will stop you. It will pop up a small message window telling you to first deselect an existing choice to ensure you provide no more than the correct number of answer selections.

But what happens if you select too few? For example, what happens when a question requires three answers but you select only two and then move on to the next question? Nothing in the system will stop you from taking that step. If you do that, you'll be leaving the question incomplete with—in this example—only two of the three required answers. You can always advance and leave any question "incomplete." However, before you can submit the exam for grading, you will be automatically presented with the summary screen at the end, in which any incomplete questions will be flagged clearly with an *I* for "incomplete." You will be able to go back and review.

When you are done with the questions and are satisfied that you have answered everything, click Exit on the summary screen. The test score will be instantly evaluated, and you may be shown your score and passing grade on the screen. If not, you'll probably be e-mailed the results within 24 hours.

At that point, pick up any papers you may have or locked bags containing your valuables such as your mobile phone, and visit the front desk of the testing center, where a clerk may provide you with a copy of your test results. The clerk can also unlock the container containing your mobile phone, which you can retrieve, and you can exit the facility knowing you have satisfied the requirements to become a happy Oracle Database SQL Certified Associate.

Oracle SQL vs. ANSI SQL

The certification exam will test you on Oracle SQL. Oracle SQL is close to, but not identical to, the standard established for SQL by the American National Standards Institute (ANSI), also known as ANSI-standard SQL. You will not be required to know the differences between them.

Oracle SQL vs. Oracle SQL*Plus

The certification exam will test you on Oracle SQL but not on Oracle's enhancements to SQL known as SQL*Plus, with two exceptions: the DESC command and substitution variables.

SQL*Plus is a set of commands, and it is also a software tool with an interface into which you can type SQL and SQL*Plus commands and monitor their execution. SQL*Plus commands include a large number of options, many of which are devoted to formatting output. Those commands are not included in the exam. You won't be studying SQL*Plus commands in this book, other than DESC and substitution variables.

Note that I will use the SQL*Plus command-line interface from time to time to demonstrate Oracle SQL commands.

SQL Fundamentals I vs. SQL Certified Associate

Since you're planning on obtaining your certification by taking the 1Z0-071 exam, then chances are you may have already looked at, or even taken, the 1Z0-051 exam, SQL Fundamentals I. The two exams share some common objectives, but 1Z0-071 goes beyond 1Z0-051. See Table 1-1 for a comparison of those objectives, including where the two exams are similar and where they are different. The table lists the objectives for 1Z0-051 on the left and 1Z0-071 on the right and lines up the rows to show where the exams share common objectives and where they vary from each other. Here are some examples:

- 1Z0-051 tests on the Cartesian product (6.4), but 1Z0-071 does not.
- Both exams test on the "Restricting and Sorting Data" objective and its three subobjectives, but 1Z0-071 adds two additional objectives to it, covering ampersand substitution and the SQL row limiting clause.
- Only 1Z0-071 tests on correlated subqueries, EXISTS, NOT EXISTS, and WITH, as well as the data dictionary, controlling user access, multitable inserts, and MERGE.
- Only 1Z0-071 tests on the objectives "Managing Objects Using Data Dictionary Views," "Controlling User Access," and "Manipulating Large Data Sets."

Those are just some examples of the information in Table 1-1. Note that Oracle does not number its objectives, so I took the liberty of assigning numbers to the objectives, respecting the sequence of the originally published list at Oracle's web site.

TABLE 1-1		Comparison of the 1Z0-051 and 1Z0-071 Exam Objectives (*Continued*)		
#	**1Z0-051, SQL Fundamentals I, Exam Objectives**	**#**	**1Z0-071, SQL Certified Associate, Exam Objectives**	
1.0	**Retrieving Data Using the SQL SELECT Statement**	**1.0**	**Oracle and Structured Query Language (SQL)**	
—		1.1	*Identify the connection between an ERD and a relational database*	
—		1.2	*Explain the relationship between a database and SQL*	
—		1.3	*Describe the purpose of DDL*	
—	*(See 9.1 for a comparable topic)*	1.4	*Describe the purpose of DML*	
1.1	*List the capabilities of SQL SELECT statements*	1.5	*Build a SELECT statement to retrieve data from an Oracle Database table*	
1.2	*Execute a basic SELECT statement*			
2.0	**Restricting and Sorting Data**	**2.0**	**Restricting and Sorting Data**	
2.1	*Limit the rows that are retrieved by a query*	2.2	*Limit the rows that are retrieved by a query*	
2.2	*Sort the rows that are retrieved by a query*	2.1	*Use the ORDER BY clause to sort SQL query results*	
—		2.3	*Use ampersand substitution to restrict and sort output at run time*	

TABLE 1-1   Comparison of the 1Z0-051 and 1Z0-071 Exam Objectives (*Continued*)

#	1Z0-051, SQL Fundamentals I, Exam Objectives	#	1Z0-071, SQL Certified Associate, Exam Objectives
—		2.4	*Use SQL row limiting clause*
3.0	**Using Single-Row Functions to Customize Output**	**3.0**	**Using Single-Row Functions to Customize Output**
3.1	*Describe various types of functions available in SQL*	3.1	*Use various types of functions available in SQL*
3.2	*Use character, number, and date functions in SELECT statements*	3.2a	*Use character, number, and date ...*
—		3.2b	*... and analytical (PERCENTILE_CONT, STDDEV, LAG, LEAD) functions in SELECT statements*
4.0	**Using Conversion Functions and Conditional Expressions**	**4.0**	**Using Conversion Functions and Conditional Expressions**
4.1	*Describe various types of conversion functions that are available in SQL*	4.1	*Describe various types of conversion functions that are available in SQL*
4.2	*Use the TO_CHAR, TO_NUMBER, and TO_DATE conversion functions*	4.2	*Use the TO_CHAR, TO_NUMBER, and TO_DATE conversion functions*
4.3	*Apply conditional expressions in a SELECT statement*	4.3	*Apply general functions and conditional expressions in a SELECT statement*
5.0	**Reporting Aggregated Data Using the Group Functions**	**5.0**	**Reporting Aggregated Data Using the Group Functions**
5.1	*Identify the available group functions*	—	
5.2	*Describe the use of group functions*	5.1	*Describe the use of group functions*
5.3	*Group data by using the GROUP BY clause*	5.2	*Group data by using the GROUP BY clause*
5.4	*Include or exclude grouped rows by using the HAVING clause*	5.3	*Include or exclude grouped rows by using the HAVING clause*
6.0	**Displaying Data from Multiple Tables**	**6.0**	**Displaying Data from Multiple Tables**
—		6.1	*Describe the different types of joins and their features*
6.1	*Write SELECT statements to access data from more than one table using equijoins and nonequijoins*	6.2	*Use SELECT statements to access data from more than one table using equijoins and nonequijoins*
6.2	*Join a table to itself by using a self-join*	6.3	*Join a table to itself by using a self-join*
6.3	*View data that generally does not meet a join condition by using outer joins*	6.4	*View data that generally does not meet a join condition by using outer joins*
6.4	*Generate a Cartesian product of all rows from two or more tables*	—	

TABLE 1-1	Comparison of the 1Z0-051 and 1Z0-071 Exam Objectives *(Continued)*

#	1Z0-051, SQL Fundamentals I, Exam Objectives	#	1Z0-071, SQL Certified Associate, Exam Objectives
7.0	**Using Subqueries to Solve Queries**	**7.0**	**Using Subqueries to Solve Queries**
7.1	*Define subqueries*	7.1	*Define subqueries*
7.2	*Describe the types of problems that the subqueries can solve*	7.2	*Describe the types of problems subqueries can solve*
7.3	*List the types of subqueries*	7.3	*Describe the types of subqueries*
—		7.4	*Query data using correlated subqueries*
—		7.5	*Update and delete rows using correlated subqueries*
—		7.6	*Use the EXISTS and NOT EXISTS operators*
—		7.7	*Use the WITH clause*
7.4	*Write single-row and multiple-row subqueries*	7.8	*Use single-row and multiple-row subqueries*
8.0	**Using the Set Operators**	**8.0**	**Using the Set Operators**
8.1	*Describe set operators*	8.1	*Describe set operators*
8.2	*Use a set operator to combine multiple queries into a single query*	8.2	*Use a set operator to combine multiple queries into a single query*
8.3	*Control the order of rows returned*	8.3	*Control the order of rows returned*
9.0	**Manipulating Data**	**9.0**	**Manipulating Data**
9.1	*Describe each data manipulation language (DML) statement*	—	*(See 1.4 for a comparable topic)*
—		9.1	*Truncate data*
9.2	*Insert rows into a table*	9.2	*Insert rows into a table*
9.3	*Update rows in a table*	9.3	*Update rows in a table*
9.4	*Delete rows from a table*	9.4	*Delete rows from a table*
9.5	*Control transactions*	9.5	*Control transactions*
10.0	**Using DDL Statements to Create and Manage Tables**	**10.0**	**Using DDL Statements to Create and Manage Tables**
10.1	*Categorize the main database objects*	—	
10.2	*Review the table structure*	—	
10.3	*List the data types that are available for columns*	10.1	*Describe data types that are available for columns*
10.4	*Create a simple table*	10.2	*Create a simple table*
10.5	*Explain how constraints are created at the time of table creation*	10.3	*Create constraints for tables*

TABLE 1-1   Comparison of the 1Z0-051 and 1Z0-071 Exam Objectives

#	1Z0-051, SQL Fundamentals I, Exam Objectives	#	1Z0-071, SQL Certified Associate, Exam Objectives
—		10.4	*Drop columns and set column UNUSED*
—		10.5	*Create and use external tables*
10.6	*Describe how schema objects work*	—	
—		**11.0**	**Managing Objects with Data Dictionary Views**
—		11.1	*Query various data dictionary views*
—		**12.0**	**Controlling User Access**
—		12.1	*Differentiate system privileges from object privileges*
—		12.2	*Grant privileges on tables and on a user*
—		12.3	*Distinguish between privileges and roles*
11.0	**Creating Other Schema Objects**	**13.0**	**Managing Schema Objects**
—		13.1	*Describe how schema objects work*
11.1	*Create simple and complex views*	13.2a	*Create simple and complex views ...*
—		13.2b	*... with visible/invisible columns*
11.2	*Retrieve data from views*	—	
11.3	*Create, maintain, and use sequences*	13.3	*Create, maintain, and use sequences*
11.4	*Create and maintain indexes*	13.4a	*Create and maintain indexes ...*
—		13.4b	*... including invisible indexes and multiple indexes on the same columns*
11.5	*Create private and public synonyms*	—	
—		13.5	*Perform flashback operations*
—		**14.0**	**Manipulating Large Data Sets**
—		14.1	*Describe the features of multitable INSERTs*
—		14.2	*Merge rows in a table*

As you can see, the SQL Certified Associate exam goes further than the topics addressed by the SQL Fundamentals I exam.

The SQL Fundamentals I exam consists of 64 questions in 120 minutes; SQL Associate consists of 73 questions within 100 minutes. At the time of this writing, the passing score requirements published at the Oracle.com web site are

- 60 percent for SQL Fundamentals I
- 63 percent for SQL Associate

However, note that passing score requirements are subject to change without notice. Oracle Corporation reserves the right to substitute one version of the test with another version, and depending on the complexity of the specific questions included in a new version, the passing score may be adjusted accordingly. Oracle publishes this notice on its web site regarding the required passing score for any given exam:

Oracle routinely publishes new versions of its Oracle Certification exams. The passing score for each exam version is set independently to maintain a consistent scoring standard across versions. For example, to maintain a consistent standard for success, a new version of an exam which contains more difficult questions than the prior version will be assigned a somewhat lower required passing score. For this reason, passing scores may vary between different exams in your certification track, and between later and earlier versions of the same exam. Oracle does not recommend an exam preparation strategy targeting the passing score, as passing scores are subject to change without notice.

In other words, study well, and don't limit your goal to simply achieving the minimal passing score requirement. Instead, do the best you possibly can to increase your chances of victory.

Subject Areas

Many questions challenge your knowledge of several facts at once. For example, I encountered one question that presented several nested scalar functions in a series of SELECT statements. I had to do the following:

- Understand clearly what each individual scalar function did
- Recognize syntax issues throughout the code
- Understand the data type transformations as one function passed on results to another
- Confirm whether the parameter positioning was accurate
- Identify two facts about the process and end result, all within the context of the given ERD

The moral to the story is that you should study this book well, understand everything listed in the certification objectives, and get all of your facts down cold. On test day, show up rested and on time and don't get distracted. With each question, seek out the actual question first and then look at the exhibits and code listings. And watch the time.

You'll be glad you did.

Confirm Appropriate Materials for Study

This section discusses some items you may want to gather as you prepare to study for the exam. If you are a seasoned veteran in the SQL business, you may not need any of it—this book will suffice. But if you'd like to put forth that extra bit of effort, it might be a good idea to get your software and documentation together as described in this section.

Software

Oracle Corporation states that it has validated the 1Z0-071 exam questions against Oracle Database 11*g* Release 2 (11.2.0.1.0) and up to 12*c* Release 1 (12.1.0.1.0). I used version 12*c*, Release 1, in preparing the SQL statements for this book.

If you don't have the software you need, you can download it from the official Oracle Corporation web site, at www.oracle.com.

If you haven't joined the Oracle Technology Network (OTN), then you should do it right away. There is no charge for it. Visit www.oracle.com/technetwork/ and sign up today. From there, you can download a great deal of Oracle software for evaluation and study, including the database itself.

If you install the personal version of Oracle, you'll probably get SQL*Plus and SQL Developer, either of which you can use for entering and executing SQL statements. If not, then be sure to download one or the other to install and use with the database. You'll need one or both of those or, if not them, then some sort of tool for entering and executing SQL commands. Chances are you already have something that you're using or else you probably wouldn't be considering certification.

Oracle's Tools for Working with SQL

Most of Oracle's various products and tools use SQL. This includes Oracle products such as Oracle Fusion Middleware, including Oracle SOA Suite, as well as Oracle APEX and others. Many development tools, such as Oracle JDeveloper, provide the ability to enter SQL statements and execute them. Two of the most commonly used tools for this purpose are Oracle's SQL*Plus command-line interface and Oracle SQL Developer.

The SQL*Plus Command-Line Interface   The SQL*Plus command-line
interface is a simple way to type SQL commands, execute them, and observe the
result. It is a universal system that operates the same way in every operating system.

See Figure 1-1 for an example of what the command-line interface looks like.

The advantage to the command-line interface is that it functions identically
in the Windows, Unix, and Linux operating systems. That is one of the many
advantages that Oracle has always offered—ease of use in any operating system.

SQL Developer   The SQL Developer interface is an interactive, point-and-click,
menu-driven graphical user interface (GUI) that is powerful and gives developers
a quick overview of the entire database. Some commands can be entered by either
typing them or using a point-and-click interaction with a graphic menu. See
Figure 1-2 for an example of what SQL Developer looks like.

There are other tools that process SQL statements:

- Oracle JDeveloper
- Oracle Application Express
- SQL Workshop
- Others

For the purposes of the certification exam, your choice of interface is irrelevant.
SQL statements execute correctly in all Oracle interfaces.

FIGURE 1-1   The SQL*Plus command-line interface

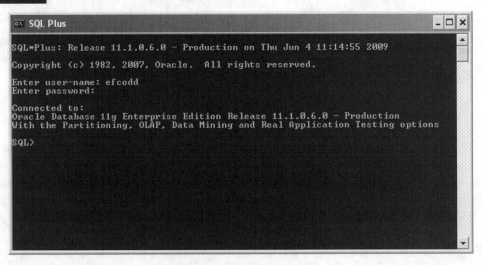

FIGURE 1-2   The SQL Developer tool

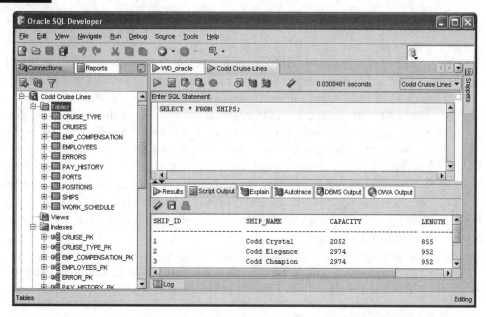

The exam will test your knowledge of the syntax of SQL, not your ability to point and click your way through a GUI. The fact that you might be able to create a SQL table using a code generator through a point-and-click interface will not help you during the exam. If you are a serious applications architect/programmer, there will come a time—probably frequently—when you need to design or program a feature as part of a larger application and design and embed SQL code into other programming languages that have no access to the nice GUI tools during application run time. Furthermore, as you'll see in numerous instances in this book,

there are many types of SQL statements in which you can combine features and clauses in such a way that they appear to be correct, execute without error, and produce lots of output—all of which can be totally erroneous. A trained eye glancing at the SQL code will recognize the mistake; an untrained eye will not even realize there is a problem. In other words, there is no alternative to having comprehensive knowledge of the syntax of SQL, neither in the world of the serious software developer nor on the certification exam. Know your syntax. As you study for this exam, type your commands, make sure they are correct, and make sure you understand them thoroughly.

Documentation

The book you have in your hands is an outstanding reference and is all you need in the way of documentation. This book is the single best guide you could possibly get to prepare you for taking the exam.

But if you crave more, you can download additional documentation from the Oracle Technology Network web site, at www.oracle.com/technetwork/. The amount of documentation is almost overwhelming, particularly to a newcomer. But one volume in particular is of interest for the purpose of the certification exam: the *SQL Language Reference Manual.* It is a huge book, with close to 2,000 pages. The size of the PDF version is more than 14MB. Its syntax charts are complex and go beyond the needs of the exam. The book contains far more information than what you'll need to pass, all of which is yet another reason why you're brilliant to have obtained this book you now have in your hands. I will refer to the *SQL Language Reference Manual* from time to time, but I will focus only on the parts that are relevant to pass the exam.

Other useful references include Oracle's Advanced Application Developer's Guide, Concepts, Security Guide, Globalization Support, and Administrator's Guide.

The questions for exam 1Z0-071 have been tested against the following:

- Oracle Database 11*g* Release 2
- Oracle Database 12*c* Release 1

I will refer to the set of manuals for Oracle Database 12*c*, Release 1, which is also referred to as 12.1.

CERTIFICATION OBJECTIVE 1.02

Identify the Connection Between an ERD and a Relational Database

For the remainder of this book, I will examine each of the objectives of the exam itself in detail. In this section I discuss the concept of an entity-relationship diagram and talk about how it is transformed into a relational database. Along the way I'll discuss business requirements, data modeling, the role of primary and foreign keys, and the concept of data normalization.

Entity-Relationship Diagrams and Data Modeling

Generally speaking, the reason a database exists is to support an existing business process or model some existing real-world system. For example, a typical business has employees who serve customers by providing some sort of product or service. If you are tasked with the responsibility of building an automated business system, you might create a data model of the business's operations. To create the data model, you identify the business's basic "things" (or *entities*). An entity might be a customer, an employee, or a product. You might add more abstract concepts as entities, such as an order, a return, a transaction, a customer's store visit, and so on.

As you identify your entities, you'll need to determine the relationships among those entities in terms of one-to-one, one-to-many, or many-to-many relationships. For example, you'll probably allow for any one customer to place zero-to-many orders. Why would you have a customer with no orders? It depends on your business rules—you may want to track potential customers who have asked for a print copy of your catalog but perhaps haven't yet ordered anything.

You'll probably want to allow for any one order to consist of multiple line items, each of which is taken from your master list of available products. Each one-line item may be returned—but no more than once and ideally not at all.

See Figure 1-3 for an example entity-relationship diagram illustrating this initial data model.

This example ERD shows five entities and the relationships between them. Each entity is a box; each relationship is a line connecting two boxes with some symbols to detail the nature of the relationship. For example, any one customer will have zero, one, or many orders. This is indicated in between Customers and Orders by the line that shows the circle (zero) with the crow's foot (many) on the side of the line connecting to Orders. The circle and crow's foot specify that there may be zero-to-many orders for any given customer.

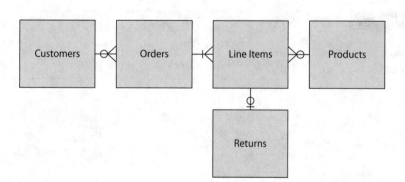

FIGURE 1-3

Entity-relationship diagram

For any one row in Orders, there may be one-to-many Line Items entries, indicated by the line (one) with the crow's foot (many) near the Line Items entity on the line from the Orders entity.

Any one Products entry may be ordered zero-to-many times as a Line Item. And a single Line Items row may be returned zero-to-one time, indicated by the circle (zero) and bar (one) at the Returns entity.

Once you've established the initial set of entities and their relationships, you might enhance your ERD with the addition of "attributes" to each entity. See Figure 1-4.

For example, for each customer you might want to track the customer's name and contact information such as an e-mail address and mailing address. For each order, you'll want to capture the order date and perhaps the terms of payment. For each line item, you'll want to know the quantity ordered and perhaps a discount for the particular line item, if appropriate.

Let's consider another example. The fictional Codd Cruise Lines is a company that provides cruise vacations to its customers. The company operates ships, and each ship is assigned to a single home port. Each ship is filled with cabins that customers reserve for their cruise vacations. The company has employees who are assigned to one ship at a time.

Figure 1-5 is an example of what an ERD for this cruise line might look like.

The example shows that for each port, there are one or more ships, and conversely, each ship is assigned to one and only one home port. Each ship has zero or more employees, suggesting that you might start tracking ships in your data model before they have employees assigned to them—perhaps while the ship is still under construction, in maintenance, and not in service. Also, each ship consists of one or more cabins.

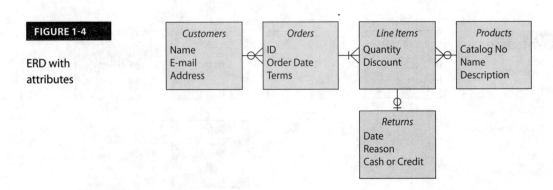

FIGURE 1-4

ERD with attributes

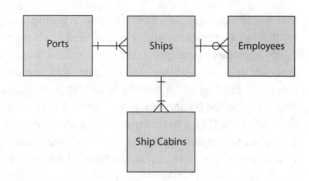

ERD for Codd
Cruise Lines,
initial

If you were to start assigning attributes to the entities, you might end up with the example shown in Figure 1-6.

For example, for each ship you might want to capture the ship's size and capacity. For each employee you might want to track the employee's name, start date, and current salary. What happens when the employee gets a raise—do you retain a record of the historic salary? Not in this example data model, but you could extend the model by adding an entity for "salary history" or something comparable and then assign that entity some attributes, such as salary amount, initial date, and final date of service at that salary, and perhaps you could even record the individual authority in the organization who granted that salary in the first place.

There is no single absolute right or wrong way to model a real-world business process. The appropriate model will vary based on what you intend to capture and how you intend to work with the system. The final authority is the set of

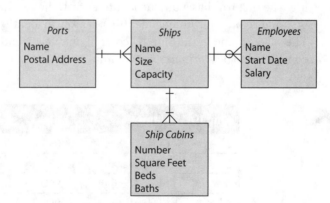

ERD for Codd
Cruise Lines, with
attributes

real-world business requirements you are supporting. Your data model is an attempt to represent those real-world business requirements.

For example, in the fictional Codd Cruise Lines, you are capturing home ports to which ships are assigned. In the real world, there exist many thousands of ports. Are you intending to capture them all? No, not in this model, because it isn't necessary for the business. Are you intending to capture every port to which your ships will travel? Not in this model. You are intending to capture only the home ports. But you could modify the model if your business requirements changed and your intended purpose of your automated system were to change. The purpose of a data model is not to represent every possibility that exists in the real world but to capture that necessary subset to which the automated system will provide support.

Relational Databases

Now let's start to use an ERD to capture some actual data. Remember that an ERD is a logical representation of a real-world system. A relational database is a physical implementation of that ERD and, as such, will need to capture actual data. The relational database builds on the entities and their relationships by specifying attributes of the entities. In the relational database, you'll add primary keys to uniquely identify each row within each entity. You may also add foreign keys to some entities to relate the rows of that entity to another entity's rows.

Let's look at how this works. Consider Table 1-2, which shows a list of ships with the fictional Codd Cruise Lines. This list is what you might use to create a database table. The list has columns for Ship ID and attributes of the Ships entity. The reason you need a Ship ID is to make sure you have a unique identifier for each row in the list. The first row has a unique identifier of 1, the second row has a unique identifier of 2, and so on. This unique identifier is a *key* to identifying a particular ship's row. The values found in the Ship ID column uniquely identify each ship. This column is considered to be a *primary key* column.

TABLE 1-2

Codd Cruise Lines Ships

Ship ID	Name	Size	Capacity
1	Codd Crystal	855	2,052
2	Codd Elegance	952	2,974
3	Codd Champion	952	2,974
4	Codd Victorious	952	2,974

TABLE 1-3	Employee ID	Name	Start Date	Salary	Ship ID
	1	Joe Smith	2016-08-20	75,000	3
Codd Cruise	2	Mike West	2015-12-01	77,000	4
Lines Employees	3	Alice Lindon	2017-04-02	85,000	3

Now, let's say you also want to create a list of employees. You'll create a primary key called Employee ID and capture all the attributes of our Employees entity, along with something additional: Ship ID. See Table 1-3.

Now, if I were to ask you to identify the ship to which Mike West was assigned, what would you say?

Naturally you would (or should) say it was the Codd Victorious, and you would determine this by looking in the list of employees, finding the record for Mike West, "relating" that record's Ship ID value to the list of ships, and finding that Ship ID 4 "relates" to the ship named Codd Victorious.

Ship ID is the *foreign key* for Employees. A foreign key for a given table points to the primary key of another table—in this case, Ships—to indicate which row relates to the current row.

These lists are what you will store in database tables. And the data contained within the lists are examples of the sort of data that a relational database might contain in tables and the sort of processing it does to "relate" data in one table to data in another table.

A typical database consists of any number of tables, many of which contain key information (such as the Employee ID and Ship ID values in the figures) that is used to *relate* rows of one table to rows of another table. The mechanism used to identify a unique row within a list is a *primary key,* and you use a *foreign key* to relate data from one table to another.

- The PRIMARY KEY is a unique identifier for a row in a particular table.
- The FOREIGN KEY is a copy of some (or all) of one table's PRIMARY KEY data in a second table so that the second table can relate to the first.

Many-to-Many Relationships

One of the most common challenges in transforming a logical model into a typical transactional physical model has to do with the situation of a many-to-many relationship between two entities. Remember that the nature of the relationship between two entities is defined by the requirements of the business model. In the earlier example of the fictional Codd Cruise Lines, the business requirement was only to track an employee's currently assigned ship. But what if the requirement were different? What if you needed to track all ships to which an employee were eligible to work? This would suggest that any one employee could be associated with zero or more ships, and any one ship could be associated with zero or more employees.

Why zero-or-more? It depends on the business logic—let's say you decide you want to start tracking ships before employees are assigned and you capture information about employees who aren't necessarily assigned to ships. Because of those business rules, you'll go with the zero-to-many relationships in both directions. However, if the business doesn't have these requirements, then you might require one-to-many relationships instead—it depends on the business requirements.

But regardless of whether these are zero- or one-to-many in either direction, this particular approach to the business results in two entities with a many-to-many relationship to each other; see Figure 1-7.

The example shows that the ships-to-employees relationship is many-to-many, meaning that you have one-to-many relationships in both directions: one employee may be assigned to multiple ships, and one ship may have multiple employees assigned to it.

The presence of a many-to-many relationship in an ERD is a major flag in a data model. The message: the data model is missing an entity. While it's fine to show a many-to-many relationship as you are in the process of building a draft model, there is never a many-to-many relationship in a finished physical model. The reason: it doesn't work. Imagine trying to transform this into the sort of lists— or tables—you just looked at in the previous example. Try to create your own lists—one of ships, another of employees. Assign primary key values to each list.

FIGURE 1-7

Many-to-many
relationship

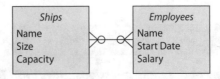

FIGURE 1-8

Many-to-many
relationship
transformed

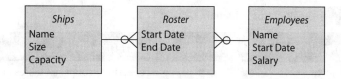

Then try to figure out how you're going to make the foreign key assignments. You could try to add one foreign key column to one table and then the other—even both. But you'll drive yourself crazy trying to list the data so that each row of ships is listed once, each employee is listed once, and there are foreign keys to represent the multiple interrelationships that might exist. It won't work.

Here's what works: a third entity. See Figure 1-8. The presence of a many-to-many relationship between two entities is always an indication that a third entity belongs in between, and it's often an entity that is more abstract in nature. In this case, name the entity Roster and use it to list each assignment of any given employee to any given ship, along with start and stop dates of when the employee is assigned to work on the ship. This enables you to list as many repeating lines as required for any given ship—once for every employee assigned—and to do the same thing in the other direction, listing every employee's assignment to ship after ship, as many as is required.

This is standard operating procedure when building an ERD and preparing to build a relational database.

Database Normalization

Good database design requires consideration for data normalization. A full analysis of the concept of database normalization is beyond the task of this book, which is to prepare you for the exam. But it is worth noting the *rules of normalization,* which are rules that drive the design of any set of tables composing a relational database.

Table 1-4 summarizes the most common levels of normalization.

A database adheres to the first normal form (1NF) when tables are structured in a one-to-many relationship. For example, in the earlier example of ships and employees, it would have been a violation of 1NF if you had instead placed all the ship names in the EMPLOYEES table and repeated each ship's name with each record of each employee that might happen to be assigned to that ship. By separating ship and employee data, you satisfied the requirement for 1NF.

Second normal form (2NF) exists when no nonkey attribute (column) is dependent upon part of a composite key.

| TABLE 1-4 | | Levels of Normalization |

Level of Normal Form	Abbreviation	Characterized By
First normal form	1NF	No repeating groups; all tables are two-dimensional.
Second normal form	2NF	1NF plus each data element is identified by one corresponding unique identifier—a *primary key*—that is not a composite and therefore cannot be subdivided into smaller bits of data.
Third normal form	3NF	2NF plus all tables contain no data other than that which describes the intent of the primary key; extraneous data is placed in separate tables.
Boyce-Codd	BCNF	A slightly modified version of 3NF designed to eliminate structures that might allow some rare logical inconsistencies to appear in the data.
Fourth normal form	4NF	BCNF plus additional logic to ensure that every multivalued dependency is dependent on a superkey.
Fifth normal form	5NF	4NF plus every join dependency for the table is a result of the candidate keys.

Third normal form (3NF) is when the one-to-many relationships within a data model are strictly respected—that is, when many-to-many relationships are each transformed into one-to-many-to-one relationships as you just did in the previous section. 3NF requires that primary key values are associated only with logically related attributes, and other data—such as lookup data—is moved to separate tables.

3NF designs are ideal where lots of data entry and updates are involved, as their design minimizes the possible duplication of data and the associated risk of data conflicts, resulting in conflicting data within the database. For example, if a customer address is stored in multiple locations and the customer contacts the organization with a new address, you don't want to run the risk that the new address is revised in one location but not elsewhere. 3NF reduces and even eliminates such risk.

1NF and 2NF favor heavy read-only use cases. For example, if you need to produce reports that connect (or join) the customer address with the customer order history and the items ordered, then the less your query has to go searching in different tables, the faster your report will execute. For systems with millions of records, lots of complex querying, and no need to add new data or update existing records, 1NF and 2NF offer faster execution without the downside risk of conflicting data that might exist in a 3NF.

For these reasons, generally speaking, most transaction-based database applications are designed to be 3NF. Data warehouses and other applications intended to support analysis and reporting are generally designed at 2NF or 1NF. Many "big data" systems are designed to work with 2NF or 1NF models.

Most data enters an organization through a transaction-based system (a 3NF) and is then moved into a data warehouse or data lake for analysis (a 2NF or 1NF). For this reason, 3NF is seen as a starting point for most data, and 1NF or 2NF models are said to be *denormalized*, which is to say that they adhere to some level of normalization below 3NF. "Big data" systems are often described as denormalized since they tend to adhere to 1NF or 2NF design.

Nothing in the exam objectives nor in my experience of having taken the exam indicates that the test involves anything other than typical third normal form scenarios.

These descriptions are merely a refresher and are not intended to be an exhaustive analysis of database normalization. For that, I refer you to other books in the Oracle Press line that deal with the fundamentals of database design.

on the **Job**   *There is no single right or wrong way to model every system. Some design decisions involve trade-offs, such as better performance (speed of response) versus less duplicate data, or an efficient data model versus a more complex application. These are just some of the challenges a data modeler or SQL developer faces.*

CERTIFICATION OBJECTIVE 1.03

Explain the Relationship Between a Database and SQL

A relational database is a physical representation of a business system. It is sometimes described as a *persistent* store, meaning that it is used to retain information that might be generated or captured when a software application is executing, but it retains that data after the application has ceased execution—the data "persists" beyond the life of a given application. A database houses data outside of the application itself and makes that data available to any authorized inquiring software application or service.

SQL is the industry-standard language for creating and interacting with a relational database. SQL is a mechanism to create and interact with the database; it is not the database itself. SQL commands can be used on a stand-alone basis, or they can be invoked from within other applications written in other languages. Most popular software languages, such Java, PHP, and others, have the capability to issue SQL statements to a relational database. Those languages will have the ability to transfer their own data into SQL statements, send the SQL statement to a database for processing, and then capture the returning data for additional processing.

A number of tools exist that enable a developer or other database user to issue SQL statements. For example, Oracle's SQL*Plus and SQL Developer tools empower a user to build and execute SQL statements to build and interact with databases. These tools issue SQL statements and receive output the same as any software language or other client application might do.

So how do you pronounce SQL? Some people pronounce it by spelling out the letters, as in "ess-cue-ell." Most of us pronounce it as "sequel." Both pronunciations are fine, and both are used by respected professionals in the industry. Whatever you do, just don't call it "squeal."

on the job

I once had a guy call the office looking for a job, and he claimed that he had five years of experience with "Squeal." He didn't get the job. Don't be that guy.

SQL is a language to

- Create databases and the objects within them
- Store data in those databases
- Change and analyze that data
- Get that data back out in reports, web pages, or virtually any other use imaginable

There are many SQL statements. Table 1-5 shows some of those that are more commonly used. For each statement shown in this table, there are many clauses, parameters, and other additional features for each one. Later in the book, you will look in great detail at each command that is covered by the exam.

All SQL statements are categorized into one of six types. Table 1-6 shows the six types of SQL statements in Oracle SQL. As you can see in the table, the exam ignores many SQL statements. Naturally you are concerned only with the exam, so in this book you will look at only three types of SQL statements: Data Definition Language, Data Manipulation Language, and Transaction Control Language.

TABLE 1-5

Some of the
More Commonly
Used SQL
Statements

SQL Command	Description
SELECT	Retrieves data from a table
INSERT	Adds new data to a table
UPDATE	Modifies existing data in a table
DELETE	Removes existing data from a table
CREATE object_type	Creates a new database object, such as a table
ALTER object_type	Modifies the structure of an object, such as a table
DROP object_type	Removes an existing database object, such as a table

TABLE 1-6   Six Types of SQL Statements in Oracle SQL

#	Abbrev.	Type of SQL Statement	SQL Statements and Reserved Words	
			Covered by the Exam	Ignored by the Exam
1	DDL	Data Definition Language	CREATE ALTER (1) DROP RENAME TRUNCATE GRANT REVOKE FLASHBACK PURGE COMMENT	ANALYZE AUDIT ASSOCIATE STATISTICS DISASSOCIATE NOAUDIT
2	DML	Data Manipulation Language	SELECT INSERT UPDATE DELETE MERGE	CALL LOCK TABLE EXPLAIN PLAN
3	TCL	Transaction Control Language	COMMIT ROLLBACK SAVEPOINT	SET TRANSACTION SET CONSTRAINT
4		Session Control Statements		ALTER SESSION SET ROLE
5		System Control Statements		ALTER SYSTEM
6		Embedded SQL Statements		Any DML, DDL, or TCL that is integrated into a third-generation language (3GL)

(1) Except ALTER SYSTEM and ALTER SESSION, which are categorized under "System Control Statements" and "Session Control Statements," respectively

CERTIFICATION OBJECTIVE 1.04

Describe the Purpose of DDL

Data Definition Language consists of those SQL statements that are used to build database objects. Specifically, DDL statements are used to

- Create, alter, and drop tables and other database objects
- Add comments on a particular object to be stored in the database and associated with that object
- Issue privileges to users to perform various tasks in the database
- Initiate performance analysis on objects using built-in tools

The following list briefly describes DDL statements that are tested by the exam:

- **CREATE**   Used to create a user, table, view, index, synonym, or other object in the database.
- **ALTER**   Used on an existing object in the database to modify that object's structure, name, or some other attribute. (Two exceptions are the uses of ALTER with the reserved words SESSION and SYSTEM. ALTER SESSION and ALTER SYSTEM are not technically considered DDL statements but fall under a different category. Neither is included on this exam.)
- **DROP**   Used to remove a database object from the database that has already been created with the CREATE statement.
- **RENAME**   Changes the name of an existing database object.
- **TRUNCATE**   Removes all the rows—in other words, data—from an existing table in the database. TRUNCATE is something of a brute-force alternative to the DELETE statement, in that TRUNCATE gives up recovery options offered by DELETE in exchange for faster performance. These differences in approach are the reason TRUNCATE is categorized as DDL while DELETE is DML.
- **GRANT**   Provides *privileges,* or rights, to user objects to enable them to perform various tasks in the database.
- **REVOKE**   Removes privileges that have been issued with the GRANT statement.
- **FLASHBACK**   Restores an earlier version of a table or database.

- **PURGE**   Irrevocably removes database objects from the recycle bin.
- **COMMENT**   Adds comments to the data dictionary for an existing database object.

Each DDL statement is rich with options and clauses. I will review and provide examples of most of these statements as you progress through the book.

SQL keywords, such as CREATE, are not really "commands" or "statements" by themselves but become commands when combined with other reserved words, as in CREATE TABLE or CREATE SEQUENCE, which are commands or statements. In practice, CREATE can be called a statement *or* command *by professionals in the field, and even by Oracle Corporation in various forms of documentation. Technically there is a difference. However, this isn't an issue on the exam. Similarly, the terms* command *and* statement *tend to be used interchangeably by Oracle's documentation. If you conduct some searches in the* SQL Language Reference Manual, *you'll find plenty of examples of SQL statements being referred to as commands. Either is fine. And none of these issues is a concern on the exam.*

CERTIFICATION OBJECTIVE 1.05

Describe the Purpose of DML

DML refers to those statements in SQL that are used to work with data in the objects. DML statements are used to add, modify, view, and delete data in a database object, such as a table.

The following list briefly describes each DML statement that is tested by the exam:

- **SELECT**   Displays data of a database table or view
- **INSERT**   Adds data to a database table, either directly or, in some situations, through a view
- **UPDATE**   Modifies existing data in a table, either directly or, in some situations, through a view
- **DELETE**   Removes existing data from a table, either directly or, in some situations, through a view
- **MERGE**   Performs a combination of INSERT, UPDATE, and DELETE statements in a single statement

The SELECT statement is rather involved and will get several chapters' worth of review. The other DML statements are reviewed in this chapter and in various sections that follow.

Transaction Control Language

In addition to these DML statements, three more SQL statements are important for working with DML. These statements are not part of DML but instead are categorized as TCL. These statements are specifically identified by Oracle within the certification objectives for DML, so I'll discuss them in this chapter. These are the statements you need to study:

- **COMMIT**   Saves a set of DML modifications performed in the current database session
- **ROLLBACK**   Undoes a set of DML modifications performed during the current database session
- **SAVEPOINT**   Marks a position in a session to prepare for a future ROLLBACK to enable that ROLLBACK to restore data at a selected point in a session other than the most recent commit event

In addition to the explicit COMMIT command, any DDL statement will cause an implied commit action to occur. In other words, if you issue an UPDATE statement on table A and then issue a GRANT statement to user B for accessing table C, an implied commit event will occur, and the data you updated to table A will be committed, even though you haven't issued an explicit COMMIT.

CERTIFICATION OBJECTIVE 1.06

Build a SELECT Statement to Retrieve Data from an Oracle Database Table

Let's look at a simple example. Consider the ships listed earlier in Table 1-2. A valid SQL command to create a table in which you could store that information might look like this:

```
CREATE TABLE SHIPS
(SHIP_ID              NUMBER,
  SHIP_NAME           VARCHAR2(20),
  CAPACITY            NUMBER,
  LENGTH              NUMBER );
```

I say "might" look like this because there are a number of options you could include here, including primary or foreign key declarations, data filtering, storage assignment, and other options that go beyond this simple example. You'll look at many of those options later in the book. But this code sample works in an Oracle SQL database.

Next, here's a SQL command to add a sample record to this table:

```
INSERT INTO SHIPS (SHIP_ID, SHIP_NAME, CAPACITY, LENGTH)
VALUES (1,'Codd Crystal', 2052, 855);
```

Again, this is a valid command, albeit a simplified version. It inserts one record of information about one ship into the new table SHIPS.

Finally, let's create a SQL command to display the contents of the newly populated SQL table.

```
SELECT     SHIP_NAME, CAPACITY, LENGTH
FROM       SHIPS;
```

If all has gone correctly, you should get a display that appears something like the display in Figure 1-9. (Note: Figure 1-9 shows the output in the Oracle tool SQL Developer.)

As you can see, the data is stored in the table, and it is still there. SELECT merely displays the data; it doesn't change the data at all. At its simplest level, this is what SQL is all about—writing statements to create database objects and then working with those objects to store and retrieve data.

FIGURE 1-9

Output of the sample SQL SELECT statement

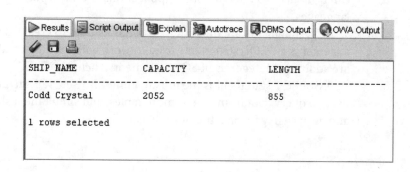

The SELECT statement is a powerful SQL statement that can be used to query data from one or more tables in a single statement. A single SELECT statement can be used to transform data, aggregate data, join multiple tables, filter out unwanted data, and much more. The rest of this book looks in detail at a variety of SQL statements as they pertain to the certification exam.

CERTIFICATION SUMMARY

The certification exam is a timed, multiple-choice exam that will test you using entity-relationship diagrams, code examples, and more. It will challenge you with questions pertaining to the correct use of syntax, the logical results of SQL statements, and the use of various functions and other capabilities of SQL. This book is the ideal tool for exam preparation. You should also have access to a functional installation of Oracle software that you can obtain from Oracle's web site.

The act of modeling a real-world business system often includes the creation of a data model, which is depicted in an entity-relationship diagram. When building a relational database, entities are transformed into tables, and an entity's attributes are implemented as the table's columns. A given entity's rows are uniquely identified using a primary key, and foreign keys can be used to establish a relationship between one table and another. Database normalization is the practice of designing your data model to serve your business application at an optimal level. The third normal form indicates your data model is free of duplicate data, uses primary keys to uniquely identify a set of attributes, and has fully transformed any many-to-many relationships into one-to-many combinations.

SQL is the most widely used language for interacting with relational databases. The language can be used to create and interact with databases. SQL statements can be issued from within other applications and incorporated with various languages.

DDL statements are those SQL statements used to create database objects. DML statements are SQL statements used to work with existing database objects. There are additional categories of SQL statements, including TCL.

A SELECT statement is the most commonly used SQL statement and can be used to query data from one or more tables, and simultaneously it can transform and even aggregate data that it returns.

TWO-MINUTE DRILL

The Exam: An Overview

- ☐ This chapter provides introductory material that is important to understand in preparing for the exam.
- ☐ The 1Z0-071 exam, Oracle Database SQL Certified Associate, which is the subject of this exam guide, has 14 certification objective categories. It shares 11 objectives with another exam, 1Z0-051, SQL Fundamentals I. But 1Z0-071 goes into more detail in those objectives and adds three more. Also, 1Z0-071 tends to emphasize the objectives and subobjectives not addressed on 1Z0-051.
- ☐ The exam includes 73 questions and allows 100 minutes to complete them. That is an average of about 82 seconds per question.
- ☐ This book will prepare you to study and successfully take and pass the exam.
- ☐ Oracle's *SQL Language Reference Manual* is overkill as an exam study guide, as it contains far more than you'll need for the exam. But it is a good reference companion to this book.

Identify the Connection Between an ERD and a Relational Database

- ☐ The ERD is a logical model of an existing business.
- ☐ The entities in an ERD are the "things" that form the basis of a business information system and that are transformed into tables in a database.
- ☐ The ERD is a logical representation of a business; the relational database is the physical model in which actual data can be housed and processed in support of the business process.

Explain the Relationship Between a Database and SQL

- ☐ A database is a persistent store of information that continues—or *persists*—beyond the execution of a given application.
- ☐ SQL is the most widely used language for interacting with a database.
- ☐ SQL statements can be issued by any one or more applications to a single database. Those applications can be written in a variety of languages that support SQL calls, including software written in languages such as Java, PHP, and others.

Describe the Purpose of DDL

☐ DDL statements include CREATE, ALTER, and DROP.

☐ DDL statements are a subset of SQL and are used to create new database objects or alter the structure of existing database objects, including removing them.

Describe the Purpose of DML

☐ DML statements include SELECT, UPDATE, and INSERT.

☐ DML statements are a subset of SQL and are used to work with existing database objects.

Build a SELECT Statement to Retrieve Data from an Oracle Database Table

☐ The SELECT statement is the most commonly used SQL statement.

☐ SELECT can be used to query data from a single table or join data together in two or more tables to return data that is logically connected.

☐ SELECT can be used with functions and other capabilities to transform data in various ways, which is discussed at length later in this book.

SELF TEST

The following questions will help you measure your understanding of the material presented in this chapter. The first five questions test you on the background information I discussed earlier to prepare you for the exam. The remaining questions begin to test you on the specific objectives of the exam itself. Furthermore, these questions are written in the style and format of the certification exam, so they can be good practice to help you get going. As is the case with the exam, some of these self test questions may have more than one correct answer, so read carefully. Choose all the correct answers for each question.

The Exam: An Overview

1. Which of the following topics are not included in the SQL Fundamentals I exam but are addressed on the SQL Associate exam? (Choose all that apply.)
   A. MERGE
   B. Conversion functions
   C. FLASHBACK
   D. External tables

2. If you focus on trying to achieve the minimum passing grade requirement for the exam, you can study more efficiently.
   A. True
   B. False

3. The exam is timed.
   A. True
   B. False

4. The 1Z0-071 exam (which is the subject of this book) has been officially validated by Oracle Corporation against which of the following versions of the Oracle database? (Choose all that apply.)
   A. Every version
   B. 9*i*
   C. 11*g*
   D. 12*c*

5. The best exam guide you could possibly get for preparing to take and pass the 1Z0-071 certification exam, SQL Associate, is which of the following? (Choose all that apply.)
   A. This book.
   B. The book you are holding right now.
   C. This here book.
   D. Don't make me tell you again.

Identify the Connection Between an ERD and a Relational Database

6. When transforming an ERD into a relational database, you often use an entity to build a database's:
   A. Table
   B. Column
   C. Attribute
   D. Relationship

7. The unique identifier of a row in a database table is a(n):
   A. ID
   B. Primary key
   C. Primary column
   D. Column

Explain the Relationship Between a Database and SQL

8. Which of the following is true of SQL?
   A. It is the most commonly used language for interacting with a database.
   B. It is the only language you can use to create a database.
   C. It is the only language you can use to interact with a database.
   D. None of the above

9. What can you use to submit SQL statements for execution? (Choose all that apply.)
   A. PHP
   B. Java
   C. SQL Developer
   D. SQL*Plus

Describe the Purpose of DDL

10. What is one of the purposes of DDL? (Choose the best answer.)
    A. Query data from a given table
    B. Issue privileges to users

    C.   Remove existing data from a database table

    D.   None of the above

11. What can DDL be used for? (Choose three.)

    A.   Add comments to a database table

    B.   Add columns to a database table

    C.   Add data to a database table

    D.   Add privileges for a user to a database table

Describe the Purpose of DML

12. Which one of the following is a DML statement?

    A.   ADD

    B.   ALTER

    C.   UPDATE

    D.   MODIFY

13. Which of the following can be used to remove data from a table? (Choose two.)

    A.   DELETE

    B.   UPDATE

    C.   MODIFY

    D.   ALTER

Build a SELECT Statement to Retrieve Data from an Oracle Database Table

14. What can a SELECT statement be used to query? (Choose the best answer.)

    A.   Only one report

    B.   Only one table

    C.   One or more reports

    D.   One or more tables

15. Which of the following is *not* a capability of the SELECT statement?

    A.   It can transform queried data and display the results.

    B.   It can remove data from a table.

    C.   It can join data from multiple tables.

    D.   It can aggregate database data.

SELF TEST ANSWERS

The Exam: An Overview

1. ☑ **A, B, C,** and **D.** See Table 1-1 for a full listing of all the topics included in both of the exams.
   ☒ All of the answers are correct.

2. ☑ **B.** Granted, it is a subjective issue, but Oracle Corporation specifically warns against this. One reason is that the published minimum requirement for a passing score can be changed without notice.
   ☒ **A** is incorrect. The statement is false.

3. ☑ **A.** Yes, the exam is timed.
   ☒ **B** is incorrect. The exam is timed, and it is imperative that you manage your time well when you take the exam.

4. ☑ **C** and **D.** The test has been officially validated against these two versions of the database and not the others.
   ☒ **A** and **B** are incorrect. The exam tests for functionality that did not exist in earlier versions of the Oracle database.

5. ☑ **A, B, C,** and **D.** Duh.
   ☒ All of the answers are correct.

Identify the Connection Between an ERD and a Relational Database

6. ☑ **A.** The table is a physical implementation of an entity.
   ☒ **B, C,** and **D** are incorrect. A column is a physical implementation of an entity's attribute. A relationship specifies how two entities relate to each other.

7. ☑ **B.** The primary key is the unique identifier in a table.
   ☒ **A, C,** and **D.** There is no particular understanding in ERDs of relational databases of an ID or a primary column. Both might be used to name a particular column or other object in the database, but they carry no particular specific meaning. A column is an attribute of an entity in a relational database.

Explain the Relationship Between a Database and SQL

8. ☑ **A.** SQL is the commonly used language for interacting with databases.
   ☒ **B, C,** and **D** are incorrect. SQL is not the only language for creating or interacting with databases, but it is the most commonly used.

9. ☑ **A, B, C,** and **D.** You can issue SQL statements from any of the listed options.
   ☒ All of the answers are correct.

Describe the Purpose of DDL

10. ☑ **B.** The GRANT statement is part of DDL and is used to issue privileges to a user.
☒ **A, C,** and **D** are incorrect. Querying data is performed using the DML statement SELECT. Use the DML statements UPDATE or DELETE to remove data from a database table. UPDATE can be used to remove data from one or more columns in a given row, and DELETE can be used to remove an entire row. "None of the above" does not apply since option **B** is correct.

11. ☑ **A, B,** and **C.** The DDL statement ALTER can be used to add columns or comments to a table. Use the DDL statement GRANT to add privileges.
☒ **C** is incorrect. There is no DDL statement to remove data from a database table. For this, use either UPDATE or DELETE. UPDATE can be used to remove data from one or more columns in a given row, and DELETE can be used to remove an entire row.

Describe the Purpose of DML

12. ☑ **C.** UPDATE is used to change data in an existing row.
☒ **A, B,** and **D** are incorrect. There is no ADD or MODIFY statement in SQL. ALTER is a DDL statement.

13. ☑ **A** and **B.** The DELETE statement is used to remove one or more rows from a given table. UPDATE is used to change data in one or more existing rows in a given table, and the change may include the removal of a value in a column, including the assignment of NULL to a given table's column value for the candidate row or rows.
☒ **C** and **D** are incorrect. There is no MODIFY statement in SQL. ALTER is a DDL statement.

Build a SELECT Statement to Retrieve Data from an Oracle Database Table

14. ☑ **D.** The SELECT statement can be used to query one or more tables.
☒ **A, B,** and **C** are incorrect. The SELECT statement does not query reports; rather, it is used to create reports. The SELECT is not limited to querying a single table.

15. ☑ **B.** The SELECT statement is not used to remove data from a table. The act of querying merely copies data out of a table for reporting and other comparable purposes, but the SELECT statement—as a stand-alone statement—always leaves the data it encounters untouched and unmodified. However, it is possible to incorporate features of the SELECT within the context of other statements, such as INSERT and UPDATE, which are described later in this book.
☒ **A, C,** and **D** are incorrect. The SELECT statement is capable of transforming data, joining data, and aggregating data.

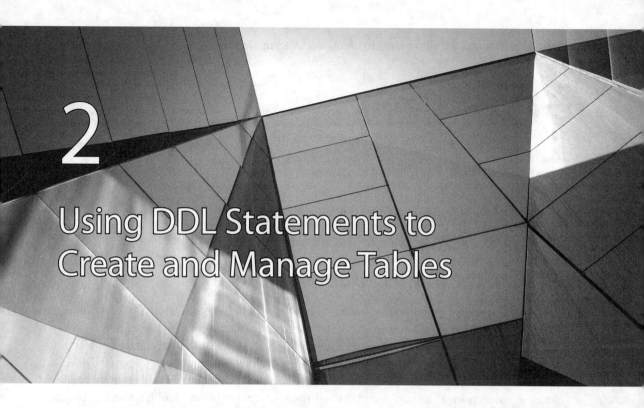

2
Using DDL Statements to Create and Manage Tables

T his chapter begins to examine tables. Tables are database objects that programmers create to store the data that populates the database.

Categorize the Main Database Objects

Database objects are the foundation of any database application. Database objects house and support everything any database application needs in order to form a working application. This section takes a high-level look at the database objects that can be created in an Oracle relational database management system (RDBMS), focusing on those objects that are tested on the exam. Here we will separate database objects into categories and discuss the relationship between objects and schemas. The rest of the book will delve into greater detail on each database object that is included in the exam.

What Are Database Objects?

You can create many different types of database objects in the Oracle RDBMS. The exam looks at eight of those objects in great detail.

The Complete List

A database consists of one or more database objects. The following list shows objects that a database developer can create in the Oracle 12c RDBMS. Those marked with an asterisk (*) are included on the exam. (Source: *SQL Language Reference Manual.*)

Clusters	Object tables
Constraints*	Object types
Contexts	Object views
Database links	Operators
Database triggers	Packages

Dimensions	*Restore points*
Directories	*Roles**
Editions	*Rollback segments*
External procedure libraries	Sequences*
Indexes*	Stored functions/procedures
Index-organized tables	Private synonyms*
Indextypes	*Public synonyms**
Java classes, etc.	Tables*
Materialized view logs	*Tablespaces*
Materialized views	*Users**
Mining models	Views*

Note: Nonschema objects are italicized; all others are schema objects. See the section "Schemas" for more information.

The exam doesn't test for all of these objects. It ignores objects such as PL/SQL program units and Java program units, as well as objects that are of more interest to database administrators. We will concern ourselves in this book only with those database objects that are included in the exam. The types of database objects on the exam are listed here, in alphabetical order:

Constraints	Synonyms
Indexes	Tables
Roles	Users
Sequences	Views

A Brief Description

Let's take a brief look at the types of objects that are the subject of the exam:

- **TABLE**   A structure that can store data. All data is stored in columns and rows. Each column's data type is explicitly defined.
- **INDEX**   An object designed to support faster searches in a table. An INDEX performs much the same way as an index to a book, by copying a relatively small, select amount of information, sorting it for speedy reference, and tying it back to locations in the table for supporting quick lookups of rows in the source table.

- **VIEW** A "filter" through which you can search a table and interact with a table but that stores no data itself and simply serves as a "window" onto one or more tables. VIEW objects can be used to mask portions of the underlying table logic for various reasons—perhaps to simplify business logic or to add a layer of security by hiding the real source of information. A VIEW can be used to display certain parts of a table while hiding other parts of the same table.

- **SEQUENCE** A counter, often used to generate unique numbers as identifiers for new rows as they are added to a table.

- **SYNONYM** An alias for another object in the database, often used to specify an alternative name for a table or view.

- **CONSTRAINT** A small bit of logic defined by you to instruct a particular table about how it will accept, modify, or reject incoming data.

- **USERS** The "owners" of database objects.

- **ROLES** A set of one or more privileges that can be granted to a user.

I will review each of these objects in greater detail throughout the book.

Each database object is considered to be either a "schema object" or a "nonschema object." This begs the question, what is a schema?

Schemas

This section describes schemas—what they are and how they relate to database objects.

What Is a Schema?

A *schema* is a collection of certain database objects, such as tables, indexes, and views, all of which are owned by a user account. You can think of a schema as being the same thing as a user account, but there is a slight difference—the user account houses the objects owned by a user, and the schema is that set of objects housed therein. One definition of schema that you'll often find in Oracle's documentation (and elsewhere) is that a schema is a "logical collection of database objects." Technically that's true, but it depends on how logical the user chooses to be when building and placing those objects within his or her user account. Ideally there should be some sense to why all those objects are in there, and ideally a "schema" shouldn't be just a random collection of objects. However, there is nothing built into the Oracle or SQL systems that prevents a user from doing just that—randomly collecting objects into a user account and thus creating a "schema" of random objects. Ideally, though, a user account should be seen and used as a logical collection of database objects, driven by business rules and collected into one organized entity—the schema.

A schema has the same name as the user account. A user account is identified by a user name and is associated with a set of privileges and roles, which are covered in Chapter 14, as well as other attributes not addressed on the exam. A user account "owns" a set of zero or more database objects, and together, these objects constitute a schema. While user accounts are often associated with a human being, it is entirely possible to create a schema (in other words, a user account) whose "owner" isn't a human being at all but perhaps is an application process, some other sort of virtual entity (perhaps a particular background process), or whatever makes sense to suit the business rules that are in force. So in other words, one user will often have one user account and therefore one schema. But the opposite isn't necessarily true. There can be more user accounts than there are actual users.

Now that you understand what a schema is and what a user account is, we can begin to look at different types of database objects, some of which are owned by a user and are thereby "schema" objects and some of which are not schema objects but are still database objects nonetheless.

Schema and Nonschema Objects

All database objects fall into one of two categories, or *types*. These types, as the Oracle documentation calls them, are *schema* and *nonschema*.

Table 2-1 shows the list of both schema and nonschema objects that are subjects of the exam.

Schema objects are those objects that can be owned by a user account. Nonschema objects cannot be owned by a user account.

TABLE 2-1	Schema Objects	Nonschema Objects
Schema vs. Nonschema Database Objects	Tables Constraints Indexes Views Sequences Private synonyms	Users Roles Public synonyms

For example, the USER object is a nonschema object. A user account cannot own itself, and it cannot be owned by another user account. Therefore, the USER object, which is a user account, is a nonschema object and is a property of the database as a whole. The same is true for ROLE objects. ROLE objects represent one or more privileges that can be granted to one or more USER objects. Thus, a ROLE inherently exists at a level outside of an individual USER account—and is therefore a nonschema object. A PRIVATE SYNONYM is owned by a user account and is therefore a schema object, but a PUBLIC SYNONYM is a variation on the SYNONYM object that is owned by the special user account PUBLIC, whose owned objects are automatically available to the entire database by definition.

All other objects are schema objects such as TABLE, INDEX, VIEW, and the others listed in Table 2-1.

CERTIFICATION OBJECTIVE 2.02

Create a Simple Table

The exam expects you to be able to recognize the correct code to create a simple table. By "simple," Oracle means that you'll be required to define the table's name, column names, data types, and any relevant constraints.

To create a table, we use the SQL command CREATE TABLE. The word CREATE is a SQL reserved word that can be combined with just about any database object (but not all) to form a SQL command. The syntax for the CREATE *objectType* statement is shown in this code listing:

```
CREATE objectType objectName attributes;
```

where

- *objectType* is a reference to an object listed in Table 2-1. Here are some exceptions:
  You cannot create a CONSTRAINT in this way. Also, while CREATE PRIVATE SYNONYM *objectName* is correct, you use simply CREATE SYNONYM *objectName* for public synonyms, never CREATE PUBLIC SYNONYM *objectName*, which is incorrect.

- *objectName* is a name you specify according to the naming rules and guidelines described later in this chapter.
- *attributes* is anywhere from zero to a series of clauses that are unique to each individual objectType, which we'll review later.

One of the most frequent usages of the SQL command CREATE is to create a TABLE. When you create a table, you'll also create the table's columns and optionally some associated objects.

Let's look at an example of a basic CREATE TABLE statement:

```
CREATE TABLE work_schedule
  (work_schedule_id  NUMBER,
   start_date        DATE,
   end_date          DATE);
```

If you were to execute this command in a schema that didn't already have a table named work_schedule (that's important), then you'd get the result shown in Figure 2-1.

Let's analyze the syntax of the preceding example of a CREATE TABLE statement:

- The reserved word CREATE.
- The reserved word TABLE.
- The name of the table, chosen by you, in accordance with the rules of naming objects, which we review next.
- A pair of parentheses, in which are a series of column declarations, each separated by a comma. Column declarations consist of the following:
  - The name of the column, chosen by you, in accordance with the rules of naming objects
  - The data type of the column, taken from the list of available data types
  - A comma to separate each column definition from the next.
- A semicolon to end the statement, as is the case with all SQL statements.

FIGURE 2-1

Results of CREATE TABLE work_schedule statement

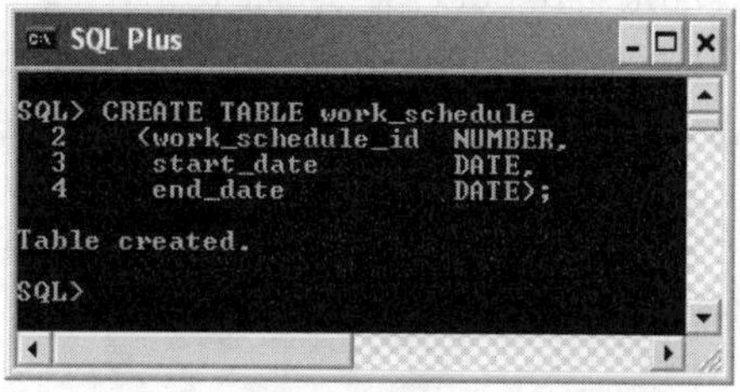

To fully understand the syntax as just described, you need to examine two important issues: the rules of naming database objects and the list of available data types. Let's look at naming rules next; after that you'll learn about data types.

Naming a Table or Other Object

Before moving on with the details of creating a table, let's take a look at the rules for naming database objects. These rules apply to tables, views, indexes, and all database objects—including a table's constraints, if any are created. The same naming rules also apply to a table's columns.

All tables have a name. Each table consists of one or more columns, and each column has a name. (For that matter, each database object in the database has its own name—each index, view, constraint, synonym, and object in the database has a name.)

When you use the SQL keyword CREATE to create a database object, you must come up with a name and assign it to the object, and sometimes—as in the case of a table—to individual components within the object, such as the columns of a table.

There is a specific set of rules for naming database objects—including tables, table columns, views—anything you must name in the database. The next section looks at those naming rules.

Naming Rules—Basics

The rules for naming tables, and any database object, include the following:

- The length of the name must be at least 1 character and no more than 30 characters.
- The first character in a name must be a letter.
- After the first letter, names may include letters, numbers, the dollar sign ($), the underscore (_), and the pound sign (#), also known as the hash mark or hash symbol. No other special characters are allowed anywhere in the name.
- Names are not case-sensitive.
- Names cannot be reserved words that are set aside for use in SQL statements, such as the reserved words SELECT, CREATE, and so on. See the following complete list of reserved words from Oracle's *SQL Language Reference Manual*. These words are off-limits when you create names for your database objects.

ACCESS	ADD	ALL
ALTER	AND	ANY
AS	ASC	AUDIT
BETWEEN	BY	CHAR
CHECK	CLUSTER	COLUMN
COLUMN_VALUE *	COMMENT	COMPRESS
CONNECT	CREATE	CURRENT
DATE	DECIMAL	DEFAULT
DELETE	DESC	DISTINCT
DROP	ELSE	EXCLUSIVE
EXISTS	FILE	FLOAT
FOR	FROM	GRANT
GROUP	HAVING	IDENTIFIED
IMMEDIATE	IN	INCREMENT
INDEX	INITIAL	INSERT
INTEGER	INTERSECT	INTO
IS	LEVEL	LIKE
LOCK	LONG	MAXEXTENTS
MINUS	MLSLABEL	MODE
MODIFY	NESTED_TABLE_ID *	NOAUDIT
NOCOMPRESS	NOT	NOWAIT
NULL	NUMBER	OF
OFFLINE	ON	ONLINE
OPTION	OR	ORDER
PCTFREE	PRIOR	PUBLIC
RAW	RENAME	RESOURCE
REVOKE	ROW	ROWID **
ROWNUM	ROWS	SELECT
SESSION	SET	SHARE
SIZE	SMALLINT	START
SUCCESSFUL	SYNONYM	SYSDATE
TABLE	THEN	TO
TRIGGER	UID	UNION

UNIQUE	UPDATE	USER
VALIDATE	VALUES	VARCHAR
VARCHAR2	VIEW	WHENEVER
WHERE	WITH	

* Reserved for use as an attribute name only.
** Unable to be used as a column name in its uppercase form. Can be used in other forms using quoted variations in case; however, it is best to avoid and is not a subject of the exam.

These rules are absolute. If you attempt to create a table or any other database object with a name that violates these rules, the attempt will fail, you'll receive an error code from the database, and your object will not exist.

Quoted Names

While not recommended by Oracle, it is possible to create database object names that are "quoted." A quoted name is surrounded with double quotes, such as the "Companies" object. Here's an example:

```
CREATE TABLE "Companies" (company_id NUMBER);
```

Quoted names must always be referenced with their quotation marks.

```
SELECT * FROM "Companies";
```

Quoted names vary from nonquoted in several ways. For example, quoted names may begin with any character. Names may include spaces.

```
CREATE TABLE "Company Employees"
  (employee_id  NUMBER,
   name         VARCHAR2(35));
```

Quoted names are case-sensitive. For example, now that I've created a table called "Company Employees", this query will work:

```
SELECT * FROM "Company Employees";
```

But the following will not:

```
SELECT * FROM "COMPANY EMPLOYEES";
```

Quoted names may include reserved words. And to reiterate, quoted names must always be referenced with their quotation marks.

Generally, most database objects are created without the use of double quotation marks, and Oracle advises against their use. But you may need to know about them anyway.

Unique Names and Namespaces

What happens if you try to create a database object with a name that matches the name of another database object that's already in the database? Can you do it? What happens to the existing database object? Will you be able to use the resulting database object? The answer is that it depends on your object's relationship to the other object that already exists, as well as on something called the *namespace*.

A namespace is a logical boundary within the database that encompasses a particular set of database objects. There are several namespaces at work at any given time, depending on the context in which you are working.

Understanding the namespace is necessary in order to understand whether you may or may not specify duplicate names for any particular database object. See Figure 2-2 for a diagram that demonstrates the namespace boundaries.

FIGURE 2-2

Diagram of namespace boundaries

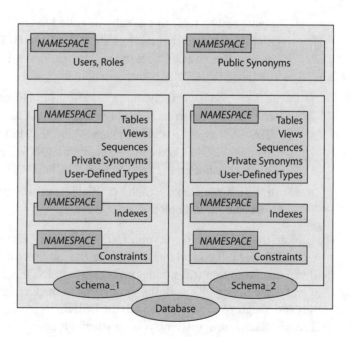

Note that each square encloses a different namespace. In Figure 2-2, there are several namespaces identified:

- USER and ROLE objects are in their own collective namespace.
- PUBLIC SYNONYM objects are in their own namespace.
- TABLE, VIEW, SEQUENCE, PRIVATE SYNONYM, and user-defined TYPE objects have their own collective unique namespace within a given schema. (Note that I haven't previously mentioned user-defined types. They aren't on the exam. I include them in this discussion to be complete, but you won't need to understand them for the exam.)
- INDEX objects have their own namespace within a given schema.
- CONSTRAINT objects have their own namespace within a given schema.

What all of this means is that you must provide unique names for an object within its own namespace. Objects that share a namespace must have unique names within that namespace. Objects in different namespaces are allowed to have identical names. Here are some examples:

- If you create a table in one schema called WORK_SCHEDULE, then you cannot create another table called WORK_SCHEDULE within that same schema. But you can do it in another schema, provided there isn't already a WORK_SCHEDULE in that schema.
- Let's say you have a schema called HR (as in Human Resources). In the HR schema, you can create a table called, say, PAYROLL. You cannot create a VIEW in that same schema called PAYROLL. But you can create an INDEX called PAYROLL. You can also create a CONSTRAINT called PAYROLL. But you cannot create a SEQUENCE called PAYROLL.
- In the entire database, each USER object must have a unique name and so must each ROLE object.

Note that later you'll see you can create a TABLE and give it a primary key CONSTRAINT. If you do this, you'll have the option of naming that CONSTRAINT. If you do, the system will automatically create an INDEX for the CONSTRAINT, and it will name the INDEX with the same name as the CONSTRAINT. You can override this and assign your own name with the USING INDEX clause of the CREATE TABLE statement, something you'll learn about later.

When naming objects, choose descriptive names that can be pronounced.
Be consistent: if your tables of EMPLOYEES, CUSTOMERS, and VENDORS each
include a reference to a person's name, make those column names all the same—
NAME, LAST_NAME, and FIRST_NAME, whatever. Just be consistent. Consider
naming all tables in plural form, since each most likely contains multiple records.
Consider using a standard prefix for every database object that's associated with
a particular application. For example, for a Human Resources application, prefix
each table with HR_, but avoid using prefixes that Oracle Corporation uses for its
system-defined objects: SYS_, ALL_, DBA_, GV$, NLS_, ROLE_, USER_, and V$.

System-Assigned Names

You'll see a bit later that you may create an object indirectly. This happens, for
example, when you create a table and within the CREATE TABLE statement you
optionally define an associated constraint, but without providing a name for the
CONSTRAINT. The language syntax of the CREATE TABLE statement allows this
to happen, as you'll soon see, and the result is not only your newly created—and
named—table, but also a newly created constraint for that table. Some developers
refer to these constraints as *anonymous,* but they aren't anonymous at all. The system
will automatically generate a name for that constraint—a name like SYS_C001234,
with a prefix of SYS_C, followed by a number generated automatically by the system.

The SQL Statement CREATE TABLE

The SQL statement CREATE TABLE is a complex statement with many clauses
and parameters. The exam tests for only some of its functionality, including how to
create columns, specify data types for those columns, and create constraints.

Here's an example of a relatively simple CREATE TABLE statement:

```
CREATE TABLE cruises
( cruise_id              NUMBER,
  cruise_type_id         NUMBER,
  cruise_name            VARCHAR2(20),
  captain_id             NUMBER NOT NULL,
  start_date             DATE,
  end_date               DATE,
  status                 VARCHAR2(5) DEFAULT 'DOCK',
  CONSTRAINT cruise_pk PRIMARY KEY (cruise_id) );
```

In this example, you are creating a table with seven columns and two constraints.
Each of the columns is given a name and a data type. The data types provide some

rules and requirements for the data that's entered into the columns. For example, only numbers can be entered into CRUISE_TYPE_ID. Only date values can be entered into START_DATE.

Note that the STATUS column has a default value of 'DOCK'. If an INSERT statement omits the value for STATUS, then 'DOCK' will be the value for STATUS.

At the end of the CREATE TABLE statement is an additional line that creates a CONSTRAINT. This particular CONSTRAINT defines the CRUISE_ID column as a *primary key,* which means that any row added to the CRUISES table must include a value for CRUISE_ID, and that value must be unique—it cannot duplicate any preexisting value for CRUISE_ID in any other row already present in the table.

There's also a NOT NULL constraint that's applied to the CAPTAIN_ID column. That CONSTRAINT isn't explicitly named, but it's a CONSTRAINT nonetheless, and it will be assigned a system-generated name.

In the remainder of this chapter, you'll learn how to review the structure of a table. You'll look at the different data types you can use to create columns in a table. The chapter will conclude by looking at constraints and how they can be created at the time you create a table.

CERTIFICATION OBJECTIVE 2.03

Review the Table Structure

Once you have created a table successfully in the database, you can review the table's structure with the DESCRIBE statement. The DESCRIBE statement, often abbreviated as DESC, isn't a SQL statement; it's a SQL*Plus statement that is unique to Oracle. (Some other product vendors have since implemented DESC in their own SQL products.) The DESC statement isn't a SQL statement—it is not described in the *Oracle Database SQL Language Reference* manual. DESC falls under the category of one of the several SQL*Plus enhancements, unique to Oracle, and documented in Oracle's *SQL*Plus User's Guide and Reference* manual, which details the DESC statement. But even though it is not considered SQL, DESC is important to understand since DESC is useful for quickly reviewing a table's structure.

One note about SQL*Plus statements: they don't require a semicolon at the end. You'll see DESC statements without a semicolon in the examples that follow. Note that a SQL*Plus statement concludes at the end of its first line unless a continuation character is placed at the end of the line to explicitly indicate that the statement continues to the next line. This is a significant difference from SQL statements, which require a semicolon at their end, and continue to multiple lines until the semicolon is encountered. The SQL*Plus use of the continuation character and the full syntax of SQL*Plus statements are beyond the scope of this book. The only point to note here is that SQL statements continue until a semicolon marks the end, spanning multiple lines if required. But a SQL*Plus statement does not behave that way and ends on its first line, with or without a semicolon, unless a continuation character is used, and we won't see the need for that in our examples that follow—we'll just see the DESC statement end without a semicolon. Also note: you can actually place a semicolon at the end of a SQL*Plus statement and—technically—it will have no effect. You won't get an error message, nor is it required. But don't forget: a semicolon is always required at the end of a SQL statement.

Let's take a look at an example of DESC. Consider the CREATE TABLE CRUISES statement you saw earlier:

```
CREATE TABLE cruises
( cruise_id              NUMBER,
  cruise_type_id         NUMBER,
  cruise_name            VARCHAR2(20),
  captain_id             NUMBER NOT NULL,
  start_date             DATE,
  end_date               DATE,
  status                 VARCHAR2(5) DEFAULT 'DOCK',
  CONSTRAINT cruise_pk PRIMARY KEY (cruise_id) );
```

Assuming this SQL statement was executed in the database successfully, resulting in the table CRUISES being stored in the database, then you could issue the following SQL*Plus command:

```
DESC cruises
```

Figure 2-3 displays the result. Notice the output list shows a three-column display.

- The first column in the output listing is titled "Name" and shows the table's column names that you specified with the CREATE TABLE statement.
- The second column in the output listing is titled "Null" and shows whether there is a NOT NULL constraint applied to that particular column in the table. In other words, will any row that's added to the database be allowed to omit this particular value?
- The third column in the output listing is titled "Type" and shows the data type for the particular table's column in question.

FIGURE 2-3

FIGURE 2-3

Result of the
command DESC
cruises

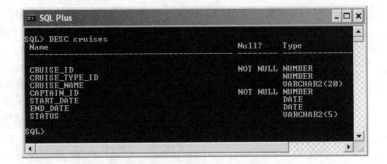

```
SQL> DESC cruises
Name                                    Null?     Type
------------------------------------    --------  -------------

CRUISE_ID                               NOT NULL  NUMBER
CRUISE_TYPE_ID                                    NUMBER
CRUISE_NAME                                       VARCHAR2(20)
CAPTAIN_ID                              NOT NULL  NUMBER
START_DATE                                        DATE
END_DATE                                          DATE
STATUS                                            VARCHAR2(5)

SQL>
```

For example, the DESC CRUISES output shows that the CRUISES table has a column titled CAPTAIN_ID, its data type is NUMBER, and it has a NOT NULL CONSTRAINT applied to it.

CERTIFICATION OBJECTIVE 2.04

List the Data Types That Are Available for Columns

This section lists and explains data types provided by Oracle that can be assigned to columns in a table. We'll look at examples in later chapters—for now we're interested only in listing and describing them.

Data types are assigned to different types of objects in the SQL database and throughout the Oracle system. In a table, each column must be assigned a data type. A column's data type defines what sort of information is—and is not—accepted as input into the column. It determines how the values in the column can be used, how they will behave when compared to other values or evaluated in expressions, and how they are sorted.

Most data types fall under one of the general categories of numeric, character, or date. There's more to it than this, but most data types fall into one of these three general categories. In addition to these three is a category referred to as large object, or LOB, data types. LOBs can include character data but cannot be included in a primary key, DISTINCT, GROUP BY, ORDER BY, or joins.

e x a m

ⓦ a t c h *Oracle's own documentation refers to data types as both* datatypes *and* data types. *These two expressions are the same thing.*

Character

Character data types are also known as text or string data types, and they include the following:

- **CHAR(n)** The name CHAR is short for "character." This is a fixed-length alphanumeric value. Any alphanumeric character is accepted as input. The n indicates how long the value will be. The CHAR(n) data type accepts valid input and pads any remaining unused space with blanks to ensure that the length of your value will always equal the value of n. For example, if you declare a column with data type of CHAR(5), then a value of, for example, "A" will be stored—and retrieved—as "A   " where A is followed by four blank spaces. Any attempt to enter a value that is longer than n will result in an error, and the value will not be accepted. When declaring a CHAR data type, the inclusion of n is optional; if it is omitted in the declaration, a value of 1 is assumed. For example, a statement of CREATE TABLE cruises (cruise_id CHAR) will result in a CRUISE_ID column with a data type of CHAR(1). The maximum allowed value for n is 2000.

- **VARCHAR2(n)** The name VARCHAR is sort of an abbreviation for "variable character." This is a variable-length alphanumeric value. The n indicates the maximum allowable length of the value stored within, but contrary to CHAR, the VARCHAR2 format will not pad its values with blanks. Its length varies according to the data it contains. Also different from the CHAR data type is that VARCHAR2 requires n to be specified. The minimum value of n is 1; the maximum allowable length of VARCHAR2 is 4000. (Note: The issue of a maximum value in VARCHAR2 is actually a bit more complex than this—the maximum is technically 4,000 bytes and not really 4,000 characters, and by default most Oracle database implementations are configured so that one character equals one byte. But it's possible to override this, which would theoretically change the maximum number you can use for n in a VARCHAR2 declaration. Furthermore, beginning with Oracle 12c, there is an initialization parameter MAX_STRING_SIZE that can be set to the value EXTENDED, enabling VARCHAR2 declarations of up to 32,767. For our purposes here it doesn't really matter—it hasn't been an issue on the exam. But keep an eye out for this; it may be introduced into the exam in the future.)

Numeric

Numeric data types include the following:

■ **NUMBER(n,m)** This data type accepts numeric data, including zero, negative, and positive numbers, where n specifies the "precision," which is the maximum number of significant digits (on either side of the decimal point), and m is the "scale," meaning the total number of digits to the right of the decimal point. Both n and m are optional; if both are omitted, both default to their maximum values. If n is specified and m is omitted, m defaults to zero. The value for n can range from 1 to 38; the value for m can range from −84 to 127. Note that these are not the largest *values* you can have but rather the largest (and smallest) specifications for values you can have—Oracle's *SQL Language Reference Manual* carefully states that the *values* accepted for a NUMBER data type range from 1.0×10^{-130} up to "but not including" 1.0×10^{126}. If a value entered into a NUMBER column has a precision greater than the specified value, an error message will result, and the value will be rejected. On the other hand, if a value is entered that exceeds the declared scale, the entered value will be rounded off (.5 is rounded up) and accepted. Also, a negative value for m identifies how many significant digits to the left of the decimal point will be rounded off. See Table 2-2 for an example of how all of this works. It's considered good

TABLE 2-2	Examples of NUMBER Precision and Scale	
Data Type	**Value Entered**	**Value Stored As**
NUMBER	4.56	4.56
NUMBER(2)	4.56	5
NUMBER(5,2)	4.56	4.56
NUMBER(5,2)	4.5678	4.57
NUMBER(4,2)	10.59	10.59
NUMBER(4,1)	10.59	10.6
NUMBER(3,2)	10.59	Nothing is stored. Instead, displays error code ORA-01438: "value larger than specified precision allowed for this column." The reason: the value has a precision of 4 (1,0,5,9—four digits), but NUMBER here is declared with a precision of 3.
NUMBER(5,−2)	1059.34	1100

practice to specify the precision and scale as part of the overall data integrity check to place some boundaries around the limits of what the business logic of the intent of the column will accept.

Date

Date data types are sometimes referred to in Oracle's documentation as *datetimes*. Each date data type consists of *fields*, and each field is a component of a date or time, such as hours, minutes, or the month value, and so on. See Table 2-3 for a list of the fields that are used in various combinations to form date data types.

The data types that support date and time information include the following:

- ■ **DATE** This accepts date and time information. The fields stored include year, month, date, hour, minute, and second. Date values may be stored as literals or using conversion functions that you'll see later in Chapter 6. Date literals are enclosed in single quotation marks and may be specified in a

TABLE 2-3   Datetime Fields

Datetime Field	Range of Valid Values
YEAR	−4712 to 9999 (excluding the year 0)
MONTH	01 to 12
DAY	01 to 31 (Limited as appropriate for months in which there are fewer than 31 days, according to the values in MONTH and YEAR.)
HOUR	00 to 23
MINUTE	00 to 59
SECOND	00 to 59.9(n), where 9(n) is the precision of time in fractional seconds. That portion—9(n)—does not apply to DATE.
TIMEZONE_HOUR	−12 to 14. Designed to accommodate changes to daylight saving time. Does not apply to DATE or TIMESTAMP.
TIMEZONE_MINUTE	00 to 59. Does not apply to DATE or TIMESTAMP.
TIMEZONE_REGION	The list of possible values here is contained in the TZNAME column of the data dictionary view V$TIMEZONE_NAMES. Examples: 'America/Chicago', 'Australia/Queensland'. Does not apply to DATE or TIMESTAMP.
TIMEZONE_ABBR	The list of possible values here is contained in the TZABBREV column of the data dictionary view V$TIMEZONE_NAMES. Examples: 'CWT', 'LMT'. Does not apply to DATE or TIMESTAMP.

number of ways. The default Oracle date format for a given calendar day is defined by the parameter NLS_DATE_FORMAT.

The initialization parameter NLS_DATE_FORMAT specifies the default date format for your database. However, it is also possible that NLS_DATE_FORMAT is not explicitly set but is instead defaulted to the associated date format of another initialization parameter, NLS_TERRITORY. To see the value specified for the initialization parameter NLS_TERRITORY in your database, use SHOW PARAMETERS NLS_TERRITORY. To see whether a value for NLS_DATE_FORMAT was specified for your database, use SHOW PARAMETERS NLS_DATE_FORMAT. Regardless of whether the NLS_DATE_FORMAT was explicitly set for your database, you can see its value with this query:

```
SELECT SYS_CONTEXT('USERENV',
                   'NLS_DATE_FORMAT') NLS_DATE_FORMAT
FROM    EMPLOYEES;
```

The NLS_DATE_FORMAT parameter can be changed with ALTER SESSION or ALTER SYSTEM, which are SQL statements that are not included on the exam. By default, installations in the United States and United Kingdom use the NLS_DATE_FORMAT of DD-MON-RR, where DD is the two-digit day, MON is the three-letter abbreviation for the month, and RR is the two-digit year, where values of RR ranging from 00 to 49 are assumed to be in the twenty-first century (2000 to 2049), while RR values ranging from 50 to 99 are assumed to be in the twentieth century (1950 through 1999). For example, '01-NOV-10' is the first of November in 2010. (Note: The same date in ANSI format is '2010-11-01'. ANSI format is 'YYYY-MM-DD', where YYYY is the four-digit year, MM is the two-digit month, and DD is the two-digit day.) See Chapter 6 for more on these topics.

- **TIMESTAMP(n)**   This is an extension of DATE that adds fractional second precision. TIMESTAMP stores year, month, day, hours, minutes, seconds, and fractional seconds. The value for n specifies the precision for fractional seconds. The range for n is 0–9. If n is omitted, it defaults to a value of 6.

- **TIMESTAMP(n) WITH TIME ZONE**   This is a variation of TIMESTAMP that adds either a time zone region name or an offset for time zone. TIMESTAMP WITH TIME ZONE is used in tracking date information across different time zones and geographical areas. The range for n is 0–9. If n is omitted, it defaults to a value of 6.

- **TIMESTAMP(*n*) WITH LOCAL TIME ZONE**   This is a variation of TIMESTAMP. The TIMESTAMP WITH LOCAL TIME ZONE differs from TIMESTAMP WITH TIME ZONE in that the time zone offset is not stored with the column's value, and the value retrieved is sent to the user in the user's local session time zone. In other words, while the offset is not stored with TIMESTAMP WITH LOCAL TIME ZONE, the system calculates the offset automatically when the value is accessed from a different time zone. End users see the time in their own local time zone, regardless of the time zone where the database server happens to reside. The offset is calculated automatically. If *n* is omitted, it defaults to a value of 6.

- **INTERVAL YEAR(*n*) TO MONTH**   This stores a span of time defined in only year and month values, where *n* is the number of digits used to define the YEAR value. The range of acceptable values for *n* is 0–9; the default for *n* is 2. This data type is useful for storing the difference between two date values.

- **INTERVAL DAY(*n1*) TO SECOND(*n2*)**   This stores a span of time defined in days, hours, minutes, and seconds, where *n1* is the precision for days, and *n2* is the precision for seconds. The range of values for *n1* is 0–9, and the default is 2. The value for *n1* specifies how many digits are accepted in declaring the size of a number for DAY to be specified. The value for *n2* is the fractional seconds precision for SECOND; the range for acceptable values is 0–9, and the default is 6. This is useful for storing the difference between two date values.

Large Objects

The exam will address your knowledge of how to use large object, or LOB, data types in SQL language syntax. LOBs can generally be used like other data types. Tables may have multiple columns with LOB data types. However, LOBs cannot be primary keys, and they cannot be used with DISTINCT, GROUP BY, ORDER BY, or joins.

LOBs include the following:

■ **BLOB** The name BLOB is an abbreviation for "binary large object." BLOB accepts large binary objects, such as image or video files. Declaration is made without precision or scale. (The maximum size is calculated by way of a formula that includes several items not on the exam, including a starting size of 4GB, something called the CHUNK parameter, and the setting for the database block size, which is a setting that affects all storage in the database.)

■ **CLOB** The name CLOB is an abbreviation for "character large object." CLOB accepts large text data elements. Declaration is made without precision or scale, and the maximum size is calculated in the same manner that it is for the BLOB data type.

■ **NCLOB** This accepts CLOB data in Unicode. The maximum size is calculated in the same manner that it is for the BLOB data type. Regarding Unicode—it is a character set that serves as an alternative to ASCII and represents a more universal standard that supports all major languages more easily than the other implementations in use today. Oracle and most other major vendors have adopted Unicode into their products, and common web technologies already support it. Given the increasing role of globalization and multilanguage support, any legacy application deployed without Unicode may inevitably require a conversion effort down the road. Oracle Corporation is officially recommending the use of Unicode as the database national character set for all new system development.

Here's an example of a table that includes a column of the CLOB data type:

```
CREATE TABLE CRUISE_NOTES
(CRUISE_NOTES_ID NUMBER,
 CRUISE_NOTES    CLOB);
```

The preceding example creates a table with two columns, the second of which is a CLOB. That column can receive extremely large text data as input.

Oracle Corporation discourages the use of the old LONG data type and encourages you to convert LONG data types to LOB data types, which have fewer restrictions. For example, you can add more than one LOB column to a table, you can select LOB columns, you can insert into tables with LOB columns, and you can delete rows with LOB values. However, as I stated earlier, you cannot use LOBs in GROUP BY or ORDER BY clauses.

All of the data types you've seen so far are built in by Oracle and included with SQL. All of these data types are known as "built-in" data types. However, it's possible for users to create their own unique "user-defined" data types. User-defined data types are created using the SQL statement CREATE TYPE. They are used in PL/SQL code and are not a subject of the exam.

CERTIFICATION OBJECTIVE 2.05

Explain How Constraints Are Created at the Time of Table Creation

You can create a CONSTRAINT to support other objects, specifically TABLE objects. But there isn't a CREATE CONSTRAINT statement; you create a CONSTRAINT as part of another statement, such as CREATE TABLE or ALTER TABLE. When you create a CONSTRAINT, you can choose to name it yourself or let the system automatically assign a name. The creation of certain constraints—PRIMARY KEY, UNIQUE, and FOREIGN KEY—will automatically trigger the creation of a corresponding index object of the same name.

Here's an example of a CREATE TABLE statement that includes the syntax to create a CONSTRAINT:

```
CREATE TABLE positions
(  position_id          NUMBER
,  position             VARCHAR2(20)
,  exempt               CHAR(1)
,  CONSTRAINT positions_pk PRIMARY KEY (position_id)
);
```

In the preceding example, we create a TABLE called POSITIONS, which consists of three columns, POSITION_ID, POSITION, and EXEMPT. After the EXEMPT column is defined, this particular example shows an additional line of code to create a CONSTRAINT. (There are other formats for creating constraints, as you will soon see.) In this example, we are choosing to name the CONSTRAINT, something that we don't necessarily have to do. The name we are assigning to this CONSTRAINT is POSITIONS_PK. We're specifying that this CONSTRAINT is of type PRIMARY KEY, and we're applying the CONSTRAINT to the column in this table that's called POSITION_ID, which we defined first.

Let's look at some specifics next.

Creating CONSTRAINTS in the CREATE TABLE Statement

There are two ways in which a CONSTRAINT can be created at the time of TABLE creation: in line and out of line.

CREATE TABLE: In-Line Constraints

Here is an example of how to create a PRIMARY KEY constraint in line:

```
CREATE TABLE PORTS
(PORT_ID    NUMBER PRIMARY KEY,
 PORT_NAME VARCHAR2(20));
```

In this example, we create a PRIMARY KEY constraint on the column PORT_ID. The constraint on PORT_ID is specified as part of the PORT_ID declaration. It is "in line" with the column upon which the constraint is applied. When I say "in line," I mean that after we declare a column to which we want to apply a constraint, we include the constraint specification (in this case, for a primary key) before the comma that separates the column specification (PORT_ID in this example) from the next column specification, which is PORT_NAME. The fact that the example happens to include the words PRIMARY KEY on the same line as PORT_ID is incidental and unnecessary to make this an "in line" format.

In this example, we omit the inclusion of a specified name for the constraint, which causes the Oracle database to generate a constraint name automatically, of the form *SYS_Cn*. Here's an example:

```
SYS_C009981
```

You'll see how you'll be able to identify the system-assigned name when you look at the data dictionary in Chapter 12.

Alternatively, you can optionally specify the constraint name at the time of creation, by preceding the reserved words PRIMARY KEY with the reserved word CONSTRAINT, followed by a name you make up according to the rules of naming database objects, like this:

```
CREATE TABLE PORTS
(PORT_ID    NUMBER CONSTRAINT PORT_ID_PK PRIMARY KEY,
 PORT_NAME VARCHAR2(20));
```

These two approaches are referred to as *in-line* constraints, since in both examples the declaration of the constraint is included with the column definition, before the comma that ends this column specification and enables a subsequent column specification.

Here's another example of in-line constraints. This example creates a table with a NOT NULL constraint:

```
CREATE TABLE VENDORS
(VENDOR_ID     NUMBER,
 VENDOR_NAME   VARCHAR2(20),
 STATUS        NUMBER(1) NOT NULL,
 CATEGORY      VARCHAR2(5));
```

The result of this constraint is to ensure that a value for STATUS must be included with each row entered into VENDORS. The value might be zero or any other single digit, but it must be provided—it cannot be left out. It cannot be unknown to the database. In other words, it cannot be NULL.

Here is the same table with a name assigned to the constraint:

```
CREATE TABLE VENDORS
(VENDOR_ID     NUMBER,
 VENDOR_NAME   VARCHAR2(20),
 STATUS        NUMBER(1) CONSTRAINT STATUS_NN NOT NULL,
 CATEGORY      VARCHAR2(5));
```

You may combine multiple constraint declarations in a single CREATE TABLE statement, like this:

```
CREATE TABLE VENDORS
(VENDOR_ID     NUMBER     PRIMARY KEY,
 VENDOR_NAME   VARCHAR2(20),
 STATUS        NUMBER(1) CONSTRAINT STATUS_NN NOT NULL,
 CATEGORY      VARCHAR2(5));
```

Each constraint specification is treated as a standalone clause of the CREATE statement. You can mix and match definition types; you can choose to name the constraint in some clauses and not in others. You can also mix and match in-line constraints with out-of-line constraints, to which we turn our attention next.

CREATE TABLE: Out-of-Line Constraints

In addition to in-line constraints, you may optionally define a constraint within a CREATE TABLE statement after the column specifications. Here's an example of a PRIMARY KEY defined with the out-of-line syntax, in this example on line 4:

```
CREATE TABLE PORTS
(PORT_ID     NUMBER,
 PORT_NAME   VARCHAR2(20),
 PRIMARY KEY (PORT_ID) );
```

After the final column is defined for the table, we include a comma, followed by the reserved words PRIMARY KEY. Notice that the out-of-line syntax requires that you indicate which column (or columns) is affected by the constraint. Since you're not "in line" with the column specification, the statement cannot know which column you're intending to constrain, unless you specifically indicate it within the clause.

Here's an out-of-line example that names the constraint:

```
CREATE TABLE PORTS
(PORT_ID    NUMBER,
 PORT_NAME  VARCHAR2(20),
 CONSTRAINT PORT_ID_PK PRIMARY KEY (PORT_ID) );
```

This example gives the constraint a name that we've chosen. As is the case with in-line constraints, any out-of-line constraint in which you do not provide a name will cause the Oracle database to automatically generate a constraint name.

Additional Ways to Create Constraints: ALTER TABLE

The CREATE TABLE statement isn't the only way to create a constraint. Constraints can also be created using the ALTER TABLE statement. For example, you can first create the PORTS table like this:

```
CREATE TABLE PORTS
(PORT_ID    NUMBER,
 PORT_NAME  VARCHAR2(20));
```

Afterward, you can ALTER the table to add a constraint by modifying the definition for a column.

```
ALTER TABLE PORTS
  MODIFY PORT_ID PRIMARY KEY;
```

In the preceding code, we're modifying the declaration of the column itself by adding the primary key and letting the system assign a name. This syntax results in the same CONSTRAINT as if we had used this instead:

```
CREATE TABLE PORTS
(PORT_ID    NUMBER PRIMARY KEY,
 PORT_NAME VARCHAR2(20));
```

In addition, you can use the data dictionary to determine what the system-generated constraint name is.

```
SELECT CONSTRAINT_NAME FROM USER_CONSTRAINTS WHERE TABLE_NAME = 'PORTS';
```

Once you learn the system-generated name of the constraint (let's say it's SYS_C0011505), then you can rename it if you wish, like this:

```
ALTER TABLE PORTS
   RENAME CONSTRAINT SYS_C0011505 TO PORT_ID_PK;
```

Those are the in-line equivalents of ALTER TABLE. Here are the out-of-line equivalents. First, here is an ALTER TABLE that adds a constraint without specifying a name:

```
ALTER TABLE PORTS
   ADD PRIMARY KEY (PORT_ID);
```

Alternatively, you can name the constraint yourself.

```
ALTER TABLE PORTS
   ADD CONSTRAINT PORT_ID_PK PRIMARY KEY (PORT_ID);
```

You'll work with the data dictionary in Chapter 12.

Warning: NOT NULL Is Different

We're about to look at the five different types of constraints, but before we do, a word of warning about the syntax variations for one particular constraint: the NOT NULL constraint is a bit different when it comes to syntax. The NOT NULL constraint cannot be created out of line. In other words, this is invalid:

```
CREATE TABLE PORTS
(PORT_ID    NUMBER,
 PORT_NAME  VARCHAR2(20),
 NOT NULL   (PORT_ID) );
```

This is also invalid:

```
CREATE TABLE PORTS
(PORT_ID    NUMBER,
 PORT_NAME  VARCHAR2(20),
 CONSTRAINT PORT_ID_NN NOT NULL (PORT_ID) );
```

Either of those will produce error messages if you try them. No table or constraint will be created. And yet, the same syntax is perfectly fine for other types of constraints. For example, here's the UNIQUE constraint:

```
CREATE TABLE PORTS
(PORT_ID    NUMBER,
 PORT_NAME  VARCHAR2(20),
 CONSTRAINT PORT_ID_UN UNIQUE (PORT_ID) );
```

And of course, this is fine, too—this is the PRIMARY KEY constraint:

```
CREATE TABLE PORTS
(PORT_ID    NUMBER,
 PORT_NAME  VARCHAR2(20),
 CONSTRAINT PORT_ID_PK PRIMARY KEY (PORT_ID) );
```

So remember, NOT NULL cannot be declared with the "out-of-line" format. The others can. But wait, there's more about NOT NULL. This won't work either:

```
ALTER TABLE PORTS
  ADD NOT NULL (PORT_NAME);
```

And this won't either:

```
ALTER TABLE PORTS
  ADD CONSTRAINT PORT_NAME_NN NOT NULL (PORT_NAME);
```

Those won't work because they are the ALTER TABLE equivalents for out-of-line declarations. But the ALTER TABLE in-line equivalents are fine.

```
ALTER TABLE PORTS
  MODIFY PORT_NAME NOT NULL;
```

And this is also fine:

```
ALTER TABLE PORTS
  MODIFY PORT_NAME CONSTRAINT PORT_NAME_NN NOT NULL;
```

The lesson: beware. NOT NULL is a bit unusual. It's a valid constraint and can be created using the other forms of syntax but not with the out-of-line format.

The list of certification objectives specifically states that you will be tested on the topic of creating constraints at the time of table creation. *This can include any one of the in-line or out-of-line combinations for any constraint. The syntax is tricky. Study it thoroughly and know it well.*

The Types of CONSTRAINTS

Several types of constraints can be applied to a table. They are PRIMARY KEY, FOREIGN KEY, NOT NULL, CHECK, and UNIQUE. (Note that the REF type is not included on the exam.) Let's explore each of these in detail.

NOT NULL

The NOT NULL constraint is simple—when applied to a column, it ensures that for any row that is added to the TABLE, the column on which the NOT NULL constraint is applied will always be provided with a value. Meanwhile, the column's data type ensures that the data entered into the column is consistent with the data type's rules.

To fully appreciate this constraint, it helps to understand what the concept of NULL is. Let's take a look.

The Concept of NULL   The reserved word NULL is, in my ever-so-humble opinion, one of the most misunderstood aspects of the SQL database. The definition of NULL is the "absence of information." Sometimes it's mischaracterized as "zero" or "blank," but that is incorrect—a "zero," after all, is a known quantity. So is a blank. But NULL is "unknown." It's the way the database acknowledges that it, the database, is merely an imperfect repository of information about some real-life business situation or some other application out there in the world, and the database is ultimately dependent on the data it's been given to mirror that real-life situation. But ultimately, it's real life—not the database—that is the final authority. So, it's entirely possible—and quite likely—that some information hasn't been provided to the database. NULL is a placeholder for where that information goes, specifically, where the database has not been given clear instruction about whether a value exists, and if it does exist, what value it might be.

For example, consider the following table containing the names of customers:

```
CREATE TABLE CUSTOMERS
( FIRST_NAME   VARCHAR2(20),
  MIDDLE_NAME VARCHAR2(20),
  LAST_NAME    VARCHAR2(30));
```

Let's add a row to this table.

```
INSERT INTO CUSTOMERS (FIRST_NAME, LAST_NAME) VALUES ('Angelina', 'Ellison');
```

Notice that no value is provided here for MIDDLE_NAME. When this happens, then in the absence of other information, the database stores a NULL in its place.

Does this mean that somewhere out there in the world is a real-life person named Angelina Ellison who has no middle name? Well, maybe she does, and maybe she doesn't. The point is that the database doesn't know whether she has a middle name or not—the value is unknown to the database.

This becomes important when it comes to such situations as mathematical expressions. Consider the following expression:

```
CRUISE_PRICE * DISCOUNT
```

Let's say that the value for CRUISE_PRICE is 300, and the value for DISCOUNT is NULL in the database. In other words, maybe there's a discount value, and maybe there isn't. The database doesn't know either way—it's unknown to the database. The value is NULL. If that's the case, then what is the answer to the equation given in this expression?

The answer for the equation of 300 times NULL is . . . what?

Give up?

The answer is NULL. The reason is simple: 300 multiplied by "I don't know" results in . . . "I don't know."

In other words, perhaps the equation really does have an answer, but if you don't know what the DISCOUNT value is, then you don't have enough information to calculate the answer of the expression. Therefore, the answer is unknown—in other words, NULL.

We'll address NULL some more in the section on functions. For now, all that we're concerned with is the NOT NULL constraint. When the NOT NULL constraint is applied to a column, you're requiring that any rows added to the table include a value for that column.

Let's go back to the earlier example. If we had applied a NOT NULL constraint to the MIDDLE_NAME column of the CUSTOMERS table, then we never would have had a row like "Angelina Ellison" with no middle name. The NOT NULL constraint, if applied to the MIDDLE_NAME column, would have required a middle name value for any row being added to the table.

on the job

In the real world, there really are people without a middle name. In such situations, an application is smart to use the NMN or No Middle Name entry to confirm that there is no middle name and thus avoid a NULL value, which is ambiguous.

By default, all columns allow NULL values when first created. You must choose to apply a NOT NULL constraint—or an equivalent—to a column if you want to require data for that column.

When I say "or an equivalent," I mean that there are alternative ways to require data in a column. One way is the PRIMARY KEY constraint, which is a NOT NULL rule combined with the UNIQUE constraint, which you'll see next.

If you apply a PRIMARY KEY constraint on a column, you do not need to also apply a NOT NULL constraint. But if there is no PRIMARY KEY constraint for a given column, the NOT NULL constraint will ensure that any rows added to the table will include a value for that particular column.

UNIQUE

The UNIQUE constraint, when applied to a column, ensures that any data added to the column in the future will be unique when compared to data already existing in the column. No other row will possess the same value for that particular column.

The following are a few notes about UNIQUE:

- A single UNIQUE constraint can be applied to one column or to multiple columns in combination. You'll learn more about this in a few sentences.
- UNIQUE, by itself, allows NULL values to be added to the column. It only restricts data that's provided for the column to being one of a kind for the column.

Note that the PRIMARY KEY constraint represents the combination of NOT NULL and UNIQUE. Use the PRIMARY KEY constraint instead of the NOT NULL and UNIQUE constraints if your intent is to create a single unique identifier for each row in the table.

Composite UNIQUE Constraint   You may create a UNIQUE constraint that applies to multiple columns simultaneously. This has the effect of requiring the combination of columns to be unique. In other words, each individual column may repeat data, but collectively the combination of data in all of the columns for any given row will have to be unique.

PRIMARY KEY

The PRIMARY KEY defines one or more columns in a table that will form the unique identifier for each row of data that is added to the table. The PRIMARY KEY constraint is a combination of the NOT NULL and UNIQUE constraints.

A table may have only one PRIMARY KEY constraint.

A single-column PRIMARY KEY is the most common form, and it ensures that for all rows of data added to the table in the future, the column upon which the PRIMARY KEY constraint has been applied will always contain a value and that value will always be unique when compared to existing values that are already in the table for that particular column.

Here is an example of a CREATE TABLE statement that creates a PRIMARY KEY constraint:

```
CREATE TABLE employees
(   employee_id          NUMBER
,   ship_id              NUMBER
,   first_name           VARCHAR2(20)
,   last_name            VARCHAR2(30)
,   position_id          NUMBER
,   CONSTRAINT employees_pk PRIMARY KEY (employee_id));
```

In the preceding example, we create a PRIMARY KEY constraint on the EMPLOYEE_ID column. In this example, we've given the constraint a name of EMPLOYEES_PK. (The PK suffix is not required; it is presented here as just one of many good design approaches that clarifies to anyone who might review a long list of database constraints later that this particular constraint is a primary key.) Now that we've created this table with the PRIMARY KEY constraint, any row that's added to the EMPLOYEES table in the future will require a unique value for each row added.

Composite Primary Keys   A multicolumn PRIMARY KEY is based on two or more columns that collectively serve the same purpose as a single-column PRIMARY KEY. In other words, the combination of column values will collectively have to be unique, and all columns—individually and collectively—will have to contain values.

See Figure 2-4 for some sample data. Notice the three columns CATEGORY, YEAR, and TICKET. Individually each shows data that repeats throughout the data listing. But together each row of combined columns represents unique data.

FIGURE 2-4

Sample data from HELP_DESK table

Category	Year	Ticket	Title
Order	2009	000001	Inkjet cartridges
Order	2009	000002	Printer paper
Bug Rpt	2009	000001	Screen fails for PDF
Order	2009	000003	Hard drive - external for conference
Bug Rpt	2009	000002	

Here's an example of a CREATE TABLE statement that would create a composite PRIMARY KEY constraint to support Figure 2-4:

```
CREATE TABLE HelpDesk
( HD_Category  VARCHAR2(8),
  HD_Year      NUMBER,
  HD_Ticket_No NUMBER,
  HD_Title     VARCHAR2(30),
  CONSTRAINT   HelpDesk_PK PRIMARY KEY (HD_Category, HD_Year, HD_Ticket_No));
```

The preceding code has the effect of creating NOT NULL and UNIQUE constraints across all three columns. For each row entered in the table HelpDesk, a value will be required in each of the three columns HD_Category, HD_Year, and HD_Ticket_No, and the combination of those three values will need to be unique for every row. As you saw in the earlier sample data, it's possible to repeat values in the individual columns, but the combination must always be unique in each row.

FOREIGN KEY

A FOREIGN KEY constraint applies to one or more columns in a particular table and works in conjunction with a referred table's PRIMARY KEY constraint. A FOREIGN KEY is the feature that helps ensure that two tables can "relate" to each other, and in many ways this really represents the "heart and soul" of what a relational database is all about.

The FOREIGN KEY constraint does the following:

- It identifies one or more columns in the current table; let's call this the *child* table.
- For each of those columns, it also identifies one or more corresponding columns in a second table; let's call this the *parent* table.
- It ensures that the parent table already has either a PRIMARY KEY or UNIQUE constraint on those corresponding columns.
- It then ensures that any future values added to the FOREIGN KEY–constrained columns of the child table are already stored in the corresponding columns of the parent table.

In other words, a FOREIGN KEY constraint on the child table, along with the PRIMARY KEY constraint on the parent table, enforces *referential integrity* between the two tables. This means that the constraints work to ensure that any future data that is added to one or both of the tables continues to support the ability to relate data from one table to another.

Note: The referenced table is not actually required to have a PRIMARY KEY constraint on the referenced columns but only a UNIQUE constraint on the referenced columns. But you'll recall that a PRIMARY KEY constraint is a combination of the UNIQUE and NOT NULL constraints, so the PRIMARY KEY satisfies the requirement for a UNIQUE constraint.

Let's look at a sample scenario. First, here is a listing of data in the PORTS table:

```
PORT_ID    PORT_NAME    COUNTRY    CAPACITY
-------    ---------    -------    --------
1          Baltimore    USA        2
2          Charleston   USA        2
3          Tampa        USA        8
4          Miami        USA        6
5          Galveston    USA        4
```

Next, here is a listing of information in the SHIPS table:

```
SHIP_ID    SHIP_NAME        HOME_PORT_ID
-------    ---------        ------------
1          Codd Crystal     1
2          Codd Elegance    3
3          Codd Champion    4
4          Codd Victorious  4
```

As you might have already surmised, the value for each ship's HOME_PORT_ID value should correspond to a PORT_ID value in the PORTS table.

To ensure that the two tables only accept data that supports this business rule (in other words, that requires all HOME_PORT_ID values to be valid PORT_ID values), you can create a PRIMARY KEY constraint on the PORTS table (or a UNIQUE constraint) and then a FOREIGN KEY constraint on the SHIPS table that correlates back to the PRIMARY KEY constraint on the PORTS table.

First, here is the PORTS table (line numbers added):

```
01   CREATE TABLE PORTS
02   (PORT_ID      NUMBER,
03    PORT_NAME    VARCHAR2(20),
04    COUNTRY      VARCHAR2(40),
05    CAPACITY     NUMBER,
06    CONSTRAINT   PORT_PK PRIMARY KEY (PORT_ID));
```

Next, here is the SHIPS table:

```
07   CREATE TABLE SHIPS
08   (SHIP_ID      NUMBER,
09    SHIP_NAME    VARCHAR2(20),
```

```
10   HOME_PORT_ID NUMBER,
11   CONSTRAINT    SHIPS_PORTS_FK FOREIGN KEY (HOME_PORT_ID)
12                               REFERENCES PORTS (PORT_ID));
```

Note that the foreign key constraint clause in the CREATE TABLE SHIPS statement starts on line 11 and continues through line 12. It references the PORTS table and the PORTS table's PORT_ID column, which already has a PRIMARY KEY constraint applied to it. If it did not already have either a PRIMARY KEY constraint or a UNIQUE constraint on it, then the CREATE TABLE SHIPS statement would result in an error and let you know that the PORTS table already must exist and must have a PRIMARY KEY or UNIQUE constraint on the PORT_ID column.

The FOREIGN KEY on SHIPS makes sure that any row added to the SHIPS table will accept values for HOME_PORT_ID only if that value already exists in the PORTS table. Note that the HOME_PORT_ID value is not required; if your goal is to ensure that the HOME_PORT_ID value is always provided, you'll have to also add a NOT NULL constraint on HOME_PORT_ID as well as FOREIGN KEY. This is one way to do that:

```
07   CREATE TABLE SHIPS
08   (SHIP_ID      NUMBER,
09    SHIP_NAME    VARCHAR2(20),
10    HOME_PORT_ID NUMBER NOT NULL,
11    CONSTRAINT    SHIPS_PORTS_FK FOREIGN KEY (HOME_PORT_ID)
12                                REFERENCES PORTS (PORT_ID));
```

In the preceding example, we create two separate constraints. Of those two constraints, one of them is on lines 11 through 12 and exists to make the HOME_PORT_ID column a foreign key, and the other constraint is at the end of line 10 and ensures that there is always a value entered for HOME_PORT_ID.

In my professional experience, I find it much easier to create foreign keys with ALTER TABLE statements instead of with CREATE TABLE statements. One reason is that the resulting code is more modular. Note that you cannot create a foreign key constraint that refers to a table that doesn't exist. If your goal is to build a script for creating (and if necessary, re-creating) your entire database and then you try to create all of your tables with foreign key constraints within your CREATE TABLE statements so that they occur after the creation of their respective primary key tables, all of that can suddenly turn into quite a puzzle of trying to ensure your CREATE TABLE statements all run in the correct order so that your referred tables already exist before you create tables with foreign key constraints against those primary key tables. Not only is such an effort difficult, it may prove to be impossible in a data model where the relationships run in both directions. All of this is an unnecessary effort when you can easily build all of your tables first, then alter those tables to add foreign keys within a series of ALTER TABLE statements, and finally place them all after your CREATE TABLE statements as a whole. The complexity just described (the "puzzle") is eliminated with that approach. Other complications you might avoid include the fact that you cannot create a foreign key within a CREATE TABLE statement that uses the "as query" approach—that approach creates the table and populates it with data using a subquery's SELECT statement all at once. In that sort of situation, the clause to create a foreign key constraint isn't allowed. Given such restrictions, I find no benefit to struggling to build a foreign key from within the CREATE TABLE statement and would just as soon use an ALTER TABLE statement where these restrictions don't exist. But . . . that's just me.

ON DELETE   The foreign key/primary key relationship between two tables introduces some additional considerations. What should be the behavior when rows are removed from the parent table for which there is a child row in a child table?

Using the earlier example of PORTS and SHIPS, a SHIPS row might contain a value for PORT_ID, indicating the home port of the ship. But what if the cruise line ceases to do business with a particular port and removes the row for that port from the PORTS table?

One option would be to manually edit SHIPS and remove all references to the PORT_ID value for the former port.

An alternative (and better) approach is to include the ON DELETE clause when we create the FOREIGN KEY constraint.

```
07   CREATE TABLE SHIPS
08   (SHIP_ID        NUMBER,
09    SHIP_NAME      VARCHAR2(20),
10    HOME_PORT_ID NUMBER,
11    CONSTRAINT     SHIPS_PORTS_FK FOREIGN KEY (HOME_PORT_ID)
12                                  REFERENCES PORTS (PORT_ID)
13                                  ON DELETE SET NULL)
14   ;
```

The previous CREATE TABLE SHIPS statement differs from the earlier example in two ways:

- The HOME_PORT_ID column (line 10) is no longer constrained by NOT NULL since we want the option of having a NULL value for HOME_PORT_ID.
- The foreign key constraint now includes the key words ON DELETE SET NULL as part of the constraint definition (note that it is within the closing parentheses that end the creation of the constraint but not the creation of the table SHIPS).

Now, when a parent row in PORTS is removed, the Oracle database will automatically inspect rows in SHIPS to see whether any SHIP specified the removed port's primary key in the HOME_PORT_ID column. If yes, any rows with a value for the removed PORT_ID will have those PORT_ID values replaced with a NULL value.

As an alternative, you could choose to remove the SHIPS row completely if a corresponding parent row in PORTS is removed.

```
07   CREATE TABLE SHIPS
08   (SHIP_ID        NUMBER,
09    SHIP_NAME      VARCHAR2(20),
10    HOME_PORT_ID NUMBER,
11    CONSTRAINT     SHIPS_PORTS_FK FOREIGN KEY (HOME_PORT_ID)
12                                  REFERENCES PORTS (PORT_ID)
13                                  ON DELETE CASCADE)
14   ;
```

This option will remove all SHIP rows assigned to a PORT row upon the PORT row's removal from the PORTS table.

CHECK

A CHECK constraint attaches an expression to a constraint. In other words, it applies a small bit of code to define a particular business rule on incoming rows of data. A CHECK constraint may, for example, restrict incoming data so that all incoming values are required to be greater than some minimum value or fall within a set of predetermined optional values. A CHECK constraint can ensure that a two-character column accepts only valid abbreviations for American states, for example, or that the date entered in one column in a table is always greater than the date entered in another column in the same table.

Here's an example of a CHECK constraint that only allows rows in the VENDORS table with a STATUS value of either 4 or 5:

```
CREATE TABLE VENDORS
(VENDOR_ID     NUMBER,
 VENDOR_NAME   VARCHAR2(20),
 STATUS        NUMBER(1) CHECK (STATUS IN (4,5)),
 CATEGORY      VARCHAR2(5));
```

While rows may be added to VENDORS with no STATUS value, they can be given a STATUS value only if it is either 4 or 5.

Any valid SQL expression may be used in a CHECK constraint, with some limitations. The CHECK condition cannot include references to the following:

- Columns in other tables (note that other columns in the same table are accepted)
- Pseudocolumns CURRVAL, NEXTVAL, LEVEL, or ROWNUM

- Subqueries and scalar subquery expressions
- User-defined functions
- Certain functions whose value cannot be known at the time of the call: SYSDATE, SYSTIMESTAMP, CURRENT_DATE, CURRENT_TIMESTAMP, DBTIMEZONE, LOCALTIMESTAMP, SESSIONTIMEZONE, UID, USER, and USERENV

For a row of data to be accepted as input to given table, any CHECK constraint present must evaluate to either TRUE or unknown, due to a NULL.

Multiple Constraints

A table may be declared with multiple constraints. Here's an example:

```
CREATE TABLE VENDORS
(VENDOR_ID      NUMBER CONSTRAINT VENDOR_ID_PK PRIMARY KEY,
 VENDOR_NAME    VARCHAR2(20) NOT NULL,
 STATUS         NUMBER(1) CONSTRAINT STATUS_NN NOT NULL,
 CATEGORY       VARCHAR2(20),
 CONSTRAINT     STATUS_CK CHECK (STATUS IN (4, 5)),
 CONSTRAINT     CATEGORY_CK CHECK
                (CATEGORY IN ('Active','Suspended','Inactive')));
```

In the preceding example, we have a single CREATE TABLE statement that creates a table along with five constraints:

- A user-named PRIMARY KEY on VENDOR_ID
- A system-named NOT NULL constraint on VENDOR_NAME
- A user-named NOT NULL constraint on STATUS
- Two CHECK constraints: one on STATUS and another on CATEGORY

Any single table may have only one PRIMARY KEY constraint. It can have any other combination of any other constraints.

Full List

Table 2-4 displays a full set of sample constraint statements for each constraint type and each statement format.

Take particular note of the FOREIGN KEY examples. The most important portion of the FOREIGN KEY constraint declaration is not the keywords FOREIGN KEY but the keyword REFERENCES. The term FOREIGN KEY appears in only one format of the statement.

| TABLE 2-4 | Constraint Review | | | |

	In Line		Out of Line	
	Named	**System Assigned**	**Named**	**System Assigned**
PRIMARY KEY	CREATE TABLE PEOPLE (ID NUMBER CONSTRAINT ID_ PK PRIMARY KEY);	CREATE TABLE PEOPLE (ID NUMBER PRIMARY KEY);	CREATE TABLE PEOPLE (ID NUMBER, CONSTRAINT ID_ PK PRIMARY KEY (ID));	CREATE TABLE PEOPLE (ID NUMBER, PRIMARY KEY (ID));
FOREIGN KEY	CREATE TABLE PETS(OWNER_ ID NUMBER CONSTRAINT PT_ PP_FK REFERENCES PEOPLE (ID));	CREATE TABLE PETS(OWNER_ ID NUMBER REFERENCES PEOPLE (ID));	CREATE TABLE PETS(OWNER_ ID NUMBER, CONSTRAINT PT_PP_FK FOREIGN KEY (OWNER_ID) REFERENCES PEOPLE (ID));	CREATE TABLE PETS(OWNER_ ID NUMBER, FOREIGN KEY (OWNER_ID) REFERENCES PEOPLE (ID));
NOT NULL	CREATE TABLE PEOPLE (ID NUMBER CONSTRAINT ID_ NN NOT NULL);	CREATE TABLE PEOPLE (ID NUMBER NOT NULL);	Not applicable	Not applicable
RUNIQUE	CREATE TABLE PEOPLE (ID NUMBER CONSTRAINT ID_ UN UNIQUE);	CREATE TABLE PEOPLE (ID NUMBER UNIQUE);	CREATE TABLE PEOPLE (ID NUMBER, CONSTRAINT ID_ UN UNIQUE (ID));	CREATE TABLE PEOPLE (ID NUMBER, UNIQUE (ID));
CHECK	CREATE TABLE PEOPLE (ID NUMBER CONSTRAINT ID_ CK CHECK (ID >10));	CREATE TABLE PEOPLE (ID NUMBER CHECK (ID >10));	CREATE TABLE PEOPLE (ID NUMBER, CONSTRAINT ID_ CK CHECK (ID >10));	CREATE TABLE PEOPLE (ID NUMBER, CHECK (ID >10));

Data Type Restrictions

There are some restrictions on some constraints. See Table 2-5 for a summary of data type restrictions on constraints. These restrictions mean that the data types identified cannot and will not receive a constraint applied against them if they are of the types indicated in the table with a "No" in the appropriate field. For

TABLE 2-5   Data Types and Constraint Restrictions (No = Not Allowed)

Data Type	NOT NULL	UNIQUE	PRIMARY KEY	FOREIGN KEY	CHECK
TIMESTAMP WITH TIME ZONE	—	No	No	No	—
BLOB	—	No	No	No	—
CLOB	—	No	No	No	—

example, the PRIMARY KEY constraint cannot include any columns with a data type of BLOB, CLOB, or TIMESTAMP WITH TIME ZONE. (Note, however, that constraints may be applied to columns that have the data type of TIMESTAMP WITH LOCAL TIME ZONE.)

CERTIFICATION OBJECTIVE 2.06

Drop Columns and Set Column UNUSED

This section looks at what you can do when you find that you have columns you no longer wish to keep in a table. You can choose to drop a column from the database or, as an alternative, you may render it UNUSED. This section looks at how to do either of these tasks.

Dropping Columns

Altering a table to drop columns that are no longer used can free up storage space and potentially improve performance of the table. Any constraints or indices on the column will also be dropped when you drop the column.

Here are two examples—one without parentheses around the column name, another with the parentheses:

```
ALTER TABLE ORDER_RETURNS DROP COLUMN CRUISE_ORDER_DATE;
ALTER TABLE ORDER_RETURNS DROP (CRUISE_ORDER_DATE);
```

Both are valid statements to drop the CRUISE_ORDER_DATE column. Note that the keyword COLUMN is required in the first variation, where the DROP clause syntax omits the parentheses. In the second variation, the keyword COLUMN is omitted, and the parentheses are used.

The first variation is limited to dropping one column per SQL statement. Using the second variation, however, you can drop multiple columns by using the keyword DROP one time, omitting the keyword COLUMN, and then including a pair of parentheses, followed by a list of the column names you wish to drop. For example:

```
ALTER TABLE ORDER_RETURNS
            DROP (CRUISE_ORDER_DATE, FORM_TYPE, NAME_SUFFIX);
```

You cannot drop all of the columns in a table. A table must have at least one column.

Restrictions

If a column is referenced by a foreign key constraint in another table, then the preceding syntax will trigger a warning message and the attempt to drop the column will fail.

For example, consider this code:

```
CREATE TABLE CRUISE_ORDERS
   (CRUISE_ORDER_ID    NUMBER,
    ORDER_DATE         DATE,
    CONSTRAINT PK_CO PRIMARY KEY (CRUISE_ORDER_ID));
CREATE TABLE ORDER_RETURNS
   (ORDER_RETURN_ID    NUMBER,
    CRUISE_ORDER_ID    NUMBER,
    CRUISE_ORDER_DATE  DATE,
    CONSTRAINT PK_OR PRIMARY KEY (ORDER_RETURN_ID),
    CONSTRAINT FK_OR_CO FOREIGN KEY
         (CRUISE_ORDER_ID)
            REFERENCES CRUISE_ORDERS (CRUISE_ORDER_ID));
```

These SQL statements will create two tables. CRUISE_ORDERS is created with a PRIMARY KEY constraint, and ORDER_RETURNS is created with a FOREIGN KEY constraint that references the primary key of CRUISE_ORDERS. See Figure 2-5 for the data model representing the relationship.

In the CRUISE_ORDERS table, we cannot simply drop the CRUISE_ORDER_ID column:

```
SQL> ALTER TABLE CRUISE_ORDERS DROP COLUMN CRUISE_ORDER_ID;
ALTER TABLE CRUISE_ORDERS DROP COLUMN CRUISE_ORDER_ID;
                                      *
ERROR at line 1:
ORA-12992: cannot drop parent key column
```

Data model for
CRUISE_ORDERS
and ORDER_
RETURNS

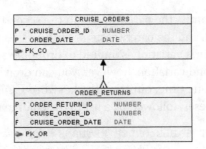

In order to drop the CRUISE_ORDER_ID column we need to address the constraint:

```
SQL> ALTER TABLE CRUISE_ORDERS DROP COLUMN CRUISE_ORDER_ID
CASCADE CONSTRAINTS;

Table altered.
```

The statement above works when we add the keywords CASCADE CONSTRAINTS to indicate that we want to drop the column and also drop any constraints on the column as well.

When using the keywords CASCADE CONSTRAINTS, note that both CONSTRAINT and CONSTRAINTS work equally well. Oracle documentation specifies the keywords in the plural: CASCADE CONSTRAINTS.

The reason we're prevented from dropping the CRUISE_ORDER_ID column in CRUISE_ORDERS is because a foreign key constraint elsewhere is depending on that column. However, the referencing table does not have the same restriction on dropping columns. For example, this will work successfully without the CASCADE CONTRAINTS keywords:

```
SQL> ALTER TABLE ORDER_RETURNS DROP COLUMN CRUISE_ORDER_ID;

Table altered.
```

The DROP COLUMN statement executes successfully, and while it may not be readily apparent, the FOREIGN KEY constraint is also dropped as a result of this statement. After all, the FOREIGN KEY constraint is based on the CRUISE_ORDER_ID column in ORDER_RETURNS, and since we've dropped the column in that table, the constraint is dropped as well, without the CASCADE CONSTRAINTS keywords. However, you may include them if you wish:

```
SQL> ALTER TABLE ORDER_RETURNS DROP COLUMN CRUISE_ORDER_ID CASCADE CONSTRAINTS;

Table altered.
```

This would have worked as well either way.

However, let's look a slight variation of this scenario and see what happens when we have a compound key as our foreign key. See below:

```
CREATE TABLE CRUISE_ORDERS
   (CRUISE_ORDER_ID     NUMBER,
    ORDER_DATE          DATE,
    CONSTRAINT PK_CO PRIMARY KEY (CRUISE_ORDER_ID, ORDER_DATE));
CREATE TABLE ORDER_RETURNS
   (ORDER_RETURN_ID     NUMBER,
    CRUISE_ORDER_ID     NUMBER,
    CRUISE_ORDER_DATE   DATE,
    CONSTRAINT PK_OR PRIMARY KEY (ORDER_RETURN_ID),
    CONSTRAINT FK_OR_CO FOREIGN KEY
              (CRUISE_ORDER_ID, CRUISE_ORDER_DATE)
     REFERENCES CRUISE_ORDERS (CRUISE_ORDER_ID, ORDER_DATE));
```

The code above creates the same two tables we saw earlier—CRUISE_ORDERS and ORDER_RETURNS. As before, there is a foreign key constraint on ORDER_RETURNS referencing CRUISE_ORDERS, but now it is a compound foreign key—this foreign key is based on two columns: CRUISE_ORDER_ID and ORDER_DATE.

If we try to drop one of those columns in ORDER_RETURNS, we get an error message:

```
SQL> ALTER TABLE ORDER_RETURNS DROP COLUMN CRUISE_ORDER_ID;
ALTER TABLE CRUISE_ORDERS DROP COLUMN CRUISE_ORDER_ID;
                                      *
ERROR at line 1:
ORA-12991: column is referenced in a multi-column constraint
```

One alternative here is to drop both foreign key columns at once:

```
SQL> ALTER TABLE ORDER_RETURNS DROP (CRUISE_ORDER_ID, CRUISE_ORDER_DATE);

Table altered.
```

FIGURE 2-6

DROP COLUMN
with CASCADE
CONSTRAINTS

Alternatively, we could stay with our original plan to drop one column, but account for the constraint in the process. If we add the keywords CASCADE CONSTRAINTS to the DROP COLUMN statement on just the CRUISE_ORDER_ ID column, the statement will execute successfully. See Figure 2-6 for an example of the results.

The effect of the CASCADE CONSTRAINT keywords with the DROP COLUMN clause is to drop the column and also to drop the associated constraints on the column that might prevent the column from being dropped.

An additional note about dropping columns: you cannot drop the final remaining column in a table; at least one column must remain in the table.

UNUSED

Instead of dropping a table column you are no longer using, you may elect to declare it *unused* and leave it in place. Once you set a column as UNUSED, it is never again available; it is as though it has been dropped. As with dropped columns, any constraints or indices on the column will also be dropped. You will never be able to recover a column that is set to UNUSED. A ROLLBACK statement will have no effect—an UNUSED column will not be recovered in a ROLLBACK operation. Once a column is set to UNUSED, you can add new columns that have the same name as any unused columns for the table.

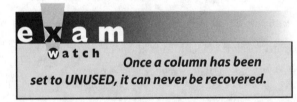

Once a column has been set to UNUSED, it can never be recovered.

So why wouldn't you just DROP a column instead of setting it to UNUSED? One reason is the performance for the DROP statement versus the SET UNUSED approach. If you're working with a very large table or set of tables, and you need to drop some columns, you may find that the system performance for executing the DROP is temporarily unacceptable, particularly for a system that is in heavy production. If this is an issue, and you need to achieve the look-and-feel of a dropped column immediately, then the SET UNUSED alternative is a welcome option. The performance is speedy, the results are—for all practical purposes—the same, and you can always schedule a time later to come back and drop the column during a period of low activity in the database.

One thing to keep in mind: there's a limit to the total number of columns any given table can have. That limit is 1,000—you cannot create more than a thousand columns in any one table. If you set a column to be UNUSED, that column will still count as part of the thousand columns toward your limit, until you eventually DROP the column—which you can do; we'll discuss how to drop an unused column in a bit.

The syntax for SET UNUSED is virtually identical to the ALTER TABLE . . . DROP syntax. Simply replace DROP with the keywords SET UNUSED, and the rest is the same. For example:

```
ALTER TABLE ORDER_RETURNS
         SET UNUSED COLUMN CRUISE_ORDER_DATE;
```

Note: in the above example, if the column CRUISE_ORDER_DATE doesn't already exist, the statement will fail with an error message. And as we saw with DROP, if the column does exist and also is constrained—if there is an existing constraint on the column—the ALTER will fail.

As with DROP, the syntax for changing multiple columns to the UNUSED state requires parentheses and eliminates the COLUMN reserved word, like so:

```
ALTER TABLE ORDER_RETURNS
         SET UNUSED (CRUISE_ORDER_DATE, FORM_TYPE, NAME_SUFFIX);
```

You can set as many columns to UNUSED as you wish. The only requirement is that you must, as you might guess, satisfy all constraints and other requirements of a table and its structure—for example, the table still must have at least one valid column at any time—so you cannot set all of its columns to UNUSED.

Tables that have any columns that are set to UNUSED can be found in the data dictionary view USER_UNUSED_COL_TABS. However, this view doesn't reveal any column names that are unused; it simply gives you the names of any and all tables that contain unused columns, and a numeric count of how many unused columns each one contains. You cannot recover the unused columns, nor can you even identify them. But you can drop them. To drop those unused columns, use this statement:

```
ALTER TABLE table_name DROP UNUSED COLUMNS;
```

For example:

```
ALTER TABLE ORDER_RETURNS DROP UNUSED COLUMNS;
```

This statement will drop all unused columns that are associated with the table ORDER_RETURNS.

CERTIFICATION OBJECTIVE 2.07

Create and Use External Tables

An external table is a read-only table that is defined within the database but exists outside of the database. In more technical terms, the external table's metadata is stored inside the database, and the data it contains is outside of the database.

External tables have a number of restrictions on them. You can query them with the SELECT statement, but you cannot use any other DML statements on them. You can't create an INDEX on them, and they won't accept constraints.

Benefits

So why would you create an external table? Their primary benefit is to create an easy-to-use bridge between SQL tables and non-database data sources. If you've ever used the Oracle tool SQL*Loader, or Data Pump, then you'll be pleased to discover that the external table feature was designed to incorporate the functionality found in those tools into a SQL context.

A great example is when you have some non-SQL data source that regularly produces information needed in the database, such as a flat file transfer, a web site reference, a spreadsheet application, a legacy 3GL application, or something comparable. If that data source is capable of providing some sort of formatted flat file, then it can be structured in such a way that it can be copied directly into a file that the SQL external table will instantly recognize and be able to query. In other words, it will create a sort of one-way data transfer into the SQL database, but using SQL SELECT statements instead of utilities such as SQL*Loader.

Creating External Tables

To create an external table, you can declare its columns and their data types. You can also populate the external table with a subquery at the time you create it.

But that's about all you can do with external tables. They are restricted in a number of ways:

- You cannot create a column with a LOB data type—no CLOB, BLOB, NCLOB, etc.
- You cannot add a constraint to an external table.
- You cannot change the column of an external table to UNUSED. If you try, SQL will process the statement but will actually drop the column.

Essentially, all you do with an external table is declare its structure and define the parameters by which the SQL database communicates with the external table. In order to establish that communication, you must first understand two subjects:

- DIRECTORY objects
- The Oracle utilities SQL*Loader and Oracle Data Pump

We'll look at those next, and then we'll create an external table.

DIRECTORY Objects

To create an external table, we'll need to identify the location in the operating system where the external file containing the table will reside. For this, we need to look at the CREATE DIRECTORY statement.

The CREATE DIRECTORY statement creates an object in the database that represents the name of a directory on the server's file system. Here's an example:

```
CREATE OR REPLACE DIRECTORY directory_name AS directory_reference;
```

where *directory_name* is a name you specify, just as you would any other database object, and *directory_reference* is a string literal, surrounded by single quotation marks, that identifies a location within your Oracle server's file system, into which you wish for external tables to be stored. For example:

```
CREATE OR REPLACE DIRECTORY BANK_FILES AS 'F:\bnk_files\trnsfr';
```

The result of this statement is that we've just created an object in the database named BANK_FILES that looks to the operating system where the Oracle server resides and assumes that the directory reference in the string literal is consistent with the syntax required for that particular operating system. In this case, we're pointing to a Windows drive "F:" and its root level directory "bnk_files", within which is the subdirectory "trnsfr"—that subdirectory is our target.

The DIRECTORY object will not parse this reference but instead will just store it as is. If it's incorrect, you won't find out until later when you try to use the DIRECTORY object.

Also, the DIRECTORY object will not create the subdirectory; the assumption here is that the subdirectory already exists. If it does not, you won't get an error message until you use the DIRECTORY object later.

The keywords OR REPLACE are optional.

In our example, the name BANK_FILES is a name we specify. This name is the name assigned to the object, and this name is how we will reference the DIRECTORY object in the future.

Once a directory has been created, the owner must grant READ and/or WRITE access to any user who may use it:

```
GRANT READ ON DIRECTORY directory_name TO username;
```

That includes users who may wish to use external tables that are built with the directory objects.

Oracle Utilities

The Oracle database provides a number of utilities that accompany their database product. Those utilities that are important to external tables include

- SQL*Loader
- Oracle Data Pump Export
- Oracle Data Pump Import

Each is documented in the Oracle Corporation reference manual titled "Oracle Utilities". Together, the utilities provide capabilities that allow external data sources to communicate with SQL objects within the database.

A complete review of their capabilities is beyond the scope of the exam and therefore this book. But it's important for the exam to recognize that a large component of the definitions associated with the declaration of an external table comes from these utilities.

Creating an External Table

Let's walk through an example. Let's say we have an external text file containing the following data about invoices:

```
ID  INV_DATE      ACCT_NO
--- ------------- --------------
701 03/15/09      CODDA009
702 03/17/09      CODDA010
703 03/18/09      CODDA011
```

We want to create an external table for this data; let's call it INVOICE_DATA.TXT.

First, we go to the file system on which the Oracle database resides, locate the same drive, and we create a subdirectory off of the root level. We'll call it "LOAD_INVOICES". Then we create the associated DIRECTORY object:

```
CREATE DIRECTORY INVOICE_FILES AS '\LOAD_INVOICES';
```

By this point, we won't necessarily have to have created the LOAD_INVOICES directory, nor to have put the INVOICE_DATA.TXT file in that directory. But for the sake of our example, now we do so, before continuing.

Next, we execute a CREATE TABLE statement that references the directory, along with the necessary clauses to tell Oracle SQL to load the external file, and how to load it:

```
01  CREATE TABLE INVOICES_EXTERNAL
02  ( INVOICE_ID      CHAR(3),
03    INVOICE_DATE    CHAR(9),
04    ACCOUNT_NUMBER CHAR(13)
05  )
06  ORGANIZATION EXTERNAL
07    (TYPE ORACLE_LOADER
08     DEFAULT DIRECTORY INVOICE_FILES
09     ACCESS PARAMETERS
10       (RECORDS DELIMITED BY NEWLINE
11        SKIP 2
12        FIELDS (INVOICE_ID      CHAR(3),
13                INVOICE_DATE    CHAR(9),
14                ACCOUNT_NUMBER CHAR(13))
15       )
16     LOCATION ('INVOICE_DATA.TXT')
17    );
```

Once this statement executes, we end up with an external table in the database called INVOICES_EXTERNAL.

■ Note lines 2 through 4 where we declared our table using the data types CHAR. You'll recall these are fixed-length data types. We did this to accommodate the transfer of rows in from the text file in lines 12 through 14. Each column's data type is set to CHAR, the fixed-length alphanumeric data type, and the counts for each data type correspond to the counts of the columns in the text file 'INVOICE_DATA.TXT', which is identified in line 16 and is in the directory stored in the directory object INVOICE_FILES, named in line 8.

■ Lines 1 through 5 form a complete CREATE TABLE statement by themselves, without the external table clause. But starting on line 6 are the keywords and clauses used to declare the external table, and together, lines 1 through 17 form the complete CREATE TABLE statement for our example.

■ Line 6 includes the keywords ORGANIZATION EXTERNAL, which are required.

■ Line 7 is where we specify that we are using ORACLE_LOADER, aka the SQL*Loader features. An alternative TYPE value here would be ORACLE_DATAPUMP.

■ Line 9 begins the set of values for ACCESS PARAMETERS, which are enclosed within the parentheses that open on line 10 and close on line 15.

■ Three ACCESS PARAMETERS are used here: RECORDS, SKIP, and FIELDS.

■ Line 10—RECORDS DELIMITED BY NEWLINE—means that each new line starts a new row of data for the INVOICES_EXTERNAL table.

■ Line 11—SKIP 2—tells ORACLE_LOADER that the first two lines of the INVOICE_DATA.TXT file are to be skipped—they just contain header information.

■ Line 12—FIELDS—starts the specifications for each column, where each column's length is carefully specified to match the length in the INVOICES_DATA.TXT file.

Many more ACCESS PARAMETERS exist that are not invoked here. I could probably write a separate book just on all the options and features that exist with the various clauses for the types ORACLE_LOADER and ORACLE_DATAPUMP. But I won't, and you shouldn't need that for the exam.

Using an External Table

Once we've created an external table, we can SELECT from it just like any other table. For example:

```
SELECT * FROM INVOICES_EXTERNAL;

INVOICE_ID INVOICE_DATE ACCOUNT_NUMBER
---------- ------------ --------------
   701       03/15/09       CODDA009
   702       03/17/09       CODDA010
   703       03/18/09       CODDA011
```

Many external tables will start with source data that is rough and unformatted. However, the first step is just to get it in the database. Once that is accomplished, you can use the various conversion functions and other features of SQL to clean up and reformat the data:

```
SELECT TO_NUMBER(INVOICE_ID),
       TO_DATE(INVOICE_DATE,'MM/DD/RR') INVOICE_DATE,
       LTRIM(ACCOUNT_NUMBER,' ') ACCOUNT_NUMBER
FROM   INVOICES_EXTERNAL;

INVOICE_ID             INVOICE_DATE               ACCOUNT_NUMBER
---------------------- -------------------------- --------------
   701                   15-MAR-09                   CODDA009
   702                   17-MAR-09                   CODDA010
   703                   18-MAR-09                   CODDA011
```

External tables can be queried like any table or view in the database.

Note the output—the numbers are reformatted, the date values are converted, the account numbers have been trimmed up, and everything looks terrific.

Remember that you cannot use INSERT, UPDATE, or DELETE statements on external tables.

CERTIFICATION SUMMARY

The main database objects that are subjects of the exam include tables, views, sequences, synonyms, indexes, constraints, users, and roles. A table stores data. A view is something that looks and acts like a table but serves as a filter onto one or more tables. A sequence is a counter, and it's often used to generate unique numbers for storing identifiers with new rows that are added to a table. A synonym is an alias for another object. An index is an object that provides lookup support to a table in order to speed up queries on the table. A constraint is a rule on a table that controls what sort of data can be stored in the table. A user is an object that defines a user account. A role represents a set of one or more privileges that are granted to a user in order for that user to have access rights to other objects.

All database objects are either schema or nonschema objects. Schema objects are owned by a user and exist within a user account. Nonschema objects exist to support the database at large. Of the main database objects you are looking at for the exam, the schema objects are table, view, sequence, private synonym, index, and constraint. The nonschema objects are user, role, and public synonym.

You use the CREATE TABLE statement to create a table, name the table, name the columns, assign data types to the columns, and optionally create various constraints to the table as well.

Objects that exist in the same namespace must have unique names. Objects that exist in different namespaces may have duplicate names. Indexes have their own namespace within a schema; so do constraints. Beyond that, a schema has one namespace for the collective set of tables, views, sequences, and private synonyms. Outside of the schema, user and role objects share a namespace for the entire database; public synonyms have their own namespace for the entire database.

Columns must be assigned a data type when they are created. Data types include character, numeric, and date data types. Character data types include CHAR and VARCHAR2; numeric data types include NUMBER and FLOAT; date data types include DATE, TIMESTAMP, TIMESTAMP WITH TIME ZONE, TIMESTAMP WITH LOCAL TIME ZONE, INTERVAL YEAR TO MONTH, and INTERVAL DAY TO SECOND. There are also large object, or LOB, data types, such as BLOB, CLOB, and NCLOB.

Constraints can be created within the CREATE TABLE statement or afterward, in the ALTER TABLE statement. They can be created in line, meaning as part of a column's definition, or out of line, meaning afterward as a separate line item within the CREATE TABLE or ALTER TABLE statement. An exception is NOT NULL, which cannot be created out of line.

The five types of constraints are NOT NULL, UNIQUE, PRIMARY KEY, FOREIGN KEY, and CHECK.

The TRUNCATE TABLE statement can be used in those special circumstances where you may want to remove all the rows of a table without firing any DML triggers or selectively removing data from any associated INDEX objects, as would happen with a DELETE statement. In such a situation, TRUNCATE TABLE is an attractive alternative to dropping and re-creating a table, since it leaves the table and its relationships intact, as well as any indexes. TRUNCATE TABLE can remove statements much more quickly with less processing overhead than DELETE. Because TRUNCATE TABLE fires no DML triggers, it is considered DDL; therefore, its use performs an implicit commit, and its results cannot be rolled back.

If TRUNCATE TABLE is applied to a table for which there exists an associated parent table with a foreign key using the ON CASCADE DELETE clause, then TRUNCATE TABLE will result in an error if there are in fact rows in that parent table that might otherwise be deleted as a result of ON CASCADE DELETE. For this situation, you must use TRUNCATE TABLE ... CASCADE to confirm your desire to remove those parent rows.

Columns can be dropped from a table. Columns that are part of a referential constraint—in other words, a FOREIGN KEY constraint—may be dropped with the CASCADE CONSTRAINTS keywords added so that the constraints are dropped as well. Columns may be set to UNUSED to render them virtually dropped, but sparing the processing overhead required to drop a column. An UNUSED column is no longer available, and it can be dropped later.

External tables exist outside of the database. The process that supports them has its roots and syntax in the SQL*Loader tool, but the result is a table that can be described just like any other. External tables can be queried but cannot receive data input via INSERT, UPDATE, or DELETE.

TWO-MINUTE DRILL

Categorize the Main Database Objects

- ☐ Tables store data.
- ☐ Views serve as a sort of "window" onto tables.
- ☐ Indexes provide lookup support to speed queries on a table, like an index to a book.
- ☐ Sequences are simple counter objects.
- ☐ Synonyms are alternative names for existing objects.
- ☐ Constraints are rules on tables.
- ☐ Users are objects that own other nonuser objects.
- ☐ Roles are sets of rights, or privileges, that can be granted to a user to give that user access to other objects.
- ☐ Objects are either schema or nonschema objects.
- ☐ Tables, views, indexes, sequences, and private synonyms are schema objects.
- ☐ Users and roles, along with public synonyms, are nonschema objects.

Create a Simple Table

- ☐ The CREATE TABLE statement is used to create a table.
- ☐ You assign a name to a table by using the rules of naming database objects.
- ☐ You also assign names to the table's columns using the same rules.
- ☐ All tables have at least one column.

Review the Table Structure

- ☐ The DESC command can be used to display a table's structure.
- ☐ The structure includes the table name, table columns, data types, and optional constraints.

List the Data Types That Are Available for Columns

- ☐ Each column must be assigned a data type.
- ☐ Data types include numeric, character, and date types, such as VARCHAR2, NUMBER, and DATE.
- ☐ Data types also include large object types, including BLOB.

Explain How Constraints Are Created at the Time of Table Creation

- ☐ The types of constraints are NOT NULL, UNIQUE, PRIMARY KEY, FOREIGN KEY, and CHECK.
- ☐ A column with a NOT NULL constraint must be assigned a value for each row that is added to the table.
- ☐ A UNIQUE constraint requires that if data is added to a column for a given row, that data must be unique for any existing value already in the column.
- ☐ A PRIMARY KEY constraint is the combination of NOT NULL and UNIQUE.
- ☐ A PRIMARY KEY may be assigned to one column or a combination of columns.
- ☐ A PRIMARY KEY assigned to a combination of columns is called a composite key.
- ☐ A single table may have only one PRIMARY KEY.
- ☐ A FOREIGN KEY correlates one or more columns in one table with a set of similar columns in a second table.
- ☐ A FOREIGN KEY requires that the second table already have either a PRIMARY KEY constraint or a UNIQUE constraint assigned to the correlated columns before the FOREIGN KEY can be created.
- ☐ Once created, the FOREIGN KEY ensures that any values added to the table will match existing values in the PRIMARY KEY columns of the second table.
- ☐ Constraints can be created with the CREATE TABLE statement or within the ALTER TABLE statement.
- ☐ Constraints can be defined as part of the column definitions (in line) or after (out of line). One exception is that NOT NULL can be created in line but not out of line.

Drop Columns and Set Column UNUSED

- ☐ The DROP clause of ALTER TABLE can be used to remove a column from a table.
- ☐ Once a column is removed with DROP, the data is lost.
- ☐ Dropping a column can consume significant processing time if the table involved contains a lot of data.
- ☐ If you drop a column with a constraint, the constraint is also dropped. The same is true for any index objects on the column; they are also dropped.

☐ SET UNUSED renders a column permanently unavailable; it cannot be recovered.

☐ The SET UNUSED clause can benefit a large table in heavy production that cannot afford the overhead processing power of a DROP.

☐ After a table has columns that are set to UNUSED, they can be dropped with the DROP UNUSED COLUMNS clause of ALTER TABLE.

Create and Use External Tables

☐ An external table is a read-only table within the database that stores data outside of the database.

☐ The communication between the external table's data storage file and database objects is based on the logic of SQL*Loader or Oracle Data Pump.

☐ You use a database object known as the DIRECTORY object as part of the definition of an external table.

SELF TEST

The following questions will help you measure your understanding of the material presented in this chapter. Choose one correct answer for each question unless otherwise directed.

Categorize the Main Database Objects

1. A table is which of the following? (Choose all that apply.)
   A. A schema object
   B. A nonschema object
   C. A role
   D. All of the above

2. Which of the following are schema objects? (Choose all that apply.)
   A. SEQUENCE
   B. PASSWORD
   C. INDEX
   D. ROLE

3. A CONSTRAINT is assigned to which of the following? (Choose all that apply.)
   A. TABLE
   B. SYNONYM
   C. SEQUENCE
   D. INDEX

Create a Simple Table

4. Which of the following are valid CREATE TABLE statements? (Choose three.)
   A. CREATE TABLE $ORDERS
      (ID NUMBER,
      NAME VARCHAR2(30));
   B. CREATE TABLE CUSTOMER_HISTORY
      (ID NUMBER,
      NAME VARCHAR2(30));
   C. CREATE TABLE "Boat Inventory"
      (ID NUMBER,
      NAME VARCHAR2(30));
   D. CREATE TABLE workSchedule
      (ID NUMBER,
      NAME VARCHAR2(30));

5. Which of the following options can be used with the reserved word CREATE to form the beginning of a complete SQL statement? (Choose three.)

   A. TABLE

   B. VIEW

   C. CONSTRAINT

   D. SEQUENCE

6. You are logged in to user FINANCE. It is currently the only schema in the entire database. The following exist in the database:

   – A VIEW named VENDORS

   – A CONSTRAINT named VENDORS

   – An INDEX named CUSTOMER#ADDRESS

   You attempt to execute the following SQL statement:

   ```
   CREATE TABLE CUSTOMER#ADDRESS
       (ID  NUMBER,
        NAME VARCHAR2(30));
   ```

   Which one of the following is true?

   A. The question is flawed because you cannot have an INDEX named CUSTOMER#ADDRESS.

   B. The question is flawed because you cannot have a VIEW and a CONSTRAINT with identical names in the same schema.

   C. The SQL statement will fail to execute and result in an error message because you cannot create a TABLE name with the # character.

   D. The SQL statement will fail to execute and result in an error message because you cannot create a TABLE that has the same name as an INDEX in the same schema.

   E. The SQL statement will execute, and the TABLE will be created.

7. You have a single database, with only one schema. The following four objects exist in the database:

   – A TABLE named PRODUCT_CATALOG

   – A TABLE named ADS

   – A USER named PRODUCT_CATALOG

   – A VIEW named CONFERENCE_SCHEDULE

   How many of the four objects are owned by the schema?

   A. 0

   B. 2

   C. 3

   D. 4

8. Which of the following is true about ROLES?
   A. Roles are schema objects but only when created from within a user account.
   B. Roles are in the same namespace as CONSTRAINTS.
   C. Roles are in the same namespace as TABLES.
   D. Roles are in the same namespace as USERS.

Review the Table Structure

9. The DESC command can be used to do which of the following?
   A. Show a table's columns and the data types of those columns
   B. Show a brief paragraph describing what the table does
   C. Show a table's name and who created it
   D. Show the data that is contained within a table

List the Data Types That Are Available for Columns

10. You attempt to execute the following SQL statement:

```
CREATE TABLE VENDORS
(VENDOR_ID    NUMBER,
 VENDOR_NAME VARCHAR2,
 CATEGORY     CHAR);
```

   Which one of the following is true?
   A. The execution fails because there is no precision indicated for NUMBER.
   B. The execution fails because there is no precision indicated for VARCHAR2.
   C. The execution fails because there is no precision indicated for CHAR.
   D. The execution succeeds, and the table is created.

11. The following SQL statements create a table with a column named A, then add a row to that table, then query the table:

```
CREATE TABLE NUMBER_TEST (A NUMBER(5,3));
INSERT INTO NUMBER_TEST (A) VALUES (3.1415);
SELECT A FROM NUMBER_TEST;
```

   What is the displayed output of the SELECT statement?
   A. 3.1415
   B. 3.142
   C. 3.141
   D. None of the above

Explain How Constraints Are Created at the Time of Table Creation

12. Which of the following SQL statements creates a table that will reject attempts to INSERT a row with NULL values entered into the POSITION_ID column?

A. `CREATE TABLE POSITIONS`
   `(POSITION_ID NUMBER(3),`
   `   CONSTRAINT POSITION_CON UNIQUE (POSITION_ID));`

B. `CREATE TABLE POSITIONS`
   `(POSITION_ID NUMBER(3),`
   `   CONSTRAINT POSITION_CON PRIMARY KEY (POSITION_ID));`

C. `CREATE TABLE POSITIONS`
   `(POSITION_ID NUMBER(3),`
   `   CONSTRAINT POSITION_CON REQUIRED (POSITION_ID));`

D. None of the above

13. Review the following SQL statement:

```
CREATE TABLE shipping_Order
( order_ID    NUMBER,
  order_Year  CHAR(2),
  customer_ID NUMBER,
 CONSTRAINT shipping_Order PRIMARY KEY (order_ID, order_Year));
```

Assume there is no table already called SHIPPING_ORDER in the database. What will be the result of an attempt to execute the preceding SQL statement?

A. The statement will fail because the data type for ORDER_YEAR is a CHAR, and CHAR data types aren't allowed in a PRIMARY KEY constraint.

B. The statement will fail because there is no precision for the ORDER_ID column's data type.

C. The table will be created, but the primary key constraint will not be created because the name does not include the _PK suffix.

D. The statement will succeed: the table will be created, and the primary key will also be created.

14. Review the following SQL statement:

```
CREATE TABLE personnel
( personnel_ID    NUMBER(6),
  division_ID     NUMBER(6),
  CONSTRAINT personnel_ID_PK PRIMARY KEY (personnel_ID),
  CONSTRAINT division_ID_PK PRIMARY KEY (division_ID));
```

Assume there is no table already called PERSONNEL in the database. What will be the result of an attempt to execute the preceding SQL statement?

- A. The statement will fail because you cannot create two primary key constraints on the table.
- B. The statement will successfully create the table and the first primary key but not the second.
- C. The statement will successfully create a single table and one composite primary key consisting of two columns.
- D. The statement will successfully create the table and two primary keys.

Drop Columns and Set Column UNUSED

15. The difference between dropping a column from a table with DROP and setting a column to be UNUSED is:
    - A. An UNUSED column can be recovered.
    - B. The UNUSED column and its data are retained within the table's storage allocation and counts against the total limit on the number of columns the table is allowed to have.
    - C. A column that is dropped with DROP no longer appears within the table's description as shown with the DESC or DESCRIBE statement, whereas a column that is set to UNUSED still appears in the table's structure as shown in the output of the DESC statement.
    - D. Nothing.

Create and Use External Tables

16. The purpose of the CREATE DIRECTORY statement is to create a named object in the database:
    - A. That lists names of user accounts that have external privileges
    - B. That contains lookup reference material for queries
    - C. That identifies the root directory of the Oracle server installation
    - D. That points to a directory you choose somewhere within the Oracle server's file system

SELF TEST ANSWERS

Categorize the Main Database Objects

1. ☑ **A.** All database objects are either schema or nonschema objects, and a table falls under the category of schema objects.
   ☒ **B, C,** and **D** are incorrect. A table, which is a schema object, is not a nonschema object. A role is another form of a database object.

2. ☑ **A** and **C.** A sequence and an index are both schema objects. They are owned by a schema.
   ☒ **B** and **D** are incorrect. A password is not a database object. A role consists of one or more privileges that are assigned to a user object, and both the user and role objects are nonschema objects.

3. ☑ **A.** A CONSTRAINT is a rule that restricts what sort of data can be added to a table.
   ☒ **B, C,** and **D** are incorrect. You cannot attach a constraint to a synonym, sequence, or index object.

Create a Simple Table

4. ☑ **B, C,** and **D.** Underscores are acceptable characters in any database table name, provided that if the name is unquoted, the first character is not an underscore. Quotation marks, when used, enable any character to be used throughout the name, including spaces, although all future references to the name will be case-sensitive and require quotation marks. Finally, mixed case can be used to create a table name, although when created, the table name will be stored and treated as uppercase. All future references to the name may continue to be in any case—SQL will perform the necessary case conversion so that the table name, on a practical level, is treated as though it is case-insensitive, even though it is stored internally in uppercase.
   ☒ **A** is incorrect. The first character in any database object name must be a letter; it cannot be a number or special character—unless the name is enclosed in double quotation marks, which this was not.

5. ☑ **A, B,** and **D.** The database objects TABLE, VIEW, and SEQUENCE can each be created directly with a CREATE reserved word to form a complete SQL statement.
   ☒ **C** is incorrect. A CONSTRAINT is not created directly with a CREATE CONSTRAINT statement but instead is created indirectly as a clause within the CREATE TABLE and ALTER TABLE statements.

6. ☑ **E.** The table name may include the # character, as long as it isn't the first character in the table name. An INDEX in the same schema is allowed to have the same name since the INDEX is inside its own namespace within the schema, separate from the namespace in which the TABLE will be created.

    ☒ **A, B, C,** and **D** are incorrect. The question is not flawed—the hash mark (#) is an acceptable character in an object name anywhere from the second character position through to the final character. You are allowed to have a VIEW and a CONSTRAINT with the same names within a single schema, since CONSTRAINTS are contained within their own unique namespace in each schema.

7. ☑ **C.** TABLE and VIEW objects are schema objects, and since you have only one schema in the database, then both have to be owned by the only schema in the database. But the USER object is a nonschema object. In fact, in this one-schema database it must be the schema that owns the other objects. It does not own itself, and it exists at the database level.

    ☒ **A, B,** and **D** are incorrect.

8. ☑ **D.** Both ROLES and USERS exist at the database level and share the same namespace.

    ☒ **A, B,** and **C** are incorrect. It doesn't matter that a ROLE is created from within a schema's user account; it's still a nonschema object and exists in the same namespace. CONSTRAINTS and TABLES both have their namespaces within a schema.

Review the Table Structure

9. ☑ **A.** DESC, or DESCRIBE, presents a display showing a table's columns and the data types of those columns.

    ☒ **B, C,** and **D** are incorrect. The DESC command doesn't show data, the creator, or a text description of the table. All of that information is available through other means, not the DESC command.

List the Data Types That Are Available for Columns

10. ☑ **B.** The VARCHAR2 data type requires precision, for example, VARCHAR2(30).

    ☒ **A, C,** and **D** are incorrect. NUMBER and CHAR can be declared without precision. But VARCHAR2 cannot, and the statement will fail.

11. ☑ **B.** The NUMBER data type has a precision of 5 and a scale of 3. The scale indicates that three digits—but no more than three digits—to the right of the decimal point are allowed. The number is rounded off, and 5 is always rounded up.

    ☒ **A, C,** and **D** are incorrect.

Explain How Constraints Are Created at the Time of Table Creation

12. ☑ **B.** The primary key constraint performs two main jobs, one of which is to ensure that the column upon which it is applied is never allowed to be NULL. The other job is to ensure that any value added to that column is UNIQUE.

☒ **A, C,** and **D** are incorrect. The UNIQUE constraint allows for NULL values. There is no such thing as a REQUIRED constraint. There is a NOT NULL constraint that essentially does what a REQUIRED constraint might do, if one existed. However, this particular form of constraint creation is the out-of-line form, and the NOT NULL constraint cannot be created with the out-of-line form, but rather the in-line form.

13. ☑ **D.** The syntax of the statement is fine. Both the table and the primary key constraint will be successfully created.

☒ **A, B,** and **C** are incorrect. It is perfectly acceptable to create a primary key in any form—single-column or composite—with the CHAR data type. NUMBER is also fine with or without precision and/or scale. The _PK suffix is not required.

14. ☑ **A.** The statement is attempting to create two different primary key constraints, but a table may have only one primary key and no more. The statement will fail with an error.

☒ **B, C,** and **D** are incorrect. The syntax is not attempting a composite primary key but rather two separate primary key constraints, and that is not allowed on any table. The entire statement will fail to execute.

Drop Columns and Set Column UNUSED

15. ☑ **B.** The UNUSED column is still stored as part of the table. There's no storage benefit to the table—no space is reclaimed from an unused column.

☒ **A, C,** and **D** are incorrect. Neither a column dropped with DROP nor an UNUSED column can be seen in the table's structure. A column, once set to UNUSED, can never be recovered. It can only be dropped.

Create and Use External Tables

16. ☑ **D.** CREATE DIRECTORY lets you create a database object name for a directory you choose. Later you can use this object for creating an external table.

☒ **A, B,** and **C** are incorrect.

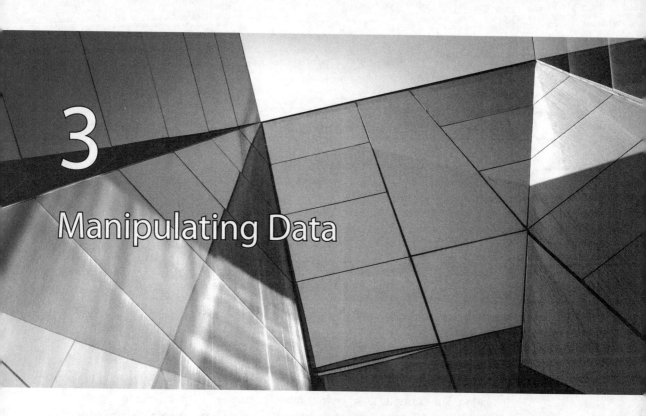

3
Manipulating Data

T his chapter begins to look at that part of SQL known as Data Manipulation Language. We'll get some perspective by looking at DML with regard to where it fits into the larger context of SQL. Then we will review DML statements and their usage and look at some specific examples. Finally we will review some supplemental statements that are used to control transactions involving DML.

CERTIFICATION OBJECTIVE 3.01

Truncate Data

Whenever you need to remove one or more rows from a table, the DELETE statement is generally your best choice. But DELETE may not be ideal in every situation. For example, let's say your table is equipped with indexes to speed up querying and with triggers to protect the logical integrity of the data in the table. Those are all great, but if your table also has a large number of rows, then a DELETE statement will invoke row-by-row processing to review and update each index and fire all appropriate triggers on a row-by-row basis. There's nothing wrong with that, of course; in fact, there's everything right about it. This is what a well-designed database might need to do, depending on its business requirements.

But in certain circumstances where you simply need to remove all the rows in the table, you may find that all that detailed processing is unnecessary; you may need to simply remove all the data.

In such a scenario, you might consider the alternative of dropping the table and then creating it again. But if you were to do that, you would also have to re-create the table's indexes and triggers. Depending on the table's relationships with other tables, the extra work required to make this all happen could grow considerably. In an attempt to bypass some unnecessary processing of a DELETE statement, you may be inadvertently creating a good amount of otherwise unnecessary rework. Yet DELETE may itself impact performance on a large production database.

This is where TRUNCATE TABLE comes in. The TRUNCATE TABLE statement does the following:

■ Removes all the rows in a given table
■ Removes all data in the associated indexes
■ Fires no DML triggers

By avoiding the DROP TABLE/CREATE TABLE approach, using TRUNCATE TABLE does the following:

- Leaves the table and index structures intact
- Leaves all dependencies intact, such as child tables

TRUNCATE TABLE also does the following:

- Does not leverage undo space like DELETE would do
- Performs an implicit commit
- Requires the DROP_ANY_TABLE privilege

Because of the implicit commit, TRUNCATE TABLE does the following:

- Cannot be rolled back
- Does not work with FLASHBACK_TABLE
- Is considered DDL

The fact that TRUNCATE TABLE is DDL is why TRUNCATE TABLE does not fire any DML triggers, such as ON DELETE, which does not apply.

The following is an example of a statement that will truncate the table VENDORS:

```
TRUNCATE TABLE VENDORS;
```

The keyword TRUNCATE is followed by the required word TABLE, which is followed by the name of the table. (The keyword TABLE is required because TRUNCATE may also be used to truncate another object called a cluster, which is not on the exam, so we are not concerned with it here.) This use of TRUNCATE TABLE will remove all the data from the VENDORS table, as well as its indexes, and automatically perform a commit to the database.

Recursively Truncate Child Tables

Oracle 12c offers a new feature with TRUNCATE TABLE, which is the option to CASCADE the truncation to dependent child tables:

```
TRUNCATE TABLE VENDORS CASCADE;
```

Earlier we looked at how a parent-child table relationship can be created with a foreign key constraint with the optional ON DELETE clause, which tells the database to take specific action on a child row if and when a parent row is removed from the parent table. The TRUNCATE TABLE statement's CASCADE works in a similar fashion.

Let's look again at the examples of the tables PORTS and SHIPS (line numbers added):

```
01   CREATE TABLE PORTS
02   (PORT_ID         NUMBER,
03    PORT_NAME       VARCHAR2(20),
04    COUNTRY         VARCHAR2(40),
05    CAPACITY        NUMBER,
06    CONSTRAINT      PORT_PK PRIMARY KEY (PORT_ID));
07
08   CREATE TABLE SHIPS
09   (SHIP_ID         NUMBER,
10    SHIP_NAME       VARCHAR2(20),
11    HOME_PORT_ID NUMBER,
12    CONSTRAINT      SHIPS_PORTS_FK FOREIGN KEY (HOME_PORT_ID)
13                                   REFERENCES PORTS (PORT_ID)
14                                   ON DELETE CASCADE)
15    ;
```

Note the ON DELETE CASCADE clause on line 14. Now let's add some rows to the tables:

```
16   INSERT INTO PORTS VALUES (315, 'Atlanta', 'USA', 100000);
17   INSERT INTO SHIPS VALUES (4000, 'Codd Land Rover', 315);
18   INSERT INTO SHIPS VALUES (4001, 'Codd Vessel Two', NULL);
```

We've created a port for Atlanta, and a ship is assigned to Atlanta. But then someone points out that Atlanta, while a beautiful city, is landlocked, so perhaps we shouldn't try to port a ship there. Clearly we need to remove Atlanta from the PORTS table.

We could simply DELETE the row:

```
19   DELETE PORTS;
```

The DELETE statement will remove all the rows from PORTS, and right now there is only the one row for the Atlanta port. But it will also delete any rows for SHIPS assigned to the Atlanta port, thanks to the ON DELETE CASCADE clause included in the SHIPS table's foreign key constraint (see line 14 in the previous code listing).

If, instead of DELETE, we needed to use TRUNCATE TABLE, then we could try this, but it will not work:

```
19   TRUNCATE TABLE PORTS;
```

With the presence of rows in PORTS for which there are corresponding HOME_PORT_ID values in SHIPS and because SHIPS is tied to PORTS using the ON DELETE CASCADE clause, this sets up the risk that rows in SHIPS may have HOME_PORT_ID values that correspond to PORT_ID values in PORTS. Sure enough, that is the case, resulting in an error message with the TRUNCATE TABLE statement earlier: "ORA-02266: unique/primary keys in table referenced by enabled by foreign keys." To get TRUNCATE TABLE to work in this situation, we need the CASCADE clause.

```
19  TRUNCATE TABLE PORTS CASCADE;
```

Without CASCADE, the Oracle database will not complete the TRUNCATE TABLE statement since the ON DELETE CASCADE clause in a separate child table would force the removal of additional rows of data beyond just the PORTS table. The TRUNCATE TABLE ... CASCADE statement tells the Oracle database to go forward with the removal of those rows anyway.

Note that we needed no such additional clause with DELETE. The presence of ON DELETE CASCADE causes the additional rows to be removed with no additional direction from the DELETE statement. But the TRUNCATE TABLE statement has the additional requirement for the CASCADE clause. Remember, this applies only to situations where a child table has the ON DELETE CASCADE clause of its foreign key constraint.

CERTIFICATION OBJECTIVE 3.02

Insert Rows into a Table

The SQL statement to add rows to a table is the INSERT statement. The INSERT statement is often used to add one row at a time, but it may also be used to add multiple rows at once by drawing them from elsewhere in the database and adding them to the target table with a single INSERT statement. INSERT may use expressions.

INSERT adds rows into a TABLE object, but it can also be used with certain VIEW objects. However, as we will see, a VIEW is simply a filter onto one or more tables, so ultimately INSERT is still adding rows to a TABLE object.

Default Column List

Let's look at an example of an INSERT statement. We're going to add a row to the CRUISES table. First, let's describe the CRUISES table so that we can see the columns—we'll need to know the names and data types of those columns so we can build our INSERT statement (see Figure 3-1).

Here's an example of an INSERT statement you could use on this table:

```
01  INSERT INTO CRUISES
02    (CRUISE_ID, CRUISE_TYPE_ID, CRUISE_NAME,
03     CAPTAIN_ID, START_DATE, END_DATE,
04     STATUS)
05  VALUES
06    (1, 1, 'Day At Sea',
07     101, '02-JAN-10', '09-JAN-10',
08     'Sched');
```

As with all SQL statements, the INSERT statement can be on a single line, or it can span multiple lines. The choice doesn't matter as far as the syntax is concerned. We separated the components of the preceding statement in order to discuss it more easily here. The statement ends with a semicolon, which is at the end of line 8 in this example.

Let's analyze the syntax for this example of INSERT:

■ **Line 1** The reserved words INSERT and INTO, followed by the name of the target table.

■ **Lines 2–4** Within a set of parentheses, a list of the table's columns. The order in which the columns appear does not need to match the order of columns in the table's structure as shown with the DESC command, nor

does it need to include all of the table's columns, as long as we provide for all of the "required" columns, in other words, those with a NOT NULL constraint or something comparable (like the PRIMARY KEY constraint). Any column assigned a DEFAULT value may be omitted from the list.

■ **Line 5**   The reserved word VALUES.

■ **Lines 6–8**   Within a set of parentheses, a series of values to be added to each of the columns listed in—in this example—lines 2–4. Values are expressions and are listed in the same order as each value's corresponding column listed in lines 2–4. For example, the first value in this list starting in line 6 will become the value for the first column identified on line 2, the second value identified in line 6 will be inserted into the second column identified in line 2, and so on.

When the INSERT statement is submitted for execution, the following steps will be performed before the statement returns any results:

■ The existence and validity of the table in line 1 will be confirmed.

■ The existence and validity of the columns in lines 2–4 will be confirmed.

■ The expressions in lines 6–8 will be evaluated.

■ The data types of the expressions in lines 6–8 will be compared against the data types of the associated columns and evaluated for compatibility.

■ The values of the expressions in lines 6–8 will be applied to any constraints that might exist in the table.

If all requirements for data entry to the target table are satisfied and the INSERT statement is determined to be valid, then the statement will execute, and the row will be inserted into the table.

In this example, the columns in our INSERT statement (lines 2–4) just happen to account for every column in the table's structure and in the default sequence of how the columns exist in the table. In this sort of situation, the column list at the beginning of the INSERT statement is not required. In other words, we could have omitted lines 2–4 in this example; the following is a valid alternative to the INSERT statement we just reviewed:

```
01   INSERT INTO CRUISES
02   VALUES
03     (1, 1, 'Day At Sea',
04      101, '02-JAN-10', '09-JAN-10',
05      'Sched');
```

This example will produce the same result because the expressions in lines 3–5 just happen to coincide with the columns in the CRUISES table, in number (there are seven) and in data type, as we saw in Figure 3-1. If that structure changes, the previous statement may fail. For example, if a new column is added to CRUISES, the previous example will fail, whereas the prior INSERT example, which names the columns, will probably continue functioning correctly.

INSERT must respect all data types and constraints in the target table.

Now you are surely asking yourself which is better: (a) to identify the column list by name or (b) to leverage the default approach, omit the list of column names, and simply account for all of the table's columns in the list of values? The answer is it depends on the situation. Generally speaking, in my experience, I tend to prefer (a), where you name each column specifically and do not depend on the default. There are several advantages to this approach. One advantage is that your code will still execute successfully if the columns in the table are altered in various ways. For example, if the table is dropped and re-created in some sort of future upgrade or maintenance effort, the columns could end up in a different sequence. That could trigger a syntax error with the default INSERT, or it could result in something worse—no syntax error but a column mismatch where the data types happen to line up and the INSERT statement works technically but isn't putting the data in the columns you originally intended.

For example, consider the SQL statements shown in Figure 3-2. Here we see a table called TEST_SCORES and an INSERT statement for it. Note that the INSERT uses the default column list. There's nothing wrong with that—technically. But now look at Figure 3-3. Notice that the TEST_SCORES columns are in a different order. Yet the same INSERT statement—with the syntax that does not list columns by name—successfully executes. Why? Because SQL sees only the data types of the list of values in the INSERT statement. In this case, both values being inserted are numeric literals, and numeric literals are acceptable in either column. So, what is

FIGURE 3-2

The TEST_
SCORES table

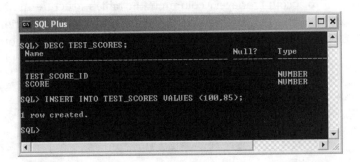

FIGURE 3-3

The TEST_
SCORES table
with a different
structure

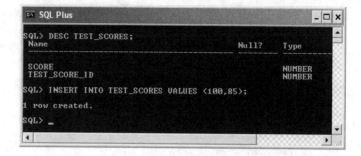

```
SQL> DESC TEST_SCORES;
 Name                                           Null?     Type

 SCORE                                                    NUMBER
 TEST_SCORE_ID                                            NUMBER

SQL> INSERT INTO TEST_SCORES VALUES (100,85);

1 row created.

SQL> _
```

the intent here? Is 100 the value for TEST_SCORE_ID and 85 the value for SCORE?
Or is it the other way around? The point is that you cannot tell in this particular
variation of INSERT statement syntax.

By always enumerating the list of column names, you can avoid any confusion.
However, there is one issue to keep in mind: if, in the future, the table into which
you are inserting values might be modified in such a way that new columns are
added to it, then you'll need to remember to revisit INSERT statements like this
and edit them if necessary. If you've enumerated a column list and the table is later
altered with the addition of new columns, then barring any constraints or triggers
that might yield a statement failure, your old INSERT statement will continue to
function normally; it just won't provide data for the new columns. But in all the
professional situations I've encountered, these types of issues are less problematic
and easier to resolve than the problem of data type matches that support illogical
data entry. The moral of this story is to always identify your column names in an
INSERT statement.

Enumerated Column List

The INSERT syntax we just reviewed assigns values to each column in the table.
It accomplishes that feat by first listing, by name, each column in the table, in the
same order in which the columns appear in the table's structure. But you are not
required to list the columns in order. Here's an example:

```
01   INSERT INTO CRUISES
02     (CRUISE_ID, CRUISE_NAME,
03      STATUS, CAPTAIN_ID, START_DATE, END_DATE)
04   VALUES
05     (2, 'Bermuda and Back',
06      'Done', 101, '07-APR-08', '14-APR-08');
```

This is a valid INSERT statement. Notice how in lines 2–3 we list the columns in a different order from the table structure. This is fine, so long as the list of expressions to be inserted (lines 5 and 6) are in the order as the column list (lines 2 and 3). They are as follows:

```
CRUISE_ID   = 2
CRUISE_NAME = 'Bermuda and Back'
STATUS      = 'Done'
CAPTAIN_ID  = 101
START_DATE  = '07-APR-08'
END_DATE    = '14-APR-08'
```

Another change with this INSERT is that we do not include every column in the table. We ignore the column CRUISE_TYPE_ID. That's also fine, provided that all required columns are included, and in this particular table, we have two columns that are NOT NULL, and both are included in this INSERT statement.

Data Type Conversion

When the INSERT statement is evaluated for syntactical correctness, the data types of the values listed in lines 5–6 will be compared to the data types of the columns identified in lines 2–3. The data types must be compatible. But the operative word here is *compatible*, not identical. For example, this works:

```
01  INSERT INTO CRUISES  (CRUISE_ID, CAPTAIN_ID)
02  VALUES (2, '101');
```

Notice that the 101 value in line 2 is in quotation marks, identifying that value as a string literal. Normally that is used for text, and in this case the text is being assigned to the column CAPTAIN_ID, which accepts only numeric data. But no error message occurs, and this INSERT will execute. The reason is that Oracle SQL is smart enough to figure out that the text contained within the literal value in this situation happens to be numeric data. The statement will execute successfully.

This feature is known in Oracle documentation as *implicit data type conversion.* Oracle Corporation formally advises that software developers avoid depending on implicit data type conversion in application development and rely instead on explicit data type conversion, which we'll look at when we review SQL conversion functions such as TO_CHAR, TO_NUMBER, and TO_DATE.

The rule of thumb is that wherever it makes sense, Oracle SQL will perform an implicit data type conversion if at all possible. Naturally it cannot convert something like 'Montana' to a DATE data type. But if you try to enter a numeric value such as 2011 into a data type such as VARCHAR2, an implicit data type conversion will convert the value of 2011 to '2011' and the statement will succeed.

INSERT and Constraints

If we happen to include data that violates a constraint, then we might get a run-time error. This point bears reiteration: violation of a constraint is a run-time error. In other words, it is not a syntax error. For example, let's say we write the following CREATE TABLE statement:

```
CREATE TABLE CRUISES
(CRUISE_ID    NUMBER,
 CRUISE_NAME VARCHAR2(30),
 START_DATE   DATE,
 END_DATE     DATE,
 CONSTRAINT   CRUISE_ID_PK PRIMARY KEY (CRUISE_ID),
 CONSTRAINT   CRUISE_NAME_CK CHECK
              (CRUISE_NAME IN ('Hawaii','Bahamas','Bermuda',
                               'Mexico','Day at Sea')
              )
);
```

This table includes a CHECK constraint that will limit any values for CRUISE_NAME to one of the listed strings: 'Hawaii', 'Bahamas', 'Bermuda', 'Mexico', or 'Day at Sea'. Anything else will be rejected.

Next, let's peek ahead a little bit and create a SEQUENCE object, like this:

```
CREATE SEQUENCE SEQ_CRUISE_ID;
```

This CREATE SEQUENCE statement creates an object that will dispense individual values, and we'll use it to generate primary key values for our INSERT statements.

Next, let's use that SEQUENCE object and issue the following INSERT statement:

```
01   INSERT INTO CRUISES
02      (CRUISE_ID, CRUISE_NAME)
03   VALUES
04      (SEQ_CRUISE_ID.NEXTVAL, 'Hawaii');
```

This INSERT statement adds a single row to the CRUISES table. The new row consists of two values. In line 4, the first value calls on the newly created SEQUENCE object and asks for the next available value from the sequence, indicated with the reserved word NEXTVAL. Given that our sequence is new and it was created with all the default settings and has never been used before, then the next available value will be 1. The second value we're inserting here is the literal string 'Hawaii', which is syntactically correct, and it also satisfies the constraint object attached to the CRUISE_NAME column in the CREATE TABLE statement.

However, had we violated the constraint, the INSERT could be syntactically correct but logically incorrect. For example, consider this variation on the same INSERT statement:

```
01  INSERT INTO CRUISES
02      (CRUISE_ID, CRUISE_NAME)
03  VALUES
04      (SEQ_CRUISE_ID.NEXTVAL, 'Hawaii and Back');
```

In this example, the string 'Hawaii and Back' violates the CHECK constraint we created for the CRUISES table. Therefore, even though this version of the INSERT statement is syntactically correct, it will fail on execution, and the CHECK constraint will reject the attempt to enter this row. See Figure 3-4 for a sample of the execution error resulting from this INSERT statement—this is shown in the SQL Developer tool instead of the SQL*Plus tool that you have seen up to now.

Note the ORA-02290 run-time error message. The CHECK constraint is identified, and you can see in this display that I'm logged in to the EFCODD_TEST user account.

It's also worth noting that even though the INSERT statement failed, the sequence generator advanced by one. Any attempt to invoke a sequence generator will advance the number count, even if the DML statement fails.

We're far from done with INSERT, and we will address more advanced concepts of INSERT in later chapters, when we look at subqueries (Chapter 9) and large data sets (Chapter 13). But first, let's look at the rest of the major DML statements.

FIGURE 3-4   Execution error for the INSERT statement

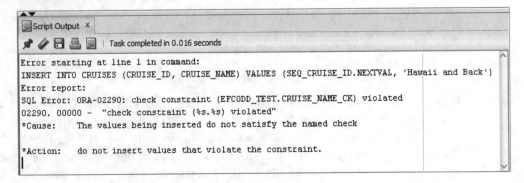

Update Rows in a Table

The UPDATE statement is a DML statement that is used to modify existing data in the database. It operates on one table at a time. It is used to modify one or more columns of data and can be used to change all the rows in a table, or it can be used to change data in only selected rows.

As with INSERT, the UPDATE statement can also work with certain VIEW objects to update data in the TABLE objects upon which the VIEW objects may be constructed. We'll look at this more later when we discuss VIEW objects.

Let's look at an example of UPDATE:

```
01   UPDATE CRUISES
02     SET  CRUISE_NAME = 'Bahamas',
03          START_DATE  = '01-DEC-11'
04   WHERE  CRUISE_ID = 1;
```

This UPDATE will look for any and all existing rows in the CRUISES table where the value for CRUISE_ID equals 1. For all of those rows, it will change the value for CRUISE_NAME to 'Bahamas' and change the value for START_DATE to '01-DEC-11'.

When we say the UPDATE statement will "change" those values, this example of UPDATE doesn't care if the column in question is already populated with data or if the existing value is NULL. Either way, UPDATE will overwrite whatever else may or may not already be there and place the new value in the column.

Let's look a little more closely at the syntax of this UPDATE statement:

- **Line 1**   The reserved word UPDATE, followed by the name of the target table
- **Lines 2–3**   One occurrence of the reserved word SET, followed by a series of one or more expressions consisting of these four elements:
  - A column name
  - The assignment operator (=)
  - An expression resulting in a value compatible with the column's data type
  - Either a comma, if additional expressions are to follow, or nothing, if the list of expressions is completed
- **Line 4**   An optional WHERE clause, defining a condition to identify rows in the table

Now that we've reviewed our sample UPDATE in detail, let's observe a few important issues about the UPDATE statement in general:

- The series of columns enumerated in the SET clause does not need to refer to the table's columns in any particular order.
- The SET clause does not need to reference all required columns—in other words, NOT NULL columns. Remember, UPDATE is not adding a row but modifying existing data. Assuming the UPDATE statement's WHERE clause specifies any existing one or more rows, those rows are already in the table, so presumably the data within each row already honors all required constraints.
- Any column names omitted from the UPDATE statement's SET clause will not be changed.
- Any attempt by UPDATE to implement a change that violates a constraint will be rejected and fail to execute.
- The WHERE clause specifies the criteria for determining which rows in the table will be updated. If no such rows are found, the UPDATE statement updates no rows, and it executes successfully with no errors.
- The WHERE clause is not required in UPDATE. If it is omitted, the UPDATE will perform on each row in the table.

Expressions

The UPDATE statement can use expressions to assign values to any given column. Expressions may include literal values, valid column references, mathematical expressions, and SQL functions. Let's look at an example to get an idea of what can be done. Here's an UPDATE statement that uses expressions in the SET clause:

```
UPDATE COMPENSATION
   SET  SALARY = SALARY * 1.03,
        LAST_CHANGED_DATE = SYSDATE
 WHERE EMPLOYEE_NUMBER = 83;
```

The preceding statement is an UPDATE statement intended to change data in a table called COMPENSATION. The UPDATE statement will change data in any and all rows with a value of 83 in the EMPLOYEE_NUMBER column. For any row that meets this WHERE criteria, UPDATE will change the values in two columns:

- The SALARY column is changed to equal itself times 1.03. This has the effect of increasing its own value by 3 percent or—if NULL—leaving the column NULL.

- The LAST_CHANGED_DATE column is set to the value of SYSDATE. SYSDATE is a built-in SQL function that contains the current date and time according to the operating system wherever the database is installed.

This example demonstrates how expressions can be used within an UPDATE statement.

Constraints

If the UPDATE statement violates any constraint on a table, the entire UPDATE statement will be rejected, and none of the modifications will be accepted for any of the rows. In other words, if the UPDATE statement attempts to change any data in any column of any row in a table and any one change results in any one constraint violation, then the entire UPDATE statement is rejected.

For example, review these SQL statements:

```
CREATE TABLE PROJECTS
(  PROJECT_ID    NUMBER PRIMARY KEY
 , PROJECT_NAME VARCHAR2(40)
 , COST          NUMBER
 , CONSTRAINT CK_COST CHECK (COST < 1000000));
INSERT INTO PROJECTS (PROJECT_ID, PROJECT_NAME, COST)
VALUES              (1,'Hull Cleaning', 340000);
INSERT INTO PROJECTS (PROJECT_ID, PROJECT_NAME, COST)
VALUES              (2,'Deck Resurfacing', 964000);
INSERT INTO PROJECTS (PROJECT_ID, PROJECT_NAME, COST)
VALUES              (3,'Lifeboat Inspection', 12000);
```

In this code, we create a table PROJECTS that includes a couple of constraints; one in particular is the CHECK constraint that limits any value in the COST column to numbers that are less than a million.

Now see Figure 3-5. Notice how we issue an UPDATE statement in which we increase the cost of each project by 20 percent. This will cause the row identified by PROJECT_ID 2 to bump up over our limitation on the COST column. The result is that the entire UPDATE statement is rejected.

However, see Figure 3-6; here we execute a slight variation of that UPDATE statement where we avoid the problem row, and the UPDATE statement executes.

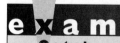

ex**a m**

ⓦatch   ***Don't get the UPDATE statement's SET clause mixed up with the "set" operators of UNION, INTERSECT, and*** ***MINUS. Those are two completely separate issues, and both are addressed on the exam. You'll study the set operators in Chapter 11.***

UPDATE
statement:
one constraint
violation rejects
the entire
statement

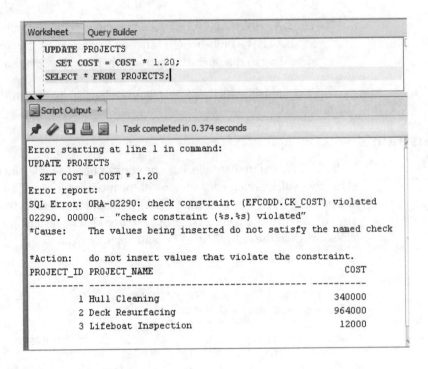

The WHERE Clause

The UPDATE statement's WHERE clause is arguably its most powerful and important feature. WHERE determines which of the existing rows in the table will be modified by the SET clause. The WHERE clause is not unique to the UPDATE statement; WHERE is also used for similar purposes with DELETE and SELECT.

UPDATE
statement: no
constraints
violated

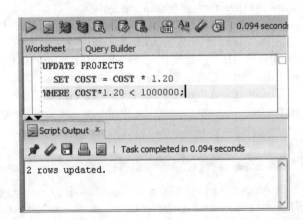

on the job

A word about terminology: UPDATE can be used only to modify existing rows in a table. On a practical level, end users may speak in terms of "adding" data to a table when all they really mean is that they want to set a value to a column within an existing row. In other words, when you are speaking with nontechnical users and they speak of "adding" data to a table, be aware that this doesn't necessarily mean you'll be using the INSERT statement; an UPDATE may actually be in order. Similarly, you can use UPDATE to "remove" values from the table by setting a given row's column to NULL. But you aren't necessarily removing a row in that situation—just modifying the contents of it. To remove a row, you need the DELETE statement. You need to keep alert to the differences between natural language and SQL syntax on the job and on the exam.

CERTIFICATION OBJECTIVE 3.04

Delete Rows from a Table

The DELETE statement is used to remove rows from tables in the database. Rows are identified by the WHERE clause of DELETE. If WHERE is omitted, DELETE removes all the rows from the table.

When DELETE identifies a row with the WHERE clause, it removes the entire row from the table, not just an individual data element from within a row. If your goal is to remove a single value from within an existing row, while retaining the row in the table, then you don't use DELETE; you use UPDATE to identify the row and set the desired value to NULL.

The DELETE clause is simple. Here's an example:

```
01  DELETE FROM PROJECT_LISTING
02  WHERE  CONSTRUCTION_ID = 12;
```

This sample deletes any and all rows in the PROJECT_LISTING table where a column called CONSTRUCTION_ID contains a value of 12. All rows that contain a 12 in the CONSTRUCTION_ID column will be deleted from the table.

Let's look at this sample statement:

- ■ **Line 1**   The required reserved word DELETE, followed by the optional reserved word FROM, followed by the required name of the target table
- ■ **Line 2**   An optional WHERE clause

As I just said, the reserved word FROM is optional. In other words, this variation of the preceding DELETE statement is also valid:

```
01   DELETE PROJECT_LISTING
02   WHERE   CONSTRUCTION_ID = 12;
```

This DELETE statement performs the same function without the reserved word FROM.

The WHERE clause for DELETE performs the same function as the WHERE clause in the UPDATE statement and in the SELECT statement, in the sense that it specifies rows for processing by the particular DML statement with which you are working. But beware: in the case of the DELETE statement, if you omit the WHERE clause, you'll delete every row in the table.

CERTIFICATION OBJECTIVE 3.05

Control Transactions

So far in this chapter, we've looked at the SQL statements INSERT, UPDATE, and DELETE. Those three statements, along with SELECT, form a set of SQL statements known as Data Manipulation Language.

There are other types of SQL statements, but one type in particular is of special importance to DML. As mentioned earlier in the chapter, that type is known as Transaction Control Language. These statements are important to any SQL session in which you use DML statements, as TCL statements provide the functionality to save or undo the changes made with DML statements.

We'll look at three TCL statements in this section: COMMIT, ROLLBACK, and SAVEPOINT:

- **COMMIT** You could think of COMMIT as SAVE. Saves changes to the database since the session began or since the most recent commit event in the session, whichever is more recent.
- **ROLLBACK** Undoes changes to the database performed within a session, back to the last "commit" point in the session.
- **SAVEPOINT** Temporarily sets an optional point, or marker, in a session to empower future "commit" or "rollback" actions by providing one or more optional points at which you may—or may not—undo changes.

Note that TCL performs changes made to the database within a session. A session begins when a single user logs in and continues as the user engages in a series of transactions, until the user disconnects from the database by either logging out or breaking the connection in some fashion. A single user may engage in multiple sessions. But the opposite is not true: only one user can engage in a given session. This discussion about TCL is concerned with sessions, including the transactions that occur within a given session and how the impact of those transactions may or may not impact other sessions.

With that in mind, let's look at each statement in more detail.

COMMIT

The SQL statement COMMIT is used to save changes made within a session to any tables that have been modified by the DML statements INSERT, UPDATE, and DELETE. COMMIT makes changes to the database permanent, and once committed, those changes can no longer be undone with a ROLLBACK statement. That isn't to say that the data cannot be changed back with additional DML statements; of course it can. But before a COMMIT is executed, changes to the database can be undone with a ROLLBACK statement. After the COMMIT, however, that option no longer exists.

A series of SQL statements is considered a *transaction* by SQL and is treated as one unit. The changes you make within a transaction are not made permanent until they are committed. A commit event completes a transaction.

There are two kinds of commit events:

- An explicit commit, which occurs when the COMMIT statement is executed
- An implicit commit, which occurs automatically when certain database events occur

Until a commit event of either type occurs, no changes that may have been performed to tables in the database are made permanent, and all changes have the potential for being undone.

Explicit commits occur when the COMMIT statement is executed. Implicit commits occur without the COMMIT statement, but instead occur when certain types of database events occur. Let's discuss both situations.

Explicit Commit

An explicit commit occurs whenever the COMMIT statement is executed. The syntax of COMMIT is simple:

```
COMMIT;
```

The COMMIT statement has a few parameters that are not required for the exam. One worth noting, however, is the optional keyword WORK, as follows:

```
COMMIT WORK;
```

The WORK keyword is included for compliance with ANSI standard SQL, but it is not required in Oracle SQL. It provides no additional functionality beyond the COMMIT statement itself.

To understand how COMMIT works, consider the following series of SQL statements:

```
01  INSERT INTO POSITIONS (POSITION_ID, POSITION_NAME)
02              VALUES (100, 'Manager');
03  SELECT POSITION_ID, POSITION_NAME
04    FROM POSITIONS;
```

In this series of statements, the change to the table made by the INSERT statement is made permanent by the COMMIT statement. Without it, the INSERT changes could be undone with a ROLLBACK statement.

Implicit Commit

An implicit commit occurs when certain events take place in the database. Those events include

- Immediately before and immediately after an attempt to execute any DDL statement, such as CREATE, ALTER, DROP, GRANT, or REVOKE. Note: Even if the DDL statement fails with an execution error (as opposed to a syntax error), the "before" implicit commit is executed and takes effect.
- A normal exit from most of Oracle's utilities and tools, such as SQL*Plus or SQL Developer. (One exception is Oracle's precompilers, which do not perform an implicit commit upon exit but instead perform a rollback.)

When these events take place, an implicit commit is automatically executed, meaning that all uncommitted changes become permanent in the same way as they would if you had executed the COMMIT statement.

Here's an example:

```
UPDATE SHIPS SET HOME_PORT_ID = 12 WHERE SHIP_ID = 31;
ALTER TABLE PORTS ADD AUTHORITY_NOTE VARCHAR2(75);
```

In this example, the change performed with the UPDATE statement has become permanent. Why? Because ALTER TABLE is a DDL statement and carries with it an implicit commit. As far as the SHIPS table is concerned, the following would have an equivalent impact:

```
UPDATE SHIPS SET HOME_PORT_ID = 12 WHERE SHIP_ID = 31;
COMMIT;
```

In both examples, the UPDATE statement is committed. The first example demonstrates an implicit commit. The second example displayed previously shows an explicit commit. From the perspective of the SHIPS table, the ultimate effect is the same—an ALTER TABLE command and a COMMIT command both result in a commit event on the changes performed by the UPDATE statement, as well as any previously performed changes that may have not yet been committed since the most recent of either a session start or another COMMIT event.

COMMIT and Multiple Sessions

Up to now, we've looked at COMMIT from the perspective of a single session. Now let's expand our perspective and discuss COMMIT and its behavior with regard to multiple sessions logged in simultaneously and accessing the same set of tables. In short, a single user, logged into a single session, can perform changes to a database using INSERT, UPDATE, DELETE, or any combination of the three, but while the resulting changes are visible in the session within which the changes were performed, they are not visible to any other login session until a COMMIT is performed. This includes additional login sessions by the same user who performed the changes. A single user can log in multiple times and open multiple login sessions, but uncommitted changes to data are visible only within the one session that performed the changes, until a commit is performed—either explicitly or implicitly.

Let's say that one user account owns a schema that includes several tables, that all users have been granted privileges to see (SELECT) data from these tables, and that only the owning user account retains the privilege of modifying any data in those tables. If that owning user executes a series of DML statements within a single session, any resulting changes will be visible within that session but will not be visible from within any other sessions—that is, not until a commit event occurs in the original session where the changes were made. Until then, other sessions will not see the changes. The owning user may perform a large series of INSERT, UPDATE, and DELETE statements and even print reports and screenshot displays showing the results of the modifications, performing SELECT statements to do it. However, unless and until a commit event occurs within the session where the changes were performed, no other session, regardless of whatever privileges might be involved, will be capable of seeing the changed data. Only after some sort of commit event occurs—either explicit or implicit—do the changes become "permanent," as Oracle likes to say, and therefore visible to all sessions.

Let's look at a variation of this scenario. Look at Figure 3-7. In this scenario, USER_1 owns a table SHIPS and has granted UPDATE privileges to USER_2. This means that USER_2, who does not own the SHIPS table, has the right to issue UPDATE statements and change that data. So, USER_2 issues an UPDATE statement on SHIPS but does not commit the changes. The result is that if USER_3 has SELECT privileges and tries to query the SHIPS table owned by USER_1, the changes made by USER_2 are not visible to anyone other than USER_2. USER_3, for example, cannot see the changed data. In this example, the value for CAPTAIN_ID is 0, and USER_2 issues a change to that value and updates it to 7. But USER_3 does not yet see the change, since it hasn't been committed to the database. For that matter, no user sees the change—other than USER_2. Not even the table owner,

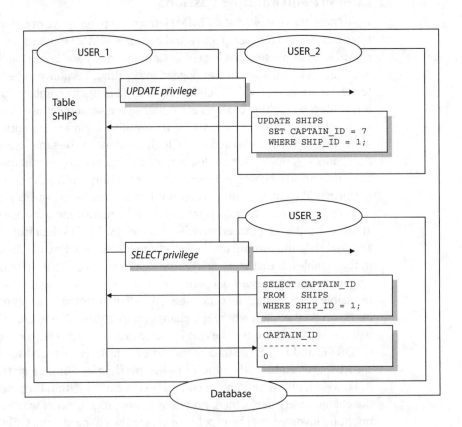

FIGURE 3-7

Uncommitted change

USER_1, will see USER_2's change unless and until USER_2 causes a commit event to occur.

Next, look at Figure 3-8. Here, USER_2 has issued a COMMIT statement to create an explicit commit event. The result is that when USER_3 queries the SHIPS table, the change issued by USER_2 is visible.

In this way, changes made prior to any commit event are in a sort of staging area, where the user can work in what is almost a "draft" mode. However, any commit event—explicit or implicit—will make changes permanent and expose the new data to all sessions.

ROLLBACK

The ROLLBACK statement is comparable to the "undo" function common to many software applications. ROLLBACK undoes changes to the database that have been performed within a given session. It does not remove any changes that have already

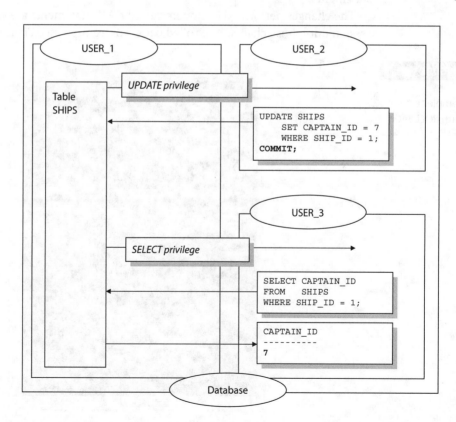

FIGURE 3-8

Committed change

been committed. The only changes that are rolled back are those changes issued within the session performing the rollback.

Here's an example:

```
COMMIT;
INSERT INTO PORTS (PORT_ID, PORT_NAME) VALUES (701, 'Chicago');
DELETE FROM SHIPS;
ROLLBACK;
```

In this example, one INSERT statement and one DELETE statement are issued. The results: we add one row to the PORTS table and delete all the rows in the SHIPS table.

But then we issue a ROLLBACK statement, and both changes are eliminated. It is as if those two DML statements never happened. The PORTS and SHIPS tables are restored to their original condition at the time of the last COMMIT event. Since none of the DML statements was committed, no other session saw the changes. The changes were observed, albeit temporarily, only by the session that issued the statements.

The changes performed by uncommitted DML statements are visible within the session until those changes are rolled back. For example, see Figure 3-9.

FIGURE 3-9

Sample session with ROLLBACK

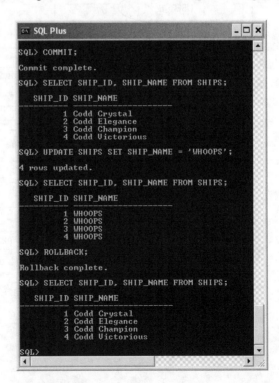

The figure shows the following series of steps:

- An explicit COMMIT statement
- A SELECT to demonstrate the data within the SHIPS table
- An UPDATE to change data in the SHIPS table
- The same SELECT statement to demonstrate the changed data
- A ROLLBACK to remove the effects of the UPDATE statement
- The same SELECT statement yet again, showing that the SHIPS table's condition has been restored

At no time during this process did any other session see the effects of the UPDATE statement. The changes were visible only to the session issuing the statements.

If a program abnormally terminates, the database will issue an implicit rollback. Uncommitted changes at the time of an abnormal termination of, for example, SQL*Plus or SQL Developer will not be committed to the database.

SAVEPOINT

So far we have looked at the TCL statements ROLLBACK and COMMIT. Let's look at a third: SAVEPOINT. The SAVEPOINT statement establishes demarcation points within a transaction to empower any following COMMIT or ROLLBACK statements to subdivide the points at which data may later be optionally saved or undone.

Without SAVEPOINT, the COMMIT and ROLLBACK statements can operate only on a sort of all-or-nothing basis. Once a series of statements have been executed, the entire series, as one large group, can be either saved or undone. But if periodic SAVEPOINTs have been issued along the way, a subsequent COMMIT or ROLLBACK can be used to save or restore data to those saved points in time marked by one or more SAVEPOINT statements, thus providing a finer level of detail at which the transaction can be controlled.

Here is an example of SAVEPOINT:

```
01   COMMIT;
02   UPDATE SHIPS SET HOME_PORT_ID = 21 WHERE SHIP_ID = 12;
03   SAVEPOINT SP_1;
04   UPDATE SHIPS SET HOME_PORT_ID = 22 WHERE SHIP_ID = 12;
05   ROLLBACK WORK TO SP_1;
06   COMMIT;
```

In this example, we start with an explicit COMMIT on line 1 and then issue an UPDATE statement. Then on line 3, we issue a SAVEPOINT statement and name it SP_1. That's followed by a second UPDATE statement. Given that we elected to issue the SAVEPOINT, we have an option on line 5 that we haven't seen yet, and that is to "undo" the previous UPDATE statement (but only that second UPDATE, not the first). We accomplish this by rolling back to the SAVEPOINT. Then we COMMIT our changes.

The result is that the value in the SHIP_ID 12 row for HOME_PORT_ID is 21.

Here's another example; see whether you can determine what the resulting value for HOME_PORT_ID will be here:

```
01   COMMIT;
02   UPDATE SHIPS SET HOME_PORT_ID = 21 WHERE SHIP_ID = 12;
03   SAVEPOINT MARK_01;
04   UPDATE SHIPS SET HOME_PORT_ID = 22 WHERE SHIP_ID = 12;
05   SAVEPOINT MARK_02;
06   UPDATE SHIPS SET HOME_PORT_ID = 23 WHERE SHIP_ID = 12;
07   ROLLBACK TO MARK_02;
08   COMMIT;
```

In this series of SQL statements, what is the resulting value of the SHIPS table's HOME_PORT_ID column where the SHIP_ID value is equal to 12? The answer: 22. That is the value committed to the database after the COMMIT statement on line 8 is executed.

In this example, we created two SAVEPOINTs—one we chose to name MARK_01, and another we chose to name MARK_02. We could have chosen any name for these savepoints that we wanted, according to the rules of naming database objects. By naming them, we reserve the right to selectively roll back to one or the other named SAVEPOINT. In this case, we chose to issue a ROLLBACK to the SAVEPOINT named MARK_02. This statement effectively restores the condition of the entire database to the point where the SAVEPOINT was executed, which, in this example, is prior to the UPDATE statement on line 6. In other words, it's as if the line 6 UPDATE statement had never been executed.

The rules for using SAVEPOINT include the following:

- All SAVEPOINT statements must include a name. The name must be specified using the same rules and limitations for naming database objects. Behind the scenes, the SAVEPOINT name you create is associated with a system change number (SCN). This is what the SAVEPOINT is marking.

- You should not duplicate SAVEPOINT names within a single transaction— and remember that a transaction is a series of one or more SQL statements ending with a commit event. If you duplicate a name, you will not receive a syntax or execution error. Instead, the new SAVEPOINT will simply override the earlier SAVEPOINT, effectively erasing it.
- Once a commit event occurs (either an explicit or implicit commit event), all existing savepoints are erased from memory. Any references to them by future TCL statements will produce an error code.

Regarding that last point, here's an example of what we're talking about:

```
01  COMMIT;
02  UPDATE SHIPS SET HOME_PORT_ID = 21 WHERE SHIP_ID = 12;
03  SAVEPOINT MARK_01;
04  COMMIT;
05  ROLLBACK TO MARK_01;
```

In the preceding example, the ROLLBACK statement on line 5 is wrong for two reasons. First, it's logically irrelevant since there is nothing to roll back— the COMMIT on line 4 permanently saved everything, and no additional SQL statements have been executed by the time the ROLLBACK is executed on line 5. Second, the ROLLBACK makes a reference to a SAVEPOINT that does not exist, so it will produce an error. Without the named savepoint reference, the ROLLBACK would execute just fine and simply have no impact on the database. But with the reference to a named SAVEPOINT that no longer exists by the time the ROLLBACK is executed, the result of line 5 is an error code.

SAVEPOINT is particularly useful when managing a large series of transactions in which incremental validation must be required, wherein each individual validation requires a complex series of DML statements that might fail but can be programmatically corrected and validated before moving on to the next increment. A great example of this occurs in the financial world. When reconciling a set of financial books for a given organization, you might find it necessary to validate an account within a larger chart of accounts. During each individual account validation process, there may be a need to roll back some statements before making some changes and attempting validation again. Then, once a given account is validated, you might want to declare that account "temporarily authorized" and then move on to attempting to validate the next account. Furthermore, you may want to defer a complete COMMIT until all accounts have been validated. SAVEPOINT is perfect for this; as each individual account is validated, a SAVEPOINT can be established so that subsequent account validation attempts that might fail can trigger a

ROLLBACK without undoing the earlier accounts that were already successfully validated. Then, when all accounts are validated—and not before—a single COMMIT can declare the full set of validated rows to the database with a permanent save.

ROLLBACK Revisited

Now that we've seen SAVEPOINT, let's take another look at the syntax for ROLLBACK and see how it can be used to roll back to a particular named SAVEPOINT.

So far, we've seen this form of the ROLLBACK statement:

```
ROLLBACK;
```

If the single word ROLLBACK is executed by itself, it will ignore any SAVEPOINT statements that may have been executed since the most recent commit event and undo any changes made by the user in the session since the time of the last commit event.

However, if ROLLBACK is intended to undo any changes since a named SCN was established by SAVEPOINT, then it can name the SCN specifically. For example, if a SAVEPOINT statement established a demarcation with an SCN named scn_01, like this:

```
SAVEPOINT scn_01;
```

then a subsequent ROLLBACK can selectively undo changes to this point like this:

```
ROLLBACK TO scn_01;
```

or alternatively like this:

```
ROLLBACK WORK TO scn_01;
```

Let's look at the components of this form of the ROLLBACK statement:

- First, the reserved word ROLLBACK
- The optional reserved word WORK
- The required reserved word TO
- The name of an SCN as named by a SAVEPOINT statement that was executed after the most recent commit event

Note that the WORK reserved word is optional. WORK is part of the ANSI standard but is not required in the Oracle implementation.

If a ROLLBACK statement is executed that names a nonexistent SAVEPOINT, SQL will display an error code warning that the rollback was attempting to roll back to a SAVEPOINT that was never established. The ROLLBACK will fail, and nothing will change regarding the state of the database. At that point, any outstanding changes will remain in an uncommitted state. At this point, uncommitted changes may still be committed or rolled back.

CERTIFICATION SUMMARY

The TRUNCATE TABLE statement can be used in those special circumstances where you may want to remove all the rows of a table without firing any DML triggers or selectively removing data from any associated INDEX objects, as would happen with a DELETE statement. In such a situation, TRUNCATE TABLE is an attractive alternative to dropping and re-creating a table, since it leaves the table and its relationships intact, as well as any indexes. TRUNCATE TABLE can remove statements much more quickly with less processing overhead than DELETE. Because TRUNCATE TABLE fires no DML triggers, it is considered DDL; therefore, its use performs an implicit commit, and its results cannot be rolled back.

If TRUNCATE TABLE is applied to a table for which there exists an associated parent table with a foreign key using the ON CASCADE DELETE clause, then TRUNCATE TABLE will result in an error if there are in fact rows in that parent table that might otherwise be deleted as a result of ON CASCADE DELETE. For this situation, you must use TRUNCATE TABLE ... CASCADE to confirm your desire to remove those parent rows.

The INSERT statement adds rows of data to a table. In its simplest form, it adds one row at a time. Its syntax starts with the reserved words INSERT INTO and the name of a single database table, followed by an optional column list, followed by the reserved word VALUES, followed by a list of values to be inserted into the table, enclosed in parentheses. The list of values is presented in the same sequential order as the column list, meaning that for the row that the INSERT statement is adding to the table, the first value in the list will be added to the first column in the column list, then the second value will be added to the second column, and so on. The data types of the values should be appropriate for the data types of the columns to which the values are being inserted. Any constraints that are not honored will cause the INSERT statement to be rejected at execution time. For example, if a column has a NOT NULL constraint, then the INSERT statement needs to provide a valid value for that particular column, or else the INSERT statement will fail and no row is added to the table. If the INSERT statement omits the column list, then the value list is assumed to be in the order of the columns according to the target table's structure, and each column is assumed to be accounted for in the values list.

The UPDATE statement is used to modify rows of data in the table. It includes the optional WHERE clause, which is used to identify which rows the UPDATE is intended to modify. If the WHERE clause is omitted, then the UPDATE statement will attempt to modify all rows in the target table. The UPDATE statement uses the reserved word SET, followed by pairs of column names and values. Each value can be substituted with an expression. Expressions may include literal values, any available table column, mathematical equations, and SQL functions.

The DELETE statement removes rows from a table. The optional WHERE clause can be used to identify which rows are to be deleted. However, if the WHERE clause is omitted, then every row in the table will be deleted.

TCL, which is separate from DML, is often used with a series of DML transactions to control whether data processed by those DML transactions will be committed to the database—in other words, made "permanent" as Oracle documentation (and others) likes to say. The TCL commands include COMMIT, ROLLBACK, and SAVEPOINT.

COMMIT makes permanent any outstanding changes to the table since the last commit event. Commits can occur explicitly or implicitly. Explicit commits occur with the simple SQL statement of COMMIT. Implicit commits occur when other events take place in the database, such as any DDL statement. A GRANT, for example, will automatically commit all changes to the database since the last COMMIT.

ROLLBACK can be used to "undo" a series of statements. ROLLBACK used by itself undoes any changes made within a session by the user to the database since the most recent commit event, implicit or explicit, took place. But if one or more SAVEPOINTs have been issued, then the ROLLBACK may optionally roll back to a particular SAVEPOINT.

SAVEPOINT names a system change number and empowers future executions of the ROLLBACK statement to go back to earlier versions of the database incrementally.

TWO-MINUTE DRILL

Truncate Data

☐ TRUNCATE TABLE removes all of a table's rows and all the data in its indexes, without firing any triggers.

☐ A TRUNCATE TABLE statement is a DDL statement. This means its use results in an implicit commit statement, and its results cannot be rolled back.

☐ If you use TRUNCATE TABLE on a child table of a parent that uses the ON DELETE CASCADE clause in its foreign key constraint, then you use the CASCADE clause with TRUNCATE TABLE, or else the existing or child rows with matching parent rows will cause the TRUNCATE TABLE statement to fail with an error.

Insert Rows into a Table

☐ The INSERT statement adds one or more rows to a table.

☐ The INSERT syntax we reviewed in this chapter consists of the reserved words INSERT INTO, the name of the table, the optional column list, the reserved word VALUES, and the list of values to be entered.

☐ If the INSERT statement is written so that the list of columns in the table is omitted, then the list of values must specify one value for each column in the table; those values will be processed in order according to the columns in the table's structure.

☐ The list of values in the INSERT statement may include expressions. Each expression must evaluate to a data type that is compatible with its target column in the table.

☐ If any value violates any constraint applied to the target table, then an execution error will result. For example, each new row added to the table must provide an appropriate value of a compatible data type for each NOT NULL column; otherwise, an execution error is issued, and the INSERT fails.

Update Rows in a Table

☐ The single UPDATE statement can modify existing data in one or more rows within a database table.

☐ The UPDATE statement syntax starts with the reserved word UPDATE and the name of the target table, the reserved word SET, and then a series of assignment expressions in which the left-side element specifies a table column, followed by the assignment operator (an equal sign), followed by an expression that evaluates to a data type appropriate for the target table's column identified on the left side of the equal sign, and finally an optional WHERE clause.

☐ If additional assignment expressions are required, each additional assignment expression is preceded by a comma.

☐ If the WHERE clause is omitted, then all the rows in the table are changed according to the series of SET values listed in the UPDATE statement.

Delete Rows from a Table

☐ The DELETE statement is used to remove rows of data from a table.

☐ The syntax starts with the reserved words DELETE and the optional FROM, then the name of the target table, then an optional WHERE clause.

☐ If the WHERE clause is omitted, all the rows in the table are deleted.

Control Transactions

☐ TCL statements include COMMIT, ROLLBACK, and SAVEPOINT.

☐ There are two types of commit events: explicit commit and implicit commit.

☐ An explicit commit occurs with the COMMIT statement.

☐ An implicit commit occurs immediately before and after certain events that take place in the database, such as the execution of any valid DDL statement, including CREATE, ALTER, DROP, GRANT, and REVOKE. Each DDL statement execution is automatically preceded and followed by an implicit commit.

☐ The COMMIT statement is used to save changes performed within the session and make those changes "permanent."

☐ If a DDL statement fails during execution, the implicit commit that preceded it still is in effect, ensuring that the commit occurred, whether the DDL statement was successful or not. The same is not true for DDL statement syntax errors.

☐ The ROLLBACK statement is used to undo changes to the database.

☐ The SAVEPOINT statement can be used to name a point within a series of SQL statements to which you may optionally roll back changes after additional DML statements are executed.

☐ Once a COMMIT is issued, all existing SAVEPOINTs are erased.

☐ Any ROLLBACK that names nonexisting SAVEPOINTs will not execute.

☐ If ROLLBACK is issued without naming a SAVEPOINT, changes made by the user during the current session are rolled back within that session to the most recent commit event.

SELF TEST

The following questions will help you measure your understanding of the material presented in this chapter. Choose the best single answer for each question unless otherwise specified.

Truncate Data

1. Review the following SQL statement:

```
TRUNCATE personnel;
```

   Which of the following is true of the previous statement? (Choose all that apply.)
   A. The statement will result in an implicit commit.
   B. The statement will remove all data from any INDEX objects associated with that table.
   C. The statement will not fire any DML triggers on the table.
   D. The statement will fail.

2. The CASCADE keyword, when used with TRUNCATE:
   A. Is required if the table has any dependent child tables
   B. Will ensure that future attempts to insert rows to the table will be rejected if they satisfy the TRUNCATE table's WHERE clause
   C. Can be used with the optional DEPENDENCY keyword
   D. None of the above

3. TRUNCATE TABLE:
   A. Cannot be used within a valid SQL statement
   B. Is a valid set of keywords to be used within a DDL statement
   C. Does not require the DROP_ANY_TABLE privilege
   D. Is a valid statement that will truncate a table called TABLE

Insert Rows into a Table

4. Review the following statement:

```
CREATE TABLE STUDENT_LIST
  (STUDENT_ID  NUMBER,
   NAME        VARCHAR2(30),
   PHONE       VARCHAR2(30));
INSERT INTO STUDENT_LIST
   VALUES (1, 'Joe Wookie', 5551212);
```

The table will create successfully. What will result from the INSERT statement?

A. The INSERT will fail because there is no list of columns after STUDENT_LIST.

B. The INSERT will fail because the literal value for PHONE is numeric and PHONE is a character data type.

C. The INSERT will execute—the table will contain one row of data.

D. None of the above.

5. Consider the following set of SQL statements:

```
CREATE TABLE INSTRUCTORS
 (INSTRUCTOR_ID  NUMBER,
  NAME           VARCHAR2(20),
  CONSTRAINT     ID_PK   PRIMARY KEY (INSTRUCTOR_ID),
  CONSTRAINT     NAME_UN UNIQUE (NAME));

INSERT INTO INSTRUCTORS (INSTRUCTOR_ID, NAME)
    VALUES (1, 'Howard Jackson');
INSERT INTO INSTRUCTORS (INSTRUCTOR_ID, NAME)
    VALUES (2, 'Trish Mars');
```

The table will create successfully. What will be the result of the two INSERT statements?

A. Neither will execute.

B. The first will execute, but the second will fail.

C. The first will fail, but the second will execute.

D. Both will execute successfully.

6. Consider the following set of SQL statements:

```
CREATE TABLE MAILING_LIST (FIRST_NAME VARCHAR2(20), LAST_NAME VARCHAR2(30));
INSERT INTO MAILING_LIST VALUES ('Smith', 'Mary');
```

What will be the result of the INSERT statement?

A. It will fail because there is no column list in the INSERT statement.

B. It will fail because there is no PRIMARY KEY in the table.

C. It will execute and create a new row in the table.

D. It will fail because the last name and first name values are reversed.

Update Rows in a Table

7. Which of the following reserved words is not required in order to form a syntactically correct UPDATE statement?

A. UPDATE

B. SET

C. WHERE

D. None of the above

8. Assume a table LAMPS that has no constraints. Which of the following is true about the UPDATE statement and the LAMPS table? (Choose all that apply.)

   A.   UPDATE can be used to add rows to LAMPS by setting values to all the columns.

   B.   UPDATE can be used to remove a row from LAMPS by setting all of the row's columns to a value of NULL.

   C.   For existing rows in LAMPS, UPDATE can add values to any column with a NULL value.

   D.   For existing rows in LAMPS, UPDATE can remove values from any column by changing its value to NULL.

9. Review the following SQL statements:

```
CREATE TABLE INSTRUCTORS
   (INSTRUCTOR_ID NUMBER,
    EXEMPT    VARCHAR2(5),
    VACATION NUMBER,
    PAY_RATE NUMBER);
INSERT INTO INSTRUCTORS VALUES (1, 'YES', NULL, 25);
INSERT INTO INSTRUCTORS VALUES (2, NULL,  NULL, NULL);
UPDATE INSTRUCTORS
   SET EXEMPT    = 'YES',
   SET VACATION  = 15
WHERE  PAY_RATE < 50;
```

What can be said of the statements listed here?

   A.   One row will be updated.

   B.   Two rows will be updated.

   C.   At least one of the statements will not execute.

   D.   None of the above.

10. Review the following SQL statements:

```
CREATE TABLE BOUNCERS
   (NIGHTCLUB_CODE NUMBER,
    STRENGTH_INDEX NUMBER);
INSERT INTO BOUNCERS VALUES (1, NULL);
UPDATE BOUNCERS
   SET STRENGTH_INDEX = 10;
```

What is the end result of the SQL statements listed here?

   A.   The BOUNCERS table will contain one row.

   B.   The BOUNCERS table will contain two rows.

   C.   The UPDATE will fail because there is no WHERE clause.

   D.   None of the above.

Delete Rows from a Table

11. Which of the following reserved words is required in a complete DELETE statement? (Choose all that apply.)

A. FROM

B. WHERE

C. DELETE

D. None of the above

12. Consider the following data in a table called PARTS:

```
PNO   PART_TITLE        STATUS
---   ----------------  -------
  1   PROCESSOR V1.0    VALID
  2   ENCASEMENT X770   PENDING
  3   BOARD CPU XER A7  PENDING
```

Which of the following SQL statements will remove the word VALID from row 1, resulting in one row with a status of NULL and two rows with a status of PENDING?

A. ```
DELETE FROM PARTS
WHERE STATUS = 'VALID';
```

B. ```
DELETE PARTS
WHERE PNO = 1;
```

C. ```
DELETE FROM PARTS
SET STATUS = NULL
WHERE PNO = 1;
```

D. None of the above

**13.** Review the following SQL statements:

```
CREATE TABLE AB_INVOICES (INVOICE_ID NUMBER, VENDOR_ID NUMBER);
ALTER TABLE AB_INVOICES ADD PRIMARY KEY (INVOICE_ID);
INSERT INTO AB_INVOICES VALUES (1,1);
DELETE AB_INVOICES WHERE INVOICE_ID = 2;
```

Which of the following best describes the results of attempting to execute the DELETE statement?

A. The DELETE statement will fail because it is missing a column list between the word DELETE and the name of the table AB_INVOICES.

B. The DELETE statement will execute, but no rows in the table will be removed.

C. The DELETE statement will produce a syntax error because it is referencing a row that does not exist in the database.

D. None of the above.
```

Control Transactions

14. Assume a schema with only two tables: one named PRODUCTS and one named ENGINEERING. Review the following SQL statements:

```
01   SELECT PRODUCT_ID FROM PRODUCTS;
02   DROP TABLE SHIP_STAFF;
03   INSERT INTO ENGINEERING (PROJECT_ID, MGR) VALUES (27,21);
04   COMMIT;
05   INSERT INTO ENGINEERING (PROJECT_ID, MGR) VALUES (400,17);
06   ROLLBACK;
```

In this series of SQL statements, which line represents the first commit event?

A. Line 1

B. Line 2

C. Line 4

D. Line 6

15. Review the SQL statements that follow, and assume that there is no table called ADDRESSES already present in the database:

```
CREATE TABLE ADDRESSES (ID NUMBER, ZONE NUMBER, ZIP_CODE VARCHAR2(5));
INSERT INTO ADDRESSES (ID, ZONE, ZIP_CODE) VALUES (1, 1, '94065');
SAVEPOINT ZONE_CHANGE_01;
UPDATE ADDRESSES SET ZONE = 2 WHERE ZIP_CODE = 94065;
ROLLBACK;
```

What will be the result of the execution of the SQL statements shown here?

A. The ADDRESSES table will have one row with a value of 1 for ZONE.

B. The ADDRESSES table will have one row with a value of 2 for ZONE.

C. The ADDRESSES table will have no rows.

D. None of the above.

SELF TEST ANSWERS

Truncate Data

1. ☑ **D.** The statement will fail. TRUNCATE TABLE is what is intended here. TRUNCATE by itself is not a valid statement.

☒ **A, B,** and **C** are incorrect. They would be correct if the statement included the keyword TABLE. But without that keyword, the statement will fail, so these options are not applicable.

2. ☑ **D.** The purpose of CASCADE is to ensure that any dependent child tables with rows that relate to the truncated rows will also be truncated.

☒ **A, B,** and **C** are incorrect. CASCADE is not required; it is optional. TRUNCATE has no effect on subsequent SQL statements, including INSERT. There is no DEPENDENCY keyword used with TRUNCATE.

3. ☑ **B.** These keywords, when combined with a valid table name, will form a valid DDL statement.

☒ **A, C,** and **D** are incorrect. These are valid keywords. TRUNCATE requires the DROP_ANY_TABLE privilege. TABLE is a keyword and required for TRUNCATE, and it requires a valid table name to follow the keyword TABLE.

Insert Rows into a Table

4. ☑ **C.** The statements are syntactically and logically correct. The INSERT statement omits the column list. This omission requires the list of values to be provided in the same sequence in which the columns appear in the table's structure, as indicated in the CREATE TABLE statement.

☒ **A, B,** and **D** are incorrect. The value provided by INSERT for the PHONE column is an expression that is compatible; the VARCHAR2 data type is a character data type, and it accepts both numeric and text data. In fact, values like phone numbers and ZIP codes are best treated as character data; otherwise, leading zeros will be truncated, and in the case of a ZIP code, that can be a disaster for a lot of addresses in the Northeastern United States.

5. ☑ **D.** The syntax is fine, and both INSERT statements will execute.

☒ **A, B,** and **C** are incorrect.

6. ☑ **C.** It will create a new row in the table. The fact that the column values are probably reversed may represent a logical error now and create problems down the road, but there's nothing about the statement that will prevent it from executing successfully.

☒ **A, B,** and **D** are incorrect. The lack of a column list in the INSERT merely requires there to be a list of values matching the number and data types of the columns in the table's structure, and this INSERT statement's list of values satisfies that requirement, albeit in an apparently illogical way, but nevertheless, the requirements for SQL are met. The lack of a PRIMARY KEY on the table probably represents poor design, but is not a problem with regard to the successful execution of the SQL statements here.

Update Rows in a Table

7. ☑ **C.** An UPDATE statement does not need to have a WHERE clause. If a WHERE clause is omitted, then every row in the target table is subject to be changed by the UPDATE statement, depending on whether any constraints exist on the table and whether they permit or reject the data changes the UPDATE statement is attempting to make.
   ☒ **A, B,** and **D** are incorrect. The reserved word UPDATE is required for a valid UPDATE statement. The same is true for the reserved word SET.

8. ☑ **C** and **D.** Adding a value to a column in an existing row is the purpose of the UPDATE statement. Setting a value to NULL is as acceptable as setting a value to some other specific value.
   ☒ **A** and **B** are incorrect. INSERT adds new rows to a table, and DELETE removes them. UPDATE doesn't remove rows from a table. The UPDATE statement can modify only existing rows. In the question of the LAMPS table, if you choose to use SET to set each column's value to NULL, then you'll still have a row in the table; it will simply consist of NULL values. But you'll still have a row. And you cannot create a new row by using SET to set values to each column; all you can do is modify existing rows. And, of course, if LAMPS were created with any NOT NULL constraints, any UPDATE statement would have to respect those constraints. But the question asserted the LAMPS has no constraints.

9. ☑ **C.** The UPDATE statement contains an extra occurrence of the reserved word SET. Only the first SET belongs; the second should be removed. Is this a tricky question? Yes, it is. So are many of the questions on the certification exam. Make sure your knowledge of syntax is strong. And read carefully.
   ☒ **A, B,** and **D** are incorrect.

10. ☑ **A.** The INSERT statement enters a single row, and the UPDATE statement modifies that single row, leaving one modified row in the table.
    ☒ **B, C,** and **D** are incorrect. There is only one row in the table—the UPDATE does not add a new row but rather changes the existing row. UPDATE does not require a WHERE clause; without it, the UPDATE statement applies its changes to all the rows in the table, and this table contains one row.

Delete Rows from a Table

11. ☑ **C.** The only required reserved word is DELETE.

☒ **A, B,** and **D** are incorrect. FROM is optional. WHERE is also optional.

12. ☑ **D** is correct. DELETE removes entire rows from the database. Removing a single value from a single column requires the use of the UPDATE statement.

☒ **A, B,** and **C** are incorrect. A and B are valid DELETE statements, either of which will remove the first row from the table, instead of just removing the value for the "status" column. Option C is an invalid statement that will trigger a syntax error—the SET reserved word has no place in the DELETE statement.

13. ☑ **B.** The syntax is fine, and the statement will execute as intended, which is to remove any rows from the table with an INVOICE_ID value of 2. It just so happens that there aren't any rows that match the stated criteria at the time the DELETE statement is issued.

☒ **A, C,** and **D** are incorrect. There is no column list in a DELETE statement before the table name. And the fact that the WHERE clause does not identify any relevant rows is not a syntax problem, nor is it a compilation problem—the statement will simply not delete any rows.

Control Transactions

14. ☑ **B.** Line 2 is a DROP statement, which falls under the type of SQL statements known as Data Definition Language. All DDL statements cause an implicit commit to occur, even if the DDL statement fails in execution.

☒ **A, C,** and **D** are incorrect. The SELECT statement has no impact on a commit event at all. Line 4 is an explicit COMMIT, and were it not for line 2, this would be the first commit event in this set of statements. Line 6 undoes the effects of line 5 and undoes the user's changes to the database since the previous commit event, which at this stage is represented by the line 4 commit.

15. ☑ **C.** The ROLLBACK statement does not reference the SAVEPOINT name, so instead it rolls all the way back to the last COMMIT event, which in this case is the implicit commit that occurred with the CREATE TABLE statement.

☒ **A, B,** and **D** are incorrect.

4

Restricting and Sorting Data

This chapter looks at various capabilities of the SELECT statement: the WHERE clause, the ORDER BY clause, ampersand substitution, and the SQL row limiting clause. The ORDER BY clause sorts the retrieved rows. It's very flexible: it can sort rows in ascending or descending order, or it can sort by expression lists or take advantage of other powerful features. The WHERE clause specifies the criteria required for a row to be included in a SQL statement. Without it, all rows in a given table are retrieved, but with it, a SQL statement can selectively target particular rows for processing. Ampersand substitution provides unique and powerful capabilities when working with Oracle SQL. The SQL row limiting clause is a flexible enhancement to the SELECT statement.

Ampersand substitution is a SQL*Plus capability on the exam. We know it is a SQL*Plus statement because it is not described in the "Oracle Database SQL Language Reference," but is detailed instead in the "SQL*Plus User's Guide and Reference." Ampersand substitution provides unique and powerful capabilities when working with Oracle's SQL, thus its inclusion on the exam.

A working knowledge of these clauses is necessary to pass the exam. Let's get started.

CERTIFICATION OBJECTIVE 4.01

Sort the Rows That Are Retrieved by a Query

This section looks at another clause in the SELECT statement, the ORDER BY clause. ORDER BY is used to sort the rows that are retrieved by a SELECT statement. It sorts by specifying expressions for each row in the table. Sorting can be performed in either ascending or descending order. SQL will sort according to the data type of the expression that is identified in the ORDER BY. You can include more than one expression. The first expression is given sorting priority, the second is given second-position priority, and so on.

ORDER BY is always the final clause in a SELECT statement. It is used only in SELECT; contrary to the WHERE clause, which can also be used in UPDATE and DELETE, the ORDER BY clause is unique to the SELECT statement and is not used in the other SQL statements.

(Note that in Chapter 9 we'll examine how you may embed a SELECT statement as a subquery within an INSERT, UPDATE, or DELETE statement—so in that regard, it is theoretically possible that an ORDER BY clause might be included in a SELECT statement that is embedded within, for example, an INSERT statement. But that is a separate issue.)

ORDER BY does not change data as it is stored in the table. Data in a table remains unchanged as a result of the ORDER BY. ORDER BY is part of the SELECT statement, and the SELECT statement is incapable of changing data in the database. Note, however, that when SELECT is embedded within other SQL statements like INSERT or UPDATE, changes to the database can result, but not because of SELECT alone. You'll see how that works in Chapter 9.

ORDER BY sorts the output of a SELECT statement for display purposes only. It is always the last step in a SELECT statement and performs its sort after all the data has been retrieved and processed by the SELECT statement.

Reference by Name

Let's look at an example of ORDER BY in action. Consider the following data listing from a table ADDRESSES:

```
ADDRESS_ID  STREET_ADDRESS              CITY            ST  COUNTRY
----------  --------------------        -------------   --  ------
         1  350 Oracle Parkway          Redwood City    CA  USA
         2  1600 Amphitheatre Parkway   Mountain View   CA  USA
         3  1 Dell Way                  Round Rock      TX  USA
         4  29 E Ohio St                Chicago         IL  USA
         5  5788 Roswell Rd NE          Atlanta         GA  USA
         6  10103 100 St NW             Edmonton        AB  Canada
         7  1221 Avenue of the Americas New York        NY  USA
         8  239 Baker Street            London              UK
         9  1 rue des Carrieres         Quebec City     QC  Canada
        10  2041 S Harbor Blvd          Anaheim         CA  USA
        11  600 N Michigan Ave          Chicago         IL  USA
        12  1515 Sheridan Rd            Wilmette        IL  USA
```

We can select this data and sort it by specifying the column name (or names) in the ORDER BY clause of the SQL statement, as follows:

```
SELECT    ADDRESS_ID, STREET_ADDRESS, CITY, STATE, COUNTRY
FROM      ADDRESSES
ORDER BY STATE;
```

Figure 4-1 shows the results. Notice in the figure that the rows are sorted in alphabetical order according to the value in the STATE column.

```
SQL Plus                                                            _ □ ✕

SQL> R
  1  SELECT    ADDRESS_ID, STREET_ADDRESS, CITY, STATE, COUNTRY
  2  FROM      ADDRESSES
  3* ORDER BY STATE

ADDRESS_ID STREET_ADDRESS                     CITY            ST COUNTRY
---------- --------------------------------- --------------- -- -------
         6 10103 100 St NW                    Edmonton        AB Canada
         2 1600 Amphitheatre Parkway          Mountain View   CA USA
         1 350 Oracle Parkway                 Redwood City    CA USA
        10 2041 S Harbor Blvd                 Anaheim         CA USA
         5 5788 Roswell Rd NE                 Atlanta         GA USA
        11 600 N Michigan Ave                 Chicago         IL USA
         4 29 E Ohio St                       Chicago         IL USA
        12 1515 Sheridan Rd                   Wilmette        IL USA
         7 1221 Avenue of the Americas        New York        NY USA
         9 1 rue des Carrieres                Quebec City     QC Canada
         3 1 Dell Way                         Round Rock      TX USA
         8 239 Baker Street                   London             UK

12 rows selected.

SQL>
```

Note that the row with a NULL value for STATE is last. The NULL value is considered the "highest" value.

As we review the output, it becomes clear that we might also want to alphabetize our information by city for each state. We can do that by modifying our ORDER BY clause ever so slightly:

```
SELECT    ADDRESS_ID, STREET_ADDRESS, CITY, STATE, COUNTRY
FROM      ADDRESSES
ORDER BY STATE, CITY;
```

In the modified version of our ORDER BY, we add a second column to the ORDER BY clause by which we want to sort. Figure 4-2 displays the results of this SELECT statement. The rows have been sorted first by STATE and then by the CITY value for each STATE.

Note that the choice of columns we include in the ORDER BY clause does not influence which columns we choose to display in the SELECT expression list. It would probably be easier to read if we put the same columns used in the ORDER BY in the same positions as the SELECT expression list. In other words, this query would probably produce a more readable output:

```
SELECT    STATE, CITY, ADDRESS_ID, STREET_ADDRESS, COUNTRY
FROM      ADDRESSES
ORDER BY STATE, CITY;
```

The output of this SELECT would draw attention to our intent, which is to sort data by STATE first and then CITY. But while this might be considered preferential

FIGURE 4-2

Results of SELECT
with ORDER BY
STATE, CITY

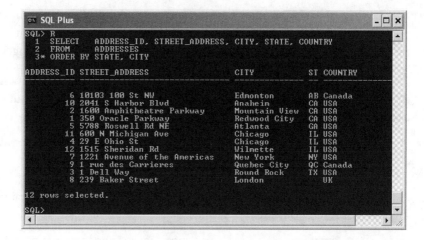

design in certain circumstances, it is by no means required within the syntax of the
SQL statement. We're not even required to include the ORDER BY columns in the
SELECT statement's expression list at all. This is another perfectly valid SELECT
statement:

```
SELECT    ADDRESS_ID, STREET_ADDRESS, COUNTRY
FROM      ADDRESSES
ORDER BY STATE, CITY;
```

Notice that we're sorting by columns that aren't included in the SELECT
statement's expression list.

Without an ORDER BY clause, there is no guarantee regarding the sequence in
which rows will be displayed in a SELECT statement's output. The rows may be
produced in a different order from one query to another. The only way to ensure
consistency to the output is to include an ORDER BY clause.

ASC and DESC

There are two reserved words that specify the direction of sorting on a given
column of the ORDER BY clause. Those reserved words are ASC and DESC.

■ ASC is short for "ascending" and indicates that values will be sorted in
ascending order. In other words, the lowest, or least, value will be listed
first, followed by values of higher, or greater, value. ASC is the default
choice and as such does not need to be specified when desired but may be
specified for clarity.

■ DESC is short for "descending" and indicates that values will be sorted in descending order. In other words, the highest, or greatest, value will be listed first, and values will continue to be listed in decreasing, or lesser, value.

As just stated, the default is ASC. You don't need to specify ASC. The ORDER BY examples you've seen so far have defaulted to ASC without our having to specify it. But you can specify ASC if you wish.

```
SELECT    SHIP_ID, PROJECT_COST, PROJECT_NAME, DAYS
FROM      PROJECTS
ORDER BY SHIP_ID ASC;
```

Here's a variation on the preceding SELECT statement that uses a combination of ASC and DESC:

```
SELECT    SHIP_ID, PROJECT_COST, PROJECT_NAME, DAYS
FROM      PROJECTS
ORDER BY SHIP_ID ASC, PROJECT_COST DESC;
```

Figure 4-3 displays the results of this SELECT. Notice that the SHIP_ID values are listed in ascending order, but that for each ship, the PROJECT_COST values are shown from the highest to the lowest values.

ASC and DESC each operate on the individual ORDER BY expressions. There is no way to assign ASC or DESC to all the ORDER BY expressions collectively; instead, you must place your choice after each individual ORDER BY expression, remembering that ASC is the default and therefore does not need to be specified.

FIGURE 4-3

PROJECTS table with ORDER BY ASC and DESC

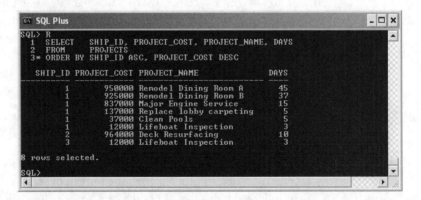

Expressions

Note that the expressions you can include in an ORDER BY clause are not limited to columns in a table. Any expression may be used. To be useful, the expression should include a value in the table; otherwise, the value may not change, and there won't be any meaningful effect on the rows in the table.

For example, here's a data listing for the PROJECTS table:

```
PROJECT_ID  SHIP_ID  PROJECT_NAME                    PROJECT_COST  DAYS
----------  -------  ------------------------        ------------  ----
         1        2  Deck Resurfacing                      964000    10
         2        3  Lifeboat Inspection                    12000     3
         3        1  Clean Pools                            37000     5
         4        1  Replace Lobby Carpeting               137000     5
         5        1  Major Engine Service                  837000    15
         6        1  Remodel Dining Room A                 950000    45
         7        1  Remodel Dining Room B                 925000    37
         8        1  Lifeboat Inspection                    12000     3
```

This data listing shows a series of projects. For each project, we see the SHIP_ID for which the project is intended, the project's total cost, and the estimated number of days it will take to complete each project.

Looking at the values for PROJECT_COST and DAYS, we see enough information to compute the average cost per day for each project.

```
PROJECT_COST / DAYS
```

For example, the per-day cost for the three-day "Lifeboat Inspection" will turn out to be 4000, or 12000 divided by 3.

What if we want to sort these rows according to the computed value of the PROJECT_COST / DAYS? No problem.

```
SELECT    *
FROM      PROJECTS
ORDER BY  PROJECT_COST / DAYS;
```

That query will achieve the result we're after. Let's vary it a bit to see more of what it is we're calculating and sorting.

```
SELECT    PROJECT_ID, PROJECT_NAME, PROJECT_COST, DAYS, PROJECT_COST/DAYS
FROM      PROJECTS
ORDER BY  PROJECT_COST/DAYS;
```

Figure 4-4 shows the results of this query. Note that the rows are ordered by a value that doesn't exist in the table but rather a value that is the result of an expression that draws values from the table.

FIGURE 4-4

PROJECTS sorted
by PROJECT_
COST / DAYS

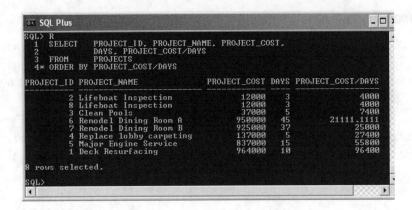

The Column Alias

As you've already seen, a SELECT statement can include expressions in the select
list. Here's an example:

```
SELECT    PROJECT_ID, PROJECT_NAME, PROJECT_COST, DAYS, PROJECT_COST/DAYS
FROM      PROJECTS
ORDER BY PROJECT_COST/DAYS;
```

Notice the output in Figure 4-4 and the default title of the fifth column. SQL has
used the expression as the title of the column.

We could have used a SQL feature called the *column alias*. Here is the same query
with a column alias (line numbers added):

```
01    SELECT    PROJECT_ID, PROJECT_NAME, PROJECT_COST,
02              DAYS, PROJECT_COST/DAYS AS PER_DAY_COST
03    FROM      PROJECTS
04    ORDER BY PER_DAY_COST;
```

Notice the PER_DAY_COST column alias at the end of line 2. The column alias
is a name you make up and place just after the column you want to alias, separated
by the optional keyword AS. In this example, the column with the column alias is
the final column in the select list. Once the column alias is used, you can reference
it from within the ORDER BY clause, as we do on line 4.

The rules for using a column alias include the following:

- Each expression in the SELECT list may optionally be followed by a
  column alias.
- A column alias is placed after the expression in the select list, separated by
  the optional keyword AS and a required space.

■ If the column alias is enclosed in double quotes, it can include spaces and other special characters.

■ If the column alias is not enclosed in double quotes, it is named according to the standard rules for naming database objects.

■ The column alias exists within the SQL statement and its results and does not exist outside of the SQL statement.

■ The column alias must be unique; it will become the new header in the output of the SQL statement.

■ The column alias can be referenced within the ORDER BY clause, but nowhere else—such as WHERE, GROUP BY, or HAVING.

Here's an example of a column alias that uses the double quotation marks. Notice the inclusion of a space in the alias.

```
01    SELECT    PROJECT_ID, PROJECT_NAME, PROJECT_COST,
02              DAYS, PROJECT_COST/DAYS "Cost Per Day"
03    FROM      PROJECTS
04    ORDER BY "Cost Per Day";
```

See the output of this query in Figure 4-5. Notice the column heading for the aliased column—the alias becomes the new heading in the SQL output.

The point of bringing up the alias here in this discussion about ORDER BY is this: you can use the column alias when referencing any column with ORDER BY, and it's particularly useful when trying to use ORDER BY with an expression from within the SELECT statement's expression list.

FIGURE 4-5

SELECT output with column alias

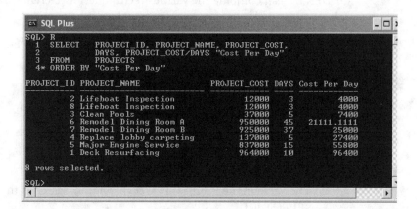

Reference by Position

Another way the ORDER BY clause can identify columns to be sorted is via the "reference by position" method. This works only if the intent of the ORDER BY is to sort rows according to information that is included in the SELECT list. Here's an example:

```
SELECT    PROJECT_ID, PROJECT_NAME, PROJECT_COST,
          DAYS, PROJECT_COST/DAYS FROM      PROJECTS
ORDER BY 5;
```

Notice that we choose to ORDER BY 5 in this SQL statement. The number 5 in this context is referencing the fifth item in the SELECT statement's select list, which is the expression PROJECT_COST/DAYS.

Any expression in the SELECT list can be referenced using its numeric position. The first expression is considered number 1, the second is number 2, and so on.

Any attempt to reference a position that doesn't exist will produce a SQL error; for example, this is invalid:

```
SELECT    PROJECT_ID, PROJECT_COST/DAYS
FROM      PROJECTS
ORDER BY 5;
```

This statement will not execute. The ORDER BY clause must identify a number that corresponds to an item that is in the SELECT list.

Combinations

ORDER BY can combine the various techniques of reference by name, reference by column alias, and reference by position. Here's an example:

```
SELECT SHIP_ID, PROJECT_COST, PROJECT_NAME "The Project", DAYS
FROM PROJECTS
ORDER BY SHIP_ID DESC, "The Project", 2;
```

This example is a valid statement. It sorts rows by

- The value of SHIP_ID, in descending order
- The value in the PROJECT_NAME column, which has a column alias in this SQL statement of "The Project"
- The value in the PROJECT_COST column, which is the second item in the SELECT list

Figure 4-6 shows the output of this query.

FIGURE 4-6

PROJECTS sorted by multiple techniques

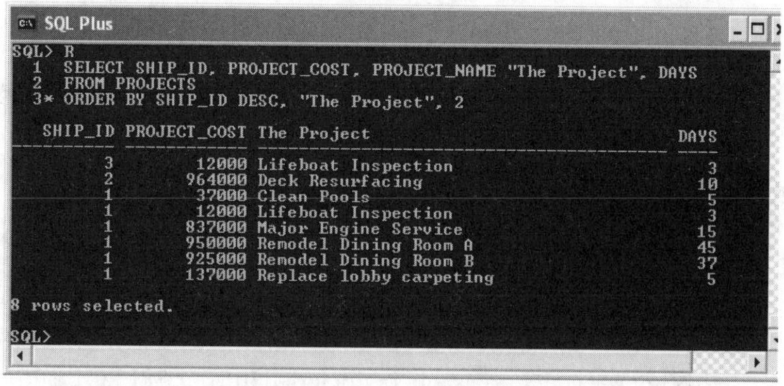

exam watch

Remember that ordering a SELECT statement by position is extremely useful in many situations that involve complex SELECT statements. Later you'll see some interesting combinations of multiple SELECT statements (such as the section that looks at using set operators that combine multiple SELECT statements into one), and in those situations, you can always reference an ORDER BY column by position.

ORDER BY and NULL

When SELECT performs a sort using ORDER BY, it treats any values that it might find to be NULL as "greater than" any other value. In other words, when you sort by a numeric data type column and that column contains NULL values, the NULL values will sort as being greater than all NOT NULL values in the list. The same is true for character data types and date data types.

CERTIFICATION OBJECTIVE 4.02

Limit the Rows That Are Retrieved by a Query

When building a SELECT statement, your first task is to identify which database table (or tables or views) contains the data you need. You also need to look at the table's structure to choose the columns that will be included in the select list of your SELECT statement. But rarely do you stop there. Most of the time you'll want to limit the rows you'll retrieve to a particular few, based on some sort of business rules. That task is accomplished with the SELECT statement's WHERE clause.

This section will look at the WHERE clause and its usage.

The WHERE Clause

The WHERE clause is one of the more important clauses of three different SQL statements: SELECT, UPDATE, and DELETE.

The purpose of the WHERE clause is to identify rows that you want to include in your SQL statement. If you're working with a SELECT, then your WHERE clause chooses which rows will be included in your SELECT output. If it's an UPDATE you're working with, the WHERE clause defines which rows will be updated. If it's a DELETE, the WHERE clause defines which rows will be deleted.

Within any SQL statement, the WHERE clause, if included, always follows the FROM clause. WHERE is optional; it is never required in order to form a complete SQL statement, but if included, it must follow the FROM clause.

The WHERE clause starts with the reserved word WHERE, which is followed by the WHERE condition. The WHERE condition consists of one or more comparisons of expressions. The ultimate goal of the WHERE condition is to determine a value of true or false for each row in the tables (and/or views) identified in the FROM clause. If the WHERE condition returns a true for a given row, that row is included in the SQL statement. If it returns a false for a given row, that row is ignored for the SQL statement.

Let's look at a simple example:

```
01    SELECT EMPLOYEE_ID
02    FROM    WORK_HISTORY
03    WHERE   SHIP_ID = 3;
```

In this example, the WHERE clause on line 3 compares two expressions:

- The first expression is the table column SHIP_ID.
- The second expression consists of the literal value 3.

The comparison operator used to compare these two expressions is the equal sign. The WHERE clause will consider each row in the tables (and/or views) identified in the FROM clause. For this WHERE clause, each row's SHIP_ID value is analyzed to determine whether its value equals 3. For each row that contains a value of 3 in the SHIP_ID column, the WHERE condition returns a value of "true" for that row, and that row is included in the SQL statement. All other rows are ignored.

Note that the SELECT statement's select list doesn't include SHIP_ID. The WHERE clause does not need to include any of the columns that are being displayed—any column in the table is available to the WHERE clause. In this particular example, the issue of whether to include a row is based on data that won't be included in the final results of the SELECT statement, and that's fine.

If you leave the WHERE clause out of a SELECT statement, then all rows of the table (or tables) are retrieved.

Here is another example of a WHERE clause:

```
01   SELECT PORT_NAME, CAPACITY
02   FROM   PORTS
03   WHERE  CAPACITY >= 5;
```

This example shows a complete WHERE clause on line 3. In this example, the SELECT statement will show the values for PORT_NAME and CAPACITY for all rows with a value in the CAPACITY column that is greater than or equal to 5.

In the next section we'll examine expressions in WHERE clauses.

Comparing Expressions

The WHERE clause uses a series of comparisons, each of which evaluates for each row to either true or false. Each comparison involves two expressions evaluated by a comparison operator. The expressions are first evaluated and then compared. For example, in the following comparison, on the left is an expression that consists solely of the column named SALARY, and on the right is an expression that multiplies two numbers together:

```
SALARY >= 50899 * 1.12
```

In this example, if the value in SALARY is greater than or equal to the result of the math equation 50899 times 1.12, the result is true. Otherwise, it's false.

The examples you've seen so far have shown column names on the left, but that's not required; any valid expression may be placed on either side—or both sides—of the comparison operator. Ideally one of the expressions should include data from the table; otherwise, what's the point? But in terms of syntax, that is not required. All that is required is a valid expression on both sides of the comparison operator.

Let's look at another example:

```
START_DATE < END_DATE
```

For a given row, if the value in the column titled START_DATE is less than the value in the column titled END_DATE, the expression is true; otherwise, it's false. (Note that when SQL compares dates, "less than" means "earlier than."

	Operator	Description
TABLE 4-1 Comparison Operators	=	Equal.
	>=	Greater than or equal to.
	>	Greater than.
	<=	Less than or equal to.
	<	Less than.
	!=	Not equal.
	<>	Not equal.
	^=	Not equal.
	IN	Compares one value on the left side of the operator to a set of one or more values on the right side of the operator. The set of values must be enclosed in parentheses. If the values are presented as constants, they are separated by commas, as in ('Maple', 'Elm', 'Main') or (2009, 2010, 2011). A query may also be used, as in (SELECT PORT_NAME FROM PORTS)—this is called a *subquery*, and we'll discuss much more on that topic in Chapter 9.
	LIKE	Enables wildcard characters. There are two wildcard characters: _ The underscore is a wildcard character representing a single character. % The percent sign is a wildcard character representing zero or more characters.
	IS	Used with NULL or NOT NULL.

For example, January 1 is less than January 2 of the same year. We'll talk more about this issue in a bit.)

The WHERE clause uses *comparison operators* to compare two expressions to each other. See Table 4-1 for a full list of the comparison operators. The operators are relatively self-explanatory, except for IN, LIKE, and IS, all of which we'll discuss in upcoming sections.

Comparing Data Types

Within a single comparison, both expressions should be the same data type for the comparison to work. There are essentially three general categories of data types to consider when performing comparisons—numeric, character string, and date. Table 4-2 lists the rules for comparing data types.

Date Type	Comparison Rules
Numeric	Smaller numbers are less than larger numbers. 1 is less than 10. −3 is less than −1. The number 0 is greater than any negative number.
Character	A is less than Z, and Z is less than a, meaning that uppercase letters are less than lowercase letters. Be careful of situations where numbers are treated as characters. For example, the string '2' is considered to be greater than the string ''10', because character strings are treated as text, not numbers, unless SQL is given explicit instructions otherwise—something we'll address later, when we discuss functions that perform data type conversions. Comparisons are case-sensitive by default.
Dates	Yesterday is less than tomorrow. Earlier dates are less than later dates.

TABLE 4-2 Rules for Data Type Comparisons

You may have noticed that I said data types "should" be the same for two expressions that are compared to each other. I say "should" because this isn't an absolute rule. Sometimes you can get away with comparing expressions of different data types provided that SQL has enough information to perform an automatic data type conversion and therefore treat both sides of the comparison as though they were the same data type, even though they are not. While this can work, it's not recommended. The results of such automatic data type conversions can be a bit tricky and relatively unpredictable, so it's best to avoid such situations. When we discuss SQL functions later, you'll see some functions that can be used to perform explicit data type conversions, which is the better choice for SQL professionals. In the meantime, don't depend on Oracle SQL's automatic data type conversion capabilities unless you love to live dangerously and don't mind if the rest of us laugh at you.

Here's an example that compares string values:

```
SELECT *
FROM    EMPLOYEES
WHERE   LAST_NAME = 'Smith';
```

This sample will show all columns in all the rows in the EMPLOYEES table where the value for the LAST_NAME column is the character string 'Smith'.

Note that text searches are case-sensitive by default. In other words, this is a different query:

```
SELECT  *
FROM    EMPLOYEES
WHERE   LAST_NAME = 'SMITH';
```

The search for employees with a value in the LAST_NAME column of 'SMITH' will not find the same rows that have a LAST_NAME value of 'Smith'. If you want to do a search on both possibilities, see Chapter 6, where we'll discuss how to handle such situations using SQL functions.

on the job

When comparing dates, I always like to remember this rhyme: "later dates are greater dates." That's my trick for remembering how the rules of date comparison work.

LIKE

The LIKE comparison operator is useful for performing wildcard searches on character data. It uses wildcard characters that you can embed within a text string. LIKE works with columns of data type CHAR and data type VARCHAR2. Technically it doesn't really work on DATE, but on a practical level it does—it performs an automatic data type conversion of the DATE values involved before performing the comparison.

The two wildcard symbols are

- The underscore (_), representing a single character
- The percent sign (%), representing zero or more characters

You use the underscore when you are referencing a fixed length of wildcard characters. Underscores can be repeated as required. For example, this query is looking for values in the PORT_NAME column that start with the string 'San', followed by a blank space, followed by any four characters:

```
01    SELECT PORT_NAME
02    FROM   PORTS
03    WHERE  PORT_NAME LIKE 'San ____';
```

In case you can't tell, that's four underscores after 'San ' in the preceding query. If you were to run this query against rows with these values:

```
San Diego
San Francisco
San Juan
```

the query will return only this value:

```
San Juan
```

That's because of the four underscores in the query (line 3), which specifically ask for four unknown characters after 'San '. No more, no less.

If you want to indicate any number of unknown characters, ranging from zero to infinity, then use the percent sign. This query,

```
SELECT  PORT_NAME
FROM    PORTS
WHERE   PORT_NAME LIKE 'San%';
```

will find all three rows in the previous example, like so:

```
San Diego
San Francisco
San Juan
```

The percent sign, combined with LIKE, indicates that any number of characters are sought.

Underscores and percent signs can be used in any combination, in any order, in any location within the pattern. Here's an example:

```
SELECT  PORT_NAME
FROM    PORTS
WHERE   PORT_NAME LIKE '_o%';
```

This query is looking for values in PORT_NAME with any one random character in the first position, followed by the lowercase letter *o* in the second position, followed by anywhere from zero to an almost infinite number of characters after the letter *o*. The following rows match the request:

```
Los Angeles
Honolulu
```

When working with LIKE, you put the wildcard character (or characters) within a string enclosed in single quotes. The string must occur after the reserved word LIKE, not before. In other words, the following is syntactically correct but doesn't perform as you might think it should:

```
SELECT PORT_NAME
FROM    PORTS
WHERE   'G_and%' LIKE PORT_NAME;
```

This query is asking whether the string literal 'G_and%' happens to match the value contained within PORT_NAME. This probably isn't what was intended. The point here is that the wildcard characters are "activated" only if the pattern containing them is on the right side of the LIKE reserved word. This is the query that was probably intended:

```
SELECT PORT_NAME
FROM    PORTS
WHERE   PORT_NAME LIKE 'G_and%';
```

This query would find a row containing a PORT_NAME value such as this:

```
Grand Cayman
```

So remember, place the pattern after LIKE, not before. Oracle won't complain if you screw it up. But your output probably won't be what you're intending.

Boolean Logic

The WHERE clause includes support for Boolean logic, whereby multiple expressions can be connected with a series of Boolean operators. This section looks at those operators, what they are, how they are used, and their order of precedence.

AND, OR

Most WHERE conditions involve more than just one comparison of two expressions. Most WHERE clauses contain several such comparisons. This is where the Boolean operators come in. Two or more comparisons of expressions can be connected by using various combinations of the Boolean operators AND and OR. There's also a third operator—NOT—and it can be used to invert an AND or OR condition. Boolean operators evaluate multiple comparison expressions and produce a single true or false conclusion from the series of comparisons. Here's an example:

```
01    SELECT EMPLOYEE_ID
02    FROM   WORK_HISTORY
03    WHERE  SHIP_ID = 3
04           AND
05           STATUS = 'Pending';
```

Let's break this down the way Oracle SQL does. Consider the following data listing:

```
WORK_HISTORY_ID   EMPLOYEE_ID   SHIP_ID   STATUS
---------------   -----------   -------   ------
             10             3         1   Pending
             11             4         4   Active
             12             7         3   Pending
```

For each row, the WHERE condition will do the following:

- Determine whether the SHIP_ID value equals 3
- Determine whether the STATUS value is equal to the string 'Pending'

The results for each row are as follows (Note: the italicized columns are not output listings, but an analysis of Boolean operator calculations):

```
WORK_HISTORY_ID   EMPLOYEE_ID   SHIP_ID   STATUS    SHIP_ID=3?   STATUS='Pending'?
---------------   -----------   -------   -------   ----------   -----------------
             10             3         1   Pending   FALSE        TRUE
             11             4         4   Active    FALSE        FALSE
             12             7         3   Pending   TRUE         TRUE
```

Now let's apply the AND operator to each row:

```
WORK_HISTORY_ID   SHIP_ID=3?          STATUS='Pending'?   RESULT
---------------   ----------          -----------------   --------
             10   FALSE        AND    TRUE                FALSE
             11   FALSE        AND    FALSE               FALSE
             12   TRUE         AND    TRUE                TRUE
```

The rules of Boolean operator evaluation are the same as they are in conventional mathematics. See Table 4-3 for a listing of all the possible results of Boolean operator expressions.

TABLE 4-3

Boolean
Expression
Combinations
and Results

Boolean Expression	Result
TRUE AND TRUE	TRUE
TRUE AND FALSE	FALSE
FALSE AND TRUE	FALSE
FALSE AND FALSE	FALSE
TRUE OR TRUE	TRUE
TRUE OR FALSE	TRUE
FALSE OR TRUE	TRUE
FALSE OR FALSE	FALSE

The rules for Booleans are

- For AND, both expressions must be true for the combination to be true. Otherwise, the answer is false.
- For OR, at least one expression needs to be true for the combination to evaluate to true. Otherwise, the answer is false.

The basic syntax for a SELECT statement with a WHERE clause that includes Booleans is as follows:

```
01   SELECT select_list
02   FROM   from_table
03   WHERE
04          expression comparison_operator expression
05          Boolean_operator
06          expression comparison_operator expression
07          termination_character
```

Lines 4 and 6 represent the same thing—a comparison of two expressions.

A single WHERE clause may include as many of these comparisons as are required, indicated on line 4 and also on line 6—provided they are each separated by a Boolean operator.

NOT

The reserved word NOT is part of the set of Boolean operators. It can be placed in front of an expression to reverse its conclusion from true to false, or vice versa.

For example, let's modify a SELECT statement you saw earlier:

```
01    SELECT  EMPLOYEE_ID
02    FROM    WORK_HISTORY
03    WHERE   SHIP_ID = 3
04            AND
05            NOT STATUS = 'Pending';
```

In this SELECT, we've added the reserved word NOT on line 5 to reverse the findings of the comparison of the string 'Pending' to the values in the column STATUS. If you were to run this version of the SELECT against the same three rows you used earlier, you'd get a very different result: no rows returned. Here is why:

WORK_HISTORY_ID	EMPLOYEE_ID	SHIP_ID	STATUS	SHIP_ID=3?	NOT STATUS='Pending'?
10	3	1	Pending	FALSE	FALSE
11	4	4	Active	FALSE	TRUE
12	7	3	Pending	TRUE	FALSE

With an AND operator still in use here, now our SELECT statement will return no rows since AND requires both sides to be true and no rows satisfy this criteria.

Let's look at another example:

```
01    SELECT  EMPLOYEE_ID
02    FROM    WORK_HISTORY
03    WHERE   NOT SHIP_ID = 3;
```

As you can see from this example, NOT can be used without any other Boolean operators. While we're at it, the use of NOT we just considered has the same effect as this:

```
01    SELECT  EMPLOYEE_ID
02    FROM    WORK_HISTORY
03    WHERE   SHIP_ID <> 3;
```

or as this:

```
01    SELECT  EMPLOYEE_ID
02    FROM    WORK_HISTORY
03    WHERE   SHIP_ID != 3;
```

Both <> and != in these contexts have the same effect as the use of the NOT operator.

If you're an experienced programmer and have used languages such as Oracle's PL/SQL, this section may have you wondering where the BOOLEAN data type fits into SQL. It doesn't. There is no BOOLEAN data type in SQL. There is in PL/SQL, but not in SQL. Instead, expressions are compared to each other to determine a Boolean condition of TRUE or FALSE, and the Boolean operators compare them to determine an answer. The concepts of TRUE and FALSE are significant throughout SQL, as we see with the WHERE condition. But there are no specific data types that represent Boolean values.

Operator Precedence

Just as there is a set of rules regarding the order of evaluating arithmetic operators within expressions, so too are there rules for evaluating Boolean operators. It's important that you remember the order in which SQL evaluates Boolean operators.

The bottom line: NOT is evaluated first. After that, AND is evaluated before OR. For example, consider the following data listing for a table called SHIP_CABINS:

```
ROOM_NUMBER   STYLE       WINDOW
-----------   ---------   ---------
        102   Suite       Ocean
        103   Stateroom   Ocean
        104   Suite       None
        105   Stateroom   Ocean
        106   Suite       None
```

Now consider this SQL statement against the data listing:

```
SELECT  ROOM_NUMBER
FROM    SHIP_CABINS
WHERE   STYLE = 'Suite'
   OR   STYLE = 'Stateroom'
  AND   WINDOW = 'Ocean';
```

How many rows do you think this query will retrieve? Are you thinking . . . three rows, by any chance? If you are, you're not alone; most people tend to think that. But, you'll really get five rows. Why? Because of the rules of Boolean operator precedence. An English-speaking person might read that query as asking for all rows with a STYLE value of either 'Suite' or 'Stateroom' and also with a value for WINDOW of 'Ocean'. But SQL sees this differently—it first evaluates the AND expression. SQL is looking for all the rows where STYLE is 'Stateroom' and

WINDOW is 'Ocean' ... OR .... any row with a STYLE value of 'Suite', regardless of its value for WINDOW. In other words, it's doing this:

ROOM_NUMBER	STYLE	WINDOW	Stateroom AND Ocean?		Suite?
102	Suite	Ocean	FALSE	OR	TRUE
103	Stateroom	Ocean	TRUE	OR	FALSE
104	Suite	None	FALSE	OR	TRUE
105	Stateroom	Ocean	TRUE	OR	FALSE
106	Suite	None	FALSE	OR	TRUE

Remember, only one side in an OR must be TRUE. And given this criterion, all five rows will evaluate to true.

You can use parentheses to override the rules of Boolean operator precedence, like this:

```
SELECT  ROOM_NUMBER
FROM    SHIP_CABINS
WHERE   (STYLE = 'Suite'
   OR   STYLE = 'Stateroom')
   AND  WINDOW = 'Ocean';
```

That query will retrieve three rows.

Additional WHERE Clause Features

The WHERE clause offers some options to streamline the readability of your code. This section describes features that are important to advanced WHERE clause usage.

IN

Sometimes you'll find yourself comparing a single column to a series of various values. Here's an example:

```
SELECT  PORT_NAME
FROM    PORTS
WHERE   COUNTRY = 'UK' OR COUNTRY = 'USA' OR COUNTRY = 'Bahamas';
```

That query is correct, but in such situations, you have the option of choosing a different style. You may choose to use the reserved word IN as an alternative. Here's an example:

```
SELECT  PORT_NAME
FROM    PORTS
WHERE   COUNTRY IN ('UK', 'USA', 'Bahamas');
```

The rules that govern the use of the IN operator include the following:

- IN can be used with dates, numbers, or text expressions.
- The list of expressions must be enclosed in a set of parentheses.
- The list of expressions must be of the same data type—or be similar enough that Oracle can perform automatic data type conversion to make them all the same.
- The list can include anywhere from one expression to several, each separated by commas.

In addition, the Boolean operator NOT may precede the IN operator, as follows:

```
SELECT  PORT_NAME
FROM    PORTS
WHERE   COUNTRY NOT IN ('UK', 'USA', 'Bahamas');
```

The use of NOT will identify rows as true if they do not contain a value from the list.

You'll see later that the reserved word IN is particularly important in the WHERE clause when we're using subqueries, which we'll discuss in Chapter 9.

BETWEEN

In addition to the formats we've seen so far, the WHERE clause supports a feature that can compare a single expression to a range of values. This technique involves the reserved word BETWEEN. Here's an example:

```
SELECT  PORT_NAME
FROM    PORTS
WHERE   CAPACITY BETWEEN 3 AND 4;
```

This is the equivalent of the following statement:

```
SELECT  PORT_NAME
FROM    PORTS
WHERE   CAPACITY >= 3
   AND  CAPACITY <= 4;
```

Notice that BETWEEN is inclusive. In other words, it doesn't simply look for values "between" the two comparison expressions, but also includes values that are equal to the comparison expressions.

The range can be specified using any valid expression.

The range should be from lowest to highest. If you specify the higher value first and the lower value second, your code will be accepted syntactically but will always return zero rows.

The NOT keyword may also be combined with BETWEEN. The following are valid statements:

```
SELECT  PORT_NAME
FROM    PORTS
WHERE   CAPACITY NOT BETWEEN 3 AND 4;


SELECT  PORT_NAME
FROM    PORTS
WHERE   NOT CAPACITY BETWEEN 3 AND 4;
```

These two examples are equivalent to each other.

IS NULL, IS NOT NULL

Remember that the NULL value represents an unknown value. NULL is the equivalent of "I don't know." Any value that's compared to "I don't know" is going to produce an unknown result—in other words, NULL. Here's an example:

```
SELECT  PORT_NAME
FROM    PORTS
WHERE   CAPACITY = NULL;
```

This SQL statement will never retrieve any rows, never ever, never ever ever. Don't believe me? Try it, I'll wait.

Told you. It will not ever retrieve any rows, not even if the value for CAPACITY is NULL within a given row. The reason is that this is asking SQL to compare CAPACITY to a value of "I don't know." But what if the value of CAPACITY in the database table is actually NULL? Shouldn't this work then? Shouldn't you be able to ask if CAPACITY = NULL? Why isn't the expression NULL = NULL true?

Well, let me ask you this: I'm thinking of two numbers, and I'm not going to tell you what either one of them is. Instead, I'm just going to ask you this: are these two numbers equal to each other? Well? Are they?

Of course you can't possibly know. I think you'd have to say the answer is "I don't know," or NULL. And NULL, in terms of Boolean logic, is always assumed to be FALSE. So, any time you create a WHERE condition that ends up as "anything" = NULL, the answer will always be FALSE, and you'll never get a row—even if the "anything" is NULL itself.

But what do you do when you really need to test the value of something like CAPACITY to determine whether it is NULL or not? There is an answer, and it's the SQL comparison condition IS NULL and its companion IS NOT NULL.

Let's redo our SELECT statement:

```
SELECT PORT_NAME
FROM    PORTS
WHERE   CAPACITY IS NULL;
```

Now you're asking for rows from the PORTS table where the value for CAPACITY is unknown in the database—which is what IS NULL asks for. That's a very different query than asking if CAPACITY happens to be identical to some number that we haven't identified yet—which is what = NULL asks.

The opposite of the IS NULL comparison operator is IS NOT NULL, like this:

```
SELECT PORT_NAME
FROM    PORTS
WHERE   CAPACITY IS NOT NULL;
```

In this query, you're asking for all rows in which the CAPACITY value is identified in the database, in other words, wherever it is not NULL.

These concepts are important. This is yet another example of one of the many ways in which SQL code might appear to be correct, might execute without any syntax or execution errors, and yet can be totally wrong.

Be sure you get this right. Don't screw it up. If you do, the problems will be subtle and potentially disastrous and might become apparent only months later after bad data and incorrect reports have been circulated. So, remember, never use this:

```
= NULL
```

There is never a good reason to use that, ever. Always use this instead:

```
IS NULL
```

Got it?

Additional Concepts

There are more ways to customize a WHERE clause than what has been presented here. Upcoming topics that will be addressed in this book—and tested on the exam—include the following:

- Subqueries
- Set operators

These and other issues are important to the WHERE clause and important to the exam. They will be covered on their own in upcoming chapters.

Use Ampersand Substitution to Restrict and Sort Output at Run Time

The inclusion of the ampersand substitution variable as an exam objective is a bit unusual in that it represents a SQL*Plus feature to be addressed. All other exam objectives focus on Oracle's implementation of the SQL language, including ANSI standard SQL as well as Oracle's enhancements, such as the DECODE function. But the ampersand substitution variable is a feature of SQL*Plus exclusively. SQL*Plus is a tool for working with Oracle's relational database by using SQL commands interactively or via batch processing, and it offers several unique commands, system variables, and other capabilities, all of which are unique to SQL*Plus. The ampersand substitution variable is one of those SQL*Plus features, but it is not part of the SQL language. You won't find a description of it in the Oracle SQL Language Reference manual, not, at least, at the time of this writing. But you will find it described in Oracle's SQL*Plus documentation.

The purpose of ampersand substitution is to provide a SQL script with a run-time parameter feature when used within SQL*Plus sessions. The value of the parameter can be set via batch before or interactively during a given SQL script's execution. Either way, the point is to decouple the value of the parameter from the script, empowering an individual script to execute in a variety of ways.

Furthermore, the substitution variable can represent any aspect of the SQL script. It can be used to specify a value in a WHERE clause, a column in a SELECT statement, the name of a table, or virtually any portion of the code within a script, including keywords, SQL commands, or data of any kind, such as input data for an INSERT or UPDATE statement, the criteria of a HAVING or GROUP BY, or anything.

To fully leverage the power of the ampersand substitution variable, you need to know more than the variable. There are a variety of surrounding commands you should understand to configure and implement the ampersand substitution variable. This section describes those supporting features, all of which may appear on the exam.

In this section, we'll look at the ampersand substitution variable itself and how to use it during execution. Next we'll predefine a value using the SQL*Plus commands DEFINE and UNDEFINE. Then we'll discuss how SQL*Plus system variables work, after which we will look at two of importance for our discussion: the VERIFY system variable and the DEFINE system variable (not to be confused with the DEFINE command). Finally, we'll discuss two additional SQL*Plus commands that you can use with substitution variables: ACCEPT and PROMPT.

&

Let's look at an example of the ampersand substitution variable by using the SHIP_CABINS table. Let's say the table contains the following rows of data:

```
ROOM_NUMBER   STYLE       WINDOW
-----------   ---------   ---------
        102   Suite       Ocean
        103   Stateroom   Ocean
        104   Suite       None
        105   Stateroom   Ocean
        106   Suite       None
```

Here is a script that will query SHIP_CABINS and use an ampersand substitution variable on the end of the third line to enable us to set the WHERE criteria at execution time:

```
SELECT    ROOM_NUMBER, STYLE, WINDOW
FROM      SHIP_CABINS
WHERE     ROOM_NUMBER = &RNO
ORDER BY ROOM_NUMBER;
```

Once we have created this script, we can execute it and specify the value for ROOM_NUMBER. Refer to Figure 4-7 to see what happens when we execute this script within a SQL*Plus client.

During execution, the presence of the ampersand substitution variable triggers an "Enter value for rno:" request from the system. In response, we type **104** and press ENTER. The system then displays the old line 3, as well as the new line 3 showing

FIGURE 4-7

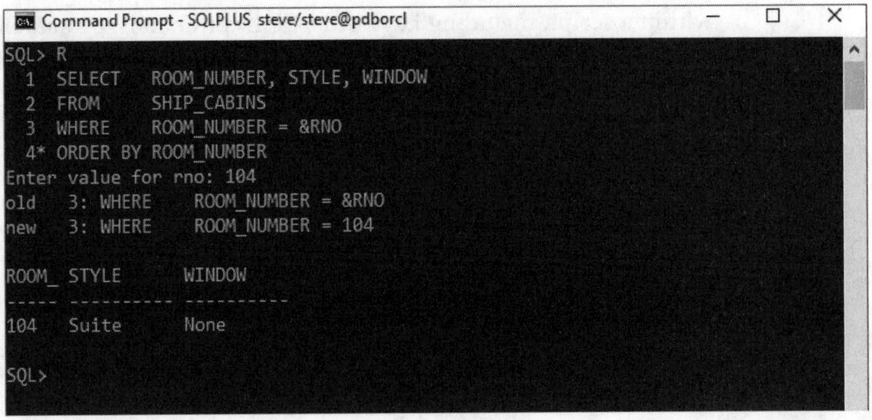

Using an ampersand variable to specify room number at run time

how the value for "rno" has been replaced with 104. Finally, the statement is executed as though 104 had been in the place of "rno" all along, and we see the result: a return of rows where ROOM_NUMBER = 104.

The ampersand substitution variable consists of the following:

- The substitution variable prefix (an ampersand)
- The substitution variable name, consisting of any subsequent contiguous set of alphanumeric characters until the next blank space

The variable name you specify will be repeated at run time in the context of a question, as you can see in the example. I used the name RNO, but you could have used something more descriptive, perhaps Room_Number or something.

In our example, we used the substitution variable to provide a value for a numeric column at run time. But what about text values? The substitution variable can be specified within quotes in the SQL statement. Here's an example:

```
SELECT     ROOM_NUMBER, STYLE, WINDOW
FROM       SHIP_CABINS
WHERE      WINDOW = '&Window_Type'
ORDER BY ROOM_NUMBER;
```

Let's see what happens when we execute this within a SQL*Plus client; see Figure 4-8.

FIGURE 4-8

Using an ampersand variable with quotes

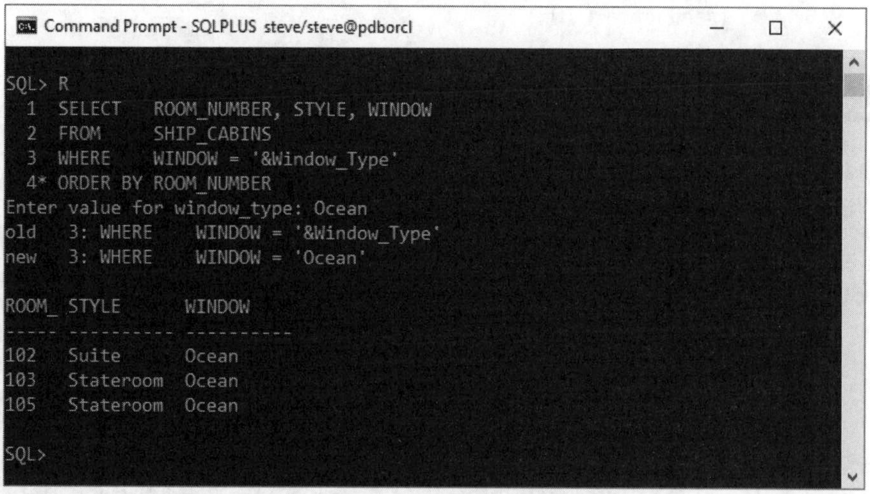

```
SQL> R
  1   SELECT     ROOM_NUMBER, STYLE, WINDOW
  2   FROM       SHIP_CABINS
  3   WHERE      WINDOW = '&Window_Type'
  4*  ORDER BY ROOM_NUMBER
Enter value for window_type: Ocean
old   3: WHERE     WINDOW = '&Window_Type'
new   3: WHERE     WINDOW = 'Ocean'

ROOM_ STYLE      WINDOW
----- ---------- ----------
102   Suite      Ocean
103   Stateroom  Ocean
105   Stateroom  Ocean

SQL>
```

FIGURE 4-9

Using an
ampersand
variable without
quotes

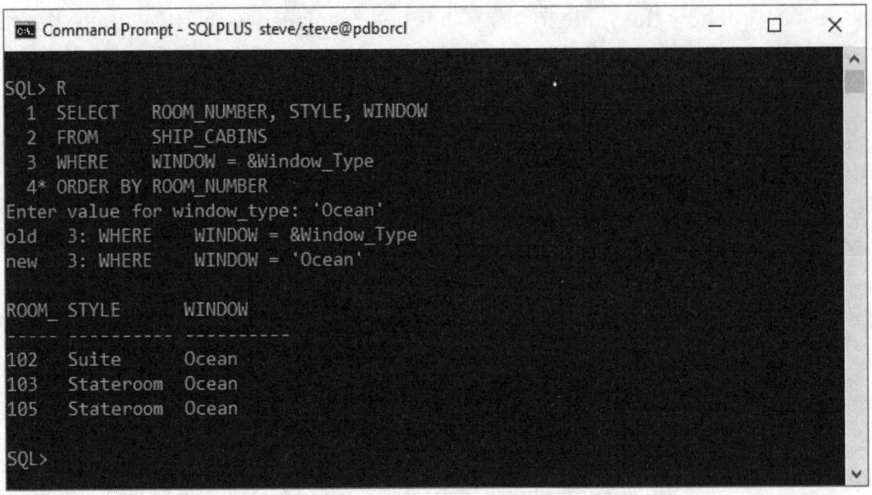

```
Command Prompt - SQLPLUS steve/steve@pdborcl                    —    □    ×

SQL> R
  1  SELECT    ROOM_NUMBER, STYLE, WINDOW
  2  FROM      SHIP_CABINS
  3  WHERE     WINDOW = &Window_Type
  4* ORDER BY ROOM_NUMBER
Enter value for window_type: 'Ocean'
old   3: WHERE     WINDOW = &Window_Type
new   3: WHERE     WINDOW = 'Ocean'

ROOM_ STYLE       WINDOW
----- ----------- ----------
102   Suite       Ocean
103   Stateroom   Ocean
105   Stateroom   Ocean

SQL>
```

As you can see in the example, the substitution variable used from within quotes works just the same. Alternatively, you can omit the quotes in the SQL and choose instead to provide the quotes at run time (see Figure 4-9).

```
SELECT    ROOM_NUMBER, STYLE, WINDOW
FROM      SHIP_CABINS
WHERE     WINDOW = &Window_Type
ORDER BY ROOM_NUMBER;
```

You can replace virtually any section of SQL code with a substitution variable; see Figure 4-10.

FIGURE 4-10

Using an
ampersand
variable with
SQL column
specifications

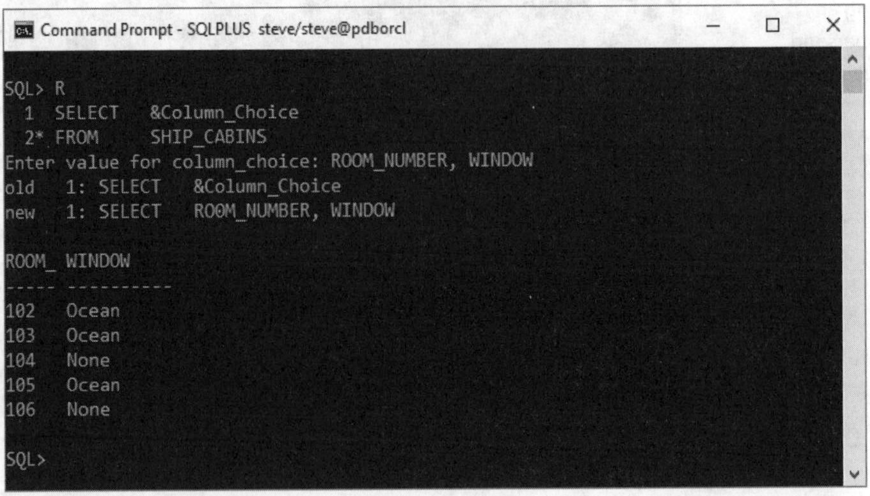

```
Command Prompt - SQLPLUS steve/steve@pdborcl                    —    □    ×

SQL> R
  1  SELECT    &Column_Choice
  2* FROM      SHIP_CABINS
Enter value for column_choice: ROOM_NUMBER, WINDOW
old   1: SELECT    &Column_Choice
new   1: SELECT    ROOM_NUMBER, WINDOW

ROOM_ WINDOW
----- ----------
102   Ocean
103   Ocean
104   None
105   Ocean
106   None

SQL>
```

Note how we just used a single substitution variable in the place of a column list of the SELECT statement. At run time, when prompted, we typed in the names of two columns, separated with a comma. These two names are substituted at run time, and the code executes accordingly.

So far we have worked with the substitution variable by specifying its value at run time. But you can predefine it as well, using the SQL*Plus command DEFINE.

DEFINE and UNDEFINE Commands

You can use a single statement on its own to define a substitution variable using the DEFINE statement so that when SQL code with a substitution variable is executed, the value you've already defined will be used. Here's an example:

```
DEFINE vWindows = Ocean
```

Note that we omit the substitution variable prefix; there is no ampersand at the beginning of the vWindows substitution variable.

To list all existing defined variables for a given session, use DEFINE on a line by itself, like this:

```
DEFINE
```

Also note: We chose to execute the SQL*Plus command DEFINE without a semicolon at the end. SQL commands require a semicolon at the end; SQL*Plus commands do not require them, yet they do accept them. So you may choose to include or omit them. SQL commands require semicolons. But for SQL*Plus commands, semicolons are optional.

The scope of the substitution variable is the session. Once defined, the variable will persist through the session or until it is "undefined."

```
UNDEFINE vWindows
```

Without an UNDEFINE, the vWindows substitution variable will persist for the duration of the login session. We will use DEFINE with a series of SQL statements to see how it works. But first let's also look at SET and SHOW.

The SET and SHOW Commands

The ampersand substitution variable is a SQL*Plus command, and its behavior is controlled by the settings of some of the SQL*Plus system variables. SQL*Plus includes a number of system variables that can be configured using the SET command. The current configuration of a system variable can be displayed using the SHOW command. For an example, see Figure 4-11.

```
Command Prompt - SQLPLUS steve/steve@pdborcl                    —  □  ×

SQL> SHOW DEFINE
define "&" (hex 26)
SQL> SHOW VERIFY
verify ON
SQL>
```

SHOW can be used with any of the SQL*Plus system variables to display the particular system variable's current state. A given system variable's current state consists of whether it is ON or OFF and optionally may include configuration details unique to the system variable.

To see the full set of all system variables and their state, use SHOW ALL.

For the purposes of working with the substitution variable, we are primarily interested in two particular substitution variables: VERIFY and DEFINE. Let's look at both in more detail.

The VERIFY System Variable

Note how SQL has been informing us of the "old" and "new" lines of code for each substitution variable. This can be turned on or off using a SET VERIFY statement.

```
SET VERIFY OFF
```

Once off, the "old" and "new" lines will no longer display. Alternatively, you can use an abbreviated version of VERIFY.

```
SET VER OFF
```

To restore VERIFY, turn it back on.

```
SET VERIFY ON
```

Setting VERIFY back to ON will ensure the "old" and "new" lines appear when using a defined variable in your SQL script.

ACCEPT and PROMPT

Two additional SQL*Plus commands are useful when working with substitution variables. PROMPT is a command to display an interactive message to an end user. ACCEPT will receive data from a user to store in a predefined variable. Together, these two commands are commonly used in interactive scripts where SQL*Plus substitution variables are in use.

For an example, let's prompt an end user to type in a number, accept the typed number as the value for a variable we'll name vRoomNumber, and then incorporate the variable into a SQL script.

```
PROMPT Welcome to our script.  This report will look up data
PROMPT using the room number you provide.
PROMPT
ACCEPT vRoomNumber PROMPT "Enter a room number: "
SELECT ROOM_NUMBER, STYLE, WINDOW
FROM   SHIP_CABINS
WHERE  ROOM_NUMBER = &vRoomNumber;
PROMPT Remember, you asked for the room number &vRoomNumber.
```

Next, we'll store the SQL script in a simple text file that we'll name The_Script .sql. We'll store the file in the default folder of our local SQL*Plus client and execute the file. See Figure 4-12 for the results.

Note that PROMPT does not require quotes when invoked as a stand-alone statement but does require them when used in conjunction with ACCEPT.

In our example, the end user provides a room number of 104, and the subsequent SQL script returns the appropriate row. Using PROMPT you can create a more meaningful question of the end user. By combining PROMPT with ACCEPT you can accept an answer from the end user and store the value in a variable you reference later in the SQL script.

An important note: We included a period at the end of our defined variable, yet the period did not display interactively. Had we added a space after the defined variable and before the period, the period would have displayed. For that matter, any additional text after the defined variable will display, provided it is separated from the defined variable with one or more spaces.

FIGURE 4-12

ACCEPT and PROMPT

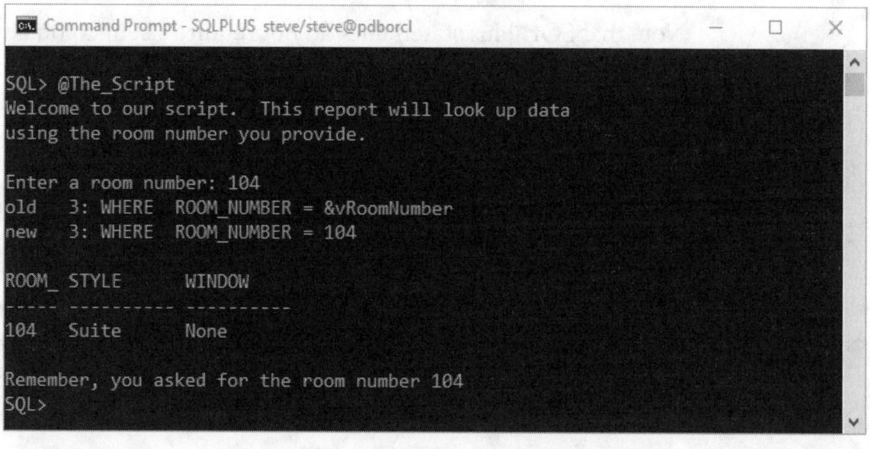

You can use any simple text editor to create batch scripts for processing by SQL*Plus. I use Notepad or UltraEdit. You should save the script in a file ending with the *.SQL suffix, but this is not required. For example, if you create a file called Run.sql and then save it on your operating system somewhere, you can invoke it from within SQL*Plus by typing @[folder location]Run, where @ tells SQL*Plus to execute the script, [folder location] is the location of the file, RUN is the file prefix, and the .SQL file suffix is assumed. Alternatively, you can use @[folder location]Run.SQL. The specific folder location is implementation specific, and you should check with your local database administrator and/or documentation to determine its location.

The DEFINE System Variable

To use the substitution variable, the DEFINE system variable must be set to ON. The default setting for DEFINE is ON for a given session, so you generally don't need to specifically set it. But to be sure, you can ensure that DEFINE is ON before you use the substitution variable by executing the following SQL*Plus statement prior to any use of a substitution variable:

```
SET DEFINE ON
```

This is particularly important if you are creating a batch script and you won't necessarily know at the time the batch script is executed whether the default ON value of DEFINE is set. It might be turned OFF. Setting it to ON explicitly when it is already ON will not trigger any complaints from the system. So, it is common practice to use SET DEFINE ON at the beginning of a batch script that uses it.

To set DEFINE to OFF, use this:

```
SET DEFINE OFF
```

Note that SQL*Plus statements do not require a semicolon at the end. You can use them if you want, but they are not required.

The exam objectives specifically refer to the substitution variable as the "ampersand substitution variable," but the ampersand itself can be changed with a variation of the SET DEFINE command that doesn't use either ON or OFF but instead resets the substitution variable prefix character. Here's an example:

```
SET DEFINE *
```

This SET DEFINE * statement will change the substitution variable prefix to an asterisk. Let's see it in action with a combination of statements. For this example, we'll set a system variable we haven't used yet, ECHO. Setting ECHO to

ON is useful when executing a series of statements in batch; ECHO ensures our statements themselves will display, not just their output, so we can see the full effect of our script.

Next, we'll set VERIFY to OFF so the "old" and "new" lines won't display whenever we invoke a substitution variable.

Next, we'll set DEFINE to OFF and use SHOW to confirm that DEFINE has in fact been turned off. But then we'll use SET DEFINE to change the prefix from the default (often an ampersand) to the asterisk. Then we will use SHOW DEFINE again to see that the default prefix has in fact been reset and that the DEFINE system variable is no longer OFF; changing the default prefix has the by-product of also turning the DEFINE system variable back to ON.

Next, we'll try to use a substitution variable with the ampersand, but since we've changed the prefix to something else, the ampersand will no longer be recognized and instead will be treated as standard text.

Finally, we'll repeat the same SQL script, but using the newly specified substitution variable's prefix of an asterisk, and we'll see that the SQL statement produces the output we're expecting.

```
SET ECHO ON

SET VERIFY OFF

SET DEFINE OFF
SHOW DEFINE
SET DEFINE *
SHOW DEFINE

SELECT ROOM_NUMBER, STYLE, WINDOW
FROM    SHIP_CABINS
WHERE   WINDOW = '&vWin';

SELECT ROOM_NUMBER, STYLE, WINDOW
FROM    SHIP_CABINS
WHERE   WINDOW = '*vWin';
```

For the results of all of this when executed as a batch script within SQL*Plus, see Figure 4-13.

Note that the substitution variable prefix is limited to one character only. Also, if DEFINE is set to OFF and you change the prefix, you will also automatically set DEFINE to ON.

FIGURE 4-13

Changing the
prefix of the
substitution
variable

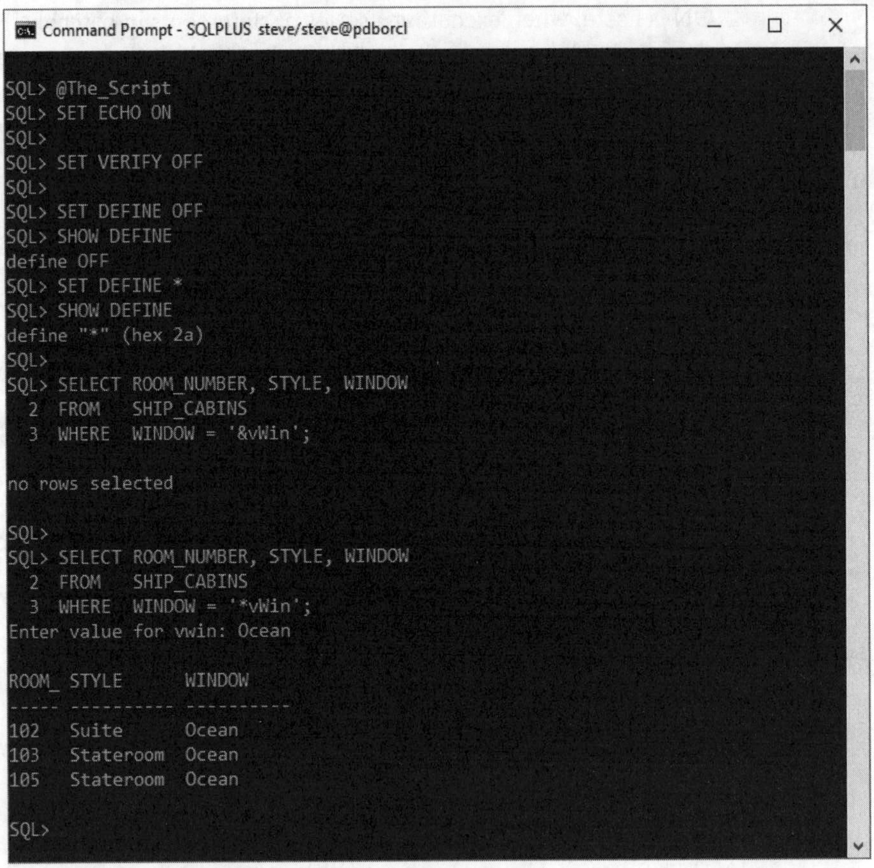

```
Command Prompt - SQLPLUS  steve/steve@pdborcl                    —    □    ✕

SQL> @The_Script
SQL> SET ECHO ON
SQL>
SQL> SET VERIFY OFF
SQL>
SQL> SET DEFINE OFF
SQL> SHOW DEFINE
define OFF
SQL> SET DEFINE *
SQL> SHOW DEFINE
define "*" (hex 2a)
SQL>
SQL> SELECT ROOM_NUMBER, STYLE, WINDOW
  2  FROM    SHIP_CABINS
  3  WHERE   WINDOW = '&vWin';

no rows selected

SQL>
SQL> SELECT ROOM_NUMBER, STYLE, WINDOW
  2  FROM    SHIP_CABINS
  3  WHERE   WINDOW = '*vWin';
Enter value for vwin: Ocean

ROOM_  STYLE       WINDOW
-----  ----------  ----------
102    Suite       Ocean
103    Stateroom   Ocean
105    Stateroom   Ocean

SQL>
```

CERTIFICATION OBJECTIVE 4.04

Use the SQL Row Limiting Clause

You can use the SQL row limiting clause to return only a subset of that data.
The SQL row limiting clause is new with Oracle 12*c*. It can be used after any
WHERE or ORDER BY clause to limit the number or percentage of rows to be
returned by a query. Granted, all WHERE criteria are already intended to limit
returned data from a logical standpoint—that's the entire purpose of the WHERE
clause. But the row limiting clause takes a much broader view. Whereas other

aspects of your query are generally focused on business logic, the row limiting clause can be used to choose, for example, only the first 10 rows of queried data, the second dozen rows, or the last 50 rows.

FETCH

Limits on the rows returned by a SELECT statement are specified by the FETCH statement. Here is an example of a single SELECT statement using the SQL row limiting clause:

```
01   SELECT * FROM ORDERS
02   FETCH FIRST 8 ROWS ONLY;
```

The keyword FETCH signifies the presence of the row limiting clause. In this example, the query will return up to eight rows and no more. For example, if only six rows exist, then all six will be returned. If 500 rows exist, only 8 will be returned.
FETCH can specify a number of rows, as we just saw, or a percentage, like so:

```
01   SELECT * FROM ORDERS
02   FETCH FIRST 50 PERCENT ROWS ONLY;
```

The FETCH clause consists of the following required keywords and options:

- The keyword FETCH (required).
- Either the keyword FIRST or the keyword NEXT (one is required). Either is acceptable, and there is no functional difference between the two; the option is available for grammatical readability only.
- A valid expression that evaluates to a number (optional).
  - If no numeric value is present but the rest of the FETCH keywords are in place, FETCH will default to one row.
  - An optional keyword PERCENT if the immediately preceding number is to be interpreted as a percentage instead of a numeric value. PERCENT will never return a partial row, and percentages are rounded up to the nearest number of rows. For example, if you specify a fetch of 1 PERCENT of four available rows, one row will be returned. If you specify 26 PERCENT of four available rows, two rows will be returned.
- Either the keyword ROW or the keyword ROWS (one is required). Just like the FIRST/NEXT keywords, either ROW or ROWS is acceptable, and there is no functional difference between the two; the option is available for grammatical readability only.

- Either the keyword ONLY or the keywords WITH TIES (one is required).
  - ONLY will return the number or percentage of rows specified and no more.
  - WITH TIES is best understood with an example, but in short, WITH TIES will return everything returned by ONLY but possibly with some additional rows. Those additional rows will be considered only if an ORDER BY clause is included in the SELECT and that ORDER BY sorts rows in such a way that there are rows remaining that were logically consistent with the particular ORDER BY clause but arbitrarily omitted to satisfy the row limit. This requires some explanation and is best illustrated with an example; see the next section.

WITH TIES

WITH TIES is "tied" to the ORDER BY clause. Without ORDER BY, WITH TIES will behave the same as ONLY.

Let's consider an example of WITH TIES. Let's say you have eight rows in a table ORDERS, five of which have a value in the LINE_ITEMS column of 2. If you sort the rows by LINE_ITEMS and then FETCH FIRST 50 PERCENT ROWS ONLY, you'll get the first four rows returned by the ORDER BY clause, as shown in Figure 4-14.

FIGURE 4-14

SELECT with FETCH

```
Command Prompt - SQLPLUS / AS SYSDBA
SQL> SELECT *
  2  FROM ORDERS
  3  ORDER BY LINE_ITEMS;

  ORDER_ID ORDER_DAT   SUBTOTAL LINE_ITEMS
---------- --------- ---------- ----------
       103 04-FEB-12        127          1
       101 01-FEB-12         23          1
       105 18-APR-12        914          2
       108 05-JAN-13         60          2
       102 02-FEB-12     219.93          2
       104 01-FEB-12         39          2
       107 10-JAN-13       75.3          2
       106 05-JAN-13         20         18

8 rows selected.

SQL>
SQL> SELECT *
  2  FROM ORDERS
  3  ORDER BY LINE_ITEMS
  4  FETCH FIRST 50 PERCENT ROWS ONLY;

  ORDER_ID ORDER_DAT   SUBTOTAL LINE_ITEMS
---------- --------- ---------- ----------
       103 04-FEB-12        127          1
       101 01-FEB-12         23          1
       105 18-APR-12        914          2
       108 05-JAN-13         60          2

SQL>
```

That makes sense because there are eight rows in total, so 50 percent—half—is four rows. However, your ORDER BY clause sorted rows by LINE_ITEMS, and the number of rows with a LINE_ITEM value of 2 doesn't conveniently break at 50 percent, so there are additional rows with a LINE_ITEM of 2 that didn't make the cut.

There's nothing inherently right or wrong about that approach. If your objective is to only get 50 percent of the rows and it doesn't matter to your business objectives that the line was arbitrarily drawn through the set of rows where LINE_ITEM=2, then you're fine.

But what if your objective requires you to include those additional rows where LINE_ITEM=2? If your objective is less concerned with an arbitrary breakpoint and more concerned with including a logically consistent set of rows, you can use the WITH TIES clause.

So, let's edit the row limiting clause to instead be FETCH 50 PERCENT ROWS WITH TIES. The result: we'll get the same 50 percent returned in the immediately preceding example plus any additional rows with the same value specified in the ORDER BY criteria, as shown in Figure 4-15.

Note that when we combine ORDER BY and a FETCH ... WITH TIES, we end up with the first 50 percent plus all rows that logically equate to the LINE_ITEM value at the cutoff point.

We said that WITH TIES is "tied" to the ORDER BY clause. What if we omitted the ORDER BY clause? See Figure 4-16.

Without ORDER BY, WITH TIES has no effect. Without ORDER BY, the use of WITH TIES produces the same result as if we had executed FETCH ... ONLY. We didn't get a syntax error. We simply received the same results as if we'd used FETCH ... ONLY.

FIGURE 4-15

SELECT with FETCH ... WITH TIES

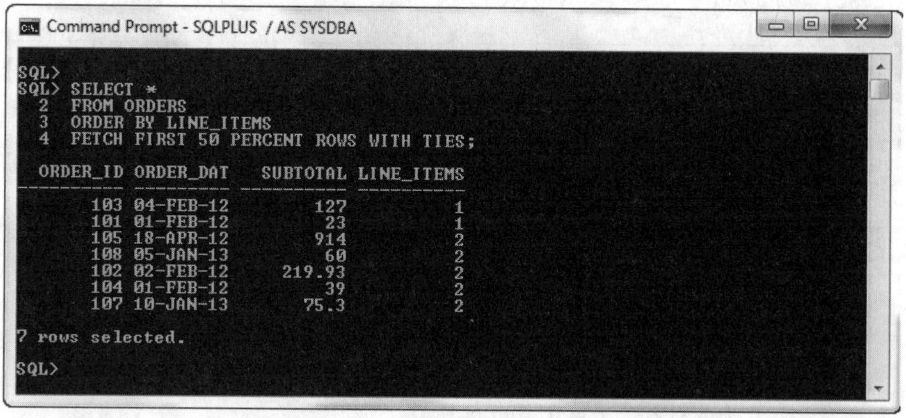

FIGURE 4-16

SELECT with
FETCH ... WITH
TIES, no ORDER
BY

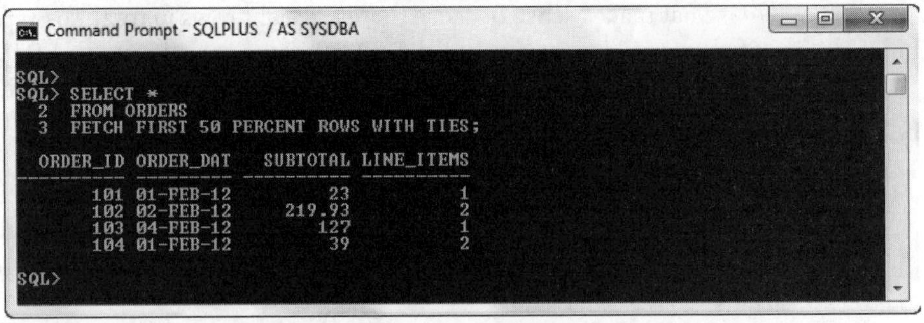

```
SQL>
SQL> SELECT *
  2  FROM ORDERS
  3  FETCH FIRST 50 PERCENT ROWS WITH TIES;

  ORDER_ID ORDER_DAT  SUBTOTAL LINE_ITEMS
---------- --------- --------- ----------
       101 01-FEB-12        23          1
       102 02-FEB-12    219.93          2
       103 04-FEB-12       127          1
       104 01-FEB-12        39          2

SQL>
```

OFFSET

By default, the row limiting clause will start with the first returned row, but you can optionally specify that the FETCH start elsewhere, at some specific number of rows into the range. Here's an example:

```
01   SELECT * FROM ORDERS
02   OFFSET 5 ROWS FETCH FIRST 2 ROWS ONLY;
```

In this example, the FETCH will skip the first five rows, start at the sixth row, and return the sixth and seventh rows, for a total of two rows returned.

The following table lists what happens with various specifications of OFFSET:

OFFSET Usage *	Note	Impact to Range
Omitted (no OFFSET clause is included	Defaults to OFFSET=0	Range begins with the first row returned by the query
OFFSET = (a negative number)	Treated as OFFSET=0	
OFFSET = 0		
OFFSET = (a positive number <= the total set of available rows)		Range begins with OFFSET row
OFFSET = (a positive number > the total set of available rows)		No rows returned

*OFFSET, if used, must be set equal to either a number or any valid expression that evaluates to a number.

CERTIFICATION SUMMARY

The ORDER BY clause of the SELECT statement is the method for sorting the rows of output returned by the SELECT statement. The ORDER BY clause is optional, but if included in a SELECT statement, it is always the final clause of the SELECT statement.

ORDER BY specifies one or more expressions. Each expression is used by ORDER BY to sort each row in the result set. Output rows are sorted first by the first expression, and for any rows that share the same value for the first expression, those rows will be subsorted for the second expression, and so on.

Expressions for ORDER BY follow the same rules as expressions in the SELECT statement's select list and the WHERE clause. Each expression should ideally reference a column in the table, but this isn't required.

The ASC and DESC reserved words can be used in an ORDER BY clause to determine the direction of sorting for each individual expression. ASC will sort values in ascending order, and DESC will sort in descending order. ASC is the default and does not need to be specified. The specification of ASC or DESC should follow each expression with a space separating them.

ORDER BY sorts values according to data types. With numeric data types, low numbers are low, and high numbers are high; with dates, yesterday is lower than tomorrow, and next week is higher than last month; with characters, Z is less than a, and the character string '10' is less than the character string '3'.

ORDER BY can specify expressions in the SELECT statement's select list by referencing the column alias, if one was created within the SELECT list. ORDER BY can also identify expressions in the SELECT list by the number corresponding to the position of the item in the SELECT list; for instance, ORDER BY 1 will sort by the first item in the SELECT list.

ORDER BY can combine all of these features into one series of order items.

A column alias, if specified in the select list, is not recognized in the WHERE, GROUP BY, or HAVING clause.

The WHERE clause is part of the SQL statements SELECT, UPDATE, and DELETE. It is used to identify the rows that will be affected by the SQL statement. For the SELECT statement, WHERE determines which rows are retrieved. For the UPDATE statement, it determines which rows will be updated. For the DELETE statement, it determines which rows will be deleted. The WHERE clause concerns itself with entire rows, not just the columns that are the subject of the particular SQL statement of which it is a part. The WHERE clause can reference columns that are not in the SELECT list.

The WHERE clause is optional. If included in a SELECT statement, it must follow the FROM clause.

The WHERE clause compares two expressions and determines whether the result of the comparison is true or false. At least one of the two expressions should include a column from whatever table the SQL statement is intended to address so that the WHERE clause is relevant to the SQL statement. The expressions are compared using comparison operators. Examples include the equal sign, the not-equal sign, and the greater-than and less-than signs.

A series of comparisons can be connected using the Boolean operators AND and OR. The NOT operator can also be included. Together, these expressions can form complex WHERE clauses.

The LIKE operator can activate the wildcard characters. The two wildcard characters are the underscore (_) and the percent sign (%).

The IN operator can compare a single value to a set of values. An expression using the IN operator will evaluate to true if that single value matches any of the values in the expression list.

When using the WHERE clause to locate rows that have a NULL value, never use the = NULL comparison; instead, always use the IS NULL or IS NOT NULL comparison operator.

The ampersand substitution variable is used within SQL*Plus to support interactive and batch processing. The ampersand is a prefix that can be configured differently with the SET DEFINE statement. The substitution variable can be turned on or off with SET DEFINE ON or SET DEFINE OFF.

You can also use SET VERIFY to turn on or off the automatic display of "old" and "new" lines of code containing the specified substitution variable value. Any SQL script can leverage the substitution variable to replace any code or value within any subsequent script.

The row limiting clause is new to Oracle 12c. Its purpose is to limit the number of rows returned by a SELECT statement. The row limiting clause is specified with FETCH and syntactically follows ORDER BY (if it is included). The FETCH clause specifies a range of rows to be returned as a subset of the SELECT statements. The range can be determined by numbers of rows or as a percentage. If no range is specified, FETCH defaults to one row. The FETCH keywords FIRST and NEXT behave the same, so do ROW and ROWS; both pairs are acceptable and exist for readability. WITH TIES can be used to include rows that have identical sorted values as specified by ORDER BY and would otherwise be arbitrarily omitted from the return set. An optional OFFSET value can be included to determine the starting point of the range. OFFSET is specified by numbers of rows (not a percentage). If omitted, OFFSET defaults to zero, and if entered as a negative number, OFFSET will be treated as though zero.

TWO-MINUTE DRILL

Sort the Rows That Are Retrieved by a Query

- ☐ ORDER BY is an optional clause used to sort the rows retrieved in a SELECT statement.
- ☐ If used, ORDER BY is always the last clause in the SELECT statement.
- ☐ ORDER BY uses expressions to direct the sorting order of the result set of the SELECT statement.
- ☐ Each expression is evaluated in order so that the first item in ORDER BY will do the initial sort of output rows, the second item listed will sort any rows that share identical data for the first ORDER BY element, and so on.
- ☐ ORDER BY can sort by columns in the table, regardless of whether the columns appear in the SELECT statement's select list.
- ☐ ORDER BY can also sort by expressions of any kind, following the same rules of expressions that you've seen with the WHERE clause and the select list.
- ☐ Numeric data is sorted by default in ascending order, from lower numbers to higher.
- ☐ Character data is sorted by default in ascending order, from *A* to *Z*.
- ☐ Date data is sorted by default in ascending order, from prior dates to later dates.
- ☐ All sorts default to ascending order, which can be specified with the optional keyword ASC.
- ☐ Sort order can be changed to descending order with the keyword DESC.
- ☐ ORDER BY can identify columns by column alias or by position within the SELECT list.

Limit the Rows That Are Retrieved by a Query

- ☐ The WHERE clause comes after the FROM clause.
- ☐ WHERE identifies which rows are to be included in the SQL statement.
- ☐ WHERE is used by SELECT, UPDATE, and DELETE.
- ☐ WHERE is an optional clause.
- ☐ Expressions form the building blocks of the WHERE clause.

☐ An expression may include references to column names as well as literal values. The WHERE clause compares expressions to each other using comparison operators and determines whether the comparisons are true or false.

☐ Boolean operators may separate each comparison to create a complex series of evaluations. Collectively, the final result for each row in the table will either be true or false. If true, the row is returned; if false, it is ignored.

☐ The Boolean operators are AND, OR, and NOT.

☐ The rules of Boolean operator precedence require that NOT be evaluated first, then AND, and then OR.

☐ Parentheses can override any Boolean operator precedence.

☐ When comparing date data types, earlier date values are considered "less" than later dates, so anything in January will be "less than" anything in December of the same year.

☐ When comparing character data types, the letter *a* is less than the letter *z*, uppercase letters are "lower than" lowercase letters, and the character representation of 3 is greater than the character representation of 22, even though the results would be different if they were numeric data types.

☐ LIKE can be used to activate wildcard searches.

☐ IN can be used to compare a single expression to a set of one or more expressions.

☐ BETWEEN can be used to see whether a particular expression's value is within a range of values. BETWEEN is inclusive, not exclusive, so that BETWEEN 2 and 3 includes the numbers 2 and 3 as part of the range.

☐ Use IS NULL or IS NOT NULL when testing a column to see whether its value is NULL.

Use Ampersand Substitution to Restrict and Sort Output at Run Time

☐ The substitution variable is used in batch or interactive SQL*Plus processing.

☐ It is not a SQL feature, but a SQL*Plus feature.

☐ The substitution variable can specify a WHERE clause parameter, ORDER BY option, column list, table name, any portion of the SQL keyword, or any portion of text within a SQL script.

☐ The substitution variable works with SELECT, INSERT, UPDATE, or other SQL statements.

☐ The ampersand can be redefined to an alternative single character.

☐ VERIFY is a system variable; when set to ON, it ensures that the use of a substitution variable will trigger the display of an "old" and "new" line of text.

☐ The DEFINE system variable specifies the prefix for use with a substitution variable.

☐ ACCEPT can be used to accept interactively specified values for a substitution variable.

☐ PROMPT can be used to issue rich prompt questions to a user during an interactive SQL*Plus session.

Use the SQL Row Limiting Clause

☐ FETCH is an optional clause that follows WHERE and ORDER BY.

☐ FETCH can specify a range in terms of a number of rows or a percentage of rows.

☐ Expressions can be used in FETCH to specify the number of rows or percentage of rows.

☐ If no range is specified, FETCH defaults to one row.

☐ An example is FETCH FIRST 20 ROWS ONLY;.

☐ The keyword FIRST can be exchanged with the keyword NEXT; both are functionally identical, but one of the two keywords is required.

☐ The keyword ROW can be exchanged with the keyword ROWS; both are functionally identical, but one of the two keywords is required.

☐ The SQL row limiting clause requires either the keyword ONLY or the keywords WITH TIES. ONLY returns rows that match the FETCH criteria only. WITH TIES returns rows that match the FETCH criteria and also satisfy the ORDER BY clause at the same FETCH logical dividing point in the range.

☐ Without ORDER BY, WITH TIES behaves like ONLY.

SELF TEST

The following questions will help you measure your understanding of the material presented in this chapter. Choose one correct answer for each question unless otherwise directed.

Sort the Rows That Are Retrieved by a Query

1. Review this SELECT statement:

```
SELECT    SHIP_NAME
FROM      SHIPS
ORDER BY SHIP_ID, CAPACITY DESC;
```

Assume that all table and column references exist within the database. What can be said of this SELECT statement?

A. The rows will sort in order by SHIP_ID and then by CAPACITY. All rows will sort in descending order.

B. The rows will sort in order by SHIP_ID in ascending order and then by CAPACITY in descending order.

C. The statement will fail to execute because the ORDER BY list includes a column that is not in the select list.

D. The statement will fail to execute because there is no WHERE clause.

2. Review this SELECT statement:

```
SELECT    PRODUCT_ID, PRODUCT_NAME, UNIT_PRICE, SHIPPING
FROM      PRODUCTS
WHERE     (UNIT_PRICE + SHIPPING) * TAX_RATE > 5
ORDER BY LIKE PRODUCT_NAME;
```

Assume all table and column references exist in the database. What can be said of this SELECT statement?

A. The statement will execute successfully and as intended.

B. The statement will execute but not sort because the ORDER BY clause is wrong.

C. The statement will fail to execute because the ORDER BY clause includes the word LIKE.

D. None of the above.

3. Which if the following is true of the ORDER BY clause? (Choose two.)

A. It is optional.

B. It can be used in the UPDATE statement as well as SELECT and DELETE.

C. It can sort rows based on data that isn't displayed as part of the SELECT statement.

D. If the list of ORDER BY expressions uses the "by position" form, then all expressions in the ORDER BY must use the "by position" form.

4. If you are using an ORDER BY to sort values in descending order, in which order will they appear?

A. If the data type is numeric, the value 400 will appear first before the value 800.

B. If the data type is character, the value 'Michael' will appear first before the value 'Jackson'.

C. If the data type is date, the value for June 25, 2010, will appear before the value for August 29, 2010.

D. If the data type is character, the value '130' will appear first before '75'.

Limit the Rows That Are Retrieved by a Query

5. Review the following data listing for a table VENDORS:

```
VENDOR_ID   CATEGORY
---------   ---------------
        1   Supplier
        2   Teaming Partner
```

Now review the following SQL statement:

```
SELECT  VENDOR_ID
FROM    VENDORS
WHERE   CATEGORY IN ('Supplier','Subcontractor','%Partner');
```

How many rows will the SELECT statement return?

A. 2

B. 1

C. 0

D. None because it will fail due to a syntax error

6. Review the following data listing for a table called SHIP_CABINS:

```
ROOM_NUMBER  STYLE     WINDOW
-----------  --------  ---------
        102  Suite     Ocean
        103            Ocean
        104
```

The blank values are NULL. Now review the following SQL statement (line numbers are added for readability):

```
01   SELECT ROOM_NUMBER
02   FROM   SHIP_CABINS
03   WHERE  (STYLE = NULL) OR (WINDOW = NULL);
```

How many rows will the SQL statement retrieve?

A. 0

B. 1

C. 2

D. None because you cannot use parentheses in line 3 to surround the expressions

7. Review the following data listing for a table SHIPS:

```
SHIP_ID  SHIP_NAME      CAPACITY  LENGTH  LIFEBOATS
-------  -------------  --------  ------  ---------
      1  Codd Crystal       2052     855         80
      2  Codd Elegance      2974     952         95
```

In the SHIPS table, SHIP_NAME has a data type of VARCHAR2(20). All other columns are NUMBER. Now consider the following query (note that line numbers have been added for readability):

```
01  SELECT  SHIP_ID
02  FROM    SHIPS
03  WHERE   CAPACITY BETWEEN 2052 AND 3000
04    AND   LENGTH IN ('100','855')
05    AND   SHIP_NAME LIKE 'Codd_%';
```

How many rows will the SELECT statement return?

A. None because of a syntax error resulting from a data type conflict in line 4

B. None because line 5 is asking for SHIP names that contain an underscore after the string 'Codd', and none do

C. 2

D. 1

8. Assume all table name and column name references in the SQL statement that follows are valid. That being said, what is wrong with the syntax of the following SQL statement?

```
SELECT SHIP_ID
FROM    SHIPS
WHERE   ((2*LIFEBOATS)+57) - CAPACITY IN (LIFEBOATS*20,
LIFEBOATS+LENGTH);
```

A. In the WHERE clause there is a syntax error before the word CAPACITY.

B. It needs to have either an equal sign or a not-equal sign.

C. In the WHERE clause there is a syntax error after the word IN.

D. There is nothing wrong with the syntax.

9. Review the following data listing for the SHIPS table:

```
SHIP_ID  SHIP_NAME        CAPACITY  LENGTH  LIFEBOATS
-------  -------------    --------  ------  ---------
      1  Codd Crystal         2052     855         80
      2  Codd Elegance        2974     952         95
```

Now review the following SQL statement (line numbers are added for readability):

```
01    SELECT SHIP_ID FROM    SHIPS
02    WHERE  SHIP_NAME IN ('Codd Elegance','Codd Victorious')
03       OR  (LIFEBOATS >= 80
04       OR   LIFEBOATS <= 100)
05      AND  CAPACITY / LIFEBOATS > 25;
```

Which of the following statements is true about this SELECT statement?

A. The syntax is correct.

B. The syntax on lines 3 and 4 is incorrect.

C. Lines 3 and 4 have correct syntax but could be replaced with OR LIFEBOATS BETWEEN 80 AND 100.

D. Line 5 is missing parentheses.

Use Ampersand Substitution to Restrict and Sort Output at Run Time

10. To list all the currently defined variables, use:

A. SHOW ALL

B. SHOW DEFINE

C. DEFINE

D. DEFINE ALL

11. You can use a substitution variable to replace:

A. A floating-point value in a WHERE clause

B. The name of a table in a SELECT statement

C. Neither

D. Both

12. Consider the following text:

```
DEFINE vRoomNumber
PROMPT "Enter a room number: "
SELECT ROOM_NUMBER, STYLE, WINDOW
FROM   SHIP_CABINS
WHERE  ROOM_NUMBER = &RNBR;
```

What will happen when this script is executed?

A. The end user will be prompted to enter a number.

B. The script will fail because vRoomNumber in the first line does not have an ampersand prefix.

C. The SELECT statement will fail because the substitution variable should not be prefixed by an ampersand since it is already defined with the DEFINE statement.

D. The DEFINE statement in line 1 should be preceded by the keyword SET.

13. To permanently delete a substitution variable named THE_NAME so that it can no longer be used, use:

A. UNDEFINE THE_NAME

B. SET DEFINE OFF

C. REMOVE THE_NAME

D. You cannot delete a substitution variable.

Use the SQL Row Limiting Clause

14. Assume you have a table ITEMS that includes a column STATUS. Which of the following statements is syntactically correct? (Choose all that apply.)

A. SELECT * FROM ITEMS FETCH NEXT 20 % ROWS ONLY;

B. SELECT * FROM ITEMS FETCH NEXT 20 PERCENT ROWS ONLY;

C. SELECT * FROM ITEMS FETCH NEXT 20 ROWS WITH TIES;

D. SELECT * FROM ITEMS ORDER BY STATUS FETCH NEXT 20 ROWS WITH TIES;

15. Consider the following statement:

```
SELECT * FROM ITEMS ORDER BY LIST_DATE
OFFSET -5 ROWS FETCH FIRST 4 ROWS ONLY;
```

Assume you have a table ITEMS with a column LIST_DATE. What is the result of an attempt to execute the statement?

A. It will sort the rows by LIST_DATE and return only the first four rows.

B. It will sort the rows by LIST_DATE and return only the last four rows.

C. It will fail with a syntax error because of the use of a negative number with OFFSET.

D. It will fail with a syntax error because of the use of FIRST and OFFSET together.

SELF TEST ANSWERS

Sort the Rows That Are Retrieved by a Query

1. ☑ **B.** The ORDER BY clause will default to ascending order for SHIP_ID, but CAPACITY is explicitly directed to sort in descending order.

    ☒ **A, C,** and **D** are incorrect. The DESC directive applies only to the CAPACITY column in the ORDER BY clause, not both items. The fact that the ORDER BY clause references columns that are not in the select list is irrelevant; it's fine to do that. The WHERE clause is not required; it's an optional clause, as is the ORDER BY clause.

2. ☑ **C.** The LIKE operator is meaningless in ORDER BY.

    ☒ **A, B,** and **D** are incorrect. The statement will certainly not execute; it will fail to parse because of the syntax error of the LIKE operator in the wrong place. Given that it won't even parse because of syntax errors, it certainly won't execute.

3. ☑ **A** and **C.** ORDER BY is optional; it is not required. It is able to sort rows in the table based on any criteria that are meaningful to the row, and when sorted, any columns may be displayed from those rows in the select list, regardless of the ORDER BY criteria.

    ☒ **B** and **D** are incorrect. It is unique to the SELECT statement and does not appear as an option or otherwise in any other SQL statement. Ordering by position is available to each individual ORDER BY expression and does not depend on or require the same format from other ORDER BY expressions.

4. ☑ **B.** If the values are characters, then *A* is less than *Z*, and if we're listing rows in descending order, then the greater value is shown first. That means the values later in the alphabet are shown first. In comparing the character strings 'Michael' and 'Jackson', the string 'Michael' is greater and will show first in the listing before 'Jackson'.

    ☒ **A, C,** and **D** are incorrect. If the values are numeric, then 400 is less than 800. That means in a descending order listing, where the higher value is listed first, 800 would be listed before 400. With regard to date data types, later dates are greater, and August 29, 2010, should list before June 25, 2010. Finally, with regard to numeric values treated as strings, you have to think about how they would appear in the dictionary—the first character is the most important, and in this case, the 7 in 75 indicates that character string is higher than 130, so in a descending pattern, the 75 would be listed before 130. If those values were treated as numeric values, it might be a different situation. But we're explicitly directed to treat them as character strings.

Limit the Rows That Are Retrieved by a Query

5. ☑ **B.** The SELECT will return one row, for VENDOR_ID 1 where the CATEGORY equals 'Supplier'.

    ☒ **A, C,** and **D** are incorrect. The second row will be ignored because even though the set of expressions within the IN clause includes a value for '%Partner' and uses the percent sign wildcard character at the beginning, the wildcard isn't activated because LIKE isn't present in the expression. Therefore, the string is treated as a literal. Had there been a value in CATEGORY of '%Partner', the row would have been returned. The failure to include LIKE is not a syntax error per se; it's just incorrect design of the SELECT statement. One way to change this query into something that is more likely the intended form would be this: SELECT VENDOR_ID FROM VENDORS WHERE CATEGORY IN ('Supplier', 'Subcontractor') OR CATEGORY LIKE '%Partner'; That approach would produce two rows and perform the query that was probably intended.

6. ☑ **A.** This query will always retrieve zero rows, no matter what they look like. The use of the = NULL expression within the WHERE clause guarantees that fact. Nothing will ever be retrieved because no SQL engine is capable of confirming that any value is equal to "I don't know."

    ☒ **B, C,** and **D** are incorrect. If line 3 had used IS NULL, as in WHERE STYLE IS NULL OR WINDOW IS NULL, then the answer would have been C, or two rows. Also, if the IS NULL were used and the OR had been AND instead, then one row would have been returned. Regardless, the parentheses are correct here; you are allowed to enclose complete expressions within parentheses within a WHERE clause.

7. ☑ **D.** The query returns the row with a value of SHIP_ID = 1, and no more. The BETWEEN range is inclusive, so the number 2052 is part of the range.

    ☒ **A, B,** and **C** are incorrect. The LENGTH value is numeric, and the set of expressions inside IN are strings. However, Oracle SQL will perform an automatic data type conversion since the strings all contain numeric data within them anyway, and the operation will succeed. It's not the best design, but it works, and you'll need to be aware of this for the exam. Also, line 5 uses the LIKE operator to activate wildcard characters within the string, and both of the available wildcards are used—the single-character underscore and the multicharacter percent sign. These combine to indicate that any row with a SHIP_NAME that starts with the string 'Codd', followed by at least one character, followed by anywhere from zero to an infinite number of additional characters, will be accepted.

8. ☑ **D.** There is nothing wrong with the syntax.

    ☒ **A, B,** and **C** are incorrect. The pair of nested parentheses before the word CAPACITY is a valid expression that multiplies the value of the LIFEBOATS column and adds the number 57 to the end of it. Then the entire result is subtracted by whatever the value for CAPACITY might be. The result of that expression will then be compared to whatever is contained in the series of expressions after the IN clause. There are two expressions there: one multiplies the LIFEBOATS value times 20, and the second adds the values of the columns named LIFEBOAT and LENGTH. All of these expressions are syntactically valid.

9. ☑ **A.** The syntax is correct. However, there are some issues involving the logic, such as the expression on lines 3 and 4, which don't really do anything. Any non-NULL value for LIFEBOATS will be found with these expressions because of the OR operator on line 4. It would make more sense for that operator to be AND, but regardless, it is syntactically correct.

☒ **B, C,** and **D** are incorrect. Lines 3 and 4 have accurate syntax, but the OR at the beginning of line 4 should probably be an AND. Since it is not, then BETWEEN would not be an equivalent substitute here since BETWEEN can test only for a range and essentially serves as a replacement of the AND combination, as in LIFEBOATS >= 80 AND LIFEBOATS <= 100. Line 5 doesn't need any parentheses. They wouldn't hurt anything necessarily; they just aren't required.

Use Ampersand Substitution to Restrict and Sort Output at Run Time

10. ☑ **C** is correct. The DEFINE command on a line by itself will display all existing variables defined for the session.

☒ **A, B,** and **D** are incorrect. The SHOW ALL command lists all system variables. SHOW DEFINE will show the current state of the DEFINE system variable. DEFINE ALL is not a valid command.

11. ☑ **D** is correct. You can use a substitution variable to replace just about any text in a SQL statement, including values and SQL keywords.

☒ **A, B,** and **C** are incorrect. While you can use a substitution variable to replace a floating-point number and also the name of a table, you can do both, so the best answer is **D**.

12. ☑ **A** is correct. The end user will be prompted to enter a number in two places. The first prompt will result from the PROMPT statement. However, PROMPT is not associated with ACCEPT, so it will neither wait for a response nor capture any input. However, the SQL script has a valid ampersand substitution variable that will prompt the user to enter a value for rnbr, at which point the end user will be able to provide a value, which will cause the SQL script to successfully execute.

☒ **B, C,** and **D** are incorrect. The DEFINE statement's reference to vRoomNumber does not require an ampersand, but nor does it assign a value to the variable vRoomNumber. The SELECT statement will not fail for the reason provided: the ampersand is correctly placed. The first line statement does not require the SET statement in front and, if it were included, would result in an error since SET DEFINE works with the keywords ON, OFF, or a single character to become the new substitution variable.

13. ☑ **A** is correct. UNDEFINE will remove a substitution variable from memory for the session.

    ☒ **B, C,** and **D** are incorrect. SET DEFINE OFF temporarily turns off the ability to reference all substitution variables. But it does not permanently remove any variables; you can SET DEFINE ON and all existing substitution variables are immediately available for reference once again. There is no REMOVE statement. To permanently delete a substitution variable, use UNDEFINE followed by the name of the particular substitution variable you want to delete.

Use the SQL Row Limiting Clause

14. ☑ **B, C,** and **D** are correct. In the case of C, the lack of an ORDER BY renders WITH TIES ineffective, but the syntax is acceptable nonetheless. There is no syntax error.

    ☒ **A** is incorrect. The percent sign cannot be used in FETCH; use the keyword PERCENT instead.

15. ☑ **A** is correct. The use of OFFSET with a negative number is treated the same as of the OFFSET were zero. The SELECT will FETCH the first row rows of the sorted row set.

    ☒ **B, C,** and **D** are incorrect. While it is tempting to think that a negative offset would start at the end of the sorted list, it does not, and instead the negative offset number is treated as though it were a zero. Syntactically the statement is correct, and it will execute. The use of FIRST is interchangeable with NEXT; one is required and either is acceptable, the choice does not change the functionality of the statement.

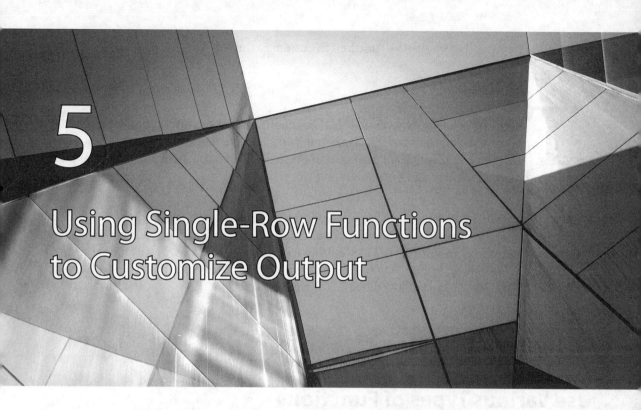

5
Using Single-Row Functions to Customize Output

This chapter looks at the topic of SQL functions. *Functions* perform unique tasks that boost the capabilities of SQL. There are many SQL functions, and it is important that you be familiar with all of them and understand how to use them individually and in various combinations in support of various real-world scenarios.

This chapter looks exclusively at *single-row* functions. Most single-row functions are known also as *scalar* functions. Scalar functions return one answer for each one row processed. There are two other categories of functions. You'll study the topic of aggregate functions and analytic functions in Chapter 7, when you study the GROUP BY clause of the SELECT statement.

CERTIFICATION OBJECTIVE 5.01

Use Various Types of Functions That Are Available in SQL

Functions have the following three characteristics:

- They may accept incoming values, or *parameters* (note that a few functions take no parameters).
- They incorporate parameter data into some sort of process; in other words, they perform some sort of task on the incoming data, such as a calculation or some other activity.
- They return one single answer as a result.

For example, here is a SQL statement that uses a function called INITCAP, which takes a single parameter:

```
SELECT LASTNAME, INITCAP(LASTNAME) FROM ONLINE_SUBSCRIBERS;
```

In this example, for each row that the SELECT statement processes, the SQL built-in function INITCAP takes the column LASTNAME and transforms the text contained within so that the first letter is displayed as a capital letter (initial capital, INITCAP, get it?) and the rest of the text is in lowercase letters. The result of the function is displayed in place of the value for the LASTNAME column.

FIGURE 5-1

Output of SELECT
with INITCAP

For each one row of data returned by the SELECT statement, INITCAP will return one value. See Figure 5-1 for an example of its output.

As you can see, a function like INITCAP isn't foolproof—notice how it does a nice transformation on the first two rows but doesn't necessarily produce a desirable result in the third row, where the third letter *L* should still be capitalized. But INITCAP performs its task; it's up to us as developers to know where best to apply it.

When a function is used in a SQL statement, it's often said that it's *called* or *invoked* from the statement.

Functions can be called from anyplace that an expression can be called. In other words, you can invoke a function from

- A SELECT statement's select list and WHERE clause
- An INSERT statement's list of values
- An UPDATE statement's SET clause and WHERE clause
- A DELETE statement's WHERE clause
  . . . and more.

There are a variety of functions available in SQL. The two major types are built-in and user-defined.

- *Built-in* functions are those that are part of the SQL language. They are available with every standard implementation of SQL.
- *User-defined* functions are those that are created by users. They are written with features that go beyond the capabilities of SQL, using languages such as PL/SQL. Their construction is beyond the scope of the exam and therefore this book. This book—and the exam—will deal only with built-in functions.

There are a great many built-in functions, and they fall into several categories. The most common categories are character, number, and data functions. We'll discuss conversion functions in Chapter 6.

Character Functions

Character functions are used to manipulate text. They can be used to perform many jobs on a given string such as analyze its length (LENGTH), pad it with extra characters (RPAD, LPAD), trim off unwanted characters (RTRIM, LTRIM, TRIM), locate a given string within a larger string (INSTR), extract a smaller string from a larger string (SUBSTR), and replace text within a string (REPLACE). It's even possible to search for strings that aren't necessarily spelled the same but that sound alike (SOUNDEX), and more. When these are combined, the possibilities are theoretically endless.

Number Functions

Number functions can perform mathematical analysis. SQL comes with many functions for determining sine (SIN, ASIN, SINH), cosine (COS, ACOS, COSH), and tangent (TAN, ATAN, ATAN2, TANH). You can determine absolute value (ABS) or determine whether a given number is positive or negative (SIGN).

A function can round off values (ROUND) and otherwise abbreviate numbers (TRUNC).

Number functions can be incorporated into expressions, and as you've already seen, expressions provide support for standard arithmetic operations of addition (+), subtraction (−), multiplication (*), and division (/). These operators are not functions but are, well, operators. The point here is that you can combine the operators with number functions to produce powerful SQL statements.

Date Functions

The set of available SQL functions includes powerful features for DATE manipulation. You can obtain the current date and time (SYSDATE, SYSTIMESTAMP), "round" off dates to varying degrees of detail (ROUND), and otherwise abbreviate them (TRUNC). You can calculate the differences between two or more dates in many ways.

Simple arithmetic operators will help determine the differences between two dates in terms of days, meaning that if you subtract one date from another, the resulting answer will be a number representing the difference in terms of days. But what if you want something else, like—the difference in terms of months? (The answer is MONTHS_BETWEEN.) There are functions that will assist in managing such tasks. You can add or subtract an entire month and account for spans of time that encompass years (ADD_MONTHS with a positive number to add or a negative number to subtract—we'll see this later).

What if you have a particular date and want to know whether that date falls on, say, a Saturday? This sort of feature can be accomplished with "conversion" functions, which we discuss in the next chapter.

Other Functions

There are some functions that don't quite fit into the categories listed here. USER is a great example—it's a standard function that takes no parameters and simply returns the value showing the name of the current user account. Other functions support advanced features, such as hierarchical queries. We'll look at those functions as we discuss various advanced features throughout the book.

Use Character, Number, Date, and Analytical (PERCENTILE_CONT, STDDEV, LAG, LEAD) Functions in SELECT Statements

This section looks in detail at many of the SQL functions. You'll learn how they work, and you'll see examples of how many of them can be used. For each function discussed here, we address

- The function's list of parameters
- Whether each parameter is required or optional
- What task the function performs
- The output from the function

Rather than present an alphabetical listing of them, I'll list the SQL functions presented in this section logically, and I'll describe related functions together. This is not an exhaustive analysis of all the functions available in SQL but is nevertheless rather comprehensive, focusing primarily on the functions that are most commonly used. Remember, functions are an exam objective. It's important to be familiar with how the major functions work. This section describes the most commonly used functions that are likely to be on the exam.

The DUAL Table

Before we get started, I need to mention the DUAL table, which is something that isn't a function issue per se but is helpful to our purposes here. It is not a "SQL" thing, nor is it necessarily a "function" thing, but it's an "Oracle" thing you should know before we continue. The DUAL table is present in every Oracle database. This special table contains just one column. The column is named DUMMY, and it has a data type of VARCHAR2(1). The DUAL table contains only one row. That row has a value in DUMMY of 'X'.

The purpose of DUAL is simple—to have something to run a SELECT statement against when you don't want to retrieve any data in particular but instead simply want to run a SELECT statement to get some other task accomplished, such as obtaining the output of a function. For example, you'll soon see in this section that there's an Oracle SQL function called SYSDATE that displays the current date according to the operating system of the server on which the Oracle database is installed. If you want to get the value of SYSDATE without wading through a bunch of table data from your application, you can simply execute the following SQL statement:

```
SELECT SYSDATE FROM DUAL;
```

The result: you'll get one response for the current value of SYSDATE, since you know the DUAL table has only one row.

We'll use the DUAL table from time to time throughout the rest of this chapter as we go through examples of the various SQL functions.

Character Functions

This section looks in detail at the more commonly used character functions. Character functions do not necessarily deal exclusively with character data—some of these functions have numeric parameters and even numeric output, like INSTR. But the overall spirit and intent of these functions is to perform the sort of data processing typically associated with text manipulation.

UPPER and LOWER

Syntax: UPPER(*s1*)
        LOWER(*s1*)
Parameters: *s1*, a required character string.
Process: Transforms *s1* into uppercase letters (UPPER) or lowercase letters (LOWER).
Output: Character string.
Example: UPPER and LOWER can be useful when you are doing a text search and aren't sure whether the data in the table is in uppercase, lowercase, or both. You can use UPPER to force a conversion of all data in the table and then compare

that result to an uppercase literal value, thus eliminating any chance of missing mixed-case text in the table.

```
SELECT  EMPLOYEE_ID
FROM    EMPLOYEES
WHERE   UPPER(LAST_NAME) = 'MCGILLICUTTY';
```

The previous query will return rows from the EMPLOYEES table where the LAST_NAME is 'McGillicutty', 'mcgillicutty', or any other combination of upper- and lowercase letters that equals the letters in the string.

e x a m
ⓦatch

Beware questions that ask you about using UPPER or LOWER when both sides of the comparison operator are variables. If your SELECT statement ends with something like WHERE LAST_NAME = FAMILY_NAME and you're concerned about case mismatch, then use UPPER or LOWER, *but on both sides of the equal signs: WHERE LOWER(LAST_NAME) = LOWER(FAMILY_NAME). Using the function on only one side might actually increase your probability of a case mismatch. Be sure to use the function to standardize the case of both values being compared.*

INITCAP

Syntax: INITCAP(*s1*)
Parameters: *s1*, a required character string.
Process: Transforms *s1* into a mixed-case string, where the first letter of each word is capitalized and each following character is in lowercase letters.
Output: Character string.

e x a m
ⓦatch

The single quote escape character activates, or enables, a single quote character to be displayed as a single quote. Without it, a string like 'O'Hearn' is *interpreted as 'O' followed by the letters 'Hearn' that appear out of context. This does not work: SELECT 'O'Hearn' FROM DUAL. But this does: SELECT 'O''Hearn' FROM DUAL.*

Example: The following is a SQL statement that invokes INITCAP three times. The first example passes in the string 'napoleon', which is translated into mixed-case letters. The second example takes the string 'Red O''Brien' as input. Notice that we need to include the single quote escape character within the string in order for a single quote character to be recognized—since the single quote mark is also the string delimiter, we need to type two single quotes in succession, which is how you instruct SQL to treat a single quote as an actual character within the string, and not the string delimiter. Without this, our string would appear to be 'Red O' followed by text that would be seen by SQL as gibberish and would result in an error message. Finally, the third example does the same thing with the string 'McDonald''s', but the results of INITCAP are less than desirable. The first *d* in McDonald's is converted to lowercase, and the *s* at the end of McDonald's is converted to uppercase because INITCAP interprets the *s* as the start of a new word.

```
SELECT INITCAP('napoleon'), INITCAP('RED O''BRIEN'), INITCAP('McDonald''s')
FROM   DUAL;

INITCAP('NAPOLEON') INITCAP('REDO''BRIEN') INITCAP('MCDONALD''S')
------------------- --------------------- ----------------------
Napoleon            Red O'Brien           Mcdonald'S
```

CONCAT and ||

Syntax: CONCAT(*s1, s2*)

  s1 || *s2*

Parameters: *s1, s2.* Both are character strings; both are required.

Process: Concatenates *s1* and *s2* into one string.

Output: Character string.

Example:

```
SELECT CONCAT('Hello, ', 'world!')
FROM   DUAL;
```

Here's the equivalent using the double vertical bars:

```
SELECT 'Hello, ' || 'world!'
FROM   DUAL;
```

While CONCAT takes only two parameters, the double vertical bar syntax can be repeated as often as is necessary. For example, this approach creates one string:

```
SELECT 'Hello, ' || 'world!' || ' Great to ' || 'see you.'
FROM   DUAL;

'HELLO,'||'WORLD!'||'GREATTO'||'SEEYOU.'
----------------------------------------
Hello, world! Great to see you.
```

Note that the result here is a single string. Here's another example:

```
SELECT FIRST_NAME || ' ' || LAST_NAME || ' of ship number ' || SHIP_ID || '.'
FROM    EMPLOYEES
WHERE   LAST_NAME = 'West';


FIRST_NAME||''||LAST_NAME||'OFSHIPNUMBER'||SHIP_ID||'.'
----------------------------------------------------------
Mike West of ship number 4.
Trish West of ship number 2.
```

LPAD, RPAD

Syntax: LPAD(*s1*, *n*, *s2*)

LPAD: RPAD(*s1*, *n*, *s2*).

Parameters: *s1* (character string—required); *n* (number—required); *s2* (character string—optional; *s2* defaults to a single blank space if omitted).

Process: Pad the left of character string *s1* (LPAD) or right of character string *s1* (RPAD) with character string *s2* so that *s1* is *n* characters long.

Output: Character string.

Example: Take a string literal 'Chapter One—I Am Born' and pad it to the right so that the resulting string is 40 characters in length.

```
SELECT RPAD('Chapter One - I Am Born',40,'.')
FROM    DUAL;


RPAD('CHAPTERONE-IAMBORN',40,'.')
-----------------------------------------
Chapter One - I Am Born.................
```

Many SQL functions are useful in and of themselves, but many become more useful when combined with each other. For example, here's a combination of RPAD and LPAD with the concatenation operators, executed against a table called BOOK_CONTENTS:

```
SELECT    RPAD(CHAPTER_TITLE || ' ',30,'.')
          ||
          LPAD(' ' || PAGE_NUMBER,30,'.') "Table of Contents"
FROM      BOOK_CONTENTS
ORDER BY PAGE_NUMBER;
```

```
Table of Contents
----------------------------------------------------------------
Introduction ............................................. 1
Chapter 1 ................................................ 5
Chapter 2 ................................................ 23
Chapter 3 ................................................ 57
Index .................................................... 79
```

Notice this example also includes three uses of the concatenation operator:

- *Once to append a single blank after the CHAPTER_TITLE value*
- *Once to put a single blank in front of the PAGE_NUMBER value*
- *Once to combine the output of RPAD and LPAD*

Also note the use of the column alias "Table of Contents", and note the ORDER BY to ensure that the rows sort according to PAGE_NUMBER.

on the **Job**

As you will see in this book, which is focused on exam preparation, SQL features a number of powerful formatting capabilities. It is worth noting, however, that reporting tools often are used to perform report formatting in a professional setting and can offer more features and ease of use. These tools may be limited to particular operating system platforms, whereas SQL's formatting capabilities exist wherever SQL is available.

e x a m
ⓦatch

If the "On the Job" code sample showing LPAD and RPAD combined with string concatenation is a mystery to you, then stop and study it. The exam may include questions about several functions combined and nested within each other, like the BOOK_CONTENTS sample shown in the sample. We will address nested functions later in this chapter.

LTRIM and RTRIM

Syntax: LTRIM(*s1*, *s2*)
         RTRIM(*s1*, *s2*)

Parameters: *s1*, *s2*—both are character strings. *s1* is required, and *s2* is optional—if omitted, it defaults to a single blank space.

Process: Removes occurrences of the *s2* characters from the *s1* string, from either the left side of *s1* (LTRIM) or the right side of *s1* (RTRIM) exclusively.
Output: Character string.
Notes: Ideal for stripping out unnecessary blanks, periods, ellipses, and so on.
Example: Remove dashes from a string. Note that we choose to include a column alias 'Result' to rename the output column for this query.

```
SELECT RTRIM('Seven thousand--------','-') Result
FROM    DUAL;

RESULT
--------------
Seven thousand
```

TRIM

Syntax: TRIM(trim_info trim_char FROM trim_source)
Parameters:
trim_info is one of these keywords: LEADING, TRAILING, BOTH—if omitted, defaults to BOTH.
trim_char is a single character to be trimmed—if omitted, assumed to be a blank.
trim_source is the source string—if omitted, the TRIM function will return a NULL.
Process: Same as LTRIM and RTRIM, with a slightly different syntax.
Output: Character string.
Example: Trim off the dashes at the end of the string 'Seven thousand--------'. Note we choose to use a column alias 'TheOutput' to rename the output column.

```
SELECT TRIM(TRAILING '-' FROM 'Seven thousand--------') TheOutput
FROM    DUAL;

THEOUTPUT
--------------
Seven thousand
```

LENGTH

Syntax: LENGTH(*s*)
Parameters: *s* is the source string (required).
Process: Identifies the length of a given string.
Output: Numeric.

Example: Determine the length of a really long and famous word.

```
SELECT  LENGTH('Supercalifragilisticexpialidocious')
FROM    DUAL;

LENGTH('SUPERCALIFRAGILISTICEXPIALIDOCIOUS')
--------------------------------------------
34
```

INSTR

Syntax: INSTR(*s1*, *s2*, *pos*, *n*)

Parameters: *s1* is the source string (required); *s2* is the substring (required); *pos* is the starting position in *s1* to start looking for occurrences of *s2* (optional, default is 1); *n* is the occurrence of *s2* to locate (optional, default is 1). If *pos* is negative, the search in *s1* for occurrences of *s2* starts at the end of the string and moves backward.

Process: Locates a string within another string (thus the name of the function: IN STRing).

Output: Numeric.

Example: Look for the string 'is' within 'Mississippi', starting at the first character position but looking for the second occurrence of 'is'.

```
SELECT  INSTR('Mississippi','is',1,2)
FROM    DUAL;

INSTR('MISSISSIPPI','IS',1,2)
-----------------------------
5
```

The INSTR function is telling us that the second occurrence of *is* starts at the fifth character in Mississippi.

SUBSTR

Syntax: SUBSTR(*s*, *pos*, *len*)

Parameters: *s* = a character string, required; *pos* = a number, required; *len* = a number, optional.

Process: Extracts a substring from *s*, starting at the *pos* character of *s* and continuing for *len* number of characters. If *len* is omitted, then the substring starts as *pos* and runs through the end of *s*. If *pos* is negative, then the function starts at the end of the string and moves backward.

Output: Character string.

Example: Starting with a source string of 'Name: MARK KENNEDY', extract a substring out of it, beginning at the seventh position and running to the end of the string.

```
SELECT SUBSTR('Name: MARK KENNEDY', 7)
FROM   DUAL;

SUBSTR('NAME:MARKKENNEDY',7)
---------------------------
MARK KENNEDY
```

SOUNDEX

Syntax: SOUNDEX(s)

Parameters: s = the source string, required.

Process: Translates a source string into its SOUNDEX code.

Output: Character string.

Notes: SOUNDEX is a coding scheme for translating English words into sound-alike patterns. A single SOUNDEX value is relatively worthless. But two combined can be surprisingly helpful. The reason is that similar-sounding words tend to generate the same SOUNDEX pattern.

Example: To generate a SOUNDEX translation for any word, the first letter remains unchanged. The next series of letters are translated into a numeric code according to the rules shown in Table 5-1. Translation is performed for each letter until three digits are generated. If any letters exist beyond that, they are ignored. For example, the last name Worthington has a SOUNDEX pattern of W635: the first letter, *W*, remains unchanged; the second letter, *o*, is ignored per the bottom row of the Table 5-1; the third letter, *r*, translates into 6 according to Table 5-1; the fourth

TABLE 5-1	Letter	SOUNDEX Code
SOUNDEX Translation Table	B, F, P, V	1
	C, G, J, K, Q, S, X, Z	2
	D, T	3
	L	4
	M, N	5
	R	6
	All other letters (A, E, H, I, O, U, W, Y)	Ignored

letter, *t*, translates into a 3; and the fifth letter, *h*, is ignored. Again, according to Table 5-1 (which also tells us to ignore the letter *i*), the letter *n* translates into 5, and now that we have one letter *W* and three numbers 635, we are done; the remaining letters in Worthington are ignored. Thus, the SOUNDEX code is W635.

So, two words that sound alike, for example, Worthington and Wurthinden, while spelled differently, will nevertheless generate the same SOUNDEX pattern. Here's an example:

```
SELECT SOUNDEX('Worthington'), SOUNDEX('Worthen')
FROM    DUAL;

SOUNDEX('WORTHINGTON') SOUNDEX('WORTHEN')
---------------------- ------------------
W635                   W635
```

Notice how the two different words produce the same SOUNDEX pattern. That means we can do queries like this:

```
SELECT EMPLOYEE_ID, FIRST_NAME, LAST_NAME
FROM    EMPLOYEES
WHERE   SOUNDEX(LAST_NAME) = SOUNDEX('Worthen');

EMPLOYEE_ID            FIRST_NAME             LAST_NAME
---------------------- ---------------------- ------------------
7                      Buffy                  Worthington
```

Notice that SOUNDEX is used twice in the WHERE clause. Using it once would probably be useless. This query will find customers with the last names of Worthington, Wurthinden, Worthan, and even Wirthen.

The concept and logic of SOUNDEX were originally developed in the early twentieth century for use with the English language, with a history of implementation in the U.S. Census and U.S. National Archives. During the late twentieth century as automated systems were developed, SOUNDEX became a popular feature to include in computer software systems, and thus we find it in SQL. Its rules are formally administered today by the National Archives and Records Administration of the United States government. But take note: It was and is designed for use with the American English language. It won't work quite as well with words originating from other languages, whose pronunciation rules and practices tend to be different. For example, the popular Vietnamese name Nguyen is pronounced "Nwen," but the SOUNDEX patterns for those two words—Nguyen and Nwen—are rather different. So, SOUNDEX is not perfect but rather useful nonetheless.

Numerical Functions

This section describes functions that deal with numeric values. Some numeric functions are pretty simple such as ABS, which takes a single numeric value and returns its absolute value. There's also SQRT, which takes a single numeric value and returns its square root.

Not all of the input parameters to numeric functions are necessarily numeric, but the overall intent of these functions is to perform numeric analysis and perform the sort of tasks typically associated with numeric manipulation and data processing.

CEIL
Syntax: CEIL(n)
Parameters: n is required and is any numeric data type.
Process: CEIL returns the smallest integer that is greater than or equal to n.

FLOOR
Syntax: FLOOR(n)
Parameters: n is required and is any numeric data type.
Process: FLOOR returns the largest integer that is less than or equal to n.

ROUND—Number
Syntax: ROUND(n, i)
Parameters: n is required, is any number, and can include decimal points. i is an integer and is optional—if omitted, it will default to 0.
Process: n is rounded depending on the value of i. If i is zero, n is rounded off to the nearest whole number, in other words, zero decimal points. If i is a positive number, n is rounded to i places to the right of the decimal point. If i is a negative number, n is rounded to i places to the left of the decimal point. The number 5 is rounded away from zero.
Output: If i is omitted, ROUND returns a value in the same numeric data type as n. If i is specified, ROUND returns a data type of NUMBER.
Example: Round off 12.355143 to two significant digits to the right of the decimal, and also round off 259.99 to the nearest "tens," in other words, one digit to the left of the decimal.

```
SELECT ROUND(12.355143, 2), ROUND(259.99,-1)
FROM DUAL;

ROUND(12.355143,2)     ROUND(259.99,-1)
---------------------  ----------------------
12.36                  260
```

TRUNC—Number

Syntax: TRUNC(n, i)

Parameters: n is required, is any number, and can include decimal points. i is an integer and is optional—if omitted, it will default to 0.

Process: TRUNC "rounds" toward zero; in other words, it truncates the numbers.

Output: If i is omitted, TRUNC returns a value in the same numeric data type as n. If i is specified, TRUNC returns a data type of NUMBER.

Example: Using the same numbers we just used with the ROUND example, truncate them instead.

```
SELECT TRUNC(12.355143, 2), TRUNC(259.99,-1)
FROM DUAL;

TRUNC(12.355143,2)     TRUNC(259.99,-1)
---------------------  ---------------------
12.35                  250
```

REMAINDER

Syntax: REMAINDER($n1$, $n2$)

Parameters: $n1$ and $n2$ are numbers. Both are required.

Process: Identifies the multiple of $n2$ that is nearest to $n1$ and returns the difference between those two values.

Output: Numeric.

Example: Test REMAINDER using three sequential numbers such as 9, 10, and 11, and compare each against the number 3. Since the first number (9) is a multiple of 3, there is no remainder, so the answer will be 0. The second number (10) represents one more number than the multiple, so the remainder is 1. Notice what happens with the third number (11)—the function doesn't return a 2 as you might expect. Instead, it returns a negative 1, because the nearest integer that's divisible by 3 is 12, which is closer to the 11 than the 9. In other words, REMAINDER identifies the closest multiple of $n2$. If the multiple is higher, REMAINDER returns a negative number to indicate that the closest multiple of $n2$ is higher than $n1$.

```
SELECT REMAINDER(9,3), REMAINDER(10,3), REMAINDER(11,3)
FROM    DUAL;

REMAINDER(9,3)       REMAINDER(10,3)      REMAINDER(11,3)
-------------------  -------------------  -------------------
0                    1                    -1
```

MOD

Syntax: MOD(*n1*, *n2*)

Parameters: *n1* and *n2* are numbers. Both are required.

Process: Performs the same task as REMAINDER, except MOD uses FLOOR instead of ROUND in its equation.

Output: Numeric.

Example: Get the MOD of the same three number pairs we tested with REMAINDER. Note the results in the third example—this might be what you would've expected with REMAINDER and didn't get—but you do get it with MOD.

```
SELECT MOD(9,3), MOD(10,3), MOD(11,3)
FROM   DUAL;

MOD(9,3)                 MOD(10,3)                MOD(11,3)
------------------------ ------------------------ ------------------------
0                        1                        2
```

Date Functions

The following section looks at functions that work primarily with DATE data types.

SYSDATE

Parameters: None

Process: Returns the current date and time according to the operating system on which the Oracle database server is installed. In other words, if your SQL statement is running on an Oracle server instance from a remote location, then regardless of the location of you or your client, SYSDATE will return the date and time of the operating system on which the server resides. Time information is contained within SYSDATE but doesn't display by default; however, it can be extracted by way of the TO_CHAR conversion function, which we will formally discuss in Chapter 6, but which we include in some of the examples throughout this chapter. (Note: It can also be altered by changing the NLS_DATE_FORMAT session parameter.)

Output: Date.

Example: Show the current date according to the operating system where the Oracle server is installed.

```
SELECT SYSDATE FROM DUAL;

SYSDATE
--------------------------
12-JUL-16
```

ROUND—Date

Syntax: ROUND(*d*, *i*)

Parameters: *d* is a date (required); *i* is a format model (optional).

Process: *d* is rounded off to the nearest date value, at a level of detail specified by *i*. *d* is required and specifies a value of the DATE data type. *i* is a format model and specifies the level of detail to which the DATE value will be rounded—in other words, to the nearest day, nearest hour, nearest year, and so on. *i* is optional; if *i* is omitted, ROUND will default to a format model that returns a value of *d* rounded to the nearest whole day. Values are biased toward rounding up. For example, when rounding off time, 12 noon rounds up to the next day. Format models are covered in Chapter 6 when we discuss the TO_CHAR conversion function. But we'll include one in the example that follows to give you an idea of what a format model is.

Output: Date.

Example: This example shows a SELECT statement with three expressions in the select list. The first is SYSDATE, which returns the current date. The second is the same date, rounded to the nearest month, as specified by the 'MM' format model. The third is the same date rounded to the nearest year, as specified by the 'RR' format model.

```
SELECT  SYSDATE  TODAY,
        ROUND(SYSDATE,'MM')  ROUNDED_MONTH,
        ROUND(SYSDATE,'RR')  ROUNDED_YEAR
FROM    DUAL;

TODAY                 ROUNDED_MONTH          ROUNDED_YEAR
--------------------  ---------------------  -------------------
03-DEC-15             01-DEC-15              01-JAN-16
```

If the optional second parameter is omitted, the DATE value will be rounded to the nearest hour.

We haven't yet covered the conversion function TO_CHAR, but we are going to use it to demonstrate how ROUND behaves when the optional format model is omitted. Without a format model, ROUND will round a date to the nearest whole date. This rounding is performed but is not necessarily obvious since, by default, values of the DATE data type don't display the hour. The value for hour is stored within a DATE data type nonetheless, as are also the values for minute and second, but you must use a conversion function to display those values. That's where TO_CHAR comes in handy.

To see how this works, we'll use the ROUND function, the upcoming TO_CHAR function (explained later in this chapter), and a technique known as *nested functions*. (We will cover nested functions in more detail later in this chapter.)

In the following example, the SELECT statement's first column takes the value of SYSDATE and uses the TO_CHAR conversion function to display the value of SYSDATE with a format model to display the date and the time.

The second column does the same thing with one change: it uses ROUND to round off the value of SYSDATE. Note the impact of ROUND.

```
SELECT  TO_CHAR(SYSDATE,'DD-MON-YY HH:MI:SS') AS RAW_DATE,
        TO_CHAR(ROUND(SYSDATE),'DD-MON-YY HH:MI:SS') AS ROUNDED_DATE
FROM    DUAL;


RAW_DATE              ROUNDED_DATE
------------------    ------------------
03-DEC-16 05:35:17    03-DEC-16 12:00:00
```

Using the TO_CHAR conversion function (explained in Chapter 6), we reveal that the current system date and time is December 3, 2016, 5:35:17 a.m., which is 5:35 in the morning. But when SYSDATE is rounded, we get December 3, 2016, 12:00:00.

This rounding is performed by ROUND regardless of whether TO_CHAR is used. The point is that ROUND works whether the results are visible or not.

ROUND is biased to round up. In the case of a date with a 12 noon time, ROUND will round the date up to the next calendar day.

```
SELECT  TO_CHAR(TO_DATE('01-AUG-16 12:00:00','DD-MON-YY HH24:MI:SS'),
                'DD-MON-YY HH:MI:SS') AS DAY_AT_NOON,
TO_CHAR(ROUND(TO_DATE('01-AUG-16 12:00:00','DD-MON-YY HH24:MI:SS')),
                'DD-MON-YY HH:MI:SS') AS ROUNDED_TO_ NEXT_DAY
FROM    DUAL;


DAY_AT_NOON           ROUNDED_TO_NEXT_DA
------------------    ------------------
01-AUG-16 12:00:00    02-AUG-16 12:00:00
```

The first column is August 1 and 12 noon. The second column starts with the same value but uses ROUND. Since the time of day is 12 noon, the result rounds up to the next whole day: August 2.

Note that we'll explore more about how DATE values and format models work when we discuss the TO_CHAR and TO_DATE conversion functions.

TRUNC—Date
Syntax: TRUNC(*d*, *i*)
Parameters: *d* is a date (required); *i* is a format model (optional).
Process: Performs the same task as ROUND for dates, except TRUNC always rounds down.
Output: Date.

Example:

```
SELECT  SYSDATE TODAY,
        TRUNC(SYSDATE,'MM') TRUNCATED_MONTH,
        TRUNC(SYSDATE,'RR') TRUNCATED_YEAR
FROM    DUAL;

TODAY      TRUNCATED TRUNCATED
---------  --------- ---------
03-DEC-15  01-DEC-15 01-JAN-15
```

NEXT_DAY

Syntax: NEXT_DAY(d, c)

Parameters: d is a date, required; c is a text reference to a day of the week, required.

Process: Returns a valid date representing the first occurrence of the c day following the date represented in d.

Output: Date.

Example: Show the first occurrence of a Saturday following May 31, 2019.

```
SELECT  NEXT_DAY('31-MAY-19','Saturday')
FROM    DUAL;

NEXT_DAY(
---------
01-JUN-19
```

LAST_DAY

Syntax: LAST_DAY(d)

Parameters: d is a date, required.

Process: Returns the last day of the month in which d falls.

Output: Date.

Example: Show the last days of February in 2020 and 2021.

```
SELECT  LAST_DAY('14-FEB-20'),  LAST_DAY('20-FEB-21')
FROM    DUAL;

LAST_DAY( LAST_DAY(
--------- ---------
29-FEB-20 28-FEB-21
```

ADD_MONTHS

Syntax: ADD_MONTHS(d, n)

Parameters: d is a date, required; n is a whole number, required.

Process: Adds n months to d and returns a valid date value for the result.

Output: Date.

Example: Add one month to January 31, 2017, and four months to November 1, 2017.

```
SELECT ADD_MONTHS('31-JAN-17',1),
       ADD_MONTHS('01-NOV-17',4)
FROM   DUAL;

ADD_MONTH ADD_MONTH
--------- ---------
28-FEB-17 01-MAR-18
```

on the job

There is no SUBTRACT_MONTHS function. Instead, use ADD_MONTHS to add a negative number of months, and you'll subtract them instead.

MONTHS_BETWEEN

Syntax: MONTHS_BETWEEN($d1, d2$)

Parameters: $d1$ and $d2$ are dates, required.

Process: Determines the number of months between the two dates. The result does not round off automatically; if the result is a partial month, MONTHS_BETWEEN shows a real number result. Whole months are counted according to the calendar months involved; if the time spans, say, a February that has 29 days, then the one month time span for that time period will be 29 days. In other words:

```
MONTHS_BETWEEN('01-JAN-17', '01-FEB-17') -1

MONTHS_BETWEEN('01-JAN-17', '01-MAR-17') -2

MONTHS_BETWEEN('10-AUG-17', '10-JUL-17') 1
```

Note that the answer may be opposite of what you might expect. You might think you could list the dates in chronological order and that MONTHS_BETWEEN would determine the difference in months. It will, but as a negative number. To get a positive number, the first parameter is expected to be the greater value; the second is expected to be the lesser. Either approach works, but be sure to consider the sign of the result; if the second parameter is the greater value, the result is a negative number.

Output: Number.

Example: Display the number of months between June 12, 2014, and October 3, 2013.

```
SELECT MONTHS_BETWEEN('12-JUN-14','03-OCT-13')
FROM    DUAL;

MONTHS_BETWEEN('12-JUN-14','03-OCT-13')
----------------------------------------
8.29032258064516129032258064516129032258
```

NUMTOYMINTERVAL

Syntax: NUMTOYMINTERVAL (*n, interval_unit*)
Parameters: *n* = number (required). *interval_unit* = one of the following values: 'YEAR' or 'MONTH'.
Process: Converts date information in numeric form into an interval value of time.
Output: A value in the INTERVAL YEAR TO MONTH data type.
Example: The following example takes the number 27 and transforms it into a value representing a time interval of 27 months, which equates to 2 years and 3 months, in the INTERVAL YEAR TO MONTH data type. The 2-3 value shows 2 years and 3 months is the amount of time that results.

```
SELECT NUMTOYMINTERVAL(27,'MONTH')
FROM    DUAL;

NUMTOYMINTERVAL(27,'MONTH')
---------------------------
2-3
```

NUMTODSINTERVAL

Syntax: NUMTODSINTERVAL (*n, interval_unit*)
Parameters: *n* = number (required). *interval_unit* = one of the following: 'DAY', 'HOUR', 'MINUTE', or 'SECOND'.
Process: Converts date information in numeric form into an interval value of time.
Output: A value of the data type INTERVAL DAY TO SECOND.
Example: The following example translates 36 hours into its formal representation of 1 day and 12 hours in the data type INTERVAL DAY TO SECOND, which displays a single number for day, followed by hours, minutes, seconds, and fractional seconds.

```
SELECT NUMTODSINTERVAL(36,'HOUR')
FROM    DUAL;

NUMTODSINTERVAL(36,'HOUR')
--------------------------
1 12:0:0.0
```

Dates and NUMBER Constants

To perform arithmetic with DATE values, use numeric literals. The number one (1) represents one day. Use literal expressions to represent hours or minutes. For example, since there are 24 hours in a day, then one hour can be represented by 1/24. There are 1,440 minutes in a day (60 minutes times 24 hours), so 1 minute can be represented by 1/1440; 12 minutes can be represented by 12/1440, and so on.

Here's an example:

```
SELECT TO_CHAR(SYSDATE,'DD-MON-YY HH:MI:SS')        AS TODAY,
       TO_CHAR(SYSDATE+1,'DD-MON-YY HH:MI:SS')      AS TOMORROW,
       TO_CHAR(SYSDATE+1/24,'DD-MON-YY HH:MI:SS')   AS ONE_HOUR_FROM_NOW,
       TO_CHAR(SYSDATE+1/1440,'DD-MON-YY HH:MI:SS') AS ONE_MIN_FROM_NOW
FROM DUAL;
TODAY              TOMORROW           ONE_HOUR_FROM_NOW  ONE_MIN_FROM_NOW
------------------ ------------------ ------------------ ------------------
03-DEC-16 07:41:27 04-DEC-16 07:41:27 03-DEC-16 08:41:27 03-DEC-16 07:42:27
```

The TIMESTAMP data type works the same way with the same results; you could replace SYSDATE in the previous example with SYSTIMESTAMP and see the same impact to the values.

Analytical Functions

There are three categories of functions tested by the exam: scalar, analytical, and aggregate functions. Scalar functions return one answer for every one row processed. Aggregate functions return one answer for a set of zero to multiple rows.

Analytical functions fall somewhere in between these. They have the ability to return multiple rows from within a group of rows. Because a given SELECT statement processes data row by row, an analytic function can operate across a window of rows. That window can be defined by numbers of rows or by logic, such as a time range. As processing moves from row to row within the SELECT statement's group of rows, the window may slide, depending on how the analytic function specifies the window.

Analytic functions are the last set of operations performed in a query prior to the ORDER BY clause, which is the final processing step. For this reason, you cannot include analytic functions anywhere other than the SELECT list or the ORDER BY clause. In other words, analytics are forbidden in the WHERE, HAVING, and GROUP BY clauses.

Let's look at some keywords commonly used with analytic functions.

OVER, PARTITION BY, and ORDER BY

To see how OVER, PARTITION BY, and ORDER BY are used with analytics, let's look at an example. First, consider the following sample data set:

```
SHIP_CABIN_ID ROOM_ WINDOW            SQ_FT
------------- ----- ----------    ----------
            1 102   Ocean                533
            2 103   Ocean                160
            3 104   None                 533
            4 105   Ocean                205
            5 106   None                 586
            6 107   Ocean               1524
```

We can use the SUM function as an aggregate function to obtain the sum total of all SQ_FT values for the entire data set, like this:

```
SQL> SELECT       SUM(SQ_FT)
  2  FROM         SHIP_CABINS;

SUM(SQ_FT)
----------
      3541
```

Alternatively, we can use SUM as an analytic function and combine it with OVER to display a running total for each row, like this (line numbers added):

```
01  SQL> SELECT        WINDOW, ROOM_NUMBER, SQ_FT
02     2         , SUM(SQ_FT) OVER (ORDER BY SQ_FT) "Running Total"
03     3         , SUM(SQ_FT) OVER (ORDER BY SQ_FT
04     4                      ROWS BETWEEN 1 PRECEDING AND
05     5                           1 FOLLOWING) "Subset"
06     6  FROM         SHIP_CABINS
07     7  ORDER BY SQ_FT;
08
09  WINDOW     ROOM_      SQ_FT Running Total    Subset
10  ---------- ----- ---------- ------------- ----------
11  Ocean      103          160           160        365
12  Ocean      105          205           365        898
13  Ocean      102          533          1431       1271
14  None       104          533          1431       1652
15  None       106          586          2017       2643
16  Ocean      107         1524          3541       2110
17
18  6 rows selected.
```

The column Running Total displays exactly what is indicated (a running total of SQ_FT values) that builds within its own window, which in this case matches the set of rows for the SELECT. The Subset column also performs the SUM operation, but over a sliding window defined as the current row, the one prior row, and the one following row. For example, the Subset value for line 13 (Room Number 104) is the combination of the SQ_FT values displayed in lines 13, 14, and 15. Why? Because of the second use of the analytic function SUM detailed on lines 3, 4, and 5.

Let's add the PARTITION BY option to perform our SUM over sets of rows by values for the WINDOW column.

```
01   SQL> SELECT       WINDOW, ROOM_NUMBER, SQ_FT
02      2          , SUM(SQ_FT) OVER (PARTITION BY WINDOW
03      3                             ORDER BY SQ_FT) "Running Total"
04      4          , SUM(SQ_FT) OVER (PARTITION BY WINDOW
05      5                             ORDER BY SQ_FT
06      6                             ROWS BETWEEN 1 PRECEDING
07      7                                AND 1 FOLLOWING) "Subset"
08      8   FROM        SHIP_CABINS
09      9   ORDER BY SQ_FT;
10
11   WINDOW        ROOM_      SQ_FT Running Total      Subset
12   ----------    -----    ---------- -------------- ----------
13   Ocean         103          160           160         365
14   Ocean         105          205           365         898
15   Ocean         102          533           898        2262
16   None          104          533           533        1119
17   None          106          586          1119        1119
18   Ocean         107         1524          2422        2057
19
20   6 rows selected.
```

The inclusion of PARTITION BY changed the way Running Total and Subset are calculated. For example, look at the values on line 16. The Running Total column restarts with a value of 533, since we've partitioned the data by WINDOW and the value for WINDOW is now None (the first example of this value and therefore the first row in a new partition). Therefore, the running total is the current value for SQ_FT and nothing more: 533.

Look at line 18. The Running Total value is 2422, which is sum of the last row for Ocean (line 15, where the value was 898) and the current value in line 18 (which is 1524). Together, 898 plus 1524 is 2422, the current value for the running total for SQ_FT for the partition defined by those rows having a value of Ocean.

Let's change the ORDER BY for the SELECT but leave the analytic functions unchanged.

```
01  SQL> SELECT         WINDOW, ROOM_NUMBER, SQ_FT
02    2         , SUM(SQ_FT) OVER (PARTITION BY WINDOW
03    3                           ORDER BY SQ_FT) "Running Total"
04    4         , SUM(SQ_FT) OVER (PARTITION BY WINDOW
05    5                           ORDER BY SQ_FT
06    6                           ROWS BETWEEN 1 PRECEDING
07    7                               AND 1 FOLLOWING) "Subset"
08    8   FROM         SHIP_CABINS
09    9   ORDER BY ROOM_NUMBER;
10
11  WINDOW      ROOM_      SQ_FT Running Total    Subset
12  ----------  -----  ---------- -------------  ----------
13  Ocean        102        533           898       2262
14  Ocean        103        160           160        365
15  None         104        533           533       1119
16  Ocean        105        205           365        898
17  None         106        586          1119       1119
18  Ocean        107       1524          2422       2057
19
20  6 rows selected.
```

Note that the SELECT statement re-sorts the rows, but the values for each row remain unchanged. For example, on line 13, Room Number 102 still shows a Subset value of 2262, just as it did in the previous query results. As you've already seen, the value for the Subset column is determined by the partition and order of rows around it, but that order wasn't changed; the analytics function on lines 4 through 7 remains unchanged. All that we changed was the sort order of the SELECT statement.

LAG, LEAD

The LAG and LEAD functions are similar to each other. For a given row within a window, LAG shows a column's value in the prior row, and LEAD shows the next value. For example, consider the following data in the SHIP_CABINS table:

```
SHIP_CABIN_ID    SHIP_ID ROOM_ WINDOW            SQ_FT
-------------  ---------- ----- ----------   ----------
            1           1 102   Ocean              533
            2           1 103   Ocean              160
            3           1 104   None               533
            4           1 105   Ocean              205
            5           1 106   None               586
            6           1 107   Ocean             1524
```

Let's use LAG and LEAD in a SELECT statement to return each row showing that row's value for SQ_FT, the prior row's SQ_FT (Lag), and the subsequent row's SQ_FT (Lead):

```
01    SQL> SELECT   WINDOW, ROOM_NUMBER, SQ_FT
02      2          , LAG(SQ_FT)  OVER (ORDER BY WINDOW, SQ_FT) "Lag"
03      3          , LEAD(SQ_FT) OVER (ORDER BY WINDOW, SQ_FT) "Lead"
04      4    FROM     SHIP_CABINS
05      5    ORDER BY WINDOW, SQ_FT;
06
07    WINDOW      ROOM_      SQ_FT        Lag         Lead
08    ----------  -----  ----------  ----------  ----------
09    None         104         533                    586
10    None         106         586         533        160
11    Ocean        103         160         586        205
12    Ocean        105         205         160        533
13    Ocean        102         533         205       1524
14    Ocean        107        1524         533
15
16    6 rows selected.
```

In this example, the LAG (line 2) and LEAD (line 3) functions are both specified to operate over a window that is sorted by WINDOW and SQ_FT. The SELECT statement uses the same ORDER BY logic (line 5). Note line 9, where the first row of output shows a NULL for the Lag value. This is because the logic in line 2 specifies logic resulting in this row (line 9) as the first row in the window (specified in line 2). Therefore, there is no prior row.

See Figure 5-2 for an illustration of these concepts. First, PARTITION BY separates the rows into sets, or groups, as specified. In our example, we specified PARTION BY WINDOW, and our sample data has two values for WINDOW, so we separate our rows into two groups—one for a WINDOW value of 'Ocean' and another for a WINDOW value of 'None'. Second, for each group, we define a window for each target row. In our example, the window consists of those rows spanning from one row prior to our target row through to one row following our target row. This means that as we step through each row, our window will slide.

Third, as we step through each row, we want the SQ_FT; the LAG(SQ_FT), which is from the prior row; and the LEAD(SQ_FT), which is from the following row. Finally, we return the output and see our results.

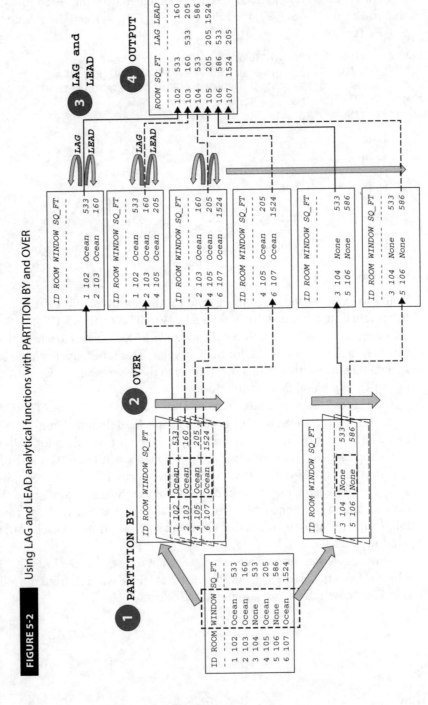

Let's change the ORDER BY logic and see whether this changes the Lag value.

```
01   SQL> SELECT    WINDOW, ROOM_NUMBER, SQ_FT
02     2          , LAG(SQ_FT)  OVER (ORDER BY WINDOW, SQ_FT) "Lag"
03     3          , LEAD(SQ_FT) OVER (ORDER BY WINDOW, SQ_FT) "Lead"
04     4   FROM     SHIP_CABINS
05     5   ORDER BY ROOM_NUMBER;
06
07   WINDOW       ROOM_       SQ_FT         Lag         Lead
08   ----------   -----   ----------   ----------   ----------
09   Ocean        102            533          205         1524
10   Ocean        103            160          586          205
11   None         104            533                       586
12   Ocean        105            205          160          533
13   None         106            586          533          160
14   Ocean        107           1524          533
15
16   6 rows selected.
```

The ORDER BY logic now sorts the output by ROOM_NUMBER. But note the output in row 11: it's the same ROW_NUMBER value of 104, and it's the same NULL value for Lag. This demonstrates how the window for LAG is defined by LAG itself, independent of the ORDER BY clause.

So far we've looked at LAG and LEAD functions that specifically return data from the one row immediately prior to (LAG) or following (LEAD) the current row. The row difference is specified by the offset, which defaults to 1 as we've seen so far but can be specified as something else. If the offset specifies a nonexisting row, the LAG or LEAD function will return a NULL value. Let's change the offset for our LAG function to 2 and see what happens.

```
01   SQL> SELECT    WINDOW, ROOM_NUMBER, SQ_FT
02     2          , LAG(SQ_FT, 2) OVER (ORDER BY WINDOW, SQ_FT) "Lag"
03     3          , LEAD(SQ_FT)   OVER (ORDER BY WINDOW, SQ_FT) "Lead"
04     4   FROM     SHIP_CABINS
05     5   ORDER BY WINDOW, SQ_FT;
06
07   WINDOW       ROOM_       SQ_FT         Lag         Lead
08   ----------   -----   ----------   ----------   ----------
09   None         104            533                       586
10   None         106            586                       160
11   Ocean        103            160          533          205
12   Ocean        105            205          586          533
13   Ocean        102            533          160         1524
14   Ocean        107           1524          205
15
16   6 rows selected.
```

In this sample listing, see line 2 for the LAG function and the offset specification of 2, immediately after the SQ_FT reference. The result appears in the rows returned. Note that both lines 9 and 10 show NULL values for LAG. This is because there are not rows at the offset for those rows. For other rows—such as line 13— you see the SQ_FT of 533, and the Lag SQ_FT value is taken from the row offset by two prior, which in this case is the row shown on line 11.

STDDEV

The STDDEV function returns the sample standard deviation of a set of numeric values. Standard deviation is a mathematical value representing the degree of distribution for a given numeric value within a larger range of values. The standard deviation for a given number is the square root of its variance. Oracle has functions for both, so the value of a given number's STDDEV is the square root of its VARIANCE, an aggregate function. Using STDDEV, you can analyze a set of numbers and determine each value's dispersion from the mean. STDDEV is useful when analyzing a set of numbers by looking for correlations among those numbers— those numbers whose STDDEV values are low are closer to the mean than those numbers with relatively higher values of STDDEV.

The mathematical formulas for calculating standard deviation and variance are simple but a bit involved. For example, consider the following set of values:

#	1	2	3	4
Value	1	2	4	13

The values are 1, 2, 4, and 13, for a total of four values.

To calculate the variance and standard deviation of our example, do the following:

- Calculate the average:
  - First, sum the values: 1 + 2 + 4 + 13 = 20
  - Next, divide the sum by the total number of values: 20 / 4 = 5. This is the average.
- For each number, determine the difference between the number and the average, then square the result.

#	1	2	3	4
Value	1	2	4	13
Average (or Mean)			5	
Difference	−4	−3	−1	8
Difference squared	16	9	1	64

■ Add up the squared differences. Take the result and divide by the total count of values less one:

   ■ $16 + 9 + 1 + 64 = 90$

   ■ $90 / (4 - 1) = 90/3 = 30$. This is the variance.

■ Calculate the square root of the variance:

   ■ $SQRT(30) = 5.477$. This is the standard deviation.

The VARIANCE and STDDEV functions will perform these calculations for you. In that context, the function will behave as an aggregate function. For example, consider the following data set:

```
SHIP_CABIN_ID ROOM_ WINDOW          SQ_FT
------------- ----- ---------- ----------
            1 102   Ocean             533
            2 103   Ocean             160
            3 104   None              533
            4 105   Ocean             205
            5 106   None              586
            6 107   Ocean            1524
```

Now let's use AVG, MEDIAN, VARIANCE, and STDDEV as aggregate functions on the full set of rows.

```
01  SQL> SELECT      AVG(SQ_FT), MEDIAN(SQ_FT), STDDEV(SQ_FT), VARIANCE(SQ_FT)
02     2  FROM       SHIP_CABINS;
03  AVG(SQ_FT) MEDIAN(SQ_FT) STDDEV(SQ_FT) VARIANCE(SQ_FT)
04  ---------- ------------- ------------- ---------------
05  590.166667           533    492.340296       242398.967
```

That is an example of using STDDEV as an aggregate function. In other words, the full set of rows as specified by the SELECT statement is considered, and a single standard deviation is computed and returned.

However, STDDEV can also be used as a single-row function in combination with a sliding window of rows. The following code calculates both the cumulative VARIANCE and the cumulative STDDEV over the same window:

```
01  SQL> SELECT      WINDOW, ROOM_NUMBER, SQ_FT
02     2             , VARIANCE(SQ_FT) OVER (ORDER BY SQ_FT) "Variance"
03     3             , STDDEV(SQ_FT)    OVER (ORDER BY SQ_FT) "Std Dev"
04     4  FROM       SHIP_CABINS
05     5  ORDER BY SQ_FT;
06
```

```
07   WINDOW      ROOM_      SQ_FT   Variance     Std Dev
08   ----------  -----  ----------  ----------  ----------
09   Ocean       103           160           0           0
10   Ocean       105           205      1012.5  31.8198052
11   Ocean       102           533  41287.5833  203.193463
12   None        104           533  41287.5833  203.193463
13   None        106           586     41385.3  203.433773
14   Ocean       107          1524  242398.967  492.340296
15
16   6 rows selected.
```

In our output, the VARIANCE and STDDEV are calculated cumulatively, and you can see the final values match the aggregate results computed in the previous example.

PERCENTILE_CONT

The PERCENTILE_CONT function uses linear interpolation between a given row's row set ceiling and floor to calculate the percentile value for that given row. The PERCENTILE_CONT function takes as input a percentage you specify, say, .4 (for 40 percent), and it analyzes a group of rows you specify; then it determines the equivalent numeric value equal to that percentage of the whole, by using linear extrapolation.

For example, let's display rows from SHIP_CABINS that show the square footage for each cabin, but for the cabins with the same type of window, consider the largest square footage, calculate 60 percent of that square footage, and display that amount.

```
01   SQL> SELECT    WINDOW, ROOM_NUMBER, SQ_FT
02    2           , PERCENTILE_CONT(.6)
03    3                WITHIN GROUP (ORDER BY SQ_FT)
04    4                OVER (PARTITION BY WINDOW) "PCT"
05    5   FROM      SHIP_CABINS
06    6   ORDER BY SQ_FT;
07
08   WINDOW      ROOM_      SQ_FT         PCT
09   ----------  -----  ----------  ----------
10   Ocean       103           160       467.4
11   Ocean       105           205       467.4
12   Ocean       102           533       467.4
13   None        104           533       564.8
14   None        106           586       564.8
15   Ocean       107          1524       467.4
16
17   6 rows selected.
```

Here is the formula used for computing the PERCENTILE_CONT.

First, we calculated the percentage by partitioning the rows by WINDOW. Our sample data has two values for Window: Ocean and None. So, we have two groups.

For every group, PERCENTILE_CONT will consider the specified percentage (P), which in our case is .60, and then count the number of rows (RN). For Ocean there are four rows, shown in the previous example on lines 10, 11, 12, and 15. Using that information, we calculate a target row (TR) using the following formula:

$$TR = (1 + (P * (RN - 1)))$$

Using our numbers, here is the calculation:

$$2.8 = (1 + (.6 * (4 - 1)))$$

Our target row number is 2.8. We have four rows for Ocean, so our target row is theoretically located between the second and third rows. Our objective is to determine the SQ_FT value that would exist on this theoretical row number 2.8. To calculate that value, we need to know the following: the CEIL and FLOOR of our target row number and the values at those rows.

For our example, this information is as follows:

- The CEIL for 2.8 is 3, and the value for the third row of Ocean is 533.
- The FLOOR for 2.8 is 2, and the value at the second row of Ocean is 205.

The formula used by PERCENTILE_CONT is as follows:

$$(CEIL - TR) * (\text{Value at the FLOOR}) + (TR - FLOOR) * (\text{Value at the CEIL})$$

In other words, here is the calculation:

$$(((3 - 2.8) * 205) + ((2.8 - 2) * 533)) = 467.4$$

The result is what you see in each row of Ocean in our output.

The intent of PERCENTILE_CONT is to compute for a group of rows the interpolated value at the specified percent (in our case, 60 percent) of the whole for that group.

exam
watch

Many more functions exist in SQL than are described in this book. Space limitations prevent me from showing descriptions and examples of all of them. Yet any of the many functions may appear on the exam. Be sure to review the Oracle Database SQL Language Reference Manual and review the lengthy description of all the SQL functions before taking the exam. Pay particular attention to the input parameters of each function, as well as the data type of each function's returned value.

Nesting Functions

When a function is placed within an expression in such a way that its output becomes the parameter value for another function of that same expression, the original function is said to be *nested*. When one function is nested within another, the nested function executes first. The nested function is also considered the *inner* function, as opposed to the *outer* function, which receives the output of the inner function as an input parameter. When functions are nested at multiple levels, the innermost functions execute first. You can nest multiple functions and at multiple levels—so you can nest a function within a function, and nest the combination within yet another function.

(Note: Once you include non-scalar functions (i.e., aggregate functions) in a SELECT statement, you begin to introduce some potential complications into the process, including with regard to nested functions. However, this chapter looks exclusively at scalar functions (single-row functions) so we'll defer concerns about nested aggregate functions until Chapter 7.

Nested Functions and Patterns

Here's an example that nests one function within another. The combination of SUBSTR and INSTR can be helpful in locating strings whose position varies within a string but varies relative to a fixed distance to another string. One often used technique is helpful when working with information about postal addresses, when you are looking for the two-letter abbreviation of one of the United States that is often found after the comma plus one blank space. See Figure 5-3 for an example.

FIGURE 5-3

SUBSTR and INSTR combined

```
SQL Plus
SQL> SELECT    ADDRESS2,
  2            INSTR(ADDRESS2, ',') THE_COMMA,
  3            SUBSTR(ADDRESS2, INSTR(ADDRESS2, ',')+2, 2) STATE
  4  FROM      ORDER_ADDRESSES
  5  ORDER BY 3;

ADDRESS2                                          THE_COMMA ST
------------------------------------------------ ---------- --
Santa Barbara, CA 93109                                  14 CA
Weeki Wachee, FL 34607                                   13 FL
Havre De Grace, MD 21078                                 15 MD
Kalamazoo, MI 49001                                      10 MI
Little Egg Harbor Township, NJ 08087                     27 NJ
Tulsa, OK 74103                                           6 OK
Pumpkin Center, OK 74451                                 15 OK
Ronks, PA 17572                                           6 PA
Woonsocket, RI 02895                                     11 RI
Bugscuffle, TN 37183                                     11 TN
Issaquah, WA 98027                                        9 WA

11 rows selected.

SQL>
```

The first column shows the column ADDRESS2 unchanged. Notice, however, that each string contains a two-letter state abbreviation and that each state is after a comma plus one blank space. We can use that consistent pattern to our advantage. The second column shows how we can use the INSTR function to find the exact location of that comma in each individual row of ADDRESS2. Finally, the third column shows how we can nest the output of each row's INSTR result within a SUBSTR function. By adding 2 to the results of INSTR (one for the comma, one for the space), we locate the precise start of the two-letter state abbreviation within each occurrence of ADDRESS2 and thus are able to extract the value for the third column, STATE.

Finally, note that we order the output by the findings of the third column. Pretty interesting that we can sort rows of data by a substring of a column whose position changes within each row of the table—but it's entirely possible thanks to the presence of a consistent pattern in the data and the use of nested functions to locate and work with those consistent patterns.

CERTIFICATION SUMMARY

SQL functions perform a wide variety of tasks, ranging from mathematical calculations to text analysis and date conversions. Functions can be called from almost any type of SQL statement and from a variety of locations within those SQL statements. SQL functions can be called from the SELECT statement's select list and WHERE clause, from the INSERT statement's value list, from the UPDATE statement's SET clause and WHERE clause, and from the DELETE statement's WHERE clause.

A function takes anywhere from zero to multiple input parameter values. Each function does some sort of processing that incorporates the input parameters, and perhaps some other data as well. Each function returns exactly one result.

Character functions perform tasks associated with string manipulation and text analysis. Character functions include UPPER, LOWER, INITCAP, CONCAT, LPAD, RPAD, LENGTH, INSTR, SUBSTR, and others. Character functions accept input parameters that may be character data and may include other data types, such as numeric parameters. And while each character function returns exactly one value, as do all functions, the character functions do not necessarily return character data as their return value. For example, LENGTH returns a number indicating the length of a given character string. But each performs a task associated with character strings.

Number functions, also referred to as numeric functions, perform analysis on numbers. They include ROUND, REMAINDER, MOD, and others.

Date functions work with date and datetime information. Date functions include SYSDATE, ROUND (for dates), TRUNC (for dates), NEXT_DAY, LAST_DAY, ADD_MONTHS, MONTHS_BETWEEN, NUMTOYMINTERVAL, NUMTODSINTERVAL, and others.

Analytical functions can be used to perform analysis on one or more sets of rows within the larger row set of a SELECT statement. Those subsets can include sliding windows that vary with each target row and can be specified by row numbers or by value range using logic. Some functions can be used as aggregates to calculate a single total value or as analytical functions within subsets of rows—like SUM, which can be used as an analytical function to calculate a running total.

Analytical functions include STDDEV, which calculates standard deviation, and PERCENTILE_CONT, which calculates a percentile value using linear interpolation within a specified set or subset of rows. Other functions perform tasks that may or may not perform processing on one or more data types.

Functions may be nested within each other so that the output of one function serves as the input parameter of another.

TWO-MINUTE DRILL

Use Various Types of Functions That Are Available in SQL

☐ Most SQL functions accept one or more input parameters. A few take no parameters.

☐ Each function returns one value; no more, no less.

☐ SQL functions perform tasks of various kinds.

☐ Functions can be included anywhere a SQL expression can be included, provided that the rules of data types are respected.

☐ Functions can be included in the WHERE clause of the SELECT, UPDATE, and DELETE statements.

☐ Functions can be included in the SELECT expression list, INSERT value list, and UPDATE SET clause.

Use Character, Number, Date, and Analytical (PERCENTILE_CONT, STDDEV, LAG, LEAD) Functions in SELECT Statements

☐ Character functions include text cleanup and conversion functions.

☐ UPPER, LOWER, and INITCAP can manage the case of a string.

☐ LPAD and RPAD can pad a string with specified characters.

☐ INSTR, SUBSTR, CONCAT, and LENGTH can be used to divide up and put together different strings.

☐ Numeric functions perform analysis and calculations.

☐ TRUNC always rounds toward zero.

☐ REMAINDER and MOD are variations on division and leftover values.

☐ PARTITION BY specifies sets of rows within the SELECT statement row set.

☐ OVER can be used to specify a sliding window of rows.

☐ The LAG and LEAD functions draw data from prior and subsequent rows.

☐ The analytical function STDDEV calculates standard deviations cumulatively.

☐ Other functions include LEAST and GREATEST.

SELF TEST

The following questions will help you measure your understanding of the material presented in this chapter. Choose one correct answer for each question unless otherwise directed.

Use Various Types of Functions That Are Available in SQL

1. Which of the following is true of functions?
   A. They never return a value.
   B. They often return a value.
   C. They always return a value.
   D. There is no consistent answer to whether they return a value or not.

2. Which of the following is true of character functions?
   A. They always accept characters as parameters and nothing else.
   B. They always return a character value.
   C. They are generally used to process text data.
   D. They generally have the letters CHAR somewhere in the function name.

3. Built-in SQL functions: (Choose three.)
   A. Can be invoked from a DELETE statement's WHERE clause.
   B. Are written by SQL developers and also known as "user-defined" functions.
   C. Are available for use from the UPDATE statement.
   D. Are available for use within a SELECT statement's WHERE clause, as well as the SELECT statement's expression list.

4. The output of a function may be used: (Choose three.)
   A. As an input parameter value to an outer function.
   B. As a column of output in a SELECT statement.
   C. As an input value within the VALUES list of an INSERT statement.
   D. As an alternative to the keyword SET in an UPDATE statement.

Use Character, Number, Date, and Analytical (PERCENTILE_CONT, STDDEV, LAG, LEAD) Functions in SELECT Statements

5. Consider the following:

```
SELECT MOD(5,3), REMAINDER(5,3) FROM    DUAL;
```

Which of the following will be the result?

A. 1, 2
B. −1, 2
C. 2, 1
D. 2, −1

6. Consider the following SQL statement:

   ```
   SELECT SOUNDEX('Donald') FROM DUAL;
   ```

   Which of the following is most likely to be the output of this SELECT statement? (Choose the best answer.)

   A. D543
   B. DON3
   C. Donalt
   D. Donalk

7. You are tasked to create a SELECT statement to subtract five months from the hired date of each employee in the EMPLOYEES table. Which function will you use?

   A. LAST_DAY
   B. SUBTRACT_MONTHS
   C. LAG
   D. None of the above

8. Review this SQL statement:

   ```
   SELECT SUBSTR('2009',1,2) || LTRIM('1124','1') FROM DUAL;
   ```

   What will be the result of the SQL statement?

   A. 2024
   B. 221
   C. 20124
   D. A syntax error

9. Review this SQL statement:

   ```
   SELECT TRUNC(ROUND(ABS(-1.7),2)) FROM DUAL;
   ```

   What will be the result of the SQL statement?

   A. 1
   B. 2
   C. −1
   D. −2

10. Review this SQL statement:

```
SELECT LASTNAME FROM CUSTOMERS WHERE LASTNAME = SOUNDEX('Franklin');
```

What is a possible result for the query?

A.   Franklyn

B.   Phrankline

C.   Ellison

D.   None of the above

11. Review this SQL statement:

```
SELECT MONTHS_BETWEEN(LAST_DAY('15-JAN-12')+1,'01-APR-12')FROM DUAL;
```

What will result from this query?

A.   > 2 (some number greater than 2)

B.   2

C.   −2

D.   < −2 (some number less than negative 2)

12. The PERCENTILE_CONT function:

A.   Returns the same result as AVG

B.   Returns the same result as VARIANCE

C.   Can be used with ROWS to specify a sliding window

D.   Can be used with PARTITION BY to specify groups of data

13. The ORDER BY in an OVER clause:

A.   Must match the ORDER BY in the SELECT statement

B.   Replaces the ORDER BY in the SELECT statement

C.   Operates independently of the ORDER BY in the SELECT statement

D.   None of the above

14. The LEAD function returns data from:

A.   A row prior to the current row as specified by the LEAD function's ORDER BY clause

B.   A row following the current row as specified by the SELECT statement's ORDER BY clause

C.   The LAG function's window's specified column

D.   The row specified by the LEAD function's offset

15. Analytic functions are processed:

A.   As the first set of operations prior to the SELECT column list processing

B.   As the first set of operations before processing the WHERE clause

C.   As the last set of operations before processing the WHERE clause

D.   As the last set of operations before processing the ORDER BY clause

SELF TEST ANSWERS

Use Various Types of Functions That Are Available in SQL

1. ☑ **C.** They always return a single value.
    ☒ **A, B,** and **D** are incorrect. Functions may or may not return a value, each function is different, and it is not possible to make a single statement that can never return a value.

2. ☑ **C.** They are generally used to process text data.
    ☒ **A, B,** and **D** are incorrect. They do not all accept characters as input parameters. Some, such as SUBSTR, take numeric input parameters. They do not always return a character value—LENGTH does not. And they do not all have CHAR in their function name.

3. ☑ **A, C,** and **D.** The functions that are reviewed in this chapter are known as built-in functions and are available to be used anywhere in SQL where an expression can be used. That includes a SELECT statement's expression list, an UPDATE statement's SET clauses, an INSERT statement's list of input values, and the WHERE clause of any SQL statement—SELECT, UPDATE, and DELETE.
    ☒ **B** is incorrect. Built-in functions and user-defined functions are separate categories. Both can be invoked from the same places—such as a SELECT statement's WHERE clause—but user-defined functions are written in languages such as PL/SQL. This chapter looked only at built-in functions.

4. ☑ **A, B,** and **C.** A nested function passes its output to the outer function as an input parameter to that outer function. A function can be used as a column in a SELECT statement, such as SELECT SYSDATE FROM DUAL. A function can be use as input for an INSERT statement.
    ☒ **D** is incorrect. A function cannot replace a keyword within a SQL statement. Having said that, it is not uncommon to write a query that produces output that is itself SQL code and then execute those dynamically generated SQL statements. The original query uses string concatenation and other features to generate output that is itself a series of SQL statements. But process requires a combination of SQL and SQL*Plus features used together to produce output that is SQL code free of output headings, titles, and other extraneous content so that the output is composed of purely SQL statements. The process can "spool" output to a file that is executable and execute that file with a SQL*Plus statement to automatically execute those statements. But that approach includes features of SQL*Plus and it is outside the scope of this book.

Use Character, Number, Date, and Analytical (PERCENTILE_CONT, STDDEV, LAG, LEAD) Functions in SELECT Statements

5.   ☑   **D.** MOD divides the first number by the second and returns the remainder relative to the first number. REMAINDER does the same thing but returns the remainder relative to the second number.

☒   **A, B,** and **C** are incorrect. **A** is incorrect for both functions. **B** would be correct if the functions were reversed. **C** is correct for MOD but is incorrect for REMAINDER.

6.   ☑   **A.** The output of SOUNDEX is a four-character code starting with the same letter of the input value, followed by a three-digit code based on the SOUNDEX logic.

☒   **B, C,** and **D** are incorrect. DON3 cannot be correct because the second, third, and fourth characters should be digits. **C** and **D** are incorrect—they are both sound-alike possibilities that might have the same SOUNDEX code, but they themselves will not be the output of SOUNDEX.

7.   ☑   **D.** None of the above. The function you want is ADD_MONTHS so that you can add negative five months to the current date.

☒   **A, B,** and **C** are incorrect. The LAST_DAY function returns the last day of a given month. There is no SUBTRACT_MONTHS function. LAG is an analytic function that shows a column's value in the prior row.

8.   ☑   **A.** The SUBSTR function will extract data from the string ('2009') starting at the first position (1) and lasting for 2 characters (2), resulting in an answer of '20'. The LTRIM function will trim off all occurrences of the 1 from the left side of '1124', resulting in 24. The two results are concatenated together for a final result of 2024.

☒   **B, C,** and **D** are incorrect. There is no syntax error present in the code. Even though the values evaluated by both functions include data that consists of numerals, both are enclosed in single quotes and therefore are treated as character data. Even if they were not enclosed in single quotes, SQL would perform an automatic data type conversion anyway.

9.   ☑   **A.** The result will be 1. The ABS function determines absolute value. As the innermost function, it will be evaluated first, resulting in an answer of 1.7. The ROUND function will process the value of 1.7 and round it to the nearest two digits to the right of the decimal point, and the result will still be 1.7. Finally, TRUNC will truncate the value down to a one.

☒   **B, C,** and **D** are incorrect. Were the ",2" omitted as the second argument in the ROUND function, option **B** would be correct, which is to say the SQL statement would return a value of 2. If both the ABS and ROUND functions were edited out and only TRUNC remained, the statement would return −1, making **C** the correct answer. Were only the ABS function removed from the statement, the statement would return −2, meaning that **D** would be the correct answer.

10. ☑ **D.** None of the above is correct.

    ☒ **A, B,** and **C** are incorrect. SOUNDEX should be applied to both the source and comparison text, but in this SELECT statement it is used on only one side of the comparison operator. Specifically, the SOUNDEX code for the text string 'Franklin' is the literal value 'F652'. Is the literal 'F652' equal to the value for LASTNAME in the CUSTOMERS table? Probably not, unless someone with a name like Freddy F652 happens to be a customer. The purpose of SOUNDEX is to convert the values themselves (in this case LASTNAME values) using SOUNDEX and then compare those converted values to a given SOUNDEX code to find sound-alikes. So if you are looking for last names that are equal to or sound like Franklin, you would want to convert the last names and then compare those converted last names to the SOUNDEX code, like this:
    WHERE SOUNDEX(LASTNAME) = 'F652'
    or like this:
    WHERE SOUNDEX(LASTNAME) = SOUNDEX('Franklin')
    To use SOUNDEX effectively, text on both sides of the comparison operator need to be SOUNDEX values.

11. ☑ **C.** The answer will be −2. First, the LAST_DAY function will transform the value of '15-JAN-12' to '31-JAN-12', and then the result of that will be added to 1, so that the first of February will result: '01-FEB-12'. The difference between that date and '01-APR-12' will be a negative 2.

    ☒ **A, B,** and **D** are incorrect. If the "+1" were removed, then the answer would be less than −2. If the dates were reversed, the answer would be greater than positive 2. There is no scenario where an obvious and minor edit would result in a value of positive 2.

12. ☑ **D.** PERCENTILE_CONT can be used with PARTITION BY to specify groups of data within a single SELECT statement.

    ☒ **A, B,** and **C** are incorrect. PERCENTILE_CONT is not the same as AVG. It uses a more complex set of logic to interpolate an answer. It does not return the same result as VARIANCE. PERCENTILE_CONT, unlike some other analytical functions, does not support sliding windows.

13. ☑ **C.** The ORDER BY in an OVER clause operates independently of the ORDER BY in the SELECT statement.

    ☒ **A, B,** and **D** are incorrect. The ORDER BY in the OVER clause does not have to match the ORDER BY in the SELECT, nor does it replace the ORDER BY in the SELECT. The two exist independently so that you can logically sort a subset in support of the calculations within analytics, particularly the row-by-row calculations.

14. ☑ **D.** The LEAD function returns data from the row specified by the LEAD function's offset. The offset defaults to 1 but may be specified within the LEAD function.

    ☒ **A, B,** and **C** are incorrect. LEAD returns data from a row following the current row, as determined by the offset and sorted by the LEAD function's ORDER BY clause. The window for LEAD is specified by LEAD, not other analytic functions, which specify their own windows.

15. ☑ **D.** Analytic functions are the last set of operations performed before the ORDER BY. For this reason, they must be specified in the SELECT list or ORDER BY only, not the WHERE, GROUP BY, or HAVING clauses.

    ☒ **A, B,** and **C** are incorrect. These options are exclusive to the correct answer, which is that the analytic functions are performed at the last set of operations prior to the ORDER BY.

6
Using Conversion Functions and Conditional Expressions

T his chapter looks at the topics of conversion functions and conditional expressions. *Conversion functions* perform data type transformation from one general type such as numeric to another such as text. Conditional expressions perform evaluations and return data using criteria you specify in the context of SQL statements. These (and other) SQL functions can be used in various portions of a SELECT statement, including the column list, the WHERE and ORDER BY clauses, within JOIN and other expressions, and more.

CERTIFICATION OBJECTIVE 6.01

Describe Various Types of Conversion Functions

The purpose of conversion functions is to convert data values from one data type to another. Conversion functions don't change values; they change the value's data type. For example, you might have financial values stored within text containing dollar signs and other symbols that a mathematical function might reject with an error message. But you could use a conversion function to convert the financial data within the text to a numeric data type, and then use whatever numeric functions you need on the converted values.

In Chapter 2 we discussed different data types. Most data types fall into one of three general categories: numeric (NUMBER), text (VARCHAR2), and dates and/ or times (DATE, TIMESTAMP, etc.). In Chapter 5 we looked at several functions that perform various operations on data, but many require that incoming data be of a particular data type. For example, math functions generally operate on numeric data type inputs. The ADD_MONTHS function uses DATE values as input.

Conversion functions can be used to transform data from one type to another. This can enable the converted data to become input to some other function requiring the converted data type. For example, a table with a column NOTE that is declared VARCHAR2(30) might contain a value of '1230'. That happens to be a number. You could perform a data type conversion on this value to first convert its data type from text to numeric. Once converted, it can be used as numeric input to a function that can accept only incoming numeric data. Alternatively, if the conversion attempt fails, that failure might indicate the value is not numeric after all; perhaps the zero at the end of '1230' is really the letter *O*. Your business rules may require such a confirmation. This is helpful when you are working in real time with data, particularly if you are coding SQL to be used on a recurring basis within an application.

Conversion functions can do more than change a value's data type. Some conversion functions also feature formatting capabilities. For example, if you have a DATE data type that contains raw information about hours, minutes, seconds, and the date on the calendar, you can transform it into a text string that spells out the entire date in detail, such as "Thursday, July the Fourth, Seventeen Seventy-Six." (See the "On The Job" after this chapter's TO_DATE section for the SQL to make that work.) Similarly, conversion functions can transform raw numeric data into financial formats that include dollar signs and symbols for other international currency, proper placement for commas and periods according to various international formats, and more.

The next section will delve into the specifics of TO_NUMBER, TO_CHAR, and TO_DATE, as well as some other conversion functions. However, before we get to that, we would be remiss if we did not also address the topic of explicit and implicit conversion—let's address that now.

Explicit and Implicit Conversion

The use of a data type conversion function is *explicit* conversion. But there is also an *implicit* conversion feature in SQL. It occurs automatically in circumstances where SQL will determine on its own that a data type conversion is required but not specified. When this happens, SQL will perform the data type conversion automatically. For example, let's say you want to concatenate a numeric value with a text string.

```
SELECT 'Chapter ' || 1 || ' . . . I am born.'
FROM    DUAL;

'CHAPTER'||1||'...IAMBORN.'
--------------------------
Chapter 1 . . . I am born.
```

Note that the second value in the SELECT list is numeric yet is included in a text function for performing string concatenation. SQL will recognize the intent and will perform the character conversion function automatically, executing the SQL statement appropriately.

SQL is generous with such automatic conversions. This characteristic is a great convenience when performing quick, ad hoc interactions with the database.

Here's another example (line numbers added):

```
01    SELECT SYSDATE,
02           ADD_MONTHS(SYSDATE,
03                      SUBSTR('plus 3 months',6,1)) PLUS_THREE
04    FROM    DUAL;
05
06    SYSDATE                    PLUS_THREE
07    -------------------------  -------------------------
08    17-FEB-16                  17-MAY-16
```

In this example, the SUBSTR function in line 3 returns a string value of 3, which is automatically converted to a numeric data type since a numeric is what is required for the ADD_MONTHS function in lines 2 and 3.

However, when your objective is to program code for reuse, it is considered good design to avoid dependence on automatic data type conversion and code your intentions explicitly. And more than simply good design and common practice, it is also the formal recommendation of Oracle Corporation to use explicit conversion where possible. The practice ensures your intent in your code is clear, documented, and supported in the future when the database conditions may change for various reasons. For example, you might code an implicit data type conversion that assumes a particular table's column will happen to contain numeric values within a VARCHAR2 column. But what if, in the future, those values change to alphabetically spelled references such as "two" and "three" instead of "2" and "3"? The error message that will result will reference the formula in which the automatic conversion was attempted. If you were to have originally used an explicit data type conversion function, then the error message would indicate the failure occurred at the attempt to convert the data type, making the true problem clear and resulting in a faster and more straightforward troubleshooting effort.

When comparing text and numeric values, such as in an IF statement, the text value will generally be converted to numeric. But not always:

```
01    SQL> SELECT 'TRUE' FROM DUAL WHERE '3' > '20';
02    'TRU
03    ----
04    TRUE
05
06    SQL> SELECT 'TRUE' FROM DUAL WHERE '3' > 20;
07
08    no rows selected
09
```

Note that the number three is not greater than the number twenty. But the first SELECT compares the two values as text values, and in the dictionary, yes, the text value '3' comes before the text value '20', where the first character defines the primary sorting criteria. When both values are treated as numeric values, obviously 20 is a larger number. When the two values are compared so that only one is numeric, an automatic data type conversion is performed on the text value, and suddenly both values are treated as numeric.

The following are some additional rules for automatic data type conversion:

- Numeric values will generally not convert automatically to dates.
- Numeric and text data will generally not convert automatically to very large sized types, such as LOB, CLOB, RAW, and others.
- Very large types will generally not automatically convert to each other, such as from BLOB to CLOB, for example. Some will, but many won't.

on the
Ojob

Explicit data type conversion is clear, is easier to read, and results in better performance; implicit conversion is not as efficient. For example, an index can speed the performance of a SELECT statement based on how the WHERE clause is phrased, but if that WHERE clause uses syntax that depends on an implicit conversion, the index might not be used or might even be used incorrectly. This doesn't affect the resulting data, of course, but it might result in performance degradation, which results in longer processing time. Additionally, Oracle's documentation warns that the behavior of implicit conversion is subject to change across software releases. The bottom line is that certain types of data type conversions are performed automatically. But don't depend on them in your code. Use explicit conversion, as we reviewed in this section.

CERTIFICATION OBJECTIVE 6.02

Use the TO_CHAR, TO_NUMBER, and TO_DATE Conversion Functions

Conversion functions convert the data type of an expression from one data type to another. Some conversion functions will also transform the format of the data at the same time.

For example, the following is an INSERT statement that attempts to store data into two columns. The CALL_ID column is of the NUMBER data type.

The CALL_DATE_TZ column is of the data type TIMESTAMP WITH TIME ZONE. Here's an attempt to insert data into that table:

```
INSERT INTO CALLS (CALL_ID, CALL_DATE_TZ)
VALUES             (1, '24-MAY-12 10:15:30');

Error starting at line 1 in command:
INSERT INTO CALLS (CALL_ID, CALL_DATE_TZ)
VALUES             (1, '24-MAY-12 10:15:30')
Error report:
SQL Error: ORA-01840: input value not long enough for date format
01840. 00000 -  "input value not long enough for date format"
```

Now let's try that same INSERT statement with a conversion function.

```
INSERT INTO CALLS (CALL_ID, CALL_DATE_TZ)
VALUES             (1, TO_TIMESTAMP_TZ('24-MAY-12 10:15:30',
                                        'DD-MON-RR HH24:MI:SS')  );

1 rows inserted
```

In this example, the TO_TIMESTAMP_TZ conversion function is used to send the same data we used in our previous INSERT. This particular conversion function uses a "format model" that describes the format of the data to the database. The format model used here is 'DD-MON-RR HH24:MI:SS'. This helps to ensure that the input data is recognized correctly.

The next section describes many conversion functions with examples of their use.

Conversion Functions

The most commonly used conversion functions are TO_NUMBER, TO_CHAR, and TO_DATE. Let's look at each of these three functions.

TO_NUMBER

Syntax: TO_NUMBER(*e1, format_model, nls_parms*)

Parameters: *e1* is an expression (required); *format_model* is the optional format model. See Table 6-1 for a complete list of elements that make up the format model.

There is an optional third parameter representing NLS settings. It allows you to identify any of the three NLS parameters defined in Table 6-2. If included, the third parameter for TO_NUMBER consists of a single string that encompasses any one or

TABLE 6-1   Number Format Elements

Element	Example	Description
, .	9,999.99	Commas and decimal points will pass through wherever they are included. Warning: Only one period is allowed per format mask.
$	$999.99	Leading dollar sign.
0	0099.99	Leading or trailing 0.
9	999	Any digit.
B	B999	Leading blank for integers.
C	C999	The ISO currency symbol as defined in the NLS_ISO_CURRENCY parameter.
D	999D99	Returns the current decimal character as defined by the NLS_NUMERIC_CHARACTERS parameter. The default value is a period.
EEEE	9.9EEE	Returns a value in scientific notation.
G	9G999	Returns the group separator (e.g., a comma).
L	L999	Returns the local currency symbol.
MI	999MI	Returns negative value with trailing minus sign; returns positive value with a trailing blank.
PR	999PR	Returns negative values in angle brackets.
RN rn	RN	Returns values in Roman numerals, uppercase. Put RN in lowercase (as in "rn") for Roman numerals in lowercase.
S (prefix)	S9999	Returns negative values with a leading minus sign, positive values with a leading positive sign. Note: Can appear only in the first or last position of a format mask.
S (suffix)	9999S	Returns negative values with a trailing minus sign, positive values with a trailing positive sign. Note: Can appear only in the first or last position of a format mask.
TM	TM	The text minimum number format model returns the smallest number of characters possible.
U	U999	Returns the Euro currency symbol or whatever is indicated by the NLS_DUAL_CURRENCY parameter.
V	999V99	Returns a value multiplied by $10n$, where n is the number of 9s after the V.
X	XXXX	Returns the hexadecimal value.

| TABLE 6-2 | The NLS Parameters |

NLS Parameter	Description
NLS_NUMERIC_CHARACTERS = 'dg'	d = decimal character (see D in Table 6-1) g = group separator (see G in Table 6-1)
NLS_CURRENCY = 'text'	text = local currency symbol (see L in Table 6-1)
NLS_ISO_CURRENCY = 'currency'	currency = international currency symbol (see C in Table 6-1)

more of those three NLS parameters. For example, the following is one example of the *nls_parms* parameter that provides a specification of two of the NLS parameters:

```
' nls_currency = ''USD'' nls_numeric_characters = '',.'' '
```

Note that since the values are enclosed in single quotes yet include single quotes themselves, each occurrence of the single quotes within the string must be preceded by the escape character—which is a single quote—to clarify that the value is in fact a single quote as part of the string, rather than the end of the overall string literal value.

These values can be used to declare nonstandard NLS parameter values within the incoming *e1* parameter.

Process: Transform *e1* from an expression, perhaps a character string, into a numeric value, using *format_model* to determine what format *e1* may take and where to extract the numeric values from among the formatting information.

Output: Numeric.

Example: In the example that follows, our starting value is a string, '$17,000.23'. This isn't a numeric data type but a character string containing a dollar sign and a comma. The format model here explains that the dollar sign is a symbol and makes it clear where the significant numeric data can be found in the source column. The 9 element in the following example is not a literal number 9 but rather an element of the format model that indicates the presence of any digit. It is repeated to indicate the upper bound of acceptable values. Finally, the output is displayed—a raw numeric value extracted from the character string '$17,000.23'.

```
SELECT TO_NUMBER('$17,000.23','$999,999.99')
FROM    DUAL;

TO_NUMBER('$17,000.23','$999,999.99')
-------------------------------------
17000.23
```

Here is a similar example showing the use of the *nls_parms* parameter:

```
SELECT TO_NUMBER('17.000,23',
                 '999G999D99',
                 'nls_numeric_characters='',.'' ')
                 REFORMATTED_NUMBER
FROM    DUAL;

REFORMATTED_NUMBER
----------------------
17000.23
```

In this example, the incoming value shows a decimal point to mark "thousands" and the comma to mark the decimal point. The *nls_parms* value clarifies this to the TO_NUMBER function, along with the format mask, and the incoming value is interpreted and translated, as shown in the displayed output.

See Table 6-1 for a complete list of the elements that can be included in a numeric format model.

TO_CHAR

The TO_CHAR function converts data from various data types to character data. There are actually three different TO_CHAR functions. They are, in the most technical of terms, three overloaded functions. An *overloaded* function is one that shares a name with one or more functions, but where each is differentiated by their respective parameter lists. Each parameter list specifies a different function, even though they might have the same name.

There are three versions of TO_CHAR: one whose first parameter is a character string, another whose first parameter is a date, and another whose first parameter is numeric.

The following sections describe each of the three TO_CHAR functions.

TO_CHAR—CHARACTER

Syntax: TO_CHAR(*c*)

Parameters: *c* is either an NCHAR, an NVARCHAR2, a CLOB, or an NCLOB.

Process: Transforms the incoming parameter into a VARCHAR2.

Output: VARCHAR2.

Example:

```
SELECT TO_CHAR('Hello') FROM DUAL;

TO_CHAR('HELLO')
----------------
Hello
```

There are situations where you'll work with data types that cannot accept, for example, CLOB data but can accept the output of TO_CHAR, such as a VARCHAR2 data type.

TO_CHAR—NUMBER

Syntax: TO_CHAR(*n*, *format_model*, *nls_parms*)

Parameters: *n* is a number (required). The parameter *format_model* is optional. A format model consists of one or more format elements, which you saw earlier listed in Table 6-1. The *nls_parms* value is the same parameter you saw earlier with the TO_NUMBER function.

Process: Transforms *n* into a character string, using the optional format model for guidance as to how to format the output with any special characters that may be desired, such as dollar signs or other financial symbols, special handling of negative numbers, and so on.

Output: Character.

Example: Format the number 198 with a dollar sign and penny specification.

```
SELECT TO_CHAR(198,'$999.99') FROM DUAL;

TO_CHAR(198,'$999.99')
----------------------
 $198.00
```

TO_CHAR—DATE

Syntax: TO_CHAR(*d*, *format_model*, *nls_parms*)

Parameters: *d* is a date or a date interval (required). The parameter *format_model* is optional and can be used to format data in a variety of ways. See Table 6-3 for details on format models for date data types. The *nls_parms* parameter is the same as you saw earlier for the TO_NUMBER function.

Output: Character.

TABLE 6-3	Date Format Elements *(Continued)*

Element	Description
AD/A.D. BC/B.C.	Anno Domini or Before Christ indicator, with or without periods.
AM/A.M. PM/P.M.	Morning or afternoon hours, with or without periods.
CC/SCC	Century.
D	Day of the week, 1 through 7.
DAY	The name of the day spelled out.
DD	Day of the month, 1 through 31.
DDD	Day of the year, 1 through 366.
DL	Long date format, as determined by the NLS_DATE_FORMAT parameter. The appearance is determined by the NLS_TERRITORY and NLS_LANGUAGE parameters. Sample AMERICAN_AMERICA output is "Saturday, July 27, 2019."
DS	Short date format. Appearance is determined by the NLS_TERRITORY and NLS_LANGUAGE parameters. Sample AMERICAN_AMERICA output is "7/27/2019."
DY	Abbreviated name of day, such as SUN, MON, TUE, and so on.
E	Abbreviated era name.
EE	Full era name.
FF	Fractional seconds.
FM	Used in combination with other elements to direct the suppression of leading or trailing blanks.
FX	Exact matching between the character data and the format model.
HH, HH12	Hour of the day, 1 through 12 (both are identical). 12 midnight is represented as 12.
HH24	Hour of the day, 1 through 24. 12 midnight is represented by 00.
IW	Week of the year, 1 through 53.
I IY IYY	Last one, two, or three digits of the ISO year.
J	Julian day, counted as the number of days since January 1, 4712 B.C.
MI	Minute. 0 through 59.
MM	Month in double digits, 01 through 12.
MON	Abbreviated name of month, such as JAN, FEB, MAR.

TABLE 6-3	Date Format Elements

Element	Description
MONTH	Name of month spelled out.
PR	If negative, numbers are enclosed within angle brackets (<>). If positive, returned with leading and trailing spaces. PR follows specification, for example: 9999PR.
Q	Quarter of year.
RM	Roman numeral month.
RR	Accepts twentieth-century dates in the twenty-first century using only two digits. 00 through 49 is interpreted as 2000 through 2049. 50 through 99 is interpreted as 1950 through 1999.
RRRR	The four-digit year. If provided a two-digit year, it returns the same value as RR.
SS	Seconds, 0 through 59.
SSSS	Seconds past midnight, 0 through 86399.
TS	The short time format. Allowable only when specified with the DL or DS format model element, separated by white space.
TZD	Abbreviated time zone with daylight saving time. Valid only in timestamp and interval formats. Examples: EST, CMT.
TZH	Time zone hour. Not valid in DATE data types; valid only in timestamp and interval formats. 00 through 12.
TZM	Time zone minute. Valid only in timestamp and interval formats. 00 through 59.
TZR	Time zone region information. Not valid in DATE data types; valid only in timestamp and interval formats. Example: America/Los_Angeles.
WW	The week of the year, 1 through 53. Week 1 starts on the first day of the year and ends on the seventh day of the year.
W	The week of the month, 1 through 5. Week 1 starts on the first day of the month and ends on the seventh day of the month.
X	Local radix character. This is the character used in a numeric representation to separate an integer from its fractional part. In base 10 notation, the radix character is a decimal point, as in 17.2, where the decimal point separates the integer 17 from its fractional part of 0.2.
Y,YYY	The year with the comma in position.
YEAR, SYEAR	The year spelled out in English. The S version causes BC dates to display with a minus sign prefix.
YYYY, SYYYY	The four-digit year. The S version causes BC dates to display with a minus sign prefix.
YYY, YY, Y	The last three digits, two digits, or one digit of the year.
- / , . ; :	Punctuation that is accepted in place and passed through as is.
"text"	Literal value. Display as is.

Example: Here's an example of the use of a date format model, as described in Table 6-3:

```
SELECT TO_CHAR(SYSDATE,'DAY, "THE" DD "OF" MONTH, RRRR')
FROM DUAL;

TO_CHAR(SYSDATE,'DAY,"THE"DD"OF"MONTH,RRRR')
-------------------------------------------
WEDNESDAY , THE 17 OF FEBRUARY , 2016
```

The FM code is a format mask that cleans up all of the trailing blanks, as follows:

```
SELECT TO_CHAR(SYSDATE,'FMDAY, "THE" DD "OF" MONTH, RRRR')
FROM DUAL;

TO_CHAR(SYSDATE,'FMDAY,"THE"DD"OF"MONTH,RRRR')
-------------------------------------------------
WEDNESDAY, THE 17 OF FEBRUARY, 2016
```

Changing the format masks to mixed case sends an implied message to mix-case the output as well.

```
SELECT TO_CHAR(SYSDATE,'FMDay, "the" Dd "of" Month, RRRR')
FROM DUAL;

TO_CHAR(SYSDATE,'FMDAY,"THE"DD"OF"MONTH,RRRR')


-------------------------------------------------
Wednesday, the 17 of February, 2016
```

Adding the th indicator introduces an additional improvement. The inclusion of th will append whatever is appropriate after the date—for 1, you'll get "1st"; for 2, you'll get "2nd"; and so on. Here's an example:

```
SELECT TO_CHAR(SYSDATE,'FMDay, "the" Ddth "of" Month, RRRR')
FROM DUAL;

TO_CHAR(SYSDATE,'FMDAY,"THE"DDTH"OF"MONTH,RRRR')
--------------------------------------------------
Wednesday, the 17th of February, 2016
```

The format model is the secret to extracting the time values from SYSDATE. Here's an example:

```
SELECT TO_CHAR(SYSDATE,'HH24:MI:SS AM') FROM DUAL;

TO_CHAR(SYSDATE,'HH24:MI:SSAM')
-------------------------------
17:48:16 PM
```

Notice in this example we can use either AM or PM to indicate where we want the morning/afternoon indicator to be located and whether we want it to include periods. Whether we use AM or PM makes no difference; the appropriate indicator will appear wherever the format model directs, as shown in the preceding example.

The SYSDATE function displays the current date by default as stored on the server on which the database is installed. But buried inside of it is also the time of day, in hours, minutes, and seconds. The full set of data can be extracted from SYSDATE with the format model parameters of the TO_CHAR function, as shown in Table 6-3. But beware, there is danger here, and it's yet another example of how tricky SQL can be. Take a look at this SQL statement:

```
SELECT TO_CHAR(SYSDATE, 'DD-MON-RRRR HH:MM:SS') "Today's Date And Time"
FROM    DUAL;
```

See anything wrong with it? Perhaps not. Most developers don't; this can trip up even the most experienced and seasoned of SQL professionals. Try it on any database instance, and it will work, and the output will probably appear to be correct. But look closely at the value displayed for that portion of the format model represented by MM. Then look at Table 6-3. MM is not minutes; it is months. If you want minutes, you need to use MI, as in HH:MI:SS. Watch this one, folks; it's tricky—the syntax is technically correct, the execution will be successful, and the test data looks correct at a glance. But it's still wrong. The sharp eye of a certified Oracle Database SQL Expert should flag this.

The YY and RR format masks interpret two-digit year representations differently. See the following query:

```
SELECT TO_CHAR(TO_DATE('01-JAN-49','DD-MON-YY'),'YYYY'),
       TO_CHAR(TO_DATE('01-JAN-50','DD-MON-YY'),'YYYY'),
       TO_CHAR(TO_DATE('01-JAN-49','DD-MON-RR'),'RRRR'),
       TO_CHAR(TO_DATE('01-JAN-50','DD-MON-RR'),'RRRR')
FROM    DUAL;

TO_C TO_C TO_C TO_C
---- ---- ---- ----
2049 2050 2049 1950
```

Note that a date entered as 50 is interpreted as 2050 by the YYYY format mask, but 1950 is entered as RRRR. See Table 6-3 for more information about YYYY and RRRR.

The hour of midnight is the starting moment of a new day. The value for midnight is stored consistently but represented differently based on the format model used. In a 24-hour format (HH24), midnight is represented as 00, but in a 12-hour format

(HH12 or HH) midnight is represented as 12. For example, we can specify a date literal at 12 midnight as a string, convert it to a DATE data type using TO_DATE, and then use TO_CHAR with a format mask to illustrate the point.

```
SELECT TO_CHAR(TO_DATE('07-JUL-16 00:00:00','DD-MON-YY HH24:MI:SS'),
            'DD-MON-YY HH24:MI:SS PM') AS MIDNIGHT_HR24,
       TO_CHAR(TO_DATE('07-JUL-16 00:00','DD-MON-YY HH24:MI:SS'),
            'DD-MON-YY HH12:MI:SS PM') AS MIDNIGHT_HR12
FROM   DUAL;


MIDNIGHT_HR24          MIDNIGHT_HR12
--------------------   --------------------
07-JUL-16 00:00:00 AM 07-JUL-16 12:00:00 AM
```

The first column takes the date literal '07-JUL-16' at midnight, converts it to a DATE data type in 24-hour format, and then converts it back to 24-hour format.

The second column starts with the same DATE value but uses TO_CHAR to display the date value with a 12-hour format. Remember that the PM format model specifies the display of PM or AM, whichever is appropriate.

The 24-hour format shows midnight as 00, and the 12-hour format shows midnight as 12. The value stored is not different. Only the representation is different, in accordance with the format model specified.

TO_DATE

Syntax: TO_DATE(c, format_model, nls_parms)

Parameters: c = a character string (required); *format_model* is a format model according to Table 6-3. The *nls_parms* value is the same parameter you saw earlier with the TO_NUMBER function.

Process: Transform the value contained within c into a valid DATE data type by structuring *format_model* to describe how the character string is formed, identifying the date information accordingly.

Output: Date.

Example: Convert a nonstandard date representation to the default format.

```
SELECT TO_DATE('2016-01-31','RRRR-MM-DD')
FROM   DUAL;


TO_DATE('2016-01-31','RRRR-MM-DD')
------------------------
31-JAN-16
```

It is common to nest conversion functions for various reasons—for example, to leverage their formatting capabilities. For example, to determine the weekday of a particular date, you can nest TO_DATE within TO_CHAR, like this: SELECT TO_CHAR(TO_DATE('04-JUL-1776'), 'Day') FROM DUAL, or for the formatted version: SELECT TO_CHAR(TO_DATE('04-JUL-1776'), 'fmDay, Month "the" Ddthsp, Year ') FROM DUAL.

Additional Conversion Functions

We have just discussed the TO_NUMBER, TO_CHAR, and TO_DATE functions, the most widely known of the conversion functions, each of which is called out as an objective on the exam. This section addresses additional conversion functions that have also been known to appear on the certification exam and are increasingly important in working with SQL data types such as TIMESTAMP, intervals, and others.

TO_TIMESTAMP

Syntax: TO_TIMESTAMP (*c, format_model, nls_parms*)

Parameters: *c* is a character data type (required); *format_model* must define the format of *c* corresponding to TIMESTAMP format model elements (optional). The default requirement is that *c* must be in the TIMESTAMP format. The *nls_parms* value is the same parameter you saw earlier with the TO_NUMBER function.

Process: Converts *c* data to the TIMESTAMP data type, which differs from DATE in that it includes fractional seconds. The *format_model* parameter defines the pattern of *c*'s date information to the function so the various elements of TIMESTAMP are identified—information for year, month, day, hours, minutes, seconds, and fractional seconds.

Output: A value in the TIMESTAMP data type.

Example: Here is a character representation of a date. The format model is included to define the pattern and inform the TIMESTAMP function where the DD information is, where the MON information is, and so on.

```
SELECT TO_TIMESTAMP('2020-JAN-01 13:34:00:093423',
                    'RRRR-MON-DD HH24:MI:SS:FF') EVENT_TIME
FROM   DUAL;

EVENT_TIME
------------------------
01-JAN-20 01.34.00.093423000 PM
```

TO_TIMESTAMP_TZ

Syntax: TO_TIMESTAMP_TZ(*c, format_model, nls_parms*)

Parameters: *c* is a character string (required). The *format_model* value must define the format of *c* corresponding to TIMESTAMP WITH TIME ZONE format model elements (optional). The default requirement is that *c* must be in the TIMESTAMP format. The optional *nls_parms* value is the same parameter you saw earlier with the TO_NUMBER function.

Process: Transforms *c* into a value of TIMESTAMP WITH TIME ZONE, where *format_model* defines the format in which *c* stores the TIMESTAMP WITH TIME ZONE information. The time zone will default to that defined by the SESSION parameter.

Output: A value in the TIMESTAMP WITH TIME ZONE data type.

Example: Convert the character string '17-04-2016 16:45:30' to a data type of TIMESTAMP WITH TIME ZONE by providing a format mask.

```
SELECT TO_TIMESTAMP_TZ('17-04-2016 16:45:30','DD-MM-RRRR HH24:MI:SS') "Time"
FROM   DUAL;

Time
-------------
17-APR-16 04.45.30.000000000 PM AMERICA/NEW_YORK
```

on the **Job**

Note that there isn't a conversion function that specifically converts values into the TIMESTAMP WITH LOCAL TIME ZONE data type. For that, use CAST, described later in this chapter.

TO_YMINTERVAL

Syntax: TO_YMINTERVAL ('*y-m*')

Parameters: *y* and *m* are numbers contained within a string (required).

Process: Transforms *y* and *m* into the years and months in a format of the data type INTERVAL YEAR TO MONTHS.

Output: A value in the INTERVAL YEAR TO MONTHS data type.

Example: Convert the character expression showing four years and six months into the data type INTERVAL YEAR TO MONTHS.

```
SELECT TO_YMINTERVAL('04-06') EVENT_TIME
FROM   DUAL;

EVENT_TIME
-----------
4-6
```

TO_DSINTERVAL

Syntax: TO_DSINTERVAL (*sql_format*, *nls_parms*)

Parameters: *sql_format* is a character string in the format required for the INTERVAL DAY TO SECOND data type, which is 'DAYS HH24:MI:SS.FF'. For example, '15 14:05:10.001' is the INTERVAL DAY TO SECOND representation for 15 days, 14 hours, 5 minutes, and 10.001 seconds. The *nls_parms* value is the same parameter you saw earlier with the TO_NUMBER function.

Process: Transforms the incoming value represented in *sql_format* to a value of the INTERVAL DAY TO SECOND data type.

Output: A value in the INTERVAL DAY TO SECOND data type.

Example: The following converts a value representing 40 days, 8 hours, 30 minutes, and 0.03225 seconds into the INTERVAL DAY TO SECOND data type:

```
SELECT TO_DSINTERVAL('40 08:30:00.03225') EVENT_TIME
FROM    DUAL;

EVENT_TIME
-----------
40 8:30:0.032250000
```

NUMTOYMINTERVAL

Syntax: NUMTOYMINTERVAL (*n*, *interval_unit*)

Parameters: *n* = number (required). *interval_unit* = one of the following values: 'YEAR' or 'MONTH'.

Process: Converts date information in numeric form into an interval value of time.

Output: A value in the INTERVAL YEAR TO MONTH data type.

Example: The following example takes the number 27 and transforms it into a value representing a time interval of 27 months, which equates to 2 years and 3 months, in the INTERVAL YEAR TO MONTH data type. The 2-3 value shows that 2 years and 3 months is the amount of time that results.

```
SELECT NUMTOYMINTERVAL(27,'MONTH')
FROM    DUAL;

NUMTOYMINTERVAL(27,'MONTH')
---------------------------
2-3
```

NUMTODSINTERVAL

Syntax: NUMTODSINTERVAL (*n*, *interval_unit*)

Parameters: *n* = number (required). *interval_unit* = one of the following: 'DAY', 'HOUR', 'MINUTE', or 'SECOND'.

Process: Converts date information in numeric form into an interval value of time.

Output: A value of the data type INTERVAL DAY TO SECOND.

Example: The following example translates 36 hours into its formal representation of 1 day and 12 hours in the data type INTERVAL DAY TO SECOND, which displays a single number for day, followed by hours, minutes, seconds, and fractional seconds.

```
SELECT NUMTODSINTERVAL(36,'HOUR')
FROM   DUAL;

NUMTODSINTERVAL(36,'HOUR')
--------------------------
1 12:0:0.0
```

CAST

Syntax: CAST(*e* AS *d*)

Parameters: *e* is an expression; *d* is a data type.

Process: Converts *e* to *d*. This is particularly useful for converting text representations of datetime information into datetime formats, particularly TIMESTAMP WITH LOCAL TIME ZONE.

Output: A value in the *d* data type.

Example: In the following, we convert a value in the default timestamp format, presented as a literal value:

```
SELECT CAST('19-JAN-16 11:35:30'
            AS TIMESTAMP WITH LOCAL TIME ZONE) "Converted LTZ"
FROM   DUAL;

Converted LTZ
-------------
19-JAN-16 11.35.30.000000000 AM
```

If we want to use a format mask for any reason, we can nest a call to, for example, the TO_TIMESTAMP conversion function, as follows:

```
SELECT CAST(TO_TIMESTAMP('19-JAN-16 14:35:30','DD-MON-RR HH24:MI:SS')
            AS TIMESTAMP WITH LOCAL TIME ZONE) "Converted LTZ"
FROM    DUAL;

Converted LTZ
-------------
19-JAN-16 02.35.30.000000000 PM
```

CERTIFICATION OBJECTIVE 6.03

Apply General Functions and Conditional Expressions in a SELECT Statement

The power of conditional expressions is well known in every software programming language, most of which feature an IF statement with some combination of ELSE, THEN, or something comparable. Conditional expressions evaluate data at the time of code execution and change the code's logical approach to processing based on certain values of data at run time. For example, processing may determine first if a particular employee is in a certain department, and if so, apply a bonus; if not, processing may assign a pay raise.

SQL does not have an IF statement, but it does feature conditional expressions. The CASE statement evaluates an expression and, based on its value, evaluates one of a series of expressions as specified in the CASE statement. The DECODE statement is similar; it is the original IF THEN ELSE of Oracle SQL. The NVL function is useful to returning rows of data that might contain NULL values where you want the NULL to be replaced with something more relevant to your immediate purposes, perhaps a numeric zero, for example. NULLIF is useful for comparing two values and returning a NULL value when both values are identical. For example, this is helpful in certain situations where you are trying to flag only variations or discrepancies between two data sets.

This section will look at these functions and expressions.

CASE

Syntax: CASE *expression1* WHEN *condition1* THEN *result1* WHEN *condition2* THEN *result2* . . . ELSE *resultfinal* END

Parameters: *expression1* can be a column in a SELECT statement's select list or any other valid expression (required). If *expression1* evaluates to a value that is equal to *condition1*, then the function returns *result1*. Additional WHEN/THEN comparison pairs may be included. The first pair is required; additional pairs are optional. An optional ELSE at the end will return the value of *resultfinal* if no WHEN/THEN comparison pair matched.

Process: Compare all the pairs to determine which value will be returned. If no values match, *resultfinal* is returned. If no values match and no ELSE clause is included, NULL is returned.

Example:

```
SELECT CASE 'option1'
        WHEN 'option1' THEN 'found it'
        WHEN 'option2' THEN 'did not find it'
        END AS "Answer"
FROM    DUAL;


Answer
----------------
found it
```

The function starts with the keyword CASE and ends with the keyword END. The CASE expression may include a column name, like this:

```
SELECT SHIP_NAME,
        CAPACITY,
        CASE CAPACITY WHEN 2052 THEN 'MEDIUM'
                      WHEN 2974 THEN 'LARGE'
                      END AS CABIN_SIZE
FROM    SHIPS
WHERE   SHIP_ID <= 4;


SHIP_NAME             CAPACITY                 CABIN_SIZE
-------------------- ------------------------ ----------
Codd Crystal         2052                     MEDIUM
Codd Elegance        2974                     LARGE
Codd Champion        2974                     LARGE
Codd Victorious      2974                     LARGE
```

Note that in this example the CASE function takes in a numeric value and returns a text string.

DECODE

Syntax: DECODE(*e, search_expression, d*)

Parameters: *e, search_expression,* and *d* are all expressions. The first two are required; the third is optional.

Process: *e* is a required expression; *search_expression* is a series of pairs of expressions, *se1* and *se2*, each separated by commas; if *e* equals *se1*, then DECODE should return *se2*. Otherwise, it should return *d*. If *d* is omitted, DECODE will return NULL.

In DECODE, two NULL values are considered to be equivalent. NULL compared to NULL will produce a TRUE result and send the corresponding value back if required. In other words, the use of NULL within DECODE is interpreted as a comparison of IS NULL as opposed to = NULL. Remember that = NULL will always return a false since NULL is unknown; think of it as "I don't know." So, is some particular value, say, 4, equal to "I don't know"? Who knows? Nobody knows, and SQL assumes FALSE in every such case. But IS NULL is asking a different question: is the value in question a NULL, or unknown, value? That's how DECODE uses NULL, in the context of the IS NULL comparison. In this case, a comparison of a NULL value will result in a true condition.

Output: If the data types of *e* and the first occurrence of *se1* are character, DECODE will return a value of data type VARCHAR2. If the data types of *e* and the first occurrence of *se1* are numeric, DECODE will return a value of numeric data type.

Example: In the example that follows, we select rows from ADDRESSES by looking at the STATE column value as is and then use DECODE to translate the values in STATE according to the *search_expression* in DECODE, which in this case looks at only two state values but could have easily been expanded to translate, or decode, all of the state values. The final item in this DECODE example is 'Other', which is assigned to all values of STATE that aren't found in our *search_expression* list—including the NULL value for STATE.

```
SELECT STATE, DECODE(STATE,'CA', 'California',
                           'IL','Illinois',
                           'Other') AS DECODED_STATE
FROM    ADDRESSES;
```

```
STATE DECODED_STATE
----- -------------
CA    California
TX    Other
IL    Illinois
AB    Other
NY    Other
      Other
QC    Other
```

The DECODE function is often referred to as the IF-THEN-ELSE of Oracle SQL.

NVL

Syntax: NVL($e1$, $e2$)

Parameters: $e1$ and $e2$ are expressions, both are required, and both should be of the same data type, but automatic data type conversion applies here, so values may be different as long as they are capable of being converted to the same data type automatically.

Process: If $e1$ has a value of NULL, then NVL returns the value for $e2$. Otherwise, it returns $e1$. The intent of NVL is to use it in a query where multiple rows are being returned and you expect that perhaps some of the rows might be NULL. There's nothing wrong with that in and of itself, but what if you are performing some sort of processing that can't take a value of NULL? For example, a single NULL value within a mathematical calculation will automatically make the answer NULL. You can use NVL to substitute something meaningful in the place of NULL—such as a zero—to satisfy the outer function.

Output: If $e1$ has a character data type, the output will be VARCHAR2. If $e1$ is numeric, the output will be numeric. If the output is NULL, then it's NULL.

Example: Note that we have three expressions in the SELECT list that follows. The first simply shows that we're using NVL to replace the literal value for NULL with a zero. This is useless by itself, but it proves the point of what the NVL function does. The second expression shows an equation in which we add 14 to NULL and subtract 4 from the result. But what is 14 plus NULL? It's NULL. So is NULL minus 4. (Remember, NULL is the absence of information. What is 14 plus "I don't know"? The answer is "I don't know," which is NULL.)

So in the third expression, we use NVL to replace NULL with a 0, and we get an answer of 10.

```
SELECT NVL(NULL,0) FIRST_ANSWER,
       14+NULL-4 SECOND_ANSWER,
       14+NVL(NULL,0)-4 THIRD_ANSWER
FROM   DUAL;

FIRST_ANSWER            SECOND_ANSWER          THIRD_ANSWER
--------------------    --------------------   --------------------
0                                              10
```

The purpose of the preceding example is to show what you can do with NVL. A more likely scenario would be something like this:

```
SELECT SQ_FT + NVL(BALCONY_SQ_FT,0)
FROM   SHIP_CABINS;
```

This SQL code adds the square feet of a ship's cabin with the square feet of its balcony. But what if there isn't a balcony and a NULL value is returned for BALCONY_SQ_FT? The entire result would be NULL, unless we use the NVL function as we do in the preceding example.

NULLIF

Syntax: NULLIF(*e1*, *e2*)

Parameters: *e1* and *e2* are both expressions (required). They must be the same data type.

Process: If *e1* and *e2* are the same, NULLIF returns NULL. Otherwise, it returns *e1*.

Output: An expression matching the data types of the input parameters.

Example: NULLIF is good for comparing multiple rows wherein an older and newer version of a particular value exist and you want to cull out those that are still not updated or perhaps have already been updated.

```
SELECT TEST_SCORE,
       UPDATED_TEST_SCORE,
       NULLIF(UPDATED_TEST_SCORE,TEST_SCORE) REVISION_ONLY
FROM   SCORES;

TEST_SCORE UPDATED_TEST_SCORE REVISION_ONLY
---------- ------------------ -------------
95         95
55         75                 75
83         83
```

In the preceding example, the column UPDATED_TEST_SCORE represents a set of values that includes older TEST_SCORE values and those that have been revised for some reason. The NULLIF function helps filter out only those values that represent changes to the older original values, as evidenced in the third SELECT column with the column alias REVISION_ONLY.

CERTIFICATION SUMMARY

Conversion functions transform values from one data type to another. The most common conversion functions are date, text, and numeric conversion functions. The use of a conversion function to perform data type conversion is considered "explicit conversion," as opposed to "implicit conversion" which may occur automatically when your code omits any use of a conversion function, yet the situation requires such a transformation and SQL language processing performs the conversion anyway. Good programming practice is to use explicit data type conversion to clarify the intent of your code and increase the odds of catching potential errors in context, which can potentially improve troubleshooting.

Certain conversion functions do more than transform values from one data type to another. Some are used to apply format models to format values for various purposes—such as to quickly generate a meaningful report, or to extract details not present in the standard default presentation of certain types of data. Date conversion functions can be used to determine the day of the week for a given date, or to be transformed into a textual presentation of the date; numeric conversion functions can be formatted with financial formats in accordance with a given locale, with commas, periods, and other special characters as appropriate.

The most commonly used conversion functions are TO_NUMBER, TO_CHAR, and TO_DATE.

Datetime conversion functions include TO_TIMESTAMP, TO_DSINTERVAL, and TO_YMINTERVAL.

The CASE and DECODE functions are like IF-THEN-ELSE logic for a SQL statement. They can be used as any other function in virtually any DML statement, subquery, SELECT list, WHERE clause, or anywhere a SQL expression can be invoked.

CASE compares a single expression to a series of WHEN conditions. If the expression evaluates to a value equal to a WHEN condition, the WHEN condition's corresponding THEN result is returned. An optional ELSE result may be included as well. The CASE statement completes with the keyword END. The complete

CASE statement is considered an expression and as such may be included anywhere in a SQL statement that an expression is permitted.

DECODE considers a single expression. If that expression evaluates to any one of a series of specified comparison expressions, that specified expression's evaluated value is returned. An optional final expression may be included as the default value to be returned in the event that none of the comparison expressions matches the evaluated expression.

The NVL function takes two parameters that are both expressions. If the first expression evaluates to a non-NULL value, it is returned as is, but if it evaluates to NULL, the second expression is returned. The purpose of the NVL function is to replace any NULL values with something you specify. For example, you might query a table of names and want to replace any missing middle names with the expression "NMN" (for no middle name). NVL is ideal for queries in which some values might return a NULL but you prefer instead to return an alternative value. One common use is in math equations. For example, within a math expression, you can use NVL to substitute any values that might be NULL with something that isn't NULL—like a zero—to enable the math equations to calculate something meaningful.

NULLIF compares a subject value with a candidate value and returns NULL if both values are identical. This is useful in reports analyzing discrepancies.

TWO-MINUTE DRILL

Describe Various Types of Conversion Functions

- ☐ Most data types fall into the categories of numeric, text, and data types.
- ☐ Conversion functions include TO_NUMBER, TO_CHAR, and TO_DATE.
- ☐ If no data type conversion function is explicitly specified, sometimes SQL will perform an implicit data type conversion if it determines that one is required.
- ☐ Implicit data type conversion can result in unpredictable outcomes. Therefore, Oracle formally advises the use of explicit data type conversions where possible.
- ☐ SQL provides explicit data type conversion functions for each data type.

Use the TO_CHAR, TO_NUMBER, and TO_DATE Conversion Functions

- ☐ TO_CHAR can convert from character, date, or numeric data and into character data.
- ☐ The conversion function TO_TIMESTAMP can convert to the TIMESTAMP data type, which is the same as DATE but adds fractional seconds.
- ☐ The functions TO_DSINTERVAL and TO_YMINTERVAL convert to interval data types INTERVAL DAY TO SECOND and INTERVAL YEAR TO MONTH.

Apply General Functions and Conditional Expressions in a SELECT Statement

- ☐ CASE and DECODE accept optional default values to return if the evaluated expression doesn't match any of the specified possible matches.
- ☐ NVL considers an expression—such as a column—and evaluates its value to determine whether the value is NULL.
- ☐ NVL is popular in math equations where the source data might be NULL but the equation requires some value, perhaps a zero.
- ☐ The expression (SALARY + BONUS) will return NULL if the value for SALARY is equal to, say, 100, but BONUS is NULL. The expression (SALARY + NVL(BONUS,0)) will return 100 if the SALARY is 100 and the BONUS is NULL.
- ☐ NULLIF returns a NULL if both parameters are equal.

SELF TEST

The following questions will help you measure your understanding of the material presented in this chapter. Choose one correct answer for each question unless otherwise directed.

Describe Various Types of Conversion Functions

1. Conversion functions:
   A. Change a column's data type so that future data stored in the table will be preserved in the converted data type.
   B. Change a value's data type in an equation to tell SQL to treat the value as that specified data type.
   C. Are similar to ALTER TABLE ... MODIFY statements.
   D. Are not required because SQL performs automatic data type conversion where necessary.

2. Which of the following statements are true? (Choose two.)
   A. You can use a data type conversion function to format numeric data to display with dollar signs and commas.
   B. The presence of an explicit data type conversion documents your intent in the code.
   C. Depending on the values, you can successfully use an explicit data type conversion to transform numeric values to text but not the other way around; you can't explicitly convert text to numeric.
   D. An implicit data type conversion performs faster than an explicit data type conversion.

3. Conversion functions cannot be used to:
   A. Format date values
   B. Convert columns to new data types
   C. Transform data
   D. Create user-defined data types

Use the TO_CHAR, TO_NUMBER, and TO_DATE Conversion Functions

4. If you want to display a numeric value with dollar signs and commas, which of the following is the best approach to take?
   A. The TO_NUMBER function with a format model
   B. The TO_CHAR function with a format model
   C. A combination of string literals that contain commas and dollar signs, along with the CONCAT function
   D. The MONEY data type

5. Which of the following SQL statements will display the current time, in hours, minutes, and seconds, as determined by the operating system on which the database server resides?
   A.   SELECT TO_CHAR(SYSDATE) FROM DUAL;
   B.   SELECT TO_CHAR(SYSDATE, 'HR:MI:SE') FROM DUAL;
   C.   SELECT TO_CHAR(SYSDATE, 'HH:MI:SS') FROM DUAL;
   D.   SELECT TO_CHAR(SYSDATE, 'HH:MM:SS') FROM DUAL;

6. Which query returns an expression of the data type INTERVAL YEAR TO MONTHS representing an interval of 1 year and 3 months?
   A.   SELECT TO_YMINTERVAL('01:03') FROM DUAL;
   B.   SELECT TO_YMINTERVAL('01-03') FROM DUAL;
   C.   SELECT TO_INTERVALYM('01:03') FROM DUAL;
   D.   SELECT TO_INTERVALYM('01-03') FROM DUAL;

7. You need to determine the day of the week for a particular date in the future. Which function will reveal this information?
   A.   TO_CHAR
   B.   DAY_OF_WEEK
   C.   TO_DATE
   D.   None of the above

8. You are tasked to create a report that displays the hours and minutes of the current date in a report. Which of the following will satisfy this requirement?
   A.   TO_DATE(SYSDATE, 'HH:MM')
   B.   TO_DATE(SYSDATE, 'HH:MI')
   C.   TO_CHAR(SYSDATE, 'HH:MM')
   D.   TO_CHAR(SYSDATE, 'HH:MI')

9. Which format mask returns the local currency symbol?
   A.   L
   B.   C
   C. $
   D.   None of the above

Apply General Functions and Conditional Expressions in a SELECT Statement

10. The purpose of NULLIF is to:
   A.   Return a NULL if a single column is NULL
   B.   Return a NULL if a single expression is NULL
   C.   Both of the above
   D.   None of the above

11. Consider the following query, its output, and a subsequent query:

```
SQL> SELECT * FROM LINE_ITEMS;
LINE_ITEM  PRICE
---------  -----
      100   4.12
      210
      184   7.07

SQL> SELECT NVL(PRICE,10) FROM LINE_ITEMS;
```

What is true of the final query shown previously?

A. It will return "no rows found" because there is no PRICE of 10.

B. It will return only the row where LINE_ITEM is 210.

C. It will return no rows because there is no PRICE of 10.

D. It will return three rows, but it will not change the price for line items 100 and 184.

12. Consider the following table listing from the table ALARM_HISTORY:

```
TRACKING_DATE   INCIDENTS
-------------   ---------
  17-OCT-2018        12
  18-OCT-2018         3
  19-OCT-2018
  20-OCT-2018
  21-OCT-2018         4
```

You are tasked to calculate the average number of alarm incidents per day in ALARM_HISTORY. You know the following query is syntactically correct:

```
SELECT AVG(INCIDENTS) FROM ALARM_HISTORY;
```

However, you are aware that the value for INCIDENTS might be NULL, and you want the AVG returned to be calculated across every day in ALARM_HISTORY, not just the non-NULL days. Which of the following queries will achieve this goal?

A. SELECT AVG(NVL(INCIDENTS)) FROM ALARM_HISTORY;

B. SELECT AVG(NVL(INCIDENTS,0)) FROM ALARM_HISTORY;

C. SELECT NVL(AVG(INCIDENTS)) FROM ALARM_HISTORY;

D. SELECT NVL(AVG(INCIDENTS,0)) FROM ALARM_HISTORY;

13. Which of the following can be said of the CASE statement?

    A. It converts text to uppercase.

    B. It uses the keyword IF.

    C. It uses the keyword THEN.

    D. Its END keyword is optional.

14. Consider the following statement:

```
01    SELECT  NVL(SHIP_NAME,'None'),
02            CASE CAPACITY WHERE 234 THEN 'OK'
03                          WHERE 999 THEN 'OK'
04            END
05    FROM  SHIPS;
```

Which of the following statements is true of the previous SELECT statement?

    A. The statement will fail with a compilation error because there is no column alias on the NVL expression (line 1).

    B. The statement will fail because of syntax errors on lines 2 and 3.

    C. The statement will fail because of the keyword END on the fourth line.

    D. The statement will execute successfully.

15. The DECODE expression always ends with:

    A. The keyword END

    B. A default expression to return if no other value matched the source expression

    C. Both of the above

    D. Neither of the above

SELF TEST ANSWERS

Describe Various Types of Conversion Functions

1. ☑ **B.** A conversion function tells SQL to treat a specified value as a specified data type for any subsequent use within a particular expression.

   ☒ **A, C,** and **D** are incorrect. Conversion functions do not change anything about a table's structure. They are not the same as ALTER TABLE ... MODIFY, which can be used to change a column's data type in a table. Conversion functions have a temporary impact; their scope is the SQL expression in which they are being used, and they leave no lasting impact beyond that. However, they are used since you cannot count on SQL's implicit data type conversion working as your business rules might require at all times. It is the formal recommendation of Oracle to use explicit data type conversion where relevant and required and to not count on implicit conversion within your production SQL code.

2. ☑ **A and B.** One of the most common uses of conversion functions is to format data, such as numeric and date formatting. The use of an explicit data type conversion function clarifies your purpose in the code and your expectation about what sort of values are contained within the various elements of your code.

   ☒ **C and D** are incorrect. You can explicitly convert numeric to text and also text to numeric; if the values make sense, then conversion will succeed. In other words, you can convert the text value '1' to the numeric value of 1. Also, explicit conversion functions perform more efficiently than a reliance on implicit conversions.

3. ☑ **B and D.** Conversion functions cannot change the data type of a column to something else. They cannot create user-defined data types.

   ☒ **A and C** are incorrect. Conversion functions are capable of formatting and transforming date, text, and numeric data as they perform data type conversions.

Use the TO_CHAR, TO_NUMBER, and TO_DATE Conversion Functions

4. ☑ **B.** The TO_CHAR function would work, along with a format model, such as TO_CHAR(rawNumber, '$999,999.99').

   ☒ **A, C,** and **D** are incorrect. The TO_NUMBER function works with format masks, but it converts from characters to numeric values, not the other way around. You may be able to use a combination of concatenation and string literals, but it would be painstakingly difficult, and people would laugh at you. Such an approach would be particularly problematic in a dynamic environment where the significant numbers involved could fluctuate. There is no MONEY data type in Oracle SQL.

5. ☑ **C.** The correct format mask is 'HH:MI:SS'.
   ☒ **A, B,** and **D** are incorrect. TO_CHAR with no format mask executes successfully but does nothing and shows the date alone. There is no SE format mask. **D** is tricky—it works and produces output, but the MM format mask indicates months, not minutes, and is logically incorrect.

6. ☑ **B.** The TO_YMINTERVAL function is correct, with the single parameter of a string containing two numbers, separated by a dash, where the first represents years in the interval, and the second represents the number of months in the interval.
   ☒ **A, C,** and **D** are incorrect. There is no TO_INTERVALYM function. The use of a colon is inappropriate in the TO_YMINTERVAL function.

7. ☑ **A.** Here's an example: SELECT TO_CHAR(SYSDATE,'Day') FROM DUAL;.
   ☒ **B, C,** and **D** are incorrect. There is no DAY_OF_WEEK function. The TO_DATE function converts text to date formats but doesn't include this sort of formatting.

8. ☑ **D.** The TO_CHAR function formats dates. The HH and MI format masks display hours and minutes, respectively.
   ☒ **A, B,** and **C** are incorrect. The TO_DATE function will not accept SYSDATE as incoming data. The TO_DATE function does perform formatting, but generally not for display in a report; instead, it can convert formats to transform incoming data into the format required for storage in the database. The TO_CHAR function is correct, but the MM format mask is used for months, not minutes.

9. ☑ **A.** L is the local currency symbol format mask.
   ☒ **B, C,** and **D** are incorrect. **C** is not a format mask. The $ specifies that the USD currency symbol should be used but will override any conflicting local currency symbol.

Apply General Functions and Conditional Expressions in a SELECT Statement

10. ☑ **D.** The purpose of NULLIF is to take two parameters, both of which are expressions, and return a NULL value if the two expressions evaluate to NULL. One common use is to analyze two sets of data and look for discrepancies; the inclusion of NULLIF can omit those expressions that are identical in order to highlight the discrepancies.
    ☒ **A, B,** and **C** are incorrect. NULLIF does not particularly care whether one expression is NULL or not; it assesses whether two expressions are identical.

11. ☑ **D.** The SELECT will return all three rows, changing only the price for line items 210 to 10, and nothing else.
    ☒ **A, B,** and **C** are incorrect. NVL is not used here to search for rows that match the specified number, which in this case is 10. It is used to transform any occurrences of NULL

values to the specified number, which, again, in this case is 10. NVL is not incorporated into the WHERE clause in this situation, so it is only filtering data within the rows, not filtering the rows themselves; therefore, it is not going to limit the rows returned, as is the case with all functions. NVL is no different in that regard.

12. ☑ **B.** The NVL function should be applied first, which means it should be the innermost nested function. NVL requires two parameters.

☒ **A, C,** and **D** are incorrect. NVL does not work with one parameter, it requires two. The NVL function should be the innermost function in order to first transform NULL

13. ☑ **C.** It uses the keyword THEN. Here's an example: SELECT CASE CAPACITY WHEN 2074 THEN 'MEDIUM' WHEN 4000 THEN 'LARGE' END FROM SHIPS;.

☒ **A, B,** and **D** are incorrect. It does not convert text; CASE is a conditional expression. It does not incorporate the IF keyword but is often said to be sort of an IF-THEN-ELSE expression. The keyword END is required.

14. ☑ **B.** The SQL statement contains the same syntax error repeated twice: the keyword WHERE is incorrect. The keyword WHEN is correct.

☒ **A, C,** and **D** are incorrect. The column alias is optional but not required. The keyword END is correct and required for CASE. The statement will not execute successfully due to the WHERE syntax conflict.

15. ☑ **D.** Neither answer is correct. The keyword END is used with CASE but never appears with DECODE. DECODE does accept a default value, but its inclusion is optional and not required.

☒ **A, B,** and **C** are incorrect.

7

Reporting Aggregated Data Using the Group Functions

I n Chapter 5, we looked at single-row functions, which process rows individually and return one answer for each row. This chapter reviews functions and features in SQL that have the ability to process zero or more rows as a logical set, analyzed together to return a single-row result. These functions are referred to as *group* functions since they accept input from groups of zero or more rows. We will also look at two new clauses in the SELECT statement: the GROUP BY clause and its companion, the HAVING clause. GROUP BY and HAVING are used with group functions. You will need to fully understand these concepts and their uses in order to pass the exam.

CERTIFICATION OBJECTIVE 7.01

Describe the Use of Group Functions

The functions we reviewed in Chapter 5 are referred to as *single-row* functions. The term *single-row* means that each function returns one value for each one row it encounters. Another term for single-row function is *scalar* function.

The focus of this chapter is the category referred to as *group* functions. A group function returns one value for each set of zero or more rows it encounters. There are two kinds of group functions: *aggregate* and *analytic* functions.

Aggregate functions are also known as *multirow* functions. Aggregate functions are typically used with a SELECT statement that selects many rows, where the aggregate function scans a set of rows and returns a single answer for all of them.

Analytic functions can consider a set of rows and process them as a single set or as varying subsets, including overlapping subsets. In other words, a single source row may be represented in more than one subsetted rows of an analytic function's output.

You've already seen the syntax of analytic functions in Chapter 5 when we looked at the STDDEV, PERCENTILE_CONT, LAG, and LEAD. We'll see that syntax again in the upcoming section about the RANK and DENSE_RANK group functions.

Many of the group functions can be used as an aggregate function and also as an analytic function, based on the syntax of the particular statement in which it is invoked. There are a few exceptions. Table 7-1 summarizes some of the more commonly used group functions available in SQL. Note that most of the functions listed can perform as either an aggregate or an analytic function; a few are limited to only one type.

Like scalar functions, group functions accept input, process that input, and return output. Also like scalar functions, group functions accept input of specific

TABLE 7-1	Commonly Used Aggregate Functions—Overview		
Function(s)	**Description**	**Aggregate**	**Analytic**
COUNT, SUM, MIN, MAX, AVG, MEDIAN	The more commonly used aggregate functions	Yes	Yes[1]
VARIANCE, VAR_POP, VAR_SAMP, COVAR_POP, COVAR_SAMP, STDDEV, STDDEV_POP, STDDEV_SAMP	Variance and standard deviation, with options for population standard deviation and cumulative standard deviation	Yes	Yes
RANK, DENSE_RANK, PERCENT_RANK PERCENTILE_CONT, PERCENTILE_ DISC, CUME_DIST, FIRST, LAST	Ranking functions and associated keywords	Yes	Yes
GROUP_ID, GROUPING, GROUPING_ID	Grouping features for use with GROUP BY . . . ROLLUP and CUBE	Yes	No

[1]Except MEDIAN—see RANK or DENSE_RANK instead.

data types and return output of specific data types, and the input and output data types are not necessarily the same, as with scalar functions. While numeric group functions (which process and return numeric data) are the most common, many group functions process data with character and date data types.

Group functions must be treated separately from scalar functions because they behave differently. A typical SELECT statement cannot invoke group functions and scalar functions at the same level of aggregation. For example, consider a table SHIP_SHOP with three rows of data. If we execute a simple SELECT statement on the table with a scalar function like ROUND, we will get one row returned for every row processed.

```
DESC ship_shop
Name                          Null?  Type
----------------------------  -----  ------------------
ID                                   NUMBER
ITEM                                 VARCHAR2(30)
PRICE                                NUMBER(5,2)

SQL> SELECT item, price, ROUND(price) FROM ship_shop;

ITEM        PRICE    ROUND(price)
----------  -------  ------------
Towel        21.99            22
Postcard      2.49             2
Mug           7.19             7
```

If we execute a simple SELECT statement against the same set of three rows using a group function like AVG (for average), we will get a one-row result showing the average value for all three rows.

```
SQL>SELECT AVG(price) FROM ship_shop;

AVG(price)
----------------
10.5566667
```

If we combine both at the same level of aggregation, we will get an error message.

```
SQL>SELECT ROUND(price), AVG(price) FROM ship_shop;

SELECT ROUND(price), AVG(price) FROM ship_shop;
                     *
ERROR at line 1:
ORA-00937: not a single-group group function
```

The problem here is that we are starting with three rows of input and trying to combine results of a scalar and group function at the same level of aggregation. The scalar (ROUND) wants to return three rows, but the group function (AVG) wants to return one row. This is not permitted together in the same SELECT output and triggers the error message.

However, we can use the two types of functions at different levels of aggregation in the same SELECT statement. For example, we could first perform the average (the group function) and then round the results (the scalar function).

```
SQL>SELECT ROUND(AVG(price)) FROM ship_shop;

ROUND(AVG(PRICE))
----------------
              11
```

Alternatively, we could round the individual values first and then take an average of the rounded numbers.

```
SQL>SELECT AVG(ROUND(price)) FROM ship_shop;

AVG(ROUND(PRICE))
----------------
       10.3333333
```

Either way, the point is that we cannot apply both scalar and group functions together onto rows at the same level of aggregation. However, we can choose to nest the function calls within a single SQL statement to process each set of rows one at a time, passing the results of one to another, combined within a single SELECT statement, by nesting the functions.

Let's look at the detailed functionality of some of the more commonly used group functions.

Group functions can be called from four places in a SELECT statement: the select list; the ORDER BY clause; and either of two additional clauses we'll look at in this chapter, namely, the GROUP BY clause and the HAVING clause.

The major group functions are described in detail in the following sections.

Note: All functions are presented in their aggregate function syntax unless otherwise specified in the text.

COUNT

Syntax: COUNT(*e1*)

Parameters: *e1* is an expression. *e1* can be any data type.

The aggregate function COUNT determines the number of occurrences of non-NULL values. It considers the value of an expression and determines whether that value is NOT NULL for each row it encounters.

For example, consider the VENDORS table, shown in Figure 7-1.

Let's look at all the rows in the VENDORS table:

```
SELECT VENDOR_NAME, STATUS, CATEGORY
FROM    VENDORS;
```

Here's the output, showing that we have two rows in the table:

```
VENDOR_NAME          STATUS                 CATEGORY
-------------------- ---------------------- ----------
Acme Steaks          17
Acme Poker Chips
```

```
                          VENDORS
P * VENDOR_ID        NUMBER
    VENDOR_NAME      VARCHAR2 (20 BYTE)
    STATUS           NUMBER (3)
    CATEGORY         VARCHAR2 (10 BYTE)
  PK_VENDOR_ID
```

We haven't selected every column here, and we don't need to for our purposes. But assume that the blank entries in the output are NULL values and not blank spaces—so that the STATUS column contains only one value, and CATEGORY has none.

Now let's look at the following SELECT statement that tries to count occurrences of data in each of these columns:

```
SELECT  COUNT(VENDOR_NAME),  COUNT(STATUS),  COUNT(CATEGORY)
FROM    VENDORS;

COUNT(VENDOR_NAME)       COUNT(STATUS)          COUNT(CATEGORY)
----------------------   --------------------   -------------------
2                        1                      0
```

The term NULL does not describe a value at all but rather the lack of a value. It is the database saying, "I don't know what this value might be, if anything." Keep this in mind each time you encounter the phrase NULL: a NULL is the lack of a value.

Notice that COUNT ignores any and all values that are NULL. Finally, we can simply count the number of rows in the entire table.

```
SELECT  COUNT(*)
FROM    VENDORS;

COUNT(*)
----------------------
2
```

COUNT will return only the number, or quantity, of non-NULL values in columns; or, when used to count rows, it returns the number of rows.

Recall that SELECT * FROM *table* is the shorthand way of asking to select all the columns in a given table. The COUNT function is often used with the asterisk in this fashion to get a quick count on all the rows in a given table using COUNT(*).

We could have mixed these functions in various combinations.

```
SELECT  COUNT(*),  COUNT(VENDOR_NAME)
FROM    VENDORS;

COUNT(*)                 COUNT(VENDOR_NAME)
----------------------   ----------------------
2                        2
```

Note that a COUNT of the asterisk is asking for a count of all rows. In the rare situation where a row contains nothing but NULL values in all of its columns, COUNT(*) will still count that row.

It's worth noting that COUNT will never return NULL. If it encounters no values at all, it will at least return a value of 0 (zero). This is not the case with all of the aggregates, but it's true with COUNT. This becomes important when working with subqueries, which we'll study in Chapter 9.

The DISTINCT and ALL operators can be used with aggregate functions. DISTINCT returns only unique values. ALL is the opposite of DISTINCT and is the default value. If you omit DISTINCT, the ALL is assumed. In other words, if you have never used DISTINCT, then you've always been implying ALL up to now and thus querying all the relevant results. So if you have three rows of PRICE values of 2.99, 3.99, and 3.99, then DISTINCT would return only 2.99 and 3.99, where ALL would return all three values, including the duplicates.

Here is an example showing DISTINCT and ALL used within a COUNT function:

```
SELECT COUNT(ALL LAST_NAME), COUNT(DISTINCT LAST_NAME)
FROM EMPLOYEES;

COUNT(ALLLAST_NAME) COUNT(DISTINCTLAST_NAME)
----------------------- -----------------------
7                         5
```

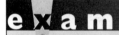

The COUNT function counts occurrences of data, ignoring NULL values. But when combined with the asterisk, as in SELECT COUNT(*) FROM VENDORS, **it counts occurrences of rows—and will include rows with all NULL values in the results.**

This example tells us that the table called EMPLOYEES has seven rows with values for LAST_NAME, of which five are unique values for LAST_NAME, so two are duplicates. Also remember that DISTINCT and ALL cannot be used with the asterisk.

SUM

Syntax: SUM(*e1*)

Parameters: *e1* is an expression whose data type is numeric.

The SUM function adds numeric values in a given column. It takes only numeric data as input. SUM adds all the values in all the rows and returns a single answer. Here's an example:

```
SELECT  SUM(SUBTOTAL)
FROM    ORDERS;
```

Such a query will add up all the values for SUBTOTAL in the ORDERS table and produce a single result. Here's another example:

```
SELECT  SUM(SUBTOTAL)
FROM    ORDERS
WHERE   TO_CHAR(ORDER_DATE, 'MON-RR') = 'APR-17';
```

This query will find any and all rows for which the order has an ORDER_DATE value sometime in the month of April 2017 and then will add up all the values in the SUBTOTAL column and produce a single answer.

MIN, MAX

Syntax: MIN(*e1*); MAX(*e1*)

Parameters: *e1* is an expression with a data type of character, date, or number.

For a given set of rows identified by a SELECT statement, MIN returns the single minimum value, and MAX returns the single maximum value. MIN and MAX can work with numeric, date, and character data, and they use the same basic logic that ORDER BY uses for the different data types, specifically:

- **Numeric** Low numbers are MIN; high numbers are MAX.
- **Date** Earlier dates are MIN; later dates are MAX. Earlier dates are less than later dates.
- **Character** A is less than Z; Z is less than a. The string value 2 is greater than the string value 100. The character 1 is less than the characters 10.

NULL values are ignored, unless all values are NULL, in which case MIN or MAX will return NULL.

For example, consider the following list of data from the table EMPLOYEES:

```
LAST_NAME
------------------------------
Hoddlestein
Smith
Lindon
West
Worthington
```

Now let's identify MIN and MAX values.

```
SELECT MIN(LAST_NAME), MAX(LAST_NAME) FROM EMPLOYEES;

MIN(LAST_NAME)                    MAX(LAST_NAME)
------------------------------    ------------------------------
Hoddlestein                       Worthington
```

Note that Hoddlestein is alphabetically the first value from the list of LAST_NAME values.

Even though the data returned by MIN and MAX represents the data found within a single row in the list, do not be tricked into thinking that this represents a single-row answer—it does not. SQL sees each response of MIN and MAX as an aggregate answer, meaning that the individual value is the answer representing the full set of rows.

AVG

Syntax: AVG(*e1*)

Parameters: *e1* is an expression with a numeric data type.

The AVG function computes the average value for a set of rows. AVG works only with numeric data. It ignores NULL values. For example, let's look at the PAY_HISTORY table; after that, we'll ask for the average value of all the values within the SALARY column.

```
SELECT PAY_HISTORY_ID, SALARY FROM PAY_HISTORY;

PAY_HISTORY_ID          SALARY
----------------------  ----------------------
1                       73922
2                       47000
3                       58000
4                       37450
5                       91379
6                       45500

SELECT AVG(SALARY) FROM PAY_HISTORY;

AVG(SALARY)
----------------------
58875.1666666666666666666666666666666667
```

While we're at it, we can nest the results of this query within the scalar function ROUND, like so:

```
SELECT ROUND(AVG(SALARY),2) FROM PAY_HISTORY;

ROUND(AVG(SALARY),2)
----------------------
58875.17
```

We can get really fancy and format the data using the TO_CHAR function and a format model.

```
SELECT TO_CHAR(ROUND(AVG(SALARY),2),'$999,999.99') FROM PAY_HISTORY;

TO_CHAR(ROUND(AVG(SALARY),2),'$999,999.99')
-------------------------------------------
  $58,875.17
```

In these last few examples of SELECT statements, we've nested a single aggregate function within two scalar, or single-row, functions. You can incorporate a single aggregate function within as many nested scalar functions as you want. The aggregate function need not be the innermost function; you can include one aggregate function with any number of scalar functions in a nested combination, provided that all of the parameter data types are respected. But if you want to include two aggregate functions within a nested combination, be careful—there are limitations on the use of nested aggregate functions. We will address that issue later in this chapter. It's more complex than it might appear.

DISTINCT and ALL are available for use with AVG. In the event that a table's data listing includes some repeated values, the use of DISTINCT will transform the results so that the average is computed only on unique occurrences of each value.

MEDIAN

Syntax: MEDIAN(*e1*)

Parameters: *e1* is an expression with a numeric or date data type.

MEDIAN can operate on numeric or date data types. It ignores NULL values. The MEDIAN function is somewhat related to AVG. MEDIAN performs as you might expect: from a set of data, MEDIAN returns either the middle value or, if that isn't easily identified, then an interpolated value from within the middle. In other words, MEDIAN will sort the values, and if there is an odd number of values, it will identify the value in the middle of the list; otherwise, if there an even number of values, it will locate the two values in the middle of the list and perform linear interpolation between them to locate a result.

Here's an example:

```
CREATE TABLE TEST_MEDIAN(A NUMBER(3));
INSERT INTO TEST_MEDIAN VALUES (1);
INSERT INTO TEST_MEDIAN VALUES (10);
INSERT INTO TEST_MEDIAN VALUES (3);
SELECT MEDIAN(A) FROM TEST_MEDIAN;
```

If you were to execute the previous SQL statements, the value returned by the SELECT statement would be 3.

RANK

RANK has to do with the numeric rank (1, 2, 3, and so on) of a value within a large group of values. When a tied set of values among rows is encountered, RANK assigns the same rank number to the tied rows but keeps count of each row and resumes counting subsequent rows with the correctly numbered position.

The analytic version of RANK returns the rankings of a set of rows. The aggregate version has one parameter of an expression pertaining to a row and returns the rank for that value. Both versions of RANK are described in the following sections.

RANK: Analytic

Syntax: RANK() OVER (PARTITION BY *p1* ORDER BY *ob1*)

Parameters: *p1* is a partition. *ob1* is an expression.

The use of PARTITION BY is optional. All other elements are required.

The RANK function calculates the rank of a value within a group of values. Ranks may not be consecutive numbers since SQL counts tied rows individually, so if three rows are tied for first, they will each be ranked 1, 1, and 1, and the next row will be ranked 4.

For example, note the use of RANK() in the following line 2 (line numbers added):

```
01  SELECT SHIP_CABIN_ID, ROOM_STYLE, SQ_FT
02       , RANK() OVER (PARTITION BY ROOM_STYLE ORDER BY SQ_FT) SQ_FT_RK
03  FROM    SHIP_CABINS
04  WHERE   SHIP_CABIN_ID <= 7
05  ORDER BY SQ_FT;
06
```

```
07  SHIP_
08  CABIN_
09     ID ROOM_STYLE   SQ_FT    SQ_FT_RK
10  ------ ----------- ------  ----------
11      2 Stateroom       160           1
12      4 Stateroom       205           2
13      7 Stateroom       211           3
14      3 Suite           533           1
15      1 Suite           533           1
16      5 Suite           586           3
17      6 Suite          1524           4
18
19  7 rows selected.
```

In the example, the values returned by RANK are in the column SQ_FT_RK. The rows are partitioned by ROOM_STYLE, so those are sorted first; then within a given partition, rows are ranked by SQ_FT. Note line 14, which is the start of a new ROOM_STYLE, and the RANK value restarts at 1. Also note that the next line, line 15, has the same value for SQ_FT, so the ranking is tied at 1. Next, line 16 is ranked 3 since this is the third row of 'Suite' ROOM_STYLES, and the SQ_FT of 586 is not tied with any other row.

RANK: Aggregate

Syntax: RANK(*c1*) WITHIN GROUP (ORDER BY *e1*)

Parameters: *c1* and *e1* are expressions.

In this format, the parameters can be repeated in such a way that for each *c1*, you can have a corresponding *e1*; for each *c2* (if included), there must be a corresponding *e2*; and so on. Each successive parameter is separated from the previous parameter by a comma, as in

```
RANK(c1, c2, c3) WITHIN GROUP (ORDER BY e1, e2, e3)
```

Also, the data type of *c1* must match the data type of *e1*, the data type of *c2* (if included) must match the data type of *e2*, and so on.

Here's an example:

```
SELECT RANK(533) WITHIN GROUP (ORDER BY SQ_FT)
FROM     SHIP_CABINS
WHERE    SHIP_CABIN_ID <= 7
ORDER BY SQ_FT;

RANK(533)WITHINGROUP(ORDERBYSQ_FT)
-----------------------------------
                                  4
```

The example shows that for a SQ_FT value of 533, the ranking is 4.

DENSE_RANK

DENSE_RANK is similar to RANK. DENSE_RANK returns the numeric rank (1, 2, 3, and so on) of a value within a large group of values. When a tie is encountered, DENSE_RANK assigns the same number to each equivalent value. But when it resumes counting after a tie, this is where DENSE_RANK differs from RANK. The DENSE_RANK function will not skip any numbers, and it will assign the next sequential number, regardless of how many tied (equivalent) values it just numbered.

DENSE_RANK: Analytic

Syntax: DENSE_RANK() OVER (PARTITION BY *p1* ORDER BY *ob1*)

Parameters: *p1* is a partition. *ob1* is an expression.

In the case of DENSE_RANK, if three rows are tied for first, they will each be ranked 1, 1, and 1, and the next row will be ranked 2.

For example, note the use of DENSE_RANK() in the following line 2:

```
01  SELECT SHIP_CABIN_ID, ROOM_STYLE, SQ_FT,
02    DENSE_RANK() OVER (PARTITION BY ROOM_STYLE ORDER BY SQ_FT) SQ_FT_DRK
03  FROM      SHIP_CABINS
04  WHERE     SHIP_CABIN_ID <= 7
05  ORDER BY SQ_FT;
06
07   SHIP_
08  CABIN_
09      ID ROOM_STYLE  SQ_FT  SQ_FT_DRK
10  ------ ----------- ------ ----------
11       2 Stateroom     160          1
12       4 Stateroom     205          2
13       7 Stateroom     211          3
14       3 Suite         533          1
15       1 Suite         533          1
16       5 Suite         586          2
17       6 Suite        1524          3
18
19  7 rows selected.
```

Note lines 16 and 17. When we used RANK, the ranks here were 3 and 4, respectively. Using DENSE_RANK, the rankings are 2 and 3. Once the two tied rows on lines 14 and 15 are returned, DENSE_RANK resumes ranking subsequent rows with the next sequential number, regardless of how many tied rows may have preceded.

DENSE_RANK: Aggregate

Syntax: DENSE_RANK(*c1*) WITHIN GROUP (ORDER BY *e1*)

Parameters: *c1* is a constant; *e1* is an expression with a data type matching the corresponding *c1* data type. Numeric and character pairs are allowed.

The rules for the aggregate form of DENSE_RANK are the same as RANK's aggregate form. The difference is that DENSE_RANK will return a value consistent with the DENSE_RANK logic as explained in the previous section; that is, if a series of tied rows is encountered, rank numbers of subsequent rows will be assigned with the next sequential number, regardless of how many tied rows preceded. So, if four rows are tied for second, they will each be ranked 2, 2, 2, and 2, and the next row will be ranked 3.

FIRST, LAST

Syntax: *aggregate_function* KEEP (DENSE_RANK FIRST ORDER BY *e1*)
 aggregate_function KEEP (DENSE_RANK LAST ORDER BY *e1*)

Parameters: *e1* is an expression with a numeric or character data type.

The functions FIRST and LAST are similar. Both are considered aggregate functions as well as analytic functions. For a given range of sorted values, each returns either the first value (FIRST) or the last value (LAST) of the population of rows defining *e1*, in the sorted order.

Here's an example:

```
SELECT    MAX(SQ_FT) KEEP (DENSE_RANK FIRST ORDER BY GUESTS)
          "Largest"
FROM      SHIP_CABINS;

Largest
--------------------
225
```

In this example, we are doing the following:

■ First, we're sorting all the rows in the SHIP_CABINS table according to the value in the GUESTS column, and we're identifying the FIRST value in that sort order, which is a complex way of saying that we're identifying the lowest value for the GUESTS column.

■ For all rows with a GUEST value that matches the lowest value we just found, determine the MAX value for SQ_FT.

- In others, display the highest number of square feet for any and all cabins that accommodate the lowest number of guests according to the GUESTS column.

on the *Job*

Experienced professionals might recognize that FIRST and LAST perform tasks that can also be done with certain usages of self-joins or views, which we examine in later chapters. While self-joins and views are beneficial for a variety of reasons, the use of FIRST or LAST as shown previously will achieve performance improvements over the alternative approaches.

Others

There are more aggregate functions than are described in this section. They include functions to work with nested tables, functions to perform linear regression analysis, and various forms of statistical analysis. These functions aren't specifically referenced in the certification exam guide objectives, so we won't review them all here. But you can find full descriptions of them in Oracle Corporation's *SQL Language Reference Manual*.

CERTIFICATION OBJECTIVE 7.02

Group Data by Using the GROUP BY Clause

The GROUP BY clause is an optional clause within the SELECT statement. Its purpose is to group sets of rows and treat each individual set as a whole. In other words, GROUP BY identifies subsets of rows within the larger set of rows being considered by the SELECT statement. In this way, it's sort of like creating a series of mini-SELECT statements within the larger SELECT statement.

GROUP BY is unique to the SELECT statement; it does not exist in other SQL statements.

Let's take another look at the SHIP_CABINS table, which now has some new columns since the last time we worked with it (see Figure 7-2).

Let's run this SELECT statement against the table, looking only at rows where SHIP_ID = 1:

```
SELECT    SHIP_CABIN_ID, ROOM_NUMBER, ROOM_STYLE,
          ROOM_TYPE,     WINDOW,      GUESTS,     SQ_FT
FROM      SHIP_CABINS
WHERE     SHIP_ID = 1;
```

FIGURE 7-2

The SHIP_CABINS
table

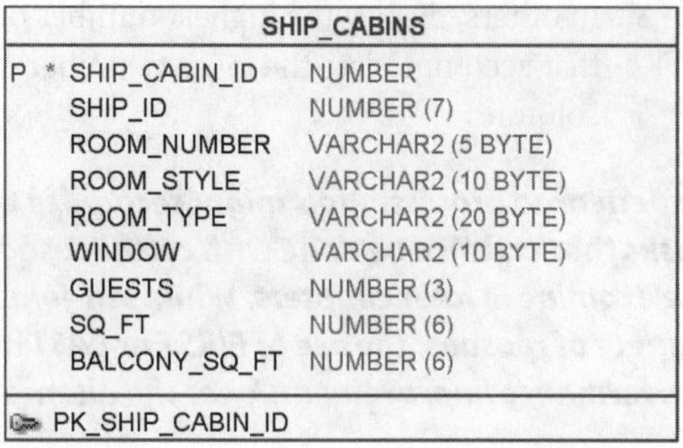

```
                        SHIP_CABINS
P  *  SHIP_CABIN_ID     NUMBER
      SHIP_ID           NUMBER (7)
      ROOM_NUMBER       VARCHAR2 (5 BYTE)
      ROOM_STYLE        VARCHAR2 (10 BYTE)
      ROOM_TYPE         VARCHAR2 (20 BYTE)
      WINDOW            VARCHAR2 (10 BYTE)
      GUESTS            NUMBER (3)
      SQ_FT             NUMBER (6)
      BALCONY_SQ_FT     NUMBER (6)

   PK_SHIP_CABIN_ID
```

The results are shown here:

```
SHIP_CABIN_ID ROOM_N ROOM_STYLE ROOM_TYPE        WINDOW GUESTS   SQ_FT
------------- ------ ---------- ---------------- ------ -------- --------
1             102    Suite      Standard         Ocean  4        533
2             103    Stateroom  Standard         Ocean  2        160
3             104    Suite      Standard         None   4        533
4             105    Stateroom  Standard         Ocean  3        205
5             106    Suite      Standard         None   6        586
6             107    Suite      Royal            Ocean  5        1524
7             108    Stateroom  Large            None   2        211
8             109    Stateroom  Standard         None   2        180
9             110    Stateroom  Large            None   2        225
10            702    Suite      Presidential     None   5        1142
11            703    Suite      Royal            Ocean  5        1745
12            704    Suite      Skyloft          Ocean  8        722
```

Take a look at the column called SQ_FT, showing the number of square feet of
each room on the ship. Let's compute the average square feet for rooms and round
off the answer:

```
SELECT   ROUND(AVG(SQ_FT),2)
FROM     SHIP_CABINS
WHERE    SHIP_ID = 1;
```

Here is the result:

```
ROUND(AVG(SQ_FT),2)
----------------------
647.17
```

That's the average for all of the cabins on the ship. But look at the data listing,
and you'll see that each of the ship's cabins seems to fall into one of two different

```
FROM       SHIP_CABINS
WHERE      SHIP_ID = 1
GROUP BY ROOM_STYLE, ROOM_TYPE
ORDER BY 3;

ROOM_STYLE ROOM_TYPE               Min    Max    Diff
---------- -------------------- ------ ------ ------
Stateroom  Standard                160    205    -45
Stateroom  Large                   211    225    -14
Suite      Standard                533    586    -53
Suite      Skyloft                 722    722      0
Suite      Presidential          1,142  1,142      0
Suite      Royal                 1,524  1,745   -221
```

Here are some details of the preceding example:

- The GROUP BY clause includes two columns from the table: ROOM_STYLE and ROOM_TYPE. The order is important: it tells SQL to group all rows first that share the same value for the ROOM_STYLE and, for each set of rows with the same ROOM_STYLE, group rows with the same ROOM_TYPE value. There are apparently six such groups, according to the output.

- The SELECT statement's select list happens to include the ROOM_STYLE and ROOM_TYPE columns in the same positions as they are in the GROUP BY clause; this is not required, but it makes the output listing easy to read.

- The ORDER BY clause tells SQL to sort the rows based on the value in the third item in the select list, which is the MIN aggregate function.

- Each of the aggregate functions is formatted with the TO_CHAR format model to include commas where appropriate and narrow the columns to a reasonable width.

- The final column in our select list is an expression that calculates the MIN and MAX values, determines the difference between them, and formats the results.

Clearly there's a lot going on in this SELECT statement, but it's a great example of a GROUP BY in action.

ORDER BY Revisited

When a GROUP BY is used in a SELECT statement, then if there is an ORDER BY clause included as well, its use will be somewhat restricted. The list of columns or expressions in an ORDER BY that is part of a SELECT statement that uses GROUP BY is limited to the following:

- Expressions specified in the GROUP BY clause
- Expressions specified in the select list, referenced by position, name, or alias
- Aggregate functions, regardless of whether the aggregate function is specified elsewhere in the SELECT statement
- The functions USER, SYSDATE, and UID

ⓦatch *A single SELECT statement must produce output at just one level of aggregation. This is why a SELECT statement cannot mix scalar and aggregate values in a select list, unless it is to nest them within each other.*

Note that when a GROUP BY is used, the ORDER BY clause must reference either columns in the table that are specified in the GROUP BY clause or the output of an aggregate function or both. Other references are not permitted. That's not the case for SELECT statements in general. In a scalar SELECT you can use ORDER BY on columns in the table whether they are included in the SELECT or not. But that's not true when a GROUP BY is involved. ORDER BY is more limited.

Nesting Functions

You might recall from our examples that we've nested functions in some of our SQL statements. The concept of nesting functions refers to the practice of positioning a function in such a way that the value it returns becomes the input parameter for another function. Here's an example:

```
SELECT TO_CHAR(MEDIAN(SQ_FT),'999.99') FROM SHIP_CABINS;
```

In this example, the MEDIAN aggregate function is nested within the TO_CHAR function. Thus, the MEDIAN function, in this example, is the inner function, and it returns a value that becomes an input parameter to the TO_CHAR conversion function, which is the outer function. As long as the data types match up, nesting is allowed. In this instance, MEDIAN can be used like this only if it is returning a value of the data type that TO_CHAR can accept.

Now, remember that there are two general types of functions: single-row, or scalar, functions; and multirow, or aggregate, functions. Scalar functions return one value for each row encountered by the SQL statement in which the scalar function is applied. Aggregate functions return one value for every zero or more rows encountered by the SQL statement.

The rules for nesting functions differ, depending on whether you are nesting aggregate or scalar functions.

Scalar functions can be nested multiple times, as long as the data types match. The reason is that scalar functions all operate on the same level of detail within the rows—for every one row, a scalar function returns one value.

Aggregate functions, on the other hand, behave differently than scalar functions when it comes to nesting. The reason is that aggregates combine data from multiple rows into a single row. Once that has been accomplished, your resulting value no longer represents the same level of detail you were originally dealing with.

For example, let's look again at the SHIP_CABINS table and consider a simple SELECT statement with a GROUP BY clause:

```
SELECT    ROOM_STYLE, ROOM_TYPE, MAX(SQ_FT)
FROM      SHIP_CABINS
WHERE     SHIP_ID = 1
GROUP BY ROOM_STYLE, ROOM_TYPE;


ROOM_STYLE ROOM_TYPE              MAX(SQ_FT)
---------- -------------------- ----------------------
Stateroom  Standard              205
Suite      Standard              586
Stateroom  Large                 225
Suite      Skyloft               722
Suite      Royal                 1745
Suite      Presidential          1142
```

This SELECT groups rows according to ROOM_STYLE and ROOM_TYPE, as we've seen, and displays the MAX value for SQ_FT within each group. The result is six rows, which tells us that we have six unique groups for ROOM_STYLE and ROOM_TYPE. It tells us nothing about the number of rows that might be found within the source data—but just so you know, it's the same data list we saw earlier in this chapter, which consisted of 12 rows.

Now let's try to compute the AVG value of these six MAX values:

```
SELECT    ROOM_STYLE, ROOM_TYPE, AVG(MAX(SQ_FT))
FROM      SHIP_CABINS
WHERE     SHIP_ID = 1
GROUP BY ROOM_STYLE, ROOM_TYPE;
```

If we try to execute this SELECT statement, this will be the result:

```
Error starting at line 1 in command:
SELECT    ROOM_STYLE, ROOM_TYPE, AVG(MAX(SQ_FT))
FROM      SHIP_CABINS
WHERE     SHIP_ID = 1
GROUP BY ROOM_STYLE, ROOM_TYPE
Error at Command Line:1 Column:9
Error report:
SQL Error: ORA-00937: not a single-group group function
00937. 00000 -  "not a single-group group function"
```

Why are we getting this error? The reason is simple: by introducing AVG into the SELECT statement's expression list, we are moving up the level of aggregation a higher degree, and we are informing SQL that we simply want one answer for all of those grouped rows. The problem: our GROUP BY is trying to display only one answer for all the rows, but there are six different ROOM_STYLE and ROOM_TYPE values for those rows. In other words, there is no single answer that can represent all six of those rows.

One solution is to modify our SELECT statement by removing items from the select list that are at inconsistent levels of detail, like this:

```
SELECT    AVG(MAX(SQ_FT))
FROM      SHIP_CABINS
WHERE     SHIP_ID = 1
GROUP BY ROOM_STYLE, ROOM_TYPE;


AVG(MAX(SQ_FT))
---------------------
770.833333333333333333333333333333333333
```

Now we get an answer, and we can see the result displays in just one row, which in turn represents the six rows from the previous query, which itself represented 12 rows. So, we have aggregated 12 rows into 6 and then 6 into 1—all with one query. In other words, this latest SELECT statement and its AVG result represent an aggregation of an aggregation.

Let's try a third level of nested aggregate:

```
SELECT    COUNT(AVG(MAX(SQ_FT)))
FROM      SHIP_CABINS
WHERE     SHIP_ID = 1
GROUP BY ROOM_STYLE, ROOM_TYPE;

Error starting at line 1 in command:
SELECT    COUNT(AVG(MAX(SQ_FT)))
FROM      SHIP_CABINS
WHERE     SHIP_ID = 1
```

```
GROUP BY ROOM_STYLE, ROOM_TYPE
Error at Command Line:1 Column:19
Error report:
SQL Error: ORA-00935: group function is nested too deeply
00935. 00000 -  "group function is nested too deeply"
```

It can't be done. Two levels deep is the furthest you can go with nested aggregate functions.

However, we are allowed to introduce nested scalar functions at any time. Here's an example:

```
SELECT    ROUND(AVG(MAX(SQ_FT)))
FROM      SHIP_CABINS
WHERE     SHIP_ID = 1
GROUP BY ROOM_STYLE, ROOM_TYPE;

ROUND(AVG(MAX(SQ_FT)))
----------------------
771
```

To sum up:

- You are allowed to nest aggregate functions up to two levels deep.
- Each time you introduce an aggregate function, you are rolling up lower-level data into higher-level summary data.
- Your SELECT statement's select list must always respect the level of aggregation and can only include expressions that are all at the same level of aggregation.

And finally, remember that scalar functions can be nested at any time and have no effect on modifying the levels of row aggregation.

CERTIFICATION OBJECTIVE 7.03

Include or Exclude Grouped Rows by Using the HAVING Clause

The HAVING clause can exclude specific groups of rows defined in the GROUP BY clause. You could think of it as the WHERE clause for groups of rows specified by the GROUP BY clause.

The HAVING clause is unique to the SELECT statement; it does not exist in other SQL statements.

The HAVING clause does not define the groups of rows themselves; those groups must already be defined by the GROUP BY clause. HAVING defines the criteria upon which each of the GROUP BY groups will be either included or excluded.

The HAVING clause can be invoked only in a SELECT statement where the GROUP BY clause is present.

If it is included, GROUP BY and HAVING must follow WHERE (if included) and precede ORDER BY (if included). Table 7-2 shows these relationships.

Here's an example:

```
01    SELECT    ROOM_STYLE,
02              ROOM_TYPE,
03              TO_CHAR(MIN(SQ_FT),'9,999') "Min"
04    FROM      SHIP_CABINS
05    WHERE     SHIP_ID = 1
06    GROUP BY ROOM_STYLE, ROOM_TYPE
07    HAVING    ROOM_TYPE IN ('Standard', 'Large')
08      OR      MIN(SQ_FT) > 1200
09    ORDER BY 3;
10
11    ROOM_STYLE ROOM_TYPE            Min
12    ---------- -------------------- ------
13    Stateroom  Standard                160
14    Stateroom  Large                   211
15    Suite      Standard                533
16    Suite      Royal                 1,524
```

Note the HAVING clause on lines 7 and 8. This particular HAVING restricts the groups identified in the GROUP BY clause to only those rows

	Sequence	Clause	Required/Optional?	Note
TABLE 7-2	1	SELECT	Required	
Clauses in a SELECT Statement	2	FROM	Required	
	3	WHERE	Optional	
	4	GROUP BY	Optional	HAVING is allowed only with a GROUP BY clause. HAVING and GROUP BY may occur in either order.
	4	HAVING	Optional	
	6	ORDER BY	Optional	

where ROOM_TYPE = 'Standard' or ROOM_TYPE = 'Large' *or* the value for MIN(SQ_FT) is greater than 1200.

As the preceding example shows, HAVING can use the same Boolean operators that WHERE does—AND, OR, and NOT. These are the only restrictions on HAVING:

- It can be used only in SELECT statements that have a GROUP BY clause.
- It can only compare expressions that reference groups as defined in the GROUP BY clause and aggregate functions.

HAVING can include scalar functions as long as these restrictions are respected. In other words, a scalar function can be incorporated into a larger expression that references a GROUP BY group or an aggregate function. Just remember that HAVING deals with groups of rows, not individual rows.

CERTIFICATION SUMMARY

Multirow functions differ from single-row functions in that they return one value for a group of rows, whereas single-row functions return one answer for each individual row. Single-row functions are also referred to as *scalar* functions; multirow functions are also referred to as *aggregate* functions. The available aggregate functions in SQL include the commonly used functions COUNT, SUM, MIN, MAX, AVG, and MEDIAN. There are aggregate functions to support standard deviation and variance, ranking, linear regression analysis, grouping with ROLLUP and CUBE, XML support, and working with nested tables.

Aggregate functions can be called from four places in a SELECT statement: the select list, the GROUP BY clause, the HAVING clause, and the ORDER BY clause.

If an aggregate function appears in the select list of the SELECT statement, then all other expressions must be at the same level of aggregation. You cannot use, in a single SELECT statement, a scalar function on one column and an aggregate function on another. The SELECT must be able to return row data that is collectively at the same level of detail.

The GROUP BY clause specifies one or more expressions that SQL is to use to group rows together. Any values displayed in the SELECT output must be displayed once for each group. In this fashion, the GROUP BY can transform a single column reference into an aggregate reference by specifying that column as a GROUP BY item.

Any column or expression specified in the GROUP BY clause can also be included in the SELECT statement's select list. However, this is not required.

The HAVING clause can be used to filter out groups that have been specified with the GROUP BY clause. HAVING works much like the WHERE clause: while the WHERE clause filters out individual rows, HAVING does the same thing for groups of rows. HAVING is allowed only if the GROUP BY clause is present.

If HAVING and GROUP BY are included in a SELECT statement, they must follow the WHERE clause (if used) and precede the ORDER BY clause (if used). GROUP BY often precedes HAVING, but HAVING is permitted to precede GROUP BY in the SELECT statement's syntax.

TWO-MINUTE DRILL

Describe the Use of Group Functions

- ☐ Group functions are also known as aggregate, or multirow, functions.
- ☐ Multirow functions return one value for every set of zero or more rows considered within a SELECT statement.
- ☐ There are group functions to determine minimum and maximum values, calculate averages, and more.
- ☐ Group functions can be used to determine rank within a group of rows.
- ☐ Aggregate and scalar data cannot be included in the same SELECT statement's select list.
- ☐ The COUNT function counts occurrences of data, as opposed to the SUM function, which adds up numeric values.
- ☐ The MIN and MAX functions can operate on date, character, or numeric data.
- ☐ The AVG and MEDIAN functions can perform average and median calculations, and they can ignore NULL values in their computations.
- ☐ Some functions such as RANK use the keywords WITHIN GROUP (ORDER BY) to process a value and identify its ranking within the overall set of rows in the data set.

Group Data by Using the GROUP BY Clause

- ☐ The GROUP BY clause is an optional clause in the SELECT statement in which you can specify how to group rows together in order to process them as a group.
- ☐ The row groups identified by GROUP BY can have aggregate functions applied to them so that the final result of the SELECT is not a single aggregate value but a series of aggregate function results, one per group.
- ☐ GROUP BY can specify columns in a table, which will have the effect of grouping rows in the SELECT that share the same values in those columns.
- ☐ Whatever you specify in the GROUP BY may also be included in the SELECT statement's select list—but this is not required.

☐ The effect of GROUP BY on a column is to change that column into an aggregate value; in other words, by grouping rows that have common data for a given column and by specifying the column in the GROUP BY, you elevate the information in the column from scalar to aggregate for the purposes of that SELECT statement.

☐ GROUP BY can specify one or more expressions.

Include or Exclude Grouped Rows by Using the HAVING Clause

☐ The HAVING clause is an optional clause for the SELECT statement that works in coordination with GROUP BY.

☐ You cannot use HAVING unless GROUP BY is present.

☐ HAVING specifies groups of rows that will be excluded in the output of the SELECT statement.

☐ HAVING performs the same function for GROUP BY that WHERE performs for the rest of the SELECT statement.

☐ HAVING specifies groups using the same expression logic and syntax that WHERE would use.

☐ The GROUP BY and HAVING clauses are not required, but if used, they must follow the WHERE clause and precede the ORDER BY clause.

☐ While GROUP BY typically precedes HAVING in common practice, this is not required, and they can appear in either order; HAVING can precede GROUP BY.

SELF TEST

The following questions will help you measure your understanding of the material presented in this chapter. Choose one correct answer for each question unless otherwise directed.

Describe the Use of Group Functions

1. Which of the following is true about aggregate functions? (Choose two.)
   A. Return one value for each group of rows specified in a SELECT statement.
   B. Are also called group functions.
   C. Will cause a run-time error when used in SELECT statements that return zero rows or one row.
   D. Can operate only with numeric data.

2. Review the following illustration:

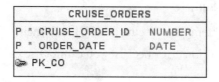

   Now review this SQL statement:

   ```
   SELECT CRUISE_ORDER_ID, COUNT(ORDER_DATE)
   FROM   CRUISE_ORDERS;
   ```

   What can be said of this statement?
   A. It will fail to execute because ORDER_DATE is a date data type, and no aggregate function can work with a date data type.
   B. It will fail to execute because it mixes scalar and aggregate data in the select list.
   C. It will execute successfully but not produce any meaningful output.
   D. There is nothing wrong with the SQL statement.

3. Which of the following aggregate functions can be used on character data? (Choose two.)
   A. COUNT
   B. MIN
   C. AVG
   D. MEDIAN

4. Examine the following data listing of a table called PERMITS:

```
PERMIT_ID    FILED_DATE    VENDOR_ID
---------    ----------    ---------
1            05-DEC-09     101
2            12-DEC-09     310903
3            14-DEC-09     101
```

Which one of the following aggregate functions could be used to determine how many permits have been filed by VENDOR_ID 101?

A. SUM

B. COUNT

C. MEDIAN

D. HAVING

5. Review the illustration from question 2, and then review the following SQL statement:

```
SELECT AVG(CRUISE_ORDER_ID), MIN(ORDER_DATE)
FROM    CRUISE_ORDERS;
```

What will result from an attempt to execute this SQL statement on the CRUISE_ORDERS table?

A. It will fail with an execution error because you cannot use the AVG function on a PRIMARY KEY column.

B. It will fail with an execution error because you cannot use the MIN function on a DATE data type.

C. It will fail with an execution error if the table contains only one row.

D. It will execute and perform as intended.

6. Review the following data listing from a table SCORES:

```
SCORE_ID    TEST_SCORE
--------    ----------
1           95
2
3           85
```

Now consider the following query:

```
SELECT  TO_CHAR(AVG(TEST_SCORE),'999,999.99') FROM SCORES;
```

What will be the result of this query?

A. It will result in a syntax error because of the TO_CHAR function.

B. It will result in an execution error.

C. 90.00.

D. 60.00.

7. Review the following illustration:

PROJECTS	
P * PROJECT_ID	NUMBER
SHIP_ID	NUMBER
PURPOSE	VARCHAR2 (30 BYTE)
PROJECT_NAME	VARCHAR2 (40 BYTE)
PROJECT_COST	NUMBER
DAYS	NUMBER
⟿ PK_PROJECT_ID	

Which of the following SQL statements will execute correctly?

A. SELECT RANK(100000) WITHIN GROUP (ORDER BY PROJECT_COST) FROM PROJECTS;

B. SELECT RANK(100,000) WITHIN GROUP (ORDER BY PROJECT_COST) FROM PROJECTS;

C. SELECT RANK(7500000) GROUP BY (ORDER BY PROJECT_COST) FROM PROJECTS;

D. SELECT RANK('Upgrade') WITHIN GROUP (ORDER BY PROJECT_COST) FROM PROJECTS;

8. Which of the following aggregate functions ignores NULL values in its calculations? (Choose all that apply.)

A. MEDIAN

B. AVG

C. SUM

D. MAX

9. An aggregate function can be called from within: (Choose two.)

A. The HAVING clause of an INSERT statement

B. The ORDER BY clause of a SELECT statement

C. The expression list of a DELETE statement

D. The select list of a SELECT statement

Group Data by Using the GROUP BY Clause

10. Review the illustration from question 7. Your task is to define a SELECT statement that groups rows according to their value for PURPOSE and, for each purpose, adds up the values stored in DAYS. Which one of the following queries will perform this task?

A.
```
SELECT SUM(DAYS), PURPOSE
FROM PROJECTS
GROUP BY PURPOSE;
```

B.
```
SELECT SUM(DAYS), PURPOSE
FROM PROJECTS
GROUP BY PURPOSE, SUM(DAYS);
```

C.
```
SELECT PURPOSE, COUNT(DAYS)
FROM PROJECTS
GROUP BY PURPOSE;
```

D.
```
SELECT PURPOSE, RANK(DAYS) ON (ORDER BY)
FROM PROJECTS
GROUP BY PURPOSE;
```

11. Review the illustration from question 2, and then look at the SQL code that follows:

```
01   SELECT   TO_CHAR(ORDER_DATE,'Q') "Quarter", COUNT(*)
02   FROM     CRUISE_ORDERS
03   WHERE    TO_CHAR(ORDER_DATE,'YYYY') = '2009'
04   GROUP BY TO_CHAR(ORDER_DATE,'Q');
```

Recall that the 'Q' format model is for quarter, so TO_CHAR using a DATE data type with the 'Q' format mask is translating the date into the quarter in which it falls—1, 2, 3, or 4. Given that, which of the following statements is true of the SQL statement?

A. It will fail because of a syntax error in line 4 since you cannot use the TO_CHAR function in the GROUP BY clause.

B. It will fail because of a syntax error in line 1 since you cannot use the TO_CHAR function with the COUNT aggregate function.

C. It will execute and show the number of orders in the CRUISE_ORDERS table for each quarter in the year 2009.

D. None of the above.

12. Review the illustration from question 7, and then look at the SQL code that follows:

```
01    SELECT     COUNT(COUNT(PROJECT_COST))
02    FROM       PROJECTS
03    GROUP BY PURPOSE;
```

What will happen if you try to execute this query on the PROJECTS table?

A. It will fail with a syntax error because line 1 is not correct.

B. It will fail with an execution error because you cannot use a VARCHAR2 column in a GROUP BY clause.

C. It will succeed and display one row for each different value in the PURPOSE column.

D. It will succeed and display one row.

Include or Exclude Grouped Rows by Using the HAVING Clause

13. Which of the following statements is true about HAVING? (Choose two.)

A. It can be used only in the SELECT statement.

B. It must occur after the GROUP BY clause.

C. It must occur after the WHERE clause.

D. It cannot reference an expression unless that expression is first referenced in the GROUP BY clause.

14. Review the illustration from question 7, and review the SQL statement that follows:

```
01    SELECT     SHIP_ID, MAX(DAYS)
02    FROM       PROJECTS
03    GROUP BY SHIP_ID
04    HAVING     AVG(PROJECT_COST) < 500000;
```

Which of the following statements is true for this SQL statement?

A. It will fail to execute because of a syntax error on line 4.

B. It will include only those rows with a PROJECT_COST value of less than 500000.

C. It will include only those groups of rows for a given SHIP_ID with an average value of PROJECT_COST less than 500000.

D. It will fail to execute because of a syntax error on line 1.

15. Review the illustration from question 7. Your assignment: create a SELECT statement that queries the PROJECTS table to show the average project cost for each PURPOSE. You know there are only two values for PURPOSE in the table: 'Upgrade' and 'Maintenance'. You want to restrict output to those rows where DAYS is greater than 3. Which of the following SELECT statements will perform this task?

A.
```
SELECT PURPOSE, AVG(PROJECT_COST)
FROM PROJECTS
WHERE DAYS > 3
GROUP BY PURPOSE;
```

B.
```
SELECT PURPOSE, AVG(PROJECT_COST)
FROM PROJECTS
GROUP BY PURPOSE
HAVING DAYS > 3;
```

C.
```
SELECT PURPOSE, AVG(PROJECT_COST)
FROM PROJECTS
GROUP BY PURPOSE, (DAYS > 3);
```

D.
```
SELECT PURPOSE, AVG(PROJECT_COST)
FROM PROJECTS
WHERE DAYS > 3
GROUP BY PURPOSE, DAYS
HAVING DAYS > 3;
```

SELF TEST ANSWERS

Describe the Use of Group Functions

1. ☑ **A** and **B.** Aggregate functions return one value for each group of rows in the SELECT statement. They are also referred to as *group* functions, or *multirow* functions.

☒ **C** and **D** are incorrect. A GROUP BY can be used in a SELECT statement that returns zero rows, one row, or multiple rows. Some aggregate functions operate on character and date data types; they are not restricted to numeric data.

2. ☑ **B.** It mixes scalar data (the CRUISE_ORDER_ID column) and aggregate data (the COUNT function applied to the ORDER_DATE column). This is not possible without a GROUP BY clause. The GROUP BY clause could be used to transform the CRUISE_ORDER_ ID column into an aggregate value by specifying GROUP BY CRUISE_ORDER_ID at the end of the statement before the semicolon termination character.

☒ **A, C,** and **D** are incorrect. Some aggregate functions can work with the date data type, and COUNT is one of them.

3. ☑ **A** and **B.** COUNT numbers occurrences of data. That data can include character, date, or numeric data types. MIN determines the minimum value but will work with character data to determine the value representing the value that would appear first in an alphabetic sorting of the candidate values.

☒ **C** and **D** are incorrect. AVG works with numeric data only; MEDIAN works with numeric and date/datetime data only.

4. ☑ **B.** COUNT will determine the occurrences of VENDOR_ID in the data listing.

☒ **A, C,** and **D** are incorrect. SUM adds numbers, which is not desired here. MEDIAN determines an average value. HAVING is not an aggregate function; it is a clause of the SELECT statement.

5. ☑ **D.** It will execute. The statement is syntactically correct.

☒ **A, B,** and **C** are incorrect. You can use AVG with a PRIMARY KEY column. It might not produce any useful information, but it's allowed. You can also use MIN with DATE data types, as well as character strings. It doesn't matter if the table has only one row; the statement will still work. You are allowed to use an aggregate function on zero, one, or more rows.

6. ☑ **C.** The AVG will compute by ignoring the NULL value and averaging the remaining values, resulting in an answer of 90.00.

☒ **A, B,** and **D** are incorrect. There is no syntax error here; the TO_CHAR function correctly formats the output to include commas if necessary. There will be no execution error, either. If the AVG function included NULL values and, say, treated them as zeros, then the answer would be 60.00. That could be accomplished with the NVL function, as in AVG(NVL(TEST_SCORE,0)). But that's not included as an option here.

7. ☑ **A.** The request to rank the literal numeric value of 100000 within the set of values for PROJECT_COST asks SQL to establish a numeric ranking for the value 100000 within the set of rows and indicate where a row containing a value of 100000 for PROJECT_COST would fall within the sorted list, if there were such a row.

   ☒ **B, C,** and **D** are incorrect. The numeric literal value cannot include a comma. In other words, within the arguments for RANK, the value of "100,000" (without quotes) is not seen as one hundred thousand but instead is seen as one hundred, followed by a second parameter of three zeros. Two parameters cannot be accepted by RANK unless there are two corresponding WITHIN GROUP expressions; there is only one in the answer provided. In **C**, the GROUP BY is misplaced. In **D**, 'Upgrade' represents an invalid data type because the data types of both RANK and ORDER BY must match, and in this example, PROJECT_COST is a numeric data type, as we see in the accompanying exhibit.

8. ☑ **A, B, C,** and **D.** All of the functions mentioned ignore null values. MAX in particular is worth emphasizing—remember that NULL values sort higher than NOT NULL values when ORDER BY sorts on a column containing NULL values. However, while that is true, only NOT NULL values are considered by the MAX function. The same is true for the other functions listed in the question.

   ☒ All of the answers are correct.

9. ☑ **B** and **D.** The SELECT statement allows an aggregate function to be called from the ORDER BY clause and the select list. If you specify an aggregate function from within an ORDER BY clause when a GROUP BY clause is present, the ORDER BY will sort the aggregate rows that each represent a group of rows.

   ☒ **A** and **C** are incorrect. There is no HAVING clause in an INSERT statement. There is no expression list in a DELETE statement.

Group Data by Using the GROUP BY Clause

10. ☑ **A.** Some might prefer to place the PURPOSE column before the SUM(DAYS) expression in the SELECT expression list, but that is not required.

    ☒ **B, C,** and **D** are incorrect. **B** is syntactically incorrect since you cannot put an aggregate function within a GROUP BY clause. **C** is incorrect because the COUNT function is used instead of SUM. COUNT would count the occurrences of data, rather than sum up the values. **D** is just a random combination of reserved words and nonsense.

11. ☑ **C.** The statement is syntactically correct and will execute.

     ☒ **A, B,** and **D** are incorrect. The TO_CHAR function is a scalar function and, as such, is not subject to the same restrictions that any aggregate function is. For example, the TO_CHAR used in the GROUP BY clause is fine. And by using the TO_CHAR expression in the GROUP BY, it can also be used in the SELECT expression list in line 1, along with the aggregate function COUNT.

12. ☑ **D.** It will succeed and display one row. The reason you know this is because line 1 shows an aggregate of an aggregate with a GROUP BY clause.

     ☒ **A, B,** and **C** are incorrect. Line 1 is correct; you are allowed to nest one aggregate within one other aggregate function. You can use GROUP BY to group any data type; there is no restriction on grouping by character data. If you were to use only one aggregate function, the result would display one row for each unique value of PURPOSE. But by nesting COUNT within COUNT, you are adding up all of those rows and displaying one aggregate answer.

Include or Exclude Grouped Rows by Using the HAVING Clause

13. ☑ **A** and **C.** HAVING is valid only in the SELECT statement, not the other SQL statements. HAVING must occur after the WHERE clause.

     ☒ **B** and **D** are incorrect. HAVING cannot be used without GROUP BY, but it is not required to follow GROUP BY. HAVING is not limited to expressions identified in the GROUP BY clause; instead, it is limited to any valid expression that addresses the groups established within the GROUP BY clause. In other words, aggregate functions can be invoked from within HAVING, whether they are called by GROUP BY or not.

14. ☑ **C.** The statement is syntactically correct and will produce a series of rows of data. Each row will represent all values for each SHIP_ID value in the table. Each row representing each SHIP_ID will have one maximum value for DAYS. Any set of rows for SHIP_ID whose average value of PROJECT_COST is less than 500000 will be included; all others will be excluded.

     ☒ **A, B,** and **D** are incorrect. There is no syntax error on line 4. The HAVING clause is not required to reference anything in the GROUP BY. HAVING can reference aggregate functions; its only limitation is that it cannot directly reference columns in the table if those columns have not been included in the GROUP BY clause. (Columns omitted from GROUP BY may be incorporated in certain expressions in HAVING but cannot be directly referenced as standalone columns.) **B** could be true only if the WHERE clause were present and filtering rows as **B** describes—the HAVING clause doesn't include or exclude rows on an individual basis but instead includes or excludes groups of rows as defined by the GROUP BY clause and the HAVING clause.

15. ☑ **A.** One of the most important aspects of understanding HAVING is to know when *not* to use it, and this is a great example of that—nothing in this question says anything about restricting groups of data, and that is the only reason why you would use HAVING. The WHERE clause achieves the task of ensuring that only rows where DAYS is greater than three will be considered.

☒ **B, C,** and **D** are incorrect. The task defined by the question doesn't require HAVING. There is no description in the question that asks for anything about the GROUPS to be excluded. **B** is syntactically incorrect because HAVING can reference only aggregate functions or columns that are identified in the GROUP BY, and this does neither. **C** is syntactically incorrect because you cannot enclose the final expression in parentheses by itself. **D** is syntactically correct but does not produce the answer that is described in the question. It will instead group all the rows by both PURPOSE and DAYS, which is not what was asked for; such a query can potentially produce many more rows than just the two expected. In other words, instead of getting one group of rows per value in PURPOSE, you'll get a finer division of detail with each set of rows containing a unique combination of both PURPOSE and DAYS, and that is something different.

8
Displaying Data from Multiple Tables

T his chapter reviews various types of joins. A *join* is a SELECT statement that retrieves data from two or more tables and connects that data to return a merged set of rows. To accomplish the join, the SELECT statement specifies data in one table that is identical to data in another table. Tables that share common data elements that support joins are said to be *related* to each other. This is why a SQL database is called a *relational database management system*; joining tables is the whole purpose of SQL database systems.

This chapter will look at

- Equijoins, which join data using the equality operator
- Non-equijoins, which join data using non-equality operators
- Inner joins
- Outer joins
- Natural joins
- Self-joins

We'll discuss the syntax of all of these forms of joins and look at the use of table aliases, as well as a number of examples.

CERTIFICATION OBJECTIVE 8.01

Describe the Different Types of Joins and Their Features

There are several types of joins in SQL. The most commonly used is the *equijoin*. Less common is the *non-equijoin*. We'll discuss both in this section.

Types of Joins

Joins are characterized in many ways. One way a join is defined is in terms of whether it is an inner join or an outer join. Another issue is that of equijoins and non-equijoins. These descriptions are not mutually exclusive.

Let's briefly look at each type of join, after which we will analyze each one in detail, with examples.

Inner Joins vs. Outer Joins

There are two major categories of syntax for creating joins in Oracle SQL:

- Inner joins connect rows in two or more tables if and only if there are matched rows in all the tables being joined.
- Outer joins connect rows in two or more tables in a way that is more inclusive—if data exists in one table that has no matching values in another, the unmatched row will still be included in the output.

Equijoins vs. Non-Equijoins

Separate from the issue of inner and outer joins is the issue of equijoin versus non-equijoin:

- Equijoins connect data in two or more tables by looking for common data among the tables' columns. In other words, an equijoin looks for an exact match of data.
- Non-equijoins connect data by looking for relationships that don't involve equality, such as "less than" or "greater than" relationships, or situations where data in one table is within a range of values in another.

Most of the joins we'll work with will be equijoins, but we'll look at non-equijoins as well.

Other Joins

There are other joins, such as self, and natural joins. We'll review each in subsequent sections of this chapter.

CERTIFICATION OBJECTIVE 8.02

Use SELECT Statements to Access Data from More Than One Table Using Equijoins and Non-Equijoins

This section looks at various forms of joins. A join is a query that associates rows of data in one table with data in another table. A two-table join is common, but you can join three or more tables. On a practical level a query that joins too many tables introduces performance and maintenance challenges. But how many tables are "too many" for a join? Most industry leaders I know say five is about the limit, but I've seen nine-table joins that made sense for a certain context on a particular project.

This section looks at inner joins, including natural joins, multitable joins, non-equijoins, and the USING clause.

Inner Joins

The first type of join we'll review is an *inner* join. An inner join returns a merged row from two or more tables if and only if there are matched values among all joined tables. For any given row, if there isn't a matched value in all tables, then no row is returned.

For example, let's connect two tables with an inner join. Every ship in the SHIPS table can be assigned a home port in the PORTS table. This is recorded in the database by assigning a HOME_PORT_ID to each row in the SHIPS table. This is why the SHIPS table includes a column called HOME_PORT_ID, which is designated a FOREIGN KEY. The FOREIGN KEY constraint references the PORT_ID column in the PORTS table so that any entry in the SHIPS table's HOME_PORT_ID will be identical to the PORT_ID for that PORT as it already exists in the PORTS table's PORT_ID column.

Let's look at our sample data in these tables. First here's the PORTS table:

```
PORT_ID                       PORT_NAME
--------------------          --------------------
1                             Baltimore
2                             Charleston
3                             Tampa
4                             Miami
```

Next, here's the SHIPS table:

```
SHIP_ID                  SHIP_NAME               HOME_PORT_ID
--------------------     --------------------    --------------------
1                        Codd Crystal            1
2                        Codd Elegance           3
3                        Codd Champion
4                        Codd Victorious         3
5                        Codd Grandeur           2
6                        Codd Prince             2
```

As you can see from these data listings, many ships have a HOME_PORT_ID that matches a PORT_ID in the PORTS table. If you were to identify the home port for, say, the Codd Elegance, you would see that it's PORT_ID 3, which is Tampa. See it? Did you look at the sample data to confirm what we just described? If you did, you compared the value of HOME_PORT_ID in SHIPS to the value of PORT_ID in PORTs. That is precisely what you have to explain in SQL syntax so that SQL can do the same thing. In other words, to join these tables together, we do the following:

- Identify both tables in the FROM clause, separated by the keywords INNER JOIN.
- Define the column from each table that is being used to join the data in the ON condition.

Here's the code for an inner join (line numbers added):

```
01  SELECT   SHIP_ID, SHIP_NAME, PORT_NAME
02  FROM     SHIPS INNER JOIN PORTS
03  ON       HOME_PORT_ID = PORT_ID
04  ORDER BY SHIP_ID;
```

The ORDER BY is something we added; it's not required for the join.

Note that the keyword INNER is not required; we can eliminate it and go with this approach:

```
01  SELECT   SHIP_ID, SHIP_NAME, PORT_NAME
02  FROM     SHIPS JOIN PORTS
03  ON       HOME_PORT_ID = PORT_ID
04  ORDER BY SHIP_ID;
```

This query is the same as the INNER JOIN query with one variation: we removed the optional keyword INNER from line 2. Everything else is the same.

Whichever syntax we use—with or without the keyword INNER—the result is the same.

SHIP_ID	SHIP_NAME	PORT_NAME
1	Codd Crystal	Baltimore
2	Codd Elegance	Tampa
4	Codd Victorious	Tampa
5	Codd Grandeur	Charleston
6	Codd Prince	Charleston

That's the output from our inner join.

Note that we can add additional WHERE clause criteria to our join. Let's say we wanted to restrict our output so that only the Charleston rows were included. Let's modify the INNER JOIN syntax:

```
01  SELECT    SHIP_ID, SHIP_NAME, PORT_NAME
02  FROM      SHIPS INNER JOIN PORTS
03  ON        HOME_PORT_ID = PORT_ID
04  WHERE     PORT_NAME = 'Charleston'
05  ORDER BY SHIP_ID;
```

The result will be to limit our results to only those ships that are ported in Charleston.

Now go back before we added the WHERE clause and look at our original output from the first inner join. Do you see something missing? Look for the Codd Champion—it isn't in the output. The reason is because the Codd Champion, aka SHIP_ID 3, has no assigned value for HOME_PORT_ID. As a result, there is no matching row in the PORTS table, and since we used an "inner join" format, we only return rows where there are matched values in the join criteria. The result is that the Codd Champion is omitted. And that's not all—we also don't see any value for the PORT_ID 4, 'Miami'. The reason is the same—there is no ship assigned to Miami as a home port.

This is why our join is an inner join. It only returns records that have matched rows in both tables. If you want to include data in our output from rows that aren't necessarily matched in all tables, use the "outer join" format. We'll look at outer joins shortly.

Older Inner Join Syntax

Before we move on to outer joins, let's review an old variation on inner join syntax. Here it is:

```
01  SELECT    S.SHIP_ID, S.SHIP_NAME, P.PORT_NAME
02  FROM      SHIPS S, PORTS P
03  WHERE     S.HOME_PORT_ID = P.PORT_ID
04  ORDER BY S.SHIP_ID;
```

(Note: This time we used table aliases. Most joins connect tables by referencing columns with identical names. In this example, the PORTS table uses PORT_ID, and the SHIPS table uses HOME_PORT_ID, so table aliases are not required. However, if SHIPS had named its foreign key PORT_ID, the use of table aliases in our example would be required. You'll learn more about table aliases in a few pages.)

In this form, the join is accomplished in lines 2 and 3, where we list the joined tables in the FROM clause and also identify the join criterion in line 3 with an equal sign. In this syntax, there is no keyword JOIN or ON. The WHERE clause can include additional criteria as any WHERE clause might. Here's an example:

```
01   SELECT    S.SHIP_ID, S.SHIP_NAME, P.PORT_NAME
02   FROM      SHIPS S, PORTS P
03   WHERE     S.HOME_PORT_ID = P.PORT_ID
04     AND     PORT_NAME = 'Charleston'
05   ORDER BY S.SHIP_ID;
```

This is the older form of an inner join that Oracle has used, and it still works. But that version, while clear, succinct, easy to use, and very popular, is nonetheless inconsistent with ANSI standards. The version we reviewed earlier—the version that uses the JOIN and ON keywords—is formally preferred and is consistent with the ANSI standard for SQL joins.

Using Table Aliases

In our examples so far, we've joined tables using columns that have had different column names. This isn't always the case, however. For example, look at the two tables in Figure 8-1.

The EMPLOYEES table and the ADDRESSES table both have a column called EMPLOYEE_ID. That column is the PRIMARY KEY in EMPLOYEES, and it's the FOREIGN KEY in ADDRESSES. Using what we've seen so far, we might try this syntax:

```
01   SELECT    EMPLOYEE_ID, LAST_NAME, STREET_ADDRESS
02   FROM      EMPLOYEES INNER JOIN ADDRESSES
03   ON        EMPLOYEE_ID = EMPLOYEE_ID;
```

There's a problem with this syntax. Look at line 1. The first item in our SELECT statement's select list is EMPLOYEE_ID, but which table's EMPLOYEE_ID are we intending here? Chances are it won't make that much of a difference with regard to data display, since both columns contain the same data—unless we use a form of OUTER JOIN, in which case there may be a difference. Regardless, that's no help to us here because SQL will reject this statement anyway because of the ambiguous column reference.

The EMPLOYEES
and ADDRESSES
tables

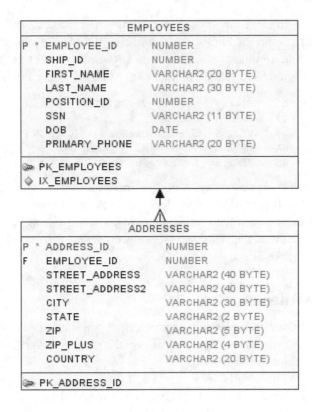

One solution is to use the full table name as a prefix to the column.

```
01  SELECT    EMPLOYEES.EMPLOYEE_ID, LAST_NAME, STREET_ADDRESS
02  FROM      EMPLOYEES INNER JOIN ADDRESSES
03  ON        EMPLOYEES.EMPLOYEE_ID = ADDRESSES.EMPLOYEE_ID;
```

We've added the full table name in front of each reference to EMPLOYEE_ID,
separated by a period, to clarify our intent. Note that we needed to make these
changes three times—once on line 1 and twice on line 3. This is perfectly acceptable
and represents clear and thorough design.

There's an alternative, however, and it's the table alias. Here's an example of the
table alias in action:

```
01  SELECT    EM.EMPLOYEE_ID, LAST_NAME, STREET_ADDRESS
02  FROM      EMPLOYEES EM INNER JOIN ADDRESSES AD
03  ON        EM.EMPLOYEE_ID = AD.EMPLOYEE_ID;
```

First look at line 2. After each table referenced in the FROM clause, we left a space, followed by a name we specify. The name needs to match the rules for naming database objects. For EMPLOYEES we chose EM, and for ADDRESSES we chose AD. We could have chosen anything within the rules of naming database objects.

Since we chose to create table aliases, we were also able to use the table alias as prefixes on lines 1 and 3. The result is a more easily readable query.

Note the scope of the table alias is the statement itself. Once the statement has completed executing, the table alias is no longer useful; it must be specified anew in any subsequent SQL statements.

There's no right or wrong answer as to which approach you should choose—the full table name prefix or the table alias prefix. Either way, you should consider the following points:

- When writing any query in which a column reference is ambiguous, you must do something to identify the column clearly to the SQL statement, using either a table prefix or a table alias. Otherwise, you'll get an error message and the SQL statement won't execute.

- The use of table prefixes and table aliases is on the exam.

The table alias is more commonly used, in my ever-so-humble opinion. But both work.

Also note that table aliases can be used in INSERT, UPDATE, MERGE, and DELETE statements, as well as SELECT.

Natural Joins

So far, many of the examples we've seen have joined tables using columns of different names, such as HOME_PORT_ID and PORT_ID. It's more common, however, for such columns to be named with the same name. In other words, when database designers create two tables and intend to link them together, it is good design to give identical names to any columns that will be linked. It's not necessarily bad design to do otherwise—it all depends on readability and intent. But the point for our discussion here on natural joins is that you will often work with tables that share identical column names, and it will be these columns upon which your joins will probably be built.

A natural join is an inner join by default, but it can also be a left outer join, right outer join, or a full outer join.

For example, review Figure 8-1 again. As we saw in the previous section, the two tables shown both have a column called EMPLOYEE_ID. This column is a FOREIGN KEY in the ADDRESSES table and the PRIMARY KEY of the EMPLOYEES table.

The natural join approach tells SQL to locate any columns in the two tables with a common name, and use them to join the tables. Here's an example:

```
01  SELECT    EMPLOYEE_ID, LAST_NAME, STREET_ADDRESS
02  FROM      EMPLOYEES NATURAL JOIN ADDRESSES;
```

Notice the use of the keywords NATURAL JOIN in line 2. Also notice that there's no keyword ON anywhere and nowhere that we establish the join between the two common columns—which in these two tables are EMPLOYEES.EMPLOYEE_ID and ADDRESSES.EMPLOYEE_ID. The NATURAL JOIN doesn't require an explicit declaration of these columns, provided that the column names are identical.

Also notice something else: see the reference to EMPLOYEE_ID in line 1? Remember that there are two EMPLOYEE_ID columns—one in EMPLOYEES and one in ADDRESSES. Normally such a reference in a join would require a table alias. But the natural join forbids such table prefixes on join column names. Their use would result in a syntax error. However, table prefixes are allowed on other columns—but not the join columns in a natural join.

Finally, a natural join defaults to an inner join, but it works with a left outer join.

```
01  SELECT    EMPLOYEE_ID, LAST_NAME, STREET_ADDRESS
02  FROM      EMPLOYEES NATURAL LEFT OUTER JOIN ADDRESSES;
```

It also works with a right outer join.

```
01  SELECT    EMPLOYEE_ID, LAST_NAME, STREET_ADDRESS
02  FROM      EMPLOYEES NATURAL RIGHT OUTER JOIN ADDRESSES;
```

Finally, it even works with a full outer join.

```
01  SELECT    EMPLOYEE_ID, LAST_NAME, STREET_ADDRESS
02  FROM      EMPLOYEES NATURAL FULL OUTER JOIN ADDRESSES;
```

The SELECT list may reference a column that is common to both tables but not qualified with a table name prefix. If this happens, which table does the value come from? The answer depends on which type of natural join is used:

- If an inner join or a left outer join is used, the leftmost table is the source of the value.
- If a right outer join is used, the rightmost table is the source.

If a full outer join is used, both tables' rows will be combined to form the output, so the value will be taken from the combination of both tables.

USING

The keyword USING is similar to the natural join, in the sense that its use depends on the presence of identically named columns in the JOIN. Like NATURAL, USING can be used with both inner and outer joins.

Let's look at an example. Following is a listing of data in the EMPLOYEES table:

```
EMPLOYEE_ID LAST_NAME   OFFICE_NAME
----------- ----------- -----------
          1 Smith       President
          2 Jones       Marketing
          3 Johnson     Marketing
          4 Smythe      Marketing
```

Next is a listing of the ADDRESS table:

```
ADDRESS_ID STREET_ADDRESS   EMPLOYEE_ID OFFICE_NAME
---------- ---------------  ----------- -----------
      1000 123 Maple #1               1 President
      1001 456 Elm #102               2 Marketing
      1001 456 Elm #103               3 Marketing
      1001 456 Elm #104               4 Marketing
      1001 123 Maple #28              4 President
```

Here's a query that joins the two tables with a USING clause that specifies the EMPLOYEE_ID column:

```
01  SELECT    EMPLOYEE_ID, LAST_NAME, STREET_ADDRESS
02  FROM      EMPLOYEES LEFT JOIN ADDRESSES
03            USING (EMPLOYEE_ID);
```

Note the syntax here—we're using a LEFT JOIN on two tables that share the same column name EMPLOYEE_ID. As we've already seen, this is a variation of an outer join. The keyword OUTER is optional and omitted from this example.

Notice the keyword USING on line 3. USING is followed by a column name enclosed in parentheses. No table name prefix is allowed before the column name—not here, and not elsewhere in the statement such as line 1.

Since the table name prefix is not allowed in line 1, how do you know which table's EMPLOYEE_ID is intended in the select list in line 1? The answer is that it may be one or the other, depending on the row. In an outer join, which is also an equijoin, the values in both tables for EMPLOYEE_ID either will be identical to each other or will include one NULL value in one of the two tables' columns. The output, therefore, will show a value if any is present in either table; otherwise, a NULL value will display. The reason this works is that the values will never conflict in an outer join. The join condition, by definition, will reject conflicting values and exclude rows with conflicting values for the join condition. The result is that if you include the join column in the select list—such as the EMPLOYEE_ID column in line 1 of the example—then the output of an outer join's "join column" specified with the USING clause will show a value wherever a value is present in either table's join column; otherwise, it will display a NULL value.

Let's extend our example.

```
01   SELECT    EMPLOYEE_ID, LAST_NAME, STREET_ADDRESS
02   FROM      EMPLOYEES LEFT JOIN ADDRESSES
03             USING (EMPLOYEE_ID, OFFICE_NAME);
```

This example assumes the presence of an additional column (OFFICE_NAME) in both tables and performs the join using the combination of EMPLOYEE_ID and OFFICE_NAME.

Multitable Joins

So far we've looked only at joins that connect two tables. But joins can connect two, three, or more tables. For example, see Figure 8-2.

These three tables can be joined in a SELECT statement like this:

```
01   SELECT   P.PORT_NAME, S.SHIP_NAME, SC.ROOM_NUMBER
02   FROM     PORTS P JOIN SHIPS S ON P.PORT_ID = S.HOME_PORT_ID
03                    JOIN SHIP_CABINS SC ON S.SHIP_ID = SC.SHIP_ID;
```

Notice the syntax for this SELECT statement that joins three tables:

- The FROM keyword appears once.
- After line 2, when the original two-table join completes, line 3 opens with the keyword JOIN.
- Line 3 continues with the third table name, followed by a table alias, followed by the explicitly defined join criteria.

Line 3 in the preceding SELECT statement can be repeated and edited as required in order to join additional tables beyond these three.

PORTS, SHIPS,
and SHIP_CABINS
tables

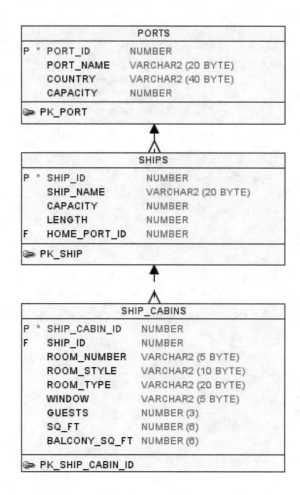

Non-Equijoins

So far, all the joins we've seen have been *equijoins*. In other words, the joins have used columns containing common data values among the join tables and have joined rows in the tables based on finding equal values in the join columns.

Non-equijoins relate one row to another by way of non-equal comparisons, such as comparisons of greater or lesser value or perhaps comparisons that look for a range of values. Such joins are unusual but important. And they are part of the certification exam criteria.

Let's look at an example. See Figure 8-3.

FIGURE 8-3

The SCORES and
GRADING tables

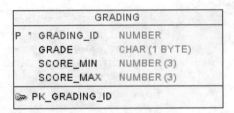

Note that these tables do not have a FOREIGN KEY relationship. As we've already noted, that is not required to join tables.

Let's look at some data in these tables. First, here's SCORES:

```
SCORE_ID                TEST_SCORE
---------------------   ----------
1                       95
2                       55
3                       83
```

Next, GRADING:

```
GRADING_ID              GRADE SCORE_MIN               SCORE_MAX
---------------------   ----- ---------------------   -----------
1                       A     90                      100
2                       B     80                      89
3                       C     70                      79
4                       D     60                      69
5                       E     50                      59
```

The idea here is that the SCORES table lists some actual scores on exams, and the GRADING table contains information about grading criteria.

In the SCORES table, we have a row of data showing that the test identified with a SCORE_ID value of 1 received a score of 95. According to the GRADING table, that should be a grade of A.

Let's create a SELECT statement that joins these tables to determine each test score's grades.

```
01  SELECT S.SCORE_ID, S.TEST_SCORE, G.GRADE
02  FROM   SCORES S JOIN GRADING G
03    ON   S.TEST_SCORE BETWEEN G.SCORE_MIN AND G.SCORE_MAX;
```

Note the syntax of this join. On line 2 we have a typical JOIN syntax, but on line 3, instead of the equijoin, we connect the two tables by comparing the value in the TEST_SCORE column of SCORES and see whether it's BETWEEN the values for the GRADING table's SCORE_MIN and SCORE_MAX columns.

Here is the output:

```
SCORE_ID                TEST_SCORE GRADE
--------------------- ---------- -----
1                       95         A
3                       83         B
2                       55         E
```

This is an example of a non-equijoin. The syntax of the ON condition in a non-equijoin is similar to the syntax for the WHERE clause in the SELECT, in that you can use comparison expressions, the greater-than or less-than operators, SQL functions, and Boolean operators to connect a series of comparisons.

CERTIFICATION OBJECTIVE 8.03

Join a Table to Itself by Using a Self-Join

A *self-join* is a table that is joined to itself. A self-join is based on the value in a column of a table as it compares to the values within another column—often a different column—in the same table. The self-join returns one or more rows from a table that are merged with other rows in the same table based on the join criteria.

(Note: Syntactically you can join a column to itself in the same table, as opposed to a different column in the same table. It doesn't do much logically, but the syntax will execute.)

Self-joins can use all the same variations on join criteria that any other table join can use. In other words, self-joins can be inner joins or outer joins, equijoins or non-equijoins, and so on.

Let's write a self-joining SELECT statement. For starters, see Figure 8-4. The POSITIONS table lists job titles within our Codd Cruises organization.

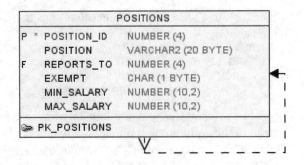

FIGURE 8-4

The POSITIONS
table

Here's a listing of some of the columns in the POSITIONS table:

```
POSITION_ID           POSITION              REPORTS_TO
--------------------  --------------------  ----------------
1                     Captain
2                     Director              1
3                     Manager               2
4                     Crew Chief            2
5                     Crew                  4
```

Note the column REPORTS_TO. It indicates that, for example, Crew Chief reports to the position of POSITION_ID 2, which is Director.

Self-Referencing Foreign Keys

The POSITIONS table is supported with a foreign key that points to itself, which is created with this SQL statement:

```
ALTER TABLE POSITIONS
ADD CONSTRAINT FK_PO_PO FOREIGN KEY (REPORTS_TO)
    REFERENCES POSITIONS (POSITION_ID);
```

Note that a foreign key is advised but not required in order to perform the self-join.

Self-Join Syntax

Now that we have our table, our data, and our optional foreign key constraint, let's look at a query that will connect all of this together. To create the self-join, we need to do the following:

- Identify the table twice in the FROM clause.
- Define our join criteria—which in this case will be an OUTER join so that we can include the highest-level position that doesn't have a REPORTS_TO value—and therefore isn't "matched" with anything.

■ Apply a table alias to all appropriate references, being careful to join the REPORTS_TO column in the first table reference to the POSITION_ID column in the second table reference.

Here's the query:

```
SELECT    A.POSITION_ID, A.POSITION, B.POSITION BOSS
FROM      POSITIONS A LEFT OUTER JOIN POSITIONS B
ON        A.REPORTS_TO = B.POSITION_ID
ORDER BY A.POSITION_ID;
```

And here's the output:

```
POSITION_ID                POSITION              BOSS
-------------------------- --------------------- --------------------
1                          Captain
2                          Director              Captain
3                          Manager               Director
4                          Crew Chief            Director
5                          Crew                  Crew Chief
```

The result is a listing of positions and the supervisor each reports to. All of this data is found in the one table POSITIONS. You can see that in the SELECT statement's output, both the POSITION column and the BOSS column contain data that is found in the POSITION column of the POSITIONS table. But the self-join returns a meaningful output display with a column alias on the second reference to POSITION.

CERTIFICATION OBJECTIVE 8.04

View Data That Generally Does Not Meet a Join Condition by Using Outer Joins

An *outer* join is a join that returns all the same data as an inner join but also returns additional rows, namely, those rows that don't have matches in all the tables that are joined together. There are three types of outer joins—LEFT, RIGHT, and FULL. Each is described here.

LEFT OUTER JOIN

To see one type of outer join in action, let's continue with our example and modify our query just a little to make it an outer join.

```
01   SELECT    SHIP_ID, SHIP_NAME, PORT_NAME
02   FROM      SHIPS LEFT OUTER JOIN PORTS
03   ON        HOME_PORT_ID = PORT_ID
04   ORDER BY SHIP_ID;
```

Notice the addition of the keywords LEFT OUTER in line 2. The following are the rows returned by this code:

```
SHIP_ID                  SHIP_NAME             PORT_NAME
---------------------    --------------------  --------------------
1                        Codd Crystal          Baltimore
2                        Codd Elegance         Tampa
3                        Codd Champion
4                        Codd Victorious       Tampa
5                        Codd Grandeur         Charleston
6                        Codd Prince           Charleston
```

By changing our FROM clause from a JOIN to a LEFT OUTER JOIN, we have changed the query from an inner join to an outer join. (Remember that JOIN defaults to INNER JOIN.) And notice that our output now includes data for SHIP_ID 3. Also notice that the row for SHIP_ID 3 shows no value for PORT_NAME, which is correct—no HOME_PORT_ID value was assigned to it.

Also note that the OUTER keyword is optional. In other words, this is just as good:

```
01   SELECT   SHIP_ID, SHIP_NAME, PORT_NAME
02   FROM     SHIPS LEFT JOIN PORTS
03   ON       HOME_PORT_ID = PORT_ID
04   ORDER BY SHIP_ID;
```

In this example, OUTER is omitted, but the effect is the same.

RIGHT OUTER JOIN

But we still don't see our PORT_NAME of Miami. So, let's change our query again.

```
01   SELECT   SHIP_ID, SHIP_NAME, PORT_NAME
02   FROM     SHIPS RIGHT OUTER JOIN PORTS
03   ON       HOME_PORT_ID = PORT_ID
04   ORDER BY SHIP_ID;
```

Note that we've replaced the keyword LEFT with the keyword RIGHT in line 2. Here is the result:

```
SHIP_ID                 SHIP_NAME               PORT_NAME
--------------------    --------------------    --------------------
1                       Codd Crystal            Baltimore
2                       Codd Elegance           Tampa
4                       Codd Victorious         Tampa
5                       Codd Grandeur           Charleston
6                       Codd Prince             Charleston
                                                Miami
```

We've now included the row for Miami. But we lost our row with the Codd Champion. That's because this RIGHT OUTER JOIN returns unmatched rows from the right side of the join, which in this example is the PORTS table (see line 2 of the SELECT statement). But we took away our LEFT OUTER JOIN to SHIPS.

As before, OUTER is optional. RIGHT JOIN will do the same thing as RIGHT OUTER JOIN.

FULL OUTER JOIN

If we want to combine the effects of a RIGHT OUTER JOIN and LEFT OUTER JOIN, we can use the FULL OUTER JOIN.

```
01   SELECT    SHIP_ID, SHIP_NAME, PORT_NAME
02   FROM      SHIPS FULL OUTER JOIN PORTS
03   ON        HOME_PORT_ID = PORT_ID
04   ORDER BY SHIP_ID;
```

Line 2 shows the use of the keywords FULL OUTER JOIN, and the output is as follows:

```
SHIP_ID                 SHIP_NAME               PORT_NAME
--------------------    --------------------    --------------------
1                       Codd Crystal            Baltimore
2                       Codd Elegance           Tampa
3                       Codd Champion
4                       Codd Victorious         Tampa
5                       Codd Grandeur           Charleston
6                       Codd Prince             Charleston
                                                Miami
```

And here we have all of our rows, merged where matched, but all returned regardless. As with all other outer join types, the keyword OUTER is optional.

For the Record: Oracle Outer Join Syntax: (+)

The LEFT, RIGHT, and FULL OUTER syntax usages are ANSI standard and featured on Oracle's exam. In addition, Oracle SQL offers an alternative outer join syntax that employs a plus sign enclosed in parentheses. This syntax is used quite a bit and long predates the ANSI standard syntax in Oracle SQL; however, the outer join plus operator is not on the exam.

Let's look at the syntax anyway. If you're a veteran Oracle professional, you might think this book is incomplete without at least a mention of the outer join plus operator. Let's restate the earlier LEFT OUTER JOIN example with the plus operator.

```
01  SELECT    SHIP_ID, SHIP_NAME, PORT_NAME
02  FROM      SHIPS, PORTS
03  WHERE     HOME_PORT_ID = PORT_ID(+)
04  ORDER BY SHIP_ID;
```

Note the special characters at the end of line 3. The plus sign in parentheses defines this query as a left outer join. It is a left outer join, but the plus sign goes on the right side; I think of the plus operator as adding fake NULL rows on the right side to enable the otherwise unmatched rows on the left to be included in the returned row set.

To create a right outer join in this syntax, you simply move the plus sign to the left side.

```
01  SELECT    SHIP_ID, SHIP_NAME, PORT_NAME
02  FROM      SHIPS, PORTS
03  WHERE     HOME_PORT_ID(+) = PORT_ID
04  ORDER BY SHIP_ID;
```

You can't really do a full outer join using this syntax, but you can use the set operator UNION to combine a left outer join and a right outer join to achieve the same result.

```
01  SELECT    SHIP_ID, SHIP_NAME, PORT_NAME
02  FROM      SHIPS, PORTS
03  WHERE     HOME_PORT_ID = PORT_ID(+)
04  UNION
05  SELECT    SHIP_ID, SHIP_NAME, PORT_NAME
06  FROM      SHIPS, PORTS
07  WHERE     HOME_PORT_ID(+) = PORT_ID
08  ORDER BY SHIP_ID;
```

(Note: Set operators are addressed in detail in Chapter 11.)

So, that's the plus operator. But it was never ANSI standard. Furthermore, Oracle Corporation formally recommends that you avoid using it from now on and stick with the keywords INNER JOIN, OUTER JOIN, and all the other related keywords. In special situations the plus operator now has some restrictions and limitations that don't pertain to the INNER JOIN and OUTER JOIN keywords.

But you won't be tested on it—you'll be tested on the newer LEFT, RIGHT, and FULL OUTER JOIN formats.

CERTIFICATION SUMMARY

There are several ways to join tables in SQL. The *inner join* compares common values in rows of two or more tables and returns data from a row only if that row has a match in the joined table. The *outer join* will show a row as output whether that row has a joined row in another table or not.

Some joins are equijoins, which means that they join rows in one table with rows in another table by looking for values in both rows that are equal to each other. Non-equijoins look for values that have some relationship other than equality, such as greater than, less than, or in between a range of values.

Primary key and foreign key relationships help protect the integrity of data in columns that are intended to join tables, but their presence is not required in order to create a successful join.

When two or more tables are joined, any of their columns may be included in the SELECT statement's select list. However, a syntax error may result if the two tables have columns that share the same name. In such situations, the table name can be placed in front of the column name as a prefix to eliminate any ambiguity. As an alternative, the table can be assigned an alias name that will last only long enough for the SELECT statement to execute. The alias can then be used as a prefix in front of any column name, and it may be required in front of the otherwise ambiguous column names.

A natural join does not specify which columns are being used to connect two or more tables together, relying instead on the assumption that the columns to form the join have the same name as each other. Natural joins are inner joins by default.

The USING keyword can do something similar to the NATURAL keyword. USING can name the common column one time, and the SELECT statement will complete the join based on that column, as well as eliminating the need for a table prefix or alias in front of the key column.

Multitable joins can be performed with any join type.

Non-equijoins use comparison operators, Boolean logic, or anything else to establish comparison logic between two or more tables in a join.

A self-join occurs when a table is joined to itself. Typically one column in the table is joined to a different column in the same table.

TWO-MINUTE DRILL

Describe the Different Types of Joins and Their Features

☐ The inner join compares a row in one table to rows in another table and returns the first table's row only if a matching row in the second table is found.

☐ The outer join compares a row in one table to rows in another table and returns the first table's row, as well as data from matching rows in the second table wherever a match is found.

☐ The equijoin identifies a particular column in one table's rows, relates that column to another table's rows, and looks for equal values in order to join pairs of rows together.

☐ The non-equijoin differs from the equijoin in that it doesn't look for exact matches but instead looks for relative matches: greater than, less than, or a range, such as one table's value that is between two values in the second table.

☐ The self-join connects a table to itself.

Write SELECT Statements to Access Data from More Than One Table Using Equijoins and Non-Equijoins

☐ A join is any SELECT statement that selects from two or more tables.

☐ A join will connect rows in one table with rows in another table.

☐ The table alias exists only for the duration of the SQL statement in which it is declared.

☐ Table aliases are necessary to eliminate ambiguity in referring to columns of the same name in a join.

☐ The natural join does not name the connecting column but assumes that two or more tables have columns with identical names and that these are intended to be the connecting, or joining, columns.

☐ The USING keyword can empower an inner, outer, or other join to connect based on a set of commonly named columns, in much the same fashion as a natural join.

☐ Joins can connect two, three, or more tables.

Join a Table to Itself by Using a Self-Join

☐ The self-join connects a table to itself.

☐ Self-join criteria compares a column in a table with the same or another column in the same table.

☐ Self-joins can also be referred to as recursive joins.

☐ Self-joins can be written as equijoins, non-equijoins, inner joins, and outer joins.

View Data That Generally Does Not Meet a Join Condition by Using Outer Joins

☐ The outer join compares rows in two tables and returns output whether there is a matching row or not.

☐ The left outer join shows all the rows in one table and only the matching rows in the second; the right outer join does the same thing in reverse.

☐ The full outer join shows all rows in both tables one way or the other—either as a matched row set or as a standalone row.

SELF TEST

The following questions will help you measure your understanding of the material presented in this chapter. Choose all the correct answers for each question.

Describe the Different Types of Joins and Their Features

1. An inner join queries from two tables (looking at values in columns and optionally using expressions that reference columns) and compares the resulting values in one set of rows with the resulting values in another set of rows, looking for:
    A. Values that match
    B. Values that may or may not match
    C. Values in the first set that are greater than values in the second set
    D. Values in the first set that are less than values in the second set

2. Which of the following symbols is most likely to be used in a SELECT statement using a non-equijoin?
    A. ! =
    B. < >
    C. < =
    D. None of the above

3. Equijoins look for:
    A. Exact data matches
    B. Ranges of data matches
    C. Comparisons using any comparison operator provided that the resulting correlations occur in both tables
    D. None of the above

Write SELECT Statements to Access Data from More Than One Table Using Equijoins and Non-Equijoins

4. Review this SQL statement:

    ```
    SELECT   V.VENDOR_ID, INV.INVOICE_DATE
    FROM     VENDORS V INNER JOIN INVOICES INV
    ON       V.VENDOR_ID = INV.VENDOR_ID;
    ```

    Which one of the following keywords in this statement is optional?
    A. JOIN
    B. INNER
    C. ON
    D. All are required

5. Review the INVOICES and VENDORS tables.

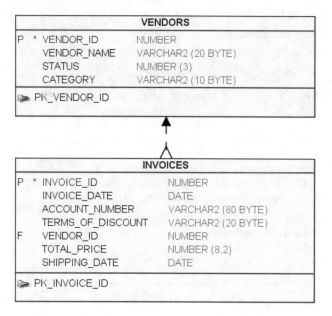

Next review the following SQL statement:

```
01   SELECT VENDOR_ID, INVOICE_DATE, TOTAL_PRICE
02   FROM   VENDORS JOIN INVOICES
03   USING (VENDOR_ID);
```

Which of the following statements is true for the SQL statement?

A. It will execute successfully.

B. It will fail with a syntax error because there is no ON clause.

C. It will fail with a syntax error on line 1 because VENDOR_ID is ambiguous.

D. It will fail with a syntax error on line 3 because of the parentheses around VENDOR_ID.

6. Review the illustration from question 5 and then review the following SQL statement:

```
01   SELECT VENDOR_ID, INVOICE_DATE, TOTAL_PRICE
02   FROM   VENDORS JOIN INVOICES
03   USING (VENDOR_ID);
```

What kind of join is this? (Choose two.)

A. INNER

B. OUTER

C. NATURAL

D. Equijoin

7. A table alias: (Choose two.)
   A. Renames a table in the database so that future joins can use the new name.
   B. Is the same thing as a database object synonym.
   C. Exists only for the SQL statement that declared it.
   D. Can be used to clear up ambiguity in the query.

8. Review the POSITIONS, EMPLOYEES, and PAY_HISTORY tables.

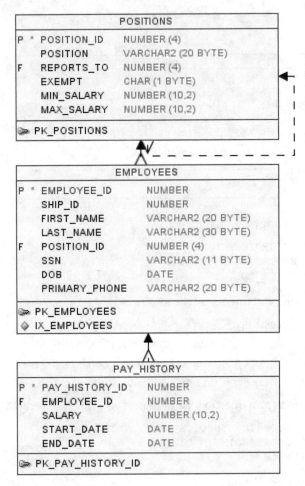

Review the following SQL statement:

```
SELECT LAST_NAME, POSITION, SALARY
FROM    POSITIONS P JOIN EMPLOYEES   E  ON P.POSITION_ID = E.POSITION_ID
                    JOIN PAY_HISTORY PH ON E.EMPLOYEE_ID = PH.EMPLOYEE_ID;
```

Which of the following is true for the SQL statement? (Choose two.)

A. It will fail because there are no table aliases.

B. It will execute successfully.

C. It is an outer join.

D. It connects three tables.

9. Review the illustration from question 8 and then review the following SQL statement:

```
01   SELECT A.EMPLOYEE_ID, B.POSITION
02   FROM   PAY_HISTORY A JOIN POSITIONS B
03     ON   A.SALARY < B.MAX_SALARY AND A.SALARY > B.MIN_SALARY;
```

Which of the following statements accurately describe the SQL statement? (Choose two.)

A. It contains a syntax error on line 3.

B. It is an inner join.

C. It is a non-equijoin.

D. It contains a syntax error on line 2 and should have an additional keyword with the JOIN keyword.

10. How many tables can be joined in a query?

A. Only two

B. As many as you like, provided they are all constrained with PRIMARY KEY and FOREIGN KEY constraints to ensure that the join condition will work

C. One, two, three, or more

D. No more than seven

11. You have two tables. One table is called CUSTOMERS. Another is called PURCHASES, and it records a list of customer transactions. Your goal is to create a SELECT statement that will show all customers by last name in alphabetical order, along with any purchases they may have made in the past two weeks, as recorded in the PURCHASES table. It's possible that many customers have made no purchases in the past two weeks, but you still want them included in the output. Both tables contain a column called CUSTOMER_ID. Which of the following will be true of the SELECT statement you'll need to create? (Choose two.)

A. It will be an inner join.

B. It will be an outer join.

C. It will be a cross-join.

D. It will be an equijoin.

Join a Table to Itself by Using a Self-Join

12. A self-join is: (Choose two.)

    A. A SELECT statement that specifies one table once in the FROM clause

    B. A SELECT statement that specifies one table twice in the FROM clause

    C. A SELECT statement that joins a table to itself by connecting a column in the table to a different column in the same table

    D. A SELECT statement that uses the SELF JOIN keywords

13. Review the illustration from question 8. Which of the following is a valid self-join statement? (Choose all that apply.)

    A.
```
SELECT P1.POSITION_ID, P1.MIN_SALARY, P1.MAX_SALARY
FROM    POSITIONS P1 JOIN POSITIONS P2
ON      P1.REPORTS_TO = P2.POSITION_ID;
```

    B.
```
SELECT P1.POSITION_ID, P1.MIN_SALARY, P1.MAX_SALARY
FROM    POSITIONS P1 SELF JOIN POSITIONS P2
ON      P1.REPORTS_TO = P2.POSITION_ID;
```

    C.
```
SELECT P1.POSITION_ID, P1.MIN_SALARY, P1.MAX_SALARY
FROM    POSITIONS P1 INNER JOIN POSITIONS P2
ON      P1.REPORTS_TO = P2.POSITION_ID;
```

    D.
```
SELECT P1.POSITION_ID, P1.MIN_SALARY, P1.MAX_SALARY
FROM    POSITIONS P1 RIGHT OUTER JOIN POSITIONS P2
ON      P1.REPORTS_TO = P2.POSITION_ID;
```

View Data That Generally Does Not Meet a Join Condition by Using Outer Joins

14. Review the illustration from question 5. Which of the following is a syntactically correct outer join query? (Choose two.)

    A.
```
SELECT VENDOR_NAME, INVOICE_DATE
FROM    VENDORS LEFT JOIN  INVOICES
ON      VENDORS.VENDOR_ID = INVOICES.VENDOR_ID;
```

    B.
```
SELECT VENDOR_NAME, INVOICE_DATE
FROM    VENDORS OUTER JOIN  INVOICES
ON      VENDORS.VENDOR_ID = INVOICES.VENDOR_ID;
```

```
C. SELECT  VENDOR_NAME,  INVOICE_DATE
   FROM     VENDORS RIGHT OUTER JOIN  INVOICES
   ON       VENDORS.VENDOR_ID = INVOICES.VENDOR_ID;
D. SELECT  VENDOR_NAME,  INVOICE_DATE
   FROM     VENDORS FULL OUTER  INVOICES
   ON       VENDORS.VENDOR_ID = INVOICES.VENDOR_ID;
```

15. The difference between an INNER and an OUTER join is:

- A. The INNER join relates a table to itself; the OUTER join relates a table to other tables.
- B. The INNER join displays rows that match in all joined tables; the OUTER join shows data that doesn't necessarily match.
- C. The OUTER join relates a table to tables in other user accounts; the INNER does not.
- D. The INNER runs on data inside the table; the OUTER runs on data outside of the table.

SELF TEST ANSWERS

Describe the Different Types of Joins and Their Features

1.   ☑   **A.** An inner join looks for values that match.
      ☒   **B, C,** and **D** are incorrect. An inner join ignores rows where values don't match; an outer join may return some of those rows. A non-equijoin may leverage matches defined by greater-than or less-than comparison operators.

2.   ☑   **C.** The non-equijoin performs comparisons using relationships that don't involve equality but where there is still some sort of matching criteria, such as less than, greater than, or values within a range.
      ☒   **A, B,** and **D** are incorrect. The not-equal signs != and <> are not what is intended with a non-equijoin. Remember, these are not "not-equal" joins but rather "non-equijoins."

3.   ☑   **A.** Equijoins look for exact data matches.
      ☒   **B, C,** and **D** are incorrect. Non-equijoins use ranges of matches. Equijoins don't use any comparison operator; they use only equal signs.

Write SELECT Statements to Access Data from More Than One Table Using Equijoins and Non-equijoins

4.   ☑   **B.** INNER is optional. When creating an INNER JOIN, you can just use the term JOIN without the reserved word INNER, and the join will be assumed to be INNER.
      ☒   **A, C,** and **D** are incorrect. JOIN is required. So is ON.

5.   ☑   **A.** It will execute successfully.
      ☒   **B, C,** and **D** are incorrect. Even though this is a JOIN, the presence of USING eliminates the need for an ON clause. With USING, a table alias is not required, nor is one allowed in the select list. The parentheses around VENDOR_ID on line 3 are fine.

6.   ☑   **A** and **D.** The INNER keyword is optional, but that is what this is by default. It's also an equijoin, in that the two tables are joined by defining values that match equally in the VENDOR_ID column—this is specified by use of the USING clause on line 3, which is equivalent to ON VENDORS.VENDOR_ID = INVOICES.VENDOR_ID.
      ☒   **B** and **C** are incorrect. It is not an OUTER join; if it were, the OUTER keyword must be specified. It is not a NATURAL join for the same reason—if it were, the NATURAL keyword must be specified.

7. ☑ **C** and **D.** The table alias goes away after the query is over. It can be used to clear up confusion in the syntax of a statement by adding it as a prefix at the beginning of any column that shares the same name with another column in a joined table.

   ☒ **A** and **B** are incorrect. The table alias is not the same as a database object synonym. The table alias survives only within the SQL statement that calls it; after that, it goes away.

8. ☑ **B** and **D.** It will execute successfully, and it connects three tables.

   ☒ **A** and **C** are incorrect. It does not require table aliases. It is an inner join, not an outer join.

9. ☑ **B** and **C.** The query is an inner join. The keyword INNER is optional and omitted in this instance. The query is a non-equijoin, wherein the ON condition compares the PAY_HISTORY table's SALARY column of values to the MAX_SALARY and MIN_SALARY of the POSITIONS table.

   ☒ **A** and **D** are incorrect. The statement contains no syntax errors.

10. ☑ **C.** You can join as many tables as you want. Remember that joining one table to itself is a self-join.

    ☒ **A, B,** and **D** are incorrect. You are not limited to two tables, nor are you required to only join tables that have constraints on them. You are not limited to seven tables.

11. ☑ **B** and **D.** The SELECT must be an outer join to include all records in the CUSTOMERS table whether or not they have a corresponding row in the PURCHASES table in the last two weeks. Also, since both tables contain a CUSTOMER_ID, you'll use an equijoin to locate exact matches between the two tables.

    ☒ **A** and **C** are incorrect. The query cannot be an inner join, because if it were, it would only show customers who have made purchases in the past two weeks. It cannot be a cross-join, which is a Cartesian product, because all that would do is connect every customer with every purchase without any regard for whether the customer actually made the purchase or someone else did.

Join a Table to Itself by Using a Self-Join

12. ☑ **B** and **C.** In a self-join, the table name is repeated twice in the FROM clause, and perhaps more than twice. A self-join is most commonly used to join a column in a table to a different column within the same table.

    ☒ **A** and **D** are incorrect. The self-join syntax names the same name twice—or more—in the FROM clause. There is no syntax in Oracle SQL involving the keywords SELF JOIN.

13. ☑ **A, C,** and **D.** All of these are valid SQL statements. The first is a typical inner join. **C** spells out the optional word INNER for the same result as **A**. **D** defines a valid outer join and is also a self-join.

    ☒ **B** is incorrect. There is no keyword SELF, as in SELF JOIN.

View Data That Generally Does Not Meet a Join Condition by Using Outer Joins

14. ☑ **A** and **C.** The LEFT JOIN . . . ON syntax is correct. So is the RIGHT OUTER JOIN . . . ON syntax. Remember that the keyword OUTER is optional.

    ☒ **B** and **D** are incorrect. The OUTER . . . ON syntax is incorrect; there is no OUTER by itself. The FULL OUTER . . . ON syntax is also incorrect. In neither of these is the required keyword JOIN present.

15. ☑ **B.** INNER shows data only when there's a row-to-row match between tables, whereas OUTER can show data for rows in one table that don't match the rows in the joined table.

    ☒ **A, C,** and **D** are incorrect. **A** describes a join that "relates a table to itself." That is a self-join, not an inner join. The fact that a table may or may not exist in other user accounts is irrelevant; you can join tables whether or not they are in the same user account. OUTER does not run on data outside of the table; all joins reference data within each of their respective referenced tables.

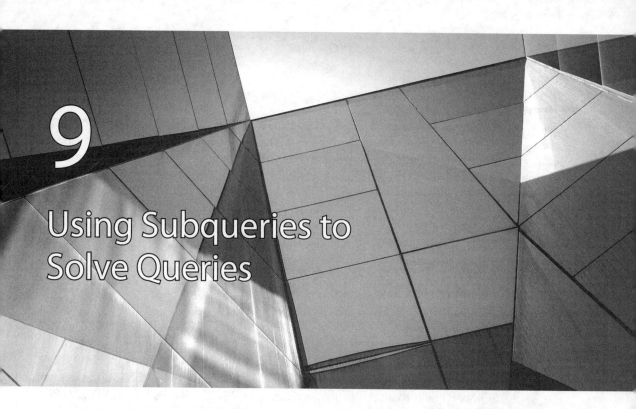

9
Using Subqueries to Solve Queries

CERTIFICATION OBJECTIVES

T his chapter looks at subqueries. A *subquery* is a SELECT statement within a larger SQL statement. The subquery concept builds on many of the features we've already looked at and combines them in a way that makes SQL quite powerful. However, subqueries introduce some complexities that are important to master. They are an important part of the certification exam.

Define Subqueries

As you've already seen, a query is a SELECT statement. A subquery is a SELECT statement that exists within another SQL statement—sort of a "sub" SQL statement. SQL statements that accept subqueries include SELECT, INSERT, UPDATE, MERGE, and DELETE. Subqueries are not limited to DML; they can also be used in a CREATE TABLE or CREATE VIEW statement.

Most subqueries are syntactically autonomous, meaning you could execute the subquery successfully on its own, separate from the parent query. However, some subqueries are not standalone queries but instead are *correlated* to the larger parent query in a way that ties the two queries together.

A subquery may return one or more columns in one or more rows. One common use of a subquery is to return data that is of use to the parent query, such as criteria within a WHERE clause, for example. A SQL statement that includes a subquery as part of its code is considered the *parent* to the subquery. A parent SQL statement may include one or more subqueries in its syntax. Subqueries may have their own subqueries. In other words, a SQL statement may have a subquery, which in turn may have another subquery within it, and on and on. The starting SQL statement in such a situation is the *top-level* query, and any subsequent subquery that contains a subquery within it is a parent to its subquery. A parent query may also be referred to as an *outer* query.

Any valid SELECT statement can qualify as a subquery of another statement. SELECT statements that can be made into a subquery include those that retrieve data from one or more tables or views; those that use complex expressions or scalar or aggregate functions; and those that include the WHERE and GROUP BY clauses, HAVING clauses, joins, or any of the other features available to SELECT statements.

A subquery is not restricted to retrieving data from the same table or tables as the parent query. In fact, subqueries often retrieve data from tables other than those specified in the parent query. The tables of the subquery are not required to have any key relationship or join or other logical relationship to the tables of the parent query. Such a relationship may exist between the parent and the subquery—but it is not required.

Subqueries can be used to solve a variety of problems.

- **Creating complex multistage queries** Subqueries can find answers to questions and then use those answers to ask new questions. In other words, in a single SELECT statement's WHERE clause, a subquery can find data based on some criteria, then use that answer to identify a secondary answer, and finally pass that answer on to the parent query, all in the same SQL statement. This can be repeated within multiple stages in ways that a standalone parent query cannot do without the use of a subquery.

- **Creating populated tables** A subquery can be incorporated into a CREATE TABLE statement to quickly create and populate a table from an existing data source at the time the table is created.

- **Manipulating large data sets** Subqueries can be incorporated into an INSERT or UPDATE statement to move large amounts of data and insert or update many rows of information by moving data from one source into another in a single SQL statement.

- **Creating named views** A subquery is used to create view objects at the time of creation.

- **Defining dynamic views** A subquery can be used to replace a table reference in a FROM clause. This form of subquery, also known as an inline view, is discussed in Chapter 10.

- **Defining dynamic expressions with scalar subqueries** There is a form of subquery that will return only one column's worth of data in one row; that is, it will return a single value. Such a subquery can be used in almost any place in a SQL statement where an expression can be used.

As you can see, subqueries are powerful, can do a wide variety of tasks, and can occur in almost any SQL statement in almost any clause. This chapter will explore many examples of these usages of subqueries.

CERTIFICATION OBJECTIVE 9.02

Describe the Types of Problems Subqueries Can Solve

Subqueries are an ideal solution to several common data challenges. Sometimes a subquery is the only solution. Subqueries are ideal for finding data that is at the top of some scale, is above average, is below average, or something comparable. You might first use a query that involves an aggregate function and then use the result of that query to find records that correlate to the result.

Let's look at an example with some code. Consider a table SALES_DATA.

```
CREATE TABLE SALES_DATA
(   ID          NUMBER
,   REP         VARCHAR2(10)
,   YEAR        NUMBER(4)
,   TOTAL_SALES NUMBER
);
```

Let's add records to the table for sales representatives showing sales by year for the years 2016 through 2018.

```
INSERT INTO SALES_DATA VALUES ( 1, 'Joe', 2018, 249);
INSERT INTO SALES_DATA VALUES ( 2, 'Joe', 2017, 178);
INSERT INTO SALES_DATA VALUES ( 3, 'Joe', 2016, 483);
INSERT INTO SALES_DATA VALUES ( 4, 'Ann', 2018, 422);
INSERT INTO SALES_DATA VALUES ( 5, 'Ann', 2017, 427);
INSERT INTO SALES_DATA VALUES ( 6, 'Ann', 2016, 245);
INSERT INTO SALES_DATA VALUES ( 7, 'Moe', 2018, 308);
INSERT INTO SALES_DATA VALUES ( 8, 'Moe', 2017, 721);
INSERT INTO SALES_DATA VALUES ( 9, 'Moe', 2016, 109);
INSERT INTO SALES_DATA VALUES (10, 'Lyn', 2018, 525);
INSERT INTO SALES_DATA VALUES (11, 'Lyn', 2017, 589);
INSERT INTO SALES_DATA VALUES (12, 'Lyn', 2016, 742);
COMMIT;
```

You are tasked with listing any and all sales reps whose sales for 2016 surpassed the sales team's average sales for the prior year of 2017.

One way to do this is to first get the average sales for 2017.

```
SELECT AVG(TOTAL_SALES) AVG_SALES
FROM    SALES_DATA
WHERE   YEAR = 2017;

AVG_SALES
---------
  478.75
```

Next, use the results to look for sales reps in 2018 who sold at a higher level.

```
SELECT  REP
FROM    SALES_DATA
WHERE   YEAR = 2018
  AND   TOTAL_SALES > 478.75;


REP
---
Lyn
```

That's one way to get the answer. But a subquery would have found the answer in a single query.

```
SELECT  REP
FROM    SALES_DATA
WHERE   YEAR = 2018
  AND   TOTAL_SALES > (SELECT AVG(TOTAL_SALES)
                       FROM    SALES_DATA
                       WHERE   YEAR = 2017);
```

You can use subqueries for many purposes.

- To populate a table using zero to more source rows within an INSERT statement or do virtually the same thing within a CREATE TABLE statement.
- To create a VIEW.
- To specify values assigned to an UPDATE statement.
- To perform comparisons against aggregated results.
- To create inline views: a subquery in a FROM clause of a SELECT statement. There is no limit to how many subqueries deep you can go within an inline view; you can have subqueries of subqueries of subqueries in this context.
- As an alternative to expressions.
- To nest other queries. A subquery in the WHERE clause of a SELECT statement is known as a nested subquery because it is nested within the larger query (the SELECT statement itself). You can nest up to 255 subqueries in this way.
- To have a correlated subquery within a SELECT, UPDATE, or DELETE.

The remainder of this chapter will explore these and other examples of subqueries.

CERTIFICATION OBJECTIVE 9.03

Describe the Types of Subqueries

There are many types of subqueries. Here are the major types:

- **Single-row subqueries**   A single-row subquery returns a single row's worth of data in its result. Single-row subqueries may include multiple columns' worth of data or a single column's worth of data.

- **Multiple-row subqueries**   A multiple-row subquery returns zero, one, or more rows in its result. It is not guaranteed to return multiple rows, but it may do so, and thus the parent query should be structured to receive multiple rows just in case in order to avoid the possibility of an execution error. For example, a parent query may use an equal sign to compare its own return values with the returned values of a subquery. An equal sign performs a comparison to a single value, so in the case of the subquery, only one row should be returned. But if the subquery returns multiple rows, the parent query (and therefore the query as a whole) will fail with an execution error—it depends on whether the subquery actually returns multiple rows. It might not, but it certainly can at any time. Therefore, the parent query to a multirow subquery typically uses a comparison operator (such as IN) that allows for multiple rows of values to be returned.

- **Multiple-column subqueries**   Multiple-column subqueries return more than one column in their result. This requires the parent query to receive multiple columns from the subquery and involves special syntax considerations, as we just discussed. A multiple-column subquery can be either a single-row subquery or a multiple-row subquery.

- **Correlated subqueries**   A correlated subquery is a subquery that specifies columns that belong to tables that are also referenced by the parent query. In a multilevel series of subqueries, subqueries within subqueries, and so on, the correlated parent query can be any number of levels higher than the subquery. The correlation involves more than the subquery merely accessing the same tables and columns through its own direct call to the table; rather, the correlated subquery performs row-by-row analysis in cooperation with the parent query, accessing data and referencing that data in its own expressions in order to coordinate row processing with the correlated parent. Correlated subqueries can exist in SELECT, UPDATE, and DELETE statements. A correlated subquery may also be a single-row, multiple-row, or multiple-column subquery.

- **Scalar subqueries** If a single-row subquery consists of only one column's worth of output, then it is known as a *scalar subquery*. Scalar subqueries can be used in almost any location that an expression can be used, which is not true for other forms of subqueries. A scalar subquery can also be correlated.

Note that the different types of subqueries aren't mutually exclusive. A single type of subquery may fall into *multiple categories of subqueries described in this chapter.*

As you can see, there are many types of subqueries. Let's begin looking at them in detail.

CERTIFICATION OBJECTIVE 9.04

Query Data Using Correlated Subqueries

A correlated subquery is a query that is integrated with a parent query. Correlated subqueries include references to elements of a parent query, and thus, they do not exist as stand-alone queries like the examples you've seen so far. Up to now, any of the subqueries you've seen could have been executed on their own. That's not the case with correlated subqueries.

Let's take a look at an example using the SHIP_CABINS table. In Chapter 7, you saw the SHIP_CABINS table in Figure 7-2, along with a data listing showing the 12 rows of information in our sample table. Each row in SHIP_CABINS shows that a cabin is of ROOM_STYLE Suite or Stateroom. Each individual room's value for SQ_FT is shown, and the values are not all the same.

Our current challenge is to create a single query that lists all the cabins in the ship whose size—as measured by the SQ_FT column—is larger than the average cabin for its ROOM_STYLE.

In other words, we need to

- Identify the average square footage for each ROOM_STYLE in SHIP_CABINS
- Use average square footage value to display each ship cabin whose SQ_FT is greater than the average for its ROOM_STYLE

Without a correlated subquery, we'd be required to create separate queries to get this information. We would need the following:

- One query to get the averages
- Another query—or queries—to compare the individual averages for each ROOM_STYLE

But with a correlated subquery, we can do it all at once. Here's the SQL (line numbers added):

```
01    SELECT    A.SHIP_CABIN_ID, A.ROOM_STYLE, A.ROOM_NUMBER, A.SQ_FT
02    FROM      SHIP_CABINS A
03    WHERE     A.SQ_FT > (SELECT AVG(SQ_FT)
04                         FROM   SHIP_CABINS
05                         WHERE  ROOM_STYLE = A.ROOM_STYLE)
06    ORDER BY A.ROOM_NUMBER;
```

Note the subquery that starts on line 3 and continues through (and includes) line 5. In particular, note the second ROOM_STYLE at the end of line 5. See the table alias of A? That is a reference to a column of the parent query—not the subquery. See line 2 to confirm that the parent query's table is aliased with the A prefix.

This is the correlation in this correlated subquery. This query is not executing as a stand-alone query and then passing back its result like noncorrelated subqueries do. Instead, the correlated subquery is executing once for each value that the parent query finds for each row, passing the value for the ROOM_STYLE column into the subquery, and determining the average square footage for that particular ROOM_STYLE. Finally, it uses the result of that query in line 3 to determine whether the row in the parent query is greater than the average of SQ_FT for the ROOM_TYPE or not.

Here's the output:

```
SHIP_CABIN_ID ROOM_STYLE ROOM_NUMBER      SQ_FT
------------- ---------- -----------  ----------
            4 Stateroom  105                 205
            6 Suite      107                1524
            7 Stateroom  108                 211
            9 Stateroom  110                 225
           10 Suite      702                1142
           11 Suite      703                1745
```

One way to validate these results would be to get a list of each ROOM_STYLE and its average value for SQ_FT. Here's a query to calculate that information:

```
SELECT    ROOM_STYLE, AVG(SQ_FT)
FROM      SHIP_CABINS
GROUP BY ROOM_STYLE;

ROOM_STYLE AVG(SQ_FT)
---------- ----------------------
Suite      969.285714285714285714285714285714
Stateroom  196.2
```

This output confirms the average SQ_FT for each ROOM_STYLE, which is information we could use to go back and confirm that our correlated subquery displayed only those room numbers whose individual SQ_FT values are higher than the average for the appropriate ROOM_STYLE. And they are.

Correlated subqueries can exist in SELECT, UPDATE, and DELETE statements. They are "correlated" by way of a column reference from the parent query within the subquery.

A table alias is not necessarily required in the subquery if no column name conflict exists. In our example, there was such a conflict, so we were required to use a table alias. But that's not necessarily required in any correlated subquery. We could have just referenced any column from the parent query, and as long as there isn't an identically named column in the subquery, no table alias is required.

It's important to note that correlated subqueries may introduce performance degradation into a query. The process of correlating rows from one or more subqueries with the outer, or parent, query or queries may consume a significant amount of processing time. However, sometimes a correlated subquery can accomplish tasks that no other form of query may accomplish.

CERTIFICATION OBJECTIVE 9.05

Update and Delete Rows Using Correlated Subqueries

Let's look at the use of correlated subqueries in an UPDATE statement and a DELETE statement.

UPDATE with a Correlated Subquery

An UPDATE statement can have a correlated subquery in these places:

- In the SET clause
- In the WHERE clause

As we saw in an earlier section, the correlated subquery will require some way to identify an expression as being from the parent query. The most common way to do this is to assign a table alias to the table name in the UPDATE and then use that same table alias within the correlated subquery.

Let's look at an example. First, review the INVOICES table shown in Figure 9-1.

Our task is to go back to our historical invoices and give a 10 percent discount to whomever placed our single biggest order for their respective quarter. So in the first quarter, we need to find the single biggest invoice and determine a 10 percent discount on that invoice, then do the same thing for the second quarter, and so on.

To accomplish this feat, we'll need to modify the invoice so that we change the value in the INVOICES table's TERMS_OF_DISCOUNT column to the string '10 PCT'—and only for the appropriate invoice record. And we'll need to do the following:

- Identify the row with the highest value for TOTAL_PRICE for any given quarter, which we can identify using the TO_CHAR format mask Q on the ORDER_DATE column
- Update an invoice only if it has the highest TOTAL_PRICE for the quarter

The INVOICES table

INVOICES	
P * INVOICE_ID	NUMBER
INVOICE_DATE	DATE
ACCOUNT_NUMBER	VARCHAR2 (80 BYTE)
TERMS_OF_DISCOUNT	VARCHAR2 (20 BYTE)
VENDOR_ID	NUMBER
TOTAL_PRICE	NUMBER (8,2)
SHIPPING_DATE	DATE
⟲ PK_INVOICE_ID	

Here's an UPDATE statement that does the trick:

```
01    UPDATE INVOICES INV
02       SET TERMS_OF_DISCOUNT = '10 PCT'
03     WHERE TOTAL_PRICE = (SELECT MAX(TOTAL_PRICE)
04                          FROM    INVOICES
05                          WHERE   TO_CHAR(INVOICE_DATE, 'RRRR-Q') =
06                                  TO_CHAR(INV.INVOICE_DATE, 'RRRR-Q'));
```

Notice the following items in the preceding query:

- We choose to create a table alias called INV, which is declared at the end of line 1 and referenced in line 6.
- The subquery starts in line 3 and runs through line 6.
- The correlation occurs in lines 5 and 6, where the subquery's reference to INVOICE_DATE is compared to the parent query's INV.INVOICE_DATE. The comparison is performed by converting both dates to the 'RRRR-Q' format, which means the year and quarter so that, for example, the date '31-MAY-17' would convert to '2017-2'.
- On line 3 is the comparison between the parent query and the subquery, which is an equal sign, indicating that the parent query is expecting a single-row subquery. Given that the subquery is returning the aggregate value MAX for TOTAL_PRICE and no GROUP BY is involved in the subquery, then the subquery will indeed return no more than one row.

Here is an example of a correlated subquery used in the SET clause of an UPDATE statement:

```
01    UPDATE PORTS P
02       SET    CAPACITY = (SELECT COUNT(*)
03                          FROM SHIPS
04                          WHERE HOME_PORT_ID = P.PORT_ID)
05     WHERE    EXISTS (SELECT *
06                      FROM SHIPS
07                      WHERE HOME_PORT_ID = P.PORT_ID);
```

In the preceding code, we do the following:

- **Lines 5 through 7** We look for records in the PORTS table that any ship calls its home port, by way of the HOME_PORT_ID column. We use the keyword EXISTS, which we will review later in this chapter. EXISTS tells us quite simply whether there are any rows returned by the subquery at all.

In other words, we're simply asking whether there are any rows in SHIPS that contain a value for HOME_PORT_ID that corresponds to a given row in the parent UPDATE statement's PORTS table. If yes, the subquery returns a TRUE.

■ **Lines 2 through 4**   Then, if we find such PORTS, we update their capacity to equal the total number of ships in the SHIPS table currently calling that port home; this is accomplished in the correlated subquery that counts the number of records in SHIPS that share the same HOME_PORT_ID value with the parent UPDATE.

Note that this example of an UPDATE uses two correlated subqueries; both of the subqueries are correlated because both include the P.PORT_ID reference in their WHERE clauses, on lines 4 and 7.

Note that a subquery of the form SELECT COUNT(*) FROM TABLE will always be a single-row subquery. If no rows are found, the subquery returns a single row with a value of zero. If multiple rows exist in the table, the subquery returns a single row with a value representing the number of rows found. This is true for queries using the COUNT function but not for queries using other aggregates, such as AVG, MIN, MAX, or SUM. This is unique to COUNT.

Next we'll look at how to use correlated subqueries in a DELETE statement.

DELETE with a Correlated Subquery

The DELETE statement can be used with a correlated subquery in the WHERE clause to determine which rows to delete from a given table. The syntax is similar to the correlated subquery syntax for SELECT and UPDATE statements.

Correlated subqueries are not limited to the SELECT statement. They can also be used in UPDATE or DELETE statements.

Let's take a look at a DELETE statement for the SHIP_CABINS table. This DELETE will remove those cabins with the smallest balcony square footage for each ROOM_TYPE and ROOM_STYLE. In other words, for a given ROOM_TYPE of Suite and a ROOM_STYLE of Ocean View, we'll remove the row for the cabin with the smallest balcony, and then we'll move on and do the same for the Stateroom with Ocean View that has the smallest balcony, and so on. Here's the query:

```
01    DELETE FROM SHIP_CABINS S1
02    WHERE  S1.BALCONY_SQ_FT =
03            (SELECT MIN(BALCONY_SQ_FT)
04             FROM   SHIP_CABINS S2
05             WHERE  S1.ROOM_TYPE  = S2.ROOM_TYPE
06               AND  S1.ROOM_STYLE = S2.ROOM_STYLE);
```

Notice that in this example, the correlation involves two columns, in lines 5 and 6.

CERTIFICATION OBJECTIVE 9.06

Use the EXISTS and NOT EXISTS Operators

The EXISTS keyword tests for the existence of any rows in a subquery. If no rows are found, the answer is FALSE. Otherwise, the subquery returns TRUE. NOT EXISTS reverses the results.

Let's look at an example. The following query looks for PORTS that have any sort of record at all in the SHIPS table with a HOME_PORT_ID value that matches any of the PORT_ID values. Here's the query:

```
01    SELECT PORT_ID, PORT_NAME
02    FROM   PORTS P1
03    WHERE  EXISTS (SELECT *
04                   FROM   SHIPS S1
05                   WHERE  P1.PORT_ID = S1.HOME_PORT_ID);
```

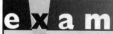

EXISTS does not compare anything to the subquery. There is no "expression equals expression" format with EXISTS. Its syntax is simple: the keywords WHERE EXISTS and the subquery. Nothing more.

Note the keyword EXISTS on line 3. The entire subquery is executed, even though EXISTS need only know whether the subquery returns any rows, so beware using EXISTS with subqueries that return large numbers of rows.

It's worth noting that this sort of query is sometimes referred to as a *semijoin*, which is a SELECT statement that uses the EXISTS keyword to compare rows in a table with rows in another table.

CERTIFICATION OBJECTIVE 9.07

Use the WITH Clause

You can use the keyword WITH to assign a name to a subquery block. Once the name is assigned, you can reference the name from elsewhere in the query. WITH is considered a clause of the SELECT statement.

Let's look at an example. We'll use WITH to declare two different subqueries. We'll name one PORT_BOOKINGS and the other DENSEST_PORT (see the following listing, lines 2 and 8) and then invoke both of them by name in a SELECT statement (lines 12 through 14). Here's the code:

```
01    WITH
02      PORT_BOOKINGS AS (
03        SELECT P.PORT_ID, P.PORT_NAME, COUNT(S.SHIP_ID) CT
04        FROM    PORTS P, SHIPS S
05        WHERE   P.PORT_ID  = S.HOME_PORT_ID
06        GROUP BY P.PORT_ID, P.PORT_NAME
07      ),
08      DENSEST_PORT  AS (
09        SELECT MAX(CT) MAX_CT
10        FROM    PORT_BOOKINGS
11      )
12    SELECT PORT_NAME
13    FROM    PORT_BOOKINGS
14    WHERE   CT = (SELECT MAX_CT FROM DENSEST_PORT);
```

exam
w a t c h

The series of one or more subquery blocks defined before the SELECT statement is referred to as the subquery factoring clause. WITH can define one subquery factoring clause; it must be defined before the SELECT statement.

Note that neither PORT_BOOKINGS nor DENSEST_PORT is a database object. They are the names of queries that exist solely within this WITH/SELECT statement.

Also note the subqueries on lines 3 through 6 and on lines 9 through 10. Also note that the only semicolon is at the end of the entire statement, not at the end of any individual SQL statement within the overall WITH statement.

Internally, Oracle SQL treats a named query within the WITH clause as a temporary table or as an inline view. (We examined inline views in Chapter 8.)

The WITH clause can be used in the top-level query of a SELECT statement and in many (but not all) subqueries of the SELECT statement, such as shown in line 14. If you use WITH to name a subquery, that name isn't recognized within the subquery itself but is recognized in most every other location in the overall query. In other words, consider line 8, where we name and specify the subquery DENSEST_PORT. We couldn't reference the name DENSEST_PORT in lines 9 through 10, but we can reference the name everywhere else.

CERTIFICATION OBJECTIVE 9.08

Write Single-Row and Multiple-Row Subqueries

In this section, we'll create subqueries that return one expression in either a single-row or multiple-row answer.

Single-Row Subqueries

A single-row subquery is a subquery that returns one row. For example, let's say you're tasked with the job of identifying the names of employees of our fictional company, Codd Cruise Lines. You're tasked to look for employees who are assigned to the same ship as an employee named Al Smith. See Figure 9-2 for the entity-relationship diagram (ERD) of the table we'll work with.

FIGURE 9-2

The EMPLOYEES table

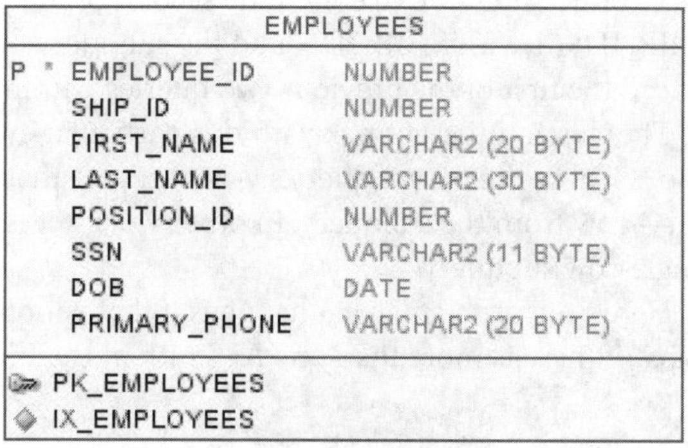

EMPLOYEES	
P * EMPLOYEE_ID	NUMBER
SHIP_ID	NUMBER
FIRST_NAME	VARCHAR2 (20 BYTE)
LAST_NAME	VARCHAR2 (30 BYTE)
POSITION_ID	NUMBER
SSN	VARCHAR2 (11 BYTE)
DOB	DATE
PRIMARY_PHONE	VARCHAR2 (20 BYTE)
➣ PK_EMPLOYEES	
◇ IX_EMPLOYEES	

You could perform this task in two steps. Step 1 is to find the SHIP_ID value of the ship on which Al Smith is assigned, like this:

```
SELECT SHIP_ID
FROM    EMPLOYEES
WHERE   LAST_NAME = 'Smith' AND  FIRST_NAME = 'Al';
SHIP_ID
-----------------------
1
```

Step 2 is to use the SHIP_ID value to locate other employees on the same ship.

```
SELECT EMPLOYEE_ID, LAST_NAME, FIRST_NAME
FROM    EMPLOYEES
WHERE   SHIP_ID = 1
  AND   NOT (LAST_NAME = 'Smith' AND  FIRST_NAME = 'Al');

EMPLOYEE_ID             LAST_NAME                     FIRST_NAME
--------------------    ------------------------      --------------------
1                       Hoddlestein                   Howard
7                       Worthington                   Buffy
```

There's an answer—in two steps. Not bad.

But a subquery could have discovered the answer in one step, like this:

```
01   SELECT EMPLOYEE_ID, LAST_NAME, FIRST_NAME
02   FROM    EMPLOYEES
03   WHERE   SHIP_ID = (SELECT SHIP_ID
04                        FROM    EMPLOYEES
05                        WHERE   LAST_NAME = 'Smith'
06                          AND   FIRST_NAME = 'Al')
07    AND  NOT (LAST_NAME = 'Smith' AND  FIRST_NAME = 'Al');
```

This one query achieves the same thing as the previous two queries. Note what we've done here—we've edited the second of the previous two queries by replacing SHIP_ID = 1 with SHIP_ID = and the subquery on lines 3 through 6. We've literally placed the first of the previous two queries within the second of those two queries.

There is an inherent risk with this particular syntax. Notice the equal sign on line 3. That's the parent query's way of saying that it is expecting one—and only one—row from the subquery. In other words, it is expecting this query to be a single-row subquery.

Here's the problem: what happens if that subquery returns more than one row? What if there is more than one Al Smith in the EMPLOYEES table?

Let's find out—let's try searching for employees who work on the same ship as anyone whose last name is Smith, regardless of first name.

```
01   SELECT EMPLOYEE_ID, LAST_NAME, FIRST_NAME
02   FROM    EMPLOYEES
03   WHERE   SHIP_ID = (SELECT SHIP_ID
04                      FROM    EMPLOYEES
05                      WHERE   LAST_NAME = 'Smith')
06   AND   NOT (LAST_NAME = 'Smith');
Error starting at line 1 in command:
Error report:
SQL Error: ORA-01427: single-row subquery returns more than one row
01427. 00000 -  "single-row subquery returns more than one row"
```

Notice the text of the error message: "single-row subquery returns more than one row." In other words, we apparently do have more than one person in the EMPLOYEES table with a last name of Smith.

This creates a problem. Our query has an equal sign on line 3, and that's why our subquery is expected to be a single-row query.

There are a few alternatives we could take here. If we want to retain the integrity of the single-row subquery, then we need to edit that subquery to ensure that it will return one, and only one, row.

There are many ways to guarantee a one-row response. For example, a subquery that uses a WHERE criterion based on a primary key or some other unique value will return only one value, like this:

```
SELECT SHIP_ID FROM EMPLOYEES WHERE EMPLOYEE_ID = 5;
```

Of course, that assumes you know the value for the appropriate EMPLOYEE_ID.

Another example would be a subquery that returns an aggregate function without a GROUP BY clause, like this:

```
SELECT MIN(SHIP_ID) FROM EMPLOYEES WHERE LAST_NAME = 'Smith';
```

Aggregate functions always return a single row, as long as no GROUP BY is involved. Logically, though, this isn't always an option to solve the particular business challenge you might be facing.

Still another example would be a subquery that uses the ROWNUM feature to limit the number of rows in the response, like this:

```
SELECT SHIP_ID FROM EMPLOYEES WHERE LAST_NAME = 'Smith' AND ROWNUM < 2;
```

Remember that the ROWNUM pseudocolumn assigns row numbers to the query's output (before processing the ORDER BY clause) and can be effective in limiting output. In this example, it ensures that we receive only a one-row response. But again, this may not logically support the original intent of your query.

The moral of the story is to use the single-row subquery when you know the result will be one row. Otherwise, you'd better use something other than the single-row subquery format or you'll run the risk of an execution error.

Also, if the subquery returns no rows at all, then no error will result. The query will execute, but the subquery will return a NULL value to the parent query.

Keep in mind that a failed execution attempt in SQL isn't necessarily a bad thing. Sometimes it's a good idea to create a single-row subquery in situations where you want to deliberately fail the parent query if multiple rows are found in the subquery. This can be a useful feature that can help flag bigger problems elsewhere in the database, such as the failure of a unique identifying mechanism like a primary key, or some other logical error beyond your immediate SQL code. When your SQL statements are embedded within some other programs that have the capabilities of handling failures, or exceptions as they are called in languages like Oracle PL/SQL and Java, you can program those systems to take evasive or corrective actions and address what might be a much bigger problem.

You can use multiple subqueries within a single WHERE clause. Here's a SQL statement with more than one subquery:

```
01    SELECT EMPLOYEE_ID, LAST_NAME, FIRST_NAME
02    FROM    EMPLOYEES
03    WHERE   SHIP_ID = (SELECT SHIP_ID FROM EMPLOYEES
04                        WHERE LAST_NAME = 'Smith' AND FIRST_NAME = 'Al')
05      AND NOT (LAST_NAME = 'Smith' AND  FIRST_NAME = 'Al')
06      AND SSN    = (SELECT SOCIAL_NUMBER FROM EMP_BENEFITS
07                        WHERE EMP_BENEFITS_ID = 17);
```

Notice in the example what is happening on line 6. In that portion of the query, we are comparing a parent column named SSN to the subquery column called SOCIAL_NUMBER. Subqueries do not have to share the same column name with the parent query. The only thing that is required is that the data types for SSN and SOCIAL_NUMBER be comparable. If the data types match up, the comparison is valid.

Table 9-1 lists the comparison conditions available for use with single-row subqueries.

TABLE 9-1	Single-Row Subquery Comparison Conditions
Comparison Conditions	**Description**
=	Equal.
<>	Not equal.
!=	Not equal.
^=	Not equal.
>	Greater than.
>=	Greater than or equal to.
<	Less than.
<=	Less than or equal to.
LIKE	Enables wildcard characters. There are two wildcard characters: _ The underscore is a wildcard character representing a single character. % The percent sign is a wildcard character representing one or more values.
IN	Compares one value on the left side of the operator to a set of zero or more values on the right side of the operator. The set of values must be enclosed in parentheses. If the values are presented as constants, they are separated by commas, as in ('Maple', 'Elm', 'Main') or (2009, 2010, 2011). A query may also be used, as in (SELECT PORT_NAME FROM PORTS).

The keyword IN deserves special attention. When the keyword IN is used, the parent query sees the subquery as potentially a multiple-row subquery, which we'll discuss in the next section.

So, single-row subqueries are useful for performing multistep queries when you can guarantee that the subquery will return a single row. But when your subquery returns multiple rows, you need to take a different approach. Let's look at that next.

Multiple-Row Subqueries

A multiple-row subquery may return more than one row of answers to the parent query. For example, we saw in our earlier example that there is apparently more than one employee in our EMPLOYEES table with a last name of Smith. Because of that fact, we couldn't use the single-row query format with a subquery that searched for rows with a LAST_NAME value of Smith. But we can use that subquery in the multiple-row format, as shown here:

```
01   SELECT     SHIP_ID, LAST_NAME, FIRST_NAME
02   FROM       EMPLOYEES
03   WHERE      SHIP_ID IN (SELECT SHIP_ID FROM EMPLOYEES WHERE LAST_NAME = 'Smith')
04   ORDER BY SHIP_ID, LAST_NAME;
```

Now our query is asking to list the employees who work on a ship with anyone named Smith and then list the Smiths themselves. But for our purposes, note line 3, where we replaced the equal sign with the reserved word IN. As a result of that one change, we no longer get an error message but instead get this:

```
SHIP_ID                    LAST_NAME                       FIRST_NAME
-----------------------    ----------------------------    -----------------
1                          Hoddlestein                     Howard
1                          Smith                           Al
1                          Worthington                     Buffy
3                          Lindon                          Alice
3                          Smith                           Joe
```

Remember from our discussion of the WHERE clause and the set of comparison operators that the keyword IN allows the WHERE clause to compare one value to a set of values. The same dynamic is at work here. IN allows the subquery to return multiple rows. The presence of the keyword IN directs the parent query to allow the subquery to be a multiple-row subquery.

Note that the subquery doesn't have to return multiple rows. The presence of IN simply allows for the possibility.

Notice we didn't get an execution error this time. Instead, we obtained output and can now see that we have an employee named Smith assigned to SHIP_ID 1 and another on SHIP_ID 3. Our SELECT statement returns rows showing employees on either ship.

Table 9-2 lists the comparison operators that can be used with a multirow subquery.

on the job

You can use greater-than or less-than comparison operators with single-row subqueries but not multirow subqueries unless those operators are combined with ALL, ANY, or SOME.

The keywords shown in Table 9-2 indicate that the parent query is expecting the subquery to be a multirow subquery. A multirow subquery can return anywhere from zero to multiple rows of answers.

TABLE 9-2	Multirow Subquery Comparison Conditions

Comparison Conditions	Description
IN	Compares a subject value to a set of zero or more values. Returns TRUE if the subject value equals any of the values in the set. Returns FALSE if the subquery returns no rows.
NOT	Used with IN to reverse the result. Returns TRUE if the subquery returns no rows. WARNING: Be careful here. If any one or more of the subquery rows returns NULL, the result of the subquery will be "no rows selected." See the discussion after the table for more about the use of NOT where NULL values may be present.
ANY	Used in combination with single-row comparison conditions (such as = or >) to compare a subject value with a multirow subquery. Returns TRUE if the subject value finds a match consistent with the comparison operator in any of the rows returned by the subquery. Returns FALSE if the subquery returns no rows.
SOME	Same as ANY.
ALL	Used in combination with single-row comparison conditions to compare a subject value with a multirow subquery. Returns TRUE if the subject value finds a match consistent with the comparison operator in all of the rows returned by the subquery. Returns FALSE if the subquery returns no rows. Example: Find all products with a price that's greater than all the products in the Luxury category: SELECT * FROM PRODUCTS WHERE PRICE > ALL (SELECT PRICE FROM PRODUCTS WHERE CATEGORY = 'Luxury');

NOT IN and NULL Values in the Subquery

Consider the following:

```
SQL> CREATE TABLE PARENT (ID NUMBER, HOUSE VARCHAR2(30));
Table created.
SQL> INSERT INTO PARENT VALUES (1, 'Oak');
1 row created.
SQL> INSERT INTO PARENT VALUES (2, 'Elm');
1 row created.
SQL> CREATE TABLE KID (KID_ID NUMBER, HOUSE VARCHAR2(30));
Table created.
SQL> INSERT INTO KID VALUES (10, 'Maple');
1 row created.
SQL> INSERT INTO KID VALUES (20, 'Elm');
```

```
1 row created.
SQL> COMMIT;
Commit complete.
SQL> SELECT * FROM PARENT WHERE HOUSE IN (SELECT HOUSE FROM KID);
        ID HOUSE
--------- ------------------------------
         2 Elm
SQL> SELECT * FROM PARENT WHERE HOUSE NOT IN (SELECT HOUSE FROM KID);
        ID HOUSE
--------- ------------------------------
         1 Oak
```

So far, so good. But let's add a NULL to the KID table and try the NOT IN again.

```
SQL> INSERT INTO KID VALUES (30, NULL);
1 row created.
SQL> SELECT * FROM PARENT WHERE HOUSE NOT IN (SELECT HOUSE FROM KID);
no rows selected
```

So what happened? When a NULL is introduced into the row set returned by the subquery, a no-win situation results. How can you know definitively whether the parent query HOUSE value is not equal to any of the values returned by the subquery when those values include NULL? Remember, NULL is not "blank." It is "I don't know"—it is an unknown value. So is the parent HOUSE value not equal to a value that isn't known by the subquery? Who could tell? It is impossible to tell, so "no rows selected."

The NOT IN comparison operator will always run the risk of this situation if the subquery includes NULL values. One approach is to exclude NULL values in the subquery when using NOT IN.

```
SQL>SELECT * FROM PARENT WHERE HOUSE NOT IN (SELECT HOUSE FROM KID WHERE HOUSE IS NOT NULL);
        ID HOUSE
--------- ------------------------------
         1 Oak
```

The result makes sense—but only if any NULL values are explicitly omitted from the subquery.

CERTIFICATION SUMMARY

A subquery is a SELECT statement that exists within a larger SQL statement. Subqueries can be included in a SELECT, INSERT, UPDATE, MERGE, or DELETE statement. Subqueries can also be used in a CREATE TABLE statement.

Subqueries can be used in WHERE clauses of SELECT, UPDATE, and DELETE statements. They can be used in the UPDATE . . . SET clause and the INSERT list of values. Some subqueries may be able to substitute for any expression almost anywhere an expression is accepted, including the SELECT list of a SELECT statement.

Subqueries can perform multiple-step queries in a single SQL statement. They can be used to reference lookup information from a given query. They can populate a table at the time of creation in a CREATE TABLE statement. They are used to create views.

There are many types of subqueries, including single-row, multiple-row, multiple-column, scalar, and correlated.

Single-row subqueries return one row of data to the parent query. Multiple-row subqueries can return anywhere from zero to one to more than one row. Multiple-column subqueries are compared to rows in the parent query using multiple columns at once. Scalar subqueries return one row and one column's worth of data at all times. Correlated subqueries contain conditions in the subquery that connect rows of data with rows in the parent query, much like a join might do.

TWO-MINUTE DRILL

Define Subqueries

- ☐ A subquery is a SELECT statement contained within a SQL statement.
- ☐ The outer SQL statement is called the parent. The outermost level is the top level.
- ☐ A top-level SQL statement containing a subquery can be a SELECT, INSERT, UPDATE, or DELETE, or else a CREATE TABLE or CREATE VIEW.
- ☐ Subqueries can be nested within other subqueries.
- ☐ Many subqueries could function as standalone queries. Some are correlated, meaning that they contain references that tie them into their parent queries.

Describe the Types of Problems Subqueries Can Solve

- ☐ Subqueries are ideal for queries based on aggregate results of other queries.
- ☐ Subqueries are used to create view objects.
- ☐ You can use a subquery in a SELECT, UPDATE, or DELETE statement.
- ☐ Subqueries can be used as alternatives to expressions.

Describe the Types of Subqueries

- ☐ A single-row subquery returns one row of data to the parent query.
- ☐ A multiple-row subquery may return more than one row of data to the parent query.
- ☐ Multiple-column subqueries return two or more columns' worth of data at once to the parent query, which must test for all the columns at once.
- ☐ Correlated subqueries use data from a parent query to determine their own result.
- ☐ Scalar subqueries always return one value, represented in one column of one row, every time.
- ☐ The multiple-column subquery may be of the single-row or multiple-row type of subquery.
- ☐ A correlated subquery might be a single-row, multiple-row, or multiple-column subquery.

Query Data Using Correlated Subqueries

☐ Correlated subqueries use data from the parent in subquery predicates to determine what data to return to the parent query.

☐ Correlated subqueries may present some performance degradation; however, they can perform tasks that could not otherwise be accomplished in a single query.

Update and Delete Rows Using Correlated Subqueries

☐ The UPDATE and DELETE statements can use correlated subqueries.

☐ The UPDATE statement can use correlated subqueries in the SET or WHERE clause.

☐ The DELETE statement can use correlated subqueries in the WHERE clause.

Use the EXISTS and NOT EXISTS Operators

☐ The EXISTS operator can be used by a parent query to test a subquery and determine whether it returns any rows at all.

☐ NOT EXISTS reverses the findings of EXISTS.

Use the WITH Clause

☐ The WITH clause can dynamically name a subquery so that the SELECT statement following the WITH clause can reference that subquery by name, treating it as a dynamic table in real time.

☐ Any subquery names assigned within the WITH clause are only good for that statement; they are not stored in the database.

Write Single-Row and Multiple-Row Subqueries

☐ The results of a single-row subquery can be compared to an expression within the parent using a scalar comparison operator, such as an equal sign or a greater-than or less-than sign.

☐ The column names are not required to match in such a comparison, but the data types must match so that the parent query can compare columns of any name to subquery columns of any name, provided the data types match.

☐ Multiple-row subqueries are compared differently to the parent query than single-row subqueries.

☐ Multiple-row subqueries are compared to expressions in the parent query by using multiple-row comparison conditions, such as IN, ANY, or ALL, in combination with single-row comparison operators such as <, >, =, !=.

☐ A multiple-row subquery cannot be compared to a parent query expression using a single-row comparison operator; if such an attempt is made, the statement will fail with an execution error message.

SELF TEST

The following questions will help you measure your understanding of the material presented in this chapter. Choose one correct answer for each question unless otherwise directed.

Define Subqueries

1. Which of the following forms of subquery never returns more than one row?
   A. Scalar
   B. Correlated
   C. Multiple-column
   D. None of the above

Describe the Types of Problems Subqueries Can Solve

2. Which of the following problems can be solved with a subquery? (Choose the two best answers.)
   A. You are tasked with determining the minimum sales for every division in a multinational corporation.
   B. You are tasked with determining which divisions in a corporation earned sales last year that were less than the average sales for all divisions in the prior year.
   C. You are tasked with creating a view.
   D. You are tasked with creating a sequence.

Describe the Types of Subqueries

3. Which of the following statements are true? (Choose two.)
   A. A single-row subquery can also be a multiple-row subquery.
   B. A single-row subquery can also be a multiple-column subquery.
   C. A scalar subquery can also be a multiple-column subquery.
   D. A correlated subquery can also be a single-row subquery.

4. Which subquery includes references to the parent query and thus cannot execute as a standalone query? (Choose the best answer.)
   A. A scalar subquery
   B. A correlated subquery
   C. A multiple-column subquery
   D. A referential subquery

5. Which of the following can a subquery be used in? (Choose all that apply.)

   A. An INSERT statement's SELECT

   B. A GRANT statement

   C. A WHERE clause in a SELECT statement

   D. An inline view

6. An inline view is a form of a subquery.

   A. True

   B. False

Query Data Using Correlated Subqueries

7. Review this WORK_HISTORY table.

```
                      WORK_HISTORY
P *  WORK_HISTORY_ID      NUMBER
     EMPLOYEE_ID          NUMBER
     START_DATE           DATE
     END_DATE             DATE
     SHIP_ID              NUMBER
     STATUS               VARCHAR2 (10 BYTE)

  PK_WORK_HISTORY
```

Your task is to create a query that will list—for each ship—all of the EMPLOYEE_ID values for all the employees who have the shortest work history for their ship. In other words, if there are two ships, you want to list all the employees assigned to the first ship who have the shortest work history, all the employees assigned to the second ship who have the shortest work history, and so on. Which of the following queries will accomplish this task? (Choose two.)

```
A. SELECT EMPLOYEE_ID FROM WORK_HISTORY W1
   WHERE ABS(START_DATE - END_DATE) =
      (SELECT MIN(ABS(START_DATE - END_DATE))
       FROM WORK_HISTORY
       WHERE SHIP_ID = W1.SHIP_ID);
B. SELECT EMPLOYEE_ID FROM WORK_HISTORY W1
   WHERE ABS(START_DATE - END_DATE) =
      (SELECT MIN(ABS(START_DATE - END_DATE))
       FROM WORK_HISTORY);
```

C.
```
SELECT EMPLOYEE_ID FROM WORK_HISTORY W1
   WHERE ABS(START_DATE - END_DATE) <= ALL
      (SELECT ABS(START_DATE - END_DATE)
       FROM WORK_HISTORY
       WHERE SHIP_ID = W1.SHIP_ID);
```

D.
```
SELECT EMPLOYEE_ID FROM WORK_HISTORY W1
   WHERE ABS(START_DATE - END_DATE) <
      (SELECT MIN(ABS(START_DATE - END_DATE))
       FROM WORK_HISTORY
       WHERE SHIP_ID = W1.SHIP_ID);
```

8. Review the PORTS and SHIPS tables.

```
                    PORTS
P *  PORT_ID        NUMBER
     PORT_NAME      VARCHAR2 (20 BYTE)
     COUNTRY        VARCHAR2 (40 BYTE)
     CAPACITY       NUMBER

  PK_PORT


                    SHIPS
P *  SHIP_ID        NUMBER
     SHIP_NAME      VARCHAR2 (20 BYTE)
     CAPACITY       NUMBER
     LENGTH         NUMBER
F    HOME_PORT_ID   NUMBER

  PK_SHIP
```

Your team is tasked with the job of creating a list of the ships with the least capacity in each port. In other words, each ship has a home port. For each port that is a home port to ships, which of each port's ships has the least capacity? Your team produces the following query in answer to this task:

```
01   SELECT S1.SHIP_NAME, (SELECT PORT_NAME
02                         FROM   PORTS
03                         WHERE  PORT_ID = S1.HOME_PORT_ID) HOME_PORT
04   FROM    SHIPS S1
05   WHERE   S1.CAPACITY = (SELECT MIN(CAPACITY)
06                          FROM   SHIPS S2
07                          WHERE  S2.HOME_PORT_ID = S1.HOME_PORT_ID);
```

Which of the following statements is true about this SQL statement?

A. The statement will fail with a syntax error because of the subquery on lines 1 through 3.

B. The statement will fail with an execution error because of the subquery on lines 1 through 3.

C. The statement will execute but will return meaningless information.

D. The statement will execute successfully as intended.

9. A correlated subquery:

A. May be used in a SELECT but not an UPDATE

B. Cannot be executed as a standalone query

C. Must use a table alias when referencing a column in the outer query

D. All of the above

Update and Delete Rows Using Correlated Subqueries

10. Which of the following can a correlated subquery be used in? (Choose three.)

A. The SET clause of an UPDATE statement

B. The WHERE clause of an UPDATE statement

C. The WHERE clause of a DELETE statement

D. The FROM clause of a DELETE statement

11. Review the illustration from question 8 and the following SQL code:

```
01  UPDATE PORTS P
02  SET     CAPACITY = CAPACITY + 1
03  WHERE   EXISTS (SELECT *
04                  FROM SHIPS
05                  WHERE HOME_PORT_ID = P.PORT_ID);
```

The PORTS table has 15 rows. The SHIPS table has 20 rows. Each row in PORTS has a unique value for PORT_ID. Each PORT_ID value is represented in the HOME_PORT_ID column of at least one row of the SHIPS table. What can be said of this UPDATE statement?

A. The value for CAPACITY will increase once for each of the 15 rows in the PORTS table.

B. The value for CAPACITY will increase by 20 for each of the 15 rows in the PORTS table.

C. The value for CAPACITY will not increase.

D. The statement will fail to execute because of an error in the syntax.

Use the EXISTS and NOT EXISTS Operators

12. Another name for an EXISTS query is:
A. Demijoin
B. Multiple-column subquery
C. Cross-join
D. Semijoin

13. Review the illustration from question 8 and the following SQL code:

```
01   DELETE FROM PORTS P
02   WHERE  PORT_ID NOT EXISTS (SELECT PORT_ID
03                              FROM   SHIPS
04                              WHERE  HOME_PORT_ID = P.PORT_ID);
```

The code is attempting to delete any row in the PORTS table that is not a home port for any ship in the SHIPS table, as indicated by the HOME_PORT_ID column. In other words, only keep the PORTS rows that are currently the HOME_PORT_ID value for a ship in the SHIPS table; get rid of all other PORT rows. That's the intent of the SQL statement. What will result from an attempt to execute the preceding SQL statement?
A. It will fail because of a syntax error on line 2.
B. It will fail because of a syntax error on line 4.
C. It will fail because of an execution error in the subquery.
D. It will execute successfully and perform as intended.

Use the WITH Clause

14. The WITH clause can be used to name a subquery. Which of the following is also true? (Choose two.)
A. The name of the subquery can be used in the SELECT statement following the WITH clause.
B. The name of the subquery can be joined to other tables in the SELECT statement following the WITH clause.
C. The name of the subquery is stored in the database by the WITH statement and can be referenced by other SQL statements in later sessions.
D. The name of the subquery can be invoked from within the subquery that is named.

15. Review the illustration from questions 8. Which of the following statements, when executed, will result in an error?

    A. ```
       WITH (SELECT SHIP_ID FROM SHIPS)
       SELECT PORT_ID
       FROM   PORTS;
       ```
    B. ```
       WITH SHIPPER_INFO AS
            (SELECT SHIP_ID FROM SHIPS)
       SELECT PORT_ID
       FROM   PORTS;
       ```
    C. ```
       WITH SHIPPER_INFO AS
            (SELECT SHIP_ID FROM SHIPS)
       SELECT PORT_ID
       FROM   PORTS, SHIPPER_INFO;
       ```
    D. ```
       SELECT WITH SHIPPER_INFO AS
            (SELECT SHIP_ID FROM SHIPS)
       SELECT PORT_ID, SHIPPER_INFO.SHIP_ID
       FROM   PORTS, SHIPPER_INFO;
       ```

Write Single-Row and Multiple-Row Subqueries

16. Which of the following comparison operators can be used with a multiple-row subquery? (Choose two.)

    A. =
    B. >= ALL
    C. LIKE
    D. IN

17. Review the PORTS and SHIPS tables:

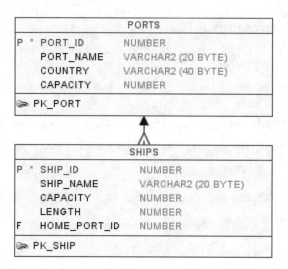

Next, review the following SQL code:

```
01    SELECT P.COUNTRY, P.CAPACITY
02    FROM   PORTS P
03    WHERE  P.PORT_ID > (SELECT S.HOME_PORT_ID
04                        FROM SHIPS S WHERE S.LENGTH > 900);
```

You know that there are five rows in the SHIPS table with a length greater than 900. What will result from an attempt to execute this SQL statement?

A. An execution error will result because the subquery will return more than one row and the parent query is expecting only one row from the subquery.

B. A syntax error will result because PORT_ID and HOME_PORT_ID in line 3 have different column names.

C. The statement will execute and produce output as intended.

D. None of the above.

18. When is a query considered a multirow subquery? (Choose the best answer.)

A. If it returns multiple rows at the time of execution

B. If it may or may not return multiple rows, as determined by its WHERE clause

C. If it returns numeric data, regardless of the number of rows of data it returns

D. All of the above

19. Which of the following is a true statement?

A. If a SELECT includes a GROUP BY clause, then any subquery used within the SELECT must also have a GROUP BY clause.

B. If a query returns multiple rows, it may not be used as a subquery for a SELECT statement that uses a GROUP BY clause.

C. A SELECT statement with a GROUP BY may use a subquery to return a value to the outermost WHERE clause.

D. The only form of subquery permitted with a GROUP BY clause is a correlated subquery.

20. Review the PORTS and SHIPS tables shown in question 7. Then review the following SQL code:

```
01   SELECT PORT_NAME
02   FROM    PORTS P
03   WHERE   PORT_ID IN (SELECT HOME_PORT_ID, SHIP_NAME
04                       FROM    SHIPS
05                       WHERE   SHIP_ID IN (1,2,3));
```

Which of the following is true of this statement?

A. The statement will fail with a syntax error because of line 3.

B. The statement will fail with a syntax error because of line 5.

C. Whether the statement fails depends on how many rows are returned by the subquery in lines 3 through 5.

D. None of the above.

SELF TEST ANSWERS

Define Subqueries

1. ☑ **A.** A scalar subquery always returns a single value, which is to say it returns only one column, one row.

   ☒ **B, C,** and **D** are incorrect. A correlated subquery may or may not return multiple rows. Multiple-column subqueries may or may not return multiple rows.

Describe the Types of Problems Subqueries Can Solve

2. ☑ **B** and **C.** The ideal query would first obtain the average sales for the prior year and then use the results to compare to the subsequent year's sales. You use a subquery to create a view.

   ☒ **A** and **D** are incorrect. The minimum sales at every division can be determined using a query with a GROUP BY. A subquery is not required or particularly necessary here, based on the information provided. You do not use a subquery to create a sequence.

Describe the Types of Subqueries

3. ☑ **B** and **D.** A single-row subquery may consist of multiple columns in its single row. And it also may be correlated.

   ☒ **A** and **C** are incorrect. A single-row subquery cannot, by definition, also be a multiple-row subquery. A scalar subquery by definition can be only one column in one row, so it cannot be a multiple-column subquery.

4. ☑ **B.** A correlated subquery is the best answer. The name indicates that the subquery is correlated to the parent query. Technically, scalar and multiple-column subqueries may also be correlated, but we asked for the best answer, and clearly that is correlated subquery.

   ☒ **A, C,** and **D** are incorrect. Technically, a scalar subquery may also be a correlated subquery, which is why the question asked you to pick the "best answer"—the term *correlated* refers specifically to the concept of referring to the parent query, whereas a scalar subquery refers specifically to a subquery's return value as being a single value. The same is true for a multiple-column subquery—that may also be a correlated subquery, but the term "multiple-column" is intended to emphasize the fact that it returns multiple columns' worth of results at once. Finally, a referential subquery isn't anything; we just made that up.

5. ☑ **A, C,** and **D.** A subquery could be used within the SELECT statement of an INSERT statement, including the SELECT statement's WHERE clause, and within an inline view.

   ☒ **B** is incorrect. A GRANT statement is a DCL statement and cannot have a subquery.

6. ☑ **A.** An inline view is called a view since it is a query that is treated like a table. That being said, its syntax is that of the subquery syntax.

   ☒ **B** is incorrect because the statement is true.

Query Data Using Correlated Subqueries

7. ☑ **A** and **C. A** is a classic correlated subquery, connecting the subquery to the parent by way of the W1.SHIP_ID value. **C** also works with the <= ALL comparison condition.

   ☒ **B** and **D** are incorrect. **B** is missing the join in the subquery that connects the subquery with the parent query. **D** compares the parent query's WHERE clause value to the subquery with a less-than sign, which won't work—the subquery is already selecting the minimum value from the subquery, so the parent query can't find anything that will be less than the minimum.

8. ☑ **D.** The statement is syntactically fine. The SELECT includes two correlated subqueries. The first, in lines 1 through 3, is an expression in the SELECT statement's select list. This subquery is correlated by way of the reference at the end of line 3. The second correlated subquery is in lines 5 through 7, and it obtains the minimum capacity value for ships belonging to each port.

   ☒ **A, B,** and **C** are incorrect. The statement will not fail, not with a syntax problem or with an execution problem. The data it returns is exactly as requested.

9. ☑ **B.** A correlated subquery cannot be executed as a stand-alone query.

   ☒ **A, C,** and **D** are incorrect. A correlated subquery can be used in a SELECT, UPDATE, or DELETE. A correlated subquery does not have to use a table alias when referencing columns unless there is a risk of ambiguity.

Update and Delete Rows Using Correlated Subqueries

10. ☑ **A, B,** and **C.** A correlated subquery can be used in any of these answers.

    ☒ **D** is incorrect. A correlated subquery cannot be used in the FROM clause of a DELETE statement. Note, however, that the question is asking specifically about correlated subqueries. While you cannot have a correlated subquery in the FROM clause of the DELETE, we'll later see that an "inline view" can be used there, and an "inline view" is essentially a subquery—but not a correlated subquery.

11. ☑ **A.** The CAPACITY will increase once for each row processed by the UPDATE if that row is found in the subquery.
    ☒ **B, C,** and **D** are incorrect.

Use the EXISTS and NOT EXISTS Operators

12. ☑ **D.** The semijoin is the correct answer.
    ☒ **A, B,** and **C** are incorrect. There is no such thing as a demijoin. A multiple-column subquery requires several columns on both sides of the comparison condition. A cross-join is a table join with no join criteria.

13. ☑ **A.** It will fail because of a syntax error on line 2—the first reference to PORT_ID should be removed. EXISTS does not compare the subquery to anything. In other words, line 2 should be **WHERE NOT EXISTS (SELECT *** without the first PORT_ID reference. Other than that, everything else about the query is fine.
    ☒ **B, C,** and **D** are incorrect. Line 4 has no syntax errors. Nor does the subquery contain any execution errors. But neither will the SQL execute, for the reasons we described for the right answer.

Use the WITH Clause

14. ☑ **A** and **B.** The name can be used in the SELECT following the WITH clause.
    ☒ **C** and **D** are incorrect. The name is not stored in the database by the WITH statement. It exists only for the WITH clause itself and is not recognized outside of the WITH clause. The one place within the WITH clause that does not recognize the subquery name is within the named subquery itself.

15. ☑ **A** and **D.** The WITH clause must name the query in order for the SELECT to be able to reference the query contained within the parentheses. The syntax of WITH does not use the SELECT preceding the WITH.
    ☒ **B** and **C** are incorrect. Each is syntactically correct. Both name the query in the WITH clause.

Write Single-Row and Multiple-Row Subqueries

16. ☑ **B** and **D.** The >=ALL syntax is "greater than or equal to all" the values returned by the subquery, which is ideal for a multiple-row query. The IN comparison operator is also useful.
    ☒ **A** and **C** are incorrect. The equal sign is restricted to only single-row subqueries. The LIKE operator is also limited to single-row subqueries.

17. ☑ **A.** The query will produce an execution error because the parent query is expecting a single-row answer from the subquery. You know this because of the comparison operator in line 3: the greater-than sign is a single-row comparison operator. The better choice here might be > ANY or > ALL, depending on the situation.

☒ **B, C,** and **D** are incorrect. There is nothing wrong with PORT_ID and HOME_PORT_ID having different column names. As long as their data types match, all is well, and you know their data types match according to the illustration provided.

18. ☑ **A.** It returns multiple rows at the time of execution.

☒ **B, C,** and **D** are incorrect. The WHERE clause is certainly important, but the query's particular form is not important. What is important is whether the query returns multiple rows at the time it executes. The presence of numeric data is not important, nor is the number of columns.

19. ☑ **C.** A subquery can be used to return a value to the WHERE clause of a SELECT statement, regardless of whether a GROUP BY is involved. The issue of whether the subquery returns one row or multiples must be handled correctly, as we've discussed elsewhere. But provided it is done correctly, a subquery can be used in this context.

☒ **A, B,** and **D** are incorrect. There is no issue with regard to GROUP BY and the use of subqueries. A SELECT with a GROUP BY is allowed the option of the use of subqueries, either single-row or multiple-row (or both) provided that the rules of the single-row and/or multiple-row subquery are handled correctly. A GROUP BY is permitted to use any form of subquery; it is not restricted to the correlated subquery.

20. ☑ **A.** The statement will fail with a syntax error because there are two columns in the subquery, but only one value is on the left side of the comparison operator IN.

☒ **B, C,** and **D** are incorrect. The syntax on line 5 is acceptable. The use of IN in line 3 ensures that the subquery will be permitted to return either one or multiple rows, and with all else being acceptable, the statement would otherwise execute successfully.

10
Managing Schema Objects

I n addition to tables, there are other important schema objects. This chapter looks at several, including views, sequences, and indexes. This chapter also addresses additional features: Flashback Table, Flashback Drop, and Flashback Query.

Describe How Schema Objects Work

As you've seen, there are several objects in the database. Many are "schema" objects, meaning they are "owned" by a user and exist in a collection within a user account. Schema objects include tables, views, indexes, and sequences. In this section, we'll look at some of the functionality of database objects and how they work with each other.

Tables

All the data in a database is stored in tables. When you create a new table, the information about that table, such as its name and columns and the data types of those columns, is all stored in a set of system-defined tables that are collectively known as the *data dictionary* and that are managed automatically by the Oracle system. (We examine the data dictionary in Chapter 12.) So, even data about your data—in other words, *metadata*—is stored in tables.

A table's columns are generally stored in the order in which they are created, but this isn't necessarily true at all times. Also, if you alter a table via ALTER and add a column to its structure, the new column will be added at the end of the list of columns in the table's structure.

Constraints

A *constraint* is a rule on a table that restricts the values that can be added to a table's columns. Note that it is not a database object, but it is listed in the data dictionary and can be named with the same naming rules of an object. You've already looked at the different types of constraints: NOT NULL, UNIQUE, PRIMARY KEY, FOREIGN KEY, and CHECK.

If a SQL statement attempts to add, modify, or delete a row to/from a table and in so doing violates a constraint, the entire SQL statement will fail with an execution error.

Views

A *view* acts like a table. It has a name. You can describe the view with DESCRIBE in the same way you would describe a table. You can run a SELECT statement on a view just as you would select from a table. Depending on the kind of view you are working with, you might even be able to execute INSERT, UPDATE, and/or DELETE statements on a view to manipulate the contents of the underlying tables.

But a view is not a table, and it stores no data. A view is nothing more than a SELECT statement that is saved in the database with a name assigned to it. The column structure that the view takes on is formed by the SELECT statement's select list. The data types for those columns are picked up automatically from the underlying table or the expressions used in the SELECT statement to create the view.

Indexes

An *index* performs the same job that a typical index in a book performs. For example, Oracle Corporation's *SQL Language Reference Manual* for Oracle 12c's R1 release is more than 1,908 pages long. What if you were looking for information on the DISTINCT clause of the SELECT statement? You have a few ways to find such information in the book. One way is to sit down and start reading the book at the first page and keep reading until you find the data you're looking for. A much more efficient way is to flip to the back of the book and find the index, which contains a summary of important topics in alphabetical order. Within a few seconds you can look up the word DISTINCT, note the page number on which it's mentioned, and flip straight to it. That's a much better approach.

The SQL INDEX object performs in much the same way. When you create an INDEX object, you are identifying one or more columns in a table that you believe will be frequently used to look up data. Then you create the index based on that column—or set of columns—and Oracle literally builds a separate object that takes a unique list of all the data currently in that column, sorts it appropriately according to data type, and then stores internal addressing information that ties the index to the source table and the rows contained within.

The result is that any future queries on the table that happen to reference any indexed data will cause the following to occur automatically:

■ Perform an analysis to determine whether the query will benefit by using the index

■ If yes, then redirect the focus temporarily to the index, search the index for any of the desired data identified by the query, and obtain direct locations of the appropriate rows

The difference in performance is potentially significant. The more data that is stored in a table, the more beneficial an index may be.

Sequences

A *sequence* is a counter, meaning that it issues numbers in a particular series, always keeping track of whatever the next number should be. If you ever watched the classic television sitcom *Seinfeld,* you might recall the episode where Jerry and Elaine go to a bakery to pick up a chocolate bobka, but don't know to take a number from the dispenser when they first arrive and lose their place in line as the bakery gets crowded. That dispenser—which issues paper tickets identifying the holder as being, say, "number 42" in line—serves the same purpose of a SEQUENCE object in the database.

The primary purpose of SEQUENCE is to support the process of adding rows to a particular table and providing the next unique value for a PRIMARY KEY for the table. That's it. There's nothing inherent in a SEQUENCE object that ties it to a particular table. There's nothing automatic in the SEQUENCE object that necessarily supports a particular table. It's up to the software developer to know how to use the SEQUENCE object correctly. We will explore this in detail later when we address the syntax for working with a SEQUENCE.

CERTIFICATION OBJECTIVE 10.02

Create Simple and Complex Views with Visible/Invisible Columns

A *view* is a SELECT statement with a name, stored in the database, and accessible as though it were a table. Earlier you saw the WITH clause that can assign a name to a query within a single SELECT statement. The view object does the same thing in a more permanent manner, meaning that the view object resides in the database alongside tables and other database objects.

Once you've created a view, you can refer to it in SELECT statements as though it were a table. Nothing about the SELECT is different—anyone looking at a given SELECT statement will not be able to determine from the SELECT statement alone if the FROM clause specifies a table or a view.

Views are useful for a variety of reasons. One benefit is security. For example, consider a typical scenario where you have a large table that contains a combination of some sensitive information along with some information that is of a general interest. You might create a view that queries the general-interest columns of the large table and then grant privileges on that view to the general population of users. Those users may now query the view and get direct access to the general information without having access to more sensitive data that exists in the underlying table. Views are a great way to mask certain data while giving access to other data in the same table.

Another benefit to views is their ability to make a complex query easier to work with. For example, you might create a view that is built on a complex join so that the complexity is built into the view. The result is a view object that appears to be a single table, which you may now query as though it were a table. You can even join the view with other tables and other views. In this situation, a view can be used to simplify the complexity of a commonly used join.

In the next section, we'll create a view object.

Creating Views

Let's look at an example. First, review Figure 10-1. We'll start with just the EMPLOYEES table—notice that it includes columns for employee ID, name, Social Security number, date of birth, and primary phone number.

So, here's a problem: what if you wanted to give access to this table so that other people in the organization can get the phone numbers of employees? Think about that sensitive information, including Social Security numbers, and you might have second thoughts about having anybody query the EMPLOYEES table.

One solution to this predicament is to use a view. Let's create a view for the EMPLOYEES table.

```
CREATE VIEW VW_EMPLOYEES AS
       SELECT EMPLOYEE_ID, LAST_NAME, FIRST_NAME, PRIMARY_PHONE
       FROM   EMPLOYEES;
```

FIGURE 10-1

Diagrams for the
EMPLOYEES and
PAY_HISTORY
tables

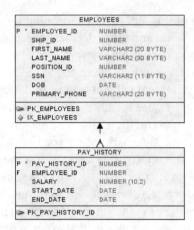

If we execute this statement in SQL, we'll get the following message:

```
VIEW VW_EMPLOYEES created.
```

(Note: This statement is the message displayed by Oracle SQL Developer. SQL*Plus will display a "View created" message.)

Now that we have this view, we can work with it just as if it were a table. For example, we can use DESCRIBE to explain it.

```
DESC VW_EMPLOYEES;
Name                               Null       Type
-------------------------------    --------   -------------
EMPLOYEE_ID                        NOT NULL   NUMBER
LAST_NAME                                     VARCHAR2(30)
FIRST_NAME                                    VARCHAR2(20)
PRIMARY_PHONE                                 VARCHAR2(20)
```

Additionally, we can select from it with SELECT as if it were a table.

```
SELECT * FROM VW_EMPLOYEES;

SELECT    FIRST_NAME || ' ' || LAST_NAME "Employee"
FROM      VW_EMPLOYEES
ORDER BY PRIMARY_PHONE;
```

The results will display just like any table. Anyone using VW_EMPLOYEES, running SELECT statements on it, describing its structure, and doing anything they might want using SQL commands may not ever realize it's not a table at all. The fact that it's a view isn't necessarily obvious. We chose to name it with a VW_ prefix for our own purposes, but we could have given it any name we wanted.

The syntax rules for creating a view are

■ The keywords CREATE VIEW

■ The optional keywords OR REPLACE

■ A name for the view, specified according to the rules for naming database objects

■ The keyword AS

■ Finally, a valid SELECT statement, with a few restrictions

One of the requirements of the CREATE VIEW statement is this: the resulting VIEW must have valid column names. This means that if you choose a SELECT statement that incorporates any complex expressions within the select list, each expression must be assigned a column alias, or column names must be assigned by the CREATE VIEW statement itself. For example, let's use the OR REPLACE option to create a new version of our VW_EMPLOYEES view (line numbers added).

```
01   CREATE OR REPLACE VIEW VW_EMPLOYEES AS
02          SELECT EMPLOYEE_ID,
03                 LAST_NAME || ', ' || FIRST_NAME,
04                 PRIMARY_PHONE
05          FROM   EMPLOYEES;
06
07   Error starting at line 1 in command:
08   CREATE OR REPLACE VIEW VW_EMPLOYEES AS
09          SELECT EMPLOYEE_ID,
10                 LAST_NAME || ', ' || FIRST_NAME,
11                 PRIMARY_PHONE
12          FROM   EMPLOYEES
13   Error at Command Line:3 Column:33
14   Error report:
15   SQL Error: ORA-00998: must name this expression with a column alias
16   00998. 00000 -  "must name this expression with a column alias"
```

What went wrong? The problem is on line 3, where we specify the expression that forms the second column in our SELECT expression list. Notice that it concatenates the column LAST_NAME with a comma, a space, and then the FIRST_NAME column. Here's the problem: what is the name of this column? There isn't one assigned, but the CREATE VIEW statement requires one. Therefore, the attempted CREATE VIEW statement fails.

To correct the problem, we can specify column names in the CREATE VIEW statement, like this:

```
01  CREATE OR REPLACE VIEW VW_EMPLOYEES (ID, NAME, PHONE) AS
02        SELECT EMPLOYEE_ID,
03               LAST_NAME || ', ' || FIRST_NAME,
04               PRIMARY_PHONE
05        FROM   EMPLOYEES;
```

Now we'll have a view consisting of three columns with the names ID, NAME, and PHONE. Alternatively, we could have used a column alias in the SELECT statement.

You can use complex queries to create views. For example, let's go back to Figure 10-1 and build a query that joins data from the PAY_HISTORY table into our view, as follows:

```
01  CREATE VIEW EMP_TREND AS
02    SELECT   EMP.SHIP_ID, MIN(SALARY) MIN_SALARY
03    FROM     EMPLOYEES EMP LEFT JOIN PAY_HISTORY PAY
04    ON       EMP.EMPLOYEE_ID = PAY.EMPLOYEE_ID
05    WHERE    END_DATE IS NULL
06    GROUP BY EMP.SHIP_ID;
```

This statement uses a SELECT statement with a join, a GROUP BY, a WHERE clause, and aggregate functions; it creates a VIEW object out of all of it.

VIEW objects can be based on SELECT statements with subqueries, functions, and more.

```
CREATE OR REPLACE VIEW SHIP_ONE_CABINS AS
      SELECT * FROM SHIP_CABINS WHERE SHIP_ID = 1;
```

The view created with this statement will consist only of the rows in the SHIP_CABINS table where the SHIP_ID value is equal to 1. The SHIP_CABINS table may contain more rows than those with a SHIP_ID of 1, but those rows won't be found by way of any query on the SHIP_ONE_CABINS view.

Also, take note again of the optional keywords OR REPLACE in the CREATE VIEW statement. These words don't work with CREATE TABLE, but they do with CREATE VIEW. Be careful with them—when included, they will give you no warning if you are or are not overwriting some existing view. They will simply overwrite what may have gone before and replace it with the new view. It's a convenient option that is powerful, so be careful with it. You have been warned.

Views and Constraints

You can create constraints on a view in the same way you can create them on a table. However, Oracle doesn't enforce them without special configuration that's available primarily to support certain data warehousing requirements. This subject is worth noting but not specifically addressed on the exam.

Updatable Views

You've seen how we can SELECT from a view. But can we also use INSERT and UPDATE and DELETE?

The answer is, it depends. If the view contains enough information to satisfy all the constraints in any underlying tables, then yes, you can use INSERT, UPDATE, or DELETE statements on the view. Otherwise, no.

Depending on the nature of the constraints, it may be possible to use some Data Manipulation Language (DML) statements but not others on the view. For example, if the view fails to include any columns from the underlying table that have NOT NULL constraints, you will not be able to execute an INSERT statement, but you may be able to issue an UPDATE or DELETE statement.

For example, let's revisit the EMPLOYEES table in Figure 10-1. Let's make a new view on that table, like this:

```
CREATE OR REPLACE VIEW EMP_PHONE_BOOK
    AS SELECT LAST_NAME, FIRST_NAME, PRIMARY_PHONE FROM EMPLOYEES;
```

This view contains just enough information to print an employee phone book, including their names and phone numbers. Once we've created this view, we can select from it, like this:

```
SELECT   LAST_NAME, FIRST_NAME, PRIMARY_PHONE
FROM     EMP_PHONE_BOOK
ORDER BY LAST_NAME, FIRST_NAME;
```

Fantastic. But wait—we just hired someone new. Her name is Sonia Sotogovernor, and we want to add her name to this view. Let's try it.

```
INSERT INTO EMP_PHONE_BOOK (LAST_NAME, FIRST_NAME, PRIMARY_PHONE)
    VALUES ('Sotogovernor', 'Sonia', '212-555-1212');

Error starting at line 1 in command:

INSERT INTO EMP_PHONE_BOOK (LAST_NAME, FIRST_NAME, PRIMARY_PHONE)
    VALUES ('Sotogovernor', 'Sonia', '212-555-1212')

Error report:
SQL Error: ORA-01400: cannot insert NULL into ("EFCODD"."EMPLOYEES"."EMPLOYEE_ID")
01400. 00000 -  "cannot insert NULL into (%s)"
```

Whoops. What's wrong here? See the error message? Remember that our underlying table is the EMPLOYEES table, and it contains a PRIMARY KEY of EMPLOYEE_ID, as shown in Figure 10-1. But our view doesn't include that column. As a result, there is no way for us to insert a value through the EMP_PHONE_BOOK view so that it will provide a value for the required column of EMPLOYEE_ID. We cannot execute an INSERT statement on this view.

However, we can execute an UPDATE statement on the view. Here's an example:

```
UPDATE EMP_PHONE_BOOK
   SET PRIMARY_PHONE = '202-555-1212'
WHERE  LAST_NAME  = 'Hoddlestein'
   AND  FIRST_NAME = 'Howard';
```

This statement works perfectly fine on the view. The reason is that the changes we're making with this UPDATE statement do not violate any underlying constraints.

If there are any constraints on the underlying table that you cannot satisfy when attempting to issue an INSERT, UPDATE, or DELETE on a view, then the statement won't work. The VIEW object must provide access to any of the underlying table's columns in such a way that the constraints can be honored to satisfy those constraints and execute the statement successfully. Otherwise, the INSERT, UPDATE, or DELETE statement will fail.

In addition, a view that is based on aggregated rows will not be updatable.

You will be prevented from using INSERT, UPDATE, or DELETE if you create a view based on a SELECT statement that includes any of the following:

- Omission of any required columns (NOT NULL) in that underlying table
- GROUP BY or any other aggregation, such as set operators

- DISTINCT
- A FROM clause that references more than one table—that is, subqueries in the SELECT or most joins

Regarding that last item, it is technically possible to execute DML changes on joins where all updatable columns belong to a key-preserved table. The details go beyond the scope of this book. For the most part, you will not be able to issue DML changes to a VIEW object based on a join.

As we've already seen, a view's SELECT statement may include expressions as part of the columns in its formation, as follows:

```
CREATE OR REPLACE VIEW EMP_PHONE_BOOK
     AS SELECT EMPLOYEE_ID,
               FIRST_NAME || ', ' || LAST_NAME EMP_NAME,
               PRIMARY_PHONE
        FROM EMPLOYEES;
```

Note that the preceding query concatenates the FIRST_NAME and LAST_NAME columns into one expression. As a result, the individual columns cannot be modified with an INSERT or UPDATE statement—there is no way to singularly refer to the individual columns unless they are added as individual items in the select list. However, EMPLOYEE_ID, the required column, is included as an individual column, so this would be a satisfactory statement:

```
INSERT INTO EMP_PHONE_BOOK (EMPLOYEE_ID, PRIMARY_PHONE)
     VALUES
     (102, '800-555-1212');
```

That statement will successfully execute on our EMP_PHONE_BOOK view and add a new row to the underlying table, assuming the primary key value for EMPLOYEE_ID is accepted as a new unique entry. But we're not able to insert a row through the view using an INSERT statement that references the EMP_NAME column alias or its component columns FIRST_NAME and LAST_NAME. We simply have to omit any references to those columns in our DML statements for our DML to execute successfully. The INSERT INTO EMP_PHONE_BOOK statement will cause a new row to be added to the EMPLOYEES table. That new row will consist of a value for EMPLOYEE_ID (102) and a value for PRIMARY_PHONE ('800-555-1212'); all other columns in the new row will show as NULL—that is, have no values. (Remember, NULL represents the absence of information.)

We may delete a row in this view. Here's an example:

```
DELETE FROM EMP_PHONE_BOOK WHERE EMPLOYEE_ID = 102;
```

This statement will successfully delete the entire row for an EMPLOYEE_ID of 102. If we issued a similar DELETE statement for any other existing value we can access, such as PRIMARY_PHONE or EMPLOYEE_ID, and the row were found, then the row—the entire row of the underlying table—would be deleted. That includes data in columns we can't even see with the view. The whole row will be deleted.

With regard to the general question of using INSERT, UPDATE, and/or DELETE on any given view, the general answer is simple: if the view provides row-level (not aggregated) access to one—and only one—table and includes the ability to access the required columns in that table, then you can use INSERT, UPDATE, and/or DELETE on the view to effect changes to the underlying table, in accordance with the restrictions listed earlier. Otherwise, you may not be able to successfully execute a change to the view's data.

on the job

Note that the INSTEAD OF trigger in PL/SQL can be used to cause a nonupdatable view to behave as though it were updatable. But PL/SQL features are not addressed on the exam.

Inline Views

An *inline view* is a subquery that is contained within a larger SELECT statement in such a way that it replaces the FROM clause of a SQL statement.

Here's an example:

```
01   SELECT *
02   FROM (SELECT * FROM DUAL);
```

In this example, the inline view is included in the parentheses at the end of line 2.

There is no limit to the number of inline views you can nest within inline views.

```
SELECT * FROM (SELECT * FROM (SELECT * FROM (SELECT * FROM DUAL)));
```

This "unlimited nesting" is different from the limit for typical subqueries, where the limit is 255 nested subqueries.

Inline views can be combined with various complex queries, such as those that use JOIN and GROUP BY clauses and more. Here's an example:

```
01   SELECT A.SHIP_ID, A.COUNT_CABINS, B.COUNT_CRUISES
02   FROM (SELECT    SHIP_ID, COUNT(SHIP_CABIN_ID) COUNT_CABINS
03          FROM      SHIP_CABINS
04          GROUP BY  SHIP_ID) A
05          JOIN
06          (SELECT   SHIP_ID, COUNT(CRUISE_ORDER_ID) COUNT_CRUISES
07          FROM      CRUISE_ORDERS
08          GROUP BY SHIP_ID) B
09     ON    A.SHIP_ID = B.SHIP_ID;
```

This statement is a single SELECT that pulls data from two inline views, one on lines 2 through 4 and the second on lines 6 through 8.

Inline views can be any valid SELECT statement, placed into a SQL statement where the FROM clause would normally go.

One great usage of an inline view is to address an issue involving the pseudocolumn ROWNUM. ROWNUM is a row number automatically assigned to each row result of a query. The challenge with ROWNUM is that it is assigned before the ORDER BY clause is processed. As a result, you cannot sort rows and then use ROWNUM as a way of displaying, for example, the line number for each row of output. The results will be mixed up since ROWNUM is determined before ORDER BY is processed. But you can move the ORDER BY clause into an inline view and then use the ROWNUM pseudocolumn on the outer query to display row numbers correctly. Here's an example:

```
SELECT ROWNUM, INVOICE_ID, ACCOUNT_NUMBER
FROM   (SELECT INVOICE_ID, ACCOUNT_NUMBER
        FROM INVOICES ORDER BY INVOICE_DATE)
WHERE ROWNUM <= 3;
ROWNUM                      INVOICE_ID              ACCOUNT_NUMBER
--------------------- ----------------------- -------------------
1                           2                       cre-kit-A1233-V01
2                           3                       ae-TRR
3                           4                       INV-PR-0101
```

In this example, we use ORDER BY in the inline view to sort our rows by INVOICE_DATE, and then we use ROWNUM in the outer query to limit our output to just the first three rows of data. We also include ROWNUM in our select list so that it appears in the output. Without the inline view, odds are that our ROWNUM values would be in an apparently random order instead of sequential.

So, why would you want to use an inline view? There are many reasons. As we've already demonstrated, inline views can be used to create complex joins built on aggregated queries. Another benefit has to do with the nature of dynamic SQL as it's used with third-generation languages. Many popular web sites are built on web pages that are dynamically formed from a combination of Java, PL/SQL, or PHP code that pulls data from the database and merges the output with the languages used to form web pages. A full example of such a scenario is beyond the scope of this book, but it's worth noting that such systems rely heavily on routines that create SQL code dynamically, during execution, in response to queries from end users. Such dynamic scenarios can benefit greatly from the ability to, for example, create a standard outer query in which the inline view can be substituted by dynamic code. An end user may perform a search that might draw data from any number of various sources yet present the output through a fixed series of data elements. The inline view can support such a situation.

ALTER VIEW

The ALTER VIEW statement is used to accomplish any of the following tasks:

- Create, modify, or drop constraints on a view
- Recompile an invalid view

The subject of constraints on a view is not something that is covered on the exam. Oracle does not enforce view constraints without special configuration (see DISABLE NOVALIDATE in Oracle's documentation).

Recompiling a view is a step you may want to take if you've created a view and then later performed some sort of modification on the underlying table or tables upon which the view is created. Depending on the change you make to the view's source table, the view may be rendered invalid as a result. Once rendered invalid, a subsequent attempt to use the view will result in one of two outcomes, depending on the nature of the change that was performed to the underlying table:

- **Outcome 1** If the change results in a situation where the original CREATE VIEW statement would have successful executed anyway, then a subsequent statement using that view will cause the view to be recompiled successfully, and the statement will successfully execute as though no problem ever existed—because it didn't.

■ **Outcome 2**   If the change results in a situation where the original CREATE VIEW statement would have not successfully executed, then subsequent attempts to use the view will fail. An example of such a change would be to alter an underlying table to drop a column that is part of a view's column list.

In Chapter 12 we'll see how you can determine whether a view is invalid or not by querying the data dictionary.

An alternative to querying the data dictionary, which is not always available to an application, is to issue an ALTER VIEW ... COMPILE statement. This statement can be used to recompile an invalid view. If the view cannot be recompiled, the ALTER VIEW ... COMPILE statement will successfully execute with a message declaring "Warning: View altered with compilation errors." The data dictionary will show the view as remaining invalid.

Here is an example of a statement that recompiles a view:

```
ALTER VIEW VW_EMPLOYEES COMPILE;
```

You cannot change a view's SELECT statement with the ALTER VIEW statement. Instead, you must drop and re-create the view.

Once compiled successfully, the view is back in working condition. If it does not compile, you know that the change to the underlying table may have fundamentally changed the nature of the view's structure. For example, if a view queries a named column from an underlying table and that column is renamed (or dropped, as I pointed out earlier), then the recompilation will not work, and you may need to re-create the view and reassess your code.

In addition, if you simply attempt to use an invalid view, it will automatically compile. If it can be compiled, the attempt to use the view will be successful, with all else being equal. However, if it cannot be recompiled, then contrary to the ALTER VIEW ... COMPILE statement, which would execute but issue a warning, any attempt to use an invalid view that cannot be automatically recompiled will result in an error.

Visible/Invisible Columns

Views are based on tables, and in Oracle 12c, a table can have columns that are either visible or invisible. How does that impact views? Let's start by looking at the use of invisible columns in tables.

Invisible Columns and Tables

The columns in a table are visible by default. New with Oracle 12c, you can specify that one or more columns be invisible. Here's an example:

```
01  CREATE TABLE SHIP_ADMIN
02  (  SHIP_ADMIN_ID       NUMBER(7) PRIMARY KEY
03   , SHIP_ID             NUMBER
04   , CONSTRUCTION_COST   NUMBER(14,2) INVISIBLE
05  );
```

Note the column CONSTRUCTION_COST, which is specified as INVISIBLE. The other columns are visible by default; only the column CONSTRUCTION_ COST is invisible.

So, what does this mean? First, let's look at displaying the table's structure with DESC. You can describe the table with DESC SHIP_ADMIN, and you will see the typical table description, but any column specified as INVISIBLE will be omitted from display.

```
SQL> DESC SHIP_ADMIN
 Name
 ---------------------
 SHIP_ADMIN_ID
 SHIP_ID
```

on the job

Note that within Oracle's SQL*Plus tool specifically, you can use the "SET COLINVISIBLE ON" statement to temporarily configure the DESC statement to return invisible columns during that particular SQL*Plus session.

You can use INSERT with a table that has invisible columns, but you have to be careful. You can use INSERT to insert values into an invisible column, but only if you specify the column names. If you omit them in the INSERT, you'll get an error message. For an example, see Figure 10-2.

Note the first INSERT statement in the figure, which uses the shorthand INSERT syntax that omits a table's columns before the VALUES clause; you'll get an error message if an invisible column is present in the table. This shorthand syntax is an implied reference to every column in the table. In this case, the SHIP_ADMIN table has three columns, but only two are visible. The final portion of this first INSERT provides values for three columns, and the table has three columns—but only two are visible. With the shorthand INSERT syntax, this statement fails. Had we used a shorthand version of INSERT that provided only two values—for the visible columns—this statement would work.

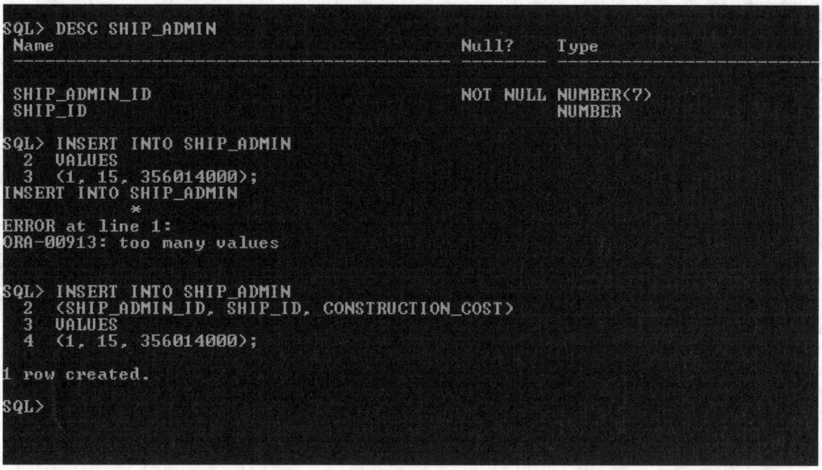

FIGURE 10-2

The INSERT
statement and
columns that
are specified as
INVISIBLE

```
SQL> DESC SHIP_ADMIN
 Name                                         Null?    Type
 ------------------------------------------   --------  --------------

 SHIP_ADMIN_ID                                NOT NULL NUMBER(?)
 SHIP_ID                                               NUMBER
SQL> INSERT INTO SHIP_ADMIN
  2   VALUES
  3   (1, 15, 356014000);
INSERT INTO SHIP_ADMIN
            *
ERROR at line 1:
ORA-00913: too many values


SQL> INSERT INTO SHIP_ADMIN
  2   (SHIP_ADMIN_ID, SHIP_ID, CONSTRUCTION_COST)
  3   VALUES
  4   (1, 15, 356014000);

1 row created.

SQL>
```

Now, note the second INSERT statement. It differs from the first only in that it specifies all three column names, including the invisible column name. This second INSERT executes successfully.

So, can you insert values into the invisible column of a table? The answer is yes, provided that you specify the column names in the INSERT statement.

Take note of this pattern; you will see it again, as we turn our attention to the use of invisible columns and VIEW objects.

Invisible Columns and Views

Remember that a view is an object built on a query of one or more tables. When we speak of a view and invisible columns, we are talking about the columns of the table or tables on which the view's query is based. Are those invisible? If so, there are several issues to address.

As you just learned, if a table has one or more columns specified as INVISIBLE, then wildcard references (with the asterisk) in an INSERT statement will not recognize the invisible column. The same issue applies to queries used to build a VIEW.

For example, let's start with the same SHIP_ADMIN table we just created. Remember, it has three columns, one of which is invisible. It also now has one row of data. See Figure 10-3.

Let's create two different views on the SHIP_ADMIN table.

For the first view, our query will use a wildcard reference to all the table's columns. Remember, the queried SHIP_ADMIN table has two visible columns and one invisible column.

FIGURE 10-3

The SHIP_ADMIN table with one row of data

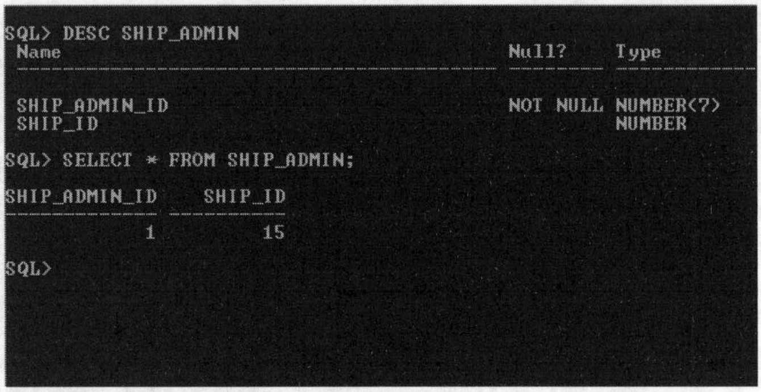

```
SQL> DESC SHIP_ADMIN
 Name                                         Null?    Type
 ------------------------------------------   -------- ----------------
 SHIP_ADMIN_ID                                NOT NULL NUMBER(7)
 SHIP_ID                                               NUMBER

SQL> SELECT * FROM SHIP_ADMIN;

SHIP_ADMIN_ID     SHIP_ID
------------- -----------
            1          15

SQL>
```

See Figure 10-4. We create the view and then describe it. The invisible column is omitted from the view's structure.

Next, we execute a SELECT statement that also uses a wildcard reference to "all" the columns, and only visible columns will be returned as output. The invisible column is not accessible. Even if we execute a SELECT that names all the columns, including any invisible columns, the invisible column is not accessible; Figure 10-4 shows the results of the attempt.

Even though the view is built on a query that uses a wildcard reference to "all" columns in the SHIP_ADMIN table, only the visible columns are included.

For our second view, let's specify the invisible column in the CREATE VIEW statement's query; see Figure 10-5.

Now we see a different outcome. This second view is based on a query that specifies an invisible column by name. In this situation, the view will see the invisible columns. The invisible column is reflected in the view's structure.

FIGURE 10-4

VW_SHIP_ADMIN view with SELECT * and SELECT column list

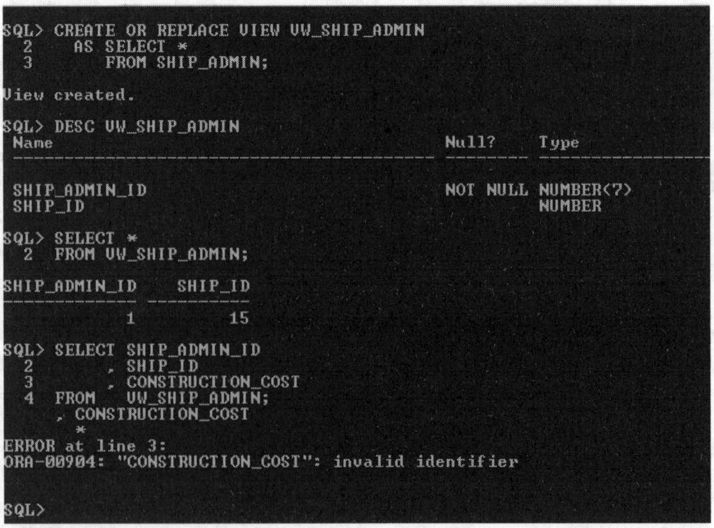

```
SQL> CREATE OR REPLACE VIEW VW_SHIP_ADMIN
  2    AS SELECT *
  3       FROM SHIP_ADMIN;
View created.
SQL> DESC VW_SHIP_ADMIN
 Name                                         Null?    Type
 ------------------------------------------   -------- ----------------
 SHIP_ADMIN_ID                                NOT NULL NUMBER(7)
 SHIP_ID                                               NUMBER

SQL> SELECT *
  2  FROM VW_SHIP_ADMIN;

SHIP_ADMIN_ID     SHIP_ID
------------- -----------
            1          15

SQL> SELECT SHIP_ADMIN_ID
  2       , SHIP_ID
  3       , CONSTRUCTION_COST
  4  FROM  VW_SHIP_ADMIN;
     , CONSTRUCTION_COST
       *
ERROR at line 3:
ORA-00904: "CONSTRUCTION_COST": invalid identifier

SQL>
```

FIGURE 10-5

VW2_SHIP_
ADMIN view
with SELECT
* and SELECT
column list

```
SQL> CREATE OR REPLACE VIEW VW2_SHIP_ADMIN
  2    AS SELECT SHIP_ADMIN_ID
  3           , SHIP_ID
  4           , CONSTRUCTION_COST
  5       FROM SHIP_ADMIN;

View created.

SQL> DESC VW2_SHIP_ADMIN
 Name                                      Null?    Type
 ───────────────────────────────────────────────────────────────────

 SHIP_ADMIN_ID                            NOT NULL NUMBER(7)
 SHIP_ID                                            NUMBER
 CONSTRUCTION_COST                                  NUMBER(14,2)

SQL> SELECT *
  2  FROM VW2_SHIP_ADMIN;

SHIP_ADMIN_ID    SHIP_ID CONSTRUCTION_COST
───────────── ────────── ─────────────────
            1         15         356014000

SQL> SELECT SHIP_ADMIN_ID
  2       , SHIP_ID
  3       , CONSTRUCTION_COST
  4  FROM   VW2_SHIP_ADMIN;

SHIP_ADMIN_ID    SHIP_ID CONSTRUCTION_COST
───────────── ────────── ─────────────────
            1         15         356014000

SQL>
```

A SELECT statement on this second view will return values from the invisible column, whether the SELECT statement (on the view) uses a wildcard reference or not, as shown in Figure 10-5. The difference is the use of the wildcard in the query that is used to create the view in the first place.

If the query used to create the view employs a wildcard column reference, invisible columns are ignored, but the view will be created successfully; it will simply omit the invisible column.

However, when working with a table consisting of one or more invisible columns, it is possible to create a view that includes those invisible columns by specifying the invisible column names in the query used to create the view. The result is a view where the column that is invisible in the table is visible to the view, both in the view's structure and in interactions with the view itself, such as SELECT statements.

CERTIFICATION OBJECTIVE 10.03

Create, Maintain, and Use Sequences

A *sequence* is an object that is predominantly used for one purpose: to generate data for primary key columns in tables. While that is the primary purpose of a sequence, there's nothing inherent in the structure of a sequence to limit you to such a purpose. You can use a sequence to generate numeric sequences for any reason. But all a sequence does is issue sequentially increasing (or decreasing) numbers, according to the rules you define when you create the sequence.

Creating and Dropping Sequences

Here's a sample of the SQL statement to create a sequence:

```
CREATE SEQUENCE SEQ_ORDER_ID;
```

This example is a complete statement and represents the simplest form of a CREATE SEQUENCE statement. The syntax is as follows:

- The required CREATE SEQUENCE keywords
- The required name of the sequence that you specify, according to the rules of naming database objects

Note that nothing in the code ties it to a particular table or other database object—nothing, that is, other than perhaps the choice of the name, which is a naming convention we use but is not required.

Here's the complete syntax for a sequence:

```
CREATE SEQUENCE sequence_name sequence_options;
```

There are several *sequence_options* that can each be specified, separated by spaces, as desired. Sequences can be set to start at any number and increment—or decrement—by any number. They can sequentially generate without ceasing or be given a range within which they continuously generate new numbers. They can be given a fixed series of numbers to generate, after which they cease generating numbers.

The sequence options include the following:

- **INCREMENT BY *integer***   Each new sequence number requested will increment by this number. A negative number indicates the sequence will descend. If omitted, the increment defaults to 1.
- **START WITH *integer***   This specifies the first number that will start the sequence. If omitted, START WITH defaults to MINVALUE (which we will discuss in a bit) for ascending sequences or MAXVALUE for descending sequences, unless NOMINVALUE or NOMAXVALUE are specified either explicitly or implicitly (by default), in which case START WITH defaults to 1.

- **MAXVALUE *integer*** This specifies the maximum number for the sequence. If omitted, then NOMAXVALUE is assumed.
- **NOMAXVALUE** This specifies that there is no MAXVALUE specified.
- **MINVALUE *integer*** This specifies the minimum number for the sequence. If omitted, NOMINVALUE is assumed, unless a MINVALUE is required by the presence of CYCLE, in which case the default is 1.
- **NOMINVALUE** This specifies that there is no MINVALUE specified.
- **CYCLE** When the sequence generator reaches one end of its range, restart at the other end. In other words, in an ascending sequence, once the generated value reaches the MAXVALUE, the next number generated will be the MINVALUE. In a descending sequence, once the generated value reaches the MINVALUE, the number generated will be the MAXVALUE.
- **NOCYCLE** When the sequence generator reaches the end of its range, stop generating numbers. NOCYCLE is the default. If no range is specified, NOCYCLE has no effect.

You can also drop a sequence, like so:

```
DROP SEQUENCE SEQ_ORDER_ID;
```

Here's another example of the CREATE SEQUENCE statement:

```
CREATE SEQUENCE SEQ_ORDER_ID START WITH 1 INCREMENT BY 1;
```

This SQL statement performs the same task as the earlier CREATE SEQUENCE statement you saw. This example explicitly specifies the default features. You can adjust those defaults if you want, like this:

```
CREATE SEQUENCE SEQ_ORDER_ID START WITH 10 INCREMENT BY 5;
```

This statement will start with the number 10 and increment each successive number by 5.

Using Sequences

Now that we've created a sequence, what do we do with it? Here's an example:

```
INSERT INTO ORDERS (ORDER_ID, ORDER_DATE, CUSTOMER_ID)
VALUES (SEQ_ORDER_ID.NEXTVAL, SYSDATE, 28);
```

In this sample INSERT statement, we insert a row into the ORDERS table that consists of three values. The first value is SEQ_ORDER_ID.NEXTVAL. This reference is to the sequence generator SEQ_ORDER_ID along with its pseudocolumn NEXTVAL, which performs the following two tasks:

■ Advances the sequence generator to the next available number
■ Returns that value

If the sequence generator SEQ_ORDER_ID had just been created and if it was created with the default values for the START WITH and INCREMENT BY, then the initial call to NEXTVAL will obtain the starting value of 1. If the next call to the sequence generator is also a call to the NEXTVAL pseudocolumn, then it will be advanced again by 1 to a value of 2.

All sequence generators have two pseudocolumns:

■ **NEXTVAL**   This increments the sequence to the next number, according to the sequence's original CREATE SEQUENCE directives. It also returns the newly incremented number.

■ **CURRVAL**   This displays the current number that the sequence is holding. However, this call is valid only from within a session in which the NEXTVAL pseudocolumn has already been invoked. You cannot use CURRVAL in your initial call to any given sequence generator within a session.

The advantage to CURRVAL becomes apparent when working with a set of tables that involve PRIMARY KEY and FOREIGN KEY relationships. Consider the entity-relationship diagram (ERD) in Figure 10-6.

Let's create a couple of sequence generators for use with these tables.

```
CREATE SEQUENCE SEQ_CRUISE_CUSTOMER_ID;
CREATE SEQUENCE SEQ_CRUISE_ORDER_ID;
```

FIGURE 10-6

ERD diagram for the CRUISE_ CUSTOMERS and CRUISE_ORDERS tables

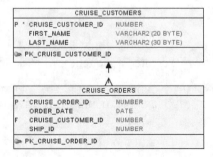

Now let's insert some new rows into these tables.

```
01   INSERT INTO CRUISE_CUSTOMERS
02     (CRUISE_CUSTOMER_ID, FIRST_NAME, LAST_NAME)
03     VALUES
04     (SEQ_CRUISE_CUSTOMER_ID.NEXTVAL, 'Joe', 'Schmoe');
05
06   INSERT INTO CRUISE_ORDERS
07     (CRUISE_ORDER_ID, ORDER_DATE, CRUISE_CUSTOMER_ID)
08     VALUES
09     (SEQ_CRUISE_ORDER_ID.NEXTVAL, SYSDATE, SEQ_CRUISE_CUSTOMER_ID.CURRVAL);
```

There are three calls to our sequence generators in the preceding code:

- In line 4 we call SEQ_CRUISE_CUSTOMER_ID.NEXTVAL to generate a new primary key.

- At the end of line 9 we call the same sequence generator with the CURRVAL pseudocolumn. This directs the sequence generator to use the same value that was just assigned in the line 4 call, ensuring that our PRIMARY KEY– FOREIGN KEY relationship between these two tables will be respected.

- At the beginning of line 9, we call SEQ_CRUISE_ORDER_ID.NEXTVAL to generate a new primary key for the CRUISE_ORDERS table.

The result of these INSERT statements and uses of the sequence generators helps to ensure that we can join our tables to produce valid and meaningful output. Here are a few important points to keep in mind about sequences:

- You cannot invoke CURRVAL in your first reference to a sequence within a given session. NEXTVAL must be the first reference.

- If you attempt to execute a statement such as an INSERT that includes the sequence reference NEXTVAL, the sequence generator will advance to the next number even if the INSERT statement fails.

- You cannot invoke CURRVAL or NEXTVAL in the DEFAULT clause of a CREATE TABLE or ALTER TABLE statement.

- You cannot invoke CURRVAL or NEXTVAL in the subquery of a CREATE VIEW statement or of a SELECT, UPDATE, or DELETE statement.

- In a SELECT statement, you cannot combine CURRVAL or NEXTVAL with a DISTINCT operator.

- You cannot invoke CURRVAL or NEXTVAL in the WHERE clause of a SELECT statement.

- You cannot use CURRVAL or NEXTVAL in a CHECK constraint.
- You cannot combine CURRVAL or NEXTVAL with the set operators UNION, INTERSECT, and MINUS.
- You can call a sequence pseudocolumn from anywhere within a SQL statement that you can use any expression.

That last point is important—a reference to a sequence must include its pseudocolumn, and such a reference is considered to be a valid expression or a component of an expression. So, assuming you're working with a table PROJECTS that has a column PROJECT_COST, you could invoke a sequence SEQ_PROJ_COST like this:

```
SELECT PROJECT_COST / (3 * SEQ_PROJ_COST.NEXTVAL) FROM PROJECTS;
```

That is valid syntax. Whether it's useful or not is up to your business rules. But SQL recognizes this syntax and will execute it successfully.

The bottom line is that references to the pseudocolumns of sequences are valid expressions.

exam
watch

Any SQL statement that is executed with a call to a sequence's NEXTVAL pseudocolumn will advance the sequence, even if the SQL statement fails.

Not even a ROLLBACK will reset a sequence; even the value of the sequence generator's CURRVAL will remain the same after a ROLLBACK.

CERTIFICATION OBJECTIVE 10.04

Create and Maintain Indexes Including Invisible Indexes and Multiple Indexes on the Same Columns

An index is an object you can create in the database, and it stores a subset of data from a table. The index is its own object; it is stored separately from the table, and it is constantly maintained with every INSERT, UPDATE, and DELETE performed on the table. For example, if you have a table SHIPS with a column CAPACITY and you create an index for the table using the column CAPACITY, then both the table and the index will store—separately—CAPACITY values. Every time a DML statement changes a value in the SHIPS table's CAPACITY column, the index will also be changed accordingly.

The purpose of an index is to support faster queries on a table. The index values are presorted. An index can be created for only one table, and it can be created on one or more of that table's columns—columns that you designate. For each column, the index also stores the address of that data from the source table. SQL can then use the index object to speed up the querying of WHERE and ORDER BY clauses. For example, if a WHERE clause references any indexed column (or columns), then SQL (or more specifically, the optimizer) will automatically consider the index as it determines the optimal query strategy for the SQL statement. The result is that queries may be significantly faster, depending on the amount of data involved and depending on the number of indexes that may be applied to a table.

Note that we say that an index "may" speed up performance. SQL statement processing is performed by a built-in function known as the Oracle Database *optimizer*. The optimizer determines how best to process any given SQL statement according to a combination of factors. Two of those factors are the presence and structure of indexes, but there are other factors as well. As SQL developers, it is our job to create the necessary resources for the optimizer to do its job, recognizing that the optimizer, in the end, makes the final decision and processes the statement. I will speak more about the optimizer in a few paragraphs.

You cannot create an index on columns of LOB or RAW data types. Given that, you can create any number of indexes, limited only with regard to certain aspects of column sets, which I will explain in a bit. However, as you add indexes, you'll eventually reach a point of diminishing returns—each index added to a table can potentially increase the workload on future INSERT, UPDATE, and DELETE statements. But let's hold off on that discussion for a bit. For now, we just want to say that the SQL system will let you create as many indexes as you want.

Remember that the WHERE clause can appear in a SELECT, UPDATE, or DELETE statement. Also note that a SELECT statement, in the form of a subquery, may appear within an INSERT statement or a variety of statements that create objects such as TABLE or VIEW. An INDEX object can potentially benefit any of these situations.

The Oracle Database Optimizer

The reason we create an index on a table is so that the Oracle Database optimizer can process SQL statements on that table faster. But what is the optimizer?

The optimizer is a built-in feature in the Oracle database that is crucial to the processing of every SQL statement issued against the database. Each SQL statement has the potential for great complexity, with instructions to join, filter, and transform data in a variety of ways. The amount of data to be processed can vary dramatically. This complexity introduces a host of challenges. The optimizer is designed to handle those challenges, and it performs very well.

For example, if you want to execute a typical SQL statement with some scalar functions and a WHERE clause, then it would be ideal if the WHERE clause executes first and the scalar functions are applied later. Why? Because the WHERE clause can first reduce the number of rows to be processed, leaving only those rows necessary on which to apply the scalar functions. The responsibility of ensuring that such prioritization is factored into SQL processing is built into the database, and the optimizer is the feature that analyzes the SQL statement and establishes an *execution plan* for processing the statement. This execution plan is accessible to you via the EXPLAIN PLAN statement, which is not a subject of the exam, but is worth investigating. If you are interested in learning more about the optimizer, look for documentation on the EXPLAIN PLAN statement, and you will learn a great deal.

For our purposes, it is enough to know that the optimizer is the built-in function that processes SQL statements and that, as part of that processing, the optimizer is the decision point where the database determines whether and how to incorporate an index in the execution of any given SQL statement.

Your goal when building indexes is to create a set of useful objects to be leveraged by the optimizer in its construction of the optimal execution plan for processing future SQL statements, whatever those may be. Your job as a developer is to anticipate the typical usage of your table and then create indexes that the optimizer will be able to use to best execute those future SQL statements. Understanding how indexes work is a necessary step toward achieving that goal—and performing well on the exam.

We will revisit the topic of the optimizer as we discuss indexes in the following sections.

Implicit Index Creation

If you create a constraint on a table that is of type PRIMARY KEY or UNIQUE, then as part of the creation of the constraint, SQL will automatically create an index to support that constraint on the column or columns, if such an index does not already exist.

For example, consider the following SQL statement:

```
CREATE TABLE SEMINARS
(SEMINAR_ID      NUMBER(11)    PRIMARY KEY,
 SEMINAR_NAME    VARCHAR2(30)  UNIQUE);
```

This statement will create the table SEMINARS, two CONSTRAINTs, and two INDEX objects. These INDEX objects will be named automatically by the SQL system. Later in this section, you'll see how to manually create these indexes. Also later, in Chapter 12, you'll see how you can query the data dictionary to see these implicitly created indexes, but for now, here's a query on the data dictionary that can confirm their creation:

```
SELECT TABLE_NAME, INDEX_NAME
FROM    USER_INDEXES
WHERE   TABLE_NAME = 'SEMINARS';


TABLE_NAME                              INDEX_NAME
----------------------------            ----------------------------------
SEMINARS                                SYS_C009932
SEMINARS                                SYS_C009931
```

In the output of this example, you can see that the system assigned the names SYS_C009932 and SYS_C009931 to the indexes.

As an alternative, you can query elsewhere in the data dictionary to see the columns that are involved in the indexes:

```
SELECT INDEX_NAME, COLUMN_NAME
FROM    USER_IND_COLUMNS
WHERE   TABLE_NAME = 'SEMINARS';


INDEX_NAME                              COLUMN_NAME
----------------------------            ----------------------------------
SYS_C009931                             SEMINAR_ID
SYS_C009932                             SEMINAR_NAME
```

In these examples, we applied each constraint to a single column. Had we created a composite PRIMARY KEY or a composite UNIQUE constraint, then all columns involved in the constraint would have also been indexed as a composite index, and the column names would be listed in the output of this second query on the data dictionary.

Single Column

Here is an example of a SQL statement that creates a single-column index:

```
CREATE INDEX IX_INV_INVOICE_DATE ON INVOICES(INVOICE_DATE);
```

This SQL statement creates a simple index called IX_INV_INVOICE_DATE, on the column INVOICE_DATE, in the table INVOICES. This will result in an object that sorts values in the INVOICE_DATE column of the INVOICES table. Once such an index exists, queries that reference INVOICE_DATE in the WHERE clause may return results significantly faster.

```
SELECT * FROM INVOICES WHERE INVOICE_DATE = '14-FEB-2017';
```

As we stated earlier, the index may or may not speed the performance of this SELECT statement. The decision is up to the optimizer. Remember that the optimizer analyzes all SQL statements to determine the best course of action for executing the statement. For any SQL statement that involves a table search or scan, such as a query with a WHERE clause or an ORDER BY clause, the optimizer will consider whether an available index on the queried table will contribute toward faster performance. The existence of an index does not guarantee its use; the optimizer determines whether or not the index will be helpful.

In our example, the SELECT statement against the INVOICES table includes a WHERE clause that specifies the INVOICE_DATE column. If, for example, all the rows in the INVOICES table have the same value for INVOICE_DATE, the index may not be used—it might contribute no performance benefit. On the other hand, if each row happens to have a unique INVOICE_DATE value, then the index most likely will be used. The difference has to do with the concept of *selectivity*. If a column tends to include data that is less repetitive and more unique, it is said to have a higher degree of selectivity, and an index on such a column would be attractive to the optimizer. But if data in a given column is relatively repetitive, it is said to have a lower degree of selectivity and will be less likely to be included in an index. The optimizer is the feature that makes that decision.

In the sample SELECT you just looked at, if the SQL optimizer determines to use the index, and if evidence is found in the index that a row of INVOICES matches the desired result, the index points the query directly to the row (or rows) in the table, and the result is achieved—much faster than otherwise would have occurred.

Usage

The Oracle Database optimizer will consider the use of an index in any query that specifies an indexed column in the WHERE clause or ORDER BY clause, depending on how the index column is specified. There are some guidelines for structuring your SQL statement so that the optimizer will be more likely to apply the index. The guidelines are as follows:

- For best results, the indexed column should be specified in a comparison of equality.
- A "greater than" or some other comparison may work.
- A "not equals" will not invoke an index.
- The LIKE comparison may invoke an index as long as the wildcard character is not in the leading position. In other words, the expression LIKE '%SMITH' will not invoke an index, but LIKE 'SMITH%' may invoke an index.
- A function on a column will prevent the use of an index—unless the index is a function-based index. (Function-based indexes are not addressed in the exam.)

Furthermore, certain types of automated data type conversions will eliminate the index.

The design of an indexing scheme is something that falls under the general category of *performance tuning*. There is no single comprehensive approach to index design for a given database application. The approach you take depends upon a variety of factors, including the amount and selectivity of data expected and the anticipated frequency and types of the various SQL statements you intend to execute on the database. A system that will not be queried much but will be heavily populated with INSERT statements would not benefit much from indexes, since each INSERT will be slower as it updates the tables and all associated INDEX objects. On such a database, infrequent queries may not justify the creation of INDEX objects and their associated performance trade-off. On the other hand, an application that involves a great deal of updating via UPDATE statements will benefit from thoughtfully designed indexes.

The optimizer will do everything it can to use an index for a given query where the index is beneficial. It avoids an index only if its use would be detrimental, such as in the case of a table with a large number of rows with an indexed column that has low selectivity.

An old rule of thumb recommends no more than five indexes on the average table in a transaction-based application. But that—again—depends on intended usage. I've implemented applications in which some tables have had as many as nine indexes applied, and the result was positive. That was a situation where queries on the table were not using primary keys so much but instead used a variety of text-based lookups.

Performance tuning is the subject of many books and is a topic that goes far beyond this book—and the exam. For the exam, it's important to understand the syntax of creating indexes—both single column and composites—and their intended purpose and general usage.

Maintenance

Indexes are automatically maintained in the background by SQL and require no effort on your part to keep their lookup data consistent with the table. However, note that this means each future INSERT, UPDATE, and DELETE statement you issue will have to work harder. Each DML statement that modifies data in a table that is indexed will also perform index maintenance as required. In other words, each index you add to a table puts more workload on each DML statement that affects indexed data.

Build the indexes that contribute to your application's overall performance, and don't build indexes unless they are necessary. Plan to periodically review your index structures to determine which indexes may no longer be needed; an existing application burdened with unnecessary indexes may benefit from removing indexes.

on the job

There are a number of performance tuning tools and techniques to assist with designing indexes. One is the EXPLAIN PLAN feature, which reveals the internal workings of a given SQL statement and provides insight into how SQL will optimize a given statement, including the use of indexes for a given SQL statement. It's a great tool. It is not a certification objective but you may want to explore one of the other books in the Oracle Press line to learn more about it.

Composite

A *composite* index is an index that is built on two or more columns of a table, like this:

```
CREATE INDEX IX_INV_INVOICE_VENDOR_ID ON INVOICES(VENDOR_ID, INVOICE_DATE);
```

In this example, the result is one single index that combines both columns. A composite index copies and sorts data from both columns into the composite index object. Its data is sorted first by the first position column, second by the second position column, and so on, for all the columns that form the composite index.

A WHERE clause that references all the columns in a composite index will cause the SQL optimizer to consider using the composite index for processing the query. For example, this query would encourage the optimizer to use the composite index IX_INV_INVOICE_VENDOR_ID to maximum advantage:

```
SELECT * FROM INVOICES WHERE VENDOR_ID = 10 AND INVOICE_DATE = SYSDATE;
```

Note that the WHERE clause in the preceding example references the columns that make up the composite INDEX object. Next, consider this query:

```
SELECT * FROM INVOICES WHERE VENDOR_ID = 10;
```

This query, which references the first column in the composite index, also invokes the index. The reason is that the composite index internally sorts data by the first column first and the second column second. Given that, the internally copied and sorted data from the indexed table is comparable in structure to a single-column index based on—in this example—the VENDOR_ID column.

But now consider this query:

```
SELECT * FROM INVOICES WHERE INVOICE_DATE = '25-MAY-2017';
```

This query references the second column in the composite query, but not the first. The composite index structure is primarily sorted on the first column of its structure, which in the example we're working with, is VENDOR_ID. But this query does not reference VENDOR_ID. Nevertheless, the SQL optimizer may still consider applying the index because of a feature known as *skip scanning*.

Skip Scanning

Thanks to skip scanning, a WHERE clause that references any columns within a composite index may invoke the index in its processing. However, the performance benefit is not identical. In skip scanning, SQL treats a composite index as a combination of several indexes. How many? That depends on the level of selectivity that results in the indexing of the first (or *leading*) column of the INDEX object. If the first column contains only a few unique values within a large number of rows, the index—if used—may be applied a relatively few number of times. On the other hand, if the leading column contains data that is relatively unique across the rows, then the index—if used—may be reviewed frequently. In other words, a skip scan will do an index scan once for each unique value in the first column. This isn't quite as beneficial as a simple one-column index, and its benefit varies, depending on the uniqueness of values in the first column. But the WHERE clause gains some benefit anyway.

The point is that a WHERE clause that references some, but not all, of the columns in a composite index may invoke the index, even if the leading column is not referenced in the WHERE clause. However, including the leading column may result in a more efficient application of the composite index and, therefore, a faster result to the query.

Unique

A *unique* index is one that helps ensure that a column in a table will contain unique information. The syntax for creating a unique index is as follows:

```
CREATE UNIQUE INDEX IX_EMP_SSN ON EMPLOYEES(SSN);
```

This SQL statement creates an index that will ensure that data entered into the SSN column of the table EMPLOYEES is unique.

This is different from the UNIQUE constraint that you can apply to a column on a table. However, note that if you create a PRIMARY KEY or UNIQUE constraint on a table, a unique index will automatically be created along with the constraint. Note that the UNIQUE constraint is more self-documenting within the database. That being said, Oracle Corporation formally recommends creating unique indexes to enforce uniqueness in a column for better results in query performance.

In practice, avoid using Social Security numbers as "unique" values. In the real world, it turns out that Social Security numbers, which are issued by the U.S. federal government, are not necessarily unique, something that many database professionals have learned the hard way. Once an SSN is no longer needed, it can be re-issued to someone else. There are many classic stories out there about application databases that started employing SSNs as primary keys on a table, only for the production database to encounter real-world data where more than one person has been issued the same SSN. It's a great argument for always making your primary keys with sequence-generated values and a lesson that SSNs in the real world aren't really unique. And don't even get me started on the issue of security and the law with regard to SSNs. Unless you are supporting a government-mandated requirement to report something with regard to Social Security taxes or payments, it is best to avoid storing the SSN at all—for security, if for no other reason.

Dropping

You can *drop* an index with the DROP INDEX statement. For example, let's drop our IX_INV_INVOICE_DATE index:

```
DROP INDEX IX_INV_INVOICE_DATE;
```

Note that if you drop a table upon which an index is based, the index is automatically dropped. If you re-create the table, you need to re-create the index.

Visible and Invisible Indexes

An index can be made to be *visible* or *invisible* to the optimizer. Only a visible index is recognized by the optimizer and, therefore, available for the optimizer to use in the processing of a SQL statement. If an index is made to be invisible, the optimizer will omit the index from consideration when creating the execution plan for the SQL statement.

An index is visible by default. You must explicitly declare an index to be invisible if that is your preference.

(There is an initialization parameter OPTIMIZER_USER_INVISIBLE_INDEXES that can be set to TRUE at the system or session level. If TRUE, the optimizer will consider all indexes regardless of visibility—or invisibility. However, initialization parameters and the statements to set them are not the subject of the exam.)

Why Use an Invisible Index?

So, why would you create an index whose sole purpose in life is to speed processing and then render it invisible so that it cannot be used to speed processing? The following sections highlight some reasons.

Index Testing on a Table   Mature applications may have a number of different indexes applied to a table. All of these indexes require maintenance. That means every time an INSERT, UDPATE, or DELETE is executed on the table, all of that table's indexes also have to be updated (or "maintained") with the same data for consistency. The requisite processing carries a price in terms of performance and storage. Is this overhead worth it? The answer depends on whether the indexes are useful. One way to find out is to temporarily change an index to invisible and then run your queries. The invisible index will be ignored by the optimizer, giving you an opportunity to assess the impact of omitting the index without having to drop it altogether. Is performance degraded when the optimizer ignores the index? If not, then the index is not improving performance. You could then choose to drop the index altogether and reduce the DML maintenance cost associated with its existence.

VISIBLE, INVISIBLE

The keywords VISIBLE and INVISIBLE specify the visibility of an index in the CREATE INDEX statement. For example, consider a table PORTS.

```
CREATE TABLE PORTS (PORT_ID NUMBER, PORT_NAME VARCHAR2(30));
```

The following code creates an invisible index on the PORT_NAME column:

```
CREATE INDEX ix1 ON PORTS(PORT_NAME) INVISIBLE;
```

Alternatively, here is how to create the same index as a visible index:

```
CREATE INDEX ix1 ON PORTS(PORT_NAME) VISIBLE;
```

VISIBLE is the default. If a CREATE INDEX statement omits the keywords VISIBLE or INVISIBLE, a visible index is what will be created.

If the index exists and you want to alter it to be invisible, use this:

```
ALTER INDEX ix1 INVISIBLE;
```

To alter an index and make it visible, use this:

```
ALTER INDEX ix1 VISIBLE;
```

If the index is already invisible (or visible) and you submit an ALTER statement to "change" it to what it already happens to be, the statement will execute successfully with no complaint or indication that the ALTER was unnecessary.

The data dictionary view USER_INDEXES includes a column VISIBILITY that reports whether an index is currently visible or invisible.

```
SELECT VISIBILITY
FROM   USER_INDEXES
WHERE  INDEX_NAME = 'IX1';
```

Remember that an index is visible by default, so if you omit the VISIBLE keyword, you still get a visible index at the time of index creation.

e x a m

ⓦ a t c h   *The data dictionary uses uppercase letters to record the names of all tables, columns, views, and other objects*   *you create, unless you enclose the name in double quotes when you create the object.*

Index Alternatives on the Same Column Set

You can create a number of indexes on a given table. However, for a given table, you are limited when creating multiple indexes on a particular column set, and by "set," we mean a set of one or more columns for that table. To create multiple indexes on a given column set, the indexes must differ with regard to one of a set of specific characteristics. However, while you can create multiple indexes within these limitations, only one of those index objects may be visible at any point in time.

To create multiple indexes on a given column set, the indexes must vary with regard to one of the following characteristics:

- **Different uniqueness** You can create a unique index on a column set and a nonunique index on the same column set.

- **Different types** The indexes we have looked at so far have been, by default, B-tree indexes. You may also create a bitmap index by adding the keyword BITMAP prior to the word INDEX, as in CREATE BITMAP INDEX, followed by the appropriate keywords to complete the index specification. A B-tree index is ideal for transactional applications where the full set of DML statements will be commonly utilized. A bitmap index is often used more in applications where heavier use of SELECT statements is anticipated. For our immediate purposes, the point is that you can create indexes on the same column set if they differ with regard to index type.

- **Different partitioning** Multiple indexes may exist on the same column set provided that certain partitioning characteristics are different:
  - Partitioning type (hash or range)
  - Local versus global partitioning
  - Partitioning versus nonpartitioning

For the purpose of the exam, the point you need to remember is that while these multiple indexes on a given column set may exist simultaneously, only one may be visible in the database at any given point in time. For example, when creating multiple indexes on a given column set, any preexisting indexes on the same column set must already be invisible, or else the attempt to create a new visible index on the same column set will fail.

One reason for toggling indexes between visibility and invisibility is to tune application performance for various purposes. Remember that the existence of an index does not guarantee the optimizer will utilize the index. However, making an index invisible guarantees the optimizer will ignore the index.

Consider the section we just reviewed. You might find it advantageous to try different types of indexes on a given type to optimize performance for transaction-based applications verses heavy querying and analytics. The details of such considerations are beyond the scope of the exam; for our purposes, it is helpful to recognize that application tuning is a useful reason to employ invisible indexes.

But remember that even if an index is invisible, it is still maintained. Any INSERT, UPDATE, or DELETE statement processed on the table will also update the index, which is a performance cost. This is true whether an index is visible or invisible.

CERTIFICATION OBJECTIVE 10.05

Perform Flashback Operations

Oracle's Flashback operations consist of a number of features that enable access to database data and objects in their past state, including objects that have already been dropped. These features have names like Flashback Table, Flashback Drop, Flashback Query, and more. The topic of Oracle's Flashback operations is quite involved. Developing a complete understanding of all of what Oracle offers with Flashback operations requires more study than what is required to pass the exam. We'll provide some background information to give you an idea of what we are talking about, and then we'll discuss the specific Flashback operations that are relevant to the exam and to this chapter's focus, which is the overall subject of managing schema objects. This book will present what you need to know for the exam, but you may want to continue your study of Flashback operations beyond what is required for the exam.

One important note: Oracle Flashback operations include some features that are available only in the Oracle Enterprise Edition. If you are using the Standard Edition, you can perform Flashback Query, but some of the features described in this section require Enterprise Edition—such as Flashback Table.

Overview

Oracle's Flashback operations include a variety of statements you can use to recover objects and/or the data contained with them, as well as dependent objects and data. The sort of tasks you can accomplish with Flashback operations include

- Recovering complete tables you may have inadvertently dropped
- Recovering data changes within one or more tables resulting from a series of DML statements
- Performing data analysis on data that's been changed over periods of time

■ Comparing data that existed at one point in time with data that existed at another point in time

■ Performing queries as of a prior time period

Flashback operations can support multiple user sessions gaining access to historical data dynamically, on any table (including the same tables) at the same time, with each user session potentially accessing different points in the history of the table simultaneously, all while the database is up and running in full operational mode.

Some Flashback operations require various configuration steps; some of those configurations can be involved and might require intervention by the database administrator. The configuration steps involved can affect system parameters, table clauses, and a feature of the database known as the undo segments, which have a purpose that goes beyond Flashback.

Recover Dropped Tables

In this chapter, we're focusing only on managing schema objects. Within the set of available Flashback operations, the feature that affects schema objects as a whole is the FLASHBACK TABLE statement. This statement can recover a previously dropped table you specify from a historical point in time that you specify. However, there are limitations. For example, you cannot flash back to a point prior to when the table's structure may have been altered.

You can identify a point in time in a variety of ways:

■ Immediately prior to when a table was dropped

■ A specific time identified by a value of data type TIMESTAMP

■ A specific transaction identified by the system change number (SCN)

■ A predetermined event identified by a database object known as the RESTORE POINT

When used to restore a table, FLASHBACK TABLE restores the dropped table with either its original name or a new name you provide with the statement. It also recovers any indexes on the table other than bitmap join indexes. All constraints are recovered, except for referential integrity constraints that reference other tables—in other words, foreign key constraints. Granted privileges are also recovered.

Note: FLASHBACK TABLE is not currently available in Oracle Database Standard Edition.

The beginning syntax of a FLASHBACK TABLE statement is as follows:

- The required keywords FLASHBACK TABLE
- One or more table names, separated by commas
- The required keyword TO

In other words:

```
FLASHBACK TABLE table_name TO ...
```

More than one table can be included in the list. Additional table names must be separated by commas:

```
FLASHBACK TABLE table1, table2, table3 TO ...
```

That's the beginning. There are several ways to complete this statement. Here is how you complete it if you want to recover a dropped table:

- The required keywords BEFORE DROP
- The optional keywords RENAME TO, followed by a new name for the table if you want to recover the dropped table into an object with a different name

Here is an example of a SQL session where we create a table, drop it, and then use FLASHBACK TABLE to restore the dropped table:

```
01    CREATE TABLE HOUDINI (VOILA VARCHAR2(30));
02    INSERT INTO HOUDINI  (VOILA) VALUES ('Now you see it.');
03    COMMIT;
04    DROP   TABLE HOUDINI;
05    FLASHBACK TABLE HOUDINI TO BEFORE DROP;
06    SELECT * FROM HOUDINI;
```

Note the FLASHBACK TABLE statement on line 5. It combines the beginning:

```
FLASHBACK TABLE HOUDINI TO
```

with the following:

```
BEFORE DROP
```

It omits the optional RENAME TO and the new name.

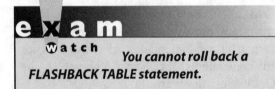

The Recycle Bin

The Flashback Drop feature recovers complete tables that are still retained in the "recycle bin," and it can do so in spite of the fact that such a change results from the DROP TABLE statement, which, by definition, is a DDL statement and therefore involves an implied COMMIT. In spite of this, we can recover the table if it is still in the recycle bin.

Tables are put into the recycle bin automatically by SQL whenever a DROP TABLE statement is issued. A table's dependent objects, such as indexes, are also placed into the recycle bin, along with the table's constraints.

The recycle bin is not counted as space that is used by a given user account.

A user account's dropped objects are retained in a separate recycle bin for each user. You can inspect the contents of your own recycle bin with the following query:

```
SELECT * FROM USER_RECYCLEBIN;
```

That query is identical to this one:

```
SELECT * FROM RECYCLEBIN;
```

RECYCLEBIN is a synonym for USER_RECYCLEBIN. In other words, the preceding two queries are identical.

There is a DBA_RECYCLEBIN, which allows user accounts with database administrator (DBA) privileges to see all dropped objects in the database.

If your user account has privileges on an object, then your user account will be able to see the object in the recycle bin in the event it is dropped.

You don't need to inspect the recycle bin before issuing a Flashback statement. But you might find it helpful.

The recycle bin is affected by the "recyclebin" initialization parameter and can be turned on or off accordingly with the following ALTER SESSION statements:

```
ALTER SESSION SET recyclebin = ON;
ALTER SESSION SET recyclebin = OFF;
```

Both of these statements take effect immediately. The initial state of the recycle bin is dependent on the setting for recyclebin in the initialization parameter file, which is controlled by the DBA.

Setting recyclebin to ON or OFF determines whether it will be used. Any objects already in the recycle bin will remain either way. To remove them, use PURGE, which is explained later in this chapter.

Dependent Objects

When a table is recovered, any associated dependent objects are also recovered, including the following:

- Indexes, except for bitmap join indexes
- Constraints, but with limitations—for example, restoring dropped tables does not recover referential constraints, meaning FOREIGN KEY constraints
- Other objects that we don't discuss in this book and that are not a subject of the exam, such as triggers

Objects that have the same name that are dropped can all be retrieved with Flashback operations. For example, if a table VENDORS was dropped and then re-created and dropped, there will be two VENDORS tables in the recycle bin. The last one dropped will be the first one retrieved.

Objects such as indexes will be recovered with system-assigned names, not the names they were originally given. You can rename each retrieved object with the RENAME TO clause of the FLASHBACK TABLE statement as it is retrieved. As of this writing, renaming retrieved objects is beyond the scope of the exam.

Statement Execution

The FLASHBACK TABLE statement operates as a single statement. If it fails, nothing in the statement succeeds. In other words, if there's an attempt to restore three tables in a single statement and the third attempt is erroneous for whatever reason, none of the tables will be restored.

PURGE

The PURGE statement permanently removes the latest version of a given item from the recycle bin—for example, to permanently remove the HOUDINI table from the recycle bin so that it cannot be recovered:

```
PURGE TABLE HOUDINI;
```

After executing this statement, the table HOUDINI cannot be recovered with the FLASHBACK TABLE statement we used earlier.

Note that the table must have first been dropped for PURGE to execute successfully. Purging may be performed automatically by the Oracle database's own automatic space reclamation operations. If that happens, the table is not in the recycle bin and cannot be recovered with Flashback operations.

You can also choose to purge the schema's recycle bin entirely.

```
PURGE RECYCLEBIN;
```

The result will be to purge all objects in the schema's recycle bin. To purge the recycle bin of the entire database, use this:

```
PURGE DBA_RECYCLEBIN;
```

The previous statement will execute successfully if the schema has the SYSDBA privilege. You can also DESCRIBE and SELECT * from the RECYCLEBIN and DBA_RECYCLEBIN.

Recovering Data Within Existing Tables over Time

This section discusses some additional ways to complete the FLASHBACK TABLE statement.

In addition to performing a Flashback operation to restore a dropped table, you can flash back an existing table to a specific point in time, showing its state prior to any committed changes that may have been transacted since the point in time of interest.

The syntax can take any of these three forms:

```
FLASHBACK TABLE HOUDINI TO SCN scn_expression;
FLASHBACK TABLE HOUDINI TO TIMESTAMP timestamp_expression;
FLASHBACK TABLE HOUDINI TO RESTORE POINT restore_point_expression;
```

The recommended form of these three is the first: the system change number. This is the mechanism that is recommended by Oracle for identifying points in time in the database. For example, let's revisit our table HOUDINI.

```
01   CREATE TABLE HOUDINI (VOILA VARCHAR2(30));
02   INSERT INTO HOUDINI  (VOILA) VALUES ('Now you see it.');
03   COMMIT;
04   EXECUTE DBMS_LOCK.SLEEP(15);
05   DELETE FROM HOUDINI;
06   COMMIT;
07   EXECUTE DBMS_LOCK.SLEEP(15);
08   FLASHBACK TABLE HOUDINI TO TIMESTAMP
09              SYSTIMESTAMP - INTERVAL '0 00:00:20' DAY TO SECOND;
```

Let's review the preceding code:

- Line 3: We commit our change to the table.
- Line 4: This is a statement that suspends processing for 15 seconds. The choice of 15 seconds is arbitrary; the intent here is to allow some time to pass.
- Line 6: We commit the deletion of one row.

■ Line 8 and line 9: This statement attempts to restore the table to where it was 20 seconds earlier. Note that line 9 contains nothing more than an expression of the TIMESTAMP data type, which in this case is a call to the SYSTIMESTAMP function minus a 20-second interval. The SYSTIMESTAMP function returns the current time as defined by the Oracle database server's operating system. Following the call to the function is the symbol for subtraction—the minus sign—followed by a literal value representing a time interval of 20 seconds.

So, what is the result of this series of statements? Here it is:

```
Error report:
SQL Error: ORA-08189: cannot flashback the table because row movement is not enabled
08189. 00000 -  "cannot flashback the table because row movement is not enabled"
*Cause:    An attempt was made to perform Flashback Table operation on a table
           for which row movement has not been enabled. Because the Flashback
           Table does not preserve the rowids, it is necessary that row
           movement be enabled on the table.
*Action:   Enable row movement on the table
```

What is wrong here? The problem is that the capability to perform Flashback operations to restore an existing table to an older state is not a capability that exists by default. It only works on tables where the ROW MOVEMENT feature has been enabled. Here's how to create the table with ROW MOVEMENT enabled:

```
CREATE TABLE HOUDINI (VOILA VARCHAR2(30))
     ENABLE ROW MOVEMENT;
```

To enable ROW MOVEMENT on a table that's already been created, use this:

```
ALTER TABLE HOUDINI ENABLE ROW MOVEMENT;
```

If we were to go back and redo our earlier series of statements with ROW MOVEMENT enabled on the table, our FLASHBACK TABLE statement would work perfectly, and we'd restore our table to its original state. Once it's restored, we could query the table and see all the data in that table as it existed at the time we specified in our FLASHBACK TABLE statement.

Data restoration is "permanent." It invokes an implicit COMMIT so that the restored data is committed. Note that ROW MOVEMENT isn't required with flashback TO BEFORE DROP.

Limitations

You cannot use the FLASHBACK TABLE statement to restore older data to an existing table if the table has been structurally altered with the ALTER TABLE statement in such a way that it can't accept the full definition of older data.

For example, if a column has been dropped or a column's data type changed, the FLASHBACK TABLE statement won't successfully restore the older data.

Marking Time

There are several ways to identify the point at which you want to restore data in the database. You saw three in the previous section, and I'll discuss them a bit more here.

SCN

The system change number is a numeric stamp that the database automatically increments for every committed transaction that occurs in the database. This includes both explicit and implicit commits, for all external or internal transactions. The SCN is automatically managed by the database in real time. Every committed transaction is assigned an SCN.

If you want to determine the current SCN at any given moment in the database, use the function DBMS_FLASHBACK.GET_SYSTEM_CHANGE_NUMBER. Here's an example:

```
01    SELECT DBMS_FLASHBACK.GET_SYSTEM_CHANGE_NUMBER FROM DUAL;
02
03    GET_SYSTEM_CHANGE_NUMBER
04    ------------------------
05    5896167
```

This example shows the request and the answer. In this case, the SCN is 5896167. If you were to hesitate a few seconds and run the same statement in line 1 again, you might get a different value returned for SCN.

on the job

The SCN can also be found with the query SELECT CURRENT_SCN FROM V$DATABASE, which is a query of the data dictionary. We'll discuss the data dictionary in Chapter 12, but for now, note that Oracle officially recommends that if your goal is to obtain an SCN from within an application or any comparable code, then you should use the DBMS_FLASHBACK .GET_SYSTEM_CHANGE_NUMBER function that we demonstrated earlier. This recommendation implies that you should steer away from tapping the V$DATABASE view for the SCN number. The DBMS_FLASHBACK.GET_SYSTEM_ CHANGE_NUMBER function is a function written in the PL/SQL language, and it is part of the DBMS_FLASHBACK package. See Oracle's reference manual on PL/SQL packages if you want to learn more—but you don't need to do that for the exam.

Each time a transaction is committed in the database, the SCN is incremented and stored with each row in each table.

The SCN for a given row can be found in the pseudocolumn ORA_ROWSCN. As is the case with any pseudocolumn, it can be included as an expression in any SELECT statement. For example, the following:

```
SELECT ORA_ROWSCN, VOILA
FROM   HOUDINI;
```

returns each row in the table HOUDINI, along with the values in the VOILA column, as well as the assigned SCN number for each row.

Timestamp

A TIMESTAMP value specifies a point in time. The TIMESTAMP data type stores the year, month, day, hour, minute, second, and fractional seconds. A literal value may be converted to the TIMESTAMP data type with the TO_TIMESTAMP function, like this:

```
SELECT TO_TIMESTAMP('2017-08-25 13:15:08.232349',
                     'RRRR-MM-DD HH24:MI:SS.FF')
FROM   DUAL;
```

This example shows the TO_TIMESTAMP function, a literal value, and a format mask that defines the location within the literal value of each component that forms a valid TIMESTAMP value. Note the use of fractional seconds, where more than two digits are accepted (up to six). Also recall that MI is the format mask for minutes—not MM, which is the format mask for months.

The FLASHBACK_TABLE function can use a TIMESTAMP value to specify a point in time in the database to within three seconds of accuracy.

If a specific point in the database is needed, don't use TIMESTAMP—use SCN instead.

If you attempt to flash back to a point in time at which the database did not exist, you'll get an error indicating "invalid timestamp specified."

If the time you're referencing closely aligns with a time at which the object or data didn't exist, and the SCN/timestamp correlation misses your target and overshoots into a time frame in which the object or data didn't exist, you may get an Oracle error.

You can use a combination of one or more conversion functions to address this discrepancy, as we discuss in the next section.

Conversion Functions

SCN numbers can be converted into their equivalent TIMESTAMP values, and vice versa. The conversions are not exact, however, because the SCN and TIMESTAMP values do not represent moments in time that are precisely identical.

The conversion functions are

- **SCN_TO_TIMESTAMP(*s1*)**   Takes an SCN expression as input; returns a TIMESTAMP value roughly corresponding to when the SCN was set
- **TIMESTAMP_TO_SCN(*t*)**   Takes a TIMESTAMP expression representing a valid past or present timestamp as input; returns an SCN value roughly corresponding to when the TIMESTAMP occurred

For example, let's perform two separate conversions of timestamp values to SCN values:

```
01   SELECT TIMESTAMP_TO_SCN(SYSTIMESTAMP) NOW,
02          TIMESTAMP_TO_SCN(TO_TIMESTAMP('01-AUG-09 09:12:23',
03                                  'DD-MON-RR HH:MI:SS')) NOT_NOW
04   FROM   DUAL;
05
06   NOW                    NOT_NOW
07   ---------------------- ----------------------
08   5911139                5639192
```

In this example, we convert the current timestamp value, as defined by SYSTIMESTAMP, to its SCN equivalent. We also convert a date in the past to its SCN equivalent. The first column's alias is NOW; the second column's alias is NOT_NOW.

Note that any time referenced must be within a range that is relevant to the database. In other words, the function recognizes times that apply to whenever the database installation has been in existence.

There is not a direct one-to-one relationship between timestamps and SCN values. For example, suppose you take a valid SCN value and convert it.

```
SELECT TIMESTAMP_TO_SCN(SCN_TO_TIMESTAMP(5895585))
FROM DUAL;

TIMESTAMP_TO_SCN(SCN_TO_TIMESTAMP(5895585))
-------------------------------------------
5895573
```

Note what happens here: one SCN goes in, and a slightly different SCN is ultimately returned.

For any work effort in which you require precision in specifying timing, Oracle recommends using SCN numbers and obtaining them with the DBMS_FLASHBACK packaged function GET_SYSTEM_CHANGE_NUMBER, which we reviewed earlier. Also note that if you want to use FLASHBACK to restore to a specific point, it is important that you obtain that point precisely. One way to do that is the RESTORE POINT object, which we discuss next.

RESTORE POINT

A restore point is an object in the database you create to represent a given moment in the database. That moment can be identified by a TIMESTAMP value or an SCN.

Here's an example of the CREATE RESTORE POINT statement:

```
CREATE RESTORE POINT balance_acct_01;
```

Once executed, you can use this as a restore point representing the moment at which the CREATE RESTORE POINT statement was executed. You can refer to the restore point either later in the current session or in a later session:

```
FLASHBACK TABLE HOUDINI TO RESTORE POINT balance_acct_01;
```

This statement restores the HOUDINI table to the point in time that correlates to the "balance_acct_01" restore point.

When you no longer need the RESTORE POINT, you can drop it:

```
DROP RESTORE POINT balance_acct_01;
```

You can find existing restore points with the data dictionary view V$RESTORE_POINT. Note that users do not "own" RESTORE POINT objects; their scope is the entire database. They exist until they are dropped or age out of the control file.

on the job

New to Oracle 12c is the ability to create a multitenant cloud architecture that includes container databases and pluggable databases, but those topics are beyond the scope of the exam. It is not possible to create a restore point from within a pluggable database. But you can create a restore point in a container database. Also, remember that the execution of a DDL statement includes an implied COMMIT. CREATE RESTORE POINT is no exception. It is DDL, and therefore its execution results in a COMMIT to the database.

CERTIFICATION SUMMARY

Tables store all the data in a database. Views are named SELECT statements. Indexes act just like an index in a book; they provide a separately stored sorted summary of the column data that is being indexed, along with addressing information that points back to the source table. Sequences provide a mechanism to count off primary key values.

Views are objects that name a query and store the query in the database. Views do not store data. They look and act like tables. Views may be built with simple or complex SELECT statements. GROUP BY, HAVING, join queries, and more are all possible in a VIEW object's SELECT statement.

A SELECT statement can be used to query a view just as it would be used to query a table. But INSERT, UPDATE, and DELETE statements will work only with certain views, not all of them—it depends on whether the view's structure allows appropriate access to the table or tables upon which the view is based. Any DML statement will work with a view based on a single table, provided that the required columns are all included in the select list of the SELECT statement used to create the view, that the rows of the view are not aggregate rows, and that all of the table's constraints are honored. A view is not necessarily required to include columns that are required by the view's underlying table, but if the view omits such columns, then an INSERT statement cannot add to the view a value that is required by the underlying table; in addition, the constraints on the underlying table will reject the INSERT, and it won't work for that view.

Any SELECT statement used to create a view must have clearly defined column names. Complex expressions must be assigned a column alias; this will become the name of the column in the resulting view object.

An inline view is a variation on a subquery, in which a SELECT statement replaces a table reference in a FROM clause of any DML statement. An inline view must be enclosed in its own set of parentheses. Once incorporated in a DML statement, the inline view behaves just like a view object would behave.

If the underlying table is modified, the view may require recompilation using the ALTER VIEW . . . COMPILE statement.

A view is built with a query, and that query may specify the names of invisible columns in a table, assuming that table consists of invisible columns. Any invisible columns in the queried table that are specified in the view's query will be accessible to DML statements executed against the view.

Views can be used to hide complexity in queries. They are beneficial for creating a series of queries, one built on another. By creating a query as a view and then publishing access to that view, the developer can retain the ability to later change that query on which the view is built so that the change is reflected in the view.

Sequence objects are counters. They dispense numbers according to the parameters established when the sequence is first created.

SQL automatically defines pseudocolumns for each sequence. The NEXTVAL pseudocolumn increments the sequence to the next available number as defined in the sequence's parameters defined at the time the sequence is created. The CURRVAL pseudocolumn refers to the last NEXTVAL reference produced in a given session. In any session with a sequence, the NEXTVAL pseudocolumn must be referenced before the CURRVAL pseudocolumn can be referenced. A reference to a sequence pseudocolumn is a valid expression and can be invoked in many places where expressions are allowed, with certain restrictions.

An index is an object that stores a subset of presorted information from a table and may be referenced automatically by SQL to speed up the processing of a given SQL statement, depending on how that SQL statement is structured and how the Oracle Database optimizer chooses to build its execution plan. An index can be built on one or more columns in a table. Once created, if a SQL statement's WHERE or ORDER BY clause references the indexed column (or set of columns), the optimizer may use the index in its execution plan to speed up the processing of the statement. An index that is built on multiple columns is known as a *composite* index. A UNIQUE INDEX can be used to enforce a unique rule on a column. An index can be rendered invisible to prevent the optimizer from including the index for consideration when forming the execution plan.

Index objects support application performance tuning. Indexes can be built on one or more columns of a table; multicolumn index objects are known as composite indexes. When a query references indexed columns in its WHERE clause, SQL will consider using the index as part of its processing strategy, and the results may be returned more quickly.

Flashback operations can restore data to a previous point in time, with some limitations. The point to which you restore data can be identified using values of data type TIMESTAMP, SCN, or RESTORE POINT. Tables that have been dropped but that are still in the recycle bin can be recovered. Any table that's been purged from the recycle bin is gone for good. Data that's been changed in existing tables can be restored to some previous point in time, provided that the table's structure hasn't been changed in such a way that the table is no longer able to receive the restored data, such as perhaps having had a column dropped.

TWO-MINUTE DRILL

Describe How Schema Objects Work

- ☐ Tables store all the data in a database.
- ☐ Views are named SELECT statements.
- ☐ You can select from a view with SELECT.
- ☐ You may be able to insert, update, and delete from a view, depending on the view's structure.
- ☐ An index speeds queries on a table by creating a presorted lookup list for the table's indexed columns, along with an address pointer back to the indexed table.
- ☐ Sequences keep track of number counters to make the job of adding primary keys and other unique values easier.

Create Simple and Complex Views with Visible/Invisible Columns

- ☐ A VIEW is a SELECT statement that is stored in the database and assigned a name.
- ☐ The columns and expressions of the SELECT statement used to create a view become the columns of the VIEW.
- ☐ You can use SELECT statements on views just as you would a table.
- ☐ You can use INSERT, UPDATE, and/or DELETE statements on some views, depending on the constraints of the view's underlying table or tables, as well as other issues such as whether the view's SELECT statement includes aggregate functions.
- ☐ An inline view is a subquery that replaces a table reference in a FROM clause of a DML statement.
- ☐ The VIEW can be treated like a table, with some limitations.
- ☐ A VIEW based on a table that is subsequently altered may require recompilation with the ALTER VIEW . . . COMPILE statement.
- ☐ A VIEW can be based on a table consisting of one or more invisible columns.
- ☐ A VIEW can include a table's invisible columns in its structure by naming the invisible columns in the VIEW's query.

Create, Maintain, and Use Sequences

- ☐ A SEQUENCE is an object that dispenses numbers according to the rules established by the sequence.
- ☐ A SEQUENCE specifies the starting number, the increment (which can be positive or negative), and an optional range of values within which the sequence can generate values.
- ☐ The starting point can be within the range or at one end of the range.
- ☐ SEQUENCES are ideal for populating primary key values.
- ☐ The NEXTVAL pseudocolumn of a sequence returns the next available number in the sequence and must be the first reference to the sequence in any given login session.
- ☐ The CURRVAL pseudocolumn can return the existing value as already defined by NEXTVAL; it can be referenced in a session only after the NEXTVAL reference has occurred.
- ☐ A pseudocolumn reference to a sequence is a valid expression and can be referenced anywhere that a valid expression is allowed.
- ☐ If a valid sequence reference to NEXTVAL occurs within a DML statement that fails, the sequence still advances.

Create and Maintain Indexes Including Invisible Indexes and Multiple Indexes on the Same Columns

- ☐ An INDEX object is built on one or more columns in a table.
- ☐ The INDEX stores data from its table's columns on which it is built and presorts that data in order to speed future queries.
- ☐ When the DML statements INSERT, UPDATE, and DELETE are executed on an indexed table so that the indexed data is changed, the index is automatically updated by Oracle, thus adding to the workload of the DML statements.
- ☐ INDEX objects are built on one or more columns. Multiple-column indexes are composite indexes.
- ☐ You use the keywords VISIBLE and INVISIBLE to specify the visibility of an INDEX. The default is VISIBLE. You can specify the visibility of an index in CREATE INDEX and ALTER INDEX statements.

Perform Flashback Operations

☐ FLASHBACK TABLE can be used to restore a table that has been dropped.

☐ If a table has been dropped, it goes into the recycle bin.

☐ You can investigate the contents of the recycle bin to determine what objects are available for use by Flashback operations.

☐ Once an object has been dropped, if it is also purged with the PURGE statement, it is no longer able to be recovered with FLASHBACK TABLE.

☐ In addition to restoring a dropped table, the FLASHBACK TABLE statement can be used to restore data within the table as of a particular time in the database.

☐ Time in the database is marked by either a system change number, a RESTORE POINT, or a timestamp.

SELF TEST

The following questions will help you measure your understanding of the material presented in this chapter. Choose one correct answer for each question unless otherwise directed.

Describe How Schema Objects Work

1. The database object that stores lookup information to speed up querying in tables is:
   A. ROWID
   B. INDEX
   C. VIEW
   D. LOOKUP

2. A SEQUENCE is
   A. Part of a table
   B. Used exclusively to create primary key values
   C. Is the only way to populate primary key values
   D. None of the above.

3. All database data is stored in:
   A. TABLES
   B. TABLES and VIEWS
   C. TABLES, VIEWS, and SEQUENCES
   D. None of the above

Create Simple and Complex Views with Visible/Invisible Columns

4. Which of the following SQL statements can always be executed on any VIEW object? (Choose all that apply.)
   A. SELECT
   B. INSERT
   C. DELETE
   D. UPDATE

5. Review the following illustration:

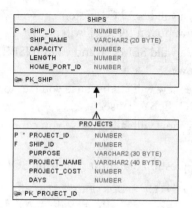

Now review the following SQL code:

```
01   CREATE OR REPLACE VIEW SHIP_CAP_PROJ AS
02   SELECT    SHIP_ID,
03             TO_CHAR(CAPACITY,'999,999'),
04             PROJECT_COST
05   FROM      SHIPS JOIN PROJECTS
06   USING     (SHIP_ID)
07   WHERE     (PROJECT_COST * 2) < 100000;
```

What will result from an attempt to execute this SQL code?

A. The statement will fail because of an error in line 3.

B. The statement will fail because of an error in line 6.

C. The statement will fail because of an error in line 7.

D. The statement will execute, and the view will be successfully created.

6. Review the illustration from question 5 and the following SQL code:

```
CREATE OR REPLACE VIEW PROJECTS_ROLLUP AS
      SELECT SHIP_NAME, CAPACITY,
             COUNT(PROJECT_ID) NUM_PROJECTS, ROUND(SUM(DAYS)) TOTAL_DAYS
      FROM   SHIPS A JOIN PROJECTS B
      ON     A.SHIP_ID = B.SHIP_ID
      GROUP BY SHIP_NAME, CAPACITY;
```

What can be said of this code?

A. After the view is created, a valid SELECT statement will work on the PROJECTS_ROLLUP view, but an INSERT will not.

B. After the view is created, a valid SELECT and valid INSERT statement will work on the PROJECTS_ROLLUP view.

C. The attempt to create the view will fail because you cannot create a VIEW with a SELECT statement that uses a GROUP BY clause.

D. The attempt to create the view will fail because you cannot create a VIEW with a SELECT statement that is a join.

7. Review the illustration from question 5 and the following SQL code:

```
01  CREATE OR REPLACE VIEW MAJOR_PROJECTS AS
02    SELECT PROJECT_ID, SHIP_ID, PROJECT_NAME, PROJECT_COST
03    FROM   PROJECTS
04    WHERE  PROJECT_COST > 10000;
05
06  INSERT INTO MAJOR_PROJECTS
07    (PROJECT_ID, SHIP_ID, PROJECT_NAME, PROJECT_COST)
08    VALUES
09    ((SELECT MAX(PROJECT_ID)+1 FROM PROJECTS),
10    (SELECT MAX(SHIP_ID) FROM SHIPS),
11    'Small Project',
12    500);
```

What will result from an attempt to execute these two SQL statements?

A. The CREATE statement will fail because it omits the PURPOSE column from the PROJECTS table.

B. The INSERT statement will fail because of an error on lines 9 and 10.

C. The INSERT statement will fail because the PROJECT_COST value being inserted is not consistent with the WHERE clause on line 4.

D. The CREATE and INSERT statements will successfully execute.

Create, Maintain, and Use Sequences

8. Which of the following keywords *cannot* be used with the CREATE SEQUENCE statement?

A. CYCLE

B. MAXVALUE

C. INCREMENT

D. JOIN

9. Review this code:

```
DROP    TABLE SHIPS CASCADE CONSTRAINTS;
DROP    SEQUENCE PROJ_ID_SEQ#;
CREATE TABLE SHIPS (SHIP_ID NUMBER PRIMARY KEY,
                    LENGTH  NUMBER);
CREATE SEQUENCE PROJ_ID_SEQ# START WITH 1 INCREMENT BY 4;
INSERT INTO SHIPS (SHIP_ID, LENGTH) VALUES (PROJ_ID_SEQ#.NEXTVAL, 'NOT A NUMBER');
INSERT INTO SHIPS (SHIP_ID, LENGTH) VALUES (PROJ_ID_SEQ#.NEXTVAL, 750);
COMMIT;
```

Note that the first INSERT statement is attempting to enter a string literal of 'NOT A NUMBER' into a column declared with a numeric data type. Given that, what will be the result of these SQL statements?

A. One row added to the SHIPS table, with a SHIP_ID value of 1.

B. One row added to the SHIPS table, with a SHIP_ID value of 5.

C. Two rows added to the SHIPS table. The first SHIP_ID is 1; the second is 5.

D. Two rows added to the SHIPS table. The first SHIP_ID is NULL; the second is 5.

10. Review this code:

```
DROP SEQUENCE PROJ_ID_SEQ#;
CREATE SEQUENCE PROJ_ID_SEQ# START WITH 1 INCREMENT BY 2;
SELECT PROJ_ID_SEQ#.CURRVAL FROM DUAL;
```

What will result from these SQL statements?

A. The SELECT statement will fail because the sequence can be referenced only in an INSERT statement.

B. The SELECT statement will fail because you cannot reference the CURRVAL pseudocolumn of a sequence until after you have referenced NEXTVAL for the sequence in a session.

C. The SELECT statement will display a value of 1.

D. The SELECT statement will display a value of 3.

Create and Maintain Indexes Including Invisible Indexes and Multiple Indexes on the Same Columns

11. Choose the best answer from the choices below. An index:

A. Stores all the data from all the columns in any given table in a separate object and sorts the data for faster lookups

B. May improve the performance of an UPDATE statement that uses a WHERE clause, if the WHERE clause performs an equality comparison on an indexed column in a table

C. Requires a separate INSERT statement each time you add data to a table—one time to add a new row to the table, another time to add the corresponding and necessary data required by the index

D. Only benefits a SELECT statement if the SELECT returns data that is indexed

12. Review the following series of SQL statements:

```
CREATE TABLE SUPPLIES_01
(  SUPPLY_ID NUMBER(7),
   SUPPLIER  VARCHAR2(30),
   ACCT_NO   VARCHAR2(50));
CREATE INDEX IX_SU_01 ON SUPPLIES_01(ACCT_NO);
DROP TABLE SUPPLIES_01;
CREATE TABLE SUPPLIES_02
(  SUPPLY_ID NUMBER(7),
   SUPPLIER  VARCHAR2(30),
   ACCT_NO   VARCHAR2(50));
CREATE INDEX IX_SU_02 ON SUPPLIES_02(ACCT_NO,SUPPLIER);
```

Assuming there are no objects already in existence named SUPPLIES_01 or SUPPLIES_02 prior to the execution of the preceding statements, what database objects will result from these statements?

A. A table called SUPPLIES_02 and nothing else

B. A table called SUPPLIES_02 and an index called IX_SU_02

C. A table called SUPPLIES_02 and two indexes called IX_SU_01 and IX_SU_02

D. None of the above

13. An invisible index is an index on one or more columns in a table:

A. Where at least one of the columns must be invisible

B. Where all the columns must be invisible

C. And is updated for any DELETE statements performed on the table

D. And is updated for any SELECT statements performed on the table

Perform Flashback Operations

14. Review the following SQL code:

```
01  DROP   TABLE PO_BOXES;
02  CREATE TABLE PO_BOXES (PO_BOX_ID NUMBER(3), PO_BOX_NUMBER VARCHAR2(10))
03                 ENABLE ROW MOVEMENT;
04  INSERT INTO PO_BOXES VALUES (1, 'A100');
05  INSERT INTO PO_BOXES VALUES (2, 'B100');
```

```
06  COMMIT;
07  EXECUTE DBMS_LOCK.SLEEP(30);
08  DELETE FROM PO_BOXES;
09  COMMIT;
10  EXECUTE DBMS_LOCK.SLEEP(30);
```

Which of the following statements could be added as line 11 and recover the deleted rows from the PO_BOXES table?

A. FLASHBACK TABLE PO_BOXES TO TIMESTAMP SYSTIMESTAMP—INTERVAL '0 00:00:45' DAY TO SECOND;

B. FLASHBACK TABLE PO_BOXES TO SYSTIMESTAMP—INTERVAL '0 00:00:45' DAY TO SECOND;

C. FLASHBACK TABLE PO_BOXES INTERVAL '0 00:00:45' DAY TO SECOND;

D. FLASHBACK TABLE PO_BOXES TO TIMESTAMP INTERVAL '0 00:00:45' DAY TO SECOND;

15. Review the following SQL code:

```
01   CREATE TABLE PO_BOXES (PO_BOX_ID NUMBER(3), PO_BOX_NUMBER VARCHAR2(10))
02                  ENABLE ROW MOVEMENT;
03   INSERT INTO PO_BOXES VALUES (1, 'A100');
04   INSERT INTO PO_BOXES VALUES (2, 'B100');
05   COMMIT;
06   DROP TABLE PO_BOXES;
07   COMMIT;
08   PURGE TABLE PO_BOXES;
09   COMMIT;
```

What statement will recover the PO_BOXES table after these statements are executed?

A. FLASHBACK TABLE PO_BOXES TO BEFORE DROP;

B. FLASHBACK TABLE PO_BOXES TO TIMESTAMP SYSTIMESTAMP—INTERVAL '0 00:00:03' DAY TO SECOND;

C. FLASHBACK TABLE PO_BOXES TO BEFORE COMMIT;

D. None of the above—the table cannot be recovered.

SELF TEST ANSWERS

Describe How Schema Objects Work

1. ☑ **B.** The INDEX stores data for speeding up querying.
   ☒ **A, C,** and **D** are incorrect. ROWID is a pseudocolumn, not a database object. A VIEW names a SELECT statement. LOOKUP is something made up; it's not a reserved word in Oracle.

2. ☑ **D.** None of the above. A SEQUENCE is a counter that is useful for populating primary keys but can be used for any purpose the developer wishes, or not.
   ☒ **A, B,** and **C** are incorrect. A SEQUENCE is a standalone object and is not part of a table. It may be used to populate primary keys or any other purpose for which the developer chooses; it is merely a number counter. Primary keys may be populated in any way, provide the values entered conform to the particular primary key's specified constraints, which are usually that the key be unique and NOT NULL.

3. ☑ **A.** All data is stored in tables. Even data about the tables you create is stored automatically by Oracle SQL in a set of system-defined and system-maintained tables.
   ☒ **B, C,** and **D** are incorrect.

Create Simple and Complex Views with Visible/Invisible Columns

4. ☑ **A.** The SELECT statement can be used against any view.
   ☒ **B, C,** and **D** are incorrect. There are many reasons why any given VIEW may reject attempts to execute the INSERT, UPDATE, or DELETE statement. For example, if the VIEW object does not contain sufficient access to its underlying tables, then it might not provide all the column access required to satisfy the underlying constraint restrictions that may exist for any INSERT, UPDATE, or DELETE statement. While many views allow all of these SQL statements to work, it's entirely possible to create a VIEW that does not.

5. ☑ **A.** The error on line 3 is the failure to give the expression a column alias. The VIEW does not assign a name to the second column, so the attempt to create the view fails.
   ☒ **B, C,** and **D** are incorrect. These are not errors. Line 6 is fine; the use of USING works well here. Line 7 is fine; the expression that calculates the result of PROJECT_COST times 2 is fine, and expressions in WHERE clauses have no restrictions in a CREATE VIEW statement.

6. ☑ **A.** The syntax for creating the view is correct, and any view can—at a minimum—work with a SELECT statement. But an INSERT will not work with this view since it consists of aggregate rows, as defined by the GROUP BY clause in the view's SELECT statement.

☒ **B, C,** and **D** are incorrect. The view will not work with an INSERT because of the GROUP BY. In other words, there is no way to add single-row values through the view since the view's access to the tables is, by definition, at the aggregate level. Also, the GROUP BY and JOIN conditions for the SELECT are fine. You can most certainly create views with those clauses in the SELECT statement—they just have the effect of limiting the capabilities of the resulting view, as we've seen. Such views won't accept INSERT or UPDATE statements.

7. ☑ **D.** The CREATE and INSERT statements will successfully execute.
   ☒ **A, B,** and **C** are incorrect. The PURPOSE column is not required to create the view—the subquery in line 2 through line 4 is a valid SELECT statement. The code on lines 9 and 10 specifies scalar subqueries and is correct. The lower PROJECT_COST value will not prevent the INSERT statement from working; however, it will prevent the row from ever being seen through the MAJOR_PROJECTS view. A SELECT statement that attempts to display this row in the future could do so by querying the original table PROJECTS, but not the view MAJOR_PROJECTS, which only sees rows with a PROJECT_COST greater than 10000 but certainly allows them to be inserted through the view into the underlying table.

Create, Maintain, and Use Sequences

8. ☑ **D.** JOIN is used in a SELECT statement that connects two or more tables. But it is not used in a CREATE SEQUENCE statement, even though its ultimate purpose may be to support the integrity of joins.
   ☒ **A, B,** and **C** are incorrect. CYCLE specifies whether the sequence will repeat a range once it reaches the end of the range. MAXVALUE specifies one end of the range. INCREMENT specifies the number by which the sequence will increment.

9. ☑ **B.** There will be one row in the table. The reason is that the first INSERT will fail because of the attempt to enter a character string into a numeric column. In the first failed INSERT statement, the PROJ_ID_SEQ# sequence generator will be invoked, and the NEXTVAL reference will use up the first number in the sequence, which will be 1. The second INSERT will succeed and grab the second number in the sequence, which will be 5.
   ☒ **A, C,** and **D** are incorrect.

10. ☑ **B.** Since the sequence was just created, NEXTVAL must be referenced before CURRVAL. This is also true if you were to log off and end the session and then log back in to restart the session—the first reference for existing sequences must be NEXTVAL.
    ☒ **A, C,** and **D** are incorrect. You are allowed to reference sequence generators in any SQL statement where expressions are allowed. If CURRVAL were replaced with NEXTVAL, the correct answer to this question would have been **C,** meaning that the SELECT statement would have displayed a value of 1.

Create and Maintain Indexes Including Invisible Indexes and Multiple Indexes on the Same Columns

11. ☑ **B.** An index can potentially speed up the WHERE clause of any DML statement, including the UPDATE statement. Comparisons of equality are ideal.

☒ **A, C,** and **D** are incorrect. An index does not store all the data from all the rows of an indexed table but instead stores only that data that is contained within the indexed column or columns. It does not require a separate INSERT statement; instead, any future INSERTs will perform automatic index maintenance as required without any extra effort from you. The SELECT statement does not need to return indexed information for the index to be useful.

12. ☑ **B.** While all the statements will execute successfully, the first DROP statement will drop the table SUPPLIES_01, which will cause the index IX_SU_01 to be dropped as well. In other words, the DROP TABLE SUPPLIES_01 statement has the effect of dropping the table SUPPLIES_01 as well as the index IX_SU_01. The tables SUPPLIES_02 and IX_SU_02 will remain at the end.

☒ **A, C,** and **D** are incorrect.

13. ☑ **C.** The index is updated for any DELETE statements performed on the table. Invisible indexes are still maintained, even though they are invisible.

☒ **A, B,** and **D** are incorrect. An invisible index has nothing to do with invisible columns in the table. The use of a SELECT statement never results in a maintenance action of an index, regardless of the visibility of the index.

Perform Flashback Operations

14. ☑ **A.** This is the correct syntax—the TO TIMESTAMP clause with the expression that starts with the current date and time and subtracts an interval of 45 seconds.

☒ **B, C,** and **D** are incorrect. Option **B** is missing the keyword TIMESTAMP. Option **C** is missing the keywords TO TIMESTAMP and includes an incomplete expression that only represents a time interval of 45 seconds. Option **D** has the keyword TIMESTAMP but also has the incomplete expression that only includes the interval value and nothing more.

15. ☑ **D.** None of the above. The PURGE statement on line 8 prevents any recovery from being possible. PURGE cleans out the recycle bin of the objects specified in the PURGE statement, from which FLASHBACK TABLE recovers objects.

☒ **A, B,** and **C** are incorrect. Were it not for the PURGE, option **A** would be correct. Option **B** is syntactically correct, except for the PURGE statement in the code sample. There is no BEFORE COMMIT option for FLASHBACK TABLE.

11
Using the Set Operators

This chapter describes the set operators in SQL. Set operators work with sets of output data from two or more SELECT statements. They combine standalone SELECT statements in ways that cannot be done with joins or other conventional methods in SQL.

Set operators are ideal for a variety of situations where a SELECT statement's output can be combined with other data that isn't necessarily related through a structured key relationship but can still be blended into one complete output data set. A series of SELECT statements combined with set operators may include a single ORDER BY clause at the end of the series of SELECT statements. Set operators should not be confused with the reserved word SET that is used with SQL statements like UPDATE. The set operators have nothing to do with the keyword SET and don't use the SET *variable_name* clause.

CERTIFICATION OBJECTIVE 11.01

Describe Set Operators

There are four set operators: UNION, UNION ALL, INTERSECT, and MINUS. Set operators combine two or more separate SELECT statements so that their output is merged in some manner. Each set operator merges the data in a different way. The set operators are described in Table 11-1 and summarized in Figure 11-1.

The UNION operator merges the resulting row sets of one SELECT statement with the resulting row sets of another so that all the rows from both SELECT statements are included in the final output. UNION also eliminates any duplicate records that might result in the combined output.

UNION ALL does the same thing as UNION, except it does not eliminate duplicate rows.

TABLE 11-1	Set Operator	Description
The Set Operators	UNION	Combines row sets. Eliminates duplicate row sets.
	UNION ALL	Combines row sets. Does not eliminate duplicate row sets.
	INTERSECT	Includes only those row sets that are present in both queries.
	MINUS	Subtracts the rows in the second row set from the rows in the first row set.

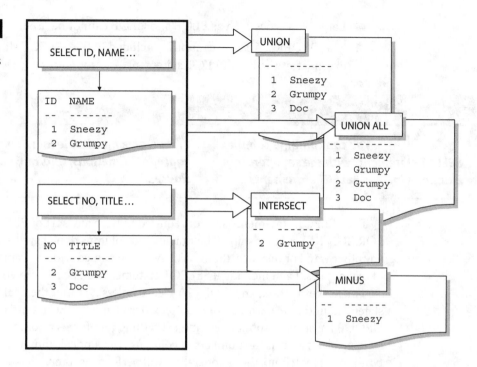

FIGURE 11-1

The set operators
in action

INTERSECT combines both sets of rows so that only those rows that were present in both SELECT statements appear in the final result.

MINUS starts with the first set of rows and then uses the second SELECT statement's row set to see whether any duplicates occur. If they do, those duplicates are completely removed, leaving only those rows that uniquely exist in the first SELECT statement's row set.

The only rules for ensuring that the SELECT statements will combine successfully with any of the set operators are as follows:

- The number of expressions selected in the select lists must be identical in each SELECT statement.

- The data types of each expression must match so that each SELECT statement's first expression shares the same data type group with the other first expressions, each second expression shares the same data type group with the other second expressions, and so on. By data type group, we mean data types that either are identical or can be made to be identical by SQL through automatic data type conversion.

- Large data types such as BLOB and CLOB cannot be used.
- The ORDER BY clause cannot be included in the SELECT statements—except after the last SELECT statement.

You can combine complex SELECT statements with the set operators. Examples include SELECT statements that involve multitable joins, subqueries, aggregate functions, and/or GROUP BY clauses.

The SELECT statements are not required to have any sort of PRIMARY KEY / FOREIGN KEY relationships. Their tables and columns don't have to be identical in any other way. For instance, they don't have to be named with the same names—none of that applies. Each individual SELECT statement can be a complete, standalone statement (but without an ORDER BY clause unless it is after the final SELECT statement in the set), with all the complexities of any SELECT statement, including GROUP BY clauses, subqueries, and everything that forms a complete SELECT statement. As long as the numbers of columns are identical, and the respective data type groups match up, the set operators will perform as intended (subject to the restrictions we just identified).

CERTIFICATION OBJECTIVE 11.02

Use a Set Operator to Combine Multiple Queries into a Single Query

Let's look at the syntax for the set operators. Each is simple—each set operator connects two SELECT statements, causing them to behave as one.

UNION

To demonstrate the use of UNION, we'll look at an exercise in which we are trying to combine e-mail addresses from different tables. First, we'll look at one of the two tables shown in Figure 11-2, the CONTACT_EMAILS table.

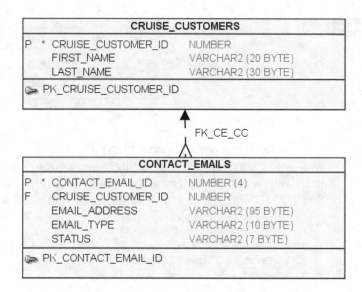

FIGURE 11-2

Diagram of
the CRUISE_
CUSTOMERS
and CONTACT_
EMAILS tables

Notice the column EMAIL_ADDRESS in the CONTACT_EMAILS table. Let's
get a data listing:

```
SELECT CONTACT_EMAIL_ID, STATUS, EMAIL_ADDRESS
FROM   CONTACT_EMAILS;

CONTACT_EMAIL_ID        STATUS  EMAIL_ADDRESS
----------------------  ------- --------------------
1                       Opt Out bubblegum@tlivecar.com
2                       Valid   nora@astann.com
3                       Valid   watcher@foursigma.org
```

Next, let's look at another table called ONLINE_SUBSCRIBERS, shown in
Figure 11-3. You can see that it has a column called simply EMAIL. Let's get a data
listing for that table as well:

```
SELECT ONLINE_SUBSCRIBER_ID, EMAIL
FROM   ONLINE_SUBSCRIBERS;

ONLINE_SUBSCRIBER_ID    EMAIL
----------------------  ----------------------------
1                       pendicott77@kasteelinc.com
2                       watcher@foursigma.org
3                       hardingpal@ckofca.com
```

FIGURE 11-3

Diagram of
the ONLINE_
SUBSCRIBERS
table

To demonstrate the set operator UNION, we'll create two SELECT statements with similar select lists—but by similar, we mean only that the select lists are identical in the number of expressions in the list and their respective data type groups. The first SELECT will include a WHERE clause to limit our rows to 'Valid' data. Let's give it a try (line numbers added):

```
01   SELECT CONTACT_EMAIL_ID, EMAIL_ADDRESS
02   FROM   CONTACT_EMAILS
03   WHERE  STATUS = 'Valid'
04   UNION
05   SELECT ONLINE_SUBSCRIBER_ID, EMAIL
06   FROM   ONLINE_SUBSCRIBERS;
```

Notice how we've structured this UNION query:

- Both SELECT statements have two expressions in their select lists (line 1 and line 5).

- The data types of each list's first expression are the same: CONTACT_EMAIL_ID (line 1) and ONLINE_SUBSCRIBER_ID (line 5). In this case, they are both numeric.

- The data types of each list's second expression are the same: EMAIL_ADDRESS (line 1) and EMAIL (line 5). In this case, they are both character strings.

Here's the output from our UNION:

```
CONTACT_EMAIL_ID          EMAIL_ADDRESS
----------------------    ------------------------------
1                         pendicott77@kasteelinc.com
2                         nora@astann.com
2                         watcher@foursigma.org
3                         hardingpal@ckofca.com
3                         watcher@foursigma.org
```

Notice the first column of output under the heading CONTACT_EMAIL_ID. The output shown includes data from both SELECT statements, which means you're seeing values from the column CONTACT_EMAIL_ID of the first SELECT statement and from the column ONLINE_SUBSCRIBER_ID of the second SELECT statement.

Logically, though, there's a problem: the values for CONTACT_EMAIL_ID and ONLINE_SUBSCRIBER_ID don't really represent the same information. Both are primary key values but for different tables, and they don't really belong in the same column—they represent totally different values. The evidence of this problem is present in the list of e-mail addresses—we only wanted a single list of unique values, but instead we have a duplication of at least one e-mail address. The reason is that UNION looks at the entire row of output from each SELECT and shows unique occurrences of the combined set of columns in the row. The first occurrence of the e-mail address "watcher@foursigma.org" has a first column value of 2, and the second has a first column value of 3, so as far as the UNION is concerned, these are unique rows of data.

Let's remove the illogical references to the first column in this example and produce something that makes more sense:

```
01    SELECT EMAIL_ADDRESS
02    FROM   CONTACT_EMAILS
03    WHERE  STATUS = 'Valid'
04    UNION
05    SELECT EMAIL
06    FROM   ONLINE_SUBSCRIBERS;
```

Here's the result:

```
EMAIL_ADDRESS
----------------------------
hardingpal@ckofca.com
nora@astann.com
pendicott77@kasteelinc.com
watcher@foursigma.org
```

The result of UNION (line 4) is a combination of the original rows, with any duplicate values removed. In this case, there were two rows for the e-mail address "watcher@foursigma.org," but only one is shown in our final result.

Notice that the output column headings display the first SELECT statement's expressions (line 1). We'll have more to say about that when we discuss ORDER BY and column references. For now, let's move on to the UNION ALL set operator.

UNION ALL

The only difference between UNION and UNION ALL is that duplicate values aren't removed from UNION ALL. If we were to execute the same SQL statement from the previous example with the UNION ALL set operator, it would look like this:

```
01   SELECT  EMAIL_ADDRESS
02   FROM    CONTACT_EMAILS
03   WHERE   STATUS = 'Valid'
04   UNION ALL
05   SELECT  EMAIL
06   FROM    ONLINE_SUBSCRIBERS;
```

Here are the results:

```
EMAIL_ADDRESS
-----------------------------
nora@astann.com
watcher@foursigma.org
pendicott77@kasteelinc.com
watcher@foursigma.org
hardingpal@ckofca.com
```

Notice that the duplicate entry is included. The value for "watcher@foursigma.org" appears in both tables, so it appears twice in the output of our UNION ALL use of the SELECT statement.

Notice also that the ordering of the rows is totally different—remember that without an explicit ORDER BY clause, you can never guarantee the ordering of rows in any SELECT statement. We'll look at how to use ORDER BY later in this chapter. First—let's look at another set operator.

INTERSECT

The set operator INTERSECT looks for common values among the rows of the SELECT statement. Let's change our example to use INTERSECT:

```
01   SELECT  EMAIL_ADDRESS
02   FROM    CONTACT_EMAILS
03   WHERE   STATUS = 'Valid'
04   INTERSECT
05   SELECT  EMAIL
06   FROM    ONLINE_SUBSCRIBERS;
```

Here are the results:

```
EMAIL_ADDRESS
-------------------------------
watcher@foursigma.org
```

Just one row was common between the two SELECT statements.

INTERSECT will eliminate duplicate rows. If one or both SELECT statement row sets contain duplicates within its own set of rows, the resulting output from INTERSECT will eliminate those duplicates.

MINUS

The final set operator is MINUS. Up to now, the results of the set operators would be the same regardless of which SELECT statement was placed first before the set operator. That's not the case with MINUS, however. MINUS will start with the first SELECT statement and remove any rows from that SELECT's output that might happen to appear in the second SELECT's output. The results may differ, depending on which SELECT is placed first and which is placed second.

Using our same example, here is the SELECT from CONTACT_EMAILS first:

```
01    SELECT  EMAIL_ADDRESS
02    FROM    CONTACT_EMAILS
03    WHERE   STATUS = 'Valid'
04    MINUS
05    SELECT  EMAIL
06    FROM    ONLINE_SUBSCRIBERS;
```

Here are the results:

```
EMAIL_ADDRESS
--------------------
nora@astann.com
```

But now let's reverse the placement of the SELECT statements:

```
01    SELECT  EMAIL
02    FROM    ONLINE_SUBSCRIBERS
03    MINUS
04    SELECT  EMAIL_ADDRESS
05    FROM    CONTACT_EMAILS
06    WHERE   STATUS = 'Valid';
```

Here are the results:

```
EMAIL
--------------------
hardingpal@ckofca.com
pendicott77@kasteelinc.com
```

Notice that the results are completely different. Notice also that the column heading is different—the column has taken the heading of the first SELECT statement, as it always does, but now the first SELECT statement is different, and along with it (in this example) so is the heading.

Combinations

The set operators may be used in multiple combinations, such as

```
SELECT...
UNION
SELECT...
INTERSECT
SELECT...
```

Such combinations can be continued indefinitely.

Set operators have equal precedence among themselves, meaning that they will all execute from start to finish in the order that they appear in the SELECT statement. To change the order of execution, use parentheses, like this:

```
SELECT...
UNION
(SELECT...
INTERSECT
SELECT...)
INTERSECT
SELECT...
```

Just be sure to use the parentheses so that:

- The code enclosed is a standalone query and does not include an ORDER BY clause.
- The enclosed code is placed into the outer query as though it were a single, standalone SELECT statement, without the ORDER BY clause.
- If an ORDER BY is desired, it must be the final clause in the entire series of statements.

Follow those rules, and you can connect as many SELECT statements together as required.

on the job

The set operators are useful for requirements to combine the data of two tables into one output result set when the two tables have no primary key/foreign key relationship with each other.

CERTIFICATION OBJECTIVE 11.03

Control the Order of Rows Returned

As with any SELECT statement, the ORDER BY clause is the only way to determine the ordering of rows that appear in output. As we already know, the ORDER BY clause determines how to sort rows by identifying a series of one or more expressions that have something to do with the table—or tables—that are involved with the SELECT statement. Often the expression is simply a column within each row, but ORDER BY also accepts complex expressions. These expressions may involve one or more columns and perform some sort of transformation on the data.

However, when set operators are involved, there's a bit of an issue. How do you identify data in the rows when there are multiple tables using different column names?

The answer is that the ORDER BY clause is a bit restricted in this situation. The clause is restricted to identifying common expression items in the select list, and nothing more. There are two ways to identify them, and we've seen these earlier—by reference and by position. The following sections show examples of these approaches with the set operators.

ORDER BY—By Position

One way to sort rows of output that result from a series of SELECT statements combined with set operators is to use the "by position" approach. Here's an example:

```
01    SELECT 'Individual',
02           LAST_NAME || ', ' || FIRST_NAME
03    FROM   CRUISE_CUSTOMERS
04    UNION
05    SELECT CATEGORY,
06           VENDOR_NAME
07    FROM   VENDORS;
```

The preceding example combines rows from two tables. The first query has two expressions:

- A string literal, 'Individual'
- A concatenation of two columns, LAST_NAME and FIRST_NAME, separated by a comma and a space

The second SELECT statement has two expressions:

- The column CATEGORY
- The column VENDOR_NAME

Here are the results:

```
'INDIVIDUAL' LAST_NAME||','||FIRST_NAME
------------ -----------------------------------------------------
Individual   Bryant, William
Individual   Gilbert, Nada
Individual   MacCaulay, Nora
Partner      Acme Steaks
Supplier     Acme Poker Chips
```

We can sort the rows with an ORDER BY that identifies the position within the select list of the expression we want to sort by, like this:

```
01   SELECT 'Individual',
02          LAST_NAME || ', ' || FIRST_NAME
03   FROM   CRUISE_CUSTOMERS
04   UNION
05   SELECT CATEGORY,
06          VENDOR_NAME
07   FROM   VENDORS
08   ORDER BY 2;
```

Here is the result:

```
'INDIVIDUAL' LAST_NAME||','||FIRST_NAME
------------ -----------------------------------------------------
Supplier     Acme Poker Chips
Partner      Acme Steaks
Individual   Bryant, William
Individual   Gilbert, Nada
Individual   MacCaulay, Nora
```

Remember, when using ORDER BY with a series of SELECT statements connected with set operators, you can use ORDER BY only once, at the end.

ORDER BY—By Reference

There is another way to use ORDER BY with set operators. ORDER BY reference is when you name one of the columns in the SELECT statement's expression list. When using set operators, the column names used in the first SELECT statement are in force. Using our earlier example, let's add column aliases to our first SELECT statement, and we'll be able to use ORDER BY:

```
01    SELECT    'Individual' CONTACT_CATEGORY,
02              LAST_NAME || ', ' || FIRST_NAME POINT_OF_CONTACT
03    FROM      CRUISE_CUSTOMERS
04    UNION
05    SELECT    CATEGORY,
06              VENDOR_NAME
07    FROM      VENDORS
08    ORDER BY POINT_OF_CONTACT;
```

Note the column alias POINT_OF_CONTACT that is specified at the end of line 2 and used in the ORDER BY in line 8. Here are the results:

```
CONTACT_CATEGORY POINT_OF_CONTACT
---------------- ------------------------------------------------------
Supplier         Acme Poker Chips
Partner          Acme Steaks
Individual       Bryant, William
Individual       Gilbert, Nada
Individual       MacCaulay, Nora
```

So, either the "by position" or "by reference" approach works with ORDER BY. Just be sure you make it the last clause of the entire series of SELECT statements.

If you combine a series of two or more SELECT statements with set operators, your ORDER BY clause must be the final clause and can specify columns by name only if it uses the column names from the first SELECT statement, regardless of how many SELECT statements might be connected with set operators.

CERTIFICATION SUMMARY

Each set operator combines rows from two independent SELECT statements. Set operators allow you to combine rows without a join by merging entire sets of rows based solely on ensuring that the number of expressions and data types involved match up.

The set operators include UNION, UNION ALL, INTERSECT, and MINUS. Each differs in how it returns rows that appear in one SELECT statement that might also appear in the other SELECT statement.

UNION combines rows from the SELECT statements and presents one unique set of rows from the combined SELECT statements. It eliminates duplicate rows that might appear as a result of the combination. UNION ALL combines both sets of rows and includes any duplicates that might occur as a result of the combination of the row sets; that is, it does not eliminate any duplicate rows. INTERSECT looks only for rows that are present in both sets of rows returned by the SELECT statements. Only the duplicates become the output from the SELECT statement. MINUS takes the set of rows from the first SELECT and removes any for which duplicates exist in the second set.

You can combine several SELECT statements with as many set operators as you want. They will execute one after the other, unless you choose to override that behavior using parentheses.

Each SELECT statement can be a complex query, with multiple joins, subqueries, and GROUP BY clauses. However, only one ORDER BY clause is allowed, and it must be at the end of the series of SELECT statements and set operators.

ORDER BY with set operators can sort rows by position or reference. If by reference, the first SELECT statement's expression names are in effect for the entire series of SELECT statements. You can use column aliases in the first (or any) SELECT statement if you want, but it is not required.

TWO-MINUTE DRILL

Describe Set Operators

- ☐ UNION combines the output of two SELECT statements, eliminating any duplicate rows that might exist.
- ☐ INTERSECT combines the output of two SELECT statements, showing only the unique occurrences of data present in both row sets and ignoring anything that doesn't appear in both sets.
- ☐ MINUS takes the first SELECT statement's output and subtracts any occurrences of identical rows that might exist within the second SELECT statement's output.
- ☐ UNION ALL does the same thing as UNION but does not eliminate duplicate rows.

Use a Set Operator to Combine Multiple Queries into a Single Query

- ☐ The set operators are placed between two SELECT statements.
- ☐ The two SELECT statements can be simple or complex and can include their own GROUP BY clauses, WHERE clauses, subqueries, and more.
- ☐ The ORDER BY clause, if used, must be the final clause of the combined SELECT statements.
- ☐ You can connect multiple SELECT statements with multiple set operators.
- ☐ The set operators have equal precedence.
- ☐ You can use parentheses to override set operator precedence.

Control the Order of Rows Returned

- ☐ If an ORDER BY clause is used, it must be placed at the end of the SQL statements.
- ☐ Multiple SELECTs that are connected with set operators may be sorted by position or reference.
- ☐ When using ORDER BY reference, the column name in force is whatever column name exists in the first SELECT statement.

SELF TEST

The following questions will help you measure your understanding of the material presented in this chapter. Choose one correct answer for each question unless otherwise directed.

Describe Set Operators

1. The set operators do *not* include which one of the following keywords?
   A. ALL
   B. SET
   C. MINUS
   D. UNION

2. You are tasked with cleaning up a database application. There are two tables in the database: ORDERS contains completed ORDERS, and ORDER_RETURNS contains duplicate information for all ORDERS that were later returned. Your goal is to find out whether any rows in ORDER_RETURNS exist that were never in the ORDERS table to begin with. Which of the following set operators should you use?
   A. ALL
   B. SET
   C. MINUS
   D. UNION

3. Review the following illustrations:

```
SELECT * FROM FURNISHING:


CAT#     ITEM_NAME     ADDED         SECTION
-----    ---------     ------        -------
1        Side table    23-DEC-09     LR
2        Desk          12-SEP-09     BR
3        Towel         10-OCT-09     BA
```

```
SELECT * FROM STORE_INVENTORY:


NUM      AISLE         PRODUCT       LAST_ORDER
----     -----         -------       ----------
77       F02           Jacket        2009-09-09
78       B11           Towel         2009-11-11
79       SP01          Lava lamp     2009-12-21
```

```
                    FURNISHINGS
P * CAT#            NUMBER
    ITEM_NAME       VARCHAR2 (15 BYTE)
    ADDED           DATE
    SECTION         VARCHAR2 (10 BYTE)
  PK_CAT#
```

```
                  STORE_INVENTORY
P * NUM            NUMBER
    AISLE          VARCHAR2 (7 BYTE)
    PRODUCT        VARCHAR2 (15 BYTE)
    LAST_ORDER     DATE
  PK_NUM
```

Next, review the following SQL code:

```
01    SELECT     TO_CHAR(A.LAST_ORDER,'RRRR-MM-DD')
02    FROM       STORE_INVENTORY A
03    ORDER BY 1
04    UNION
05    SELECT     ADDED
06    FROM FURNISHINGS;
```

What will result from an attempt to execute this SQL statement?

A. It will fail with a syntax error because of the TO_CHAR conversion function on line 1.

B. It will fail because of the table alias in lines 1 and 2, which cannot be used in this context.

C. It will fail with a syntax error on line 3 because you cannot use an ORDER BY in this context.

D. It will execute successfully.

4. When combining two SELECT statements, which of the following set operators will produce a different result, depending on which SELECT statement precedes or follows the operator?

A. MINUS

B. UNION ALL

C. INTERSECT

D. UNION

5. Which of the following statements about set operators is true? Choose the best answer.

A. If you add the reserved word ALL to the end of any set operator, it will change the behavior of the set operator by removing duplicate rows.

B. Set operators can be used to combine INSERT statements.

C. You can connect two SELECT statements with one set operator.

D. The UNION set operator has precedence over the others.

Use a Set Operator to Combine Multiple Queries into a Single Query

6. Review the first two illustrations from question 3, and then review this SQL code:

```
SELECT NUM, PRODUCT FROM STORE_INVENTORY
INTERSECT
SELECT CAT#, ITEM_NAME   FROM FURNISHINGS;
```

How many rows will result from this query?

A. 0

B. 1

C. 3

D. 6

7. Review the first two illustrations from question 3, and then review this SQL code:

```
01    SELECT '--', SECTION
02    FROM   FURNISHINGS
03    WHERE  CAT# NOT IN (1,2)
04    UNION ALL
05    SELECT TO_CHAR(LAST_ORDER,'Month'), AISLE
06    FROM   STORE_INVENTORY;
```

How many rows will result from this query?

A. 0

B. 4

C. 6

D. It will not execute because it will fail with a syntax error.

8. Review the first two illustrations from question 3, and then review this SQL code:

```
(  SELECT PRODUCT   FROM STORE_INVENTORY
   UNION ALL
   SELECT ITEM_NAME FROM FURNISHINGS
)
INTERSECT
(  SELECT ITEM_NAME FROM FURNISHINGS WHERE ITEM_NAME = 'Towel'
   UNION ALL
   SELECT ITEM_NAME FROM FURNISHINGS WHERE ITEM_NAME = 'Towel'
);
```

How many rows will result from this code?

A. 1

B. 2

C. 4

D. 6

9. Review the first two illustrations from question 3, as well as the ONLINE_SUBSCRIBERS table in Figure 11-3, and then review this SQL code:

```
01    SELECT COUNT(*)
02    FROM   ONLINE_SUBSCRIBERS
03    WHERE  SUB_DATE IN
04               (SELECT LAST_ORDER FROM STORE_INVENTORY
05                UNION
06                SELECT ADDED      FROM FURNISHINGS);
```

What will happen when this SQL statement is executed?

A. It will fail with a syntax error because you cannot use an aggregate function like COUNT(*) in line 1 in this context.

B. It will fail with a syntax error starting at line 4.

C. It will execute, but it will not perform as intended because the second SELECT statement within the subquery on line 6 will not execute; only the first SELECT in the subquery on line 4 will execute.

D. It will execute successfully.

10. Review the first two illustrations from question 3, as well as the ONLINE_SUBSCRIBERS table in Figure 11-3, and then review this SQL code:

```
01    SELECT  (SELECT LAST_ORDER FROM STORE_INVENTORY
02                UNION
03                SELECT ADDED "Date Added" FROM FURNISHINGS)
04    FROM    ONLINE_SUBSCRIBERS
05    ORDER BY 1;
```

What will happen when this SQL statement is executed?

A. It will fail with an execution error on line 1.

B. It will execute, but the UNION will not work as expected.

C. It will execute and display one column under the "Date Added" heading.

D. It will execute and display one column under the "LAST_ORDER" heading.

11. Review the first two illustrations from question 3, as well as the ONLINE_SUBSCRIBERS table in Figure 11-3, and then review this SQL code:

```
01    SELECT    (SELECT PRODUCT FROM STORE_INVENTORY
02              INTERSECT
03              SELECT ITEM_NAME FROM FURNISHINGS)
04    FROM      ONLINE_SUBSCRIBERS;
```

What will happen when this SQL statement is executed?

A. It will fail with a general syntax error.

B. It will fail with an execution error.

C. It will execute, but the INTERSECT will not work correctly.

D. It will execute and repeat the value 'Towel' for each row of the ONLINE_SUBSCRIBERS table.

12. Review the first two illustrations from question 3, as well as the ONLINE_SUBSCRIBERS table in Figure 11-3, and then review this SQL code:

```
01    SELECT    A.SUB_DATE, COUNT(*)
02    FROM      ONLINE_SUBSCRIBERS A JOIN
03                  (SELECT LAST_ORDER, PRODUCT FROM STORE_INVENTORY
04                  UNION
05                  SELECT ADDED, ITEM_NAME FROM FURNISHINGS) B
06    ON        A.SUB_DATE = B.LAST_ORDER
07    GROUP BY A.SUB_DATE;
```

Which of the following are true about this SQL statement? (Choose two.)

A. The GROUP BY clause on line 7 is not allowed here.

B. The B.LAST_ORDER reference at the end of line 6 refers to data included in the ADDED column referred to in line 5.

C. The JOIN at the end of line 2 is not allowed in this context.

D. The statement is syntactically correct and will execute successfully.

Control the Order of Rows Returned

13. Review the first two illustrations from question 3, as well as the ONLINE_SUBSCRIBERS table in Figure 11-3, and then review this SQL code:

```
01    SELECT    A.SUB_DATE, COUNT(*)
02    FROM      ONLINE_SUBSCRIBERS A JOIN
03                  (SELECT LAST_ORDER, PRODUCT FROM STORE_INVENTORY
04                  UNION
05                  SELECT ADDED, ITEM_NAME FROM FURNISHINGS) B
06    ON        A.SUB_DATE = B.LAST_ORDER
07    GROUP BY A.SUB_DATE;
```

Where can you add an ORDER BY to this code? (Choose two.)

A. At the end of line 5 before the right parenthesis

B. Between lines 5 and 6

C. After line 7

D. Nowhere

14. The ORDER BY clause can be included in a SELECT with set operators if:

A. It follows the first SELECT statement.

B. It follows the final SELECT statement.

C. It is used in each SELECT statement and its ORDER BY expressions match in data type.

D. The ORDER BY clause cannot be used in a SELECT with set operators.

15. Review the first two illustrations from question 3; then review this SQL code:

```
01   SELECT '--' "Order Date", SECTION
02   FROM   FURNISHINGS
03   WHERE  CAT# NOT IN (1,2)
04   UNION ALL
05   SELECT TO_CHAR(LAST_ORDER,'Month') "Last Order", AISLE
06   FROM   STORE_INVENTORY;
```

Which of the following are valid ORDER BY clauses for this query? (Choose two.)

A. ORDER BY AISLE

B. ORDER BY "Last Order"

C. ORDER BY SECTION

D. ORDER BY 1

SELF TEST ANSWERS

Describe Set Operators

1. ☑ **B.** The keyword SET is not used with the set operators.
   ☒ **A, C,** and **D** are incorrect. ALL is part of the UNION ALL clause. MINUS and UNION are both set operators.

2. ☑ **C.** MINUS is what you would use. That is the set operator with which you can remove rows from one table that are also present in the second table, resulting in output that shows rows from the first table that are not present in the second.
   ☒ **A, B,** and **D** are incorrect. ALL is not a full set operator; it works with UNION ALL but is not a set operator on its own. SET is not a set operator. UNION would combine records from both tables, which is not what is desired here.

3. ☑ **C.** The ORDER BY of the first SELECT statement in line 3 is incorrect and causes the statement to fail.
   ☒ **A, B,** and **D** are incorrect. The TO_CHAR conversion function in line 1 is correct syntax. It ensures that the data types for LAST_ORDER and ADDED correspond to each other. The table alias on lines 1 and 2 is fine. But the entire statement will not execute for the reason explained for the correct answer.

4. ☑ **A.** The only set operator that changes its end result based on which SELECT statement precedes or follows the set operator is MINUS.
   ☒ **B, C,** and **D** are incorrect.

5. ☑ **C.** You can connect two SELECT statements with one set operator.
   ☒ **A, B,** and **D** are incorrect. The reserved word ALL works only with UNION. Set operators can combine only SELECT statements, not other SQL statements. All set operators have equal precedence; only parentheses can be used to override set operator precedence.

Use a Set Operator to Combine Multiple Queries into a Single Query

6. ☑ **A.** No rows will result. The reason is that we're trying to intersect rows, which means to show only those rows that are common between the two row sets. While both tables share a value of 'Towel', the SELECT statements are including the NUM and CAT# columns from the two tables. In the two rows for Towel, the values for NUM and CAT# don't match. The result is that neither row that includes 'Towel' is a complete match.
   ☒ **B, C,** and **D** are incorrect.

7. ☑ **B.** The first select will produce one row. The second will produce three rows. The UNION ALL set operator will combine the results and return four rows.

☒ **A, C,** and **D** are incorrect. The syntax is fine and the statement will execute.

8. ☑ **A.** Only one row will result, as explained next.

☒ **B, C,** and **D** are incorrect. It might be tempting to have chosen option B, since the first and second SELECT statement combinations with the UNION ALL will produce two rows containing the value 'Towel', and so will the second UNION ALL. But the INTERSECT will eliminate duplicate rows and return one row for 'Towel'.

9. ☑ **D.** It will execute successfully. Set operators are perfectly acceptable in a subquery.

☒ **A, B,** and **C** are incorrect.

10. ☑ **A.** Since we know from the data listings that the results of the SELECT statements with the set operator UNION will produce multiple rows, the statement will fail, since a scalar subquery is what is expected here by the outer query.

☒ **B, C,** and **D** are incorrect. UNION is fine, but the end result caused a problem for reasons unrelated to the UNION. The column heading issues don't apply, but if the subquery had not produced the execution error, options **C** and **D** would still be incorrect—the heading would be a concatenated version of the entire string of characters forming the subquery.

11. ☑ **D.** We can tell from the data listing that the subquery will return one value representing the INTERSECT of both queries. That, and the fact that the subquery will return just one column in that one row, makes this a scalar subquery, albeit a risky one, since there's no guarantee that it will always execute as a scalar subquery. But it will work given the data listings, and the subquery will perform as though it were a literal value within the outer SELECT, returning the same result for each row of the ONLINE_SUBSCRIBERS table.

☒ **A, B,** and **C** are incorrect. There is nothing wrong syntactically with the SQL statement, and as we discuss in describing the correct choice, because of the data listings we are provided with, we can tell that there will be no execution errors either. The INTERSECT will perform just fine.

12. ☑ **B** and **D.** This is a valid SQL statement that will execute successfully. The subquery on lines 3 through 5 is the complete UNION and is treated as an inline view in this context. As such, it behaves like any other inline view and is perfectly fine in this context. At the end of line 5 is a table alias B that is given to the inline view, and that table alias is used in line 6 to identify the column of the inline view called LAST_ORDER, which represents the first column of the combined SELECT statements, including the ADDED column.

☒ **A** and **C** are incorrect. GROUP BY is allowed, as is the JOIN, for reasons explained under the correct choice.

Control the Order of Rows Returned

13. ☑ **A** and **C.** The ORDER BY can go at the end of the inline view or at the end of the entire SQL statement.

☒ **B** and **D** are incorrect.

14. ☑ **B.** The ORDER BY is optional, but if used, it must be the last clause in the entire series of SELECT statements.

☒ **A, C,** and **D** are incorrect. ORDER BY cannot be used in any SELECT statements within a series of SELECT statements connected by set operators. It can be placed at the end only, following the final SELECT statement.

15. ☑ **C** and **D.** Any ORDER BY that uses the "by reference" technique must reference column names of the first SELECT statement. So, ORDER BY SECTION is valid. Also, the "by position" is accepted, so ORDER BY 1 is good.

☒ **A** and **B** are incorrect. The AISLE column name isn't recognized, since it isn't a column in the first SELECT statement. The same is true for the "Last Order" column alias.

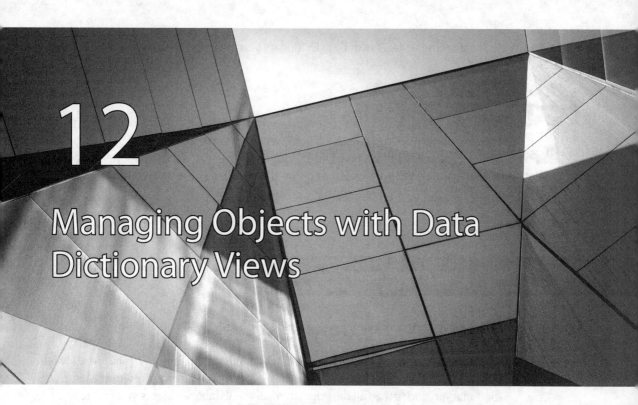

12

Managing Objects with Data Dictionary Views

T his chapter describes a valuable tool that all Oracle professionals should understand. The data dictionary is Oracle's built-in real-time reference source for all information about the applications that you build in your database. Armed with the full capabilities of the data dictionary, you can obtain information on the database objects that have been created within your database, who created them, when, and much more.

CERTIFICATION OBJECTIVE 12.01

Query Various Data Dictionary Views

The *data dictionary* is a collection of database tables and views. It is automatically built and populated by the Oracle database. The information stored in the data dictionary includes the full description of all the database objects you create as part of your application, including tables, views, indexes, constraints, sequences, and more. In other words, the result of each Data Definition Language (DDL) statement you've studied in this book is recorded in the dictionary, and the information is automatically maintained by the Oracle system in real time as you change database objects and their structures.

The information stored in the data dictionary includes (but is not limited to):

- The names of database objects, their owners, and when they were created
- The names of each table's columns, along with data types, precision, and scale
- Any constraints
- Views, indexes, and sequences

This chapter will explore how the data dictionary is structured and what sort of information is contained within it. We'll go through some examples of how to extract valuable information and use the data dictionary to assist you as you build your applications.

The data dictionary is often referred to as *metadata*, which means "data about data." That is what the data dictionary is—it's a comprehensive detailed database that tracks everything there is to know about the database applications you create within the Oracle system. Every time you create a database object, the Oracle

Database works in the background to record that object's name and structure and makes that information available to you by way of the data dictionary. Every object created by every user is documented within the data dictionary.

Structure

The data dictionary consists of tables and views that are owned by the user account SYS. As owner, SYS has full privileges over these tables and views. No user should ever alter data owned by SYS or else the integrity of the database may be compromised.

on the job

The SYS account is one of a few powerful accounts that comes with every implementation of the Oracle database. The SYS account is something of a "super user" account, with master privileges to virtually everything in the database. Generally, no developer uses the SYS account for anything other than database system maintenance, and often it's the database administrator (DBA) who possesses exclusive access to the SYS account.

All data dictionary information is stored in tables, but much of that data is presented to users through views. In other words, users generally don't get direct access to the tables of the data dictionary; they get access to the views, which provide somewhat limited access in order to protect the integrity of the data dictionary.

In addition, many data dictionary objects are renamed via public synonyms, and those are the names by which you know the data. In other words, there are multiple levels of abstraction that separate users from the underlying data. No matter—the ability to read the information in the data dictionary is a great asset to all SQL professionals.

Every DDL statement that is issued throughout the database causes an automatic update to the data dictionary. That update is handled by the Oracle system and applied to the base tables that form the foundation of the data dictionary. Users do not explicitly update any information in the dictionary.

(Note: There is one exception to this. Users may optionally choose to add comments, which you'll explore later in this chapter.)

As of this writing, there are more than 2,000 views in the data dictionary. One in particular is a good starting point: DICTIONARY. This view contains information about the views that compose the data dictionary. It includes the name of each view, along with a brief explanation of each view. You'll look at it a bit later.

The USER_TABLES view contains information about the tables owned by the current user account. In other words, no matter which account you log in to, you can query the USER_TABLES view and get detailed information about the tables owned by whatever account you are logged in with.

A full description of the USER_TABLES view would show that it consists of over 50 columns. Some of the columns include

- **TABLE_NAME** The name of the table.
- **STATUS** Indicates whether the table is currently valid and therefore available for use.
- **ROW_MOVEMENT** Indicates whether ROW MOVEMENT has been enabled for the table. (See our discussion in Chapter 10 about the FLASHBACK TABLE statement for more information about enabling and disabling ROW_MOVEMENT.)
- **AVG_ROW_LEN** The average length of the rows currently stored in the table.

These are just some of the several dozen columns that are in the USER_TABLES view.

What if you want to see information about tables other than your own? Well, it just so happens there are two other views in the data dictionary that have almost the identical set of columns as USER_TABLES.

- **ALL_TABLES** Shows all the same table information but for tables to which the current user has privileges, regardless of owner
- **DBA_TABLES** Shows all the same table information but for all the tables in the entire database, regardless of owner or table privileges

These other two views also have an additional column:

- **OWNER** The owner of the table in question

And that makes sense—there is no need for OWNER in the USER_TABLES view since that view shows information about only one owner, namely, the current owner.

This naming pattern of using one of these three prefixes (USER_, ALL_, DBA_) is a pattern that is used throughout the data dictionary. Many of the data dictionary views that store information about objects in the database have names that start with one of these three prefixes. An overview of these data dictionary views is presented in Table 12-1. As you can see from the table, the vast majority of data dictionary views have a prefix of USER_, ALL_, or DBA_. A set of three views

TABLE 12-1   Prefixes of Some of the Data Dictionary Views

Prefix	# of Views[1]	Description
USER_	462	Objects owned by the current user accessing the view.
ALL_	417	Objects owned by any user in the database to which the current user has privileges.
DBA_	948	All objects in the database.
V_$ (for views) V$ (for public synonyms)	768	Dynamic performance views, each of which has a public synonym counterpart. Stores information about the local database instance.
GV_$ (for views) GV$ (for public synonyms)	638	Global dynamic performance views.
Other SM$, AUDIT_, CHANGE_, TABLE_ CLIENT_, COLUMN_, DICT_, DATABASE_, DBMS_, GLOBAL_, INDEX_, LOGSTDBY_, NLS_, RESOURCE_, ROLE_, SESSION_, CLIENT_RESULT_CACHE_STATS$, or no prefix, etc.	41	The remaining views of the data dictionary have a variety of prefixes and unique individual names.

[1] View counts were determined using an Oracle 12.1.0.2.0 container database (CDB). Other versions may vary.

that have the USER_, ALL_, and DBA_ prefix and share the same suffix, such as TABLES, draw their data from a single data dictionary table. For example, USER_CONSTRAINTS, ALL_CONSTRAINTS, and DBA_CONSTRAINTS share the same data dictionary table. Table 12-2 shows the most common USER_ views you'll use on a regular basis.

Note that public synonyms are not listed in the USER_SYNONYMS view, which shows only private synonyms. Even if you're logged in to a user account that created a particular public synonym object, you'll still not find it listed in the USER_SYNONYMS view. Instead, you'll find it in ALL_SYNONYMS and DBA_SYNONYMS.

Dynamic Performance Views

Table 12-1 includes references to a set of views that begin with the prefixes V_$ and GV_$. These are defined as the dynamic performance views and the global dynamic performance views.

TABLE 12-2	Selected Data Dictionary Views Showing Objects Owned by the Current User

Suffix	Description
USER_CATALOG	All tables, views, synonyms, and sequences owned by USER
USER_COL_PRIVS	Grants on columns of tables owned by USER
USER_CONSTRAINTS	Constraints on tables owned by USER
USER_CONS_COLUMNS	Accessible columns in constraint definitions for tables owned by USER
USER_DEPENDENCIES	Dependencies to and from a user's objects
USER_ERRORS	Current errors on stored objects owned by USER
USER_INDEXES	Indexes owned by USER
USER_IND_COLUMNS	Columns in user tables used in indexes owned by USER
USER_OBJECTS	Objects owned by USER
USER_SEQUENCES	Sequences owned by USER
USER_SYNONYMS	Private synonyms owned by USER (public synonyms are displayed in ALL_SYNONYMS and DBA_SYNONYMS)
USER_TABLES	Tables owned by USER
USER_TAB_COLUMNS	Columns in USER's own tables and views
USER_TAB_PRIVS	Grants on objects owned by USER
USER_VIEWS	Views owned by USER

Dynamic performance views display information about current database activity in real time. They receive data dynamically from the database through mechanisms that go beyond the scope of this book. For our purposes, it's important to know that they are maintained automatically by the system and are available for querying—with some limitations.

The dynamic performance views start with the prefix V_$. There are public synonyms created for each of the views, and they have similar names but begin with the prefix V$.

Simple queries on dynamic performance views are accepted, but complex queries, with or without joins, require some special attention. Oracle formally recommends that the dynamic nature of these views does not guarantee read consistency for anything other than the simplest of single-view queries, so it's advised that you perform complex joins and/or queries by

- Creating a set of temporary tables to mirror the views
- Copying the data out of the views and into a set of temporary tables
- Performing the join on the temporary tables

This way, you'll avoid getting bad results caused by a lack of read consistency.

Some of the dynamic performance synonyms (which point to views that point to tables) include the following:

- **V$DATABASE**   Includes information about the database itself, including the database name, the date created, the current operating system platform, and much more
- **V$INSTANCE**   Includes the instance name, the host name, the startup time, and much more
- **V$PARAMETER**   The current settings for system parameters, such as NLS_LANGUAGE, NLS_DATE_LANGUAGE, NLS_CURRENCY, NLS_TIME_FORMAT, NLS_TIME_TZ_FORMAT, NLS_TIMESTAMP_TZ_FORMAT, SQL_TRACE, and much more
- **V$SESSION**   Many current settings for each individual user session, showing active connections, login times, machine names that users are logged in to, the current state of transactions, and much more

- **V$RESERVED_WORDS**   Current list of reserved words, including information indicating whether the keyword is always reserved, and if not, under what circumstances it is reserved
- **V$OBJECT_USAGE**   Useful for monitoring the usage of INDEX objects
- **V$TIMEZONE_NAMES**   Includes two columns: TZNAME, which is time zone region, and TZABBREV, which is the time zone abbreviation

Reading Comments

The data dictionary is rich with comments that help describe the intent of the various views of the data dictionary and the columns within them. In addition to the comments that are provided in the DICTIONARY view for each of the individual data dictionary views, you can view comments about the columns within those views or about any object stored anywhere in the database:

- **ALL_TAB_COMMENTS**   Displays comments for all objects in the database
- **ALL_COL_COMMENTS**   Displays comments for all columns of all tables and views in the database

Say you're looking at a data dictionary view like USER_SYNONYMS and you want to learn more about its columns. Here's a query that will help you:

```
SELECT '*TABLE: ' || TABLE_NAME, COMMENTS
FROM    ALL_TAB_COMMENTS
WHERE   OWNER = 'SYS'
  AND   TABLE_NAME = 'USER_SYNONYMS'
UNION
SELECT 'COL: ' || COLUMN_NAME, COMMENTS
FROM    ALL_COL_COMMENTS
WHERE   OWNER = 'SYS'
  AND   TABLE_NAME = 'USER_SYNONYMS' ;
```

That's the query; here are the results:

```
'*TABLE:'||TABLE_NAME      COMMENTS
----------------------     ---------------------------------------------
*TABLE: USER_SYNONYMS      The user's private synonyms
COL: DB_LINK               Database link referenced in a remote synonym
COL: SYNONYM_NAME          Name of the synonym
COL: TABLE_NAME            Name of the object referenced by the synonym
COL: TABLE_OWNER           Owner of the object referenced by the synonym
```

As you can see, we're using the data dictionary to study the data dictionary. The right-side listing under COMMENTS is helpful in describing the contents of the view in the data dictionary. You can use this technique to inspect all of the contents of the data dictionary.

Adding Comments

You can add your own comments to the data dictionary to add notes and descriptions about the tables and columns you create. The COMMENT statement is what we use to add comments to the data dictionary for a particular database object. Its syntax is as follows:

```
COMMENT ON objectType fullObjectName IS c1;
```

where:

- *objectType* is one of the keywords TABLE, COLUMN, or some other objects that are not subjects of the certification exam, such as INDEXTYPE, OPERATOR, MATERIALIZED VIEW, and others.
- *fullObjectName* is the name of the object for which you want to add a comment. If it's a TABLE, name the table. But if it's a column, use the TABLE.COLUMN syntax.
- *c1* is the full text of the comment you want to add.

When you add a comment to the table, the comment will be displayed in the data dictionary views USER_TAB_COMMENTS, ALL_TAB_COMMENTS, and DBA_TAB_COMMENTS.

When you add a comment to a column in a table, the comment will be displayed in the data dictionary views USER_COL_COMMENTS, ALL_COL_COMMENTS, and DBA_COL_COMMENTS.

For example, let's say we want to add a comment to the data dictionary about the PORTS table. Here's an example:

```
COMMENT ON TABLE PORTS
        IS 'Listing of all ports of departure and arrival.';
```

To see the results, you could use this query:

```
SELECT COMMENTS
FROM   USER_TAB_COMMENTS
WHERE  TABLE_NAME = 'PORTS';


COMMENTS
----------------------------
Listing of all ports of departure and arrival.
```

Here's an example of adding a comment to a table's column:

```
COMMENT ON COLUMN PORTS.CAPACITY
        IS 'Maximum number of passengers (exclusive of crew).';
```

You can't really drop a comment from the data dictionary. Instead, you change it to a blank, like this:

```
COMMENT ON TABLE PORTS IS '';
```

Let's take a look at some useful examples of the data dictionary in action.

DICTIONARY

The DICTIONARY view is a great starting point for any investigation of the data dictionary. If we DESCRIBE the view, we get the following:

```
DESC DICTIONARY;

Name                                Null     Type
----------------------------------- -------- ----------------------------
TABLE_NAME                                   VARCHAR2(30)
COMMENTS                                     VARCHAR2(4000)
```

There are just two columns in the DICTIONARY view, but note that the second column can potentially hold a great deal of information.

In our current installation of the Oracle database (using a container database), we're showing 3,228 entries in this view. You can run a simple query to list all of its contents in your own user account.

```
SELECT    TABLE_NAME, COMMENTS
FROM      DICTIONARY
ORDER BY TABLE_NAME;
```

The output is too much to list here, and it's generally the same here as it will be on your own Oracle database implementation, depending on which version you're using. You might want to run this query in your own user account and review its output. If you're looking for something specific, such as anything that addresses index objects, you might try a query like this:

```
SELECT    TABLE_NAME, COMMENTS
FROM      DICTIONARY
WHERE     UPPER(COMMENTS) LIKE '%INDEX%'
ORDER BY TABLE_NAME;
```

That query will locate anything in the DICTIONARY table that mentions "index" in the comments. The result will include the name of the data dictionary view that lists all of the indexes, the one that lists all of the columns upon which an index is based, and so on.

Then, if you locate a particular entry in the dictionary you want to know more about—for example, USER_DEPENDENCIES—you can run the following query to get comments on that particular view and its columns:

```
SELECT COLUMN_NAME, COMMENTS
FROM    ALL_COL_COMMENTS
WHERE   OWNER = 'SYS'
  AND   TABLE_NAME = 'USER_DEPENDENCIES';
```

Those queries should help to zero in on helpful information in the data dictionary.

Identifying a User's Owned Objects

There are a variety of data dictionary views from which you might gather data about your own user account's objects. Two views in particular are a good starting point: USER_CATALOG and USER_OBJECTS.

USER_CATALOG

The USER_CATALOG view displays a summary listing of tables, views, synonyms, and sequences owned by the user. See Figure 12-1 for a description of the view.

FIGURE 12-1

Description
of the USER_
CATALOG data
dictionary view

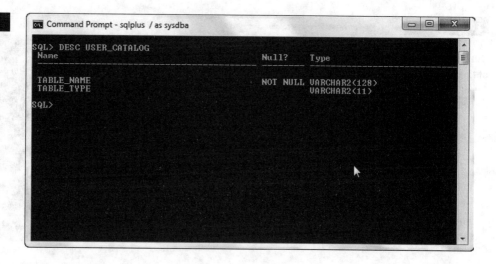

```
Command Prompt - sqlplus / as sysdba

SQL> DESC USER_CATALOG
 Name                                      Null?    Type
 ---------------------------------------- -------- ----------------------------
 TABLE_NAME                                NOT NULL VARCHAR2(128)
 TABLE_TYPE                                         VARCHAR2(11)

SQL>
```

Here's a sample query to get a quick overview of what a particular user account
may own:

```
SELECT TABLE_TYPE, COUNT(*)
FROM   USER_CATALOG
GROUP BY TABLE_TYPE;

TABLE_TYPE   COUNT(*)
-----------  ----------------------
SEQUENCE     21
TABLE        35
VIEW         2
SYNONYM      1
```

There are only two columns in USER_CATALOG; they are TABLE_TYPE and
TABLE_NAME, where TABLE_NAME is actually the name of the table, view,
sequence, or synonym object.

A synonym for USER_CATALOG is CAT.

**Be sure you have at least a
basic working knowledge of each of the data
dictionary views that track the basic objects
in the database—tables, views, sequences,**
**synonyms, sequences, constraints—and the
difference for each with regard to the USER_,
DBA_, and ALL_ prefixes.**

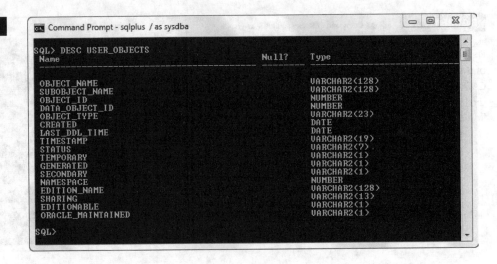

FIGURE 12-2

Description of the USER_OBJECTS data dictionary view

USER_OBJECTS

The USER_OBJECTS view contains information about all objects owned by the user. A synonym for USER_OBJECTS is OBJ. See Figure 12-2 for a description.

Inspecting Tables and Columns

The USER_TABLES table (synonym TABS) is helpful for inspecting table metadata, as is its companion USER_TAB_COLUMNS (synonym COLS). This section will look at USER_TAB_COLUMNS in particular.

Let's get column information for the table shown in Figure 12-3.

FIGURE 12-3

Diagram of the INVOICES table

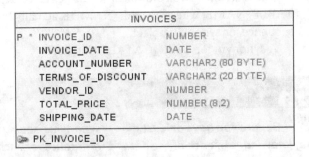

Here is a SELECT statement that will pull information from the data dictionary about the columns of INVOICES:

```
SELECT
  COLUMN_NAME,
  DECODE(
    DATA_TYPE,
    'DATE'    , DATA_TYPE ,
    'NUMBER'  , DATA_TYPE || DECODE(DATA_SCALE,
                NULL,
                NULL,
                '(' || DATA_PRECISION || ',' || DATA_SCALE || ')'),
    'VARCHAR2', DATA_TYPE || '(' || DATA_LENGTH || ')', NULL)
    DATA_TYPE
FROM    USER_TAB_COLUMNS
WHERE   TABLE_NAME = 'INVOICES';
```

Here's the output:

```
COLUMN_NAME                          DATA_TYPE
------------------------------------ ----------------------
INVOICE_ID                           NUMBER
INVOICE_DATE                         DATE
ACCOUNT_NUMBER                       VARCHAR2(80)
TERMS_OF_DISCOUNT                    VARCHAR2(20)
VENDOR_ID                            NUMBER
TOTAL_PRICE                          NUMBER(8,2)
SHIPPING_DATE                        DATE
```

Note: For the record, the preceding SELECT statement isn't totally perfect. It only addresses data types of DATE, NUMBER, and VARCHAR2, and in the event a NUMBER data type has a precision but no scale, the formatting won't come out looking quite right. The point here is to illustrate the sort of query you might want to do in order to extract data dictionary information from the database.

Compiling Views

One of the many useful tasks you can accomplish with the data dictionary is to check for the status of a view that you've created. Remember from Chapter 10 that a view is a named query based on a table and that after the view has been created, if the table is altered for any reason, you may have to recompile the view. For example, if a table's structure is altered, such as by a change to a column's data type or perhaps if a column is dropped from the table altogether (a column that is used by the view), then it may change the status of the view to INVALID.

You can check the data dictionary's USER_OBJECTS view to determine the status of any of your views, like this:

```
SELECT    STATUS, OBJECT_TYPE, OBJECT_NAME
FROM      USER_OBJECTS
WHERE     STATUS = 'INVALID'
ORDER BY OBJECT_NAME;
```

In our case, here is the output:

```
STATUS   OBJECT_TYPE         OBJECT_NAME
-------  ------------------  --------------------
INVALID VIEW                 EMP_PHONE_BOOK
INVALID VIEW                 VW_EMPLOYEES
```

So now we know we need to recompile these views. See Chapter 10 for details about how to recompile a view.

The data dictionary contains a lot of information about views, including the query upon which the view is based, which can be found in the USER_VIEWS view and its TEXT column. Here's a query on the data dictionary that asks for the query that was used to create the view VW_EMPLOYEES:

```
SELECT TEXT
FROM    USER_VIEWS
WHERE   VIEW_NAME = 'VW_EMPLOYEES';
```

Here is the output:

```
TEXT
--------------------------------------------------------------
SELECT EMPLOYEE_ID,
          LAST_NAME || ', ' || FIRST_NAME EMP_NAME,
          PRIMARY_PHONE
      FROM    EMPLOYEES
```

In summary, all the metadata for your database is stored in the data dictionary and is available for display and inspection.

Checking Privileges

Privileges are discussed in Chapter 14, when we discuss user access. For now, note that privileges can be inspected using the following views:

- **USER_SYS_PRIVS**   System privileges granted to the current user
- **USER_TAB_PRIVS**   Granted privileges on objects for which the user is the owner, grantor, or grantee
- **USER_ROLE_PRIVS**   Roles granted to the current user

- **DBA_SYS_PRIVS**   System privileges granted to users and roles
- **DBA_TAB_PRIVS**   All grants on objects in the database
- **DBA_ROLE_PRIVS**   Roles granted to users and roles
- **ROLE_SYS_PRIVS**   System privileges granted to roles
- **ROLE_TAB_PRIVS**   Table privileges granted to roles
- **SESSION_PRIVS**   Session privileges that the user currently has set

Each can be inspected by the user to determine the current state of privileges and roles. See Chapter 14 for a full discussion of user access, privileges, and roles, including sample queries of these data dictionary views.

Inspecting Constraints

The USER_CONSTRAINTS view is one of the more useful views. Here's a query you might run to check the current state of constraints on a table CRUISES:

```
SELECT CONSTRAINT_NAME, CONSTRAINT_TYPE, R_CONSTRAINT_NAME, STATUS
FROM   USER_CONSTRAINTS
WHERE  TABLE_NAME = 'CRUISES';
```

Here is an example of the output:

```
CONSTRAINT_NAME            CONSTRAINT_TYPE R_CONSTRAINT_NAME   STATUS
-------------------------- --------------- ------------------- -------
PK_CRUISE                  P                                   ENABLED
FK_CRUISES_CRUISE_TYPES    R               PK_CRUISE_TYPE_ID   ENABLED
FK_CRUISES_SHIPS           R               PK_SHIP             ENABLED
FK_CRUISES_EMPLOYEES       R               PK_EMPLOYEES        ENABLED
```

The output lists all the constraints on the CRUISES table. We're seeing four: one primary key and three foreign keys.

How do you know which constraint is a PRIMARY KEY and which is a FOREIGN KEY? The answer is by the CONSTRAINT_TYPE column. Some of the possible entries in the CONSTRAINT_TYPE column are

- P = PRIMARY KEY
- R = FOREIGN KEY (the R is for "referential integrity")
- U = UNIQUE
- C = CHECK or NOT NULL constraint

Note: There are additional constraints; these are beyond the scope of the exam. The DELETE_RULE column shows whether a foreign key constraint was created with ON DELETE CASCADE or ON DELETE SET NULL.

The SEARCH_CONDITION column is particularly useful for inspecting CHECK constraint criteria. Here's an example:

```
SELECT SEARCH_CONDITION
FROM   USER_CONSTRAINTS
WHERE  CONSTRAINT_NAME = 'CK_PROJECT_COST'
   AND CONSTRAINT_TYPE = 'C';

SEARCH_CONDITION
------------------------
PROJECT_COST < 1000000
```

Take note of the constraints with unexpected values for CONSTRAINT_TYPE: R for FOREIGN KEY, and C for NOT NULL as well as for CHECK.

The data dictionary provides additional information about constraints in the USER_CONS_COLUMNS data dictionary view. That view contains all the information about which columns in CRUISES are constrained and what the names are of the referenced tables and columns that make up the FOREIGN KEY constraints.

Finding Columns

Here is one type of data dictionary query I find useful:

```
SELECT TABLE_NAME
FROM   USER_TAB_COLUMNS
WHERE  COLUMN_NAME = 'EMPLOYEE_ID';
```

That's a query that looks for all tables in the current user account that happen to have a particular column—in this case, one named EMPLOYEE_ID. I find it helpful to search for particular column names across all tables or views in a given user account (i.e., a schema).

on the job

There are many helpful software tools available that will extract data dictionary information—such as comments—and provide a nice point-and-click interface to make it easy to navigate. That's all very helpful. But sometimes you'll find yourself in a situation where you simply don't have access to those tools. You might even realize that a particular application you're developing could benefit by programmatically accessing data dictionary information by way of SQL statements to draw data into your application for some project requirement. The point is that the data dictionary is a certification exam objective for a good reason; a comfortable understanding of its information and an ability to navigate it easily is important for any serious SQL professional.

CERTIFICATION SUMMARY

The data dictionary is a powerful tool. It consists of a series of tables and views that are automatically maintained by the Oracle system to document the state of every object in the database. Whenever a DDL statement is executed, the data dictionary is updated in some fashion.

The data dictionary is often referred to as metadata, a term that means "data about data." The data dictionary contains information about the database objects you create—their structures, names, status, and more.

The SYS account owns the data dictionary's base tables, which cannot be changed directly by users. Instead, all of the tables have views and, in some cases, public synonyms that have been created, and it is these the user accesses in a read-only mode.

Many of the data dictionary views follow a prefix pattern that indicates the contents of the view. Views with a prefix of USER_ show data about objects owned by the user accessing the view. ALL_ is the prefix for objects that exist anywhere in the database to which the current user has access. DBA_ is the prefix for views that show data about all objects in the database, regardless of who owns them or what privileges may be granted to them.

Information in the data dictionary includes the names of tables and their columns, including each column's data type, along with its precision, scale, and/or length where applicable. All of the database objects are listed in the data dictionary, including all tables, views, indexes, sequences, constraints, and more.

Views that have a prefix of V$ or some variation are dynamic performance views and show real-time database performance information. Oracle cannot guarantee the read consistency of these views, so it's recommended that for dynamic performance views you limit your access to single-table queries. If more complex queries and/or joins are required, you are advised to first copy data out of the views into your own temporary tables and then query those tables for better results and data integrity.

You can add comments to the entries in the data dictionary for your own tables and columns using the COMMENT statement. You cannot delete comments but instead update comments with a blank string.

The data dictionary can be used to perform a variety of useful tasks, such as obtaining information about time zones, determining whether a view requires recompilation, identifying any privileges that are currently granted, and much more.

TWO-MINUTE DRILL

Query Various Data Dictionary Views

- [ ] The data dictionary is made of tables that store data about the database.
- [ ] The data dictionary contains the metadata for your database.
- [ ] It contains information about tables, views, constraints, indexes, sequences, roles, privileges, and any and all other objects you might create in the database.
- [ ] It keeps track of all the users in the database and which user account owns which objects, who has privileges on which object, the status of each object, and more.
- [ ] Oracle automatically updates and maintains the data dictionary views with each DDL statement executed throughout the database.
- [ ] The data dictionary views that begin with the prefix USER_ contain information about objects owned by the user accessing the view.
- [ ] The ALL_ prefix indicates a data dictionary view that contains information about objects that might be owned by any user in the database but to which the accessing user has privileges.
- [ ] The DBA_ prefix is affixed to all views that contain data about all objects in the database.
- [ ] The V$ or GV$ prefix identifies views that are part of the set of dynamic performance tables and views, which show real-time performance data about the database.
- [ ] Most (but not all) of the data dictionary views are stored with comments that provide brief descriptions about each view and what it contains; many of the columns of the views also have comments.
- [ ] You can add comments of your own alongside the data dictionary record for your own objects that you've created.
- [ ] The COMMENT statement is how you store a comment in the data dictionary for any table you own and for its associated columns.
- [ ] The DICTIONARY view is a great starting point for finding what you might be looking for in the data dictionary.

- ☐ The USER_CATALOG view contains a summary of information about some of the major objects owned by your user account.
- ☐ The USER_OBJECTS view is similar to USER_CATALOG but with much more information.
- ☐ You can get a full listing from the data dictionary for your tables; their columns; and associated data types, lengths, precision, and scale.
- ☐ The status of objects is also stored; for example, the data dictionary flags views that are invalid and might need recompilation.
- ☐ All roles and privileges of all users on all objects are stored somewhere in the data dictionary.
- ☐ If you have the name of a column and aren't sure which table it might be part of, use the ALL_TAB_COLUMNS data dictionary view.

SELF TEST

The following questions will help you measure your understanding of the material presented in this chapter. Choose one correct answer for each question unless otherwise directed.

Query Various Data Dictionary Views

1. One place to get a master list of all the views that form the data dictionary is:
   A. DICTIONARY
   B. DATA_DICTIONARY
   C. CATALOG
   D. USER_CATALOG

2. You are tasked with querying the data dictionary view that lists only those sequences to which you currently have privileges but don't necessarily own. To do this, you log in to your own user account and query the data dictionary view called:
   A. ALL_SEQUENCES
   B. DBA_SEQUENCES
   C. USER_SEQUENCES
   D. USER_PRIV_SEQUENCES

3. Which of the following actions will *not* cause the contents of the data dictionary to be changed in some way?
   A. Create a new table
   B. Modify the data type of an existing column
   C. Execute a valid COMMENT statement
   D. None of the above

4. The data dictionary is owned by:
   A. PUBLIC
   B. SYS
   C. SYSTEM
   D. Each individual user

5. You can add your own comments to the data dictionary with the COMMENT statement using which of the following? (Choose two.)
   A. INDEX
   B. COLUMN
   C. SEQUENCE
   D. TABLE

6. You need to get information about columns in a table you do not own, nor do you have privileges to it. Which view can you query to get this information?

A. DBA_TAB_COLUMNS

B. ALL_TAB_COLUMNS

C. ALL_COLUMNS

D. Can't be done

7. Which among the following is considered an acceptable query with V$DATAFILE?

A. A join with two other objects in the data dictionary

B. A complex GROUP BY with multiple levels of aggregation

C. A query that displays rows from the table with no joins

D. All of the above

8. You are tasked with the job of adding a comment to the data dictionary to accompany the column PIER in the table MARINA. Which of the following will execute successfully?

A. COMMENT ON COLUMN (MARINA.PIER) IS 'Number of piers';

B. COMMENT ON COLUMN MARINA.PIER IS 'Number of piers';

C. COMMENT ON COLUMN MARINA(PIER) IS 'Number of piers';

D. COMMENT ON TABLE COLUMN MARINA.PIER IS 'Number of piers';

9. Now you have changed the purpose of the PIER column in the MARINA table and want to remove the comment you just created in the previous question. Which of the following statements will remove the comment?

A. COMMENT ON COLUMN MARINA.PIER DROP;

B. COMMENT ON COLUMN MARINA.PIER IS NULL;

C. COMMENT ON COLUMN MARINA.PIER SET UNUSED;

D. COMMENT ON COLUMN MARINA.PIER IS '';

10. When you're looking for a particular bit of data and you're not sure where in the data dictionary it might be, a good starting point is: (Choose the best answer.)

A. SELECT * FROM V$DATABASE;

B. SELECT * FROM GV_$START_HERE;

C. SELECT * FROM DICTIONARY;

D. SELECT * FROM V$RESERVED_WORDS;

11. The USER_CONSTRAINTS view in the data dictionary lists FOREIGN KEY constraints in the CONSTRAINT_TYPE column with which of the following single-letter abbreviations?

A. K

B. R

C. F

D. G

12. You are tasked to work with a view. The view's underlying table has been altered. What information can the data dictionary provide at this point? (Choose all correct answers.)
    A. The status of the view so that you can determine whether the view requires recompilation
    B. The current state of the table
    C. The query that was used to create the view
    D. The names of columns in the underlying table

13. The term *metadata* means:
    A. Data about data
    B. Global data that is accessible throughout the database
    C. Data that is automatically updated and maintained by the database system
    D. Distributed data

14. Which of the following data dictionary views does not have an OWNER column?
    A. USER_TABLES
    B. ALL_INDEXES
    C. DBA_CONS_COLUMNS
    D. All of the above

15. If an ALTER TABLE . . . DROP COLUMN statement is executed against an underlying table upon which a view is based, the status of that view in the data dictionary changes to:
    A. COMPILE
    B. INVALID
    C. ALTERED
    D. FLAG

SELF TEST ANSWERS

Query Various Data Dictionary Views

1. ☑ **A.** DICTIONARY. You can run the DESC DICTIONARY command to see the two columns that form DICTIONARY and then query it for additional information.

   ☒ **B, C,** and **D** are incorrect. There is no system view called DATA_DICTIONARY. CATALOG is also incorrect; there is a CATALOG view included with Oracle for backward compatibility with version 5, but Oracle officially discourages its use. On the other hand, there is a view in the data dictionary called USER_CATALOG; it's a recommended resource for finding information about tables, views, and other database objects the current user owns.

2. ☑ **A.** ALL_SEQUENCES will list any sequences in the database, regardless of owner, to which your account has been granted access.

   ☒ **B, C,** and **D** are incorrect. DBA_SEQUENCES will list all sequences in the database, regardless of who owns them and regardless of who has privileges on them. USER_SEQUENCES will list only those sequences that your user account currently owns. There is no view called USER_PRIV_SEQUENCES.

3. ☑ **D.** None of the above.

   ☒ **A, B,** and **C** are incorrect. All of these will enact some sort of change to the information in the data dictionary. Any DDL that creates or modifies objects will update the object listings in the data dictionary. The COMMENT statement adds to the data dictionary a comment about a particular object.

4. ☑ **B.** SYS is the owner of the data dictionary.

   ☒ **A, C,** and **D** are incorrect. Neither PUBLIC nor SYSTEM owns the data dictionary, although both are valid users in the system.

5. ☑ **B and D.** TABLE and COLUMN objects are supported by the COMMENT statement.

   ☒ **A and C** are incorrect. You cannot add comments of your own to the data dictionary for an INDEX or SEQUENCE object.

6. ☑ **A.** DBA_TAB_COLUMNS is the view that contains information about columns in tables, and because of the DBA_ prefix, you know it contains information about tables and columns that exist anywhere in the database, regardless of owner or privileges granted.

   ☒ **A, C,** and **D** are incorrect. ALL_TAB_COLUMNS would be correct if you were limiting your search to tables and columns to which you've been granted privileges because that is what the ALL_ prefix indicates. There is no ALL_COLUMNS view in the data dictionary.

7. ☑ **C.** The V\$ prefix indicates that V\$DATAFILE is a public synonym for a dynamic performance view, for which Oracle Corporation does not guarantee read consistency. Therefore, you are recommended to limit your direct access of V\$ objects to simple queries.
☒ **A, B,** and **D** are incorrect. Oracle Corporation officially advises against using any of the V\$ objects in complex queries and/or joins.

8. ☑ **B.** The correct syntax is to use the keywords COMMENT ON COLUMN, followed by the table name and column name, separated by a period, and the keyword IS, followed by the string.
☒ **A, C,** and **D** are incorrect. Parentheses are not part of the COMMENT statement. The keyword TABLE is used only when adding a comment to a table.

9. ☑ **D.** There really isn't a statement to explicitly drop a comment or delete it. The practice is to overwrite the old comment with an empty string.
☒ **A, B,** and **C** are incorrect. None of these options is a valid statement. They contain bits and pieces of valid reserved words from other statements but do not apply to COMMENT.

10. ☑ **C.** The DICTIONARY view summarizes the names of tables and views in the data dictionary, along with detailed comments about each one.
☒ **A, B,** and **D** are incorrect. The V\$DATABASE and V\$RESERVED_WORDS objects are valid public synonyms for data dictionary views, but these are part of the set of dynamic performance tables and not good for getting an overview of the dictionary as a starting point. There is no such object in the Oracle data dictionary called GV_\$START_HERE.

11. ☑ **B.** R is the answer. R stands for "referential integrity" and indicates the presence of a FOREIGN KEY constraint in the CONSTRAINT_TYPE column of the USER_CONSTRAINTS data dictionary view.
☒ **A, C,** and **D** are incorrect. It's not K or G. And you'd think it would be F, but it's not. R makes sense, though, when you think about it.

12. ☑ **A, B, C,** and **D.** The data dictionary can assist with all of the answers listed.
☒ None are incorrect.

13. ☑ **A.** Metadata is "data about data."
☒ **B, C** and **D** are incorrect.

14. ☑ **A.** USER_TABLES does not have or need an OWNER column since the view only presents a set of tables owned by the user accessing them.
☒ **B, C,** and **D** are incorrect. Even if you haven't looked in detail at these views, you can rely on the fact that views that start with ALL_ and DBA_ have a column showing OWNER information since they contain, by definition, objects owned by—potentially—more than one user.

15. ☑ **B.** It changes to INVALID. Recompiling the view could restore the status of the view to VALID.
☒ **A, C,** and **D** are incorrect.

13
Manipulating Large Data Sets

This chapter looks at features and operations that are useful for working with large groups of data. We cover two operations in particular. The first consists of additional features to the INSERT statement that enable you to use one INSERT statement to add multiple rows of data to a given table or to several tables, with and without conditional logic. Later in the chapter we'll cover the SQL statement MERGE, which is a powerful statement that enables you to combine the features of multiple Data Manipulation Language (DML) statements into a single SQL statement.

CERTIFICATION OBJECTIVE 13.01

Describe the Features of Multitable INSERTs

The multitable INSERT statement is a variation on the INSERT statement syntax you've already seen. A multitable INSERT statement repeats the INTO clause of the INSERT statement to insert data into more than one table. Each INTO clause applies to just one table, but by repeating the INTO clause, you can add data to multiple tables. The multitable INSERT must have a subquery to select rows for inserting.

Multitable INSERT statements can accomplish a variety of tasks, including the following:

- Query data from one table and insert the data into multiple tables with conditional logic, such as transforming data into a series of archive tables.

- Exchange data between two similar systems of different requirements— perhaps between a transaction-based application and a data warehouse optimized for analysis.

- Support logical archiving at any level of detail with logical decision points embedded in the INSERT statements.

- Integrate complex queries with GROUP BY, HAVING, set operators, and more, all while moving any number of rows dynamically, distributing output into multiple data targets, and programming logical decision points to control data distribution.

- Transform data that is stored in rows and levels into a cross-tabulation output, the type you would typically see in a spreadsheet application.

There are two general types of multitable INSERT statements: unconditional and conditional.

- Unconditional multitable INSERT statements process each of the INSERT statement's one or more INTO clauses, without condition, for all rows returned by the subquery.

- Conditional multitable INSERT statements use WHEN conditions before INTO clauses to determine whether the given INTO clause (or clauses) will execute for a given row returned by the subquery. In other words, for each row returned by the INSERT statement's subquery, each WHEN condition's expression is considered and evaluates to either a true or false condition. If true, the associated INTO clause (or clauses) will execute. If false, it will not. Finally, an optional ELSE clause can include an alternative INTO clause that can be executed if none of the WHEN conditions is true.

Let's look at the overall syntax for the multitable INSERT statement. First, we'll examine an unconditional multitable INSERT statement. The syntax repeats the INTO statement from one to many times as required.

```
INSERT ALL
   INTO tab1 VALUES (col_list1)
   INTO tab2 VALUES (col_list2)
   INTO tab3 VALUES (col_list3)
   . . .
subquery;
```

The unconditional multitable INSERT statement syntax just shown assumes the following:

- The keyword ALL is required in an unconditional multitable INSERT. Note, however, that while the presence of the keyword ALL is indicative of a multitable INSERT, it doesn't necessarily indicate the unconditional multitable INSERT, as you'll see in the next section.

- Following the keyword ALL, there must be at least one INTO clause.

- You can include multiple INTO clauses.

- Each INTO may have its own VALUES clause.

- Each VALUES list is optional; if omitted, the select list from the subquery will be used.

- The *subquery* is a SELECT statement that can stand alone.

The conditional multitable INSERT statement syntax is similar but adds the WHEN condition, like this:

```
INSERT option
   WHEN expression THEN
      INTO tab1 VALUES (col_list1)
   WHEN expression THEN
      INTO tab2 VALUES (col_list2)
   . . .
   ELSE
      INTO tab3 VALUES (col_list3)
subquery;
```

For each row returned by the subquery, each WHEN condition is evaluated and determined to be either true or false. If true, then the WHEN condition's associated set of one or more INTO clauses is executed; otherwise, processing skips over the INTO clauses to the next WHEN condition. If none of the WHEN conditions evaluates to true, the ELSE clause is processed, and its associated set of one or more INTO clauses is executed.

The conditional multitable INSERT statement syntax just shown is used as follows:

- The *option* is one of two keywords: ALL or FIRST.
- ALL is the default and may be omitted.
- FIRST is the alternative keyword; it indicates that the only set of INTO clauses that will execute are those that follow the first WHEN clause that evaluates to true.
- You can include multiple WHEN conditions.
- Each WHEN condition is followed by one or more INTO clauses.
- Each INTO may have its own VALUES clause; if omitted, the subquery's select list must match the number and data types of the INTO table's columns.
- Each *expression* evaluates to true or false and should involve one or more columns from the subquery.
- The *tab* and *col_list* are the components of the INSERT statement that will execute if the WHEN expression evaluates to true.
- The optional ELSE . . . INTO clause, if included, must be last.
- The *subquery* is required and must be a valid SELECT statement.

A conditional multitable INSERT statement will process each row returned by the subquery.

The multitable INSERT statement always uses a subquery. As you know, a subquery may return anywhere from zero to many rows. For each row returned by a subquery, processing does a pass through the set of WHILE ... INTO clauses. But the way it processes the WHILE ... INTO clauses differs based on whether the keyword ALL or FIRST is used.

If the keyword ALL is specified, then all the WHEN conditions will be evaluated for each row returned by the subquery. For each WHEN condition that evaluates to true, the corresponding INTO clause (or clauses) that follow the WHEN will be executed. For each WHEN condition that evaluates to false, the corresponding INTO clause (or clauses) will not be executed. All the WHEN conditions are evaluated if the keyword ALL is specified at the beginning of the multitable INSERT statement.

On the other hand, if the keyword FIRST is used, then for each row returned by the subquery, WHEN conditions are evaluated until the first true condition is encountered. As soon as a WHEN condition is determined to be true, the corresponding set of one or more INTO clauses that follows the WHEN will be executed. Processing will then skip over the remaining WHEN conditions for that row of the subquery.

In either situation—INSERT FIRST or INSERT ALL—if no WHEN condition was found to be true and if the optional ELSE clause is present, then the ELSE clause's INTO clause will be executed for the row. Then processing moves on to the next row returned by the subquery.

Note that for the conditional multitable INSERT statement—which is to say any multitable INSERT with a WHEN condition—ALL is the default keyword. If no WHEN condition is used, then the multitable INSERT is unconditional, and the ALL keyword must be present.

In other words, you may not omit the keyword in an unconditional multitable INSERT, like this:

```
INSERT
  INTO ... VALUES ...
  INTO ... VALUES ...
  subquery;
```

The preceding statement shows incorrect syntax since it omits the ALL option and yet has no WHEN condition. Therefore, it is syntactically incorrect. However, you may do something like this:

```
INSERT ALL
   INTO ... VALUES ...
   INTO ... VALUES ...
   subquery;
```

The preceding unconditional multitable INSERT correctly shows the ALL keyword.

The conditional multitable INSERT allows you to omit the keyword, like this:

```
INSERT
   WHEN ... THEN
      INTO ... VALUES ...
   WHEN ... THEN
      INTO ... VALUES ...
   subquery;
```

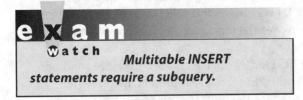

Multitable INSERT statements require a subquery.

The default keyword is ALL. In all forms of the multitable INSERT, the subquery is required; it is not optional. And as is always the case with any INSERT that uses a subquery, the INSERT statement will execute once for each row returned by the subquery.

Note that if any one INTO clause fails with an execution error for any one row returned by the subquery, then the entire statement fails for all rows of the subquery, and no data change results.

Use the Following Types of Multitable INSERTS: Unconditional and Conditional

Let's look at some examples of the multitable INSERT statement in action. First up are unconditional multitable INSERTs, followed by conditional examples. Then we'll consider the unique and useful approach to perform the equivalent of a spreadsheet pivot, a common use of the multitable INSERT.

Unconditional

As we discussed, the unconditional multitable INSERT statement omits conditional logic, in other words, the WHEN clause. For example, consider the CRUISE_ORDERS table, as shown in Figure 13-1.

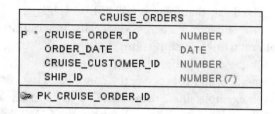

Diagram for the
CRUISE_ORDERS
table

In addition to the CRUISE_ORDERS table, our example uses three identically structured tables named CO_2018, CO_ELCARO, and CO_ARCHIVED, each with the same columns as the table CRUISE_ORDERS. The three identically structured tables are used for archiving and analyzing the CRUISE_ORDERS table data.

Here is an example of a valid SQL statement that queries the CRUISE_ORDERS table and inserts the output into each of our three archive tables (line numbers added):

```
01   INSERT ALL
02       INTO CO_2018      (CRUISE_ORDER_ID, ORDER_DATE,
03                          CRUISE_CUSTOMER_ID, SHIP_ID)
04       VALUES            (CRUISE_ORDER_ID, ORDER_DATE,
05                          CRUISE_CUSTOMER_ID, SHIP_ID)
06       INTO CO_ELCARO    (CRUISE_ORDER_ID, ORDER_DATE,
07                          CRUISE_CUSTOMER_ID, SHIP_ID)
08       VALUES            (CRUISE_ORDER_ID, ORDER_DATE,
09                          CRUISE_CUSTOMER_ID, SHIP_ID)
10       INTO CO_ARCHIVED  (CRUISE_ORDER_ID, ORDER_DATE,
11                          CRUISE_CUSTOMER_ID, SHIP_ID)
12       VALUES            (CRUISE_ORDER_ID, ORDER_DATE,
13                          CRUISE_CUSTOMER_ID, SHIP_ID)
14       SELECT CRUISE_ORDER_ID, ORDER_DATE, CRUISE_CUSTOMER_ID, SHIP_ID
15       FROM   CRUISE_ORDERS;
```

Note that we have three INTO clauses here. If the subquery returns, for example, three rows, then the result of this INSERT statement will be to insert nine rows: three into the CO_2018 table (line 2), three into the CO_ELCARO table (line 6), and three into the CO_ARCHIVED table (line 10).

As we see in the preceding example, the unconditional INSERT statement uses the keyword ALL (line 1), followed by one or more INTO clauses (lines 2, 6, and 10), each of which specifies a table and the columns into which we are inserting data, followed by the VALUES list.

The VALUES list can specify expressions found in the subquery's select list. In our example, in line 4 we specify CRUISE_ORDER_ID as the first expression in the VALUES list to be inserted into the CO_2018 table. This corresponds to the CRUISE_ORDER_ID column in the subquery select list in line 14. The other

VALUES lists that refer to CRUISE_ORDER_ID (line 8 and line 12) are specifying that same column. Each VALUES list in a multitable INSERT can specify any column names or expressions that are in the subquery select list.

On the other hand, the column references within each INTO list (each starting at lines 2, 6, and 10) specify the columns of the tables named for the INTO clause. In our example, line 2 names the CO_2018 table, and the INTO list that follows on line 2 and line 3 specifies columns in the CO_2018 table.

You'll recall that in a standard INSERT statement, the list of values in the VALUES expression list must match in number and in data type (or be able to be automatically converted to a matching data type) with the columns specified in the INTO clause. The same is true here for each pair of INTO and VALUES lists.

Each VALUES expression list may use any complex expression in specifying the value to be inserted into its corresponding table and column. Here's an example:

```
01    INSERT ALL
02         INTO CO_2018      (CRUISE_ORDER_ID, ORDER_DATE,
03                            CRUISE_CUSTOMER_ID, SHIP_ID)
04         VALUES            (CRUISE_ORDER_ID, SYSDATE, 14, 1)
05         INTO CO_ELCARO    (CRUISE_ORDER_ID, ORDER_DATE,
06                            CRUISE_CUSTOMER_ID, SHIP_ID)
07         VALUES            (CRUISE_ORDER_ID, ORDER_DATE+30, 15, 1)
08         INTO CO_ARCHIVED  (CRUISE_ORDER_ID, ORDER_DATE,
09                            CRUISE_CUSTOMER_ID, SHIP_ID)
10         VALUES            (CRUISE_ORDER_ID, ORDER_DATE,
11                            CRUISE_CUSTOMER_ID, SHIP_ID)
12      SELECT CRUISE_ORDER_ID, ORDER_DATE, CRUISE_CUSTOMER_ID, SHIP_ID
13      FROM   CRUISE_ORDERS;
```

In this example, we are choosing to insert some values that are different from what the subquery is returning. For the CO_2018 table, in lines 2 through 4, we are defining the ORDER_DATE value for all rows to be SYSDATE, the CRUISE_CUSTOMER_ID value to be the literal value of 14, and the SHIP_ID value to be a literal value of 1. For the CO_ELCARO table, in lines 5 through 7, we are giving each row an ORDER_DATE value that is 30 days beyond the incoming value in the subquery, and we're assigning the number 15 to each CRUISE_CUSTOMER_ID and assigning 1 to each SHIP_ID. For the CO_ARCHIVED table, in lines 8 through 11, we are choosing to pass through values from the subquery unchanged.

As the example shows, the VALUES list can specify column names and expressions from the subquery's select list, but may also define any valid SQL expression. The INTO column list must specify columns in the table into which the INTO statement is inserting data.

If the VALUES list is omitted, the columns of the subquery become the de facto VALUES list and therefore must match the columns of the corresponding INTO clause. By "match," we mean that they must match in number and in data type, or be of such data types that an automatic data type conversion may be performed.

If there is no column list in the INTO clause, the subquery's select list must match the columns in the table of the INTO clause.

Conditional

Conditional multitable INSERT statements use conditional logic to determine which INTO clause or clauses to process. Each row that is returned by the subquery is processed through a series of one or more WHEN conditions. Each WHEN condition is followed by a set of one or more INTO clauses.

For each row returned by the subquery, each WHEN condition is evaluated to be either true or false. If true, the following set of one or more INTO clauses is executed. If false, the set of one or more INTO clauses is skipped, and the next WHEN condition is evaluated.

An ELSE clause may optionally be included in the conditional multitable INSERT statement. If present, it must define its own set of one or more INTO clauses, and the ELSE/INTO clauses must follow all WHEN conditions/INTO clause combinations. If all WHEN conditions are skipped for any given row, then the ELSE clause's INTO will be processed. Otherwise, it will be skipped for that row.

Each row returned by the subquery is processed according to these rules we have just reviewed.

Let's look again at our table INVOICES and the archive table INVOICES_ARCHIVED, in which we stored invoice records that are more than a year old. See Figure 13-1 for the INVOICES table, and see Figure 13-2 for the INVOICES_ARCHIVED table.

FIGURE 13-2	INVOICES_ARCHIVED	
	INVOICE_ID	NUMBER
Diagram for	INVOICE_DATE	DATE
the INVOICES_	ACCOUNT_NUMBER	VARCHAR2 (80 BYTE)
ARCHIVED table	TERMS_OF_DISCOUNT	VARCHAR2 (20 BYTE)
	VENDOR_ID	NUMBER
	TOTAL_PRICE	NUMBER (8,2)
	SHIPPING_DATE	DATE

FIGURE 13-3

Diagram for the
WO_INV table

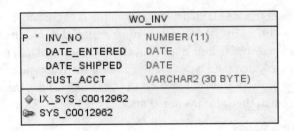

Let's say our organization is engaged in a merger and we are tasked with the job of integrating data from another application. The newly acquired company has provided us with the table WO_INV, as shown in Figure 13-3.

We need to create an INSERT statement that will

- Pull data from the WO_INV table
- Insert WO_INV's invoice information from within the past year into our INVOICES table
- Insert WO_INV's invoice information that is more than a year old into our INVOICES_ARCHIVED table

It's a perfect task for a conditional multitable INSERT statement, as follows:

```
01    INSERT FIRST
02      WHEN (DATE_SHIPPED < (ADD_MONTHS(SYSDATE,-12))) THEN
03        INTO INVOICES_ARCHIVED (INVOICE_ID, INVOICE_DATE,
04                                    SHIPPING_DATE, ACCOUNT_NUMBER)
05        VALUES (INV_NO, DATE_ENTERED, DATE_SHIPPED, CUST_ACCT)
06      ELSE
07        INTO INVOICES (INVOICE_ID, INVOICE_DATE,
08                                    SHIPPING_DATE, ACCOUNT_NUMBER)
09        VALUES (INV_NO, DATE_ENTERED, DATE_SHIPPED, CUST_ACCT)
10      SELECT INV_NO, DATE_ENTERED, DATE_SHIPPED, CUST_ACCT
11      FROM  WO_INV;
```

In this statement, we see the following:

- A subquery on lines 10 through 11. Note the subquery includes a column DATE_SHIPPED.
- Line 2 compares the DATE_SHIPPED value in a WHEN condition.

■ If line 2 evaluates to true for a given row from the subquery, the INSERT statement will take that row's data and insert it into the INVOICES_ ARCHIVED table, as specified on line 3. The columns in the INVOICES_ ARCHIVED table are specified in lines 3 and 4.

■ Line 5 defines the values from the subquery that will be inserted if the WHEN clause on line 2 is true. For example, the subquery's column INV_NO (line 5) will be inserted into the target table's column INVOICE_ID (line 3).

■ Line 6 is an ELSE clause that will execute for each row that does not satisfy the WHEN condition in line 2.

In the example we just reviewed, there was one WHEN condition and one ELSE condition. Let's look at an example with multiple WHEN conditions. Let's say you had three archive tables, named INVOICES_THRU_2019, INVOICES_ THRU_2018, and INVOICES_THRU_2017, and wanted to insert rows from the incoming table into each archived table based on the year of the DATE_SHIPPED value. Note that each table is not mutually exclusive; for example, the INVOICES_ THRU_2019 table will contain invoices from 2019, 2018, and 2017, as well as earlier. One row returned by the subquery might be inserted into all three tables.

To accomplish this task, you could use the following INSERT statement:

```
01    INSERT
02      WHEN (TO_CHAR(DATE_SHIPPED,'RRRR') <= '2019') THEN
03        INTO INVOICES_THRU_2019 (INVOICE_ID, INVOICE_DATE,
04                                  SHIPPING_DATE, ACCOUNT_NUMBER)
05        VALUES (INV_NO, DATE_ENTERED, DATE_SHIPPED, CUST_ACCT)
06      WHEN (TO_CHAR(DATE_SHIPPED,'RRRR') <= '2018') THEN
07        INTO INVOICES_THRU_2018 (INVOICE_ID, INVOICE_DATE,
08                                  SHIPPING_DATE, ACCOUNT_NUMBER)
09        VALUES (INV_NO, DATE_ENTERED, DATE_SHIPPED, CUST_ACCT)
10      WHEN (TO_CHAR(DATE_SHIPPED,'RRRR') <= '2017') THEN
11        INTO INVOICES_THRU_2017 (INVOICE_ID, INVOICE_DATE,
12                                  SHIPPING_DATE, ACCOUNT_NUMBER)
13        VALUES (INV_NO, DATE_ENTERED, DATE_SHIPPED, CUST_ACCT)
14      SELECT INV_NO, DATE_ENTERED, DATE_SHIPPED, CUST_ACCT
15      FROM    WO_INV;
```

Notice that there is no keyword FIRST or ALL in this example. Therefore, the statement will default to ALL. Since there are three WHEN conditions, each with an associated INTO clause, each and every WHEN condition that evaluates to true will execute. Also, this example omits the ELSE clause, so if any row from the subquery does not satisfy a WHEN condition, then no action will be taken for that particular row returned by the subquery.

After any WHEN condition, you may include more than one INTO clause. For example, let's say we have a table INVOICES_CLOSED that takes any invoice rows that shipped prior to 2018. We might modify our example like this:

```
01    INSERT
02       WHEN (TO_CHAR(DATE_SHIPPED,'RRRR') <= '2019') THEN
03          INTO INVOICES_THRU_2019 (INVOICE_ID, INVOICE_DATE,
04                                   SHIPPING_DATE, ACCOUNT_NUMBER)
05          VALUES (INV_NO, DATE_ENTERED, DATE_SHIPPED, CUST_ACCT)
06       WHEN (TO_CHAR(DATE_SHIPPED,'RRRR') <= '2018') THEN
07          INTO INVOICES_THRU_2018 (INVOICE_ID, INVOICE_DATE,
08                                   SHIPPING_DATE, ACCOUNT_NUMBER)
09          VALUES (INV_NO, DATE_ENTERED, DATE_SHIPPED, CUST_ACCT)
10          INTO INVOICES_CLOSED   (INVOICE_ID, INVOICE_DATE,
11                                   SHIPPING_DATE, ACCOUNT_NUMBER)
12          VALUES (INV_NO, DATE_ENTERED, DATE_SHIPPED, CUST_ACCT)
13       WHEN (TO_CHAR(DATE_SHIPPED,'RRRR') <= '2017') THEN
14          INTO INVOICES_THRU_2017 (INVOICE_ID, INVOICE_DATE,
15                                   SHIPPING_DATE, ACCOUNT_NUMBER)
16          VALUES (INV_NO, DATE_ENTERED, DATE_SHIPPED, CUST_ACCT)
17       SELECT INV_NO, DATE_ENTERED, DATE_SHIPPED, CUST_ACCT
18       FROM   WO_INV;
```

Note the new INTO clause, lines 10 through 12. This INTO is subject to the WHEN condition in line 6. In other words, if DATE_SHIPPED is in the year 2018 or before, the INSERT statement will add the candidate row to both the INVOICES_THRU_2018 table and the INVOICES_CLOSED table. One WHEN condition is the gateway to both INTO clauses.

What this example shows us is that any WHEN condition can have multiple INTO clauses that follow it. If the WHEN condition evaluates to true, all of its INTO clauses will execute. If the WHEN condition evaluates to false, execution will skip over the INTO clauses and move on directly to either the next WHEN condition, an ELSE if it is present, or the next row in the subquery.

The INSERT ALL will evaluate each and every WHEN condition and process all INTO clauses for all WHEN conditions that evaluate to true. Therefore, the INSERT ALL may result in a single row being added to more than one table.

The INSERT FIRST will evaluate every WHEN condition until one of them evaluates to true. It will then process that WHEN condition's INTO and skip the remaining WHEN conditions. The INSERT FIRST will process only zero or one

WHEN condition; however, it may also result in a single row being added to more than one table, but only if the first true WHEN condition has more than one INTO clause.

Table aliases in the subquery of a multitable INSERT are not recognized in the rest of the INSERT. For example, you can't reference them from within a WHEN condition or INTO statement. If a subquery's column reference depends on a table alias, be sure to use a column alias for the column and then reference the column alias if you want to reference that column from elsewhere within the INSERT statement—outside of the subquery. For example, see Figure 13-4.

In a query that queries rows from the POSITIONS table and conditionally inserts them into the SALARY_CHART table, we cannot use this query:

```
01    INSERT
02       WHEN (B.MAX_SALARY - A.MAX_SALARY < 10000) THEN
03       INTO SALARY_CHART (EMP_TITLE, SUPERIOR,
04                             EMP_INCOME, SUP_INCOME)
05       VALUES            (A.POSITION, B.POSITION,
06                           A.MAX_SALARY, B.MAX_SALARY)
07    SELECT A.POSITION,
08           B.POSITION,
09           A.MAX_SALARY,
10           B.MAX_SALARY
11    FROM   POSITIONS A JOIN POSITIONS B
12      ON   A.REPORTS_TO = B.POSITION_ID
13    WHERE  A.MAX_SALARY > 100000;
```

FIGURE 13-4

Diagram of the POSITIONS and SALARY_CHART tables

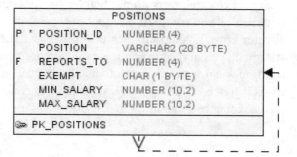

SALARY_CHART	
ORG_ID	NUMBER (7)
EMP_TITLE	VARCHAR2 (30 BYTE)
EMP_INCOME	NUMBER (10,2)
SUPERIOR	VARCHAR2 (30 BYTE)
SUP_INCOME	NUMBER (10,2)

POSITIONS		
P *	POSITION_ID	NUMBER (4)
	POSITION	VARCHAR2 (20 BYTE)
F	REPORTS_TO	NUMBER (4)
	EXEMPT	CHAR (1 BYTE)
	MIN_SALARY	NUMBER (10,2)
	MAX_SALARY	NUMBER (10,2)
PK_POSITIONS		

This statement will not work. Here is the result:

```
Error at Command Line:6 Column:35
Error report:
SQL Error: ORA-00904: "B"."MAX_SALARY": invalid identifier
00904. 00000 -  "%s: invalid identifier"
```

Notice how the subquery is a self-join and uses table aliases to identify each table and column reference. These table aliases are perfectly fine in the subquery but are not recognized beyond the subquery. In other words, the attempts to reference each table alias from within the WHEN condition or VALUES clause are invalid.

So, what do we do? The solution is to specify a column alias to any column names within the subquery that use a table alias and then reference the column alias from the rest of the conditional INSERT statement, like we do in the following lines 5 and 6:

```
01   INSERT
02     WHEN (BOSS_SALARY - EMPLOYEE_SALARY < 10000) THEN
03     INTO SALARY_CHART (EMP_TITLE, SUPERIOR, EMP_INCOME,      SUP_INCOME)
04     VALUES            (EMPLOYEE,  BOSS,     EMPLOYEE_SALARY, BOSS_SALARY)
05   SELECT A.POSITION   EMPLOYEE,
06          B.POSITION   BOSS,
07          A.MAX_SALARY EMPLOYEE_SALARY,
08          B.MAX_SALARY BOSS_SALARY
09   FROM   POSITIONS A JOIN POSITIONS B
10     ON   A.REPORTS_TO = B.POSITION_ID
11   WHERE  A.MAX_SALARY > 100000;
```

Note that this version has done more than is required; it applies column aliases to each column in the subquery and then references those column aliases from the WHEN and VALUES clauses. We only needed column aliases on A.POSITION and B.POSITION in lines 5 and 6, so we can reference the column aliases in line 4. Either way, this version of the conditional INSERT is syntactically correct.

You cannot execute a multitable INSERT on a view; it can be used only with a table.

Sequence generators do not behave consistently in a multitable INSERT statement. If you try to use a sequence generator within the subquery, you'll get a syntax error. If you try to include one within the expression list of the INTO statement, you may or may not get the functionality you want—the NEXTVAL function will not advance as you might expect. The reason is that a multitable insert is treated as a single SQL statement. Therefore, if you reference NEXTVAL with a sequence generator, Oracle's documentation warns that NEXTVAL will be incremented once in accordance with the sequence generator's parameters and stay that way for the duration of a pass through the multitable insert. In other words, a conditional INSERT with a single INTO, one that invokes a single sequence generator once with a NEXTVAL, will increment the sequence once for each row returned by the subquery—regardless of whether the WHEN condition is true. Consider this example:

```
01    INSERT
02        WHEN (TO_CHAR(DATE_ENTERED,'RRRR') <= '2019') THEN
03          INTO INVOICES_ARCHIVED (INVOICE_ID, INVOICE_DATE)
04          VALUES (SEQ_INV_NUM.NEXTVAL, DATE_ENTERED)
05        SELECT INV_NO, DATE_ENTERED FROM   WO_INV;
```

e x a m

ⓦ**a t c h**
Remember, a table alias defined in a subquery of a multitable INSERT is not recognized throughout the rest of the INSERT statement. Also, if a multitable INSERT statement fails for any reason, the entire statement is rolled back, and no rows are inserted in any of the tables.

The sequence generator in line 4 will increment for each row returned by the subquery, regardless of whether the WHEN condition is true. For this example, assume the sequence generator has just been created and has never been used and that it has the default settings of an initial value of 1 and an increment of 1. Given that, if the subquery returns ten rows and if, for instance, the final row alone causes the WHEN condition in line 2 to be true, then the one row inserted into the INVOICES_ARCHIVED table will be assigned a value of 10 for the INVOICE_ID column.

If this statement contained additional calls to the same sequence generator in additional INTO clauses, they would not cause the sequence generator to increment. The sequence generator increments with each row of the subquery returned—no more, no less—regardless of additional calls to NEXTVAL.

Oracle's documentation warns that "you cannot specify a sequence in any part of a multitable insert statement." The only place you'll get the syntax error is in the subquery, but know that attempts to invoke a sequence generator from the WHEN or INTO clause of the INSERT may produce undesirable results.

Using Multitable INSERT to Perform a Pivot

You can use a conditional multitable INSERT statement to transform data from a spreadsheet structure to a rows-and-columns structure. This section describes the technique.

First, let's start with the following data listing:

```
ROOM_TYPE              OCEAN             BALCONY            NO_WINDOW
-------------------    ----------------  ---------------    ---------
ROYAL                  1745              1635
SKYLOFT                722               722
PRESIDENTIAL           1142              1142               1142
LARGE                  225                                  211
STANDARD               217               554                586
```

This is the sort of data you might find in a typical spreadsheet display. Let's say this spreadsheet has been stored in an external table. Figure 13-5 shows the table's structure.

Next, you're given the task of moving this data into the table, as shown in Figure 13-6.

This isn't a straightforward row-for-row insert with a subquery. This data must be transformed so that each column from the spreadsheet is transformed into an individual row in the new table.

The following query will accomplish the task:

```
01   INSERT ALL
02     WHEN OCEAN IS NOT NULL THEN
03        INTO SHIP_CABIN_STATISTICS (ROOM_TYPE, WINDOW_TYPE, SQ_FT)
04        VALUES (ROOM_TYPE, 'OCEAN', OCEAN)
05     WHEN BALCONY IS NOT NULL THEN
06        INTO SHIP_CABIN_STATISTICS (ROOM_TYPE, WINDOW_TYPE, SQ_FT)
07        VALUES (ROOM_TYPE, 'BALCONY', BALCONY)
08     WHEN NO_WINDOW IS NOT NULL THEN
09        INTO SHIP_CABIN_STATISTICS (ROOM_TYPE, WINDOW_TYPE, SQ_FT)
10        VALUES (ROOM_TYPE, 'NO WINDOW', NO_WINDOW)
11   SELECT ROWNUM RN, ROOM_TYPE, OCEAN, BALCONY, NO_WINDOW
12     FROM SHIP_CABIN_GRID;
```

FIGURE 13-5

Diagram of the
SHIP_CABIN_
GRID table

SHIP_CABIN_GRID	
ROOM_TYPE	VARCHAR2 (20 BYTE)
OCEAN	NUMBER
BALCONY	NUMBER
NO_WINDOW	NUMBER

FIGURE 13-6

Diagram of the
SHIP_CABIN_
STATISTICS table

SHIP_CABIN_STATISTICS	
SC_ID	NUMBER (7)
ROOM_TYPE	VARCHAR2 (20 BYTE)
WINDOW_TYPE	VARCHAR2 (10 BYTE)
SQ_FT	NUMBER (8)

Note how each row of the subquery is considered three times. For a given row returned by the subquery, each of three columns of the row is individually considered. If any one of the three columns OCEAN, BALCONY, and NO_WINDOW is not NULL, then a row is inserted into the target table. It's possible that some individual rows returned by the subquery will result in three new rows being added to the target table SHIP_CABIN_STATISTICS.

Let's take a look at the results:

```
SELECT    ROOM_TYPE, WINDOW_TYPE, SQ_FT
FROM      SHIP_CABIN_STATISTICS
ORDER BY ROOM_TYPE, WINDOW_TYPE;


ROOM_TYPE                WINDOW_TYPE SQ_FT
-------------------- ----------- ---------------------
LARGE                    NO WINDOW   211
LARGE                    OCEAN       225
PRESIDENTIAL             BALCONY     1142
PRESIDENTIAL             NO WINDOW   1142
PRESIDENTIAL             OCEAN       1142
ROYAL                    BALCONY     1635
ROYAL                    OCEAN       1745
SKYLOFT                  BALCONY     722
SKYLOFT                  OCEAN       722
STANDARD                 BALCONY     554
STANDARD                 NO WINDOW   586
STANDARD                 OCEAN       217
```

In this example, the conditional multitable INSERT transformed incoming data from a spreadsheet summary style into a row-by-row structure, all within a single SQL statement. In this way, the conditional multitable INSERT statement "pivots" the data by changing columns into rows.

on the job

Note that this pivot technique is different from SQL operations that use the keyword PIVOT or UNPIVOT. What we've described here is a technique that uses the conditional multitable INSERT to pivot data. The keyword PIVOT, while somewhat similar in function, is a separate feature. Note that Oracle's published material, including documents published in connection SQL certification exams, have described this multitable INSERT style as a pivot and makes a distinction between this pivot approach and the PIVOT keyword.

CERTIFICATION OBJECTIVE 13.02

Merge Rows into a Table

The MERGE statement is a SQL DML statement that can combine the functionality of INSERT, UPDATE, and DELETE, all into a single SQL statement. There isn't anything you can do with MERGE that you cannot already do with some combination of those three DML statements. However, if it's possible to use MERGE as an alternative to executing two or more DML statements, then MERGE is preferable since it combines multiple DML actions into a single SQL statement, resulting in a single pass through the database. In other words, it will perform more efficiently. In many situations, such as applications built with distributed architectures, MERGE may be an invaluable weapon in your arsenal to build optimally efficient professional applications.

The syntax of MERGE follows:

```
01    MERGE INTO table
02    USING table | subquery
03    ON condition
04    WHEN MATCHED THEN UPDATE SET col = expression | DEFAULT
05        where_clause
06        DELETE where_clause
07    WHEN NOT MATCHED THEN INSERT (col, col2)
08        VALUES (expr1, expr2 | DEFAULT)
09        where_clause
10    WHERE condition;
```

Note the following:

- **Line 1** INTO specifies the target into which you are either inserting or updating rows; it can be a table or an updatable view. This line is required.

- **Line 2** USING identifies the source of the data, which can be a table, view, or subquery. This line is required.

- **Line 3** The ON condition for MERGE behaves essentially like a WHERE clause. It determines how to compare each row in the USING data source with each row in the MERGE INTO data target. The ON condition can use Boolean operators and expressions to form complex comparisons. In practice, the ON condition is often limited to comparing primary key values, but this is not required. This line is required.

FIGURE 13-7

Diagram of the
WWA_INVOICES
table

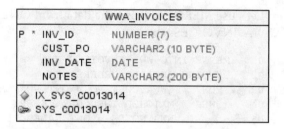

WWA_INVOICES		
P * INV_ID	NUMBER (7)	
CUST_PO	VARCHAR2 (10 BYTE)	
INV_DATE	DATE	
NOTES	VARCHAR2 (200 BYTE)	
◇ IX_SYS_C0013014		
⌷ SYS_C0013014		

- **Lines 4 through 6** These lines are considered the "update clause" and identify the logic by which the MERGE will update target rows; it cannot update a column in the ON condition.

- **Lines 7 through 9** These lines are considered the "insert clause" and identify the logic by which the MERGE will insert rows into the target table.

As you can see, it's an involved statement. Let's look at an example in action. Let's say you are responsible for an application that uses the WWA_INVOICES table (see Figure 13-7) and you have been tasked to bring in data from an outside table, ONTARIO_ORDERS (see Figure 13-8).

The data listing for the WWA_INVOICES table follows:

```
INV_ID                         CUST_PO    INV_DATE             NOTES
------------------------------ ---------- -------------------- -----
10                             WWA-200    17-DEC-19
20                             WWA-001    23-DEC-19
```

The data listing for the ONTARIO_ORDERS table follows:

```
ORDER_NUM                      PO_NUM                SALES_REP
------------------------------ --------------------- --------------------
882                            WWA-001               C. Nelson
883                            WWA-017               J. Metelsky
884                            NBC-201               D. Knight
```

FIGURE 13-8

Diagram of
the ONTARIO_
ORDERS table

ONTARIO_ORDERS		
P * ORDER_NUM	NUMBER (11)	
PO_NUM	VARCHAR2 (20 BYTE)	
SALES_REP	VARCHAR2 (20 BYTE)	
◇ IX_SYS_C0013015		
⌷ SYS_C0013015		

Let's use MERGE to bring the data from ONTARIO_ORDERS into the WWA_INVOICES table.

```
01   MERGE INTO WWA_INVOICES WWA
02     USING ONTARIO_ORDERS ONT
03     ON    (WWA.CUST_PO = ONT.PO_NUM)
04     WHEN  MATCHED THEN UPDATE SET
05           WWA.NOTES = ONT.SALES_REP
06     WHEN  NOT MATCHED THEN INSERT
07           (WWA.INV_ID, WWA.CUST_PO, WWA.INV_DATE, WWA.NOTES)
08           VALUES
09           (SEQ_INV_ID.NEXTVAL,
10                       ONT.PO_NUM, SYSDATE, ONT.SALES_REP)
11     WHERE SUBSTR(ONT.PO_NUM,1,3) <> 'NBC';
```

The preceding MERGE statement includes the following features:

- **Line 1**   Here we specify that we are going to merge rows into the table WWA_INVOICES. Also, we assign a table alias WWA to the table WWA_INVOICES.
- **Line 2**   Here we specify the ONTARIO_ORDERS table as the data source and give that table an alias of ONT.
- **Line 3**   Here we define the ON condition, indicating that the columns CUST_PO and PO_NUM are where the common information exists that will "join" the rows logically in order to associate them with each other for the merge.
- **Lines 4 through 5**   These lines are the "update clause."
- **Lines 6 through 10**   These lines are the "insert clause."
- **Line 11**   This line is the WHERE clause for the MERGE, filtering out rows from the USING data source—in this case, ONTARIO_ORDERS.

The result of our MERGE is to merge rows from ONTARIO_ORDERS into WWA_INVOICES. If we query the WWA_INVOICES table, here are the results, after the MERGE:

```
SELECT * FROM WWA_INVOICES;

INV_ID                    CUST_PO    INV_DATE           NOTES
------------------------- ---------- ------------------ ---------
10                        WWA-200    17-DEC-19
20                        WWA-001    23-DEC-19          C. Nelson
40                        WWA-017    30-JUL-19          J. Metelsky
```

Notice the following:

■ We updated the row where CUST_PO equals WWA-001.

■ We added the row where CUST_PO equals WWA_017.

■ Our MERGE statement's WHERE clause correctly ignored the row where the PO_NUM was NBC-201.

MERGE is a useful and efficient DML statement. In this example, you saw how we performed an INSERT and UPDATE statement in a single MERGE statement.

Our example did not make use of the DELETE feature of the "update clause" within MERGE. But we could have included one, like this:

```
01    MERGE INTO WWA_INVOICES WWA
02      USING ONTARIO_ORDERS ONT
03      ON    (WWA.CUST_PO = ONT.PO_NUM)
04      WHEN  MATCHED THEN UPDATE SET
05            WWA.NOTES = ONT.SALES_REP
06            DELETE WHERE WWA.INV_DATE < TO_DATE('01-SEP-09')
07      WHEN  NOT MATCHED THEN INSERT
08            (WWA.INV_ID, WWA.CUST_PO, WWA.INV_DATE, WWA.NOTES)
09            VALUES
10            (SEQ_INV_ID.NEXTVAL,
11                      ONT.PO_NUM, SYSDATE, ONT.SALES_REP)
12    WHERE SUBSTR(ONT.PO_NUM,1,3) <> 'NBC';
```

In this example, we've added line 6, which contains the "delete clause" for the MERGE. But take note:

■ The "delete clause" affects only rows that are a result of the completed "update clause" and remain in the target table—which in this instance is WWA_INVOICES.

■ Rows added as a result of the "insert clause" are unaffected by the "delete clause."

So, MERGE represents a combination of the UPDATE and INSERT DML statements and, to a lesser and somewhat limited extent, the DELETE statement.

CERTIFICATION SUMMARY

The INSERT statement can be augmented with a number of clauses to introduce conditional logic into its execution and to add data to more than one table from within a single INSERT statement. Conditional logic can be added with a WHEN condition and optionally the ELSE keyword. The INSERT ALL form will test incoming data against each WHEN condition, and the INSERT FIRST form will stop at the first WHEN condition that evaluates to true. In either situation, the optional ELSE clause can define an insert that will execute if all previous WHEN conditions failed. Conditional INSERT statements may be used to "pivot" data from columns into rows and back again.

The MERGE statement does not do anything you cannot otherwise do with a series of other DML statements, but its advantage is its powerful ability to perform multiple operations from within a single SQL statement and therefore a single execution and single pass through the database.

TWO-MINUTE DRILL

Describe the Features of Multitable INSERTs

☐ Multitable inserts are useful for applying conditional logic to the data being considered for insertion.

☐ Conditional logic can evaluate incoming rows of data in a series of steps, using several evaluation conditions, and can offer alternative strategies for adding data to the database, all in a single SQL statement.

☐ Multitable INSERT statements offer flexibility and performance efficiency over the alternative approaches of using multiple SQL statements.

☐ Multitable INSERT statements may use conditional operations such as the WHEN condition and the ELSE clause.

☐ A WHEN condition can be used to evaluate incoming data and determine whether it should be inserted into the database, and if yes, which table and which columns are to be inserted.

☐ The ELSE clause is a last alternative choice that will execute if no WHEN condition evaluated to true.

☐ Both WHEN and ELSE are associated with their own unique INSERT statement directives; depending on which conditions apply, the appropriate INSERT statement directives will execute.

☐ Each condition can INSERT data in different ways into different tables.

☐ The INSERT FIRST statement tests each WHEN condition and executes the associated INSERT statement directives with the first WHEN condition that evaluates to true.

☐ The INSERT ALL statement executes all the WHEN conditions that evaluate to true.

☐ The ELSE clause executes for either the INSERT FIRST or INSERT ALL statement when none of the WHEN conditions has executed.

☐ The subquery of a multitable INSERT determines the data that will be considered in the insert logic; it can be a complex query and can include joins, GROUP BY clauses, set operators, and other complex logic.

Merge Rows in a Table

☐ The MERGE statement is one of the SQL DML statements, alongside SELECT, INSERT, UPDATE, and DELETE.

☐ MERGE replicates some of the functionality found in INSERT, UPDATE, and DELETE and combines it all into a single statement that executes with a single pass through the database.

☐ MERGE doesn't do anything new that you cannot already do with existing DML statements, but it does them more efficiently in combination.

☐ The MERGE statement includes an "update clause" and an "insert clause."

☐ The WHEN MATCHED THEN UPDATE keywords form the "update clause."

☐ The WHEN NOT MATCHED THEN INSERT keywords form the "insert clause."

☐ The DELETE clause of the MERGE statement only deletes rows that were first updated with the "update clause" and remain after a successful update; they must also meet the WHERE condition of the "delete clause."

SELF TEST

The following questions will help you measure your understanding of the material presented in this chapter. Choose one correct answer for each question unless otherwise directed.

Describe the Features of Multitable INSERTs

1. What can an INSERT statement do? (Choose two.)
   A. Add rows into more than one table
   B. Add data into more than one column in a table
   C. Delete rows by overwriting them
   D. Join tables together

2. A multitable INSERT statement:
   A. Can accomplish tasks that cannot otherwise be done in any combination of SQL statements
   B. Will create any tables in which it attempts to INSERT but that do not yet exist
   C. Can use conditional logic
   D. Is capable of inserting rows into nonupdatable views

3. Review the following diagrams of the SPARES table:

SPARES	
SPARE_ID	NUMBER (8)
PART_NO	VARCHAR2 (30 BYTE)
PART_NAME	VARCHAR2 (80 BYTE)
◇ IX_01	

Also examine the diagrams of the tables PORT_INVENTORY, STORE_INVENTORY, and SHIP_INVENTORY, shown here.

STORE_INVENTORY	
P * NUM	NUMBER
AISLE	VARCHAR2 (7 BYTE)
PRODUCT	VARCHAR2 (15 BYTE)
LAST_ORDER	DATE
⟱ PK_NUM	

SHIP_INVENTORY	
P * NUM	NUMBER
AISLE	VARCHAR2 (7 BYTE)
PRODUCT	VARCHAR2 (15 BYTE)
LAST_ORDER	DATE
⟱ PK_SHIP_INV_NUM	

PORT_INVENTORY	
P * NUM	NUMBER
AISLE	VARCHAR2 (7 BYTE)
PRODUCT	VARCHAR2 (15 BYTE)
LAST_ORDER	DATE
⟱ PK_PORT_INV_NUM	

Now consider the following SQL statement:

```
01   INSERT ALL
02      WHEN (SUBSTR(PART_NAME,1,4) = 'MED-') THEN
03        INTO STORE_INVENTORY (NUM, AISLE, PRODUCT, LAST_ORDER)
04        VALUES (SPARE_ID, 'Back', PART_NAME, SYSDATE)
05        INTO SHIP_INVENTORY (NUM, AISLE, PRODUCT, LAST_ORDER)
06        VALUES (SPARE_ID, 'Back', PART_NAME, SYSDATE)
07      WHEN (SUBSTR(PART_NAME,1,4) = 'ARR-') THEN
08        INTO PORT_INVENTORY (NUM, AISLE, PRODUCT, LAST_ORDER)
09        VALUES (SPARE_ID, 'Back', PART_NAME, SYSDATE)
10   SELECT SPARE_ID, PART_NO, PART_NAME
11   FROM    SPARES;
```

Regarding this SQL statement, which of the following statements is true?

A. The statement will fail because there is no ELSE clause.

B. The statement will fail because it is missing a WHEN condition.

C. The statement will add a row returned from the SPARES table to the SHIP_INVENTORY table only if the WHEN condition on line 2 evaluates to true.

D. The statement will add every row returned from the SPARES table to the SHIP_INVENTORY table.

4. Review the SQL statement in the preceding question. If one of the INTO clauses executed on a table and resulted in a constraint violation on that table, what would result?

A. The row would not be inserted, and the INSERT statement would skip to the next row returned by the subquery and perform another pass through the WHEN conditions.

B. The row would not be inserted, and the INSERT statement would stop. No additional rows would be returned by the subquery or processed, but rows that have already been processed are unaffected.

C. The row would not be inserted, the INSERT statement would stop, and all rows affected by the INSERT statement would be rolled back, as if the INSERT statement had never been executed.

D. None of the above.

5. Review the diagrams in question 3, and consider the following SQL statement:

```
01   INSERT FIRST
02      WHEN (SUBSTR(PART_NAME,5,3) = 'OPS') THEN
03       INTO STORE_INVENTORY (NUM, AISLE, PRODUCT, LAST_ORDER)
04         VALUES (SEQ_NUM.NEXTVAL, 'Back', PART_NAME, SYSDATE)
05      WHEN (SUBSTR(PART_NAME,1,4) = 'PAN-') THEN
06        INTO SHIP_INVENTORY (NUM, AISLE, PRODUCT, LAST_ORDER)
07         VALUES (SEQ_SHIP_NUM.NEXTVAL, 'Back', PART_NAME, SYSDATE)
08      ELSE
09        INTO PORT_INVENTORY (NUM, AISLE, PRODUCT, LAST_ORDER)
10         VALUES (SEQ_PORT_NUM.NEXTVAL, 'Back', PART_NAME, SYSDATE)
11      SELECT SPARE_ID, PART_NO, PART_NAME
12      FROM    SPARES
13      WHERE   LENGTH(PART_NO) > 2;
```

Which one of the following answers correctly identifies data that, if present in the SPARES table, will be inserted by this conditional INSERT statement into the table—or tables—identified by the answer?

A. PART_NO = 123; PART_NAME = 'BAH-OPS', in both STORE_INVENTORY and PORT_INVENTORY

B. PART_NO = 401; PART_NAME = 'PAN-OPS', in both SHIP_INVENTORY and PORT_INVENTORY

C. PART_NO = 170; PART_NAME = 'TRA-OPS', in STORE_INVENTORY

D. PART_NO = 4; PART_NAME = 'PAN-OPS', in both STORE_INVENTORY and SHIP_INVENTORY

6. Review the diagrams in question 3, and examine the following statement:

```
01    INSERT
02      WHEN (PART_NO < 500) THEN
03       INTO STORE_INVENTORY (NUM, PRODUCT)
04        VALUES (SPARE_ID, PART_NAME)
05       INTO PORT_INVENTORY (NUM, PRODUCT)
06        VALUES (SPARE_ID, PART_NAME)
07      WHEN (PART_NO >= 500) THEN
08        INTO SHIP_INVENTORY (NUM, PRODUCT)
09        VALUES (SPARE_ID, PART_NAME)
10      SELECT SPARE_ID, PART_NO, PART_NAME
11      FROM   SPARES;
```

Which of the following statements is true for this SQL statement?

A. If the first WHEN condition in line 2 is true, the INTO clause in line 3 and line 4 will be executed, after which processing will skip to the next row returned by the subquery.

B. If the first WHEN condition in line 2 is true, the WHEN condition in line 7 will not be evaluated.

C. No matter which WHEN condition is true, the INTO clause in line 5 will be executed regardless.

D. Regardless of whether the first WHEN condition is true, the second WHEN condition will be evaluated.

Merge Rows in a Table

7. The MERGE statement includes a USING clause. Which of the following statements is *not* true of the USING clause?

A. It can be used to specify a subquery.

B. The data it identifies remains unchanged after the MERGE statement executes.

C. The USING clause is optional.

D. It can be used to specify an inline view.

8. See the diagrams in question 3. You want to merge rows from the PORT_INVENTORY table into the SHIP_INVENTORY table. You start with the following SQL statement:

```
01    MERGE INTO SHIP_INVENTORY A
02    USING PORT_INVENTORY B
03    ON (A.NUM = B.NUM)
04    WHEN NOT MATCHED THEN INSERT
05       (A.NUM, A.AISLE, A.PRODUCT, A.LAST_ORDER)
06       VALUES
07       (B.NUM, B.AISLE, B.PRODUCT, B.LAST_ORDER)
08    WHERE TO_CHAR(A.LAST_ORDER,'RRRR') = '2019';
```

What will this SQL statement do?

A. It will fail with a syntax error because you must have an ELSE clause.

B. It will fail with a syntax error because you cannot reference the target table (SHIP_INVENTORY) in the WHERE clause in line 8.

C. It will add rows from PORT_INVENTORY to SHIP_INVENTORY that do not already exist in SHIP_INVENTORY, limited to LAST_ORDER values from the year 2019.

D. It will add rows from PORT_INVENTORY to SHIP_INVENTORY that do not already exist in SHIP_INVENTORY, regardless of the value for LAST_ORDER.

9. Examine the SQL syntax in question 8. Which of the following two alternatives for line 3 are syntactically correct?

```
OPTION 1:   ON (A.NUM = B.NUM AND A.AISLE = B.AISLE)
OPTION 2:   ON (A.LAST_ORDER < B.LAST_ORDER)
```

A. Only option 1

B. Only option 2

C. Both option 1 and option 2

D. Neither option 1 nor option 2

10. Which of the following statements is false?

A. It is possible to merge into two or more tables.

B. It is possible to merge into a view.

C. The USING clause can reference two or more tables.

D. You cannot perform an update to a column that is referenced in the ON clause.

SELF TEST ANSWERS

Describe the Features of Multitable INSERTs

1. ☑ **A** and **B.** INSERT statements can add rows to more than one table using conditional and unconditional logic. INSERT statements can also add data to more than one column in any given table.

   ☒ **C** and **D** are incorrect. INSERT cannot overwrite data; it adds new rows to a table. INSERT does not perform joins.

2. ☑ **C.** Multitable INSERT statements can use conditional logic, with statements such as WHEN and ELSE.

   ☒ **A, B,** and **D** are incorrect. Multitable INSERTS do not do anything you couldn't otherwise do with one or more SQL statements. Their advantage is that they can accomplish complex SQL tasks in a single pass that might otherwise require multiple passes through the database, thus yielding performance advantages. And nothing can add rows into a nonupdatable view—if it's not updatable, it's not updatable.

3. ☑ **C.** The WHEN condition in line 2 determines whether the INTO clauses in lines 3, 4, 5, and 6 will execute.

   ☒ **A, B,** and **D** are incorrect. The ELSE clause is not required. No particular WHEN condition is required. The INTO clause for SHIP_INVENTORY is subject to the WHEN condition in line 2.

4. ☑ **C.** The entire statement fails, and all inserted rows are rolled back. It is as if the statement had never been executed. Had this statement included any calls to a sequence generator and its NEXTVAL pseudocolumn would have advanced the count in the generator, that effect would remain unchanged. However, this example does not include any sequence generators, so that particular exception does not apply.

   ☒ **A, B,** and **D** are incorrect.

5. ☑ **C.** The PART_NO of 170 has a length of 3, and that is longer than 2, so the WHERE clause in line 13 is found to be true, and the row will be evaluated by the rest of the INSERT FIRST statement. Next, the PART_NAME of PAN-OPS will cause the first WHEN condition to be true, and since this is an INSERT FIRST statement, no other WHEN condition will be considered.

   ☒ **A, B,** and **D** are incorrect. These answers result from various interpretations of the WHEN conditions and ELSE. In an INSERT FIRST statement, the first WHEN condition that evaluates to true is the only condition that is executed. All others are ignored. If no WHEN is found to be true, then the optional ELSE clause will be processed.

6. ☑ **D.** Both WHEN conditions will be evaluated because the conditional INSERT is an INSERT ALL statement.

   ☒ **A, B,** and **C** are incorrect. If the first WHEN condition is true, both INTO clauses that follow it will be executed—that includes the INTO on line 5 through line 6. Whether the first WHEN condition is true or false, the second will also be evaluated since this is an INSERT ALL statement. The INTO in line 5 through line 6 will be evaluated only if the first WHEN condition is true.

Merge Rows in a Table

7. ☑ **C.** The USING clause is not optional; it is required in the MERGE statement.

   ☒ **A, B,** and **D** are incorrect. USING can identify a table, view, or subquery. An inline view is also acceptable. It identifies the source of data to be merged; the source data remains unchanged after the MERGE statement is executed.

8. ☑ **B.** It will fail because the WHERE clause references something that is not in the source table. The WHERE clause is an extension of USING, which specifies the target table. The A table alias reference is meaningless and will fail.

   ☒ **A, C,** and **D** are incorrect. There is no ELSE clause in MERGE, so it is not only not required, it is not accepted.

9. ☑ **C.** Both options are acceptable. The ON condition can be any comparison of expressions, and it can include Boolean operators.

   ☒ **A, B,** and **D** are incorrect.

10. ☑ **A.** You cannot MERGE into two or more tables. Only one is permitted.

    ☒ **B, C,** and **D** are incorrect. You can MERGE into a view provided the view is updateable. The USING clause can reference two or more tables by way of a join or subquery. You cannot change the values of a join criteria during the join, so you cannot update columns that are referenced in an ON clause.

14
Controlling User Access

CERTIFICATION OBJECTIVES

T his chapter explores the subject of user access and the privileges associated with performing actions in the database. Every action performed by any user account requires a corresponding privilege or set of privileges to perform that action. There are two categories of privileges. *System* privileges are required to perform a task in the database; *object* privileges are required to use those system privileges on any given database object in particular. Privileges may be granted to a user account or to another database object called a *role*. A role, in turn, can be granted to a user account, which effectively grants the set of privileges collected within the role. Once granted, privileges and roles can later be revoked. Together, privileges and roles are the mechanism for managing and controlling access to the database by user accounts. This chapter looks at how to create and manage privileges and roles.

A word of warning about the sample code contained in this chapter: some of it has the ability to change your database permanently with results that may be undesirable. Some of our code samples will look at SQL code that uses the SYSTEM user account, an important account that should be controlled by experienced database administrators in any production database. You should always check with your database administrator (DBA) before trying any code samples from any book, but this chapter in particular includes code that you should not execute in a professional installation without first checking with your DBA.

CERTIFICATION OBJECTIVE 14.01

Differentiate System Privileges from Object Privileges

Throughout this book, we've looked at how a user account can use SQL statements to create and use a variety of database objects. However, before any user account can execute a SQL statement, it must be granted the privilege to execute that SQL statement. Furthermore, once a database object has been created, any user account that will use the database object must first be granted privileges to do so.

There are three general categories of privileges, as described in Table 14-1. We'll review each of the items listed in Table 14-1 in this chapter.

TABLE 14-1   Types of Privileges

Type of Privilege	Description
System privilege	The ability to perform a particular task in the database
Object privilege	The ability to perform a particular task on a particular database object
Role	A collection of one or more system privileges and/or object privileges and/or other roles

System Privileges

System privileges are the right to perform some task in the database. For example, to log in to the database, a user account is granted the system privilege CREATE SESSION. To create a table, a user account must be granted the system privilege CREATE TABLE.

There are more than 100 different system privileges that can be granted to a user account. Table 14-2 lists some of the system privileges that are required to perform the tasks we've discussed in this book.

TABLE 14-2   Some System Privileges

System Privilege	Description
CREATE SESSION	Connect to the database.
CREATE TABLE	Create a table in your user account. Includes the ability to use ALTER and DROP TABLE. Also includes the ability to use CREATE, ALTER, and DROP INDEX on objects.
CREATE VIEW	Create a view in your user account. Includes ALTER and DROP.
CREATE SEQUENCE	Create a sequence in your user account. Includes ALTER and DROP.
CREATE SYNONYM	Create a synonym in your user account. Includes ALTER and DROP. Does not include PUBLIC synonyms (see CREATE PUBLIC SYNONYM).
CREATE ROLE	Create a role. Includes ALTER and DROP.
CREATE PUBLIC SYNONYM	Create a synonym in the PUBLIC account. Does not include DROP, which is separate.
DROP PUBLIC SYNONYM	Drop a synonym from the PUBLIC account.

TABLE 14-2	Some System Privileges (*Continued*)
System Privilege	**Description**
CREATE ANY TABLE	Create a table within any user account.
ALTER ANY TABLE	Alter a table within any user account.
DELETE ANY TABLE	Delete from any table within any user account.
DROP ANY TABLE	Drop or truncate any table within any user account.
INSERT ANY TABLE	Insert into any table within any user account.
SELECT ANY TABLE	Select from any table within any user account.
UPDATE ANY TABLE	Update any table within any user account.
CREATE ANY VIEW	Create a view in any user account.
DROP ANY VIEW	Drop a view from any user account.
CREATE ANY INDEX	Create an index in any user account.
ALTER ANY INDEX	Alter an index in any user account.
DROP ANY INDEX	Drop an index from any user account.
CREATE ANY SEQUENCE	Create a sequence in any user account.
ALTER ANY SEQUENCE	Alter a sequence in any user account.
DROP ANY SEQUENCE	Drop a sequence from any user account.
SELECT ANY SEQUENCE	Select from a sequence in any user account.
CREATE ANY SYNONYM	Create a synonym in any user account.
DROP ANY SYNONYM	Drop a synonym from any user account.
CREATE ANY DIRECTORY	Create a directory in any user account.
DROP ANY DIRECTORY	Drop a directory from any user account.
ALTER ANY ROLE	Alter a role in the database.
DROP ANY ROLE	Drop any role in the database.
GRANT ANY ROLE	Grant any role in the database.
FLASHBACK ANY TABLE	Perform flashback operations on any table in the database.
CREATE USER	Create a user account.
ALTER USER	Alter a user account.
DROP USER	Drop a user account.
GRANT ANY PRIVILEGE	Grant any system privilege to any user account in the database.
GRANT ANY OBJECT PRIVILEGE	Grant, to any other user account in the database, any object privilege that the object's owner is also able to grant.

System privileges differ from object privileges in that system privileges are what a user account must have to create database objects, among other things. Then, once a database object has been created, object privileges on that database object can be granted to other users.

For example, the right to execute the SQL statement CREATE TABLE and create a new database table is a system privilege. But the ability to change rows of data in, for example, a table called BENEFITS owned by a user account named EUNICE is an object privilege. In other words, an object privilege is the right to do something to a particular object.

As an analogy, consider the concept of a driver's license. A driver's license is sort of like a system privilege; it's the right to drive a car in a general sense. Once you have a driver's license, if you get a car, you can drive it. But you don't have the right to drive anyone's car in particular unless the owner specifically authorizes you to do so.

The right to drive someone else's car is like an object privilege. You need both of these privileges in order to drive a car and to be in full compliance with the law. The same is true in the database: you need system privileges to perform particular tasks, and you need object privileges to perform those tasks on an object in particular.

Let's look at some of the syntax for granting privileges. Note that for some of the upcoming examples, we'll use the SQL*Plus tool and some SQL*Plus commands. These SQL*Plus commands do not require the semicolon termination character that is required in SQL statements.

We'll use the SQL*Plus command CONNECT to log in to another user account. You can also use the SQL*Plus command SHOW USER to confirm which account is currently active in the session. SQL*Plus commands are helpful to use in your SQL sessions. But they are not on the exam.

Prerequisites

Before we get started with GRANT and REVOKE statements, let's review some supporting statements that aren't specifically included in the exam objectives but are useful for demonstrating system privileges, object privileges, roles, and their capabilities.

CREATE, ALTER, and DROP USER

Let's look at how to create a user account. Any SQL user with the CREATE USER system privilege may execute the CREATE USER statement, whose syntax looks like this:

```
CREATE USER username IDENTIFIED BY password;
```

In this statement, *username* is a name you specify according to the rules for naming database objects. The *password* follows the same rules. (Note that passwords are case sensitive by default starting with Oracle 11*g*.)

For example, this statement will create a user name JOAN with the password DEMERY:

```
CREATE USER JOAN IDENTIFIED BY DEMERY;
```

You can use the ALTER USER statement to change the password, like this:

```
ALTER USER JOAN IDENTIFIED BY HAWAII;
```

Finally, you can remove a user from the database using the DROP USER statement, like this:

```
DROP USER username;
```

If a user account owns any database objects, the preceding statement won't work, and you'll need to use this:

```
DROP USER username CASCADE;
```

The CASCADE option directs SQL to drop the user account and all of the objects it owns.

Once a user object has been created, it can be granted privileges, as you'll see in an upcoming section.

CONNECT

The CONNECT statement is not a SQL statement but a SQL*Plus enhancement you can use within the Oracle SQL*Plus tool. Once you've started SQL*Plus, you can use CONNECT to log in or switch login sessions from one user account to another. If, for example, you are using the SQL*Plus tool and have logged in to the EFCODD account and created the user account JOAN, you can log in to the JOAN account directly from EFCODD with this statement:

```
CONNECT JOAN/HAWAII
```

This assumes the user account JOAN is still using the password HAWAII. It also assumes that JOAN has been granted the minimum system privileges to log in, such as CREATE SESSION.

Again, a semicolon termination character is not required in SQL*Plus statements. It is accepted but not required. The semicolon termination character is required in SQL statements but is optional in SQL*Plus statements.

Tablespaces

In the course of setting up a new user account, the topic of tablespaces must be addressed. However, the topic of tablespaces goes beyond our scope and is not included in the exam objectives, so we'll show the simple way to address the tablespace requirement, as follows:

```
GRANT UNLIMITED TABLESPACE TO username;
```

This would probably not be something that your typical production DBA would do. Tablespaces are controlled by database administrators. A typical DBA generally creates uniquely named tablespaces and carefully allocates space quotas to them. We, however, aren't concerned with any of that for this book or for the exam. So for us, the preceding statement is what we'll include. If you want to learn more, we encourage you to check out any of the outstanding books from Oracle Press on the topic of database administration. In the meantime, if you're working on your own test system on your own personal machine, this particular statement that grants UNLIMITED TABLESPACE is more than adequate for our purposes going forward. If you're using these at work, check with your DBA before trying any of the code samples in this chapter.

GRANT and REVOKE

Now let's get down to business. System privileges are granted with the GRANT statement. Here's an example of a SQL session that logs in to the Oracle SYSTEM account, creates a new user, and grants the new user account some initial system privileges using three GRANT statements (line numbers added):

```
01    CONNECT SYSTEM/MANAGER
02    CREATE USER HAROLD IDENTIFIED BY LLOYD;
03    GRANT CREATE SESSION TO HAROLD;
04    GRANT UNLIMITED TABLESPACE TO HAROLD;
05    GRANT CREATE TABLE TO HAROLD;
```

In these statements, here is what we are doing:

- **Line 1** We establish a user session with the user account SYSTEM, with a password of MANAGER. The SYSTEM account is installed with every Oracle database, and the DBA installing Oracle assigns the password. (Warning: Do not try this on a production system. No self-respecting production system should have a SYSTEM account password set to a value of MANAGER anyway, but the point is that if you have installed your own version of the

Oracle database on your own local machine and it is not used for production work, then you can try this, but if you're trying things out within a system at your workplace or somewhere comparable, then be sure to check with your database administrator before trying this.)

■ **Line 2** We create a new user account called HAROLD, with the password LLOYD.

■ **Line 3** We use the SQL statement GRANT to give the CREATE SESSION privilege to user HAROLD. This is a minimum requirement for us to be able to log in to the database with the HAROLD user account; without this GRANT statement, we couldn't successfully log in with the user account HAROLD.

■ **Line 4** This is one way to ensure that HAROLD can create objects. See our earlier discussion about tablespaces in the previous section.

■ **Line 5** Using GRANT, we give the system privilege CREATE TABLE to user account HAROLD.

See Figure 14-1 for the results of these statements in the SQL*Plus window.

Now let's log in to HAROLD and try out what we've done. For that, we'll try the following SQL statements:

```
CONNECT HAROLD/LLOYD
CREATE TABLE CLOCKTOWER (CLOCK_ID NUMBER(11));
CREATE SEQUENCE SEQ_CLOCK_ID;
```

See Figure 14-2 for the results. Note that we aren't able to create the sequence because we haven't been granted sufficient privileges to do so. For that, we'll need

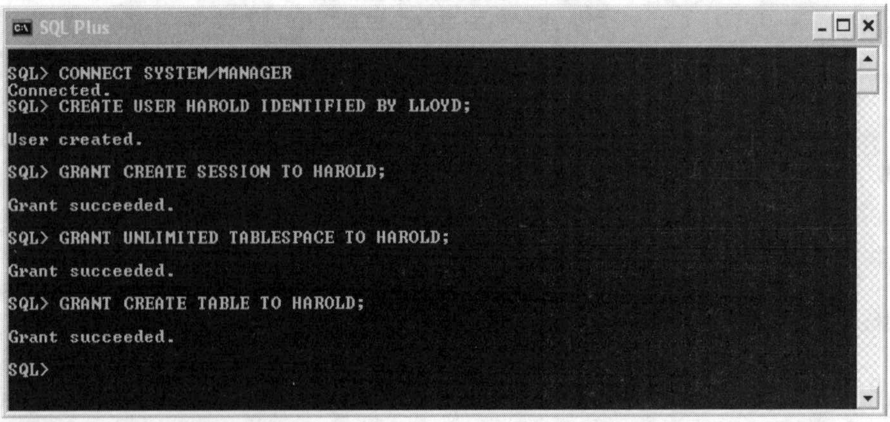

FIGURE 14-1

SQL*Plus session: GRANT statements

```
SQL> CONNECT SYSTEM/MANAGER
Connected.
SQL> CREATE USER HAROLD IDENTIFIED BY LLOYD;

User created.

SQL> GRANT CREATE SESSION TO HAROLD;

Grant succeeded.

SQL> GRANT UNLIMITED TABLESPACE TO HAROLD;

Grant succeeded.

SQL> GRANT CREATE TABLE TO HAROLD;

Grant succeeded.

SQL>
```

SQL*Plus session:
testing system
privileges

```
SQL> CONNECT HAROLD/LLOYD
Connected.
SQL> CREATE TABLE CLOCKTOWER (CLOCK_ID NUMBER(11));

Table created.

SQL> CREATE SEQUENCE SEQ_CLOCK_ID;
CREATE SEQUENCE SEQ_CLOCK_ID
*
ERROR at line 1:
ORA-01031: insufficient privileges

SQL>
```

to log back in to the SYSTEM account and grant the system privilege CREATE
SEQUENCE to HAROLD. Once that has been accomplished, we can log back in to
HAROLD and create the sequence (see Figure 14-3).

In these examples, we have been logged in to the SYSTEM account to grant
these privileges, but any qualified DBA account will do and is preferable in any
serious installation with multiple Oracle users. In such a situation, the less time a
developer or DBA spends in the SYSTEM account—or the other restricted default
DBA accounts in the Oracle database such as SYS—the less likely a mistake will
accidentally cause some serious damage to the database.

The basic syntax for the GRANT statement is simple.

```
GRANT privilege TO user options;
```

Here, *privilege* is one of the several dozens of system privileges that are already
defined in the database (see the *Oracle Database SQL Language Reference Manual*
for a complete list). Multiple privileges can be granted at once by separating each
additional privilege with a comma, as in GRANT *privilege, privilege*. (We'll discuss
option in an upcoming section.)

SQL*Plus session:
creating the
sequence

```
SQL> CONNECT SYSTEM/MANAGER
Connected.
SQL> GRANT CREATE SEQUENCE TO HAROLD;

Grant succeeded.

SQL> CONNECT HAROLD/LLOYD
Connected.
SQL> CREATE SEQUENCE SEQ_CLOCK_ID;

Sequence created.

SQL>
```

The basic syntax for REVOKE is comparable.

```
REVOKE privilege FROM user;
```

Note that you grant TO and you revoke FROM.

Once a system privilege is revoked from a user, the effect is immediate. However, any actions taken prior to the revocation stand. In other words, if a user account has been granted the system privilege CREATE TABLE and then creates some tables but then has the CREATE TABLE system privilege revoked, the created tables already in existence remain in place. They do not disappear. But the owning user may not create additional tables while the CREATE TABLE system privilege is revoked.

We've looked at a few system privileges, and we've said that they are somewhat like a driver's license. Now let's extend the analogy a little bit: imagine what would happen if you could get a universal driver's license that carried with it the ability to drive anyone's car legally without the car's owner express permission. Such a concept exists within the Oracle database, and it's embodied in the keyword ANY. Let's look at that next.

ANY

Some system privileges include the keyword ANY in the title. For example, there is a system privilege CREATE ANY TABLE, which is the ability to create a table in any user account anywhere in the database. Let's look at a sample session that involves this privilege.

```
CONNECT SYSTEM/MANAGER

CREATE USER LAUREL IDENTIFIED BY POKE;
GRANT CREATE SESSION TO LAUREL;
GRANT UNLIMITED TABLESPACE TO LAUREL;
GRANT CREATE TABLE TO LAUREL;

CREATE USER HARDY  IDENTIFIED BY CLOBBER;
GRANT CREATE SESSION TO HARDY;
GRANT UNLIMITED TABLESPACE TO HARDY;
GRANT CREATE ANY TABLE TO HARDY;

CONNECT LAUREL / POKE
CREATE TABLE MOVIES (MOVIE_ID NUMBER(7));

CONNECT HARDY / CLOBBER
CREATE TABLE LAUREL.TVSHOWS (TVSHOW_ID NUMBER(7));
```

The result of the preceding SQL statements is that two user accounts will be created. Also, two tables will be created, with one table called MOVIES and another table called TVSHOWS. Both tables will exist in the user account LAUREL. The first table was created by LAUREL, but the second table, TVSHOWS, was created by user account HARDY and was created as a table that is owned by LAUREL. The user account HARDY will contain no tables. The official "owner" of both tables is LAUREL, as the data dictionary confirms.

```
SELECT OWNER, TABLE_NAME
FROM   DBA_TABLES
WHERE  OWNER IN ('HARDY','LAUREL');

OWNER                              TABLE_NAME
------------------------------     ------------------------------
LAUREL                             MOVIES
LAUREL                             TVSHOWS
```

When a system privilege includes the keyword ANY in its title, it means that the privilege will authorize a user to perform the task as though they were any user account. In this example, user HARDY was able to create a table and place it in the LAUREL account, a task typically reserved only for user LAUREL. However, since user HARDY has the system privilege CREATE ANY TABLE, then HARDY can create any table in any user account.

ADMIN OPTION

In a previous section we said we would look at the *option* in the GRANT statement's syntax we examined. Here it is: the *option* is an additional clause that may be included with the GRANT statement, as follows:

```
GRANT privilege TO user WITH ADMIN OPTION;
```

When any system privilege is granted with the WITH ADMIN OPTION option, then the recipient receives the system privilege itself, along with the right to grant the system privilege to another user (see Figure 14-4).

The REVOKE statement does not use the WITH ADMIN OPTION clause. Whenever a system privilege is revoked, the entire system privilege is revoked.

If a user—let's call it the first user—grants a system privilege to a second user WITH ADMIN OPTION and the second user uses the admin option to grant that same system privilege to a third user, then the third user retains the privilege until it is explicitly revoked from the third user. In other words, once the second user has

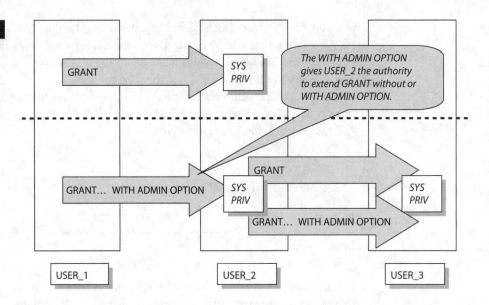

FIGURE 14-4

GRANT versus
GRANT WITH
ADMIN OPTION

granted the third user with the system privilege, it stays with the first user, even if the first user—or any other qualified user—revokes the system privilege from the second user. If that happens, the third user still has the system privilege. The only way the third user will lose the system privilege is if any qualified user revokes the system privilege explicitly from the third user with a REVOKE statement. In other words, the REVOKE statement for system privileges does not "cascade." It applies only to the user to whom the revocation is applied.

ALL PRIVILEGES

As an alternative to granting specific system privileges, a qualified user account, such as SYSTEM or some other DBA qualified account, can issue the following statement:

```
GRANT ALL PRIVILEGES TO user;
```

This statement has the effect of granting all system privileges to the user. The WITH ADMIN OPTION clause may be used with this as well.

Needless to say, this should be done with great caution, if at all. It is not easily reversible. In other words, the following is not an exact counterpart:

```
REVOKE ALL PRIVILEGES FROM user;
```

This statement will reverse all system privileges granted to the user, assuming that all system privileges have been granted to the user. If not, an error message will result.

PUBLIC

The PUBLIC account is a built-in user account in the Oracle database that represents all users. Any objects owned by PUBLIC are treated as though they are owned by all the users in the database, present and future.

The GRANT statement will work with the keyword PUBLIC in the place of a user account name. Here's an example:

```
GRANT CREATE ANY TABLE TO PUBLIC;
```

This statement grants the CREATE ANY TABLE privilege to every user in the database. The CREATE ANY TABLE privilege gives every user the ability to create any table in any other user account. In other words, it's mass hysteria—or something like it. Mind you, we're not recommending you do this, but it's syntactically possible, and you need to be aware of it. While this sort of an example is unlikely, granting to PUBLIC may be useful with a selected number of object privileges, which we'll discuss a bit later.

Note that if you come to your senses and decide to revoke a system privilege from PUBLIC, you can do so without revoking any other system privileges. In other words, consider this statement:

```
REVOKE CREATE ANY TABLE FROM PUBLIC;
```

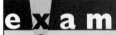

Note that if you want to grant all privileges, you use the keywords ALL PRIVILEGES. But if you want to grant certain privileges to all users, you do not use the keyword ALL. Instead, you grant to PUBLIC.

This statement will reverse the GRANT ... TO PUBLIC that we issued a few paragraphs earlier and thankfully will not revoke any individually granted CREATE ANY TABLE system privileges held by any user accounts. It will revoke only the GRANT to PUBLIC.

If you're even thinking about using GRANT ALL PRIVILEGES TO PUBLIC WITH ADMIN OPTION, you can put that thought out of your mind right this second.

CERTIFICATION OBJECTIVE 14.02

Grant Privileges on Tables and on a User

Any user with the system privilege CREATE TABLE can create a table. The table, once created, is owned by the user who created it. The owner does not require any explicitly granted privileges on the table. The table owner can use DML to add rows, change data in the table, query the data in the table, and remove rows from the table. But other users do not have that privilege automatically. Other users must have explicitly granted privileges on the object, which, in this case, is a table.

(Note: The exception, of course, is those users who have the system privileges that allow them to run any DML statements on any table in the database, regardless of who owns it. Those system privileges, as we saw in the previous section, include SELECT ANY TABLE, INSERT ANY TABLE, UPDATE ANY TABLE, and DELETE ANY TABLE.)

Any user who owns a table—or any other database object—may grant object privileges on their database object to other users in the database.

Object privileges exist for all DML statements—SELECT, INSERT, UPDATE, and DELETE—as well as any DDL statement that is relevant to an existing object, such as ALTER, for example. Note that there is no separate set of object privileges for the MERGE statement.

Object privileges on a table include all the DML statements that can be executed against a table. For example, if a user account LISA has the system privilege CREATE TABLE, then LISA can create a table. If LISA takes advantage of this system privilege and creates a table WEBINARS, then LISA can access the new table, but other users are not automatically able to see the table (unless, as we stated earlier, those users possess one of the ANY system privileges, such as SELECT ANY TABLE). To ensure that other user accounts can execute SQL statements on the table, user account LISA will have to grant object privileges on WEBINARS to other users.

See Figure 14-5 for a SQL*Plus session in which we connect to the SYSTEM account, where we create two user accounts, LISA and HENRY. We give LISA sufficient privileges to connect (CREATE SESSION) and create tables. Note how we combined multiple system privileges in a single GRANT statement. Also, we give HENRY sufficient privileges to create a session—but nothing more.

FIGURE 14-5

Creating,
granting, and
testing object
privileges—part 1

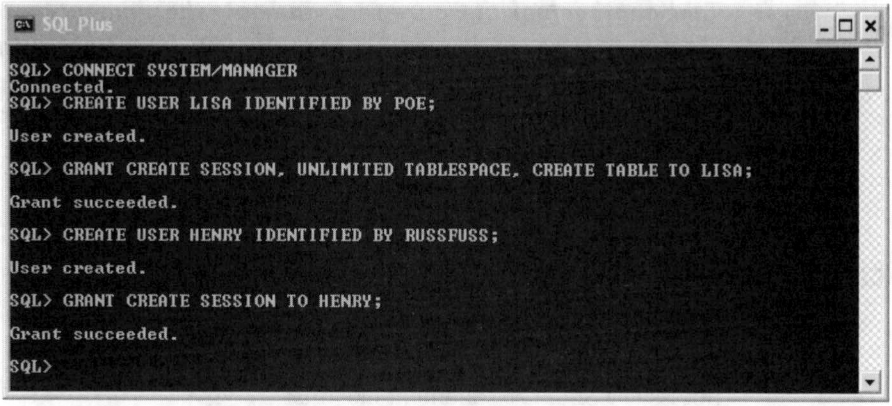

```
SQL> CONNECT SYSTEM/MANAGER
Connected.
SQL> CREATE USER LISA IDENTIFIED BY POE;
User created.
SQL> GRANT CREATE SESSION, UNLIMITED TABLESPACE, CREATE TABLE TO LISA;
Grant succeeded.
SQL> CREATE USER HENRY IDENTIFIED BY RUSSFUSS;
User created.
SQL> GRANT CREATE SESSION TO HENRY;
Grant succeeded.
SQL>
```

We continue in Figure 14-6, where we connect to the LISA account and create a table, add data to it, and then grant privileges on the table to HENRY. Then we connect to HENRY, where we can issue SELECT and UPDATE statements but not INSERT—that particular privilege wasn't granted to HENRY.

FIGURE 14-6

Creating,
granting, and
testing object
privileges—part 2

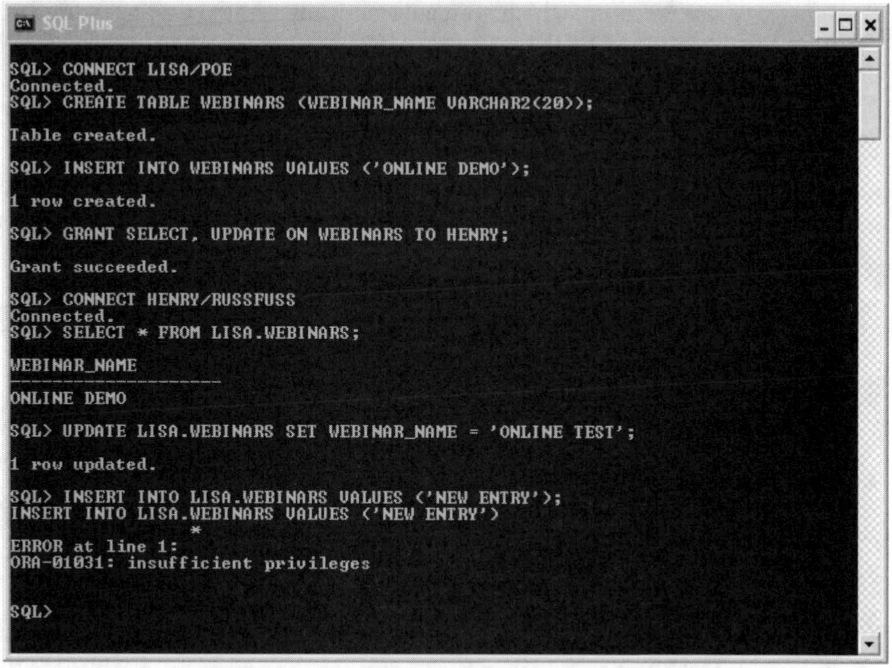

```
SQL> CONNECT LISA/POE
Connected.
SQL> CREATE TABLE WEBINARS (WEBINAR_NAME VARCHAR2(20));
Table created.
SQL> INSERT INTO WEBINARS VALUES ('ONLINE DEMO');
1 row created.
SQL> GRANT SELECT, UPDATE ON WEBINARS TO HENRY;
Grant succeeded.
SQL> CONNECT HENRY/RUSSFUSS
Connected.
SQL> SELECT * FROM LISA.WEBINARS;

WEBINAR_NAME
--------------------
ONLINE DEMO

SQL> UPDATE LISA.WEBINARS SET WEBINAR_NAME = 'ONLINE TEST';
1 row updated.
SQL> INSERT INTO LISA.WEBINARS VALUES ('NEW ENTRY');
INSERT INTO LISA.WEBINARS VALUES ('NEW ENTRY')
            *
ERROR at line 1:
ORA-01031: insufficient privileges

SQL>
```

on the Job

Take another look at Figure 14-6, and note the moment that the GRANT statement is issued. Remember that any DDL statement carries with it an implicit commit event. In other words, the GRANT statement has the effect of making the results of the INSERT statement permanent in the database. Once that GRANT has executed, the option to roll back the INSERT statement with ROLLBACK is no longer available.

Schema Prefixes

Note in Figure 14-6 that when HENRY references a table owned by LISA, HENRY must use the schema prefix to make the reference. In other words, HENRY could not issue a SELECT statement like this:

```
SELECT * FROM WEBINARS;
```

Instead, HENRY uses this sort of reference:

```
SELECT * FROM LISA.WEBINARS;
```

A SYNONYM is an object in the database that is an alternative name for a database object. A PUBLIC SYNONYM is a SYNONYM that is owned by the PUBLIC user account, which is an automatically created user account that is maintained by the Oracle database. The PUBLIC user isn't intended to be an account into which you log in to get access. Instead, PUBLIC is a mechanism by which you can create globally owned objects. Specifically, anything that is owned by PUBLIC is automatically owned by all users in the database. The same is true for PUBLIC SYNONYMS.

In our earlier example, the user SYSTEM could have given user LISA the system privilege to create public synonyms by issuing the following statement:

```
GRANT CREATE PUBLIC SYNONYM TO LISA;
```

Then, later, the user LISA could have used that system privilege to create a PUBLIC SYNONYM like this:

```
CREATE PUBLIC SYNONYM WEBINARS FOR LISA.WEBINARS;
```

Finally, once user HENRY got around to issuing DML statements on the WEBINARS table, HENRY could have omitted the schema prefix and instead simply executed this statement:

```
SELECT * FROM WEBINARS;
```

In this instance, HENRY would be specifying the WEBINARS object PUBLIC SYNONYM, which in turn points to the object LISA.WEBINARS. Note that no object privilege had to be granted on the PUBLIC SYNONYM object to HENRY. All objects owned by PUBLIC are automatically available and accessible to all users in the database, present and future. However, privileges must be granted to whatever object for which the PUBLIC SYNONYM serves as an alias. It's one thing to have privileges on a PUBLIC SYNONYM that references a table, but it's another thing to have privileges on the table it references. All users have privileges automatically on any object owned by PUBLIC; they do not have automatically granted privileges on anything a PUBLIC SYNONYM references; such privileges must be granted explicitly.

This sort of usage is the most common purpose of the PUBLIC SYNONYM object.

Note that to create PUBLIC SYNONYM objects, a user account must have the CREATE PUBLIC SYNONYM system privilege.

Name Priority, Revisited

You may recall our discussion in Chapter 2 about a concept called *namespace*. When a user makes a reference to an object by name, SQL will use that name to search for that object as follows:

- First, SQL looks in the local namespace, which contains objects owned by the user account: tables, views, sequences, private synonyms, and something called user-defined types (these objects are beyond the scope of the exam).
- Next, SQL looks in the database namespace, which contains users, roles, and public synonyms.

This concept was demonstrated graphically in Figure 2-2.

WITH GRANT OPTION

If you want to grant another user a particular object privilege and include the ability for the user to grant that same object privilege to yet another user, then include the WITH GRANT OPTION clause in the GRANT statement. Here's an example:

```
CONNECT LISA/POE
GRANT SELECT, UPDATE ON WEBINARS TO HENRY WITH GRANT OPTION;
```

This grant gives user HENRY the ability to issue SELECT and UPDATE statements on table WEBINARS, along with the ability to grant those privileges to other users. HENRY is not obligated to grant the set of privileges together; HENRY can choose to be selective.

```
CONNECT HENRY/RUSSFUSS
GRANT SELECT ON LISA.WEBINARS TO HAROLD WITH GRANT OPTION;
```

Now user HAROLD has the ability to issue SELECT statements on LISA. WEBINARS, as well as the ability to grant that privilege to others. But HENRY did not pass along the UPDATE privilege.

REVOKE

User LISA may choose to revoke privileges from HENRY, like this:

```
REVOKE SELECT, UPDATE ON WEBINARS FROM HENRY;
```

If user LISA does this, then HENRY and HAROLD lose all privileges, as does anyone to whom they extended privileges with their WITH GRANT OPTION option.

In other words, the revocation of object privileges "cascades." Note that this is different from system privilege revocation, which does not cascade, as we stated earlier in this chapter.

Note that the REVOKE statement does not require the WITH GRANT OPTION clause. REVOKE doesn't care whether that option had been included; it just revokes all specified privileges and cascades the change throughout all user accounts as required.

ALL PRIVILEGES

The ALL PRIVILEGES option works with granting and revoking object privileges in much the same way it does with system privileges, with some differences. Here's an example:

```
GRANT ALL PRIVILEGES ON WEBINARS TO HENRY;
```

This statement gives all privileges on the object WEBINARS to HENRY, except for the ability to grant privileges. To grant the ability to grant, use this:

```
GRANT ALL PRIVILEGES ON WEBINARS TO HENRY WITH GRANT OPTION;
```

The keyword PRIVILEGES is not required when granting object privileges.

```
GRANT ALL ON WEBINARS TO HENRY;
```

The same is true with REVOKE when used with object privileges.

```
REVOKE ALL PRIVILEGES ON WEBINARS FROM HENRY;
```

The following is also good:

```
REVOKE ALL ON WEBINARS FROM HENRY;
```

This shorthand way of revoking object privileges spares the effort of identifying all the individual object privileges that may have already been granted to HENRY on the WEBINARS table and revokes them all at once.

Note that the keyword PRIVILEGES is optional when working with object privileges, but not when working with system privileges.

If you use REVOKE ALL to revoke object privileges from a user and no object privileges exist on the object for that user, then no error message results, and the statement executes successfully with no practical effect.

Dependent Privileges

If user A owns a view, which is based on a table that user A also owns, and user A grants privileges on the view to user B, then user B can access the view without privileges to the underlying table.

If user A creates a table and a public synonym, then user B has immediate visibility of the public synonym because the synonym is owned by PUBLIC and all users have visibility of all objects owned by PUBLIC. However, user B still requires privileges on the table for which the public synonym is an alias. If the public synonym references a view that user A owns, then user B must have object privileges on the view, but is not required to have access to its underlying table.

e**x**a m
watch
If you grant privileges on a table and then drop the table, the privileges are dropped with the table. If you later re-create the table, you must also grant the privileges again. However, if you restore a dropped table with the FLASHBACK TABLE ... BEFORE DROP statement, you will recover the table, its associated indices, and the table's granted privileges, and you will not need to grant the privileges again.

View Privileges in the Data Dictionary

We've already looked at the data dictionary and seen how it provides information about the state of objects in the database, as well as providing some historic information.

There are many views in the data dictionary that present information about system privileges and object privileges. See Table 14-3 for a listing of some of these views.

TABLE 14-3   Data About Privileges in the Data Dictionary

Data Dictionary View	Explanation
USER_SYS_PRIVS	System privileges granted to current user
DBA_SYS_PRIVS	System privileges granted to users and roles
USER_TAB_PRIVS	Grants on objects for which the user is the grantor, grantee, or owner
ALL_TAB_PRIVS	Grants on objects for which the user is the grantor, grantee, owner, or an enabled role or PUBLIC is the grantee
DBA_TAB_PRIVS	Grants on all objects in the database
ALL_TAB_PRIVS_RECD	Grants on objects for which the user, PUBLIC, or enabled role is the grantee
SESSION_PRIVS	Privileges that are enabled to the user

For example, to see what system privileges are granted to your current user account, you can query the data dictionary view USER_SYS_PRIVS. Here's what the results might look like from user account LISA:

```
SELECT   PRIVILEGE, ADMIN_OPTION
FROM     USER_SYS_PRIVS
ORDER BY PRIVILEGE;

PRIVILEGE                                       ADMIN_OPTION
---------------------------------------------   ------------
CREATE PUBLIC SYNONYM                           NO
CREATE SESSION                                  NO
CREATE TABLE                                    NO
UNLIMITED TABLESPACE                            NO
```

The equivalent data dictionary view DBA_SYS_PRIVS allows you to see the same information for other users.

exam watch

A privilege may be granted directly as a privilege or indirectly as part of a role. If you intend to drop a privilege from a user, use the data dictionary to determine whether that same privilege is granted to a role that is also granted to the same user. If so, then the privilege you dropped directly is still granted to the user indirectly through the role.

To see all the object privileges that your current user account may have granted to others or that may have been granted by others, you can use the following query. This is what the results might look like within the user account LISA:

```
SELECT   GRANTOR, OWNER, GRANTEE, TABLE_NAME, PRIVILEGE, GRANTABLE
FROM     USER_TAB_PRIVS
ORDER BY GRANTOR, OWNER, GRANTEE, TABLE_NAME, PRIVILEGE;


GRANTOR      OWNER       GRANTEE     TABLE_NAME    PRIVILEGE       GRANTABLE
----------   ----------  ----------  ------------  -------------   ---------
EFCODD       EFCODD      LISA        PORTS         DELETE          NO
EFCODD       EFCODD      LISA        PORTS         INSERT          NO
EFCODD       EFCODD      LISA        PORTS         SELECT          NO
EFCODD       EFCODD      LISA        PORTS         UPDATE          NO
EFCODD       EFCODD      LISA        SHIPS         ALTER           NO
EFCODD       EFCODD      LISA        SHIPS         DELETE          NO
EFCODD       EFCODD      LISA        SHIPS         INSERT          NO
EFCODD       EFCODD      LISA        SHIPS         SELECT          NO
EFCODD       EFCODD      LISA        SHIPS         UPDATE          NO
LISA         LISA        HENRY       WEBINARS      SELECT          NO
LISA         LISA        HENRY       WEBINARS      UPDATE          NO
```

Note that the first several rows show object privileges granted by EFCODD to LISA. The final two rows show object privileges granted by LISA to HENRY.

These are just a few examples of the sort of information the data dictionary provides about system privileges and object privileges that have been granted to and from user accounts within the database.

on the **Job**

When inspecting data dictionary views like DBA_TAB_PRIVS or DBA_SYS_PRIVS to see what privileges have been granted to a particular user account, you can check the GRANTEE column for the appropriate USER name. However, don't forget to also check for rows where GRANTEE = 'PUBLIC'; these privileges are also available to your user account.

Grant Roles

A role is a database object that you can create and to which you can assign system privileges and/or object privileges. You can also assign other roles to a given role. Once it is created, you can grant a role to a user just as you can grant privileges to a user. The user is then automatically granted any privileges contained within the role. A role is an excellent way to manage the various privileges required for performing different tasks in the database and to organize the process of granting and revoking privileges.

You may grant the role to as many user accounts as you want.

If any privilege is subsequently revoked from the role, it is also revoked from any users to whom the role has been granted. In other words, changes to roles cascade to the users to whom the role is granted.

Three roles in particular have historically been associated with standard Oracle databases, but they are being phased out. On a practical level, though, it's good to know about them, if you don't already. The three roles are CONNECT, RESOURCE, and DBA. The CONNECT role consists of the CREATE SESSION system privilege, intended for the typical generic end user. RESOURCE is a collection of system privileges intended for the typical application developer. DBA is intended for the typical database administrator. Each can be seen in detail in the data dictionary view DBA_SYS_PRIVS (see Table 14-4 for details). All three roles are still included in each implementation of the Oracle database as of this writing, but Oracle has stated formally that the use of these roles is now officially discouraged, and their inclusion in future database implementations is not guaranteed. Oracle Corporation's official position is that you should create your own set of roles as required.

You can refer to the data in Table 14-4 to get an idea of the kind of system privileges you may want to include in your ROLE objects.

To create a role, a user account needs the CREATE ROLE system privilege.

	Role	Privilege
TABLE 14-4 The Classic Roles CONNECT, RESOURCE, and DBA	CONNECT	CREATE SESSION
	RESOURCE	CREATE TRIGGER CREATE SEQUENCE CREATE TYPE CREATE PROCEDURE CREATE CLUSTER CREATE OPERATOR CREATE INDEXTYPE CREATE TABLE
	DBA	More than 100 system privileges, including the following: CREATE ANY TABLE CREATE PUBLIC SYNONYM CREATE ROLE CREATE SYNONYM CREATE SEQUENCE CREATE USER CREATE VIEW GRANT ANY PRIVILEGE

For example, the user account EFCODD owns several tables and wants to grant privileges on these tables to some users in the database. Some of these users will be performing queries on the tables and nothing more. Others will be responsible for performing changes to the data. Therefore, we want to create two different roles and grant them the necessary privileges.

```
CONNECT EFCODD/FOUNDER

CREATE ROLE CRUISE_ANALYST;
GRANT SELECT ON SHIPS       TO CRUISE_ANALYST;
GRANT SELECT ON PORTS       TO CRUISE_ANALYST;
GRANT SELECT ON EMPLOYEES TO CRUISE_ANALYST;

CREATE ROLE CRUISE_OPERATOR;

GRANT SELECT, UPDATE, INSERT, DELETE ON SHIPS       TO CRUISE_OPERATOR;
GRANT SELECT, UPDATE, INSERT, DELETE ON PORTS       TO CRUISE_OPERATOR;
GRANT SELECT, UPDATE                 ON EMPLOYEES TO CRUISE_OPERATOR;
```

In the preceding code, we create two ROLE objects: one called CRUISE_ANALYST, to which we grant some SELECT privileges on tables, and another called CRUISE_OPERATOR, to which we grant some other privileges. Once they are created, we can grant these roles to user accounts in the database.

```
GRANT CRUISE_OPERATOR TO LISA;
GRANT CRUISE_ANALYST  TO HENRY;
```

Once a role is granted, a user has access to all of the privileges within it.
A role can be granted to another role.
A role can be granted WITH ADMIN OPTION to empower the recipient to grant the role to yet another user. Here's an example:

```
GRANT CRUISE_OPERATOR TO LISA WITH ADMIN OPTION;
```

If a user grants a role to another user and uses WITH ADMIN OPTION, the second user may further grant the same role to a third user. If the first user revokes the role from the second user, the third user retains the role until it is explicitly revoked from the third user by a qualified user.

Table 14-5 lists some of the data dictionary views that provide information about existing roles in the database.

Roles exist in a namespace that resides outside of any user account. Therefore, you can create roles with names that are the same as objects within a user account, such as tables and views. That's not necessarily a good idea, but it's allowed in the database.

A user account may be granted multiple roles at once.

TABLE 14-5

Data Dictionary Views with Information About ROLE Objects

Data Dictionary View	Explanation
DBA_ROLES	All roles that exist in the database
DBA_ROLE_PRIVS	Roles granted to users and roles
DBA_SYS_PRIVS	System privileges granted to users and roles
DBA_TAB_PRIVS	All grants on objects to users and roles
ROLE_ROLE_PRIVS	Roles that are granted to roles
ROLE_SYS_PRIVS	System privileges granted to roles
ROLE_TAB_PRIVS	Table privileges granted to roles
SESSION_ROLES	Roles that are enabled to the user

exam
ⓦatch

Let's say you create an object, then grant a privilege on that object to a role, and then grant the role to a user. If you drop the object, then you also drop the granted object privilege to the role. However, the role still exists, and the grant of the role to the user still exists. If you subsequently re-create the object and then grant the object privilege to the role once again, then you've re-created the situation before the object was dropped. In other words, you do not need to re-create the role or grant the role to the user once again since neither was affected by the act of dropping the object on which the privilege had originally been granted.

CERTIFICATION OBJECTIVE 14.03

Distinguish Between Privileges and Roles

A role object does not represent privileges in and of itself. It is merely a collection of zero or more privileges. A role exists independently of the privileges it may—or may not—contain. Furthermore, the relationship a user account has to a granted role is separate from any privileges that may have been granted directly to the user account. In other words, if a user account already has any object privileges granted directly to it as a result of earlier GRANT statements and then later is granted a role that duplicates any of those privileges, then the role exists separately from those originally granted privileges, which exist independently of the role. If the role is later revoked, that revocation does not adversely affect any separately granted privileges given directly to the user account.

If user HENRY were already granted a privilege that happens to be duplicated within the role CRUISE_ANALYST and then subsequently the role is granted but then is revoked, like this:

```
REVOKE CRUISE_ANALYST FROM HENRY;
```

then any object privileges granted directly to HENRY still exist.

For example, examine the following code:

```
01    GRANT SELECT ON INVOICES TO HENRY;
02    CREATE ROLE CRUISE_ACCOUNTANT;
03    GRANT SELECT ON INVOICES TO CRUISE_ACCOUNTANT;
04    GRANT CRUISE_ACCOUNTANT TO HENRY;
05    REVOKE CRUISE_ACCOUNTANT FROM HENRY;
```

User HENRY still has SELECT on INVOICES because of line 1, in spite of lines 2 through 5.

Similarly, if the role is restored but the direct object privilege is revoked, HENRY still has access through the role. Here's an example:

```
01    GRANT SELECT ON INVOICES TO HENRY;
02    CREATE ROLE CRUISE_ACCOUNTANT;
03    GRANT SELECT ON INVOICES TO CRUISE_ACCOUNTANT;
04    GRANT CRUISE_ACCOUNTANT TO HENRY;
05    REVOKE SELECT ON INVOICES FROM HENRY;
```

HENRY still has privileges on INVOICES in spite of line 5. The reason is the CRUISE_ACCOUNTANT role, from lines 2 through 4.

However, if the object privilege revoked from HENRY in line 5 were also to be revoked from the CRUISE_ACCOUNTANT role, then the object privilege would be removed from HENRY altogether.

CERTIFICATION SUMMARY

A system privilege is the right to perform a task in the database, using a DDL, DCL, or DML statement on objects in general. The right to perform those tasks on a particular object in the database is an object privilege. Finally, a role combines privileges into a single object so that a combination of privileges can be managed as a group.

The SQL statements GRANT and REVOKE are used to issue system privileges and object privileges and to take them away. Privileges are given to—or taken away from—user accounts. Any user in the database must have privileges to perform any task. The act of logging in requires the CREATE SESSION system privilege. Other privileges include CREATE PUBLIC SYNONYM and CREATE TABLE.

The ANY keyword in a system privilege indicates the ability to work with objects that are owned by any user account.

A user account, by default, has object privileges on the objects it owns. Object privileges are required for a user to be able to interact with objects it does not own.

Instead of granting privileges to a user, you may create a role, then grant privileges to a role, and then grant the role to one or more users. The advantage is that if you have multiple users, a role is much easier to change since you can grant or revoke privileges as desired after the role has been assigned to any number of users, and all of the users will automatically have the new privileges granted or revoked automatically.

The data dictionary provides information about system privileges, object privileges, and roles from the perspective of both the grantor and the grantee.

TWO-MINUTE DRILL

Differentiate System Privileges from Object Privileges

☐ The right to use any given SQL statement and/or to generally perform a task in the database is a system privilege.

☐ The right to perform some task on a specific existing object in the database is an object privilege.

☐ Both system and object privileges are granted to and revoked from users in the database.

☐ System privileges may be granted WITH ADMIN OPTION, which provides the ability for the recipient to grant the same privilege to yet another user.

☐ When a system privilege is revoked, the revocation does not cascade, meaning that it is revoked only from the user from whom it is being revoked, not from other users to whom the revoked user may have extended the privilege.

☐ The ALL PRIVILEGES keywords can be used to grant or revoke all privileges to or from a user.

Grant Privileges on Tables and on a User

☐ Object privileges correspond to DML statements and to DDL statements that are relevant to existing objects.

☐ Object privileges may be granted WITH GRANT OPTION, which provides the ability for the recipient to grant the same privilege to yet another user.

☐ When an object privilege is revoked, the revocation cascades, meaning that it is revoked from the user from whom it is being revoked, as well as from other users to whom the revoked user may have extended the privilege.

☐ When a user has been granted access to an object, the object name will require a schema name prefix to be correctly identified.

☐ A PUBLIC SYNONYM can provide an alternative name for the schema-prefixed version of the granted object.

☐ The ALL PRIVILEGES keywords can be used to grant or revoke all privileges to or from a user.

☐ A variety of data dictionary views provide information about system and object privileges.

☐ Users may see privileges granted to them, or granted by them to others, by querying the data dictionary.

☐ A role is created with the CREATE ROLE statement.

☐ Roles may be granted WITH ADMIN OPTION, which provides the ability for the recipient to grant the same role to yet another user.

☐ Roles exist in a namespace outside of an individual user account.

☐ A role is a collection of privileges and other roles.

☐ A role may be granted to another role.

Distinguish Between Privileges and Roles

☐ A privilege granted directly to a user exists independently from a privilege granted to a role.

☐ If you revoke a privilege directly from a user who also has been granted a role containing the same privilege, the role remains unchanged, and the user still has privileges by way of the role.

☐ The same situation is true with regard to revoking privileges directly from roles; if you revoke a privilege from a role that a user already has through a direct grant, the direct grant stays in force.

SELF TEST

The following questions will help you measure your understanding of the material presented in this chapter. Choose one answer for each question, unless otherwise directed.

Differentiate System Privileges from Object Privileges

1. Which of the following SQL statements will authorize the user account JESSE to create tables in each and every user account in the database?
    A.   GRANT CREATE ALL TABLE TO JESSE;
    B.   GRANT CREATE PUBLIC TABLE TO JESSE;
    C.   GRANT CREATE ANY TABLE TO JESSE;
    D.   GRANT CREATE TABLE TO JESSE WITH PUBLIC OPTION;

2. You are logged in to user account FRED and have been tasked with granting privileges to the user account ETHEL. You execute the following SQL statements:

    ```
    GRANT CREATE ANY TABLE TO ETHEL WITH ADMIN OPTION;
    REVOKE CREATE ANY TABLE FROM ETHEL;
    ```

    Assuming both statements execute successfully, what is the result?
    A.   ETHEL does not have the system privilege CREATE ANY TABLE or the right to grant the CREATE ANY TABLE system privilege to any other user.
    B.   ETHEL has the system privilege CREATE ANY TABLE because the WITH ADMIN OPTION clause wasn't included in the REVOKE statement.
    C.   ETHEL no longer has the system privilege CREATE ANY TABLE but still has the right to grant the CREATE ANY TABLE system privilege to any other user, since the WITH ADMIN OPTION clause was omitted from the REVOKE statement. However, ETHEL may not grant the CREATE ANY TABLE privilege to herself.
    D.   ETHEL no longer has the system privilege CREATE ANY TABLE but still has the right to grant the CREATE ANY TABLE system privilege to any other user since the WITH ADMIN OPTION clause was omitted. Furthermore, ETHEL may grant the CREATE ANY TABLE privilege to herself because of the WITH ADMIN OPTION clause.

3. Which of the following is the system privilege that is required as a minimum to allow a user account to log in to the database?
    A.   CREATE ANY LOGIN
    B.   CREATE ANY SESSION
    C.   CREATE SESSION
    D.   CREATE TABLE

4. Which of the following is the system privilege that empowers the grantee to create an index in his or her own user account but not in the accounts of others?

   A. CREATE TABLE

   B. CREATE ANY TABLE

   C. CREATE INDEX

   D. CREATE ANY INDEX

Grant Privileges on Tables and on a User

5. Your user account owns a table BACK_ORDERS, and you want to grant privileges on the table to a user account named CARUSO, which already has the system privileges CREATE SESSION and UNLIMITED TABLESPACE. Examine the following SQL statement:

   ```
   GRANT SELECT ON BACK_ORDERS TO CARUSO;
   ```

   Once this statement has been executed, which of the following statements will be true for user CARUSO?

   A. CARUSO will have SELECT privileges on BACK_ORDERS but not the ability to give other users SELECT privileges on BACK_ORDERS.

   B. CARUSO will have SELECT privileges on BACK_ORDERS, as well as the ability to give other users SELECT privileges on BACK_ORDERS.

   C. CARUSO will have SELECT, INSERT, UPDATE, and DELETE privileges on BACK_ORDERS but not the ability to give other users those same privileges on BACK_ORDERS.

   D. CARUSO will have SELECT and ALTER TABLE privileges on BACK_ORDERS but not the ability to give other users those same privileges on BACK_ORDERS.

6. Your user account owns an updatable view, BACKLOG, which is based on the table PROJECTS. You are tasked to give SELECT and UPDATE capabilities to another user account named MARINO. Currently, MARINO has no privileges on either the table or the view. You want for MARINO to have the ability to grant SELECT on the view to other users as well. Examine the following SQL code:

   ```
   GRANT SELECT ON BACKLOG TO MARINO WITH GRANT OPTION;
   GRANT UPDATE ON BACKLOG TO MARINO;
   ```

   Which of the following statements is true?

   A. The statements will fail, and MARINO will not be able to use the view.

   B. The statements will execute successfully, but MARINO will not be able to SELECT from the view because the PROJECTS table has not been granted to MARINO.

   C. The statements will execute successfully, and MARINO will be able to SELECT from the view but not UPDATE the view.

   D. The statements will execute successfully and perform as intended.

7. User account MUSKIE owns a table called CBAY. Which of the following statements can be executed by MUSKIE and enable user ONEILL to execute UPDATE statements on the CBAY table? (Choose three.)
   A. GRANT ALL ON CBAY TO ONEILL;
   B. GRANT ALL PRIVILEGES TO ONEILL;
   C. GRANT ALL TO ONEILL;
   D. GRANT INSERT, UPDATE ON CBAY TO ONEILL;

8. Examine the following two claims:
   [1] The DBA_TAB_PRIVS data dictionary view allows a user account to see object privileges it has granted to other user accounts.
   [2] The DBA_TAB_PRIVS data dictionary view allows a user account to see object privileges granted by other user accounts to itself.
   Which of these claims is true?
   A. Only 1
   B. Only 2
   C. Both 1 and 2
   D. Neither 1 nor 2

9. Which of the following data dictionary views contains information about grants on tables that have been made by other users to your user account, as well as grants on tables that have been made by your user account to other user accounts?
   A. USER_TAB_COLUMNS
   B. USER_TAB_PRIVS
   C. USER_TABLES
   D. ALL_TAB_PRIVS_RECD

10. What can be granted to a role? (Choose all that apply.)
    A. System privileges
    B. Object privileges
    C. Roles
    D. None of the above

11. Which of the following statements will grant the role OMBUDSMAN to user JOSHUA in such a way that JOSHUA may grant the role to another user?
    A. GRANT OMBUDSMAN TO JOSHUA WITH ADMIN OPTION;
    B. GRANT OMBUDSMAN TO JOSHUA WITH GRANT OPTION;
    C. GRANT OMBUDSMAN TO JOSHUA WITH ROLE OPTION;
    D. GRANT OMBUDSMAN TO JOSHUA CASCADE;

12. User HARDING owns a table TEAPOT. User HARDING then executes the following SQL statements to give access to the table to user ALBERT:

```
CREATE PUBLIC SYNONYM TEAPOT FOR HARDING.TEAPOT;
CREATE ROLE DOME;
GRANT DOME TO ALBERT;
GRANT SELECT ON TEAPOT TO DOME;
```

Which of the following statements can user ALBERT now execute on the TEAPOT table?

A.   SELECT * FROM DOME.HARDING.TEAPOT;

B.   SELECT * FROM HARDING.DOME.TEAPOT;

C.   SELECT * FROM HARDING.TEAPOT;

D.   None of the above

Distinguish Between Privileges and Roles

13. A role:

A.   Takes the place of privileges automatically so that any privilege granted to a role supersedes any grants that have already been granted directly to a user

B.   Cannot be given the same name as a table

C.   Can be granted to a user, who can be granted only one role at a time

D.   Can be created by a user only if that user has the CREATE ROLE system privilege

14. You have a table FURNISHINGS and are told to grant DELETE privileges on the table to user HEARST. Examine the following SQL statements:

```
GRANT DELETE ON FURNISHINGS TO HEARST;
CREATE ROLE MGR;
GRANT DELETE ON FURNISHINGS TO MGR;
GRANT MGR TO HEARST;
```

Now you are told to change the privileges given to HEARST so that HEARST can no longer execute DELETE statements on the FURNISHINGS table. Which of the following will accomplish the goal? (Choose the best answer.)

A.   REVOKE DELETE ON FURNISHINGS FROM HEARST;

B.   REVOKE DELETE ON FURNISHINGS FROM MGR;

C.   REVOKE DELETE ON FURNISHINGS FROM HEARST, MGR;

D.   None of the above

15. Assume a database with three valid users: NEIL, BUZZ, and MICHAEL. Assume all users have the appropriate privileges they require to perform the tasks shown here. Assume NEIL owns a table called PROVISIONS. Examine the following code (assume all password references are valid):

```
01    CONNECT NEIL/neilPassword
02    GRANT SELECT ON PROVISIONS TO BUZZ, MICHAEL;
03
04    CONNECT BUZZ/buzzPassword
05    CREATE VIEW PROVISIONS AS SELECT * FROM NEIL.PROVISIONS;
06    GRANT SELECT ON PROVISIONS TO MICHAEL;
07    CREATE PUBLIC SYNONYM PROVISIONS FOR BUZZ.PROVISIONS;
08
09    CONNECT MICHAEL/michaelPassword
10    CREATE SYNONYM PROVISIONS FOR NEIL.PROVISIONS;
11    SELECT * FROM PROVISIONS;
```

What object is identified in line 11 by the name PROVISIONS?

A. The public synonym created in line 7

B. The synonym created in line 10

C. Nothing, because user NEIL did not include WITH GRANT OPTIONS in the GRANT SELECT ON PROVISIONS TO BUZZ statement

D. Something else not listed above

SELF TEST ANSWERS

Differentiate System Privileges from Object Privileges

1. ☑ **C.** The system privilege CREATE ANY TABLE is the system privilege that you're looking for in this question. The keyword ANY is found in many system privileges to indicate that the user authorized with the system privilege may perform the task as though it were any user account in the database.

   ☒ **A, B,** and **D** are incorrect. There is no ALL keyword in this context, and PUBLIC does not apply here. There is no system privilege with the WITH PUBLIC OPTION keywords.

2. ☑ **A.** The WITH ADMIN OPTION clause is not allowed nor needed in the REVOKE statement.

   ☒ **B, C,** and **D** are incorrect. They are all interesting ideas, but they are all wrong.

3. ☑ **C.** The CREATE SESSION system privilege is the minimum requirement.

   ☒ **A, B,** and **D** are incorrect. There is no system privilege CREATE ANY LOGIN or CREATE ANY SESSION. CREATE TABLE is not required to establish a user session.

4. ☑ **A.** The CREATE TABLE privilege also includes the ability to create an index. Remember that a CREATE TABLE statement may include the PRIMARY KEY or UNIQUE constraint, which—if created—will automatically cause the creation of an index to support each constraint.

   ☒ **B, C,** and **D** are incorrect. There isn't a CREATE INDEX system privilege. The ability is included with CREATE TABLE. CREATE ANY TABLE empowers the grantee the ability to create tables in the accounts of others, which potentially may also create indices in those same accounts. CREATE ANY INDEX is a valid system privilege for creating index objects in user accounts other than your own.

Grant Privileges on Tables and on a User

5. ☑ **A.** GRANT SELECT ON *table* TO *user* gives the user the ability to SELECT on the table and nothing more.

   ☒ **B, C,** and **D** are incorrect. To give CARUSO the ability to SELECT on the table as well as to grant other users SELECT, the WITH GRANT OPTION clause would need to have been included with the GRANT statement, as in GRANT SELECT ON BACK_ORDERS TO CARUSO WITH GRANT OPTION. To grant the other DML statements on the table, each would have to have been included, as in GRANT SELECT, INSERT, UPDATE, DELETE ON BACK_ORDERS TO CARUSO. To grant SELECT and ALTER, both would have to have been named, as in GRANT SELECT, ALTER ON BACK_ORDERS TO CARUSO.

6. ☑ **D.** The statements are syntactically correct and will perform as intended.
☒ **A, B,** and **C** are incorrect. The PROJECTS table does not need to be granted to MARINO since the VIEW has been granted. Since the VIEW is updatable, then the UPDATE privilege will work as well.

7. ☑ **A, B,** and **D.** All three forms result in the UPDATE privilege being granted to user ONEILL for the CBAY table.
☒ **C** is incorrect. This statement is an invalid SQL statement. It either needs for the keyword PRIVILEGES to grant all system privileges to ONEILL or needs to name an object for which ALL privileges should be granted. The question is specifically asking about granting privileges on the CBAY table, so the ALL PRIVILEGES form would not work.

8. ☑ **C.** The data dictionary view DBA_TAB_PRIVS allows a user to see privileges that have been granted to itself or by itself to others.
☒ **A, B,** and **D** are incorrect.

9. ☑ **B.** USER_TAB_PRIVS is the correct answer.
☒ **A, C,** and **D** are incorrect. USER_TAB_COLUMNS has no information about grants. Neither does USER_TABLES. The ALL_TAB_PRIVS_RECD view contains data about incoming grants only.

10. ☑ **A, B,** and **C.** Both system and object privileges, as well as other roles, can be granted to any given role.
☒ **D** is incorrect.

11. ☑ **A.** WITH ADMIN OPTION is what is used for roles.
☒ **B, C,** and **D** are incorrect. WITH GRANT OPTION works for object privileges but not roles. There is no such clause as WITH ROLE OPTION. CASCADE does not apply here.

12. ☑ **C.** The schema name prefix correctly identifies the table. In addition, since the public synonym TEAPOT references the table, then DESC TEAPOT would also have worked—but that was not one of the options listed.
☒ **A, B,** and **D** are incorrect. You cannot use the role as a prefix or any other component of the name of a database object.

Distinguish Between Privileges and Roles

13. ☑ **D.** The CREATE ROLE privilege is required to create a role.
☒ **A, B,** and **C** are incorrect. A role does not replace privileges but instead is granted alongside of them. A role may be used to replace privileges as a management choice, and in fact such an approach is advisable, but it is not done automatically. Roles exist in a different namespace from tables and may duplicate table names. A user may be granted multiple roles at any given time.

14. ☑ **C.** This SQL statement accomplishes the goal in one statement.

☒ **A, B,** and **D** are incorrect. **A** and **B** are helpful but do not completely accomplish the task. **D** is incorrect because **C** is correct.

15. ☑ **B.** From within the MICHAEL user account, SQL first searches the local namespace and then searches the database namespace. The local namespace contains the private synonym, and that will be found first, before SQL looks in the database namespace.

☒ **A, C,** and **D** are incorrect. The GRANT statement issued by NEIL does not require WITH GRANT OPTION for the synonyms to function.

A

About the CD-ROM

T he CD-ROM included with this book comes complete with Total Tester customizable practice exam software with 140 practice exam questions and a secured PDF copy of the book.

System Requirements

The software requires Windows Vista or higher and 30MB of hard disk space for full installation, in addition to a current or prior major release of Chrome, Firefox, Internet Explorer, or Safari. To run, the screen resolution must be set to 1024 × 768 or higher. The secured book PDF requires Adobe Acrobat, Adobe Reader, or Adobe Digital Editions to view.

Installing and Running Total Tester Premium Practice Exam Software

From the main screen you may install the Total Tester software by clicking the Total Tester Practice Exams button. This will begin the installation process and place an icon on your desktop and in your Start menu. To run Total Tester, navigate to Start | (All) Programs | Total Seminars, or double-click the icon on your desktop.

To uninstall the Total Tester software, go to Start | Control Panel | Programs And Features, and then select the Total Tester program. Select Remove, and Windows will completely uninstall the software.

Total Tester Premium Practice Exam Software

Total Tester provides you with a simulation of the Oracle Database SQL exam (Exam 1Z0-071). Exams can be taken in Practice Mode, Exam Mode, or Custom Mode. Practice Mode provides an assistance window with hints, references to the book, explanations of the correct and incorrect answers, and the option to check your answer as you take the test. Exam Mode provides a simulation of the actual exam. The number of questions, the types of questions, and the time allowed are intended to be an accurate representation of the exam environment. Custom Mode allows you to create custom exams from selected domains or chapters, and you can further customize the number of questions and time allowed.

To take a test, launch the program and select Oracle Database SQL from the Installed Question Packs list. You can then select Practice Mode, Exam Mode, or Custom Mode. All exams provide an overall grade and a grade broken down by domain.

Secured Book PDF

The entire contents of the book are provided in secured PDF format on the CD-ROM. This file is viewable on your computer and many portable devices.

- **To view the PDF on a computer**, Adobe Acrobat, Adobe Reader, or Adobe Digital Editions is required. A link to Adobe's web site, where you can download and install Adobe Reader, has been included on the CD-ROM.

Note: For more information on Adobe Reader and to check for the most recent version of the software, visit Adobe's web site at www.adobe.com and search for the free Adobe Reader or look for Adobe Reader on the product page. Adobe Digital Editions can also be downloaded from the Adobe web site.

- **To view the book PDF on a portable device**, copy the PDF file to your computer from the CD-ROM and then copy the file to your portable device using a USB or other connection. Adobe offers a mobile version of Adobe Reader, the Adobe Reader mobile app, which currently supports iOS and Android. For customers using Adobe Digital Editions and an iPad, you may have to download and install a separate reader program on your device. The Adobe web site has a list of recommended applications, and McGraw-Hill Education recommends the Bluefire Reader.

Technical Support

For questions regarding the Total Tester software or operation of the CD-ROM, visit **www.totalsem.com** or e-mail **support@totalsem.com**.

For questions regarding the secured book PDF, visit **http://mhp.softwareassist .com** or e-mail **techsolutions@mhedu.com**.

For questions regarding book content, e-mail **hep_customer-service @mheducation.com**. For customers outside the United States, e-mail **international_cs@mheducation.com**.

1GL   First-generation language. The 1s and 0s that computers use to communicate. Binary language.

2GL   Second-generation language. Assembler language.

3GL   Third-generation language. A general category of computer programming languages that tend to support structured or object-oriented programming in a manner that is closer to the spoken word than 2GLs. Common 3GLs are Java, C++, JavaScript, and PHP.

4GL   Fourth-generation language. Closer to the spoken word than 3GLs. The most well-known and widely used 4GL is SQL.

administrator   *See* database administrator.

aggregate   A single value representing any number of other values.

alias   An alternative name for something. For example, Joe is an alias for Joseph.

alphabetic   Describes the letters of the alphabet.

alphanumeric   Describes the letters of the alphabet and numbers.

ALTER   A SQL statement that modifies the structure, the name, or some other attribute of an existing object in the database. (Note: There are exceptions to this definition that occur when ALTER is combined with the keyword SESSION or STATEMENT.)

analytic functions   Functions that operate on a group of rows (known as a *window*) and return multiple rows for each group. Sometimes called *analytical* functions.

ANSI   American National Standards Institute. An organization that oversees a number of voluntary committees that set standards for many industries, including software development and information technology.

attribute   A property or characteristic. Examples might include a name, ZIP code, or entry date. Corresponds to a column in a table. *See also* entity.

BLOB   Binary Large Object. A data type that stores unstructured binary data, up to 128 terabytes. BLOB data types can be rolled back or committed as part of any database transaction. Suitable for storing multimedia data.

Boolean   Refers to the valuation of expressions as either true, false, or unknown and using the logical operators AND, OR, and NOT. Named after the mathematician George Boole.

built-in   Already present. SQL built-in functions are those that come already installed in a database, as opposed to user-defined functions that you can create yourself and add to the set of available functions in a database.

Cartesian product   The combination of each row in one table with every row in another table. The result of two or more tables joined together with no specified join criteria. Also known as a *cross-join*.

case insensitive   Without regard for whether a letter is in uppercase or lowercase form. For example, when performing a case-insensitive comparison of the letter *A* and the letter *a*, the two are equal.

case sensitive   With regard for whether a letter is in uppercase or lowercase form. For example, when performing a case-sensitive comparison of the letter *A* and the letter *a*, the two are not equal.

character   The symbols of a writing system.

character class   Also known as POSIX character classes. Shorthand references in regular expressions for specifying a range of characters.

character set   An encoding system for representing characters in bytes.

CHECK constraint   A rule on a table that filters incoming data. Only data that satisfies that rule will be accepted by the table. Also known as a CHECK integrity constraint.

child   A row or record that is one level below another level in a hierarchical data relationship. For example, if one table contains "orders" and another contains the "line items" that each order contains, then a table containing those "line items" would be said to be the *child table*. A child table is one that typically has a foreign key relationship with a parent table so that rows in the parent table are one level higher in the hierarchy than the rows in the child table. *See also* orphan; parent.

clause   A subset within a larger construct, such as a portion of a statement or command.

CLOB   Character Large Object. A data type that stores large amounts of character data, up to 128 terabytes. CLOB data types can be rolled back or committed as part of any database transaction.

Codd   The last name of Dr. E.F. Codd, the person credited with forming the original ideas that led to the creation of modern-day relational database programming.

column   A vertical space in a database table. Columns have a name and a data type.

command   A directive.

COMMENT   A SQL statement to add comments to the data dictionary for database objects you have created.

commit   To cause changes within the current session to be made permanent.

COMMIT   A SQL statement to save data to the database.

condition   An expression that evaluates to a meaningful result to indicate the next course of action. Conditions are used to determine whether a statement will take a particular action or not; the decision hinges on whether the condition evaluates to true or false.

conditional   A situation that depends on the evaluation of a condition.

connect   Establish a user session with the database.

constant   *See* literal.

constraint   A rule defining how data is to be processed. A table can have one or more constraints that may restrict it to having certain kinds of data and rejecting others. *See also* referential integrity.

conversion   The act of transforming something from one form to another. Conversion functions in SQL can change data from one data type to another data type.

correlated subquery   A subquery that uses, as part of its execution logic, data from an outer query.

CREATE   A reserved word that starts one of many SQL statements, used to create database objects such as tables, views, indexes, sequences, and synonyms.

cross-join   *See* Cartesian product.

data dictionary   A set of tables and views automatically maintained by the Oracle system for documenting the characteristics and status of all objects in the database.

data file   A physical file in the file system for storing data, located either in the operating system file system or in an Automated Storage Management disk group.

data type   A set of rules defining a subset of data.

database   An organized collection of information.

database administrator   Often abbreviated DBA. The job of administering the database. The DBA often is tasked with installing the database software and configuring it for use, performing backups, generally making the database system available for use, maintaining optimal performance, and taking steps to protect against loss of data.

date   A calendar date.

datetime   Any of the set of data types DATE, TIMESTAMP, TIMESTAMP WITH TIME ZONE, or TIMESTAMP WITH LOCAL TIME ZONE.

daylight saving time   Time defined as a 1-hour offset from standard time to provide more daylight at the end of the working day during seasons in which daylight is limited.

DBA   *See* database administrator.

DBMS   Database management system.

DDL   Data Definition Language. A subset of SQL. Refers to the set of SQL statements that is used to create database objects, modify their structure, and remove them from the database.

default   When used in association with a parameter, "default" is the value of that parameter when no specific value is assigned. *See* parameter.

DEFINE   A reserved word used in pattern matching to specify pattern variables.

DELETE   A SQL statement used to remove data from the database.

deprecated   Said of a feature that may still exist but is no longer officially supported and whose use is officially discouraged.

developer   An individual engaged in the job of creating applications.

development   The act of creating applications.

DML   Data Manipulation Language. A subset of SQL. Refers to the set of SQL statements used to query existing data in database objects, add data to existing database objects, modify that data, and remove data from the database.

DROP   A reserved word used to start one of many SQL statements, all of which are used to remove certain existing database objects from the database.

Ellison   The last name of Larry Ellison, founder of Oracle Corporation, the first company to release a commercial RDBMS product.

entity   An organized collection of attributes in a data model. Corresponds to a table. *See also* attribute; ERD.

equijoin   A join that uses an equality operator (the equal sign) in the join condition.

ERD   Entity-relationship diagram. A diagram that shows entities and how they relate to each other. *See also* entity.

escape character   A single character that can take on an alternative purpose separate from its character's standard meaning. For example, a single quotation mark is an escape character when preceding another single quotation mark in a text string delimited by single quotes so that strings such as 'O"Brian' will be correctly interpreted as *O'Brian* in the database, rather than the truncated string *'O'* followed by the characters *Brian'*—which would be meaningless in any SQL statement and would result in a syntax error.

explicit commit   The COMMIT statement.

expression   A combination of literal values, operators, variables, and functions, with the intent of computing a value of a particular data type.

external table   A SQL table that stores table metadata in the database but stores the table's data outside of the database.

FIRST   A reserved word that refers to the first row in a sequence of rows.

FLASHBACK   A SQL statement used to restore older versions of database objects.

flashback operations   A set of operations using undo data to support data recovery and the analysis of historical data over time.

foreign key   A referential integrity constraint in a table. A foreign key specifies one or more attributes in one entity that relate to one or more attributes in another entity. Values entered in the foreign key's attributes must already exist in the referenced table's corresponding attributes. *See also* referential integrity; constraint.

function   A set of code that performs a particular task and returns a single result. A SQL function can be used within a SQL expression. A function is one type of subprogram, also known as a program unit. There is another form known as a procedure, which is not included on the exam.

GRANT   A SQL statement used to give system privileges or object privileges to a user account.

hierarchical query   A query that specifies multiple levels of relationship. Typically built on a self-join. Note that a typical join of two tables in a parent-child relationship can be said to be a two-level *hierarchy*; technically that would be accurate. But the term *hierarchical query* in Oracle SQL is generally understood to indicate a particular type of query based on a data model that is capable of supporting more than two levels.

IEEE   Institute of Electrical and Electronics Engineers. A nonprofit organization with the mission to advance technology as it relates to the use of electricity.

implicit commit   A commit event other than the COMMIT statement. The execution of DDL code will result in an implicit commit.

index   A database object that copies a subset of data from a table, presorted, and intended to support faster querying on the indexed table.

inline view   A subquery that performs like a view in support of a single SQL statement.

inner join   A join of two or more tables in which a join condition is specified, and the result consists exclusively of rows in one table that match rows in the other table according to the join condition. If a row in one table has no matching counterpart in the other table, it is not included in the results. *See also* outer join.

INSERT   A SQL statement used to store data in a database table.

instance   One set of Oracle background processes and memory structures used to access a database.

integrity constraint   *See* constraint.

interpolation   A method for calculating one or more values within a range of known values.

invisible column   An invisible column in a table is not visible, but its values are available to be referenced by SQL statements, including INSERT and SELECT statements, and including VIEW objects based on the table.

invisible index   An index that can be made invisible to the Oracle Database Query Optimizer to omit the inclusion of that index from the execution plan of a given SQL statement.

join   The act of connecting rows in one table with rows in one or more other tables, based on some criteria that determine how the data in the tables correlates to each other.

key   One or more attributes—or columns—used in the definition of an integrity constraint. Keys include primary keys, foreign keys, and unique keys.

keyword   A special word used in a SQL command or serving some other special purpose. Keywords are often reserved words, but they are not necessarily reserved.

LAST   A reserved word that refers to the last row in a sequence of rows.

linear   Refers to a straight-line numeric pattern, as opposed to exponential patterns. For example, linear interpolation considers known values in a range and computes interim values, assuming a linear relationship among all values.

literal   A fixed data value. Also called a constant.

LOB   Large Object. Any of a number of data types that store large amounts of information. *See also* BLOB; CLOB; NCLOB.

lowercase   The letters of the alphabet in miniscule form, in other words, *a*, *b*, and so on.

MERGE   A SQL statement that performs a combination of INSERT, UPDATE, and/or DELETE statement functionality.

metacharacter operators   Used to define patterns in regular expressions.

metadata   Data about data. For example, is the "account number" at a given organization a numeric value, or is it an alphanumeric value? Or perhaps alphabetic? Metadata describes data in high-level terms.

multitable insert   A SQL INSERT statement that is able to add rows of data to one or more tables. Multitable inserts can be conditional or unconditional.

namespace   A virtual location within the database in which no database objects may share the same name. All names must be unique within a given namespace.

natural join   A join in which the join criteria are implied based on common names of columns in the tables being joined.

NCLOB   National Character Set Large Object. A data type that stores large amounts of character data in a national database character set. Stores up to 128 terabytes. NCLOB data types can be rolled back or committed.

NEXT   A reserved word that refers to the next row in a sequence of rows.

NLS   National Language Support.

NLS parameters   Variables that customize the behavior of the database in accordance with a given locale. NLS_SORT is an example.

non-equijoin   A join condition that uses operators other than the equality operator to specify the join condition—such as greater-than or less-than operators.

normalization   A specific series of processes intended to support the design of a database to maximize efficiency.

NoSQL   Refers to "not only SQL" databases.

NULL   Unknown. The absence of information.

number   A digit.

numeric   Said of a set of data types that accept number data.

object   An item in the database. Objects have properties of structure and security.

object privilege   The right to perform a particular task on a particular object in the database. *See also* system privilege.

OFFSET   A reserved word used with FETCH to limit rows returned by a query, starting after the number of rows specified by OFFSET.

ONE ROW PER MATCH   Reserved words used when performing analytics across multiple rows of data.

operator precedence   The rules defining the order in which operators within an expression are processed.

operators   Symbols that perform tasks on values within an expression.

optimizer   A feature built into the Oracle database that evaluates processing within the database to improve speed and optimizer performance of SQL statements.

ORA_ROWSCN   A conservative upper bound of the latest commit time for the transaction that last changed the row. The actual commit SCN of the transaction can be somewhat earlier. *See also* system change number (SCN).

Oracle   The leading RDBMS product on the market today.

Oracle Corporation The first company to produce a commercial RDBMS product.

orphan A child row in a child table for which there is no corresponding parent row in the corresponding parent table.

outer join A join of two or more tables in which a join condition is specified, and the result consists of rows in one table that match rows in the other table according to the join condition, as well as rows that do not match. If a row in one table has no matching counterpart in the other table, it may be included in the results. *See also* inner join.

parameter A variable that is passed to or from a function or procedure.

parent A row or record that is one level above another level in a hierarchical data relationship. For example, if one table contains "orders" and another contains the "line items" that each order contains, then a table containing those "orders" would be said to be the *parent table*. A parent table is one that is referenced by a foreign key in a child table so that rows in the parent table are one level higher in the hierarchy than the rows in the child table. *See also* orphan; child.

parse To analyze code for syntactic accuracy. SQL code that is submitted for execution is parsed first and then executed upon successful completion of the parsing process.

PARTITION BY Reserved words used to specify a subset of rows within a larger query.

pattern variables A pattern variable is a name you create and associate with a condition you specify. Pattern variables are used to search for matches by comparing data across multiple rows of data with comparison operators.

POSIX Portable Operating System Interface (for Unix). A set of IEEE standards for defining standards and interoperability on a number of issues.

precedence A logical prioritization of a set of items.

precision Part of the definition of a numeric data type. Precision specifies the number of significant digits in the numeric value. *See also* scale.

predicates These compare one expression to another to produce a true, false, or NULL result. Can be combined with Boolean operators AND, OR, and NOT.

PREV A reserved word that refers to the previous row in a sequence of rows.

primary key A unique non-NULL attribute in an entity, or a unique non-NULL column in a table.

private synonym A synonym that is not a PUBLIC synonym. There is no PRIVATE keyword.

privilege The right to perform a task in the database. *See also* object privilege; system privilege.

procedure A set of code that performs a particular task. A procedure may return anywhere from zero to multiple results. Procedures cannot be used within a SQL expression but instead are often invoked in statements by themselves.

production Professional use. Database applications in "production" are actively storing data for an ongoing organization, as opposed to database applications that are in development or testing.

projection The concept of querying a subset of columns from a table.

pseudocolumns Values that are defined automatically by the Oracle system for certain objects in the database, such as tables and sequences. Pseudocolumns can be selected like a column in a table.

PUBLIC A special database user automatically maintained by the database. PUBLIC represents all users in the database. Granting privileges to PUBLIC has the effect of granting them to all users.

PURGE A SQL statement to remove objects from the recycle bin.

query   A SELECT statement. A request of the database for some of the data contained within it.

RDBMS   Relational database management system.

read consistency   The ability for data in the database to be read and joined in a manner that is accurate. Read consistency represents a view of data that is "frozen" in an instant of time. Read consistency becomes important when joining tables that are being modified in real time so that as the database queries one table and then another, the combined records reflect what was intended.

record   A set of data elements related to each other and representing a meaningful collection of information. One row can be a record; joined rows might also be a record.

recycle bin   The structure in the SQL database into which dropped objects are tracked.

redo logs   A set of operating system files that record all changes made to a database, whether those changes have been committed or not.

referential integrity   A constraint, or rule, on one table's column that requires any value to be stored in that column to be already present in another particular table's column. *See also* foreign key.

regular expression   A language of pattern matching. Not to be confused with expressions. Oracle's support for regular expressions is consistent with the POSIX and Unicode standards.

relational   Having a relation or being related. A database is said to be relational when it is built on data objects that can be joined together based on common criteria within and among the objects.

RENAME   A SQL statement used to change the name of certain objects in the database.

reserved word   Special words set aside for special use and not available for application development. You cannot use reserved words as the names of database objects or variables.

restore point   A marked point in time, to be recorded for possible future reference in support of flashback operations.

REVOKE   A SQL statement to remove system privileges or object privileges that have been granted to a user account.

role   A collection of one or more privileges.

rollback   An action that restores the database to the most recent commit within the current session.

ROLLBACK   A SQL statement used to restore the database to an earlier state. Cancels the effects of a transaction in progress.

row   One set of values for the columns of a table.

savepoint   A marked point in time, to be recorded for possible future rollback.

SAVEPOINT   A SQL statement that marks a point in a session. Future uses of the ROLLBACK statement may choose to restore the database to the point marked by a SAVEPOINT statement.

scalar subquery   A subquery that returns one column in one row as its output—in other words, a single value, as opposed to rows of values or columns of values.

scale   Part of the definition of a numeric data type. Scale specifies where rounding will occur in the numeric data type. *See also* precision.

schema   A collection of tables owned by a user account.

SCN   *See* system change number (SCN).

segment   A level of logical database storage.

SELECT   A SQL statement used to query one or more database tables.

selection   The ability to query a subset of rows from a table.

selectivity   The degree of uniqueness of values in a column. If all values in the column are identical, selectivity is said to be low. If the values are all unique, selectivity is said to be high.

self-join   A join that connects rows in a table with other rows in the same table.

semijoin   A query that returns rows that match an EXISTS subquery.

sequence   A number generator. A database object.

session   A user process in which the user interacts with the database.

set operator   Any of the operators UNION, UNION ALL, INTERSECT, or MINUS.

SKIP   A reserved word used in pattern matching. May be combined with other keywords to form keyword phrases, for example, AFTER MATCH SKIP TO NEXT ROW.

SQL   *See* Structured Query Language.

standard deviation   When used with numeric analysis, standard deviation is a quantified degree of variation of individual values within a large set of values. The formula for standard deviation takes the square root of the variance. See *variance* for more information.

standard time   Also known as winter time zones. Time as defined by UTC.

statement   A command.

string   A series of characters.

Structured Query Language   A worldwide standard language for interacting with a database.

subquery A SELECT statement contained within another (outer) SELECT statement so that the data of the subquery feeds into the processing of the outer query.

superaggregate An aggregation of aggregate values.

synonym An alias, or alternative name, for something in the database. A synonym is itself an object in the database.

syntax The rules for forming a statement, a command, or some other language construct.

SYS A built-in user account with DBA privileges that comes with all Oracle installations. SYS owns the data dictionary.

SYSTEM A built-in user account with DBA privileges that comes with all Oracle installations.

system change number (SCN) A marker that specifies a committed version of the database at a particular point in time. Each committed transaction is assigned an SCN. *See also* transaction.

system privilege The right to perform a particular task in the database. *See also* object privilege.

table A storage unit in the database that consists of columns and rows.

tablespace A mechanism in the database that is home to one or more tables and stores that data in one or more data files.

TCL Transaction Control Language. A subset of SQL. Refers to the set of SQL statements that is used to control a user's session in which DML statements are used. TCL determines whether the results of a DML statement are allowed to be made permanent or whether they are undone from the database.

text Character-based data.

time zone   A region of the earth that uses uniform standard time as an offset from UTC. There are currently 24 such regions defined in the earth, divided roughly by longitudinal lines. Also known as *time zone region*.

time zone name   The name of a time zone region. Examples are Pacific/Auckland and America/Indianapolis.

time zone offset   A time difference between the local time and UTC.

timestamp   A value representing the date and time.

transaction   A series of one or more SQL statements executed between commit events.

TRUNCATE   A SQL statement used to remove data from a database quickly but without recoverability.

unconditional   Without restriction.

undo segments   Segments that are maintained automatically by the database to support rollback operations, to assure read consistency, and to otherwise recover from logical corruptions.

Unicode   An industry standard that attempts to create a standardized encoding of every character of every language in existence.

unique   One of a kind.

unique identifier   An unambiguous reference to something, leaving no doubt what is being referenced.

UPDATE   A SQL statement used to modify data in a database table.

uppercase   The letters of the alphabet in majuscule form, also known as capital letters, such as *A*, *B*, and so on.

user account   A process that provides password-protected access to and ownership of a set of database objects and privileges.

UTC   Coordinated Universal Time. The new name for Greenwich Mean Time. The universal standard for measuring time internationally. UTC measures time as it exists at the Royal Observatory of Greenwich, London.

variable   A small unit of storage, represented by a name and a data type, for holding values that can be changed.

variance   When used with numeric analysis, variation quantifies the degree of variation of individual values within a large set of values. Variance is determined by averaging a set of values, subtracting each value from the average, squaring each difference, and summing the result.

view   A named query that is stored in the database.

window   When used with analytic functions, a window is a group of rows surrounding a target row. Analytics may perform operations on the target row by leveraging data from throughout the window.

winter time zone   *See* standard time.

INDEX

analytic functions. *See also* aggregate functions
    defined, 570
    DENSE_RANK, 291
    FIRST and LAST, 292–293
    group functions used as, 280
    LAG and LEAD, 226–230
    OVER, PARTITION BY, and ORDER BY, 224–226
    overview of, 223
    PERCENTILE_CONT, 232–233
    RANK, 289–290
    STDDEV, 230–232
AND operator, Boolean
    HAVING clause with, 304–305
    operator precedence, 168–169
    overview of, 164–167
ANSI (American National Standards Institute), 7, 570
ANY comparison operator, multi-row subquery, 371
ANY keyword, system privileges, 538–539
AS keyword, create views, 395
ASC reserved word, ascending sort in ORDER BY, 151–152
asterisk, COUNT function, 284–285
attributes
    * reserved for naming, 50
    building relational database, 20–21
    create simple table, 46–47
    in database normalization, 23–24, 32
    defined, 570
    entity-relationship diagram with, 18–19
autonomous, subqueries as, 352
AVG function, 287–288, 295

B

batch scripts, 180
BEFORE DROP, recover dropped tables, 426
BETWEEN reserved word, WHERE clause, 170–171
BLOB (binary large object) data types
    constraint restrictions, 80
    defined, 570
    overview of, 62

Boolean
    defined, 570
    HAVING clause, 304–305
    limit rows retrieved by query, 164–169
    NOT operator, 166–168
    operator precedence, 168–169
    AND/OR operators, 164–166
built-in
    data types, 61
    defined, 570
    functions, 203

C

calling functions, SQL statement, 203
Cartesian product, 8, 570
CASCADE clause, 107–109, 534
CASCADE CONSTRAINTS, dropped columns, 82–84
CASE conditional expression, 265
case insensitive
    defined, 570
    table/object names as, 48
case sensitive
    character data type comparisons as, 161
    data dictionary names, 422
    defined, 571
    object names in data dictionary as, 422
    passwords as, 534
    quoted names as, 50
    text searches as, 162, 206–207
case, strings
    INITCAP managing, 207–209
    UPPER and LOWER managing, 206–207
CAST conversion function, 263–264
CD-ROM, accompanying this book, 566–567
CEIL numerical function, 215
CHAR data type, 57
character class (POSIX character class), 571
character data types
    list of, 57
    MIN and MAX group functions for, 286–287
    ORDER BY and NULL, 157

N

U

V

Beta Test Oracle Software

Get a first look at our newest products—and help perfect them. You must meet the following criteria:

- ✔ Licensed Oracle customer or Oracle PartnerNetwork member

- ✔ Oracle software expert

- ✔ Early adopter of Oracle products

Please apply at: pdpm.oracle.com/BPO/userprofile

Join the Largest Tech Community in the World

 Download the latest software, tools, and developer templates

 Get exclusive access to hands-on trainings and workshops

 Grow your professional network through the Oracle ACE Program

 Publish your technical articles – and get paid to share your expertise

Join the Oracle Technology Network
Membership is free. Visit community.oracle.com

@OracleOTN facebook.com/OracleTechnologyNetwork

 ORACLE®

Push a Button
Move Your Java Apps to the Oracle Cloud

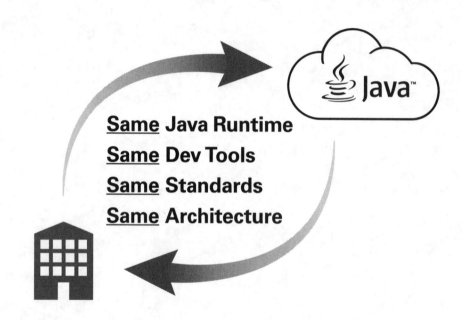

Same Java Runtime
Same Dev Tools
Same Standards
Same Architecture

... or Back to Your Data Center

cloud.oracle.com/java

Oracle Learning Library

Created by Oracle Experts
FREE for Oracle Users

- ✔ Vast array of learning aids
- ✔ Intuitive & powerful search
- ✔ Share content, events & saved searches
- ✔ Personalize your learning dashboard
- ✔ Find & register for training events

ORACLE®

oracle.com/oll

Reach More than 640,000 Oracle Customers with Oracle Publishing Group

Connect with the Audience that Matters Most to Your Business

Oracle Magazine
The Largest IT Publication in the World
Circulation: 325,000
Audience: IT Managers, DBAs, Programmers, and Developers

Profit
Business Insight for Enterprise-Class Business Leaders to Help Them Build a Better Business Using Oracle Technology
Circulation: 90,000
Audience: Top Executives and Line of Business Managers

Java Magazine
The Essential Source on Java Technology, the Java Programming Language, and Java-Based Applications
Circulation: 225,00 and Growing Steady
Audience: Corporate and Independent Java Developers, Programmers, and Architects

For more information or to sign up for a FREE subscription: Scan the QR code to visit Oracle Publishing online.